Lecture Notes in Artificial Intelligence   9324

Subseries of Lecture Notes in Computer Science

LNAI Series Editors

Randy Goebel
University of Alberta, Edmonton, Canada
Yuzuru Tanaka
Hokkaido University, Sapporo, Japan
Wolfgang Wahlster
DFKI and Saarland University, Saarbrücken, Germany

LNAI Founding Series Editor

Joerg Siekmann
DFKI and Saarland University, Saarbrücken, Germany

More information about this series at http://www.springer.com/series/1244

Steffen Hölldobler · Markus Krötzsch
Rafael Peñaloza · Sebastian Rudolph (Eds.)

KI 2015: Advances in Artificial Intelligence

38th Annual German Conference on AI
Dresden, Germany, September 21–25, 2015
Proceedings

 Springer

Editors
Steffen Hölldobler
Technische Universität Dresden
Dresden
Germany

Markus Krötzsch
Technische Universität Dresden
Dresden
Germany

Rafael Peñaloza
Free University Bozen-Bolzano
Bozen-Bolzano
Italy

Sebastian Rudolph
Technische Universität Dresden
Dresden
Germany

ISSN 0302-9743　　　　　　　ISSN 1611-3349　(electronic)
Lecture Notes in Artificial Intelligence
ISBN 978-3-319-24488-4　　　ISBN 978-3-319-24489-1　(eBook)
DOI 10.1007/978-3-319-24489-1

Library of Congress Control Number: 2015949317

LNCS Sublibrary: SL7 – Artificial Intelligence

Springer Cham Heidelberg New York Dordrecht London

Printed on acid-free paper

Springer International Publishing AG Switzerland is part of Springer Science+Business Media
(www.springer.com)

Preface

This volume contains the conference proceedings of the 38th German Conference on Artificial Intelligence, KI 2015, which was held 21–25 September 2015 in Dresden, Germany. Starting as German Workshop on AI (GWAI) in 1975, this annual event traditionally brings together academic and industrial researchers from all areas of AI, providing a premier forum for exchanging news and research results on theory and applications of intelligent system technology.

This year, the conference was preceded by an international summer school on reasoning organized by the International Center for Computational Logic. Nine workshops with their own proceedings were held on the first two days of the conference. In addition, a doctoral consortium provided doctoral researchers the opportunity to obtain feedback on their work. The research outlines are included in the KI proceedings.

The conference received 59 submissions (involving authors from 22 countries), of which 48 were research papers (RPs), and 11 were technical communications (TCs), a more concise paper format that was introduced for the first time this year. TCs provide the opportunity to present a wider range of results and ideas that are of interest to the KI audience, including reports about researchers' own recent publications, position papers, and previews of ongoing work. In a rigorous reviewing process, 15 research papers were selected for publication (31% of 48 submitted RPs), while another 14 submissions were accepted as TCs. On top of these conference papers, the volume also features the four accepted contributions to the KI 2015 Doctoral Consortium.

We thank all Program Committee members and additional reviewers for their invaluable effort in thoroughly assessing and discussing the submitted contributions. Special thanks are due to Riccardo Rosati, who acted as an External Program Chair, in order to coordinate the review of all papers that involved authors from TU Dresden.

For KI 2015 we were happy to secure the participation of three distinguished scientists as keynote speakers: Molham Aref (LogicBlox, USA) delivered a talk about declarative probabilistic programming, Ross D. King (University of Manchester) provided insights into his work with robot scientists, and Francesca Rossi (University of Padova) addressed safety and ethical issues in systems for collective decision making. Abstracts of each invited talk are included in this volume.

A number of people were involved in the organization of this conference. We would like to thank our Sponsorship Chair, Saartje Brockmans, our Publicity Chair, Simone Paulo Ponzetto, as well as the local organization team, in particular Emmanuelle-Anna Dietz, Norbert Manthey, and Peter Steinke. We further thank our Workshop Chair, Anni-Yasmin Turhan, and all workshop organizers. We also gratefully acknowledge the support of our sponsors. In particular, we thank the main conference sponsors *arago* (platinum) and *STI Innsbruck* (gold), as well as all other sponsors and partners as mentioned on the following pages. Moreover, we appreciate the assistance and professional service provided by the Springer LNCS editorial and publishing teams. Finally, thanks are due to all authors and participants of KI 2015; we hope that their stay in Dresden was most profitable and enjoyable.

September 2015   Steffen Hölldobler
                                                                 Markus Krötzsch
                                                                 Rafael Peñaloza
                                                                 Sebastian Rudolph

Organization

General Chair

Steffen Hölldobler   TU Dresden, Germany

Program Chairs

Markus Krötzsch   TU Dresden, Germany
Sebastian Rudolph   TU Dresden, Germany

Doctoral Consortium Chair

Rafael Peñaloza   FU Bozen-Bolzano, Italy

Workshop Chair

Anni-Yasmin Turhan   TU Dresden, Germany

External Program Chair

Riccardo Rosati   Sapienza University of Rome, Italy

Sponsorship Chair

Saartje Brockmans   Volz Innovation GmbH, Germany

Publicity Chair

Simone Paolo Ponzetto   University of Mannheim, Germany

Local Organization

Emmanuelle-Anna Dietz   TU Dresden, Germany
Norbert Manthey   TU Dresden, Germany
Peter Steinke   TU Dresden, Germany

Program Committee

Sven Behnke   University of Bonn, Germany
Ralph Bergmann   University of Trier, Germany
Mehul Bhatt   University of Bremen, Germany

Chris Biemann	TU Darmstadt, Germany
Philipp Cimiano	Bielefeld University, Germany
Johannes Fürnkranz	TU Darmstadt, Germany
Christopher Geib	Drexel University, USA
Christian Guttmann	Ivbar Institute AB, Sweden
Barbara Hammer	Clausthal University of Technology, Germany
Malte Helmert	University of Basel, Switzerland
Gabriele Kern-Isberner	Technische Universität Dortmund, Germany
Oliver Kramer	Universität Oldenburg, Germany
Ralf Krestel	Hasso Plattner Institute for Software Systems Engineering, Germany
Volker Lohweg	Hochschule Ostwestfalen-Lippe, Germany
Robert Mattmüller	University of Freiburg, Germany
Ralf Möller	Universität zu Lübeck, Germany
Till Mossakowski	University of Magdeburg, Germany
Justus Piater	Universität Innsbruck, Austria
Maria Silvia Pini	University of Padova, Italy
Marco Ragni	University of Freiburg, Germany
Achim Rettinger	Karlsruhe Institute of Technology, Germany
Stephan Schiffel	Reykjavík University, Iceland
Malte Schilling	Bielefeld University, Germany
Ute Schmid	University of Bamberg, Germany
Lars Schmidt-Thieme	University of Hildesheim, Germany
Lutz Schröder	FAU Erlangen-Nürnberg, Germany
Marija Slavkovik	University of Bergen, Norway
Daniel Sonntag	German Research Center for Artificial Intelligence (DFKI), Germany
Marc Stamminger	FAU Erlangen-Nürnberg, Germany
Hannes Strass	Leipzig University, Germany
Heiner Stuckenschmidt	University of Mannheim, Germany
Thomas Stützle	Université Libre de Bruxelles (ULB), Belgium
Michael Thielscher	The University of New South Wales, Australia
Matthias Thimm	Universität Koblenz-Landau, Germany
Ingo J. Timm	University of Trier, Germany
Toby Walsh	NICTA and UNSW, Australia
Stefan Woel	University of Freiburg, Germany

Additional Reviewers

Darko Anicic	Siemens AG, Germany
Darina Benikova	TU Darmstadt, Germany
Stefan Borgwardt	TU Dresden, Germany
Federico Cerutti	University of Aberdeen, UK
Marc Chee	University of New South Wales, Australia
Laura Diosan	Babeş-Bolyai University, Romania
Francesco M. Donini	Università della Tuscia, Italy

Manfred Eppe	University of California at Berkeley, USA
Justin Heinermann	Universität Oldenburg, Germany
Andreas Hertle	Universität Freiburg, Germany
Matthias Innmann	FAU Erlangen-Nürnberg, Germany
Sarah Kohail	TU Darmstadt, Germany
Ayush Kumar	Indian Institute of Technology, Patna, India
Oliver Kutz	Free University of Bozen-Bolzano, Italy
Mona Lange	Universität zu Lübeck, Germany
Domenico Lembo	Sapienza University of Rome, Italy
Maurizio Lenzerini	Sapienza University of Rome, Italy
András Lőrincz	Eötvös Loránd University, Hungary
Thomas Lukasiewicz	University of Oxford, UK
Carsten Lutz	University of Bremen, Germany
Rene Mandiau	Université de Valenciennes et du Hainaut Cambrésis, France
Aditya Mogadala	Karlsruhe Institute of Technology, Germany
Chifumi Nishioka	Kiel University, Germany
Özgur Özcep	Universität zu Lübeck, Germany
Steffen Remus	TU Darmstadt, Germany
Fabrizio Riguzzi	Università di Ferrara, Italy
Uli Sattler	The University of Manchester, UK
Ansgar Scherp	Kiel University, Germany
Sam Schreiber	Mountain View, California, USA
Lukas Schweizer	TU Dresden, Germany
Bariş Sertkaya	Frankfurt University of Applied Sciences, Germany
Michael Siebers	University of Bamberg, Germany
Christian Siegl	FAU Erlangen-Nürnberg, Germany
Peter Steinke	TU Dresden, Germany
Jakob Suchan	University of Bremen, Germany
Steffen Thoma	Karlsruhe Institute of Technology, Germany
Praveen Tirupattur	TU Kaiserslautern, Germany
Yongxin Tong	Hong Kong University of Science and Technology, Hong Kong
Takumi Toyama	German Research Center for Artificial Intelligence (DFKI), Germany
Claudia Wagner	GESIS Leibniz Institute for Social Sciences, Germany
Markus Weber	Zuse Institute Berlin, Germany
Martin Wehrle	University of Basel, Switzerland
Wolfgang Wörndl	TU München, Germany
Zhiqiang Zhuang	Griffith University, Australia

Sponsors and Patronage

Platinum

Gold

Silver

Bronce

Partners

Keynotes

Declarative Probabilistic Programming

Molham Aref

LogicBlox, Atlanta, USA
molham.aref@logicblox.com

Abstract. I will summarize our work on a declarative programming language that offers native language support for expressing predictive (e.g. machine learning) and prescriptive (e.g. combinatorial optimization) analytics. The presentation gives an overview of the platform and the language. In particular, it focuses on the important role of integrity constraints, which are used not only for maintaining data integrity, but also, for example, for the specification of complex optimization problems and probabilistic programming.

Molham Aref is the founder and CEO of LogicBlox and Predictix. He has over 23 years of experience leading teams that deliver high value predictive and prescriptive analytics solutions to some of the world's largest enterprises. Previously, he was CEO of Optimi (acquired by Ericsson), a leader in wireless network simulation and optimization and has held senior leadership positions at Retek (now Oracle Retail) and HNC Software (now FICO). He received his Bachelors in Computer Engineering, M.S. in Electrical Engineering, and M.S in Computer Science from Georgia Tech.

Automating Chemistry and Biology Using Robot Scientists

Ross D. King

School of Computer Science
University of Manchester, Manchester, UK
ross.king@manchester.ac.uk

"When my metaphysical friends tell me that the data on which the astronomers made their calculations ... were necessarily obtained originally through the evidence of their senses, I say 'No'. They might, in theory at any rate, be obtained by automatic calculating machine set in motion by the light falling upon them without admixture of the human senses at any stage"

Winston Churchill (1930)

Abstract. Science is an excellent application area for AI. Scientific problems are abstract, which suits AI reasoning, but they also involve the complexity of the real-world. Scientific problems are also restricted in scope, which again suits AI reasoning there is no need to know about "Cabbages and Kings". Nature is also honest and this simplifies reasoning as there is no need to consider malicious agents. Finally, Nature is a worthy object of our study, and the generation of scientific knowledge is a public good.

A Robot Scientist is a physically implemented robotic system that utilises techniques from artificial intelligence to execute cycles of automated scientific experimentation. A Robot Scientist can automatically execute cycles of: hypothesis formation, selection of efficient experiments to discriminate between hypotheses, execution of experiments using laboratory automation equipment, and analysis of results. The aim of developing Robot Scientists is to better understand science, and to make scientific research more efficient.

The Robot Scientist "Adam" was the first machine to autonomously hypothesise and experimentally confirm novel scientific knowledge: Adam generated functional genomics hypotheses about the yeast *Saccharomyces cerevisiae*, and experimentally tested these hypotheses using laboratory automation. Adams conclusions were then confirmed by manual experiments. To describe Adams research, we have developed an ontology and logical language. The resulting formalization involves over 10,000 different research units in a nested treelike structure, 10 levels deep, that relates the 6.6 million biomass measurements to their logical description. This formalisation describes how a machine contributed to scientific knowledge.

The Robot Scientist "Eve" was developed to automate and integrate drug discovery: drug screening, hit conformation, and QSAR development. Eve executes library-screening, hit-confirmation, and lead generation through cycles of quantitative structure activity relationship learning and testing. Using econometric modelling it was shown that the selection of compounds by Eve is more cost efficient than standard drug screening. Eve has repositioned several drugs against specific targets in parasites that cause tropical diseases. One validated discovery is that the anti-cancer compound TNP-470 is a potent inhibitor of dihydrofolate reductase from the malaria-causing parasite *Plasmodium vivax*.

My colleagues and I are currently working on a number of extensions/refinements to Eve. We are improving Eves AI reasoning through integration of nonmonotonic abductive inductive learning, and probabilistic relational learning. We are also investigating how Eve can plan new types of experiments to test hypotheses through intelligent use of a set of available laboratory automation equipment, rather than just applying formulaic experiments. We are also currently extending the biological application area of Eve to investigate cancer. This involves modifying Eve to be able to work with mammalian cells, and the AI to be able to use background knowledge about signaling networks.

I believe that in the future advances in computer hardware and software will drive the development of ever-smarter Robot Scientists. The improved collaboration between Human and Robot Scientists will produce better science than either can alone. The resulting improved productivity of science will lead to societal benefits: better food security, better medicines, etc. The Physics Nobel Laureate Frank Wilczek is on record as saying that in 100 years time the best physicist will be a machine. Time will tell.

References

1. King, R.D., Whelan, K.E., Jones, F.M., Reiser, P.G.K., Bryant, C.H., Muggleton, S.H., Kell, D.B., Oliver, S.G.: Functional genomic hypothesis generation and experimentation by a robot scientist. Nature **427**, 247–252 (2004)
2. King, R.D., Rowland, J., Oliver, S.G., Young, M., Aubrey, W., Byrne, E., Liakata, M., Markham, M., Pir, P., Soldatova, L.N., Sparkes, A., Whelan, K.E., Clare, C.: The automation of science. Science **324**, 85–89 (2009)
3. Williams K., Bilsland E., Sparkes A., Aubrey W., Young M., Soldatova L.N., De Grave K., Ramon J., de Clare M., Sirawaraporn W., Oliver S.G., King R.D.: Cheaper faster drug development validated by the repositioning of drugs against neglected tropical diseases. Royal Soc. Interface. DOI: 10.1098/rsif.2014.1289 (2015)

Safety Constraints and Ethical Principles in Collective Decision Making Systems

Francesca Rossi

University of Padova, Padua, Italy

This extended abstract describes a research project funded by the Future of Life Institute, 2015–2018.
Joint work with J. Greene (Harvard Univ.), J. Tasioulas
(King's College London),
K. B. Venable (Tulane Univ. and IMHC), B. Williams (MIT).

Abstract. The future will see autonomous machines acting in the same environment as humans, in areas as diverse as driving, assistive technology, and health care. Think of self-driving cars, companion robots, and medical diagnosis support systems. We also believe that humans and machines will often need to work together and agree on common decisions. Thus hybrid collective decision making systems will be in great need.

In this scenario, both machines and collective decision making systems should follow some form of moral values and ethical principles (appropriate to where they will act but always aligned to humans'), as well as safety constraints. In fact, humans would accept and trust more machines that behave as ethically as other humans in the same environment. Also, these principles would make it easier for machines to determine their actions and explain their behavior in terms understandable by humans. Moreover, often machines and humans will need to make decisions together, either through consensus or by reaching a compromise. This would be facilitated by shared moral values and ethical principles.

Contents

Technical Communications

Doctoral Consortium Contributions

Keynote

Safety Constraints and Ethical Principles in Collective Decision Making Systems

Francesca Rossi$^{(\boxtimes)}$

University of Padova, Padua, Italy
frossi@math.unipd.it

Abstract. The future will see autonomous machines acting in the same environment as humans, in areas as diverse as driving, assistive technology, and health care. Think of self-driving cars, companion robots, and medical diagnosis support systems. We also believe that humans and machines will often need to work together and agree on common decisions. Thus hybrid collective decision making systems will be in great need. In this scenario, both machines and collective decision making systems should follow some form of moral values and ethical principles (appropriate to where they will act but always aligned to humans'), as well as safety constraints. In fact, humans would accept and trust more machines that behave as ethically as other humans in the same environment. Also, these principles would make it easier for machines to determine their actions and explain their behavior in terms understandable by humans. Moreover, often machines and humans will need to make decisions together, either through consensus or by reaching a compromise. This would be facilitated by shared moral values and ethical principles.

1 Introduction

The future will see autonomous agents acting in the same environment as humans, over extended periods of time, in areas as diverse as driving, assistive technology, and health care. In this scenario, such agents should follow moral values and ethical principles (appropriate to where they will act), as well as safety constraints. When directed to achieve a set of goals, agents should ensure that their goal achieving actions do not violate these principles and values overtly, or through negligence, by performing risky actions. It would be easier for humans to accept and trust agents who behave as ethically as other humans in the same environment. Also, these principles would make it easier for agents to determine their actions and explain their behavior in terms understandable by humans. Moreover, often agents and humans will need to make decisions together, either through consensus or by reaching a compromise. This would be facilitated by shared moral values and ethical principles.

This extended abstract describes a research project funded by the Future of Life Institute, 2015-2018.

Joint work with J. Greene (Harvard Univ.), J. Tasioulas (King's College London), K. B. Venable (Tulane Univ. and IMHC), B. Williams (MIT).

We believe it is important to study the embedding of safety constraints, moral values, and ethical principles in agents, within the context of collective decision making systems in societies of agents and humans.

Collective decision making involves a collection of agents who express their preferences over a shared set of possible outcomes, and a preference aggregation rule which chooses one of the options to best satisfy the agents' preferences. However, aggregating just preferences may lead to outcomes that do not follow any ethical principles or safety constraints. To embed such principles/constraints in a collective decision making system, we need to understand how to model them, how to reason with them at the level of a single agent, and how to embed them into collective decision making.

Just like individual humans, each agent who operate in a multi-agent context needs to be have an internal representation of moral values and ethical principles, as well as an ethical reasoning engine. Otherwise it would not able to explain its behaviour to others.

We claim that there is a need to adapt current logic-based modelling and reasoning frameworks, such as soft constraints, CP-nets, and constraint-based scheduling under uncertainty, to model safety constraints, moral values, and ethical principles. More precisely, we study how logic-based preference modelling frameworks can be adapted to model both (explicit) ethical principles and (implicit) moral values, as sophisticated constraints over possible actions. The constraints may be unconditional ("hard") constraints, or soft, overridable if the consequences of an individual bad action can still lead to overall good. We propose to replace preference aggregation with an appropriately developed value/ethics/preference *fusion*, an operation designed to ensure that agents' preferences are consistent with their moral values and do not override ethical principles

For ethical principles, we use hard constraints specifying the basic ethical "laws", plus some form of common-sense morality expressed as sophisticated prioritised and possibly context-dependent constraints over possible actions, equipped with a conflict resolution engine. To avoid reckless behavior in the face of uncertainty, we proposed to bound the risk of violating these ethical laws in the form of chance constraints, and we propose to develop stochastic constraint solvers that propose solutions that respect these risk bounds, based on models of environmental uncertainty. We also propose to replace preference aggregation with an appropriately developed constraint/value/ethics/preference *fusion*, an operation designed to ensure that agents' preferences are consistent with the system's safety constraints, the agents' moral values, and the ethical principles. We will leverage previous experience in developing single and multi-agent preference/constraint reasoning engines.

Today, techniques exist to enable agents to make decisions, such as scheduling activities, while satisfying some safety concerns, e.g. by using techniques from constraint-based optimization. For instance, in many critical scenarios, such as space missions where a malfunction can endanger the whole mission, activities are scheduled in such a way to maximise robustness against possible problems.

We believe that these techniques can provide an inspiration to handle ethical concerns. However, we think that a much more explicit model and reasoning engine for ethical principles and moral values is needed in order to deal with them satisfactorily and allow them to evolve over time.

We also propose to study *safe moral learning*, that is, how agents autonomously modify their moral values and ethical principles based on their interactions with other agents / humans, and through observation of collective decisions, while respecting safety constraints. Machine learning techniques have traditionally been successfully developed for "lower level" perception tasks such as vision and speech understanding. We believe that adapting these techniques to ("higher level", symbolic) moral learning tasks will be a significant challenge but will build on the defines formal model of moral values. It will be important to ensure that resulting modified behaviors remain *explainable* (to humans) in moral and ethical terms. We will investigate several approaches including logic-based inductive learning ones.

2   Which Ethical Principles for Intelligent Agents?

An intelligent agent should have capability to autonomously make good decisions, based on available data and preferences, even in the context of uncertainty, missing or noisy information, as well as incorrect input, and should be able to learn from past experience or from available historical data. Even more importantly, intelligent agents should have the ability to interact with humans, make decisions together with them, and achieve goals by working together.

An agent with these capabilities poses several crucial ethical questions. Ethical principles guide humans' behaviour. They tell us what is regarded as right or wrong. They come from values that we regards as absolute, guiding our whole life. If we want intelligent agents to enhance human capabilities, or to collaborate with humans, or even just to live and act in the same society, we need to embed in them some ethical guidelines, so they can act in their environment following values that are aligned to the human ones. Or maybe we need different values and ethical principles for agents, since they are inherently different from humans?

As Issac Asimov famously illustrated in his *I, Robot* series, explicitly programming ethical behavior is surprisingly challenging. Moral philosophy – the field that has studied explicit ethical principles most extensively – suggests three general approaches, corresponding to the three major schools of Western moral thought.

The *deontological* approach (most closely associated with Immanuel Kant) regards morality as a system of *rights* and *duties*. Here the focus is on categories of *actions*, where different actions are deemed impermissible, permissible, or obligatory based on a set of explicit rules.

The *consequentialist* approach (most closely associated with Jeremy Bentham and John Stuart Mill) aims to produce the best aggregate consequences minimizing costs and maximizing benefits according to a pre-specified value function.

For example, a classical utilitarian approach aims to maximize the total amount of happiness.

The *virtue-* or *character-*based approach (most closely associated with Aristotle) regards ethical behavior as the product of an acquired set of behavioral dispositions that cannot be adequately summarized as an adherence to a set of deontological rules (concerning actions) or to as a commitment to maximizing good consequences.

These three approaches are well known and have been the starting point for nearly all discussions of machine ethics [5,12,23]. Each approach has limitations that are well known. Deontological principles are easily to implement but may be rigid. Consequentialist principles require complex calculations that may be faulty. Virtue is opaque and requires extensive training with an unknown teaching criterion. There is, however, a more general problem faced by all three approaches, which is that implementing them may depend on solving daunting, general computation problems that have not been solved and may not be solved for some time.

For example, a "simple" deontological rule such as "don't lie" or "don't kill" is not specified in terms of machine movements. Rather, the machine must understand which acts of communication would constitute lying and which body movements would constitute killing in a given context. A consequentialist system would require a machine to represent all of the actions available to it, and a virtue based system would have to recognize the present situation as one with a variety of features that, together, call for one action rather than another. In other words, all three approaches, when fully implemented, seem to require something like general intelligence, which would enable the machine to represent its current situation in rich conceptual terms. Indeed, this speculation is consistent with recent research on the cognitive neuroscience of moral judgment indicating that moral judgment depends on a variety of neural systems that are not specifically dedicated to moral judgment [10]. This includes systems that enable the general representation of value and the motivation of its pursuit, visual imagery, cognitive control, and the representation of complex semantic representations. Unfortunately for Commander Data, humans have no "ethical subroutine". Real human moral judgment uses the whole brain.

What, then, can be done? Here, the human brain may nevertheless offer some guidance [20]. Is it morally acceptable to push someone off of a footbridge in order to save five lives [21]? A simple deontological response says no ("Don't kill"). A simple consequentialist response says yes ("Save the most lives"), and most humans are at least somewhat conflicted about this, but err on the side of the deontological response (in this particular case). We now know that the deontological response depends on a classically emotional neural structure known as the amygdala (reflecting emotional salience) and that the application of the consequentialist maximizing principle depends on a classically "cognitive" structure known as the dorsolateral prefrontal cortex. It seems that healthy humans engage both responses and that there is a higher-order evaluation process that depends on the ventromedial prefrontal cortex, a structure that across domains attaches emotional weight to decision variables. In other words, the brain seems to make both types of judgment (deontological and consequentialist) and then makes a higher order judgment about which lower-order judgment to trust, which may be viewed as a kind of wisdom (reflecting virtue or good character).

Such a hierarchical decision system might be implemented within an agent, or across agents. For example, some agents may apply simple rules based on action features. Others may attempt to make "limited" cost-benefit calculations. And collectively, the behavior of these agents may be determined by a weighting of these distinct, lower-level evaluative responses. Such as system might begin by following simple deontological rules, but then, either acquire more complex rules through learning, or learn when it can and cannot trust its own cost-benefit calculations. Starting with action-based rules and simple cost-benefit calculations substantially reduces the space of possible responses. Learning to trade-off between these two approaches adds some flexibility, but without requiring intractable cost-benefit calculations or lifelong moral education.

We offer this approach as just one example strategy. Of course, if we knew how we were going to solve this problem, there would be no need to bring together people with diverse expertise. What we wish to convey is twofold: First, that we are aware of the scope of the challenge and the strengths and limitations of the extant strategies. Second, that we have some preliminary ideas for hybrid approaches that leverage insights from human moral cognition.

Another important aspect of the project would be to consider the extent to which morality could be reduced to a set of rules that is capable of being applied in a fairly straightforward way to guide conduct , e.g. 'Do not kill', 'Keep one's promises', 'Help those in need', etc. We already know that much of common sense morality is codifiable in this way, thanks to the example of the law.

However, even if we could achieve an adequate codification of ordinary moral consciousness, at least within some domain, problems would arise. Two cases are especially worth highlighting: (a) cases where the strict application of a given rule generates an unacceptable outcome, often but not always characterisable as such by reference to some other rule that has been violated in adhering to the first, and (b) cases where the strict application of the given set of rules is unhelpfully 'silent' on the problem at hand, because it involved circumstances not foreseen by the rules.

Both of phenomena (a) and (b) raise the question of when and how the strict application of a rule needs to be modified or supplemented to resolve the problem of perverse results or gaps. One important source of thinking about these issues is Aristotle's discussion of justice and equity in the Nicomachean Ethics. According to Aristotle, the common sense morality codified in law, although capable of being a generally a good guide to action, will nonetheless on occasion breakdown along the lines of (a) and (b). For Aristotle, this means that the virtuous judge will need to possess, in addition to a propensity to follow legal rules, the virtue of equity. This enables the judge to use their independent judgment to correct or supplement the strict application of legal rules in cases of type (a) or (b). A key topic involves the clarification of the notion of equity, with its rule and judgment structure, as a prelude to a consideration of how this might be embedded in autonomous agents.

3   Designing Ethical Agents

No matter which approach we will choose to express ethical principles and moral values in intelligent agents, we need to find a suitable way to model it in computational terms, which is expressive enough to be able to represent all we have in mind in its full generality, and which can be reasoned upon with computational efficiency.

Ethical principles may seem very similar to the concepts of constraints [7,16] and preferences [17], which have already received a large attention in the AI literature. Indeed, constraints and preferences are a common feature of everyday decision making. They are, therefore, an essential ingredient in many reasoning tools. In an intelligent agent, we need to specify what is not allowed according to the principles, thus some form of constraints, as well as some way to prioritise among different principles, that some form of preference.

Representing and reasoning about preferences is an area of increasing theoretical and practical interest in AI. Preferences and constraints occur in real-life problems in many forms. Intuitively, constraints are restrictions on the possible scenarios: for a scenario to be feasible, all constraints must be satisfied. For example, if we have an ethical rule that says we should not kill anybody, all scenarios where people are killed are not allowed. Preferences, on the other hand, express desires, satisfaction levels, rejection degrees, or costs. For example, we may prefer an action that solves reasonably well all medical issues in a patient, rather than another one that solves completely one of them but does not address the other ones. Moreover, in many real-life optimization problems, we may have both constraints and preferences.

Preferences and constraints are closely related notions, since preferences can be seen as a form of "relaxed" constraints. For this reason, there are several constraint-based preference modeling frameworks in the AI literature. One of the most general of such frameworks defines a notion of *soft* constraints [11], which extends the classical constraint formalism to model preferences in a quantitative way, by expressing several degrees of satisfaction that can be either totally or partially ordered. The term soft constraints is used to distinguish this kind of constraints from the classical ones, that are usually called *hard* constraint. However, hard constraints can be seen as an instance of the concept of soft constraints where there are just two levels of satisfaction. In fact, a hard constraint can only be satisfied or violated, while a soft constraint can be satisfied at several levels.When there are both levels of satisfaction and levels of rejection, preferences are usually called bipolar, and they can be modeled by extending the soft constraint formalism [4].

Preferences can also be modeled in a qualitative (also called *ordinal*) way, that is, by pairwise comparisons. In this case, soft constraints (or their extensions) are not suitable. However, other AI preference formalisms are able to express preferences qualitatively, such as CP-nets[6]. More precisely, CP-nets provide an intuitive way to specify conditional preference statements that state the preferences over the instances of a certain feature, possibly depending on some other features. For example, we may say that we prefer driving slow to driving fast if we are in a country road. CP-nets and soft constraints can be combined, providing a single environment where both qualitative and quantitative preferences can be modeled and handled. Specific types of preferences come with their own reasoning methods. For example, temporal preferences are quantitative preferences that pertain to the position and duration of events in time. Soft constraints can be embedded naturally in a temporal constraint framework to handle this kind of preference.

An intuitive way to express preferences consists of providing a set of goals, each of which is a propositional formula, possibly adding also extra information such as priorities or weights. Candidates in this setting are variable assignments, which may satisfy or violate each goal. A weighted goal is a propositional logic formula plus a real-valued weight. The utility of a candidates is then computed by collecting the weights of satisfied and violated goals, and then aggregating them. Often only violated goals count, and their utilities are aggregated with functions such as sum or maximin. In other cases, we may sum the weights of the satisfied goals, or we may take their maximum weight. Any restriction we may impose on the goals or the weights, and any choice of an aggregation function, give a different language. Such languages may have drastically different properties in terms of their expressivity, succinctness, and computational complexity.

In the quantitative direction typical of soft constraints, there are also other frameworks to model preferences, mostly based on utilities. The most widely used assumes we have some form of independence among variables, such as mutual preferential independence. Preferences can then be represented by an additive utility function in deterministic decision making, or utility independence, which assures an additive representation for general scenarios. However, this assumption often does not hold in practice since there is usually some interaction among the variables. To account for this, models based on interdependent value additivity have been defined which allows for some interaction between the variables while preserving some decomposability. This notion of independence, also called generalized additive independence (GAI), allows for the definition of utility functions which take the form of a sum of utilities over subsets of the variables. GAI decompositions can be represented by a graphical structure, called a GAI net, which models the interaction among variables, and it is similar to the dependency graph of a CP-net or to the junction graph of a Bayesian network. GAI decompositions have been used to provide CP-nets with utility functions, obtaining the so-called UCP networks.

In this project we intend to investigate the use of existing or new formalisms to model and reason with ethical principles in intelligent agents.

4 Preferences and Ethical Principles in Collective Decision Making Systems

If agents and humans will be part of a hybrid collective decision making system, and thus will make collective decisions, based on their preferences over the possible outcomes, can ethical principles for such decision system be modelled just like the preferences of another dummy agent, or should they be represented and treated differently? Are the knowledge representation formalisms that are usually used in AI to model preferences suitable to model values as well, or should we use something completely different? A very simple form of values could be modelled by constraints, so that only feasible outcomes can be the results of a collective decisions process. But values and ethical principles could often take a graded form, thus resembling a kind of preference. Also, should individual and collective ethical principles be modelled differently?

We believe that some of the answers to these questions may exploit the existing literature on preference aggregation [17]. Indeed, an important aspect of reasoning about preferences is preference aggregation. In multi-agent systems, we often need to combine the preferences of several agents. More precisely, preferences are often used in collective decision making when multiple agents need to choose one out of a set of possible decisions: each agent expresses its preferences over the possible decisions, and a centralized system aggregates such preferences to determine the "winning" decision. Preferences are also the subject of study in social choice, especially in the area of elections and voting theory [1]. In an election, the voters express their preferences over the candidates and a voting rule is used to elect the winning candidate. Economists, political theorist, mathematicians, as well as philosophers have invested considerable effort in studying this scenario and have obtained many theoretical results about the desirable properties of the voting rules that one can use.

Since the voting setting is closely related to multi-agent decision making, it is not surprising that in recent years the area of multi-agent systems has witnessed a growing interest in trying to reuse social choice results in the multi-agent setting. However, it soon became clear that an adaptation of such results is necessary, since several issues, which are typical of multi-agent settings and AI scenarios, usually do not occur, or have a smaller impact, in typical voting situations. In a multi-agent system, the set of candidates can be very large with respect to the set of voters. Usually in social choice, it is the opposite: there are many voters and a small number of candidates. Also, in many AI scenarios, the candidates often have a combinatorial structure. That is, they are defined via a combination of features. Moreover, the preferences over the features are often dependent on each other. In social choice, usually the candidates are tokens with no structure. In addition, for multi-issue elections, the issues are usually independent of each other. This combinatorial structure allows for the compact modelling of the preferences over the candidates. Therefore, several formalisms have been developed in AI to model such preference orderings. In social choice, little emphasis is put on how to model preferences, since there are few candidates, so one can usually explicitly specify a linear order. In AI, a preference ordering is not necessarily linear, but it may include indifference and incomparability. Moreover, often uncertainty is present, for example in the form of missing or imprecise preferences. In social choice, usually all preferences are assumed to be present, and a preference order over all the candidates is a linear order that is explicitly given as a list of candidates. Finally, multi-agent systems must consider the computational properties of the system. In social choice this usually has not been not a crucial issue.

It is therefore very interesting to study how these two disciplines, social choice and AI, can fruitfully cooperate to give innovative and improved solutions to aggregating preferences of multiple agents. In this project, since we intend to deal with ethical issues in collective decision making, we need to understand what modifications to the usual preference aggregation scenario should be done to account for them, and how they can be handled satisfactorily when making collective decisions. Collective decision making in the presence of feasibility constraints is starting to be considered in the literature [9]. However, ethical principles and safety constraints will be much more complex than just a set of constraints, so we need to understand the computational and expressiveness issues arising in this scenario.

5   Safety Constraints vs. Ethical Principles

It is crucial that computational agents offer guarantees that they will act in a manner that is both safe and ethical. Achieving safe and ethical behavior each is an exceptional challenge in its own right. However, we can leverage the fact that these two concepts are closely intertwined. For example, a person commits the crime of reckless endangerment when the action of that person creates a substantial risk of serious physical injury to another person. That is, the action of one individual is unsafe to another. An example is the case when the death of a pedestrian results from running a traffic light. This is distinguished from accidental death, for example, in which the driver is operating safely, but a child is killed after jumping out between two parked cars. While a tragedy the drivers actions are not deemed unethical.

The legal system differentiates between a range of these behaviors with such terms as voluntary versus involuntary manslaughter, and constructive versus criminally negligent manslaughter. Each category offers insight into the behaviors that we should expect of computational agents. In this proposal effort we will codify and design algorithms to satisfy the constraints underlying several of these category.

The example of accidental death versus reckless endangerment highlights several key points that our research must address. First, while an ethical principle, such as thou shalt not kill, appears to be a crisp logical constraint (at least in a civilian context), the concept of accidental death highlights that the act of killing is not considered by society to be a crime or unethical behavior in all cases. Second, the underlying reason for this is that the world is uncertain, and as a consequence, many of our every day actions, although considered ethical, have some non-zero probability of exacting harm. Risk of harm is often unavoidable; hence we cannot consider lack of harm to be a hard constraint for ethical behavior. Third, reckless endangerment acknowledges that it is criminal to act in a manner that incurs unacceptably high risk of doing harm, as deemed by societal norms. Finally, we assert that associated with safety and ethical constraints is an upper bound on the probability of failure. This provides a dividing line between acceptable and unacceptable risk.

Carrying these observations over to computational agents, we likewise argue that it is both unsafe and unethical for an agent to take action that incurs excessive risk of doing harm. Unfortunately, many of the automated decision making methods being deployed today do not bound the risk of failure of their actions, and are at risk of performing acts of reckless endangerment.

Specifically, many decision-making systems frame and solve their problem as an instance of a deterministic constraint optimization problem, where constraints include safety constraints. These methods generate an optimal solution without considering uncertainty due to the environment and inaccuracies in their knowledge. The reason this can be reckless is that optimal solutions typically lie along one of the constraint boundaries that separate feasible (safe) and infeasible (hazardous) solutions. Intuitively, the highest utility solution often pushes a system to its limits. A small disturbance in one of the random variables is then likely to push a solution into a hazardous state.

In summary, decision methods based on deterministic optimization offer no bound on the risk of failure, and worse, gravitate towards solutions with high failure rates. To avoid this, the standard practice is to have a user insert a safety margin [2,22] into the problem formulation, in order to compensate for uncertainty. This, however, shifts the burden of ethical behavior onto the user, who often has insufficient knowledge and experience of the algorithms operation to set these margins effectively.

A wide range of probabilistic decision-making algorithms have been developed that reason about uncertainty. The dominant approach is an algorithm that maximizes expected utility [3,15]. In this case risk of failure is incorporated within a utility function. This devalues risky behavior but does not prevent excessive risk. Arbitrarily high levels of reward can result in behaviors that incur arbitrary levels of risk, and hence are still reckless.

Instead we argue that computational agents should be designed to ensure that their safety and ethical constraints are violated with a probability that is always below a maximum probability of acceptable failure. This requires methods that learn these thresholds of acceptable risk, methods that learn models that capture environmental uncertainty, and decision-making algorithms that operate on these models, safety and ethical constraints, and thresholds.

To solve these decision problems, we note that the concept of a constraint with bounded risk, called a *chance constraint*, is fundamental to the field of stochastic optimization [14]. Stochastic optimization is a branch of mathematical programming, where constraint optimization problems include random variables with unbounded uncertainty and constraints include a maximum probability of violation. The solution to a stochastic optimization problem is one that maximizes expected utility with acceptable risk of failure, as defined by the chance constraint.

Likewise, we propose that, first, the ethical principles and safety constraints of agents be expressed as chance-constraints; second, agents learn failure thresholds that reflect social norms; third, agents learn stochastic models of their own actions and their environment; fourth, agents learn models of the reliability and accuracy of these models; fifth, agents then generate courses of action that they can prove do not have excessive risk of violating these safety and ethical constraints, and finally, that agents are able to explain that their actions incur acceptable risk.

Existing stochastic programming formalisms [19] are not up to expressing or solving the tasks that our agents are needed to perform. First, real-world agents leverage a diverse set of constraint representations to describe their goals, safety and ethical constraints and world models, including temporal logics, finite domain constraints, temporal and resource constraints, and a range of automata models. Our project starts by defining appropriate constraint representations that are essential for capturing ethical and safety constraints for a representative computational agent, such as an autonomous vehicle.

Second, we will explore the development of decision procedures for planning and monitoring based on subclasses of these chance-constrained models, with a particular focus on handling constraints appropriate for expressing safety and ethical constraints. A significant challenge is to develop decision procedures that respond quickly to changing environmental conditions and goals. Stochastic optimization algorithms are typically based on sampling based methods, such as scenario trees, and can be quite slow. The MIT team has developed a range of algorithms based on the concept of *risk-allocation* that demonstrate fast runtime performance for a range of constraint formulations, including finite domain [18], temporal [8] and dynamical constraints [13]. We will extend this work to handle the appropriately identified ethical and safety constraints.

Chance-constrained variants for combinations of these constraint representations and corresponding decision procedures need to be developed. In this proposed effort we will start be defining appropriate constraint representations that are essential for capturing ethical and safety constraints for some of the most pervasive instances of computational agents.

Finally, as humans an important aspect of responsible behavior involves identifying when our actions could be unsafe, and calling for help, such as asking a sober friend to drive home from a party. Computational agents are limited by the accuracy of their models, and the performance of their procedures. Responsible agents should know their limits, by analyzing the potential risks of up coming actions, and inaccuracies in their knowledge, and develop appropriate contingencies, including engaging human involvement [24]. This engagement requires offering the human sufficient lead-time to transfer authority safely, and explanatory capabilities that facilitate this transition.

6 Concluding Remarks

The future of our society will see a tight interconnection between humans and intelligent agents. These two "species" will augment and extend each other form of intelligence. Humans will be greatly helped by the computational and cognitive power of intelligent agents, that will be able to solve many of the planets' problems, eradicate several diseases, and save many lives. However, to do that, intelligent agents have to be able to make autonomous decisions in their functioning.

Humans will trust them to make autonomous decisions only if they are built in a way to follow ethical principles which are aligned to human ones. For example, a companion robot that keeps company to an elderly person and check on his/her health state, needs to have some level of empathy and other social skills. Also, a self-driving car needs to handle critical situations, where lives may be at risk, in a way that is similar to what a human would do.

If the project is successful, and we can embed (or learn) ethical principles into intelligent agents and (hybrid) collective decision making systems, such agents and systems will be trusted by humans and therefore serve as the building blocks of a very strong cooperation between humans and machines. The impact that we envision is huge. Intelligent machines will behave in a safe way, and thus humans and machines will be able to actively cooperate to solve many essential problems of our civilisation.

Of course this is not enough to ensure that no undesired effect will emerge from the use of intelligent agents. Issues like validation and security must still be considered and work in those areas needs to complement the one carried on in this project.

References

1. Arrow, K.J., Sen, A.K., Suzumara, K.: Handbook of Social Choice and Welfare. North-Holland, Elsevier (2002)
2. Bemporad, A., Morari, M.: Robust model-predictive control: a survey. In: Garulli, A., Tesi, A. (eds.) Robustness in Identification and Control. LNCS, vol. 245, pp. 207–226. Springer, London (1999)
3. Bertsekas, D.P.: Dynamic Programming and Stochastic Control. Academic Press (1976)
4. Bistarelli, S., Pini, M.S., Rossi, F., Venable, K.B.: Bipolar preference problems: framework, properties and solving techniques. In: Azevedo, F., Barahona, P., Fages, F., Rossi, F. (eds.) CSCLP. LNCS (LNAI), vol. 4651, pp. 78–92. Springer, Heidelberg (2007)
5. Bostrom, N.: Superintelligence: Paths, Dangers, Strategies. Oxford University Press (2014)
6. Boutilier, C., Brafman, R.I., Domshlak, C., Hoos, H.H., Poole, D.: CP-nets: A tool for representing and reasoning with conditional ceteris paribus preference statements. J. Artif. Intell. Res. (JAIR) 21, 135–191 (2004)
7. Dechter, R.: Constraint Processing. Morgan Kaufmann (2003)

8. Fang, C., Yu, P., Williams, B.C.: Chance-constrained probabilistic simple temporal problems. In: Proc. AAAI 2014. AAAI Press (2014)
9. Grandi, U., Luo, H., Maudet, N., Rossi, F.: Aggregating CP-nets with unfeasible outcomes. In: O'Sullivan, B. (ed.) CP 2014. LNCS, vol. 8656, pp. 366–381. Springer, Heidelberg (2014)
10. Greene, J.D.: The cognitive neuroscience of moral judgment and decision-making. MIT Press (2014)
11. Meseguer, P., Rossi, F., Schiex, T.: Soft constraints. In: Handbook of constraint programming, chapter 9, pp. 281–328. Elsevier (2006)
12. Moor, J.H.: What is computer ethics? Metaphilosophy **16**(4), 266–275 (1985)
13. Ono, M., Blackmore, L., Williams, B.: Chance constrained finite horizon optimal control with nonconvex constraints. In: Proc. American Control Conference (2010)
14. Prekopa, A.: Stochastic Programming. Kluwer (1995)
15. Puterman, M.L.: Markov Decision Processes. Wiley (1994)
16. Rossi, F., Van Beek, Walsh, T.: Handbook of Constraint Programming. Elsevier (2006)
17. Rossi, F., Venable, K.B., Walsh, T.: A Short introduction to preferences: between artificial intelligence and social choice. In: Synthesis Lectures on Artificial Intelligence and Machine Learning. Morgan & Claypool Publishers (2011)
18. Santana, P.H.R.Q.A., Williams, B.C.: Chance-constrained consistency for probabilistic temporal plan networks. In: Proc. AAAI 2014. AAAI Press (2014)
19. Schwarm, A., Nikolaou, M.: Chance-constrained model-predictive control. AlChE Journal **45**, 1743–1752 (1999)
20. Shenhav, A., Greene, J.D.: Integrative moral judgment: dissociating the roles of the amygdala and ventromedial prefrontal cortex. The Journal of Neuroscience **34**(13), 4741–4749 (2014)
21. Thomson, J.J.: The trolley problem. Yale Law Journal **94**, 1395 (1985)
22. Vidal, T., Fargier, H.: Handling contingency in temporal constraint networks: from consistency to controllabilities. Journal of Experimental and Theoretical Artificial Intelligence **11**, 23–45 (1999)
23. Wallach, W., Allen, C.: Moral machines: Teaching robots right from wrong. Oxford University Press (2008)
24. Yu, P., Fang, C., Williams, B.C.: Resolving over-constrained probabilistic temporal problems through chance constraint relaxation. In: Proc. AAAI 2015. AAAI Press (2015)

Full Technical Papers

Complexity of Interval Relaxed Numeric Planning

Johannes Aldinger[✉], Robert Mattmüller, and Moritz Göbelbecker

Institut Für Informatik, Albert-Ludwigs-Universität, 79110 Freiburg, Germany
{aldinger,mattmuel,goebelbe}@informatik.uni-freiburg.de

Abstract. Automated planning is computationally hard even in its most basic form as STRIPS planning. We are interested in numeric planning with instantaneous actions, a problem that is not decidable in general. Relaxation is an approach to simplifying complex problems in order to obtain guidance in the original problem. We present a relaxation approach with intervals for numeric planning and show that plan existence can be decided in polynomial time for tasks where dependencies between numeric effects are acyclic.

1 Motivation

Automated planning can be used to solve many real world problems where a *goal* is reached by applying *operators* that change the *state* of the world. In classical planning, the world is modeled with Boolean variables. Modeling of physical properties (e.g. velocity) or resources (e.g. fuel level) requires real-valued variables instead. Unlike classical planning, which is PSPACE-complete [4], numeric planning is *undecidable* [7]. Even though completeness of numeric planning algorithms can therefore not be achieved in general, numeric planners can find plans or an assurance that the problem is unsolvable for many practical tasks.

Heuristic search is a predominant approach to solve planning problems. One way to obtain heuristic guidance is to ignore negative interactions between the operators. The underlying assumption of a *delete relaxation* is that propositions which are achieved once during planning can not be invalidated (deleted). More recent planning systems are usually not restricted to propositional state variables. Instead they use the SAS+ formalism [2], which allows for (finite-domain) multi-valued variables and a "delete relaxation" corresponds to variables that can attain a *set* of values at the same time. Extending this concept for numeric planning relaxes the set representation even further. A memory efficient approach to capture possibly infinitely many values of a numeric variable is to consider the interval that encloses the reached values. The methods to deal with intervals have been studied in the field of interval arithmetic [10], which has been used in mathematics for decades [9] and enables us to deal with intervals in terms of basic numeric operations.

Extending classical delete relaxation heuristics to numeric problems has been done before, albeit only for a subset of numeric tasks, where numeric variables

© Springer International Publishing Switzerland 2015
S. Hölldobler et al. (Eds.): KI 2015, LNAI 9324, pp. 19–31, 2015.
DOI: 10.1007/978-3-319-24489-1_2

can only be manipulated in a restricted way. The Metric-FF planning system [8] tries to convert the planning task into a *linear numeric* task, which ensures that variables can "grow" in only one direction. When high values of a variable are beneficial to fulfill the preconditions, *decrease* effects are considered harmful. Another approach to solve *linear* numeric planning problems is to encode numeric variables in a linear program and solve constraints with an LP-solver. Coles et al. [5] analyze the planning problem for consumers and producers of resources to obtain a heuristic that ensures that resources are not more often consumed than produced or initially available. The RANTANPLAN planner [3] uses linear programs in the context of planning as satisfiability modulo theories. In contrast, we are interested in approaching numeric planning supporting all arithmetic base operations by generalizing relaxation heuristics.

2   Basics

In this section, we outline numeric planning with instantaneous actions, which is expressible in PDDL2.1, layer 2 [6]. We describe interval arithmetic, the technique we use to extend delete relaxation heuristics to numeric planning.

2.1   Numeric Planning with Instantaneous Actions

Given a set of variables $\mathcal{V}$ with domains $\mathrm{dom}(\mathsf{v})$ for all $\mathsf{v} \in \mathcal{V}$, a *state* s is a mapping of variables v to their respective domains. Throughout the paper, we denote the value of a variable v in state s by $s(\mathsf{v})$. Whenever the state s is not essential, we use the same letter in different fonts to distinguish a variable or expression (sans-serif) and its value or evaluation (italic), e.g. $s(\mathsf{x}) = x$.

A numeric planning task $\Pi = \langle \mathcal{V}_P, \mathcal{V}_N, \mathcal{O}, \mathcal{I}, \mathcal{G} \rangle$ is a 5-tuple where $\mathcal{V}_P$ is a set of propositional variables $\mathsf{v_p}$ with domain $\{true, false\}$. $\mathcal{V}_N$ is a set of numeric variables $\mathsf{v_n}$ with domain $\mathbb{Q}^\infty := \mathbb{Q} \cup \{-\infty, \infty\}$. $\mathcal{O}$ is a set of operators, $\mathcal{I}$ the initial state and $\mathcal{G}$ the goal condition. A *numeric expression* $\mathsf{e_1 \circ e_2}$ is an arithmetic expression with operators $\circ \in \{+, -, \times, \div\}$ and expressions $\mathsf{e_1}$ and $\mathsf{e_2}$ recursively defined over variables $\mathcal{V}_N$ and constants from $\mathbb{Q}$. A *numeric constraint* $(\mathsf{e_1 \bowtie e_2})$ compares numeric expressions $\mathsf{e_1}$ and $\mathsf{e_2}$ with $\bowtie \in \{\leq, <, =, \neq\}$. A *condition* is a conjunction of propositions and numeric constraints. A *numeric effect* is a triple $(\mathsf{v_n} \mathrel{\circ=} \mathsf{e})$ where $\mathsf{v_n} \in \mathcal{V}_N$, $\mathrel{\circ=} \in \{:=, +=, -=, \times=, \div=\}$ and e is a numeric expression. Operators $o \in \mathcal{O}$ are of the form $\langle \mathrm{pre} \rightarrow \mathrm{eff} \rangle$ and consist of a condition pre and a set of effects $\mathrm{eff} = \{\mathrm{eff}_1, \dots, \mathrm{eff}_n\}$ containing at most one numeric effect for each numeric variable and at most one truth assignment for each propositional variable.

The semantics of a numeric planning task is straightforward. For constants $c \in \mathbb{Q}$, $s(c) = c$. Numeric expressions $(\mathsf{e_1 \circ e_2})$ for $\circ \in \{+, -, \times, \div\}$ are recursively evaluated in state s: $s(\mathsf{e_1 \circ e_2}) = s(\mathsf{e_1}) \circ s(\mathsf{e_2})$. Satisfaction of conditions in a state s is defined as follows: for propositional variables $\mathsf{v_p} \in \mathcal{V}_P$, $s \vDash \mathsf{v_p}$ iff $s(\mathsf{v_p}) = true$, for numeric constraints $(\mathsf{e_1 \bowtie e_2})$, with expressions $\mathsf{e_1}$, $\mathsf{e_2}$ and $\bowtie \in \{\leq, <, =, \neq\}$,

$s \models (e_1 \bowtie e_2)$ iff $s(e_1) \bowtie s(e_2)$ and finally, for conjunctive conditions $s \models p_1 \wedge p_2$ iff $s \models p_1$ and $s \models p_2$.

An operator $o = \langle \text{pre} \rightarrow \text{eff} \rangle$ is applicable in s iff $s \models \text{pre}$ and if for none of its numeric effects a division by zero occurs. The successor state $\text{app}_o(s) = s'$ resulting from an application of o is defined as follows: if $\text{eff}_i \in \{\text{eff}_1, \ldots, \text{eff}_n\}$ is a numeric effect $v_n \circ= e$ with $\circ= \in \{+=, -=, \times=, \div=\}$, then $s'(v_n) = s(v_n) \circ s(e)$. If eff_i is a numeric effect $v_n := e$, then $s'(v_n) = s(e)$. If eff_i is a propositional effect $v_p := e_p$ with $e_p \in \{true, false\}$, then $s'(v_p)$ is the new truth value e_p. Finally, if a variable v does not occur in any effect, then $s'(v) = s(v)$.

A plan π is a sequence of actions that leads from $\mathcal{I}$ to a state satisfying $\mathcal{G}$ such that each action is applicable in the state that follows by executing the plan up to that action. We intend to relax numeric planning with the help of intervals. The next section recalls the foundations of interval arithmetic.

2.2   Interval Arithmetic

Interval arithmetic uses an upper and a lower bound to enclose the actual value of a number. Closed intervals $[\underline{x}, \overline{x}] = \{q \in \mathbb{Q}^\infty \mid \underline{x} \leq q \leq \overline{x}\}$ contain all rational numbers from $\underline{x}$ to $\overline{x}$. Throughout this paper we refer to the lower bound of an interval x by $\underline{x}$ and to the upper bound by $\overline{x}$. The set $\mathbb{I}_c = \{[\underline{x}, \overline{x}] \mid \underline{x} \leq \overline{x}\}$ contains all closed intervals. Numbers q can be identified with the degenerate interval $[q, q]$. In interval arithmetic, the basic operations are given as:

- addition: $[\underline{x}, \overline{x}] + [\underline{y}, \overline{y}] = [\underline{x} + \underline{y}, \overline{x} + \overline{y}]$,
- subtraction: $[\underline{x}, \overline{x}] - [\underline{y}, \overline{y}] = [\underline{x} - \overline{y}, \overline{x} - \underline{y}]$,
- multiplication: $[\underline{x}, \overline{x}] \times [\underline{y}, \overline{y}] = \left[\min(\underline{xy}, \underline{x}\overline{y}, \overline{x}\underline{y}, \overline{xy}), \max(\underline{xy}, \underline{x}\overline{y}, \overline{x}\underline{y}, \overline{xy})\right]$,
- division: $[\underline{x}, \overline{x}] \div [\underline{y}, \overline{y}] = \left[\min\left(\underline{x}/\underline{y}, \underline{x}/\overline{y}, \overline{x}/\underline{y}, \overline{x}/\overline{y}\right), \max\left(\underline{x}/\underline{y}, \underline{x}/\overline{y}, \overline{x}/\underline{y}, \overline{x}/\overline{y}\right)\right]$
  if $0 \notin [\underline{y}, \overline{y}]$. Otherwise, at least one of the bounds diverges to $\pm\infty$. We do not explicate all cases of $\underline{x}, \overline{x}, \underline{y}$ and $\overline{y}$ being positive, zero or negative, which determine which of the bounds diverge and refer to the literature [9].

Analogously we define open intervals $(\underline{x}, \overline{x}) = \{q \in \mathbb{Q}^\infty \mid \underline{x} < q < \overline{x}\}$ and the set of open intervals $\mathbb{I}_o = \{(\underline{x}, \overline{x}) \mid \underline{x} < \overline{x}\}$, as well as half open intervals $[\underline{x}, \overline{x}) = \{q \in \mathbb{Q}^\infty \mid \underline{x} \leq q < \overline{x}\}$ and $(\underline{x}, \overline{x}] = \{q \in \mathbb{Q}^\infty \mid \underline{x} < q \leq \overline{x}\}$ and the respective sets $\mathbb{I}_{co} = \{[\underline{x}, \overline{x}) \mid \underline{x} < \overline{x}\}$ and $\mathbb{I}_{oc} = \{(\underline{x}, \overline{x}] \mid \underline{x} < \overline{x}\}$. Finally the set of mixed-bounded intervals is given as $\mathbb{I}_m = \mathbb{I}_c \cup \mathbb{I}_o \cup \mathbb{I}_{oc} \cup \mathbb{I}_{co}$. Open and mixed-bounded intervals follow the same arithmetic rules as closed intervals. Whenever open and closed bounds contribute to the new interval bound, the bound is open.

Definition 1. *Let* $x, y \in \mathbb{I}_m$ *be intervals. The* convex union $u = x \sqcup y$ *is the interval with* $\underline{u} = \min(\underline{x}, \underline{y})$ *and* $\overline{u} = \max(\overline{x}, \overline{y})$. *Whether the bounds of* u *are open or closed depends on whether those of* x *and* y *are open or closed.*

If $x \cap y = \emptyset$, u also includes intermediate values not present in either x or y.

3 Delete Relaxation

In this section, we discuss extensions of delete relaxation to numeric planning. The idea behind delete relaxation is that values of a variable that are achieved once remain achieved. We discuss several ways to extend this concept to numeric planning.

Accumulation Semantics. In the accumulation semantics, instead of *changing* their values, variables *accumulate* all values achieved so far. The number of accumulated values after k parallel steps is finite, but generally exponential in k. Therefore, it quickly becomes infeasible to maintain the set of possible values, as can be seen in the task with $o_1 = \langle \emptyset \to \{x \mathrel{+}= 1\}\rangle$, $o_2 = \langle \emptyset \to \{x \mathrel{\div}= 2\}\rangle$ and $\mathcal{I}(x) = 0$. Denoting by x_k, $k = 0, \ldots, 3$, the possible values of x after k parallel steps, we get $x_0 = \{0\}$, $x_1 = \{0, 1\}$, $x_2 = \{0, \frac{1}{2}, 1, 2\}$ and $x_3 = \{0, \frac{1}{4}, \frac{1}{2}, 1, \frac{3}{2}, 2, 3\}$. Besides this observation for *bounded* plan existence, one can also show that *unbounded* plan existence wrt. the accumulation semantics is still undecidable. To see this, we can adapt the undecidability proof for numeric planning by Helmert [7]. A reduction of the search for solutions to Diophantine equations to numeric planning wrt. the accumulation semantics shows that the latter problem is undecidable, since solutions to Diophantine equations have to be integers and the delete relaxation does not relax this property.

Accumulation Semantics for Positive Tasks. One possible approach to dealing with the exploding number of accumulated values is the restriction to tasks where higher values are always better. Then, instead of storing *all values* a variable has attained so far, it is sufficient to store (an upper bound on) the *highest value*. A sufficient criterion for this is that all preconditions and goals have the form $(x > c)$ or $(x \geq c)$, where x is a numeric variable and c a constant, and that all numeric effects only add or subtract a positive constant to or from a variable. The Metric-FF planner uses this type of relaxation, and Hoffmann [8] shows that a large class of problems can be compiled into the required linear normal form.

Interval Relaxation. One can handle a larger class of tasks with higher precision by only making the assumption that one of the *extreme* values, the highest or lowest, is best. This necessitates keeping track of two values for each variable, a lower bound $\underline{x}$ and an upper bound $\overline{x}$. As long as preconditions and goals are comparisons of variables to constants and effects only add or subtract constants, it is insubstantial whether one considers the values between $\underline{x}$ and $\overline{x}$ reached or not. By considering the entire interval reached in a relaxed sense, one can handle even more expressive tasks. In particular, when allowing divisions in effects, besides "higher values are better" and "lower values are better", one also has the objective "values closer to c are better" for constants c. Then, if c is in the interval between $\underline{x}$ and $\overline{x}$, one may assume that values arbitrarily close to c can be reached, whereas otherwise, one can assess the proximity to c achieved so far. Since the algebraic base operations that are allowed in PDDL are also supported by interval arithmetic, we consider interval relaxation a viable approach and focus on it in the following section.

4   Interval Relaxation

This section elaborates on interval relaxation for numeric planning tasks. We discuss the complexity of the plan existence problem for the presented semantics.

The interval relaxation of a numeric planning task differs only marginally from the original task description on a syntactic level. The domains of variables are change and propositional variables can now be both true and false at the same time whereas numeric variables are mapped to closed intervals.

Definition 2. *Let Π be a numeric planning task. The* interval delete relaxation *$\Pi^+ = \langle \mathcal{V}_P^+, \mathcal{V}_N^+, \mathcal{O}^+, \mathcal{I}^+, \mathcal{G}^+ \rangle$ of Π is a 5-tuple where $\mathcal{V}_P^+$ are the propositional variables from Π with the domains replaced by $\mathrm{dom}(v_p) = \{true, false, both\}$ and $\mathcal{V}_N^+$ are the numeric variables with the domains replaced by closed intervals $\mathrm{dom}(v_n) = \mathbb{I}_c$ for all $v_n \in \mathcal{V}_N^+$. The initial state $\mathcal{I}^+$ is derived from $\mathcal{I}$ by replacing numbers $\mathcal{I}(v_n)$ with degenerate intervals $\mathcal{I}^+(v_n) = [\mathcal{I}(v_n), \mathcal{I}(v_n)]$ and $\mathcal{I}^+(v_p) = \mathcal{I}(v_p)$. Operators $\mathcal{O}^+ = \mathcal{O}$ and the goal condition $\mathcal{G}^+ = \mathcal{G}$ remain unchanged.*

The semantics of Π^+ draws on interval arithmetic. *Numeric expressions* are defined recursively. Constant expressions are interpreted as $s^+(c) = [c, c]$ and compound expressions e_1 and e_2 as $s^+(e_1 \circ e_2) = s^+(e_1) \circ s^+(e_2)$ for $\circ \in \{+, -, \times, \div\}$ where "$\circ$" now operates on intervals. For (goal and operator) conditions, the relaxed semantics is defined as follows: let $v_p \in \mathcal{V}_P^+$ be a propositional variable, then $s^+ \vDash v_p$ iff $s^+(v_p) \in \{true, both\}$. For numeric constraints let e_1 and e_2 be numeric expressions, and $\bowtie \in \{<, \leq, =, \neq\}$ a comparison operator. Then $s^+ \vDash (e_1 \bowtie e_2)$ iff $\exists q_1 \in s^+(e_1), \exists q_2 \in s^+(e_2)$ with $q_1 \bowtie q_2$. This implies that two intervals can be "greater" and "less" than each other at once.

The "values remain achieved" idea for numeric effects $v_n \circ= e$ is obtained by the semantics in that v_n keeps its old value and gains all values up to the new value, which is an interval in the relaxation. The state $\mathrm{app}_o^+(s^+) = s'^+$ resulting from an application of o is then $s'^+(v_n) = s^+(v_n) \sqcup (s^+(v_n) \circ s^+(e))$ if $\mathrm{eff}_i \in \{\mathrm{eff}_1, \dots, \mathrm{eff}_n\}$ is a numeric effect. As we use the convex union from Definition 1, $s'^+(v_n)$ contains all values between the old value of v_n and the evaluated expression $(s^+(v_n) \circ s^+(e))$. For propositional effects, $s'^+(v_p) = both$ if the effect changes the truth value $\mathrm{eff}_i(v_p) \neq s^+(v_p)$ of v_p, and $s'^+(v_p) = s^+(v_p)$ otherwise. Again, $s'^+(v) = s^+(v)$ if v occurs in no effect. A relaxed plan is defined in the obvious way.

Example 1. Applying $o = \langle \emptyset \rightarrow \{x \times= e\} \rangle$ in a state with $x = [8, 10]$ and $e = [-\frac{1}{2}, \frac{1}{2}]$ leads to $s'(x) = [8, 10] \sqcup ([8, 10] \times [-\frac{1}{2}, \frac{1}{2}]) = [8, 10] \sqcup [-5, 5] = [-5, 10]$.

To compute relaxed plans, we can proceed as in classical planning: there, a relaxed plan can be found by iteratively applying all applicable operators to the current relaxed state in parallel, and terminating if either a fix-point is reached or the current relaxed state satisfies the goal condition. As no effect can invalidate any condition in the relaxed task, the number of iterations is restricted by the number of operators in the task. A serialized plan can be obtained by ordering parallel actions arbitrarily.

For interval relaxed numeric planning, we have to take into account that numeric operators may have to be applied arbitrarily often. Our idea is to transform the planning task into a semi-symbolic representation that captures repeated application of operators with numeric effects. We define *repetition relaxed* planning tasks, where we simulate the behavior of applying numeric effects arbitrarily often *independently*. As we will see later, the independence assumption is not justified for numeric effects $v_n \circ= e$ where the expression of e depends on the affected variable v_n. However, we can find plans for tasks with *acyclic dependencies* in polynomial time with our approach.

Repetition relaxed planning tasks use mixed-bounded intervals to capture the attainable values of a numeric variable. We are interested in the behavior of numeric effects in the limit. If an operator o has an additive effect $x \pm= e$ for $\pm= \in \{+=, -=\}$ that can extend a bound of x once, it can extend that bound to any value by applying o multiple times. The result of applying an additive effect arbitrarily often in a state s only depends on whether e can be negative, zero or positive. The behavior of multiplicative effects $*= \in \{\times=, \div=\}$ is slightly more complex. Multiplicative effects $x *= e$ can *contract* or *expand* depending on whether e contains elements with absolute value greater one and switch signs if e contains negative elements, resulting in up to seven different behaviors of e.

Definition 3. *Let Π^+ be an interval relaxed planning task. The* repetition relaxation *of Π^+ is a 5-tuple $\Pi^\# = \langle V_P^+, V_N^\#, \mathcal{O}^\#, \mathcal{I}^\#, \mathcal{G}^\# \rangle$ with propositional variables V_P^+ from Π^+. The domains of numeric variables $\mathrm{dom}(v_n) = \mathbb{I}_m$ for $v_n \in V_N^\#$ are extended to mixed-bounded intervals. The initial state $\mathcal{I}^\#$ maps variables to the same truth (for propositional variables v_p) respectively the same closed degenerate interval (for numeric variables v_n) from $\mathcal{I}^+$. Operators $\mathcal{O}^\# = \mathcal{O}^+$ and the goal condition $\mathcal{G}^\# = \mathcal{G}^+$ remain unchanged.*

Again, the relaxations differ mainly in the semantics of numeric effects. The semantics of *numeric expressions* is transferred directly from the interval relaxation as interval arithmetic operations are also defined for mixed-bounded intervals. The interpretation of a numeric expression is given as $s^\#(e_1 \circ e_2) = s^\#(e_1) \circ s^\#(e_2)$ for expressions e_1 and e_2 and $\circ \in \{+, -, \times, \div\}$. The semantics of conditions is $s^\# \models v_p$ iff $s^\#(v_p) \in \{true, both\}$ for propositions $v_p \in V_P^\#$. For numeric constraints, where e_1 and e_2 are expressions and $\bowtie \in \{<, \leq, =, \neq\}$ is a comparison operator, $s^\# \models (e_1 \bowtie e_2)$ iff $\exists q_1 \in s^\#(e_1), \exists y \in s^\#(e_2)$ with $q_1 \bowtie q_2$.

The semantics of *numeric effects* captures the repeated application of actions. We first define the *repetition relaxed* semantics of $x \circ= e$ for intervals x and e with $\circ= \in \{:=, +=, -=, \times=, \div=\}$. Let $x_0 = x$ and $x_{k+1} = x_k \sqcup (x_k \circ e)$ for $k \geq 0$ where $(x : e)$ is defined as e for assign effects. Let $\mathrm{succ}_\circ(x, e) = \bigcup_{k=0}^{\infty} x_k$. We are interested in the result of applying an operator arbitrarily often individually for each effect, where the interval e is fixed even if the expression e depends on x. As $x_{k+1} \supseteq x_k$ by definition of the convex union and because all x_k are convex, the resulting set $\mathrm{succ}_\circ(x, e)$ is an interval. However, open intervals can be generated in the limit. The state $\mathrm{app}_o^\#(s^\#) = s'^\#$ resulting from an application of o with effect $\mathrm{eff} = \{\mathrm{eff}_1, \ldots, \mathrm{eff}_n\}$ is again $s'^\#(v) = s^\#(v)$ if v

Table 1. Partial behaviors for numeric effects

$+\!=$	$\tilde{e}$		
	$(-\infty,0)$	$\{0\}$	$(0,\infty)$
$\tilde{x}\ (-\infty,\infty)$	$(-\infty,\overline{x}\rangle$	$\langle\underline{x},\overline{x}\rangle$	$\langle\underline{x},\infty)$

$-\!=$	$\tilde{e}$		
	$(-\infty,0)$	$\{0\}$	$(0,\infty)$
$\tilde{x}\ (-\infty,\infty)$	$\langle\underline{x},\infty)$	$\langle\underline{x},\overline{x}\rangle$	$(-\infty,\overline{x}\rangle$

$\times\!=$	$\tilde{e}$						
	$(-\infty,-1)$	$\{-1\}$	$(-1,0)$	$\{0\}$	$(0,1)$	$\{1\}$	$(1,\infty)$
$\tilde{x}$ $(-\infty,0)$	$(-\infty,\infty)$	$\langle\underline{x},-\underline{x}\rangle$	$\langle\underline{x},\underline{x}\times\underline{e}\rangle$	$\langle\underline{x},0]$	$\langle\underline{x},0)$	$\langle\underline{x},\overline{x}\rangle$	$(-\infty,\overline{x}\rangle$
$\{0\}$	$[0,0]$						
$(0,\infty)$	$(-\infty,\infty)$	$\langle-\overline{x},\overline{x}\rangle$	$\langle\overline{x}\times\underline{e},\overline{x}\rangle$	$[0,\overline{x}\rangle$	$(0,\overline{x}\rangle$	$\langle\underline{x},\overline{x}\rangle$	$\langle\underline{x},\infty)$

$\div\!=$	$\tilde{e}$						
	$(-\infty,-1)$	$\{-1\}$	$(-1,0)$	$\{0\}$	$(0,1)$	$\{1\}$	$(1,\infty)$
$\tilde{x}$ $(-\infty,0)$	$\langle\underline{x},\underline{x}\div\overline{e}\rangle$	$\langle\underline{x},-\underline{x}\rangle$	$(-\infty,\infty)$	undefined	$(-\infty,\overline{x}\rangle$	$\langle\underline{x},\overline{x}\rangle$	$\langle\underline{x},0)$
$\{0\}$	$[0,0]$			undefined	$[0,0]$		
$(0,\infty)$	$\langle\overline{x}\div\overline{e},\overline{x}\rangle$	$\langle-\overline{x},\overline{x}\rangle$	$(-\infty,\infty)$	undefined	$\langle\underline{x},\infty)$	$\langle\underline{x},\overline{x}\rangle$	$(0,\overline{x}\rangle$

occurs in no effect, $s'^{\#}(v_p) = both$ if $\mathrm{eff}_i(v_p) \neq s^{\#}(v_p)$ is a propositional effect changing the truth value of v_p and $s'^{\#}(v_p) = s^{\#}(v_p)$ otherwise. For numeric effects $\mathrm{eff}_i = (v_n \circ\!\!=\, e)$, $s'^{\#}(v_n) = \mathrm{succ}_\circ(s^{\#}(v_n), s^{\#}(e))$. Repetition relaxed plans are defined in the obvious way.

Fixing expressions e of numeric effects to the interval e they evaluate to in the previous state is beneficial to compute the successor, as changes in the assignment (which can be an arbitrary arithmetic expression) do not have to be considered immediately. The repetition relaxation $\Pi^{\#}$ of a planning task relaxes Π^{+} further and plans for Π^{+} are still plans for $\Pi^{\#}$. The reason is that each operator application can only extend the interval of affected numeric variables.

We want to use the fix-point algorithm that applies all operators of a planning task in parallel until a fix-point is reached to find a repetition relaxed plan. The successors $\mathrm{succ}_\circ(x,e)$ of numeric effects are defined by the limit $\bigcup_{i=0}^{\infty} x_i$ and we are interested in determining the result of such an effect in constant time. The result only depends on which of up to 21 symbolic *behavior classes* are covered by x and e. The *behavior classes* for x are $\mathcal{B}_x = \{(-\infty,0), \{0\}, (0,\infty)\}$, and for e they are $\mathcal{B}_e = \{(-\infty,-1), \{-1\}, (-1,0), \{0\}, (0,1), \{1\}, (1,\infty)\}$. We decompose e and x into the behavior classes they hit, i.e, where $e \cap \tilde{e} \neq \emptyset$ for a behavior class $\tilde{e} \in \mathcal{B}_e$ and $x \cap \tilde{x} \neq \emptyset$ for a behavior class $\tilde{x} \in \mathcal{B}_x$, respectively. Table 1 contains partial behaviors $\mathcal{T}_\circ(x,e)$ for $\circ\!\!=\, \in \{+\!=, -\!=, \times\!=, \div\!=\}$ where $\mathcal{T}_\circ(x,e)$ is only defined if $x \subseteq \tilde{x} \in \mathcal{B}_x$ and $e \subseteq \tilde{e} \in \mathcal{B}_e$ and $\mathcal{T}_\circ(x,e)$ is the table entry with column $\tilde{x}$ and row $\tilde{e}$ in the table with the corresponding $\circ\!\!=$ operator. We use "indeterminate" parentheses $(\lfloor\cdot, \bar{\cdot}\rceil)$ to denote intervals whose openness is determined by the contributing terms. For assignment effects $:=$ we do not need a table as $\mathcal{T}_{:}(x,e) = (\!\lceil\min(\underline{x},\underline{e}), \max(\overline{x},\overline{e})\rceil\!)$ for all classes. Division by zero is undefined for degenerate intervals $[0,0]$. Otherwise, the union over partial behaviors can ignore "undefined" entries. If a division by zero would occur in the original problem, the causing operator is not applicable. Therefore, actual division by zero neither occurs in the relaxation.

Theorem 1. *The partial behaviors* $\mathcal{T}_\circ(x, e)$ *equal* $\mathrm{succ}_\circ(x, e)$ *for* $x \subseteq \tilde{x} \in \mathcal{B}_x$ *and* $e \subseteq \tilde{e} \in \mathcal{B}_e$. $\qquad\qquad\qquad\qquad\qquad\qquad\qquad\qquad\qquad\qquad\qquad\square$

Theorem 1 is shown exemplarily for "$\times=$", $\tilde{x} = (0, \infty), \tilde{e} = (0, 1)$ and for "$\div=$", $\tilde{x} = (-\infty, 0)$ and $\tilde{e} = (-\infty, -1)$ in the workshop version of this paper [1]. For each $q \in \mathcal{T}_\circ(x, e)$, we obtain a number of iterated assignments sufficient to reach q as a byproduct of the proof.

With such a decomposition, numeric effects can now be computed in constant time. Unfortunately, the union of the partial behaviors of an effect does not equal the succeeding interval according to the semantics.

Hypothesis 1. *The successor* $\mathrm{succ}_\circ(x, e)$ *of an effect* $x \circ = e$ *is the union of the successors obtained by decomposition of the effect into behavior classes, i.e.* $\bigcup_{\tilde{x}\in\mathcal{B}_x,\tilde{e}\in\mathcal{B}_e} \mathrm{succ}_\circ(x \cap \tilde{x}, e \cap \tilde{e}) = \mathrm{succ}_\circ(x, e)$ *for* $\mathrm{succ}_\circ(\emptyset, e) = \mathrm{succ}_\circ(x, \emptyset) = \emptyset$.

Hypothesis 1 does not hold in general, as the following example illustrates. The successor can grow into behavior classes which were not covered initially:

Example 2. Let $o = \langle \emptyset \rightarrow \{x \times = e\} \rangle$ have an effect on x in a state with $x = [1, 4]$ and $e = [-\frac{1}{2}, 2]$. The partial behaviors are $\mathrm{succ}_\times(x, [-\frac{1}{2}, 0)) = [-2, 4]$, $\mathrm{succ}_\times(x, [0, 0]) = [0, 4]$, $\mathrm{succ}_\times(x, (0, 1)) = (0, 4]$, $\mathrm{succ}_\times(x, [1, 1]) = [1, 4]$ and finally $\mathrm{succ}_\times(x, (1, 2]) = [1, \infty)$. However, the union $\bigcup_{\tilde{x}\in\mathcal{B}_x,\tilde{e}\in\mathcal{B}_e} \mathrm{succ}_\times(x\cap\tilde{x}, e\cap\tilde{e})$ $= [-2, \infty)$, differs from $\mathrm{succ}_\times(x, e) = (-\infty, \infty)$.

However, the number of behavior classes is restricted, and therefore, new classes can only be hit a restricted number of times. We correct the hypothesis by including the partial behaviors $\mathcal{T}_\circ(x, e)$ of the classes hit by x in a nested fix-point iteration: Let $x_0 = x$ and $x_{j+1} = \bigcup_{\tilde{x}\in\mathcal{B}_x,\tilde{e}\in\mathcal{B}_e} \mathrm{succ}_\circ(x_j \cap \tilde{x}, e \cap \tilde{e})$ with $\mathrm{succ}_\circ(\emptyset, e) = \mathrm{succ}_\circ(x, \emptyset) = \emptyset$ for $j \geq 0$. Let $\widetilde{\mathrm{succ}}_\circ(x, e) = \bigcup_{j=0}^{\infty} x_j$. Now, newly attained behavior classes become part of the decomposition in the next iteration.

Example 3. Recall Example 2 starting with $x_0 = x = [1, 4]$ where the successor $\mathrm{succ}_\times(x_0 \cap \tilde{x}, e \cap \tilde{e})$ equals $[-2, \infty)$. The decomposition over the newly achieved behavior classes with $x_1 = [-2, \infty)$ and $e = [-\frac{1}{2}, 2]$ contains among others the successor $\mathrm{succ}_\times([-2, 0), (1, 2]) = (-\infty, 0)$. The union still contains partial behaviors that set the upper bound to ∞, so $\mathrm{succ}_\times(x_1 \cap \tilde{x}, e \cap \tilde{e}) = (-\infty, \infty)$. Now, a fix-point is reached and $\widetilde{\mathrm{succ}}_\circ(x, e) = \mathrm{succ}_\circ(x, e)$.

Lemma 1. *The sequence of* x_j *converges to* $\widetilde{\mathrm{succ}}_\circ(x, e)$ *after at most 3 steps.*

Proof sketch. The number of behaviors in each class is restricted to $|\mathcal{B}_x| = 3$ and $|\mathcal{B}_e| = 7$. Most partial behaviors $\mathcal{T}_\circ(x, e)$ either set a new bound to a certain value (0 or $\pm\infty$), or leave a bound of x unchanged. The only unsafe cases are multiplications or divisions of a bound with -1 or e. However, none of these cases is problematic because e is fixed: $\mathcal{T}_\times(x, e)$ with $x \subseteq \tilde{x} = (-\infty, 0)$ and $e \subseteq \tilde{e} = (-1, 0)$ sets a new upper bound $\underline{x} \times \underline{e} > 0$. However, for all classes $\mathcal{T}_\times(x, e)$ with $x \subseteq \tilde{x} = (0, \infty)$, the upper bound is either set to ∞ or it remains the same. Therefore no problematic interactions occur. The same reasoning holds for $\mathcal{T}_\times(x, e)$ with $x \subseteq \tilde{x} = (0, \infty)$ and $e \subseteq \tilde{e} = (-1, 0)$ as well as $\mathcal{T}_\div(x, e)$ with $e \subseteq \tilde{e} = (-\infty, -1)$. As e remains fixed x can change at most 3 times. □

We reformulate the feasibility of the decomposition to the following Theorem:

Theorem 2. *The successor* $\mathrm{succ}_\circ(x, e)$ *of an effect* $x \circ = e$ *is the fix-point of the convex union of the successors obtained by decomposition of the effect into behavior classes, i.e.* $\widetilde{\mathrm{succ}}_\circ(x, e) = \mathrm{succ}_\circ(x, e)$.

Proof sketch. To see that $\widetilde{\mathrm{succ}}_\circ(x, e) \subseteq \mathrm{succ}_\circ(x, e)$ consider the first iteration determining $\widetilde{\mathrm{succ}}_\circ(x, e)$: all partial behaviors $\mathrm{succ}_\circ(x \cap \tilde{x}, e \cap \tilde{e})$ are operations on subsets of x and e. As we use the convex union for effects, $\mathrm{succ}_\circ(x, e)$ is monotone in both arguments i.e. $x_1 \subseteq x_2 \wedge e_1 \subseteq e_2 \Rightarrow \mathrm{succ}_\circ(x_1, e_1) \subseteq \mathrm{succ}_\circ(x_2, e_2)$. During each iteration determining $\widetilde{\mathrm{succ}}_\circ(x, e)$, the decomposition can only grow to behavior classes that were part of $\mathrm{succ}_\circ(x, e)$ in the first place. The converse direction $\widetilde{\mathrm{succ}}_\circ(x, e) \supseteq \mathrm{succ}_\circ(x, e)$ is shown by contradiction. Let $q \in \mathrm{succ}_\circ(x, e)$ but not in $\widetilde{\mathrm{succ}}_\circ(x, e)$. Both successor functions are defined recursively starting with $x_0 = x$. Therefore, $q \notin x_0$. Let $x_0, x_1, \ldots$ be the sequence of intervals defining $\mathrm{succ}_\circ(x, e)$. There has to be a $k > 0$ with $x_{k+1} = x_k \sqcup (x_k \circ e)$ so that $x_k \subset \widetilde{\mathrm{succ}}_\circ(x, e)$ but $x_{k+1} \not\subset \widetilde{\mathrm{succ}}_\circ(x, e)$. After k steps, the bound of the successor is extended beyond the decomposition $\widetilde{\mathrm{succ}}_\circ(x, e)$ for the first time. Obviously, the new bound does not originate in x_k but the new interval x_{k+1} is obtained from $(x_k \circ e)$. The resulting interval depends on $\underline{x_k}, \overline{x_k}, \underline{e}, \overline{e}$ and in case of division also on whether $0 \in e$. Each combination of these extreme bounds is contained in one partial behavior $\mathcal{T}_\circ(x_k, e)$. If $(x_k \circ e)$ hits a new behavior class or extends the bounds within a behavior class, this is a contradiction to $\widetilde{\mathrm{succ}}_\circ(x, e)$ being a fix-point. If $(x_k \circ e)$ stays within a behavior, this is a contradiction to $\mathcal{T}_\circ(x_k, e)$ being well defined (Theorem 1). Thus, such a k cannot be found, and therefore, it is impossible for $q \in \mathrm{succ}_\circ(x, e)$ but not $q \in \widetilde{\mathrm{succ}}_\circ(x, e)$. □

With the help of the decomposed successor $\widetilde{\mathrm{succ}}_\circ(x, e)$ we can compute the result of applying an operator $\mathrm{app}_o^\#$ with the repetition relaxed semantics in constant time. This allows us to use the parallel fix-point algorithm from the classical case analogously: apply all applicable operators in parallel until a fix-point is reached.

Theorem 3. *The parallel fix-point algorithm for repetition relaxed planning is sound, i.e. if the algorithm outputs an alleged plan, it is indeed a plan for* $\Pi^\#$.

Proof. Operators are only applied if the precondition is fulfilled. □

Unfortunately, the algorithm does not necessarily terminate. In the definition of the semantics of a repetition relaxed planning task, we fix the effect e even if it depends on x. However, this implicit independence assumption is not justified. Inspecting the entries in Table 1 reveals critical entries (marked in bold gray) for multiplicative effects that contract x and flip the arithmetic sign at the same time. The same is true for assignment effects $\mathcal{T}_:(x, e) = (\!|\min(\underline{x}, \underline{e}), \max(\overline{x}, \overline{e})|\!)$. In these cases, the new value of x can have a different behavior, if e also depends on x. As e can change when x changes, the algorithm does not necessarily terminate.

Example 4. Let $o = \langle \emptyset \rightarrow \{x \times = e\}\rangle$ in a state with $x = [-1, -1]$, $e = -\frac{x+1}{2}$ and goal $\mathcal{G} = \{x \geq 1\}$. Applying the operator arbitrarily often according to the repetition semantics yields the progression for k operator applications depicted to the right. Obviously, interval x does *not* only change a restricted number of times, so the fix-point algorithm for interval relaxed numeric planning will not terminate.

k	x	e
0	$[-1, -1]$	$[0, 0]$
1	$[-1, 0]$	$[-0.5, 0]$
2	$[-1, 0.5]$	$[-0.75, 0]$
3	$[-1, 0.75]$	$[-0.875, 0]$
4	$[-1, 0.875]$	$[-0.9375, 0]$
$\vdots$	$\vdots$	$\vdots$

If we succeeded in directly computing the fix-point to which the intervals converge with a symbolic interval we could continue the fix-point algorithm from here. In Example 4 we would set $x = [-1, 1)$ and $e = (-1, 0]$. Unfortunately, the authors did not succeed in finding a general approach to do so (or to prove that such a general approach does not exist). Instead, we restrict the problem to planning tasks where the aforementioned problem does not occur. The problem in Example 4 is that e depends on x. Thus, we restrict planning tasks to contain only effects where the assigned expression is independent from the affected variable. We show that such planning tasks are solvable in polynomial time.

Definition 4. *A numeric variable v_1 is* directly dependent *on a numeric variable v_2 in task Π if there exists an $o \in \mathcal{O}$ with a numeric effect $v_1 \circ = e$ so that e contains v_2. A planning task with acyclic direct dependency relation is an* acyclic dependency *task.*

Note that a variable can be *directly dependent* on itself. Also, the definition of *direct dependence* does not consider operator applicability.

Theorem 4. *The parallel fix-point algorithm for repetition relaxed planning terminates for acyclic dependency tasks.*

Proof. As the planning task has *acyclic dependencies*, the *direct dependency* relation induces a topology. Let a *phase* of the algorithm be a sequence of parallel operator applications, where no new operator becomes applicable. During each *phase*, we consider numeric effects in topological order concerning the dependency graph. Let $V_N^{\#l} \subseteq V_N^\#$ be the variables in dependency layer l. We iterate over the layers $k \geq 0$ of the topology assuming that a fix-point is reached for all variables $V_N^{\#k}$. Variables $V_N^{\#k+1}$ only depend on variables $V_N^{\#l}$ with $0 \leq l \leq k$ or on constants. A fix-point is reached for all those variables by induction hypothesis. Inductively, we can assume that the expressions of numeric effects that alter the variables of layer $V_N^{\#k+1}$ are fixed. Therefore, the successor $succ_o(x, e)$ of an effect $(x \circ = e)$ with $x = s^\#(x)$ and $e = s^\#(e)$ does not change the variable more than once (or more than 3 times, if we also consider the variable updates of the nested fix-point iteration from Lemma 1).

The number of *phases* is restricted, with the same argument as for the fix-point algorithm in the classical case. Preconditions cannot be invalidated and during each phase at least one previously inapplicable operator must become applicable. The number of phases is therefore restricted to the number of operators in the planning task.   □

Theorem 5. *The fix-point algorithm for repetition relaxed planning is complete for* acyclic dependency *tasks.*

Proof. We prove completeness by contradiction and show that it is impossible that the algorithm terminates and reports unsolvable although a plan exists. Now assume there is a plan, but the algorithm terminates and reports unsolvable. All operators are applied as soon as they are applicable, so a satisfiable condition must have been unsatisfied. For propositional conditions, this is impossible, as $s^{\#}(v_p) \vDash v_p$ if $v_p \in \{true, both\}$ and no effect can set propositional variables to *false*. Therefore, a satisfiable numeric constraint was not achieved by the algorithm. This implies that an effect $(v_n \circ= e)$ would have been able to assign a value to a variable that was not reached by our algorithm. Therefore, the successor defined by the semantics $\text{succ}_{\circ}(s^{\#}(v_n), s^{\#}(e))$ has to be different from the successor computed by the algorithm $\widehat{\text{succ}}_{\circ}(s^{\#}(v_n), s^{\#}(e))$, which is impossible for numeric tasks with Theorem 2, a contradiction.   □

Until now we have an algorithm which can compute parallel plans for repetition relaxed planning tasks in polynomial time for acyclic dependency tasks. As intervals can only grow by applying an operator, the plan can be serialized by applying parallel operators from the same layer in an arbitrary order. Beneficial effects may make the application of some operators unnecessary, but it cannot harm conditions. We are interested in plans for the interval relaxation without the symbolic description of numeric variables. We will now show that we can derive interval relaxed plans π^+ from repetition relaxed plans $\pi^{\#}$.

Theorem 6. *Let $\langle o_1, o_2, \ldots, o_n \rangle$ be a repetition relaxed plan. Then, there exist $k_1, \ldots, k_n \in \mathbb{N}^+$ such that $\langle o_1^{k_1}, o_2^{k_2}, \ldots, o_n^{k_n} \rangle$ is an interval relaxed plan, where $o_i^{k_i}$ denotes a sequence of k_i repetitions of operator o_i.*   □

A proof of Theorem 6 can be found in the workshop version of this paper [1]. The idea is to explicate the number of operator applications from a plan obtained by the fix-point algorithm for repetition relaxed planning. For each numeric constraint we determine a target value in the open intervals, which is sufficient to satisfy that constraint. The number of required operator applications k_i to reach the target value is obtained from the proof of Theorem 1.

Example 5. Let $x = [0, 1)$, $y = [0, 1)$ and $z = (1.7, 3]$ be the symbolic values of variables x, y and z with a condition $x+y > z$. From $e_a = x+y \mapsto [0, 2)$ and $e_b = z$ we choose an arbitrary $q_a = 1.9 \in s^{\#}(e_a)$ and an arbitrary $q_b = 1.8 \in s^{\#}(e_b)$ from within the expression intervals so that the constraint is satisfied. We have to recursively find appropriate q_x and q_y in the sub-expressions. A leeway of $2 - 1.9 = 0.1$ can be distributed to the target values of the sub-expressions. We could continue with target values 0.95 for x and y each. Let $x = [0, 1)$ be obtained from a repetition relaxed operator $o_1 = \langle \emptyset \rightarrow \{x := (a + 1)\} \rangle$, $a = [-1, -1]$, which induces a target value of -0.05 for a. Let now $o_2 = \langle \emptyset \rightarrow \{a \div= 2\} \rangle$ be the operator that manipulated a in the repetition relaxed plan. The explicated number of operator applications for o_2 is obtained by solving $-0.05 = -1 \div 2^k$ so $k \approx 4.3$ and o_2 has to be applied 5 times.

Theorem 7. *The problem to generate an interval relaxed numeric plan is in P for tasks with* acyclic dependencies.

Proof. The fix-point algorithm for repetition relaxed planning tasks is sound (Theorem 3), complete (Theorem 5) and terminates in polynomial time (Theorem 4). Thus, generating a repetition relaxed plan $\pi^\#$ is in P. An interval relaxed plan π^+ can be constructed from $\pi^\#$ (Theorem 6) in polynomial time.   □

The definition of a relaxation is *adequate* [8] if it is *admissible*, i.e. any plan π for the original task Π is also a relaxed plan for Π^+, if it offers *basic informedness*, i.e. the empty plan is a plan for Π iff it is a plan for Π^+ and finally the plan existence problem for the relaxation is in P.

Theorem 8. *The* interval relaxation *is adequate for* acyclic dependency *tasks*.

Proof. Admissibility: After each step of the original plan π, the propositional variables are either equal in the relaxed and in the original state, or they assign to *both*, which cannot invalidate any (goal or operator) conditions. For numeric variables, the value of the original task is contained in the mapped interval. Admissibility follows from the semantics of comparison constraints that hold if they do for any pair of elements from the two intervals. *Basic informedness:* No (goal or operator) conditions are dropped from the task. Relaxed numeric variables are mapped to degenerate intervals that only contain one element. Therefore, conditions in the original task $x \bowtie y$ correspond to interval constraints $[x, x] \bowtie [y, y]$, which are satisfied iff they are satisfied in the relaxed task. *Polynomiality:* As a corollary to Theorem 7, we can also conclude that interval relaxed numeric plan existence is in P for tasks with *acyclic dependencies*.   □

5   Conclusion and Future Work

We presented interval algebra as a means to carry the concept of a delete relaxation from classical to numeric planning. We proved that this relaxation is adequate for *acyclic dependency tasks*, tasks where the expressions of numeric effects do not depend on the affected variable. The proposed relaxation advances the state of the art even though adequacy of interval relaxation was only shown for the restricted set of *acyclic dependency* tasks. However, the requirement of acyclic dependency for numeric expressions is a proper generalization of expressions e being required to be constant, a requirement for other state-of-the-art approaches, e.g. [8], which is met in many practically relevant problems. The complexity of the approach for arbitrary interval relaxed planning problems remains an open research issue, though. It is imaginable that the fixpoint reached by arbitrary operator repetitions can be found in polynomial time.

In the future, we intend to adapt the well-known heuristics from classical planning, h_{max}, h_{add} and h_{FF}, to the interval relaxation framework.

Acknowledgments. This work was supported by the DFG grant EXC1086 BrainLinks-BrainTools and the DFG grant SFB/TR 14 AVACS to the University of Freiburg, Germany.

References

1. Aldinger, J., Mattmüller, R., Göbelbecker, M.: Complexity issues of interval relaxed numeric planning. In: Proceedings of the ICAPS-15 Workshop on Heuristics and Search for Domain-Independent Planning (HSDIP 2015), pp. 4–12 (2015)
2. Bäckström, C., Nebel, B.: Complexity results for SAS$^+$ planning. In: Proceedings of the 13th International Joint Conference on Artificial Intelligence (IJCAI 1993), pp. 1430–1435 (1993)
3. Bofill, M., Arxer, J.E., Villaret, M.: The RANTANPLAN planner: system description. In: Proceedings of the ICAPS-15 Workshop on Constraint Satisfaction Techniques for Planning and Scheduling Problems (COPLAPS 2015), pp. 1–10 (2015)
4. Bylander, T.: The Computational Complexity of Propositional STRIPS Planning. Artificial Intelligence **69**, 165–204 (1994)
5. Coles, A., Fox, M., Long, D., Smith, A.: A hybrid relaxed planning graph-LP heuristic for numeric planning domains. In: Proceedings of the 20th International Conference on Automated Planning and Search (ICAPS 2008), pp. 52–59 (2008)
6. Fox, M., Long, D.: PDDL2.1 : An Extension to PDDL for Expressing Temporal Planning Domains. Journal of Artificial Intelligence Research (JAIR) **20**, 61–124 (2003)
7. Helmert, M.: Decidability and undecidability results for planning with numerical state variables. In: Proceedings of the 6th International Conference on Artificial Intelligence Planning and Scheduling (AIPS 2002), pp. 303–312 (2002)
8. Hoffmann, J.: The Metric-FF Planning System: Translating 'Ignoring Delete Lists' to Numeric State Variables. Journal of Artificial Intelligence Research (JAIR) **20**, 291–341 (2003)
9. Moore, R.E., Kearfott, R.B., Cloud, M.J.: Introduction to Interval Analysis. Society for Industrial and Applied Mathematics (2009)
10. Young, R.C.: The Algebra of Many-valued Quantities. Mathematische Annalen **104**, 260–290 (1931)

Oddness-Based Classifiers for Boolean or Numerical Data

Myriam Bounhas[1,2]([✉]), Henri Prade[3,4], and Gilles Richard[3,4]

[1] LARODEC Laboratory, ISG de Tunis, 41 Rue de la Liberté,
2000 Le Bardo, Tunisia
myriam_bounhas@yahoo.fr
[2] Emirates College of Technology, P.O. Box: 41009,
Abu Dhabi, United Arab Emirates
[3] IRIT – CNRS, 118, Route de Narbonne, Toulouse, France
{prade,richard}@irit.fr
[4] QCIS, University of Technology, Sydney, Australia

Abstract. The paper proposes an oddness measure for estimating the extent to which a new item is at odds with a class. Then a simple classification procedure based on the minimization of oddness with respect to the different classes is proposed. Experiments on standard benchmarks with Boolean or numerical data provide good results. The global oddness measure is based on the estimation of the oddness of the new item with respect to the subsets of the classes having a given size.

1 Introduction

It is a commonsense principle to consider that a class cannot be reasonably assigned to a new item if this item would appear to be odd with respect to the known members of the class. On the contrary, the item should be even with respect to these class members for entering the class. A particular implementation of this principle has been recently explored in [3] by judging to what extent the item conforms with the majority of elements in any triple of members of the class. The idea of considering triples as a basis for estimating the evenness of the item with respect to the class has been motivated by two facts. First, triples are the only subsets where when the new item conforms with the minority, there is no longer any majority (with respect to a given feature) in the triple augmented with the new item. Second, being odd with respect to three other elements is closely connected with the idea of heterogeneous logical proportions, themselves dual of the homogeneous logical proportions where analogical proportion is a prominent case [9] (also used successfully in classification [4,7]).

Although, rather competitive results have been obtained for Boolean data on benchmarks, it is unclear how to extend the above evenness-based approach to numerical data. In this paper, we propose a slightly different view of the estimation of oddness, which in the case of triples can still be related to heterogeneous logical proportions, but may apply as well to subsets of any size, and can be

© Springer International Publishing Switzerland 2015
S. Hölldobler et al. (Eds.): KI 2015, LNAI 9324, pp. 32–44, 2015.
DOI: 10.1007/978-3-319-24489-1_3

extended to numerical features in a straightforward manner. Good results can be then obtained for both Boolean and numerical data, as we shall see.

Our paper is structured as follows. In Section 2, we first provide a brief background about logical proportions and we demonstrate the ability of heterogeneous proportions to identify an intruder among a set of 4 elements. Their weakness is also highlighted when it comes to deal with multi-valued logic. Moreover, inspired by heterogeneous proportions, we define a new logical formula acting as a marker for the oddness of a fourth item with respect to a set of 3 elements. Oddness is expressed by a concise formula in the Boolean and multi-valued settings, since the Boolean expression easily extends to numerical data. In Section 3, we show that the proposed oddness measure extends to subsets of any size, and can be the basis for estimating the oddness of an item with respect to a whole class for a given set of features. In Section 4, we investigate a way to design classifiers based on this new oddness measure. Section 5 is devoted to a set of experiments on standard benchmarks coming from the UCI repository. Finally, we provide some hints for future works and concluding remarks in Section 6.

2   Heterogeneity of an Item with Respect to a Triple

We recall the semantics of heterogeneous proportions in terms of oddness of an item among a set of 4 items. Then, using heterogeneous proportions, we propose a new logical formula, more suitable for expressing oddness, first in the Boolean case, and then in the multiple-valued case.

2.1   Heterogeneous Proportions

Heterogeneous proportions are a particular case of logical proportions. Logical proportions have been defined and studied in [8]. Considering 2 Boolean variables a and b representing a given feature attached to 2 items A and B, $a \wedge b$ and $\overline{a} \wedge \overline{b}$ indicate that A and B behave similarly w.r.t. the given feature ("similarity" indicators), $a \wedge \overline{b}$ and $\overline{a} \wedge b$ the fact that A and B behave differently ("dissimilarity" indicators). When we have 4 items A, B, C, D, for comparing their respective behavior in a pairwise manner, we are led to consider logical equivalences between similarity, or dissimilarity indicators, such as $a \wedge b \equiv c \wedge d$ for instance. A logical proportion T involves 4 items and is the conjunction of two equivalences between indicators such as, for instance:

$$((a \wedge \overline{b}) \equiv (c \wedge \overline{d})) \wedge ((\overline{a} \wedge b) \equiv (\overline{c} \wedge d))$$

It has been established that there are 120 syntactically and semantically distinct logical equivalences. A property which appears to be paramount in many reasoning tasks is *code independency*: there should be no distinction when encoding information positively or negatively. In other words, encoding truth (resp. falsity) with 1 or with 0 (resp. with 0 and 1) is just a matter of convention, and should not impact the final result. When dealing with logical proportions, this property is called *code independency* and can be expressed as

$$T(a, b, c, d) \implies T(\overline{a}, \overline{b}, \overline{c}, \overline{d})$$

We have only 8 code independent proportions, but only 4 among these proportions make use of similarity and dissimilarity indicators by mixing these types of indicators inside one equivalence: for this reason, these 4 proportions denoted H_1, H_2, H_3, H_4 are called *heterogeneous proportions*. Their logical expressions are given below.

$$\mathbf{H_1}: ((a \wedge \overline{b}) \equiv (c \wedge d)) \wedge ((\overline{a} \wedge b) \equiv (\overline{c} \wedge \overline{d}))$$

$$\mathbf{H_2}: ((\overline{a} \wedge b) \equiv (c \wedge d)) \wedge ((a \wedge \overline{b}) \equiv (\overline{c} \wedge \overline{d}))$$

$$\mathbf{H_3}: ((a \wedge b) \equiv (c \wedge \overline{d})) \wedge ((\overline{a} \wedge \overline{b}) \equiv (\overline{c} \wedge d))$$

$$\mathbf{H_4}: ((a \wedge b) \equiv (\overline{c} \wedge d)) \wedge ((\overline{a} \wedge \overline{b}) \equiv (c \wedge \overline{d}))$$

The index i in H_i refers to a position inside the formula $H_i(a, b, c, d)$. The truth tables for heterogeneous proportions are shown below where only the patterns leading to 1 (which make the logical proportion true) are given. Note that every

Table 1. Heterogeneous proportions valid patterns

$\mathbf{H_1}$	$\mathbf{H_2}$	$\mathbf{H_3}$	$\mathbf{H_4}$
1 1 1 0	1 1 1 0	1 1 1 0	1 1 0 1
0 0 0 1	0 0 0 1	0 0 0 1	0 0 1 0
1 1 0 1	1 1 0 1	1 0 1 1	1 0 1 1
0 0 1 0	0 0 1 0	0 1 0 0	0 1 0 0
1 0 1 1	0 1 1 1	0 1 1 1	0 1 1 1
0 1 0 0	1 0 0 0	1 0 0 0	1 0 0 0

H_i is stable w.r.t. any permutation which does not affect position i. Apart from code independency property, heterogeneous proportions have a remarkable semantics which can be seen from their truth tables. H_i is valid iff there is an *intruder* among the 4 parameters a, b, c, d and the value at position i is not this intruder. For instance, $H_1(a, b, c, d)$ implies that the first value a is not an intruder and there is an intruder among the remaining values. It can be checked that $H_1(a, b, c, d)$ is false when there is no intruder (even number of 0 among the values of a, b, c, d) or when a is the intruder. In other words, this means that either b or c or d is at odds with respect to the 2 remaining values and a that are equal together (e.g. $c = 1$ while $a = b = d = 0$). But H_i taken alone does not provide precise knowledge about the position of the intruder. This is why we investigate in the following section a proper formula able alone to do this job.

2.2   An Oddness Measure for Boolean Data

In the following, we proceed in two steps: first, we define a new measure to capture *oddness* in a set of Boolean values via the heterogeneous proportions introduced in the previous section. Then, we extend it to multi-valued logic in the next subsection.

Let us remember that each proportion H_i provides a piece of knowledge on the intruder and when combined with other pieces, we can pick out which one is the "intruder" among a, b, c and d. For example $H_1(a, b, c, d) = H_2(a, b, c, d) = H_3(a, b, c, d) = 1$ means that there is an intruder which is out of the set $\{a, b, c\}$. Then we define the oddness of d w.r.t. $\{a, b, c\}$ with the following formula:

$$odd(\{a, b, c\}, d) =_{def} H_1(a, b, c, d) \wedge H_2(a, b, c, d) \wedge H_3(a, b, c, d)$$

Due to the permutation properties of the H_i's, the right hand side of this definition is stable w.r.t. permutation of a, b, c then the set notation on the left hand side is justified. The truth table of *odd* is given in Table 2. It is clear

Table 2. H_1, H_2, H_3 and *odd* truth values

$a\ b\ c\ d$	H_1	H_2	H_3	odd
0 0 0 0	0	0	0	0
0 0 0 1	1	1	1	1
0 0 1 0	1	1	0	0
0 0 1 1	0	0	0	0
0 1 0 0	1	0	1	0
0 1 0 1	0	0	0	0
0 1 1 0	0	0	0	0
0 1 1 1	0	1	1	0
1 0 0 0	0	1	1	0
1 0 0 1	0	0	0	0
1 0 1 0	0	0	0	0
1 0 1 1	1	0	1	0
1 1 0 0	0	0	0	0
1 1 0 1	1	1	0	0
1 1 1 0	1	1	1	1
1 1 1 1	0	0	0	0

that *odd* holds only when the value of d is seen as *odd* among the other values: d is the intruder. Moreover *odd* does not hold in the opposite situation where there is a majority among values in a, b, c, d and d belongs to this majority (e.g. $odd(\{0, 1, 0\}, 0) = 0$) or there is no majority at all (e.g. $odd(\{0, 1, 1\}, 0) = 0$). A simple observation of Table 2 shows that

$$odd(\{a, b, c\}, d) \equiv ((a \vee b \vee c) \not\equiv d) \wedge (a \wedge b \wedge c) \not\equiv d)) \quad (1)$$

More precisely, given a set of 3 identical Boolean values a, b, c, $odd(\{a, b, c\}, d)$ can act as a flag indicating if the 4th value d is different from the common value of a, b, c. Then the value d is at odds w.r.t. the other values.

2.3   Extension to Numerical Data

As we are also dealing with numerical data in this paper, it is necessary to extend the previous *oddness* measure to handle variables with graded values (i.e. variables whose values belong to $[0, 1]$ after suitable normalization of numerical data). For now, this oddness is just 0 or 1 (i.e. the truth value of $odd(\{a, b, c\}, d)$), but we would like to consider tuples such as $(0.1, 0.2, 0.1, 0.8)$ and still consider that the 4th value is somewhat odd w.r.t. the 3 other ones.

A direct translation of formula (1), taking min for $\wedge$, max for $\vee$, and $1 - |\cdot - \cdot|$ for $\equiv$ as in Łukasiewics logic, leads to:

$$odd(\{a, b, c\}, d) = \min(|\max(a, b, c) - d|, |\min(a, b, c) - d|) \quad (2)$$

Let us examine some examples to get a precise understanding of the formula for numerical data and to check that this *oddness* measure fits with the intuition.

- We see that $odd(\{u, u, u\}, v) = |u - v|$. Indeed, if $u = v$ then obviously the 4th value is not an intruder. The larger $|u - v|$, the more v is at odds w.r.t the 3 values equal to u.
- We see also that $odd(\{v, u, u\}, v) = 0$ which is consistent with the expected semantics of *odd*.
- More generally, $odd(\{u, v, w\}, \max(u, v, w)) = odd(\{u, v, w\}, \min(u, v, w)) = 0$, and in any case, $odd(\{u, v, w\}, u) \leq 0.5$.
- Let us now consider a numerical pattern with 4 different values: $(\{0, 0.1, 0.2\}, 0.9)$. We feel that $d = 0.9$ appears as an intruder in the set $(\{0, 0.1, 0.2\})$. This is still consistent with the truth value provided by $odd(\{0, 0.1, 0.2\}, 0.9) = 0.7$ while $odd(\{0, 0.1, 0.1\}, 0.9) = 0.8$ and $odd(\{0, 0.1, 0.3\}, 0.9) = 0.6$.
- The pattern $(\{0.7, 1, 1\}, 0.9)$ does not strongly suggest 0.9 as an intruder value. Indeed $odd(\{0.7, 1, 1\}, 0.9) = 0.1$. Note that $odd(\{0.9, 1, 1\}, 0.7) = 0.2$, which is a bit higher, as expected since we have moved towards more uniformity among a, b, c and slightly increased the differences between d and the elements of $\{a, b, c\}$. Moreover, note that $odd(\{0.7, 1, 1\}, 0.9) = 0.1$, and $odd(\{0, 0, 1\}, 0.9) = 0.1$, since the two cases illustrate two different ways of not being really an intruder. Indeed, although 0.9 is close to the majority value in $\{0.7, 1, 1\}$ in the first case, and far from the majority value in $\{0, 0, 1\}$ in the second case, closeness to majority value in $\{a, b, c\}$ is not at all what *odd* estimates. Rather it is expected to find similar estimates in the two above cases, since they are respectively close to $odd(\{1, 1, 1\}, 1) = 0$ and to $odd(\{0, 0, 1\}, 1) = 0$ as shown in Table 2.
- Finally, $odd(\{a, b, c\}, d)$ does not always behave as $|d - average(\{a, b, c\})|$: the cases $\{a, b, c\} = \{0.5, 0.5, 0.5\}$, $d = 0.5$, and $\{a, b, c\} = \{0, 0.5, 1\}$, $d = 0.5$ cannot be distinguished by the second average-based expression, but, with our definition, $odd(\{0.5, 0.5, 0.5\}, 0.5) = 0$, while $odd(\{0, 0.5, 1\}, 0.5) = 0.5$.

From the previous examples, we understand that the proposed definition fits with the initial intuition and provides high truth values when d appears *odd* w.r.t. the set $\{a, b, c\}$ and low truth values in the opposite case where d is not very different from the other values. On top of that, the expression of odd given here is not the conjunction of the multiple-valued extensions of H_1, H_2, H_3 as given in [9], which would lead to a less satisfactory measure of oddness. Indeed, we are here interested in the oddness of d w.r.t. a set $\{a, b, c\}$, and not in picking out an intruder in the set $\{a, b, c, d\}$ as in [9].

3   Oddness of an Item with Respect to a Class

The previous measure of oddness is not limited to subsets $\{a, b, c\}$ with 3 elements, and can be extended to a measure of oddness $odd(S, x)$ of an item x w.r.t. a subset S of any size, as discussed below. Then we extend $odd(S, x)$ to multiple features. Finally, we build up a global oddness measure of an item x w.r.t. a class by cumulating the measure $odd(S, x)$ for all subsets S of the same size in the class.

3.1   Oddness with Respect to Subsets of Various Size

In view of the above definition for oddness, we can naturally extend to subsets S of values in $[0, 1]$ of any finite size, as follows:

$$odd(S, x) = \min(|\max(S) - x|, |\min(S) - x|)$$

As can be seen, we compare x to the upper and lower values in S. When S becomes large, $odd(S, x)$ does not take precisely into account a large number of values between the min and max of S. Then, $odd(S, x)$ is more informative for small sets S with 2, 3, 4 elements that we shall consider in our experiments.

The particular case where S is a singleton is worth of interest as we will see below.

3.2   Oddness Measure for Vectors

When it comes to real life application, it is not enough to represent individuals with a single Boolean or real value. Generally, individuals are encoded by a set of features, That is why we have to define an oddness measure for vectors. When dealing with vectors $\overrightarrow{x} \in [0, 1]^n$, Boolean vectors are also covered as a particular case. The odd measure, defined by (1) and extended by (2) is used to estimate to what extent a value x can be considered as odd among a set S of values. Thanks to the latter formula, assuming the independence of features, it is natural to compute the $oddity$ of a vector $\overrightarrow{x}$ as the sum of the $oddities$ for each feature $x_i \in \overrightarrow{x}$, as follows:

$$Odd(\overrightarrow{S}, \overrightarrow{x}) =_{def} \Sigma_{i=1}^n odd(S_i, x_i) \in [0, n]$$

where x_i is the i-th component of $\overrightarrow{x}$ and S_i is the subset gathering the i-th components of the vectors in $\overrightarrow{S}$.

If $Odd(\overrightarrow{S}, \overrightarrow{x}) = 0$, no feature indicates that $\overrightarrow{x}$ behaves as an intruder and there is no obstacle for $\overrightarrow{x}$ to join the set $\overrightarrow{S}$. On the contrary, high values of $Odd(\overrightarrow{S}, \overrightarrow{x})$ (close to n) means that, for *many* features, $\overrightarrow{x}$ appears as an intruder and may reduce the homogeneity when going from $\overrightarrow{S}$ to the set $\overrightarrow{S} \cup \{\overrightarrow{x}\}$.

3.3   Global Oddness Measure

Given a set $\mathcal{C}$ of vectors belonging to the same class and a non nul integer m, we can compute $Odd(\overrightarrow{S}, \overrightarrow{x})$ for each distinct subset $\overrightarrow{S} \subseteq \mathcal{C}$ of cardinal m. The oddness measure of the vector $\overrightarrow{x}$ in the class $\mathcal{C}$ is simply the sum of all these elementary values as follows:

$$ODD_m(\mathcal{C}, \overrightarrow{x}) = \Sigma_{\overrightarrow{S} \subseteq \mathcal{C} s.t. |\overrightarrow{S}| = m} Odd(\overrightarrow{S}, \overrightarrow{x})$$

To take into account the relative size of the different classes $\mathcal{C}$, it is fair to introduce a normalization factor. Namely to consider the number of subsets $\overrightarrow{S}$ available, as an increasing function of $|\mathcal{C}|$, we have to divide the above oddness measure by $\binom{|\mathcal{C}|}{m}$ which, for large values of $|\mathcal{C}|$ and small values of m, has $|\mathcal{C}|^m$ as order of magnitude So it is relevant to consider the normalized version of ODD as follows:

$$ODD_m^*(\mathcal{C}, \overrightarrow{x}) = \frac{1}{|\mathcal{C}|^m} ODD_m(\mathcal{C}, \overrightarrow{x})$$

When $m = 2$, it means we deal with pairs, when $m = 3$, we deal with triple, etc. When $m = 1$, we deal with singletons $\overrightarrow{S} = \{\overrightarrow{s}\}$, and $Odd(\{\overrightarrow{s}\}, \overrightarrow{x}) = \Sigma_{i=1}^n odd(s_i, x_i) = \Sigma_{i=1}^n |s_i - x_i|$, which is just the Hamming distance between $\overrightarrow{s}$ and $\overrightarrow{x}$. Then $ODD_1^*(\mathcal{C}, \overrightarrow{x})$ is the average distance between $\overrightarrow{x}$ and the elements in $\mathcal{C}$.

4   An Oddness-Based Classifier

In this section, we propose a family of classifiers based on the above global oddness measure and indexed by the size of the subsets used in the comparison process.

4.1   Algorithm

Let TS be a training set composed of instances $(\overrightarrow{z}, cl(\overrightarrow{z}))$, where $\overrightarrow{z} \in \mathbb{B}^n$ or $\mathbb{R}^n$, $cl(\overrightarrow{z})$ is the label of $\overrightarrow{z}$. Given the set $\mathcal{C}$ of instances in TS having the same label c, and a new instance $\overrightarrow{x} \notin TS$ without label, in order to allocate a label to $\overrightarrow{x}$ we look for the class that better maintains its homogeneity when $\overrightarrow{x}$ is added to it. More formally, we want to check if $\mathcal{C} \cup \{\overrightarrow{x}\}$ may be more heterogeneous than $\mathcal{C}$ itself. Based on the *oddness* measure defined before, the idea is then to assign to $\overrightarrow{x}$ the label corresponding to the class minimizing the oddness when $\overrightarrow{x}$ is added. Implementing this idea leads to the following algorithm:

Algorithm 1. Oddness-based algorithm A

Input: a training set TS of examples $(\overrightarrow{z}, cl(\overrightarrow{z}))$
       a non nul integer m
       a new item $\overrightarrow{x}$,
Partition TS into sets C of examples having the same label c. ▷ c is the label of the class C
for each C **do**
    Compute $ODD_m^*(C, \overrightarrow{x})$
end for
$cl(\overrightarrow{x}) = argmin_c(ODD_m^*(C, \overrightarrow{x}))$
return $cl(\overrightarrow{x})$

For a given value of m, we will denote A_m the corresponding algorithm, using ODD_m^* as oddness measure. In order to reduce the complexity of A_m, we have chosen, for the subsets of size m, to take one element as a k nearest neighbor of the new item $\overrightarrow{x}$. So the oddness measure that will be used in practice is:

$$ODD_m^k(C, \overrightarrow{x}) = \frac{1}{|C|^{m-1}} ODD_m(C, \overrightarrow{x})$$

Our approach might appear somehow similar to k-nearest neighbors (k-nn) methods. However, the proposed method relies on the comparison of a newcomer with respect to subsets S involving $m = 2, 3$, or more elements, which are not singletons, while k-nn methods compare the newcomer with examples taken one by one. Obviously, this has a greater computational cost, since in the basic method, we have to consider all the subsets of size m in the training set.

5   Experimentations and Discussion

In order to evaluate the efficiency of the proposed classifier when applied to Boolean and numerical data, we have tested our algorithm A_m on 13 data sets (6 datasets having a Boolean coding and 7 datasets having a numerical coding) taken from the UCI machine learning repository [6]. A brief description of these data sets is given in Table 3. In terms of classes, we deal with a maximum number of 7 classes. In order to apply our Boolean and multiple-valued semantics framework, all discrete attributes are binarized and all numerical attributes are normalized in a standard way to get numbers in $[0,1]$: a real value is thus changed into a number that may be understood as a truth value. In terms of protocol, we apply a standard 10 fold cross-validation technique to build the training and testing sets and we run our tests on 4 different sizes of subsets: subsets of one, two, tree or four items to compute the oddness measure, leading to algorithms A_1, A_2, A_3, A_4.

In Table 4, we provide mean accuracies and standard deviations obtained with the three first implemented options using A_1, A_2 and A_3. For A_2 and A_3 alternatives, we also test different values of k (k being the number of nearest

Table 3. Description of datasets

Datasets	Instances	Nominal Att.	Binary Att.	Numerical Att.	Classes
Balance	625	4	20	-	3
Car	743	6	21	-	4
Spect	267	-	22	-	2
Monk1	432	6	15	-	2
Monk2	432	6	15	-	2
Monk3	432	6	15	-	2
Diabetes	768	-	-	8	2
W. B. Cancer	699	-	-	9	2
Heart	270	-	-	13	2
Iris	150	-	-	4	3
Wine	178	-	-	13	3
Satellite Image	1090	-	-	36	6
Glass	214	-	-	9	7

neigbours used). Let us note that when we have less than k elements in a given class, we do not check the version of our algorithm for the value k: this is the case for *Glass* and $k = 11$.

Table 5 shows classification results obtained with A_4. Since this is a time consuming option, we limit our tests to datasets with small size. In Tables 4 and 5, we notice that:

Table 4. Classification accuracies given as mean and standard deviation with A_1, A_2 and A_3

Datasets	A_1	A_2				A_3			
value of k		1	3	5	11	1	3	5	11
Balance	83,67±3,82	49,81±6,39	76,93±5,02	**87,34±3,17**	86,29±3,45	52,05±6,98	74,99±3,59	87,16±2,71	86,63±2,90
Car	57,89±7,73	83,99±4,10	87,34±3,25	**91,72±2,81**	91,04±2,91	83,96±3,67	86,90±3,64	91,12±3,26	89,57±3,07
Spect	44,02±6,63	78,68± 6,96	83,72± 6,17	83,11± 6,06	83,19± 5,27	80,97±6,80	84,13±4,99	**84,30± 4,34**	**84,30± 4,35**
Monk1	75,01±6,53	99,12±1,49	99,77±0,51	**99,86±0,33**	99,68±1,29	99,63±0,71	97,15±3,46	98 ± 2,46	91,99±6,40
Monk2	50,74±9,11	34,52±6,70	36,57±6,21	43,37±4,70	**58,98±4,13**	34.28±7.29	37.05±6.44	41.91±7.57	55.32±7.21
Monk3	97,23±1,78	99,96±0,13	100	100	100	100	100	99.77± 0.68	99.32± 2.05
Diabetes	74,85±4,39	69,95±4,16	73,81±4,42	74,28±4,70	75,73±3,77	70,31±4,06	74,03±3,75	74,55±4,25	**76,41±4,32**
W. B. Cancer	94,23±2,58	96,80±1,69	97,2± 1,66	**97,43±1,76**	97,31± 1,71	96,10±2,35	97,03± 1,94	97,08±1,87	97,03± 1,85
Heart	**83,18±7,74**	78,89± 7,63	81,70± 6,87	82,22± 6,53	81,85± 6,81	77,63 ±7	81,26± 5,63	82 ± 6,75	82,44± 6,28
Iris	94,53±6,15	93,87± 5,41	94,67± 4,96	94,80± 4,81	95,06± 4,55	94,93± 5,22	94,79±4,81	94,66± 4,76	**95,73± 5,07**
Wine	93,25±5,59	97,97± 3,44	97,98± 2,87	**98,34± 2,53**	97,52± 3,21	95,77± 4,35	97,4± 3,56	96,58± 3,92	96,48± 4,25
Sat. Image	87,15±2,95	**95,17±1,77**	95,06±2,16	95,04±1,97	94,33 ±2,12	94,12± 1,90	94,18±2,08	94,18±2,30	93,51±2,36
Glass	35,93±9,51	75,15±8,00	**76,53 ±7,71**	74,77±7,62	-	70,12± 6,06	74,26± 6,42	72,44± 7,23	-

Table 5. Classification accuracies given as mean and standard deviation obtained with A_4

Datasets	A_4			
value of k	1	3	5	11
Spect	81.28± 5.2	**84.2± 5.11**	**84.2± 3.89**	**84.2± 3.89**
Monk1	99.55± 0.91	96.28± 4.31	90.07± 4.37	
Heart	71.48± 7.95	78.89± 4.7	79.26± 5.79	80.37± 5.25
Iris	95 ± 5,68	95,67± 5,01	95,50± 4,98	**96,34± 4,84**
Wine	92,89± 6,15	94,58± 5,75	94,20± 5,52	94,83± 4,75

Table 6. Comparison with classification results of other classifiers

Datasets	C4.5	SVM Poly-Kernel	SVM PUK-Kernel	JRip	IBK (k=1, k=10)	Analogy1 [4] (k=5,l=n)	Analogy2 [2] (Algo2:A,k=11)	Evenness [3] (k=5, l=n)
Balance	78	90	89	76	83, 83	87	-	83
Car	95	91	87	91	92, 92	94	-	92
Spect	81	81	83	81	75, 81	41	-	84
Monk1	99	75	100	98	100, 100	99	-	100
Monk2	95	67	67	73	44 , 64	99	-	58
Monk3	100	100	100	100	100, 99	99	-	100
Diabetes	74	77	77	76	70, 71	-	73	-
Cancer	96	97	96	96	96 , 97	-	97	-
Heart	77	84	81	81	75, 81	-	82	-
Iris	96	96	96	95	95, 96	-	97	-
Wine	94	98	99	93	95, 95	-	98	-
Sat. Image	94	94	95	93	95, 94	-	94	-
Glass	66	58	71	69	70, 64	-	72	-

- A_1 seems to be significantly less efficient than all other subset sizes for most data-sets. The worst accuracy for this option is noted for datasets: Car, Spect, Sat.Image, Wine and Glass having large number of attributes and/or classes. In fact, this option remains close to the basis of k-nn algorithm since both compute the distance to the training examples in an independent way without any further investigation on the relationship between these training data. Moreover, since this option computes the mean oddness measure to elements of classes, this makes it less informative than other options.
- For most datasets, best results are obtained with large values of k (k=5 or 11) for the three alternatives using A_2, A_3 or A_4, except in the case of Monk1 where small values of k provide better accuracy for A_3 and A_4. Since subsets of pairs are generally less informative than subsets of triples or quadruples, it is better to consider, for this option, large values of k to take advantage of a larger variety of data. It remains to investigate what is the suitable k for a target dataset.
- If we compare A_2 to the other A_i's for $k = 5$, we note that this option provides the best accuracy for all datasets except for Spect., where it performs slightly worse than A_3 and A_4.
- A_4 performs generally worse than A_2 and A_3 for all datasets expect for the Iris where it is slightly better. Especially for datasets Heart and Wine, the accuracy strongly decreases with A_4. This may reinforce the intuition that pairs and triples are appropriate to evaluate oddness.
- It is quite clear that the proposed classifier, especially A_2, is able to classify numerical as well as Boolean data sets almost in the same way. These results highlight that the proposed multi-valued oddness measure correctly extends the Boolean case.

In order to evaluate the efficiency of the oddness-based classifiers, we compare their accuracy to existing classification approaches. Table 6 includes classification results of some machine learning algorithms: C4.5 for decision trees, SVMs, JRip an optimized propositional rule learner, and IBk a k-nearest neighbors procedure for k=1, k=10. To test the SVMs, we use two types of kernels: the polynomial kernel and the Pearson VII function-based universal kernel denoted respectively

Poly-Kernel and PUK-Kernel. Accuracy results for C4.5, SVMs, JRip and IBk are obtained by using the free implementation of Weka software to the datasets described in Table 3. The columns Analogy1, Analogy2 and Evenness in Table 6 refer to the results obtained respectively with analogy-based classifiers [4] in the case of Boolean data, [2] in the case of numerical data and evenness-based classifier [3] (using heterogeneous proportions) in the case of Boolean data. We note that:

- Table 6 highlights the fact that our oddness-based classifier performs more or less in the same way as the best known algorithms. Especially, A_2 outperforms all other classifiers for data sets Spect., Monk1, Monk3, Cancer, Sat. Image and Glass and has performances similar to SVM based Poly-Kernel for datasets Car.
- A_2 shows high efficiency to classify datasets Balance, Car, Sat.Image and Glass (which have multiple classes) which demonstrates its ability to deal with multiple class data sets.
- The oddness-based classifier seems to be also efficient when classifying data sets with a large number of instances and attributes as in the case of Car and Sat.Image for instance.
- If we compare the best results obtained with A_2 in Table 4 with those obtained with the analogy-based classifier for numerical data [2], we can notice that the two classifiers perform similarly for most datasets, with maybe the exception of Iris. In that latter case, the analogy is significantly better, while for Diabetes the converse is observed.
- We notice that both oddness-based and analogy-based classifiers Analogy1 [4] in the case of Boolean datasets, exhibit good results for Balance, Car, Monk1 and Monk3, comparable to those obtained by classifiers like IBK or SVM. The results of oddness-based classifier A_2 are also comparable to those of the evenness-based classifier [3]
- Regarding Monk2, it is known that the underlying function ("having exactly two attributes with value 1") is more complicated than the functions underlying Monk1 and Monk3, and involves all the attributes (while in the two other functions only 3 attributes among 6 are involved in the discrete coding). We suspect that the existence of a large discontinuity in the classification of data (a nearest neighbor y of x will not generally be labelled with the same class $cl(\overrightarrow{x})$) may be too difficult to apprehend using oddness (or heterogeneous proportions Evenness in Table 6). Moreover, for this dataset, we expect that the classifier needs to consider more neighbors k to get better results. Thus, we also tested the approach using pairs with bigger values of k for Monk2 data set, we get an accuracy equal to 64.83 ± 2.06 for $k = 17$.

Lastly, on Table 6, we also observe that A_2 with $k = 5$ significantly outperforms IBK on datasets Balance, Spect., Diabetes, Heart, Wine, Sat. Image and Glass and has similar results for Monk1, Monk3. This is confirmed by the Wilcoxon Matched-Pairs Signed-Ranks Test as proposed by Demsar [5]. This test is a nonparametric alternative to the paired t-test enabling to compare two classifiers over multiple data sets. In our case, the null hypothesis, states that the two compared algorithms performs in the same way. Table 7 summarizes the results of the computed p-values for each pair of compared classifiers. The null hypothesis has to be rejected when the p-value is *less* than the threshold 0.05. These values are highlighted in bold in Table 7. We add a * to each significant p-value (< 0.05) if the classifier given in the row significantly outperforms the classifier given in the column. There is no * for any significant p-value if the classifier given in the column is rather statistically better than the classifier given in the row. From the computed p-values, we can draw the following conclusions:

- As expected, A_1 is statistically less efficient than IBK, A_2 and A_3.
- If we compare with A_3, the p-value confirms that A_2 is more efficient than A_3.
- A_2 is also significantly better than IB1. Our proposed algorithm statistically outperforms IB10 *only* if we remove Monk2 from the list of compared datasets for the Wilcoxon Ranks test (note that A_2 performs as IB10 for $k = 17$).

Table 7. Results for the Wilcoxon Matched-Pairs Signed-Ranks Test, the * means that the classifier in the row in statistically better than the classifier on the column

		A_1	A_3 (k=5)	IB1	IB10
A_1	Without Monk2	-	-	**0.049**	**0.022**
	With Monk2	-	-	0.1	**0.013**
A_2 (k=5)	Without Monk2	**0.0076***	0,061	**0.026***	**0.0229***
	With Monk2	**0.023***	**0,034***	**0.034***	0.1158
A_3 (k=5)	Without Monk2	**0.0076***	-	0.091	0.1823
	With Monk2	**0.027***	-	0.136	0.463

6   Conclusion

In this paper, we have defined a family of classifiers based on a oddness measure, which compares the new item to be classified with elements of subsets, having fixed size, from the training set. More precisely, it appears that the algorithm performing the best is the one using pairs of elements in the comparison process. On Boolean datasets, the performance of A_2 are quite similar to an algorithm based on triples using a so-called evenness measure based on heterogeneous logical proportions. This should not come as a surprise since oddness measure is high when the new item is similar to both elements in the pairs, while the evenness measure is high when the new item is similar to at least 2 of the 3 elements in the triples. The interest of the oddness-based view becomes striking for numerical datasets, where the evenness-based approach has no counterpart to offer. It is also worth noticing that oddness-based classifiers go beyond nearest neighbors algorithms.

Several issues are still to investigate. Algorithm A_2 has been tested for pairs including a nearest neighbor. It would be interesting to relax this constraint to any kind of pairs. Besides, the link with a formal setting as in [11] would also be of interest. Approaches to classification where a compression-based similarity measure is used (in place of the oddness measure presented here) have been also proposed [1,10], which would be worth comparing.

References

1. Benedetto, D., Caglioti, E., Loreto, V.: Language trees and zipping. Phys. Review Lett. 88(4) (2002)
2. Bounhas, M., Prade, H., Richard, G.: Analogical classification: handling numerical data. In: Straccia, U., Calì, A. (eds.) SUM 2014. LNCS, vol. 8720, pp. 66–79. Springer, Heidelberg (2014)
3. Bounhas, M., Prade, H., Richard, G.: A new view of conformity and its application to classification. In: Destercke, S., Denoeux, T. (eds.) ECSQARU 2015. LNAI, vol. 9161. Springer, Heidelberg (2015)
4. Bounhas, M., Prade, H., Richard, G.: Analogical classification: a new way to deal with examples. In: ECAI 2014–21st European Conference on Artificial Intelligence, 18–22 August 2014, Prague, Czech Republic. Frontiers in Artificial Intelligence and Applications, vol. 263, pp. 135–140. IOS Press (2014)
5. Demsar, J.: Statistical comparisons of classifiers over multiple data sets. Journal of Machine Learning Research 7, 1–30 (2006)
6. Mertz, J., Murphy, P.: Uci repository of machine learning databases (2000). ftp:// ftp.ics.uci.edu/pub/machine-learning-databases
7. Miclet, L., Bayoudh, S., Delhay, A.: Analogical dissimilarity: definition, algorithms and two experiments in machine learning. JAIR 32, 793–824 (2008)
8. Prade, H., Richard, G.: From analogical proportion to logical proportions. Logica Universalis 7(4), 441–505 (2013)
9. Prade, H., Richard, G.: Homogenous and heterogeneous logical proportions. IfCoLog J. of Logics and their Applications 1(1), 1–51 (2014)
10. Sculley, D., Brodley, C.E.: Compression and machine learning: a new perspective on feature space vectors. In: Proc. of the Data Compressing Conference DCC, pp. 332–341. IEEE (2006)
11. Vovk, V., Gammerman, A., Saunders, C.: Machine-learning applications of algorithmic randomness. Int. Conf. on Machine Learning, pp. 444–453 (1999)

Packing Irregular-Shaped Objects for 3D Printing

Stefan Edelkamp$^{(\boxtimes)}$ and Paul Wichern

Faculty 3—Mathematics and Computer Science, University of Bremen,
PO Box 330 440, 28334 Bremen, Germany
edelkamp@tzi.de

Abstract. This paper considers solving a problem in combinatorial search: the automated arrangement of *irregular-shaped* objects for industrial 3D printing. The input is a set of triangulated models; the output is a set of location and orientation vectors for the objects. The proposed algorithm consists of three stages: (1) translation of the models into an octree; (2) design of an efficient test for pairwise intersection based on sphere trees; and (3) computation of an optimized placement of the objects using simulated annealing. We compare several sphere-tree construction methods and annealing parameter settings to derive valid packings.

1 Introduction

Additive manufacturing (AM) has an increasing range of applicability. Compared to classical manufacturing it shows several advantages. Previously impossible shapes and structures are available, leading to prototypes that can be produced without a large supply or production chain. Hence, the manufacturing of new products is accelerated, the according costs are reduced, and a wide range of user-specified products can be produced. Given the 3D model of the product, it can be produced overnight and delivered to the consumers. While 3D printing (3DP) is one particular AM technique (processes that sequentially deposit material onto a powder bed with inkjet printer heads), nowadays, both terms used as umbrella terms for several technologies, which include laser stereo lithography (SL), selective laser sintering/melting (SLS/SLM), electron beam melting (EBM), layer laminate manufacturing (LLN), and fused layer modeling (FLM).

To save production time and cost, the joint print of several objects is crucial. A valid *packing* for a set of objects $(o_1, \ldots, o_n)$ into a box $B = [0..x, 0..y, 0..z]$ with $(x, y, z) \in I\!R^3$ subject to objective function f is a sequence of location coordinates $(x_i, y_i, z_i) \in I\!R^3$ (e.g., for the centers of mass of o_i) and rotation angles $(\alpha_i, \beta_i, \gamma_i) \in [0, 2\pi)^3$, $1 \leq i \leq n$, which is collision-free (for all $1 \leq i \neq j \leq n$ objects o_i and o_j do not overlap), fits completely in box B; and optimizes f. Packing algorithms should: 1) be robust to overcome inaccuracies in the input model, 2) support general user-supplied objective functions, 3) preserve a minimal pairwise distance between the objects.

© Springer International Publishing Switzerland 2015
S. Hölldobler et al. (Eds.): KI 2015, LNAI 9324, pp. 45–58, 2015.
DOI: 10.1007/978-3-319-24489-1_4

Fig. 1. Levels of a sphere tree (all figures best be viewed in colors on screen).

A number of research papers on the efficient packing of objects for 3D print-ing have been published: [24] separates the work into two classes: 3D packing and searching for an optimal orientation, which we consider in common; [11] applies genetic algorithms to place the models close to the working space cen-ter using a hierarchical structure of axis-aligned bounding boxes (AABB) for collision detection; [17] improves manufacturing time, surface quality and the volume of support also using genetic algorithms for the optimization; [18] opti-mizes average surface quality and manufacturing time, comparing particle swarm optimization with genetic algorithms for finding the Pareto optimum; [2] pro-vides an overview on AABB algorithms, while [5] is concerned about heuristically packing concave/convex bodies, assuming no noise in the input; [24] optimizes height, surface quality and support volume, also genetic algorithms and octrees for AABB collision detection, thus, being limited to rotations of 90 degrees.

Packing squares into rectangles has been studied in [12,13], discrete rectan-gles in [8] and high-precision rectangles in [9,15]. A new method for packing boxes grows an arrangement of objects from multiple sides of the container [14]. Industrial tools with restricted functionality for packing irregular-shaped object in the context of 3D printing include Magics Sintermodule and NetFab Profes-sional Other tools (CAMWorks, MOSAIX, Nest++, ProNest, Nshaker& NEsti-mate) are limited to 2D.

2   Sphere-Tree Construction

Bounding volume hierarchies (BVHs) are recursive tree data structures that at the leaf nodes include a primitive volume data type. There are various sorts of BVHs, e.g., based on AABBs, OBBs (oriented bounded boxes), cones, ellipsoids, and convex hulls. With *sphere trees* (Fig. 1) we chose BVHs for which translation, rotation and intersection are fast: a collision of spheres A and B with resp. origins c_A and c_B and radii r_A and r_B is detected by evaluating $\|c_A - c_B\|_2 < r_A + r_B$. If there is no intersection on a coarser level of granularity higher up in the tree, there will be none on finer level.

For the subsequent construction of a sphere tree, in Alg. 1.2 a sphere is generated for each internal cell (see Fig. 2).

Algorithm 1.1. Procedure InOutOctree(T, b_T, c_{min})

1: $O \leftarrow$ octree of T with smallest cube around b_T as root
2: **for** $c \in$ cells of O **do**
3:     mark c as INTERNAL
4: $c_{start} \leftarrow$ corner leaf cell of O
5: $BreadthFirstMark(O, c_{start}, \text{EXTERNAL})$
6: **return** O

Algorithm 1.2. Procedure SphereByOctree(T, b_T, c_{min})

1: $O \leftarrow InOutOctree(T, b_T, c_{min})$
2: $S_{tree} \leftarrow O \setminus \{o \in O \mid o \text{ marked as EXTERNAL}\}$
3: replace every cube in S_{tree} by its surrounding sphere
4: **return** S_{tree}

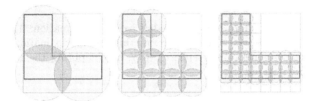

Fig. 2. Conversion of an octree into a sphere tree.

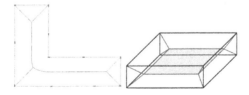

Fig. 3. Exact medial axes in 2D and 3D.

The equation of the sphere of coplanar points (x_i, y_i, z_i), $1 \leq i \leq 4$ (that can be transformed to a standard form for determining the midpoint) is given by

$$
det \begin{vmatrix} x^2 + y^2 + z^2 & x & y & z & 1 \\ x_1^2 + y_1^2 + z_1^2 & x_1 & y_1 & z_1 & 1 \\ x_2^2 + y_2^2 + z_2^2 & x_2 & y_2 & z_2 & 1 \\ x_3^2 + y_3^2 + z_3^2 & x_3 & y_3 & z_3 & 1 \\ x_4^2 + y_4^2 + z_4^2 & x_4 & y_4 & z_4 & 1 \end{vmatrix} = 0
$$

Octree. The simplest algorithm to construct a sphere tree is by extending the corresponding octree [19]. Alg. 1.1 distinguishes in- and outside leaf cells in the

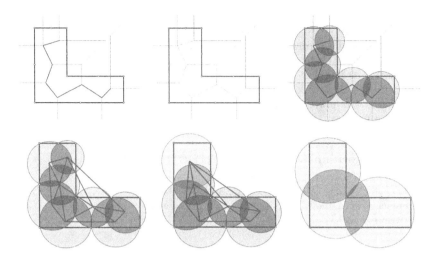

Fig. 4. Constructing a sphere tree via medial axis approximation: 1) computing a Voronoi diagram of the object vertices, 2) extracting the approximation of the medial axis of the object, 3) generating a sphere cover, 4) computing the triangulation of centers, 5) merging spheres.

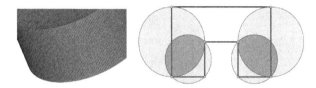

Fig. 5. Curved object (left), and one, where all vertices, but not all edges are covered (right).

octree, with T as the set of object triangles and b_T as its bounding box, and c_{min} as minimal cell size. It marks cells in breadth-first order, starting with an initial external one. All remaining cells belong to the interior of the object.

Medial Axis. Another sphere-tree construction method links to the *medial axis* [1,10], a generalized Voronoi nearest-boundary distance diagram data structure residing in the interior of objects (see Fig. 3). As the exact medial axis can be complex, computational approaches for its construction usually resort to its approximation [10]. By the limited set of available empirical results [1], studying the efficiency of medial axes for sphere tree intersection and 3D printing was our key research question.

Sphere-tree construction via the medial axis operates in stages (illustrated in Fig. 4). In the first stage, an initial 3D Voronoi diagram *for the object vertices* is constructed that approximates the exact medial axis. The Voronoi edges/faces

Fig. 6. Problem of grid sampling (left) and recursive construction of coverage points (right).

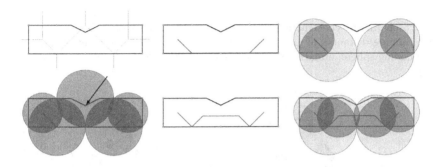

Fig. 7. Steps in *ImprovedAdaptiveSampling*: 1) Voronoi diagram, 2) medial axis approximation, 3) spheres constructed, 4) new point generated (red), 5) and updated axis, 6) final sphere cover.

that do not cross the object boundaries are the building blocks of the medial axis skeleton. Together with the distance to the boundary they define the set of spheres to cover the object. Then, with the help of a triangulation of the centers (red), we incrementally merge spheres that have been constructed. Too aggressive merging strategies, however, negatively influence the runtime and are avoided.

For complex objects (see Fig. 5), the Voronoi diagram is *extended by sampling random points on the object surface* [20]. Such *adaptive sampling* starts with a set of points on the surface of the object, and is extracted from the medial axis approximation. One sampling option [10] is to exploit an underlying grid, but on curved boundaries with small but lengthy triangles, cells might still not be sampled. Therefore, we decided to recursively construct coverage points (see Fig. 6).

In contrast to [1] that calls the algorithm of [6], we applied coarse sampling for the initial Voronoi diagram, and insert the additional set of *coverage* points on the surface for the resulting spheres (Fig. 7) in a refinement step. Followed by this, an error value is computed, which denotes how far a sphere exceeds the surface. For all spheres that have a value that is too large, the medial axis is refined, until no sphere remaining in the result set exceeds the error threshold. Eventually, all sample points and the model itself were finally covered with spheres. Depending on the density of the sampling [10], the approximation can be made arbitrarily exact. 3D Voronoi diagrams are the geometric dual of the

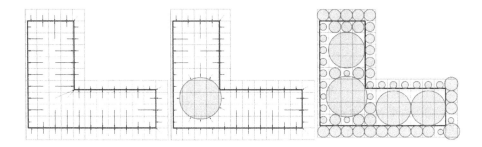

Fig. 8. Steps in the construction of a sphere packing (top to bottom, left to right): 1) determining distances of grid centers to the nearest boundary point, 2) drawing a corresponding sphere, updating the distance information, 3) final result of iterating the process

Fig. 9. Robustness issues: wrong orientation & holes (left), self-intersection (right).

according Delaunay tessellations, which are more convenient to compute [22]; we used the algorithm of Bowyer and Watson [7]. For querying points in such nearest-neighbor database, randomized data structures and random walk algorithms are recommended [3,16].

Sphere Packing. The sphere packing algorithm operates in voxel space, which is a discretized grid representation of the work space. The input is the set of octree cells that have been identified as being inside. The algorithm incrementally adds a sphere in the cell that has the largest distance to the surface [23]. Next, all distances are updated and the algorithm iterates (see Fig. 8). As the result of the algorithm needs to be a cover, spheres have to be inflated. As before, iterative merging of spheres yields a sphere tree.

3   Robustness Considerations

Fig. 9 illustrates subtle but important aspects that affect the robustness of the packing algorithms, namely orientation, holes and self-intersections. Other issues are: isolated triangles, open and multiple edges, or degenerated triangles.

Objects may have inverse orientation, defined by the normals of the triangles. As an example, in our visualization the model *bunny* (left) is shown in red,

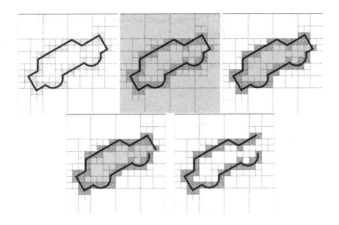

Fig. 10. Separating in- from exterior octree cells (top), impact of small and large holes (bottom).

Algorithm 1.3. Procedure EvaluateState(M, S_{trees}, e, F, δ)

1: $c_{collisions} \leftarrow 0$
2: **for** $s_{tree} \in S_{trees}$ **do**
3:     $c_{collisions} \leftarrow c_{collisions}$ + number of leaves in s_{tree} not completely inside e
4: **for** $a_{tree}, b_{tree} \in S_{trees}, a_{tree} \neq b_{tree} \wedge$ index of $a_{tree} <$ index of b_{tree} **do**
5:     $c_{collisions} \leftarrow c_{collisions} + CollisionCount(a_{tree}, b_{tree})$
6: **return** $\delta \cdot c_{collisions} + \sum_{i=1}^{n} f_i(M)$

illustrating that its orientation is reversed. Our algorithm is robust wrt. this artifact.

For interior detection Fig. 10 shows that small holes may be captured correctly, but for larger holes semantic problems might appear. Our approach of imposing a minimal cell size for an object boundary aligns with the observation that a 3D printer assumes that even a flat surface has some positive volume.

Exact computation is wanted, but negatively influences the runtime, so that good trade-offs between running time and robustness are needed. For illustration purpose, we conducted a benchmark (with very large coordinates) for sphere computation that with data type *float* (IEEE Standard 754) took 0.11s and produced 50,006 errors, with data type *double* took 0.12s and produced 481 errors, with data type *SoftFloat128* we got 1.21s and 6 errors, and with *BigIntegers/Rationals* 51,53s and no error. We used a combination of the data types with a quick check of validity that achieves the acceptable trade-off with 0.43s, while producing no error.

Algorithm 1.4. Procedure *CollisionCount*(*a*, *b*).

1: **if** *a* and *b* do not overlap **then**
2:    **return** 0
3: **else if** *a* and *b* are leaves **then**
4:    **return** 1
5: **else**
6:    $c \leftarrow 0$
7:    **for** $a_{child} \in$ children of *a* **do**
8:       **for** $b_{child} \in$ children of *b* **do**
9:          $c \leftarrow c + CollisionCount(a_{child}, b_{child})$
10:    **return** *c*

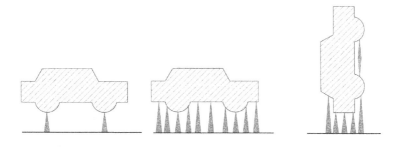

Fig. 11. 3D printing support of different granularity and object orientation.

4   Cost Functions and Global Optimization

For evaluating a state in Alg. 1.3 we assume a set of models M, a set of their sphere trees S_{trees}, a build envelope e, a set of evaluation functions $F = \{f_1, \ldots, f_n\}$, and an evaluation value of colliding leaf spheres δ.

Alg. 1.4 recursively computes the number of intersections of spheres tree leaves, which is combined with the overall objective function (such as maximizing centrality and minimizing height). For more advanced optimizations functions, the user can supply own evaluation function. For example, additional support (see Fig. 11) is dependent on the rotation of the object and needed not only for stabilization of the object but also for the transport of heat. Its cost has to be carefully implemented in the user-defined objective function.

Given the neighborhood relation and the evaluation function, an initial packing can be optimized. We choose simulated annealing (SA, see Alg. 1.5) as the global optimization process. It allows sub-optimal decisions with a probability that is decreasing with the temperature *temp*. Different to the research of finding an optimal 3D AABB packing [4,21] we used simulated annealing wrt. minimal translation step size $q_{stepsize}$ and rotation stepsize q_{angle}. Using sphere trees the search primitives for checking intersection and translation are fast, so that SA converges more effectively to a good solution.

Algorithm 1.5. Procedure $SimulatedAnnealing(s, f, c)$

1: $i \leftarrow 0$
2: $u \leftarrow u_{best} \leftarrow s$
3: $temp \leftarrow 1$
4: **while** $temp > 0$ **do**
5:    $u_{next} \leftarrow ExpandRandom(u, temp)$
6:    **if** $f(u_{next}) < f(u)$ **then**
7:      $u \leftarrow u_{next}$
8:      **if** $f(u) < f(u_{best})$ **then**
9:        $u_{best} \leftarrow u$
10:    **else**
11:      $r \leftarrow Random(0, 1)$
12:      **if** $r < e^{(f(u_{next}) - f(u))/temp}$ **then**
13:        $u \leftarrow u_{next}$
14:    $i \leftarrow i + 1$
15:    $temp \leftarrow Cooling(temp, i, c)$
16: **return** u_{best}

Table 1. Complexity of SA, assuming octree construction.

Algorithm	Run-Time Complexity
INOUTOCTREE	$O(|T|)$
SPHERETREEBYOCTREE	$O(|T|)$
COLLISIONCOUNT	$O(n_1 n_2)$
EVALUATESTATE	$O(m^2 n_{max}^2)$
SIMULATEDANNEALING	$O(cm^2 n_{max}^2)$
Total	$O(m|T| + cm^2 n_{max}^2)$

5   Complexity Considerations

Collision counting has a worst-case time complexity of $O(n_1 n_2)$ for two shere trees of size n_1 and n_2, but is faster in practice.

Assuming m to be the number of models, $|T|$ to be the number of input triangles, n to be the number of cells in the octree, c to be the number of cooling steps, n_1, n_2 to be the number of nodes in two sphere trees, and n_{max} to be the number of nodes in the largest sphere tree, we get the worst-case run-time complexities shown in Table 1. For the sake of brevity, we assume sphere tree generated directly from the octree. Finding the exterior cells may take $O(|T|)$ time, which dominates sphere-tree construction.

SA terminates, if the temperature after c steps has reached zero. The running time of one step heavily depends on EVALUATESTATE, which is supplied by the user and, therefore, may be arbitrary complex. Therefore, in Alg. 1.3 we chose a default implementation for the evaluation function based on collision counting. The implementation of EVALUATESTATE has a worst-case bound of $O(m^2 n_{max}^2)$ so that the overall complexity amounts to $O\left(m|T|n + cm^2 n_{max}^2\right)$ (see Table 1).

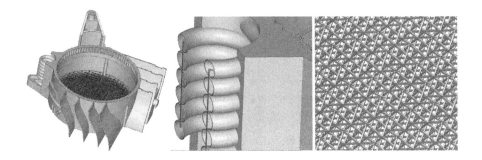

Fig. 12. Complex 3D object with magnified parts.

Fig. 13. Sphere trees constructed via medial axes, octrees, and sphere packings.

6   Experimental Results

We conducted our experiments on an Intel Core i5 2500K PC with 16GB DDR RAM. We selected publically available 3D CAD models, including the model *cow* of the University of North Carolina (with 5 804 triangles), the model *bunny* of the Stanford University (69 451), and the model *ShowPart* from Renishaw (250 934, see Fig. 12). Further models are *angel, dragon, hand, buddha* and belong to the Stanford 3D Scanning Repository and Greg Turk's Large Geometric Models Archive.

Table 2 compares some selected sphere tree construction algorithms For the sphere tree computed via medial axis, we also measure the impact of a larger branching factor of interior nodes. A visualization for applying three different construction algorithms to the *cow* model is shown in Fig. 13.

For the initial state we placed the objects on a sphere around the center, and started the simulated annealing process (maximizing centrality or minimizing height, see Fig. 14). As expected, the octree construction was by far the fastest, but in all but one case (bunny) the medial axis yielded fewer leaf nodes of the sphere tree. Decreasing the branching factor further slows down sphere-tree construction.

Besides changing the user-supplied optimization function we experimented with different branching strategies in the simulated annealing algorithm: trans-

Table 2. Sphere-tree construction (b: branching factor).

Model	Approach	Leaves	Depth	Time
ShowPart	Octree	105 027	8	0,95s
	Medial Axis ($b = 16$)	33 483	6	44,27s
	Medial Axis ($b = 8$)	33 483	8	45,64s
	Medial Axis ($b = 4$)	33 483	11	53,45s
	Medial Axis ($b = 2$)	33 483	24	78,58s
Bunny	Octree	14 095	7	0,20s
	Medial Axis ($b = 16$)	25 755	6	23,86s
	Medial Axis ($b = 8$)	25 755	8	25,07s
	Medial Axis ($b = 4$)	25 755	11	27,14s
	Medial Axis ($b = 2$)	25 755	21	36,91s
Cow	Octree	8 142	7	0,03s
	Medial Axis ($b = 16$)	1 634	4	1,70s
	Medial Axis ($b = 8$)	1 634	6	1,76s
	Medial Axis ($b = 4$)	1 634	8	1,80s
	Medial Axis ($b = 2$)	1 634	17	2,10s
Angel	Octree	28 790	8	1,44s
	Medial Axis ($b = 16$)	7 875	5	14,75s
	Medial Axis ($b = 8$)	7 875	7	15,24s
	Medial Axis ($b = 4$)	7 875	10	15,98s
	Medial Axis ($b = 2$)	7 875	20	18,57s
Dragon	Octree	14 394	7	2,06s
	Medial Axis ($b = 16$)	13 961	6	23,64s
	Medial Axis ($b = 8$)	13 961	7	24,24s
	Medial Axis ($b = 4$)	13 961	11	25,10s
	Medial Axis ($b = 2$)	13 961	21	31,58s
Hand	Octree	5 390	7	1,38s
	Medial Axis ($b = 16$)	3 866	5	12,54s
	Medial Axis ($b = 8$)	3 866	6	12,99s
	Medial Axis ($b = 4$)	3 866	9	13,23s
	Medial Axis ($b = 2$)	3 866	18	14,23s
Buddha	Octree	48 428	8	3,00s
	Medial Axis ($b = 16$)	15 080	5	32,31s
	Medial Axis ($b = 8$)	15 080	7	33,65s
	Medial Axis ($b = 4$)	15 080	11	34,24s
	Medial Axis ($b = 2$)	15 080	22	44,22s

lation and/or rotation on one/all axis and of one/all models, the best results were obtained with translating or rotation of one model and one axis at a time. Dynamically adapting the cooling process to the number of rotational and translational steps was fortunate (see Fig. 16).

Despite the considerably larger number of leaves, the intersection test for sphere trees based on the octree data structure was the fastest. As indicated in Fig. 15 with tight upper and lower bounds for the cover, a possible reason for this unexpected behavior is that the spheres in the octree have a smaller over-

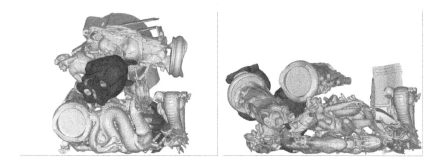

Fig. 14. Arrangement of 3D objects, maximizing centrality (left) and total height (right).

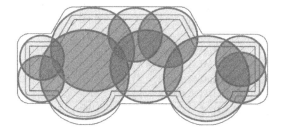

Fig. 15. Min. (blue) and max. distance (red) of medial axis sphere-tree cover of object (green).

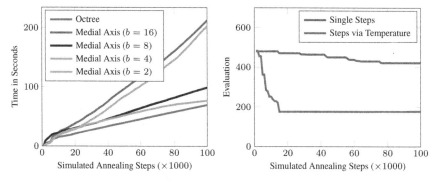

Fig. 16. Result of the optimization process.

lap than for the construction via the medial axis. Moreover, in the optimization algorithm we did not aim at the Boolean decisions, but computed the number of intersecting spheres. For sphere trees constructed via the medial axis computation, we obtained the best performance, with a sweet-spot branching factor $b \approx 4$.

7   Conclusion and Outlook

In the area of combinatorial search there is a large body of AI research on packing regular-shaped objects (squares, rectangles, boxes). In this paper we have seen an approach to solve the packing problem of irregular-shaped objects, which has practical implications for 3D printing in saving both production time and cost. The goal was to find a collision-free arrangement preserving a minimal distance between the objects, and optimizing a user-defined objective function.

The algorithm is practical and its refined implementation is used in industrial practice, which has direct implications to the software's flexibility and quality. The user can add requirements to the objective function, like a small height, a high surface quality, a low number of supports, less stretch, small distances for the laser travel. Advanced topics are stability and extractability. For the concurrent print we allow flexible change to the objective function as the evaluation changes quickly wrt. customer demands, varying hardware, and chosen materials.

The research interest is studying the data structure for engineering the efficiency of the optimization algorithm, which boils down to frequently computing some score for the intersection of objects. Our experimental study reveals that there might not be a uniformly best intersection routine. While medial axis and sphere packings produce a smaller number of spheres, computing the intersection volume is often slower than by using sphere trees extracted straight from the octrees.

The packings we found at the end of the simulated annealing process were all valid. The results were better, if the step size was dynamically adjusted to the temperature parameter. Our simple evaluation function relied on counting the number of intersections (as an indicator for computing the volume of the sphere tree intersection area) in order to improve the arrangement of objects. Other global optimization procedures only need efficient intersection tests for reducing the set of possible successor candidates. Hence, one future resarch avenue is to apply recent advances in Monte-Carlo tree search, which amounts to sample random packings, while incrementally learning their best arrangement [4].

References

1. Bradshaw, G., O'Sullivan, C.: Adaptive medial-axis approximation for sphere-tree construction. ACM Transactions On Graphics **23**(1), 1–26 (2004)
2. Crainic, T.G., Perboli, G., Tadei, R.: Recent Advances in Multi-Dimensional Packing Problems. InTech (2012)
3. Devillers, O., Pion, S., Teillaud, M.: Walking in a triangulation. In: Symposium on Computational Geometry, pp. 106–114 (2001)
4. Edelkamp, S., Gath, M., Rohde, M.: Monte-carlo tree search for 3D packing with object orientation. In: German Conference on Artificial Intelligence, pp. 285–296 (2014)
5. Egeblad, J., Nielsen, B.K., Odgaard, A.: Fast neighborhood search for two- and three-dimensional nesting problems. Europ. Journ. of Oper. Res. **183**(3), 1249–1266 (2007)

6. Gärtner, B.: Fast and robust smallest enclosing balls. In: Nešetřil, J. (ed.) ESA 1999. LNCS, vol. 1643, pp. 325–338. Springer, Heidelberg (1999)

7. Guibas, L.J., Knuth, D.E., Sharir, M.: Randomized incremental construction of Delaunay and Voronoi diagrams. Algorithmica **7**(4), 381–413 (1992)

8. Huang, E., Korf, R.E.: Optimal rectangle packing on non-square benchmarks. In: AAAI (2010)

9. Huang, E., Korf, R.E.: Optimal packing of high-precision rectangles. In: SOCS (2011)

10. Hubbard, P.M.: Collision detection for interactive graphics applications. IEEE Transactions on Visualization and Computer Graphics **1**(3), 218–230 (1995)

11. Ikonen, I., Biles, W.E., Kumar, A., Wissel, J.C., Ragade, R.K.: A genetic algorithm for packing three-dimensional non-convex objects having cavities and holes. In: International Conference on Genetic Algorithms, pp. 591–598 (1997)

12. Korf, R.E.: Optimal rectangle packing: Initial results. In: ICAPS, pp. 287–295 (2003)

13. Korf, R.E.: Optimal rectangle packing: new results. In: ICAPS, pp. 142–149 (2004)

14. Lim, A., Ying, W.: A new method for the three dimensional container packing problem. In: IJCAI, pp. 342–347 (2001)

15. Moffitt, M.D., Pollack, M.E.: Optimal rectangle packing: a Meta-CSP approach. In: ICAPS, pp. 93–102 (2006)

16. Mücke, E.P., Saias, I., Zhu, B.: Fast randomized point location without preprocessing in two- and three-dimensional delaunay triangulations. In: Symposium on Computational Geometry, pp. 274–283 (1996)

17. Nezhad, A.S., Vatani, M., Barazandeh, F., Rahimi, A.R.: Multi objective optimization of part orientation in stereolithography. In: International Conference on Simulation, Modelling and Optimization, pp. 36–40 (2009)

18. Padhye, N., Deb, K.: Multi-objective optimisation and multi-criteria decision making for FDM using evolutionary approaches. In: Multi-objective Evolutionary Optimisation for Product Design and Manufacturing, pp. 219–247 (2011)

19. Palmer, I.J., Grimsdale, R.L.: Collision detection for animation using sphere-trees. Computer Graphics Forum **14**(2), 105–116 (1995)

20. Turk, G.: Generating random points in triangles. In: Glassner, A.S. (ed.) Graphics Gems, pp. 24–28. Academic Press Professional Inc. (1990)

21. van den Bergen, G.: Efficient collision detection of complex deformable models using AABB trees. Journal of Graphics, GPU, & Game Tools **2**(4), 1–13 (1997)

22. Watson, D.F.: Computing the n-dimensional delaunay tessellation with application to Voronoi polytopes, 24(2) (1981)

23. Weller, R., Frese, U., Zachmann, G.: Parallel collision detection in constant time. In: Workshop on Virtual Reality Interactions and Physical, pp. 61–70 (2013)

24. Wu, S., Kay, M., King, R., Vila-Parrish, A., Warsing, D.: Multi-objective optimization of 3D packing problem in additive manufacturing. In: Industrial and Systems Engineering Research Conference (2014)

Deciding Subsumers of Least Fixpoint Concepts w.r.t. general $\mathcal{EL}$-TBoxes

Shasha Feng[1], Michel Ludwig[2]([⊠]), and Dirk Walther[2]

[1] Jilin University, Changchun, China
fengss@jlu.edu.cn
[2] Theoretical Computer Science, TU Dresden, Dresden, Germany
{michel,dirk}@tcs.inf.tu-dresden.de

Abstract. In this paper we provide a procedure for deciding subsumptions of the form $\mathcal{T} \models \mathcal{C} \sqsubseteq E$, where $\mathcal{C}$ is an $\mathcal{ELU}_\mu$-concept, E an $\mathcal{ELU}$-concept and $\mathcal{T}$ a general $\mathcal{EL}$-TBox. Deciding such subsumptions can be used for computing the logical difference between general $\mathcal{EL}$-TBoxes. Our procedure is based on checking for the existence of a certain simulation between hypergraph representations of the set of subsumees of $\mathcal{C}$ and of E w.r.t. $\mathcal{T}$, respectively. With the aim of keeping the procedure implementable, we provide a detailed construction of such hypergraphs deliberately avoiding the use of intricate automata-theoretic techniques.

1 Introduction

Description Logics (DLs) are popular KR languages [3]. Light-weight DLs such as $\mathcal{EL}$ with tractable reasoning problems in particular are commonly used ontology languages [1,2]. The notion of logical difference between TBoxes was introduced as a logic-based approach to ontology versioning [10]. Computing the logical difference between $\mathcal{EL}$-TBoxes can be reduced to fixpoint reasoning w.r.t. TBoxes in a hybrid μ-calculus [8,13]. This involves subsumptions of the form $\mathcal{T} \models \mathcal{C} \sqsubseteq \mathcal{D}$, where $\mathcal{C}$ is an $\mathcal{ELU}_\mu$-concept, i.e. $\mathcal{EL}$-concepts enriched with disjunction and the least fixpoint operator, $\mathcal{D}$ an $\mathcal{EL}_\nu$-concept, i.e. $\mathcal{EL}$-concepts enriched with the greatest fixpoint operator, and $\mathcal{T}$ an $\mathcal{EL}$-TBox. Such subsumptions can be reduced to finding an $\mathcal{ELU}$-concept E such that $\mathcal{T} \models \mathcal{C} \sqsubseteq E$ and $\mathcal{T} \models E \sqsubseteq \mathcal{D}$. Here E acts as an *interpolant* between the fixpoint concepts $\mathcal{C}$ and $\mathcal{D}$ w.r.t. $\mathcal{T}$. In this paper, we only focus on deciding the former type of subsumption, whose decision procedure is arguably more involved than the one for the latter type of subsumption. Deciding the existence of a suitable $\mathcal{ELU}$-concept E, however, will be handled in another paper. Unfortunately, the fact that the required fixpoint reasoning can be solved using automata theoretic techniques does not mean that one can immediately derive a practical algorithm from it [4,9,13]. We therefore aim to develop a procedure that can be implemented more easily by following our hypergraph-based approach to the logical difference problem as introduced in [6]

The second and third authors were supported by the German Research Foundation (DFG) within the Cluster of Excellence 'Center for Advancing Electronics Dresden'.

© Springer International Publishing Switzerland 2015
S. Hölldobler et al. (Eds.): KI 2015, LNAI 9324, pp. 59–71, 2015.
DOI: 10.1007/978-3-319-24489-1_5

and further extended in [12]. The idea here is to solve the subsumption problem by checking for the existence of a certain simulation between hypergraphs that represent the set of subsumees of C and of E w.r.t. $\mathcal{T}$, respectively.

We proceed as follows. In the next section we start with reviewing the basic DL $\mathcal{EL}$ together with its extensions with disjunction and the least fixpoint operator. In Section 3 we present a three-step procedure for computing a normal form of C and of E w.r.t. $\mathcal{T}$ in detail, which is then used in Section 4 to decide the subsumption problem $\mathcal{T} \models C \sqsubseteq E$. Finally in Section 5, we conclude the paper with a discussion on how the $\mathcal{ELU}$-concept E can be characterised as a most-consequence preserving subsumer, which is a more general version of the notion of least common subsumer [7].

2   Preliminaries

We start by briefly reviewing the lightweight description logic $\mathcal{EL}$ together with the extensions of $\mathcal{EL}$ that we consider in this paper.

Let $\mathsf{N_C}$, $\mathsf{N_R}$, and $\mathsf{N_V}$ be mutually disjoint sets of concept names, role names, and variable names, respectively. We assume these sets to be countably infinite. We typically use A, B to denote concept names, r, s to indicate role names, and x, y to denote variable names.

The sets of $\mathcal{EL}$-concepts C, $\mathcal{ELU}$-concepts D, $\mathcal{ELU}_V$-concepts E, and $\mathcal{ELU}_\mu$-concepts $\mathcal{F}$ are built according to the following grammar rules:

$$C ::= \top \mid A \mid C \sqcap C \mid \exists r.C$$
$$D ::= \top \mid A \mid D \sqcap D \mid D \sqcup D \mid \exists r.D$$
$$E ::= \top \mid A \mid E \sqcap E \mid E \sqcup E \mid \exists r.E \mid x$$
$$\mathcal{F} ::= \top \mid A \mid \mathcal{F} \sqcap \mathcal{F} \mid \mathcal{F} \sqcup \mathcal{F} \mid \exists r.\mathcal{F} \mid x \mid \mu x.\mathcal{F}$$

where $A \in \mathsf{N_C}$, $r, s \in \mathsf{N_R}$, and $x \in \mathsf{N_V}$. We use calligraphic letters to denote concepts that may contain a least fixpoint operator. We denote with L the set of all L-concepts, where $L \in \{\mathcal{EL}, \mathcal{ELU}, \mathcal{ELU}_V, \mathcal{ELU}_\mu\}$. For an $\mathcal{ELU}_\mu$-concept $\mathcal{C}$, the set of *free variables* in $\mathcal{C}$, denoted by $\mathrm{FV}(\mathcal{C})$ is defined inductively as follows: $\mathrm{FV}(\top) = \emptyset$, $\mathrm{FV}(A) = \emptyset$, $\mathrm{FV}(\mathcal{D}_1 \sqcap \mathcal{D}_2) = \mathrm{FV}(\mathcal{D}_1) \cup \mathrm{FV}(\mathcal{D}_2)$, $\mathrm{FV}(\mathcal{D}_1 \sqcup \mathcal{D}_2) = \mathrm{FV}(\mathcal{D}_1) \cup \mathrm{FV}(\mathcal{D}_2)$, $\mathrm{FV}(\exists r.\mathcal{D}) = \mathrm{FV}(\mathcal{D})$, $\mathrm{FV}(x) = \{x\}$, $\mathrm{FV}(\mu x.\mathcal{D}) = \mathrm{FV}(\mathcal{D}) \backslash \{x\}$. An $\mathcal{ELU}_\mu$-concept $\mathcal{C}$ is *closed* if $\mathcal{C}$ does not contain free occurrences of variables, i.e. $\mathrm{FV}(\mathcal{C}) = \emptyset$. In the following we assume that every $\mathcal{ELU}_\mu$-concept $\mathcal{C}$ is *well-formed*, i.e. every subconcept of the form $\mu x.\mathcal{D}$ occurring in $\mathcal{C}$ binds a fresh variable x.

An $\mathcal{EL}$-*TBox* $\mathcal{T}$ is a finite set of axioms, where an axiom can be a *concept inclusion* $C \sqsubseteq C'$, or a *concept equation* $C \equiv C'$, for $\mathcal{EL}$-concepts C, C'.

The semantics of $\mathcal{ELU}_\mu$ is defined using interpretations $\mathcal{I} = (\Delta^{\mathcal{I}}, \cdot^{\mathcal{I}})$, where the domain $\Delta^{\mathcal{I}}$ is a non-empty set, and $\cdot^{\mathcal{I}}$ is a function mapping each concept name A to a subset $A^{\mathcal{I}}$ of $\Delta^{\mathcal{I}}$ and every role name r to a binary relation $r^{\mathcal{I}} \subseteq \Delta^{\mathcal{I}} \times \Delta^{\mathcal{I}}$. Interpretations are extended to concepts using a function $\cdot^{\mathcal{I},\xi}$ that is parameterised by an *assignment function* that maps each variable $x \in \mathsf{N_V}$ to a set $\xi(x) \subseteq \Delta^{\mathcal{I}}$. Given an interpretation $\mathcal{I}$ and an assignment ξ, the extension of an $\mathcal{ELU}_\mu$-concept is defined inductively as follows: $\top^{\mathcal{I},\xi} := \Delta^{\mathcal{I}}$, $x^{\mathcal{I},\xi} := \xi(x)$ for $x \in N_V$, $(\mathcal{C}_1 \sqcap \mathcal{C}_2)^{\mathcal{I},\xi} := \mathcal{C}_1^{\mathcal{I}} \cap \mathcal{C}_2^{\mathcal{I}}$, $(\exists r.\mathcal{C})^{\mathcal{I},\xi} := \{ x \in \Delta^{\mathcal{I}} \mid \exists y \in \mathcal{C}^{\mathcal{I},\xi} : (x,y) \in r^{\mathcal{I}} \}$, and $(\mu x.\mathcal{C})^{\mathcal{I},\xi} = \bigcap \{ W \subseteq \Delta^{\mathcal{I}} \mid \mathcal{C}^{\mathcal{I},\xi[x \mapsto W]} \subseteq W \}$, where $\xi[x \mapsto W]$ denotes the assignment ξ modified by mapping x to W.

For $\mathcal{ELU}_\mu$-concepts $\mathcal{C}$ and $\mathcal{D}$, an interpretation $\mathcal{I}$ *satisfies* $\mathcal{C}$, an axiom $\mathcal{C} \sqsubseteq \mathcal{D}$ or $\mathcal{C} \equiv \mathcal{D}$ if, respectively, $\mathcal{C}^{\mathcal{I},\xi_\emptyset} \neq \emptyset$, $\mathcal{C}^{\mathcal{I},\xi_\emptyset} \subseteq \mathcal{D}^{\mathcal{I},\xi_\emptyset}$, or $\mathcal{C}^{\mathcal{I},\xi_\emptyset} = \mathcal{D}^{\mathcal{I},\xi_\emptyset}$, where $\xi_\emptyset(x) = \emptyset$ for every $x \in N_V$. We write $\mathcal{I} \models \alpha$ iff $\mathcal{I}$ satisfies the axiom α. An interpretation $\mathcal{I}$ *satisfies* a TBox $\mathcal{T}$ iff $\mathcal{I}$ satisfies all axioms in $\mathcal{T}$; in this case, we say that $\mathcal{I}$ is a *model* of $\mathcal{T}$. An axiom α *follows* from a TBox $\mathcal{T}$, written $\mathcal{T} \models \alpha$, iff for all models $\mathcal{I}$ of $\mathcal{T}$, we have that $\mathcal{I} \models \alpha$. Deciding whether $\mathcal{T} \models C \sqsubseteq C'$, for two $\mathcal{EL}$-concepts C and C', can be done in polynomial time in the size of $\mathcal{T}$ and C, C' [1,5].

A signature Σ is a finite set of symbols from N_C and N_R. The signature $\mathsf{sig}(\mathcal{C})$, $\mathsf{sig}(\alpha)$ or $\mathsf{sig}(\mathcal{T})$ of the concept $\mathcal{C}$, axiom α or TBox $\mathcal{T}$ is the set of concept and role names occurring in $\mathcal{C}$, α or $\mathcal{T}$, respectively. Analogously, $\mathsf{sub}(\mathcal{C})$, $\mathsf{sub}(\alpha)$, or $\mathsf{sub}(\mathcal{T})$ denotes the set of subconcepts occurring in $\mathcal{C}$, α or $\mathcal{T}$, respectively.

An $\mathcal{EL}$-TBox $\mathcal{T}$ is *normalised* if it only contains $\mathcal{EL}$-concept inclusions of the forms $\top \sqsubseteq B$, $A_1 \sqcap \ldots \sqcap A_n \sqsubseteq B$, $A \sqsubseteq \exists r.B$, or $\exists r.A \sqsubseteq B$, where $A, A_i, B \in N_C$, $r \in N_R$, and $n \geq 1$. Every $\mathcal{EL}$-TBox $\mathcal{T}$ can be normalised in polynomial time in the size of $\mathcal{T}$ with a linear increase in the size of the normalised TBox w.r.t. $\mathcal{T}$ such that the resulting TBox is a conservative extension of $\mathcal{T}$ [10].

3   Normal Form Computation

Our aim is to check whether $\mathcal{T} \models \mathcal{C} \sqsubseteq \mathcal{D}$ holds with the help of simulations, where $\mathcal{T}$ an $\mathcal{EL}$-TBox, $\mathcal{C}$ is an $\mathcal{ELU}_\mu$-concept, and $\mathcal{D}$ an $\mathcal{ELU}$-concept. Simulations are typically used to characterise properties between two graph structures, e.g. behavioural equivalence. To be able to apply simulations to our subsumption problem, we represent the unfoldings of $\mathcal{C}$ and the subsumees of $\mathcal{D}$ w.r.t. $\mathcal{T}$ in two separate hypergraphs. Intuitively, in such a hypergraph every node v together with its outgoing hyperedges represents a disjunction of the form $\bigsqcup_{i=1}^{m} A_i \sqcup \bigsqcup_{j=1}^{n} \exists r_j.C_j$ where the A_i and r_j are pairwise different, respectively. A hyperedge e in such a hypergraph is labelled with role names and it connects one source node with several target nodes. A hyperedge $e = (v_0, \{v_1, \ldots, v_\ell\})$ $(\ell \geq 1)$ labelled with a role r represents an existential restriction $\exists r.\varphi$ where φ stands for the conjunction of the nodes $v_1, \ldots, v_\ell$. A crucial condition is that for every role r, a node has at most one outgoing hyperedge labelled with r as otherwise our simulation notion is not applicable. In this sense, the hypergraph can be seen to be *deterministic*. To obtain such a deterministic hypergraph, it is necessary to merge disjunctively connected existential restrictions involving the same role name. We therefore design the hypergraphs to be a conjunctive normal form representation of the set of respective subsumees as it becomes immediate to identify the existential restrictions that have to be merged. The hypergraph for an $\mathcal{ELU}$-concept is a tree, whereas the hypergraph for an $\mathcal{ELU}_\mu$-concept, or for an $\mathcal{ELU}$-concept w.r.t. a cyclic TBox, may contain cycles.

A related normal form, later called *automaton normal form* [4], was introduced in [9] for the full modal μ-calculus with the difference that disjunctive normal form was used. In particular it is shown that every modal μ-calculus formula is equivalent to a formula in normal form. The transformation of a formula into automaton normal form is based on an involved, non-trivial construction using parity automata [4,9]. For our purposes, however, it was not immediate how to derive a practical algorithm from such a construction.

Our construction is essentially based on applying the following three equivalences as rewrite rules to transform $\mathcal{ELU}_\mu$-concepts into the desired format.

(i) $\mathcal{C} \sqcup (\mathcal{D}_1 \sqcap \mathcal{D}_2) \equiv (\mathcal{C} \sqcup \mathcal{D}_1) \sqcap (\mathcal{C} \sqcup \mathcal{D}_2)$
(ii) $(\exists r.\mathcal{C}) \sqcup (\exists r.\mathcal{D}) \equiv \exists r.(\mathcal{C} \sqcup \mathcal{D})$
(iii) $\mu x.\mathcal{C} \equiv \mathcal{C}[x \mapsto \mu x.\mathcal{C}]$

Equivalence (i) is used to transform every "existential level" of the $\mathcal{ELU}_\mu$-concept into conjunctive normal form, (ii) to regroup and merge existentials that involve the same role, and (iii) to unfold fixpoint variables. However, due to the unfolding of fixpoints, a straightforward rewriting of concepts using these equivalences may not terminate, and it is not clear how to formulate a termination condition based on the sequence of concept rewritings.

In the following sections we present a detailed construction of our normal form, and show how termination can be ensured. Our procedure consists of the following three steps:

(1) construct a finite labelled tree representing the successive applications of the equivalences (i)–(iii);
(2) transform the tree that was obtained in the previous step into an hypergraph by removing superfluous nodes, introducing hyperedges that represent existential restrictions over conjunctions, and possibly form cycles;
(3) simplify the hypergraph obtained in the previous step by pruning nodes that can safely be removed while preserving equivalence and that our simulation notion (Section 3.3) cannot handle correctly.

Before presenting the three steps, we introduce the following auxiliary notions. An $\mathcal{ELU}$-concept C is said to be *atomic* iff $C = \top$, $C = A \in \mathsf{N_C}$, or $C = \exists r.D$ for some $\mathcal{ELU}$-concept D. We denote with $\mathrm{Atoms}(S)$ the set of atomic concepts from a set S of $\mathcal{ELU}_\mu$-concepts.

Definition 1 (μ-Suppression). *Let $\mathcal{C}$ be an $\mathcal{ELU}_\mu$-concept. We define an $\mathcal{ELU}_V$-concept $\mathcal{C}^\dagger$ inductively as follows:* $\top^\dagger := \top$, $A^\dagger := A$ *for* $A \in \mathsf{N_C}$, $x^\dagger := x$ *for* $x \in \mathsf{N_V}$, $(\mu x.\mathcal{D})^\dagger := x$, $(\mathcal{C}_1 \sqcap \mathcal{C}_2)^\dagger := (\mathcal{C}_1^\dagger) \sqcap (\mathcal{C}_2^\dagger)$, $(\mathcal{C}_1 \sqcup \mathcal{C}_2)^\dagger := (\mathcal{C}_1^\dagger) \sqcup (\mathcal{C}_2^\dagger)$, *and* $(\exists r.\mathcal{D})^\dagger := \exists r.(\mathcal{D}^\dagger)$ *for $\mathcal{ELU}_\mu$-concepts $\mathcal{C}_1, \mathcal{C}_2, \mathcal{D}$.*

Example 1. Let $\mathcal{C} = (\exists s.\top) \sqcap (\exists r.\mu x.\mathcal{C}_1)$ for $\mathcal{C}_1 = A \sqcup \exists r.\mu y.\mathcal{C}_2$ and $\mathcal{C}_2 = B \sqcup \exists s.y \sqcup x$. Then $\mathcal{C}^\dagger = (\exists s.\top) \sqcap (\exists r.x)$, $(\mathcal{C}_1)^\dagger = A \sqcup \exists r.y$ and $(\mathcal{C}_2)^\dagger = B \sqcup \exists s.y \sqcup x$.

Definition 2 (Variable Expansion Function). *Let $\mathcal{C}$ be a closed $\mathcal{ELU}_\mu$-concept. A variable expansion function for $\mathcal{C}$ is a partial function $\xi_\mathcal{C} : \mathcal{ELU}_V \to 2^{\mathcal{ELU}_V}$ defined as follows: for every $x \in var(\mathcal{C})$,*

$$\xi_\mathcal{C}(x) := \{\, \mathcal{D}^\dagger \mid \mu x.\mathcal{D} \in \mathrm{sub}(\mathcal{C}) \,\}.$$

Note that since $\mathcal{C}$ is well-formed, $\xi_\mathcal{C}(x)$ is a singleton set for every $x \in \mathrm{dom}(\xi_\mathcal{C})$.

Example 2. Let $\mathcal{C}$ be defined as in Example 1. Then we obtain the following variable expansion function $\xi_\mathcal{C}$ for $\mathcal{C}$: $\xi_\mathcal{C} = \{x \mapsto A \sqcup \exists r.y, y \mapsto B \sqcup \exists s.y \sqcup x\}$.

Definition 3 (TBox Expansion Function). *Let $\mathcal{T}$ be a normalised $\mathcal{EL}$-TBox and let D be an $\mathcal{ELU}$-concept. A TBox expansion function for $(D, \mathcal{T})$ is a partial function $\xi_{(D,\mathcal{T})} : \mathcal{ELU}_V \to 2^{\mathcal{ELU}}$ defined as follows: for every $\varphi \in \mathrm{sub}(\mathcal{T}) \cup \mathrm{sub}(D)$,*

$$\xi_{(D,\mathcal{T})}(\varphi) := \{\, \psi \in \mathrm{sub}(\mathcal{T}) \cup \mathrm{sub}(D) \mid \mathcal{T} \models \psi \sqsubseteq \varphi \,\}.$$

Example 3. Let $\mathcal{T} = \{A \sqsubseteq Z, \exists r.X \sqsubseteq Z, Z \sqsubseteq \exists r.Y, \exists r.Y \sqsubseteq X, B \sqsubseteq Y\}$ and $D = \top$. Then we obtain the following TBox expansion function for $\mathcal{T}$: $\xi_{(D,\mathcal{T})} = \{\, \top \mapsto \{\top\}, A \mapsto \{A\}, B \mapsto \{B\}, Y \mapsto \{B, Y\}, Z \mapsto \{A, Z, \exists r.X\}, X \mapsto \{A, X, Z, \exists r.X, \exists r.Y\}, \exists r.X \mapsto \{\exists r.X\}, \exists r.Y \mapsto \{A, Z, \exists r.X, \exists r.Y\} \,\}$.

3.1 Step 1

We start with a tableau-like procedure to produce a finite labelled tree, called *concept expansion tree*. The tree is iteratively constructed using four expansion rules. For an $\mathcal{ELU}_\mu$-concept $\mathcal{C}$ we start from a root node labelled with the $\mathcal{ELU}_V$-concept $\mathcal{C}^\dagger$ using the variable expansion function $\xi_\mathcal{C}$ in the expansion rules, whereas for an $\mathcal{ELU}$-concept D and an $\mathcal{EL}$-TBox $\mathcal{T}$ the root node is labelled with $D^\dagger = D$ and the TBox expansion function $\xi_{(D,\mathcal{T})}$ is used instead. The tree structure and the expansion rules are defined as follows.

Definition 4 (Concept Expansion Tree). *Let $\mathcal{C}$ be a closed $\mathcal{ELU}_\mu$-concept, and let $\xi : \mathcal{ELU}_V \to 2^{\mathcal{ELU}_V}$ be a TBox or variable expansion function. A concept expansion tree for $\mathcal{C}$ w.r.t. ξ is a finite labelled tree $T = (\mathcal{V}, \mathcal{E}, \mathcal{L})$, where $\mathcal{V}$ is a finite, non-empty set of nodes, $\mathcal{E} \subseteq \mathcal{V} \times \mathcal{V}$ is a set of edges and $\mathcal{L}$ is a labelling function mapping every node $v \in \mathcal{V}$ to a subset $\mathcal{L}(v)$ of $\mathrm{sub}(\mathcal{C}) \cup \mathrm{sub}(\mathrm{ran}(\xi))$. We say that a node $v \in \mathcal{V}$ is blocked iff there exists an ancestor v' of v in T such that $\mathcal{L}(v) = \mathcal{L}(v')$.*

A concept expansion tree $T = (\mathcal{V}, \mathcal{E}, \mathcal{L})$ for $\mathcal{C}$ w.r.t. ξ is initialised with a single node v_0 with $\mathcal{L}(v_0) = \{\mathcal{C}^\dagger\}$ and T is expanded using the following rules which are only applied on leaf nodes $v \in \mathcal{V}$ that are not blocked, and the rule (Exists) is only applied when no other rule is applicable.

(Disj) *if $C_1 \sqcup \ldots \sqcup C_n \in \mathcal{L}(v)$ and $\{C_1, \ldots, C_n\} \not\subseteq \mathcal{L}(v)$, add the node v' with $\mathcal{L}(v') = \mathcal{L}(v) \cup \{C_1, \ldots, C_n\}$ as a child of v;*

(Conj) *if $C \sqcap D \in \mathcal{L}(v)$ and $\{C, D\} \cap \mathcal{L}(v) = \emptyset$, add the two nodes v_1, v_2 with $\mathcal{L}(v_1) = \mathcal{L}(v) \cup \{C\}$, $\mathcal{L}(v_2) = \mathcal{L}(v) \cup \{D\}$ as children of v;*

(Expansion) *if $\varphi \in \mathcal{L}(v)$, $\varphi \in \mathrm{dom}(\xi)$, and $\xi(\varphi) \not\subseteq \mathcal{L}(v)$, add the node v' with $\mathcal{L}(v') = \mathcal{L}(v) \cup \xi(\varphi)$ as a child of v;*

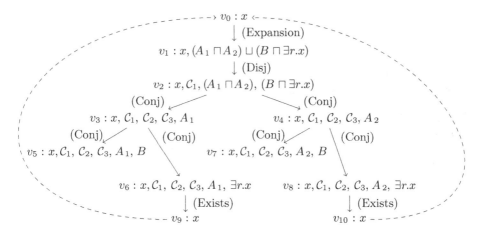

Fig. 1. Fully-expanded concept expansion tree for Example 4

(Exists) *if Atoms($\mathcal{L}(v)$)* $= \{A_1, \ldots, A_m\} \cup \{\exists r_1.C_1, \ldots, \exists r_n.C_n\}$, *then for every* $r \in \{r_1, \ldots, r_n\}$, *add the node* v_r *with* $\mathcal{L}(v_r) = \{C_i \mid r_i = r, 1 \leq i \leq n\}$ *as a child of* v.

A concept tree is said to be fully expanded *iff none of the expansion rules is applicable.*

The rule (Disj) is responsible for splitting disjunctions and adding the disjuncts to the respective node label. The rule (Conj) splits conjunctions and distributes the conjuncts over new successor nodes. The (Expansion) rule handles the expansion of fixpoint variables and TBox entailments. The rule (Exists) adds one (and only one) successor for every role occurring in some existential restriction contained in the node label. In this sense, the resulting expansion tree can be seen to be deterministic. The rule (Exists) ensures that all the subconcepts of existential restrictions over the same role are included disjunctively into the successor node dedicated to that role. For instance, if $\{\exists r.C_1, \exists r.C_2\} \subseteq \mathcal{L}(v)$ for some node v, then the concepts C_1, C_2 will be added to the label of the successor node of v for r. We assume that the rule (Exists) has the least priority among all expansion rules, i.e. (Exists) is only applied when no other rule is applicable. During the expansion process, every rule is applied on leaf nodes that are not blocked. A node is blocked if there exists an ancestor node with the same label.

Example 4. Let $\mathcal{C} = \mu x.\mathcal{C}_1$ where $\mathcal{C}_1 = \mathcal{C}_2 \sqcup \mathcal{C}_3$ and $\mathcal{C}_2 = A_1 \sqcap A_2$, $\mathcal{C}_3 = B \sqcap \exists r.x$.

The fully expanded concept expansion tree $T = (\mathcal{V}, \mathcal{E}, \mathcal{L})$ for $\mathcal{C}$ is shown in Figure 1. The nodes together with their labels are represented in the form '$v : \mathcal{L}(v)$' for $v \in \mathcal{V}$. Edges are represented as arrows between nodes. Arrows are additionally labelled by the expansion rule that was applied. Blocked nodes are indicated using dashed arrows.

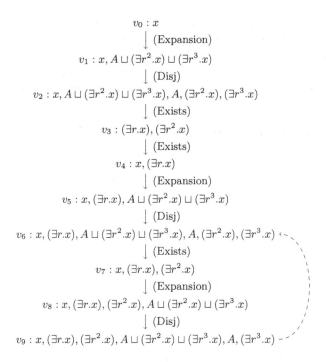

Fig. 2. Fully-expanded concept expansion tree for Example 5

Example 5. Let $\mathcal{D} = \mu x.(A \sqcup (\exists r.\exists r.x) \sqcup (\exists r.\exists r \exists r.x))$. The fully expanded concept expansion tree for $\mathcal{D}$ is depicted in Figure 2.

3.2 Step 2

In the second step of our normalisation procedure the concept expansion tree that was obtained in the previous step is transformed into an *expansion hypergraph*.

Definition 5 (Expansion Hypergraph). *Let S be a finite set of atomic $\mathcal{ELU}_V$-concepts. An* expansion hypergraph *over S is a finite labelled directed hypergraph $(\mathcal{V}, \mathcal{E}, \mathcal{L}, \mathcal{R})$ with a dedicated set $\mathcal{R}$ of root nodes, where*

- *$\mathcal{V}$ is a finite, non-empty set of nodes;*
- *$\mathcal{E} \subseteq \mathcal{V} \times 2^{\mathcal{V}}$ is a set of directed hyperedges;*
- *$\mathcal{L} \colon \mathcal{V} \cup \mathcal{E} \to 2^S \cup 2^{N_R}$ is a labelling function, mapping nodes $v \in \mathcal{V}$ to subsets $\mathcal{L}(v) \subseteq S$, and mapping edges $e \in \mathcal{E}$ to sets of role names $\mathcal{L}(e) \subseteq \mathsf{sig}(S) \cap N_R$;*
- *$\mathcal{R} \subseteq \mathcal{V}$ is a non-empty set of root nodes,*

such that if $\mathcal{L}(v) = \mathcal{L}(v')$ for some $v, v' \in \mathcal{V}$, then $v = v'$.

Nodes in such hypergraphs are labelled with sets of atomic concepts and sets of roles occurring in the outermost existential restrictions of such concepts are the labels of hyperedges. Expansion hypergraphs have a dedicated set of root nodes, indicating a starting point for concept unfoldings, which will be defined later. Note also that in expansion hypergraphs all the nodes have different labels, which ensures that only finitely many expansion hypergraphs over S exist.

We now describe how a fully expanded concept expansion tree can be transformed into an expansion hypergraph over the set of atomic concepts occurring in the node labels of the concept expansion tree.

Definition 6 (Concept Expansion Tree Transformation). *Let* $T = (\mathcal{V}, \mathcal{E}, \mathcal{L})$ *a fully expanded concept expansion tree for a closed* $\mathcal{ELU}_\mu$*-concept* C *w.r.t. a TBox or variable expansion function* ξ *with root node* v_0. *Let* $\mathcal{V}_\exists \subseteq \mathcal{V}$ *be the set of nodes on which the (Exists)-rule was applied. For every* $v \in \mathcal{V}_\exists$ *let* $succ_r(v) \in \mathcal{V}$ *such that* $(v, succ_r(v)) \in \mathcal{E}$ *and* $\mathcal{L}(succ_r(v)) = \{\, C \mid \exists r.C \in \mathcal{L}(v)\,\}$.

First, given $v \in \mathcal{V}$, *let* $\chi(v) \subseteq \mathcal{V}$ *be the smallest set closed under the following conditions:*

- *if* $v \in \mathcal{V}_\exists$, *let* $\chi(v) := \{v\}$;
- *if* v *is a leaf that is not blocked, let* $\chi(v) := \{v\}$;
- *if* v *is blocked by an ancestor* v', *let* $\chi(v) := \chi(v')$;
- *otherwise, let* $\chi(v) := \bigcup\{\, \chi(v_i) \mid (v, v_i) \in \mathcal{E}\,\}$.

We now define the expansion hypergraph $\mathcal{G}'_T = (\mathcal{V}', \mathcal{E}', \mathcal{L}', \mathcal{R}')$ *for* T *as follows:*

- $\mathcal{V}' = \chi(v_0) \cup \bigcup\{\, \chi(succ_r(v)) \mid v \in \mathcal{V}_\exists, \exists r.C \in \mathcal{L}(v)\,\}$;
- $\mathcal{E}' = \{\, (v, \chi(succ_r(v))) \mid \exists r.C \in \mathcal{L}(v)\,\}$;
- $\mathcal{L}' = \{\, (v, Atoms(\mathcal{L}(v))) \mid v \in \mathcal{V}'\,\} \cup$
  $\qquad \{\, (e, M) \mid e = (v, \chi(v')), M = \{\, r \mid v' = succ_r(v)\,\}\,\}$;
- $\mathcal{R}' = \chi(v_0)$.

We obtain the required hypergraph $\mathcal{G}_T$ *from* $\mathcal{G}'_T$ *by taking the quotient of* $\mathcal{G}'_T$ *w.r.t. equal node labels, i.e. all nodes* $v_1, v_2 \in \mathcal{V}'$ *such that* $\mathcal{L}'(v_1) = \mathcal{L}'(v_2)$ *are unified.*

The expansion hypergraph of a closed $\mathcal{ELU}_\mu$*-concept* C *is the expansion hypergraph* $\mathcal{G}_{T_C}$ *for a fully expanded concept expansion tree* T_C *for* C *w.r.t. the variable expansion function* ξ_C *for* C. *Similarly, the expansion hypergraph of an* $\mathcal{ELU}$*-concept* D *w.r.t. a TBox* $\mathcal{T}$ *is the expansion hypergraph* $\mathcal{G}_{T_{(D,\mathcal{T})}}$ *for a fully expanded concept expansion tree* $T_{(D,\mathcal{T})}$ *for* D *w.r.t. the TBox expansion function* $\xi_{(D,\mathcal{T})}$.

For a node $v \in \mathcal{V}$, the set $\chi(v)$ consists of leaf nodes and nodes on which the (Exists)-rule was applied that are reachable from v in T without walking along an edge that was produced by the (Exists)-rule. In this way the set $\chi(v)$ can be seen as representing the conjunctive normal form of the concepts in $\mathcal{L}(v)$.

The function χ is used to define the node set and the set of root nodes of the resulting expansion hypergraph. Note that not necessarily all nodes of T are nodes in the expansion hypergraph for T. The hyperedges connect a node with a set of nodes. Every node is labelled with a set of atomic concepts, and every hyperedge with a set of roles.

Example 6. Let $\mathcal{C}$ and T be defined as in Example 4. The expansion hypergraph for T is shown below. The root nodes are underlined. We have: $\chi(v_0) = \chi(v_1) = \chi(v_2) = \chi(v_{10}) = \{v_5, v_6, v_7, v_8\}$, $\chi(v_3) = \{v_5, v_6\}$, and $\chi(v_4) = \{v_7, v_8\}$.

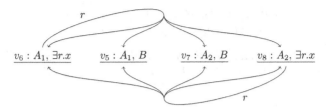

Example 7. Let $\mathcal{D}$ and T be defined as in Example 5. The expansion hypergraph for T is shown below. Note that only v_2 is a root node.

$$v_2 : A, (\exists r^2.x), (\exists r^3.x)$$
$$\downarrow r$$
$$v_3 : (\exists r.x), (\exists r^2.x)$$
$$\downarrow r$$
$$v_6 : A, (\exists r.x), (\exists r^2.x), (\exists r^3.x) \curvearrowleft$$
$$r$$

We now define how to obtain the $\mathcal{EL}$-concepts that are represented by an expansion hypergraph.

Definition 7 ($\mathcal{EL}$-Concept Unfoldings of an Expansion Hypergraph).
Let $\mathcal{G} = (\mathcal{V}, \mathcal{E}, \mathcal{L}, \mathcal{R})$ be an expansion hypergraph over a finite set S of atomic $\mathcal{ELU}_\mathcal{V}$-concepts. First, let $Unfold_\mathcal{G} \subseteq \mathcal{V} \times \mathcal{EL}$ be the smallest set closed under the following conditions:

- *if $v \in \mathcal{V}$, $\varphi = A \in \mathcal{L}(v)$ or $\varphi = \top \in \mathcal{L}(v)$, then $(v, \varphi) \in Unfold_\mathcal{G}$;*
- *if $e = (v, \{v_1, \ldots, v_n\}) \in \mathcal{E}$, $r \in \mathcal{L}(e)$, $(v_i, C_i) \in Unfold_\mathcal{G}$ for every $1 \le i \le n$, then $(v, \exists r. \bigsqcap_{i=1}^n C_i) \in Unfold_\mathcal{G}$.*

We set $Unfold(\mathcal{G}) = \{ \bigsqcap_{v \in \mathcal{R}} C_v \mid (v, C_v) \in Unfold_\mathcal{G} \}$.

Example 8. Let $\mathcal{G}_\mathcal{C}$ be the expansion hypergraph for $\mathcal{C}$, and let $\mathcal{G}_\mathcal{D}$ be the expansion hypergraph for $\mathcal{D}$, where $\mathcal{C}$, $\mathcal{D}$ are defined as in Examples 4 and 5. Then $Unfold(\mathcal{G}_\mathcal{C}) = \{A_1 \sqcap A_2, A_1 \sqcap A_2 \sqcap B, A_1 \sqcap \exists r.(A_1 \sqcap A_2), \ldots\}$ and $Unfold(\mathcal{G}_\mathcal{D}) = \{A, \exists r^2.A, \exists r^3.A, \exists r^4.A, \ldots\}$.

3.3   Step 3

The last step of our normalisation procedure removes superfluous nodes from the expansion hypergraph obtained in the previous step to ensure the correctness of our simulation check. Here, a node is superfluous if it does not yield an $\mathcal{EL}$-concept unfolding (cf. Definition 7).

Definition 8 (Simplifying Expansion Hypergraphs). *Let* $\mathcal{G} = (\mathcal{V}, \mathcal{E}, \mathcal{L}, \mathcal{R})$ *be an expansion hypergraph over a finite set S of atomic $\mathcal{ELU}_V$-concepts.*

Let $\mathcal{V}_{red} \subseteq \mathcal{V}$ be the smallest set closed under the following conditions:

- *for every $v \in \mathcal{V}$ with $\mathcal{L}(v) \cap \mathsf{N_C} \neq \emptyset$ or $\top \in \mathcal{L}(v)$, we have $v \in \mathcal{V}_{red}$;*
- *if $v_1, \ldots, v_n \in \mathcal{V}_{red}$ and $(v, \{v_1, \ldots, v_n\}) \in \mathcal{E}$, then $v \in \mathcal{V}_{red}$.*

The simplified *expansion graph of $\mathcal{G}$ is the expansion graph $\mathcal{G}'$ such that $\mathcal{G}' = (\{v\}, \emptyset, \{v \mapsto \emptyset\}, \{v\})$ if $\mathcal{V}_{red} \cap \mathcal{R} = \emptyset$; and otherwise, $\mathcal{G}' = (\mathcal{V}', \mathcal{E}', \mathcal{L}', \mathcal{R}')$ where*

- $\mathcal{V}' = \mathcal{V}_{red}$;
- $\mathcal{E}' = \{ (v, \{v_1, \ldots, v_n\}) \mid v \in \mathcal{V}', \{v_1, \ldots, v_n\}) \subseteq \mathcal{V}' \}$;
- $\mathcal{L}' = \{ (v, \mathcal{L}_v(v)) \mid v \in \mathcal{V}' \} \cup \{ (e, \mathcal{L}_e(e)) \mid e \in \mathcal{V}' \}$; *and*
- $\mathcal{R}' = \mathcal{R} \cap \mathcal{V}'$.

Intuitively, an expansion hypergraph is simplified by starting from nodes containing concept names or $\top$ in their labels and by collecting the nodes and hyperedges encountered while following hyperedges backwards. Note that we only walk an edge $(v_0, \{v_1, \ldots, v_n\})$ to the node v_0 when all the nodes v_i have been visited already (i.e. they are contained in $\mathcal{V}_{red}$). This condition corresponds to the intuition that for building a concept for v_0 it must be possible to construct at least one concept for every node v_i.

Example 9. Let $\mathcal{C} = A \sqcup \mu x.(\exists r.x))$. We obtain the following concept expansion hypergraph for $\mathcal{C}$. The concept expansion hypergraph for $\mathcal{C}$ and its simplification are respectively shown on the left-hand and right-hand side below.

We can now state the correctness property of our normal form transformation, i.e. all the $\mathcal{EL}$-concepts that are subsumed by the initial closed $\mathcal{ELU}_\mu$-concept $\mathcal{C}$ or by an $\mathcal{ELU}$-concept D w.r.t. a TBox $\mathcal{T}$ are preserved.

In the following we write $S_1 \equiv S_2$, for two sets S_1, S_2 of $\mathcal{EL}$-concepts, to denote that for every $C_1 \in S_1$ there exists $C_2 \in S_2$ with $\models C_1 \sqsubseteq C_2$, and that for every $D_2 \in S_2$ there exists $D_1 \in S_1$ with $\models D_2 \sqsubseteq D_1$.

Theorem 1. *Let $\mathcal{T}$ be a normalised $\mathcal{EL}$-TBox, let $\mathcal{C}$ be a closed $\mathcal{ELU}_\mu$-concept, and let D be an $\mathcal{ELU}$-concept. Then the expansion hypergraph $\mathcal{G}(\mathcal{C})$ for $\mathcal{C}$ and the expansion hypergraph $\mathcal{G}_{\mathcal{T}}(D)$ for D w.r.t. $\mathcal{T}$ can be computed in exponential time w.r.t. the size of $\mathcal{C}$, or D and $\mathcal{T}$, respectively. Moreover, the following two statements hold:*

- *(i)* $Unfold(\mathcal{G}(\mathcal{C})) \equiv \{ E \in \mathcal{EL} \mid \emptyset \models E \sqsubseteq \mathcal{C} \}$;
- *(ii)* $Unfold(\mathcal{G}_{\mathcal{T}}(D)) \equiv \{ E \in \mathcal{EL} \mid \mathcal{T} \models E \sqsubseteq D \}$.

4   Simulation

We are now ready to characterise the subsumption $\mathcal{T} \models \mathcal{C} \sqsubseteq D$ in terms of simulations between the respective expansion hypergraphs. In this way we obtain a practical decision procedure for the subsumption $\mathcal{T} \models \mathcal{C} \sqsubseteq D$.

Definition 9 (Expansion Graph Simulation). *Let $\mathcal{G}_1 = (\mathcal{V}_1, \mathcal{E}_1, \mathcal{L}_1, \mathcal{R}_1)$, $\mathcal{G}_2 = (\mathcal{V}_2, \mathcal{E}_2, \mathcal{L}_2, \mathcal{R}_2)$ be two expansion graphs.*

We say that $\mathcal{G}_1$ can be simulated by $\mathcal{G}_2$, written $\mathcal{G}_1 \hookrightarrow \mathcal{G}_2$, iff there exists a binary relation $S \subseteq \mathcal{V}_1 \times \mathcal{V}_2$ which fulfills the following conditions:

(i) if $(v_1, v_2) \in S$ and $\top \notin \mathcal{L}_2(v_2)$, then $\mathcal{L}_1(v_1) \cap (\mathsf{N_C} \cup \{\top\}) \subseteq \mathcal{L}_2(v_2)$;
(ii) if $(v_1, v_2) \in S$, $\top \notin \mathcal{L}_2(v_2)$, and $e_1 = (v_1, H_1) \in \mathcal{E}_1$, then for every $r \in \mathcal{L}_1(e_1)$ there exists $e_2 = (v_2, H_2) \in \mathcal{E}_2$ such that $r \in \mathcal{L}_2(e_2)$ and for every $v_2' \in H_2$ there exists $v_1' \in H_1$ with $(v_1, v_1') \in S$; and
(iii) for every $v_2 \in \mathcal{R}_2$ there exists $v_1 \in \mathcal{R}_1$ such that $(v_1, v_2) \in S$.

The simulation Condition (i) ensures that all the concept names contained in the label of v_1 must also be present in the label of v_2 (if the label of v_2 does not contain $\top$). Condition (i) is a *local* condition in the sense that it does not depend on other nodes to be contained in the simulation. Condition (ii) propagates the simulation conditions along hyperedges (if the label of v_2 does not contain $\top$), and in contrast to Condition (i) it imposes constraints on other nodes. Condition (iii) enforces that the root nodes are present in the simulation.

For a more detailed explanation of the simulation conditions, we refer the reader to [6,12], where a similar simulation notion between hypergraphs and its connection to reasoning has been established.

We note that without Step 3 in our normal form transformation it would be impossible to establish for $\mathcal{C} = \mu x.(\exists r.x)$ and $D = A$ that $\mathcal{T} \models \mathcal{C} \sqsubseteq A$ holds (as $\mathcal{C}^{\mathcal{I},\emptyset} = \emptyset$ in every interpretation $\mathcal{I}$). Condition (ii) would require the hypergraph $\mathcal{G}_\mathcal{T}(D)$ to contain edges labelled with r, which it does not have.

Example 10. Let $\mathcal{T} = \{\exists s.X \sqsubseteq Y, \exists r.Y \sqsubseteq X, A \sqsubseteq X\}$ and let $\mathcal{C} = B \sqcap \mu x.(A \sqcup \exists r.\exists s.x)$. Then $\mathcal{T} \models \mathcal{C} \sqsubseteq A \sqcup \exists r.\exists s.X$. The simplified expansion hypergraph $\mathcal{G}(\mathcal{C})$ for $\mathcal{C}$ and the simplified expansion hypergraph $\mathcal{G}_\mathcal{T}(\mathcal{D})$ for $\mathcal{D}$ w.r.t. $\mathcal{T}$ are shown in Figure 3.

We have that $S = \{(v_1, v_0'), (v_2, v_1'), (v_1, v_2'), (v_2, v_3')\}$ is a simulation between $\mathcal{G}(\mathcal{C})$ and $\mathcal{G}_\mathcal{T}(D)$.

We can now state our main result, linking the existence of a simulation between simplified expansion hypergraphs with subsumption.

Theorem 2. *Let $\mathcal{T}$ be an $\mathcal{EL}$-TBox, let $\mathcal{T}'$ be its normalisation, let $\mathcal{C}$ be a closed $\mathcal{ELU}_\mu$-concept, and let D be an $\mathcal{ELU}$-concept. Additionally, let $\mathcal{G}(\mathcal{C})$ be the simplified expansion hypergraph for $\mathcal{C}$ and let $\mathcal{G}_\mathcal{T}(D)$ be the simplified expansion hypergraph for $\mathcal{D}$ w.r.t. $\mathcal{T}'$. Then the following two statements are equivalent:*

(i) $\mathcal{T}' \models \mathcal{C} \sqsubseteq D$;
(ii) $\mathcal{G}(\mathcal{C}) \hookrightarrow \mathcal{G}_{\mathcal{T}'}(D)$.

The subsumption $\mathcal{T} \models \mathcal{C} \sqsubseteq D$ can be decided in exponential time in the size of $\mathcal{T}, \mathcal{C},$ and D.

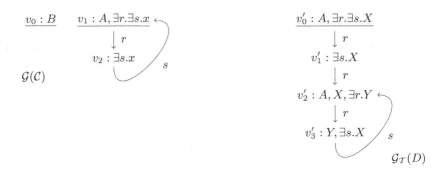

Fig. 3. Simplified expansion hypergraphs for Example 10

5   Conclusion and Discussion

We have provided a procedure for deciding subsumptions of the form $\mathcal{T} \models \mathcal{C} \sqsubseteq D$, where $\mathcal{C}$ is an $\mathcal{ELU}_\mu$-concept, D an $\mathcal{ELU}$-concept and $\mathcal{T}$ an $\mathcal{EL}$-TBox. Our procedure is based on checking for the existence of a certain simulation between hypergraph representations of the unfoldings of $\mathcal{C}$ and the subsumees of D w.r.t. $\mathcal{T}$, respectively. We have presented in detail how the hypergraphs can be built in three steps from $\mathcal{C}$ and D, $\mathcal{T}$, not relying on automata-theoretic techniques.

We plan to apply our procedure for solving the logical difference problem between $\mathcal{EL}$-TBoxes and for checking the existence of uniform interpolants of $\mathcal{EL}$-TBoxes. In this context an evaluation of the procedure will be required.

Applying our procedure for solving $\mathcal{T} \models \mathcal{C} \sqsubseteq D$ to the logical difference problem between $\mathcal{EL}$-TBoxes requires finding a suitable $\mathcal{ELU}$-concept D, which acts as an interpolant between $\mathcal{C}$ and an $\mathcal{EL}_\nu$-concept w.r.t. $\mathcal{T}$ (cf. Section 1). The notion of the *least common subsumer* (lcs) appears to lend itself as a candidate for such concepts D [7]. For our purposes we would consider the following notion. An $\mathcal{ELU}$-concept D is the *least common subsumer* of an $\mathcal{ELU}_\mu$-concept $\mathcal{C}$ w.r.t. an $\mathcal{EL}$-TBox $\mathcal{T}$ (written $\mathsf{lcs}_\mathcal{T}(\mathcal{C})$) if it satisfies the following two conditions: (i) $\mathcal{T} \models \mathcal{C} \sqsubseteq D$, and (ii) $\mathcal{T} \models D \sqsubseteq E$, for all $\mathcal{ELU}$-concepts E with $\mathcal{T} \models \mathcal{C} \sqsubseteq E$. Intuitively, $\mathcal{C}$ stands for a disjunction of infinitely many concept descriptions which are to be approximated by an $\mathcal{ELU}$-concept. However, such an lcs does not always exist. For instance, let $\mathcal{C} = \mu x.(A \sqcup \exists r.x)$ and $\mathcal{T}' = \{A \sqsubseteq Y, \exists r.Y \sqsubseteq Y\}$. For $\varphi_0 = Y$, $\varphi_1 = A \sqcup \exists r.Y$, $\varphi_2 = A \sqcup \exists r.(A \sqcup \exists r.Y)$, etc., it holds that $\mathcal{T}' \models \mathcal{C} \sqsubseteq \varphi_i$ and $\mathcal{T}' \models \varphi_{i+1} \sqsubseteq \varphi_i$ for $i \geq 0$. Then, for every $\mathcal{ELU}$-concept E with $\mathcal{T}' \models \mathcal{C} \sqsubseteq E$ we have that $\mathcal{T}' \not\models E \sqsubseteq \varphi_i$ for some $i \geq 0$.

As an alternative to an lcs of a least fixpoint concepts w.r.t. a background TBox, we say that an $\mathcal{ELU}$-concept D is a *most-consequence preserving subsumer* (mcps) of an $\mathcal{ELU}_\mu$-concept $\mathcal{C}$ for $\mathcal{EL}$-consequences w.r.t. an $\mathcal{EL}$-TBox $\mathcal{T}$ iff the following conditions hold: (i) $\mathcal{T} \models \mathcal{C} \sqsubseteq D$, and (ii) there does not exist an $\mathcal{ELU}$-concept E with $\mathcal{T} \models \mathcal{C} \sqsubseteq E$ and $\{F \in \mathcal{EL} \mid \mathcal{T} \models D \sqsubseteq F\} \subsetneq \{F \in \mathcal{EL} \mid \mathcal{T} \models E \sqsubseteq F\}$. Continuing the example above, every φ_i is an mcps of $\mathcal{C}$ w.r.t. $\mathcal{T}$ as $\{F \in \mathcal{EL} \mid \mathcal{T}' \models \varphi_i \sqsubseteq F\} = \{Y\}$ and $\{F \in \mathcal{EL} \mid \mathcal{T}' \models \mathcal{C} \sqsubseteq F\} = \{Y\}$.

We plan to investigate the notion of an mcps further and possibly apply it to finding interpolants of least and greatest fixpoint concepts w.r.t. TBoxes.

References

1. Baader, F., Brandt, S., Lutz, C.: Pushing the EL envelope. In: Proceedings of IJCAI-05: the 19th International Joint Conference on Artificial Intelligence, pp. 364–369. Morgan-Kaufmann Publishers (2005)
2. Baader, F., Brandt, S., Lutz, C.: Pushing the EL envelope further. In: Proceedings of the OWLED 2008 DC Workshop on OWL: Experiences and Directions (2008)
3. Baader, F., Calvanese, D., McGuinness, D.L., Nardi, D., Patel-Schneider, P.F. (eds.): The description logic handbook: theory, implementation, and applications. Cambridge University Press, 2nd edition (2010)
4. Bradfield, J., Stirling, C.: Modal μ-calculi. In: Blackburn, P., van Benthem, J., Wolter, F. (eds.) Handbook of Modal Logic, Studies in Logic and Practical Reasoning, vol. 3, pp. 721–756. Elsevier (2007)
5. Brandt, S.: Polynomial time reasoning in a description logic with existential restrictions, GCI axioms, and–what else? In: Proceedings of ECAI-04: the 16th European Conference on Artificial Intelligence, pp. 298–302. IOS Press (2004)
6. Ecke, A., Ludwig, M., Walther, D.: The concept difference for EL-terminologies using hypergraphs. In: Proceedings of DChanges-13: the International Workshop on (Document) Changes: Modeling, Detection, Storage and Visualization. CEUR-WS, vol. 1008 (2013)
7. Baader, F., Küsters, R., Molitor, R.: Computing least common subsumers in description logics with existential restrictions. In: Proceedings of IJCAI-99: the 16th International Joint Conference on Artificial Intelligence, pp. 96–101. Morgan-Kaufmann Publishers (1999)
8. Feng, S., Ludwig, M., Walther, D.: The logical difference for EL: from terminologies towards TBoxes. In: Proceedings of IWOST-15: the 1st International Workshop on Semantic Technologies. CEUR-WS (2015)
9. Janin, D., Walukiewicz, I.: Automata for the modal mu-calculus and related results. In: Wiedermann, J., Hájek, P. (eds.) Mathematical Foundations of Computer Science 1995. LNCS, vol. 969, pp. 552–562. Springer, Heidelberg (1995)
10. Konev, B., Ludwig, M., Walther, D., Wolter, F.: The logical difference for the lightweight description logic EL. Journal of Artificial Intelligence Research (JAIR) **44**, 633–708 (2012)
11. Kozen, D.: Results on the propositional μ-calculus. Theoretical Computer Science **27**(3), 333–354 (1983)
12. Ludwig, M., Walther, D.: The logical difference for ELHr-terminologies using hypergraphs. In: Proceedings of ECAI-14: the 21st European Conference on Artificial Intelligence. Frontiers in Artificial Intelligence and Applications, vol. 263, pp. 555–560. IOS Press (2014)
13. Sattler, U., Vardi, M.Y.: The hybrid mgr-calculus. In: Goré, R.P., Leitsch, A., Nipkow, T. (eds.) IJCAR 2001. LNCS (LNAI), vol. 2083, p. 76. Springer, Heidelberg (2001)

Towards a More Efficient Computation of Weighted Conditional Impacts for Relational Probabilistic Knowledge Bases Under Maximum Entropy Semantics

Marc Finthammer$^{(\boxtimes)}$ and Christoph Beierle

Department of Computer Science, FernUniversität in Hagen, Hagen, Germany
marc@finthammer.de

Abstract. While the complexity of the optimization problem to be solved when computing the Maximum Entropy distribution $P_{\mathcal{R}}^*$ of a knowledge base $\mathcal{R}$ grows dramatically when moving to the relational case, it has been shown that having the weighted conditional impacts (WCI) of $\mathcal{R}$ available, $P_{\mathcal{R}}^*$ can be computed much faster. Computing WCI in a straightforward manner readily gets infeasible due to the size of the set Ω of possible worlds. In this paper, we propose a new approach for computing the WCI without considering the worlds in Ω at all. We introduce the notion of *sat-pairs* and show how to determine the set $\mathcal{CSP}$ of all possible combinations of sat-pairs by employing combinatorial means. Using $\mathcal{CSP}$ instead of Ω for computing the WCI is a significant performance gain since $\mathcal{CSP}$ is typically much smaller than Ω. For a start, we focus on simple knowledge bases consisting of a single conditional. First evaluation results of an implemented algorithm illustrate the benefits of our approach.

1 Introduction

There is a long tradition of enriching propositional logic with probabilities ([8,17,19]), and relational probabilistic logics (e.g. [7,9,12,20,22]) provide a strong means to model uncertain knowledge about relations among individual objects. Here, we are especially interested in relational probabilistic conditionals.

Example 1. A movie actor can be awarded with certain awards (e. g. Oscar, Palme d'Or) and depending on that, a movie director might consider engaging that actor with a probability of 0.3. This scenario could be modeled by the relational probabilistic conditional $(considerEngagement(X, Z)|awardedWith(X, Y))[0.3]$ where the variable X stands for some actor, Y for some award, and Z for some movie director.

A set of relational probabilistic conditionals is called a knowledge base $\mathcal{R}$ and there generally exist many probability distributions which satisfy $\mathcal{R}$. Recently, several semantics for relational probabilistic conditionals have been introduced which employ the principle of maximum entropy (ME) to select the distribution

© Springer International Publishing Switzerland 2015
S. Hölldobler et al. (Eds.): KI 2015, LNAI 9324, pp. 72–86, 2015.
DOI: 10.1007/978-3-319-24489-1_6

which represents $\mathcal{R}$ in the most unbiased way, i.e. by adding as little information as possible (cf. [10,11,18,23]). Computing the ME distribution $P_{\mathcal{R}}^*$ of $\mathcal{R}$ requires solving an optimization problem whose complexity grows dramatically when moving from a propositional to a first-order setting. In [4], the well-known technique of generalized iterative scaling (GIS) [2] is used to develop an algorithm computing the ME distribution $P_{\mathcal{R}}^*$ under aggregating semantics [13] for the relational case. In [5], it is shown that $P_{\mathcal{R}}^*$ can be computed much faster by an algorithm which works on the so-called *weighted conditional impacts* (WCI) of $\mathcal{R}$ instead of the exponentially large set Ω of possible worlds. Equivalence classes of worlds are used for probabilistic logics, e.g. in [6,10,12,15,21], and WCI provide a more abstract view on these equivalence classes and their cardinalities. That way, WCI comprise the essential information about worlds and their interaction with the logical part of the conditionals in $\mathcal{R}$ in a condensed form. Thus, $P_{\mathcal{R}}^*$ can be computed more efficiently once the WCI have been determined. Since the WCI do not consider the given probabilities of the conditionals in $\mathcal{R}$, the WCI can also be reused when the probabilities in $\mathcal{R}$ are changed. However, computing the WCI straightforwardly requires to consider each world in Ω once which readily becomes infeasible due to the size of Ω.

In this paper, we propose a new approach for computing the WCI without considering the worlds in Ω at all. This approach abstracts from concrete worlds and from the concrete ground atoms satisfied by worlds. Instead, we focus on the possible numbers of ground atoms which in principle can be satisfied by some worlds. So we do not care which worlds cause a certain number of satisfied ground atoms, but we just make sure that we determine the particular numbers which are actually possible. We introduce the concept of *sat-pairs*, i.e. pairs of numbers which represent satisfiable numbers of ground atoms. We extend that concept to *combinations of sat-pairs* and show that the set $\mathcal{CSP}$, consisting of all possible combinations of sat-pairs and generally being much smaller then Ω, is a viable replacement for the set Ω. As a start, we focus on simple knowledge bases consisting of a single conditional, and point out possible extensions.

Section 2 briefly recalls the required background, Section 3 analyzes the WCI of atomic conditionals, Section 4 shows how to compute the WCI combinatorially, Section 5 presents the results of a practical algorithm, and Section 6 concludes.

2   Background

Relational Probabilistic Conditional Logic. Let $\mathcal{L}$ be a quantifier-free first-order language defined over a many-sorted first-order signature $\Sigma = (Sort, Const, Pred)$, where $Sort$ is a set of sorts, $Const$ is a finite set of constants, and $Pred$ a set of predicates. The language $(\mathcal{L}|\mathcal{L})^{prob}$ consists of *probabilistic conditionals* of the form $(B(\boldsymbol{X})|A(\boldsymbol{X}))[d]$ with $\boldsymbol{X}$ containing the variables of the formulas A and B, and where $d \in [0,1]$ is a probability; A finite set $\mathcal{R} \subseteq (\mathcal{L}|\mathcal{L})^{prob}$ is called a *knowledge base*; we always implicitly consider $\mathcal{R}$ together with some appropriate signature Σ.

$\mathcal{H}$ denotes the *Herbrand base*, i. e. the set containing all ground atoms over Σ, and $\Omega = \mathfrak{P}(\mathcal{H})$ is the set of all possible worlds (i. e. *Herbrand interpretations*), where $\mathfrak{P}$ is the power set operator. The satisfaction relation between a world $\omega \in \Omega$ and a ground atom at is defied as $\omega \models at$ iff $at \in \omega$ and extended to ground formulas in the usual way. $\Theta(\mathcal{V})$ denotes the set of all ground substitutions w. r. t. a set of variables $\mathcal{V}$. $A(\boldsymbol{a})$ denotes a ground instance of $A(X)$, where $\boldsymbol{a}$ contains the particular constants which substitute the variables in $\boldsymbol{X}$. The expression $\mathrm{gnd}(r)$ denotes the set of ground instances of a conditional $r = (B(\boldsymbol{X})|A(\boldsymbol{X}))[d]$, and we write $r(\boldsymbol{a})$ for a ground instance $(B(\boldsymbol{a})|A(\boldsymbol{a}))[d] \in \mathrm{gnd}(r)$. The *probabilistic interpretations* for $(\mathcal{L}|\mathcal{L})^{prob}$ are given by the set *Prob* of all probability distributions $P : \Omega \rightarrow [0,1]$ over possible worlds. P is extended to ground formulas $A(\boldsymbol{a})$ by defining $P(A(\boldsymbol{a})) := \sum_{\omega \models A(\boldsymbol{a})} P(\omega)$. The *aggregation semantics* [13] extends P to conditionals and resembles the definition of a conditional probability by summing up the probabilities of all respective ground formulas; it defines the satisfaction relation $\models_{\odot}$ for $r = (B(\boldsymbol{X})|A(\boldsymbol{X}))[d]$ by

$$P \models_{\odot} r \quad \textit{iff} \quad \frac{\sum_{r(\boldsymbol{a}) \in \mathrm{gnd}(r)} P(A(\boldsymbol{a})B(\boldsymbol{a}))}{\sum_{r(\boldsymbol{a}) \in \mathrm{gnd}(r)} P(A(\boldsymbol{a}))} = d \tag{1}$$

where $\sum_{r(\boldsymbol{a}) \in \mathrm{gnd}(r)} P(A(\boldsymbol{a})) > 0$. If $P \models_{\odot} r$ holds, we say that P *satisfies* r or P *is a model of* r. P *satisfies* a set of conditionals $\mathcal{R}$ if it satisfies every element of $\mathcal{R}$.

The principle of *maximum entropy* (*ME*) chooses the distribution P where the entropy $H(P)$ is maximal among all distributions satisfying $\mathcal{R}$ [10,18]. The ME model $P_{\mathcal{R}}^*$ for $\mathcal{R}$ based on aggregation semantics is uniquely defined [13] by the solution of the convex optimization problem $P_{\mathcal{R}}^* := \arg\max_{P \in Prob : P \models_{\odot} \mathcal{R}} H(P)$.

Weighted Conditional Impacts. For $r \colon (B(\boldsymbol{X})|A(\boldsymbol{X}))$, the *counting functions* (cf. [4,14]) $\mathrm{app}, \mathrm{ver} : \Omega \rightarrow \mathbb{N}_0$ are:

$$\mathrm{app}(\omega) := \big|\{r(\boldsymbol{a}) \in \mathrm{gnd}(r) \mid \omega \models A(\boldsymbol{a})\}\big| \tag{2}$$

$$\mathrm{ver}(\omega) := \big|\{r(\boldsymbol{a}) \in \mathrm{gnd}(r) \mid \omega \models A(\boldsymbol{a})B(\boldsymbol{a})\}\big| \tag{3}$$

For $\omega \in \Omega$, $\mathrm{app}(\omega)$ yields the number of ground instances of r which are *applicable* w. r. t. ω, and $\mathrm{ver}(\omega)$ yields the number of ground instances of r *verified* by ω.

Definition 1 (va-Pair). *The function* $\mathrm{va}_\Omega : \Omega \rightarrow \mathbb{N}_0 \times \mathbb{N}_0$ *with*

$$\mathrm{va}_\Omega(\omega) := \langle \mathrm{ver}(\omega), \mathrm{app}(\omega) \rangle \tag{4}$$

w. r. t. a conditional r *is called the* va-pair function *of* r. *A function value* $\mathrm{va}_\Omega(\omega)$ *is called the* va-pair *of* r *with respect to* ω. *The image of* va_Ω *is denoted by*

$$\mathcal{VA} := \{\langle v, a \rangle \in \mathbb{N}_0 \times \mathbb{N}_0 \mid \langle v, a \rangle = \mathrm{va}_\Omega(\omega), \ \omega \in \Omega\} \tag{5}$$

and called the set of va-pairs *of* r, *and a pair* $\langle v, a \rangle \in \mathcal{VA}$ *is called a* va-pair *of* r.

For example, if for some $\omega \in \Omega$, ten ground instances of a conditional r are applicable and six ground instances are verified, then we have $\text{app}(\omega) = 10$ and $\text{ver}(\omega) = 6$ and consequently $\langle 6, 10 \rangle$ is a va-pair of r.

Definition 2 (Conditional Impact). *The function* $\gamma_{\mathcal{R}} : \Omega \to (\mathbb{N}_0 \times \mathbb{N}_0)^m$ *with*

$$\gamma_{\mathcal{R}}(\omega) := \left[\text{va}_{\Omega,1}(\omega), \ldots, \text{va}_{\Omega,m}(\omega) \right] \tag{6}$$

is called the conditional impact function *of* $\mathcal{R}$. *The value* $\gamma_{\mathcal{R}}(\omega)$ *is called the* conditional impact caused by ω *on the ground instances of* $\mathcal{R}$. *The image of* $\gamma_{\mathcal{R}}$ *is denoted by*

$$\Gamma_{\mathcal{R}} := \gamma_{\mathcal{R}}(\Omega) = \{ \gamma \in (\mathbb{N}_0 \times \mathbb{N}_0)^m \mid \gamma = \gamma_{\mathcal{R}}(\omega) \ for \ some \ \omega \in \Omega \} \tag{7}$$

and called the set of conditional impacts *of* $\mathcal{R}$,
and a tuple $\gamma = \left[\langle v_1, a_1 \rangle, \ldots, \langle v_m, a_m \rangle \right] \in \Gamma_{\mathcal{R}}$ *is called a* conditional impact of $\mathcal{R}$.

For example, a conditional impact of a set $\mathcal{R}$ consisting of 4 conditionals could be $\gamma = \left[\langle 6, 10 \rangle, \langle 1, 8 \rangle, \langle 0, 6 \rangle, \langle 5, 9 \rangle \right]$. Conditional impacts were introduced by Kern-Isberner [10] as *conditional structures* in a propositional setting, using a free Abelian group construction. In the propositional case, each va-pair is $\langle 0, 0 \rangle$, $\langle 0, 1 \rangle$, or $\langle 1, 1 \rangle$.

Definition 3 (WCI). *The function* $\text{wgt}_{\mathcal{R}} : \Gamma_{\mathcal{R}} \to \mathbb{N}_0$ *with*

$$\text{wgt}_{\mathcal{R}}(\gamma) := \left| \gamma_{\mathcal{R}}^{-1}(\gamma) \right| = \left| \{ \omega \in \Omega \mid \gamma_{\mathcal{R}}(\omega) = \gamma \} \right|$$

is called the weighting function of $\mathcal{R}$. *The pair* $(\Gamma_{\mathcal{R}}, \text{wgt}_{\mathcal{R}})$ *is called the* **weighted** conditional impacts (WCI) *of* $\mathcal{R}$.

Proposition 1 ([5]). *The ME-distribution* $P_{\mathcal{R}}^*$ *can be computed by a GIS-algorithm which solely works on the WCI of* $\mathcal{R}$ *and does not refer to* Ω *at all.*

ME-Computation on Weighted Conditional Impacts. Since the WCI are in general much smaller than Ω, the adopted GIS-algorithm computes the ME-distribution $P_{\mathcal{R}}^*$ much faster and requires much less space than a comparable algorithm working on Ω directly. So the WCI comprise the essential information about the qualitative part of $\mathcal{R}$ and the worlds in Ω in a most condensed form. Once determined, the WCI can also be reused together with different probabilities for the conditionals in $\mathcal{R}$. A drawback of the generic algorithm WCI_{gen} [5] computing the WCI is that is has to consider each world from Ω once for determining the WCI. However, note that once the WCI are available, the set Ω does not have to be considered anymore in the whole process of determining the ME-distribution $P_{\mathcal{R}}^*$ according to Prop. 1. Thus, our objective is to a develop a more efficient approach to compute the WCI without considering the set Ω at all.

3   Basic Case: WCI of a Single Conditional

Since analyzing the WCI for a whole set $\mathcal{R}$ of m conditionals is a much too complex task to begin with, we focus on the WCI of single conditional, i.e. we consider a set $\mathcal{R} = \{r\}$ throughout the rest of this paper. That way, we do not have to consider conditional impacts in terms of m-tuples of va-pairs as $\gamma_\mathcal{R}$ in Def. 2, but we can just consider the va-pairs of r themselves. That is, the set of conditional impacts under consideration is $\Gamma_\mathcal{R} = \{[\langle v, a\rangle] \mid \langle v, a\rangle \in \mathcal{VA}\}$ with $\mathcal{VA}$ being the set of va-pairs of r. Analogously to $\mathrm{wgt}_\mathcal{R}$ (Def. 3), the function $\mathrm{wgt} : \mathcal{VA} \to \mathbb{N}$ with

$$\mathrm{wgt}(\langle v, a\rangle) := \mathrm{wgt}_\mathcal{R}([\langle v, a\rangle]) = |\mathrm{va}_\Omega^{-1}(\langle v, a\rangle)| \tag{8}$$

is the weighting function of r. This allows us to denote the WCI of a single conditional r more directly as $(\mathcal{VA}, \mathrm{wgt})$ when investigating va-Pairs of r and their weights in the following. Since we will often refer to the number of ground instances of r, we define the compact notation $G := |\mathrm{gnd}(r)|$.

Note that when discussing values depending on r, the values of $\mathcal{VA}$, wgt, G, etc. also depend on the number of constants in the given signature Σ.

Proposition 2 (Upper Bound for $|\mathcal{VA}|$). *The number of va-pairs of a conditional is bounded by its number of ground instances by* $|\mathcal{VA}| \le va_{\mathrm{lim}}(G)$ *with:*

$$va_{\mathrm{lim}}(G) = \sum_{a=0}^{G}\sum_{v=0}^{a} 1 = \sum_{a=0}^{G} a + 1 = \sum_{a=1}^{G+1} a = \frac{(G+1) \cdot (G+2)}{2} = \frac{G^2 + 3G + 2}{2} \tag{9}$$

For instance, a conditional with 20 ground instances can have at most 231 va-pairs.

Atomic Conditionals. Since the set $\mathrm{gnd}(r)$ plays an important role when considering the constitution of the set $\mathcal{VA}$ of a conditional r, we want to take a closer look at the syntactical structure of the ground instances arising from r. Here, we focus on a simple syntactical structure, already covering many relevant aspects:

Definition 4 (Atomic Conditional). *Let* Cons *and* Ante *be atoms of different predicates. Then* $r = (\,\mathrm{Cons} \mid \mathrm{Ante}\,)$ *is called an* atomic conditional.

The atoms Ante and Cons can have an arbitrary number of arguments, being either a variable or a constant. For the rest of this paper, we focus on an atomic conditional r with only variables, since constants do not have any further effect when constructing the ground instances of $\mathcal{R} = \{r\}$.

Example 2 (Atomic Conditionals). Some examples for atomic conditionals are

$$r_{X|X} : (c(X)|a(X)) \quad r_{X|XY} : (c(X)|a(X,Y))$$
$$r_{Z|Y} : (c(Z)|a(Y)) \quad r_{XZ|X} : (c(X,Z)|a(X)) \quad r_{XZ|XY} : (c(X,Z)|a(X,Y))$$

Note that the conditional given in Ex. 1 corresponds to the schema used in $r_{XZ|XY}$.

The above atomic conditionals just differ in the numbers and positions of their variables. We introduce the following notation to refer to the respective sets of variables of an atomic conditional $r = ($ Cons $|$ Ante $)$:

- $C \cap A$: variables appearing in both Cons and Ante
- $A\backslash C$: variables appearing exclusively in Ante
- $C\backslash A$: variables appearing exclusively in Cons

Accordingly, with $\Theta_{C \cap A}(r)$, $\Theta_{A\backslash C}(r)$, and $\Theta_{C\backslash A}(r)$ we denote the corresponding sets of substitutions with respect to the particular sets of variables, and with

$$G_{C \cap A} := |\Theta_{C \cap A}(r)|, \quad G_{A\backslash C} := |\Theta_{A\backslash C}(r)|, \quad G_{C\backslash A} := |\Theta_{C\backslash A}(r)|$$

we denote the respective number of substitutions. Since $\Theta_{C \cap A}(r) \cup \Theta_{A\backslash C}(r) \cup \Theta_{C\backslash A}(r) = \Theta(r)$ and since the three sets of substitutions are pairwise disjoint, we have $G = G_{C \cap A} \cdot G_{A\backslash C} \cdot G_{C\backslash A}$. Note that each of the sets $C \cap A$, $A\backslash C$, and $C\backslash A$ may be empty for a particular atomic conditional; however $G_{C \cap A} \geq 1$, $G_{A\backslash C} \geq 1$, and $G_{C\backslash A} \geq 1$ always hold, since $\Theta(\emptyset)$ contains the empty substitution. The next example illustrates these definitions by an atomic conditional $r_{X_s Z_u | X_s Y_t}$ covering all three kinds of appearances of variables (cf. Ex. 1 for some practical interpretation of such a conditional):

Example 3. For $\Sigma = (Sort, Const, Pred)$ with $Sort = \{S, T, U\}$, $Pred = \{a/(S, T), c/(S, U)\}$, and $Const = Const_{(S)} \cup Const_{(T)} \cup Const_{(U)}$ with

$$Const_{(S)} = \{s_1, \ldots, s_3\}, \; Const_{(T)} = \{t_1, \ldots, t_4\}, \; Const_{(U)} = \{u_1, \ldots, u_5\}$$

together with the conditional $r_{X_s Z_u | X_s Y_t} \colon (c(X, Z) | a(X, Y))$ we have:

$$C \cap A = \{X\}, \quad A\backslash C = \{Y\}, \quad C\backslash A = \{Z\}$$
$$\Theta_{C \cap A}(r_{X_s Z_u | X_s Y_t}) = \{\{X/s_1\}, \{X/s_2\}, \{X/s_3\}\}$$
$$\Theta_{A\backslash C}(r_{X_s Z_u | X_s Y_t}) = \{\{Y/t_1\}, \{Y/t_2\}, \{Y/t_3\}, \{Y/t_4\}\}$$
$$\Theta_{C\backslash A}(r_{X_s Z_u | X_s Y_t}) = \{\{Z/u_1\}, \{Z/u_2\}, \{Z/u_3\}, \{Z/u_4\}, \{Z/u_5\}\}$$
$$G_{C \cap A} = |\Theta_{C \cap A}(r_{X_s Z_u | X_s Y_t})| = |Const_{(S)}| = 3$$
$$G_{A\backslash C} = |\Theta_{A\backslash C}(r_{X_s Z_u | X_s Y_t})| = |Const_{(T)}| = 4$$
$$G_{C\backslash A} = |\Theta_{C\backslash A}(r_{X_s Z_u | X_s Y_t})| = |Const_{(U)}| = 5$$

The total number of ground instances is $G = G_{C \cap A} \cdot G_{A\backslash C} \cdot G_{C\backslash A} = 3 \cdot 4 \cdot 5 = 60$; all these ground instances are depicted in Tab. 1. According to (9), an upper bound for number of va-pairs is $|\mathcal{VA}| \leq va_{\lim}(60) = 1{,}891$. Computing the set $\mathcal{VA}$ gives us the actual size $|\mathcal{VA}| = 348$. However, the number of worlds is:

$$|\Omega| = 2^{|\mathcal{H}|} = 2^{3 \cdot 4 + 3 \cdot 5} = 2^{27} = 134{,}217{,}728$$

So the set $\mathcal{VA}$, which emerges from Ω according to (5), is indeed much smaller than the original set Ω:

$$|\Omega| = 134{,}217{,}728 \gg |\mathcal{VA}| = 348$$

Table 1. Complete ground-instance-table of $r_{X_s Z_u | X_s Y_t}$

$c(s_1,Z) \mid a(s_1,Y)$	$c(s_2,Z) \mid a(s_2,Y)$	$c(s_3,Z) \mid a(s_3,Y)$
$c(s_1,u_1) \mid a(s_1,t_1)$	$c(s_2,u_1) \mid a(s_2,t_1)$	$c(s_3,u_1) \mid a(s_3,t_1)$
$c(s_1,u_2) \mid a(s_1,t_1)$	$c(s_2,u_2) \mid a(s_2,t_1)$	$c(s_3,u_2) \mid a(s_3,t_1)$
$c(s_1,u_3) \mid a(s_1,t_1)$	$c(s_2,u_3) \mid a(s_2,t_1)$	$c(s_3,u_3) \mid a(s_3,t_1)$
$c(s_1,u_4) \mid a(s_1,t_1)$	$c(s_2,u_4) \mid a(s_2,t_1)$	$c(s_3,u_4) \mid a(s_3,t_1)$
$c(s_1,u_5) \mid a(s_1,t_1)$	$c(s_2,u_5) \mid a(s_2,t_1)$	$c(s_3,u_5) \mid a(s_3,t_1)$
$c(s_1,u_1) \mid a(s_1,t_2)$	$c(s_2,u_1) \mid a(s_2,t_2)$	$c(s_3,u_1) \mid a(s_3,t_2)$
$c(s_1,u_2) \mid a(s_1,t_2)$	$c(s_2,u_2) \mid a(s_2,t_2)$	$c(s_3,u_2) \mid a(s_3,t_2)$
$c(s_1,u_3) \mid a(s_1,t_2)$	$c(s_2,u_3) \mid a(s_2,t_2)$	$c(s_3,u_3) \mid a(s_3,t_2)$
$c(s_1,u_4) \mid a(s_1,t_2)$	$c(s_2,u_4) \mid a(s_2,t_2)$	$c(s_3,u_4) \mid a(s_3,t_2)$
$c(s_1,u_5) \mid a(s_1,t_2)$	$c(s_2,u_5) \mid a(s_2,t_2)$	$c(s_3,u_5) \mid a(s_3,t_2)$
$c(s_1,u_1) \mid a(s_1,t_3)$	$c(s_2,u_1) \mid a(s_2,t_3)$	$c(s_3,u_1) \mid a(s_3,t_3)$
$c(s_1,u_2) \mid a(s_1,t_3)$	$c(s_2,u_2) \mid a(s_2,t_3)$	$c(s_3,u_2) \mid a(s_3,t_3)$
$c(s_1,u_3) \mid a(s_1,t_3)$	$c(s_2,u_3) \mid a(s_2,t_3)$	$c(s_3,u_3) \mid a(s_3,t_3)$
$c(s_1,u_4) \mid a(s_1,t_3)$	$c(s_2,u_4) \mid a(s_2,t_3)$	$c(s_3,u_4) \mid a(s_3,t_3)$
$c(s_1,u_5) \mid a(s_1,t_3)$	$c(s_2,u_5) \mid a(s_2,t_3)$	$c(s_3,u_5) \mid a(s_3,t_3)$
$c(s_1,u_1) \mid a(s_1,t_4)$	$c(s_2,u_1) \mid a(s_2,t_4)$	$c(s_3,u_1) \mid a(s_3,t_4)$
$c(s_1,u_2) \mid a(s_1,t_4)$	$c(s_2,u_2) \mid a(s_2,t_4)$	$c(s_3,u_2) \mid a(s_3,t_4)$
$c(s_1,u_3) \mid a(s_1,t_4)$	$c(s_2,u_3) \mid a(s_2,t_4)$	$c(s_3,u_3) \mid a(s_3,t_4)$
$c(s_1,u_4) \mid a(s_1,t_4)$	$c(s_2,u_4) \mid a(s_2,t_4)$	$c(s_3,u_4) \mid a(s_3,t_4)$
$c(s_1,u_5) \mid a(s_1,t_4)$	$c(s_2,u_5) \mid a(s_2,t_4)$	$c(s_3,u_5) \mid a(s_3,t_4)$

Syntactical Structure of Ground Instances. In the following, we employ Ex. 2 to explain the general concepts. The tabular representation of the ground instances of $r_{X_s Z_u | X_s Y_t}$ in Tab. 1 is called the *ground-instance-table* of $r_{X_s Z_u | X_s Y_t}$ and consists of $3 = G_{C \cap A}$ sub-tables. Each of these sub-tables emerges from one particular substitution for the variable $X \in C \cap A$ (cf. the respective table-headers).

The ground atoms appearing in each sub-table are pairwise disjoint due to the different substitutions for X, and our results will apply to each of the sub-tables in the same way. Thus, we continue our analysis with the first sub-table, which contains all ground instances emerging from the substitution X/s_1; we refer to that table as the s_1-table. The ground instances in the sub-table are divided into $4 = G_{A \backslash C}$ blocks (represented by horizontal lines), whereas each block considers a particular substitution for the variable $Y \in A \backslash C$. Finally, each block contains $5 = G_{C \backslash A}$ ground instances emerging from the substitutions for the variable $Z \in C \backslash A$.

Note that, apart from the concrete example, the ground-instance-table of every atomic conditional has such a three-leveled block-structure, which is a direct consequence of the three sets $C \cap A$, $A \backslash C$, and $C \backslash A$. In particular, this also holds for any atomic conditional with more than three variables.

Table 2. General block-structure of a sub-table

Table 3. Atoms satisfied by ω'

Table 4. Atoms satisfied by ω''

$c(s_1,Z)$	$a(s_1,Y)$
$c(s_1,u_1)$	$a(s_1,t_1)$
$c(s_1,u_2)$	$a(s_1,t_1)$
$c(s_1,u_3)$	$a(s_1,t_1)$
$c(s_1,u_4)$	$a(s_1,t_1)$
$c(s_1,u_5)$	$a(s_1,t_1)$
$c(s_1,u_1)$	$a(s_1,t_2)$
$c(s_1,u_2)$	$a(s_1,t_2)$
$c(s_1,u_3)$	$a(s_1,t_2)$
$c(s_1,u_4)$	$a(s_1,t_2)$
$c(s_1,u_5)$	$a(s_1,t_2)$
$c(s_1,u_1)$	$a(s_1,t_3)$
$c(s_1,u_2)$	$a(s_1,t_3)$
$c(s_1,u_3)$	$a(s_1,t_3)$
$c(s_1,u_4)$	$a(s_1,t_3)$
$c(s_1,u_5)$	$a(s_1,t_3)$
$c(s_1,u_1)$	$a(s_1,t_4)$
$c(s_1,u_2)$	$a(s_1,t_4)$
$c(s_1,u_3)$	$a(s_1,t_4)$
$c(s_1,u_4)$	$a(s_1,t_4)$
$c(s_1,u_5)$	$a(s_1,t_4)$

Table 3 and Table 4 contain the same sub-table structure with different highlighting:

$c(s_1,Z)$	$a(s_1,Y)$		$c(s_1,Z)$	$a(s_1,Y)$
$c(s_1,u_1)$	$a(s_1,t_1)$		$c(s_1,u_1)$	$a(s_1,t_1)$
$c(s_1,u_2)$	$a(s_1,t_1)$		$c(s_1,u_2)$	$a(s_1,t_1)$
$c(s_1,u_3)$	$a(s_1,t_1)$		$c(s_1,u_3)$	$a(s_1,t_1)$
$c(s_1,u_4)$	$a(s_1,t_1)$		$c(s_1,u_4)$	$a(s_1,t_1)$
$c(s_1,u_5)$	$a(s_1,t_1)$		$c(s_1,u_5)$	$a(s_1,t_1)$
$c(s_1,u_1)$	$a(s_1,t_2)$		$c(s_1,u_1)$	$a(s_1,t_2)$
$c(s_1,u_2)$	$a(s_1,t_2)$		$c(s_1,u_2)$	$a(s_1,t_2)$
$c(s_1,u_3)$	$a(s_1,t_2)$		$c(s_1,u_3)$	$a(s_1,t_2)$
$c(s_1,u_4)$	$a(s_1,t_2)$		$c(s_1,u_4)$	$a(s_1,t_2)$
$c(s_1,u_5)$	$a(s_1,t_2)$		$c(s_1,u_5)$	$a(s_1,t_2)$
$c(s_1,u_1)$	$a(s_1,t_3)$		$c(s_1,u_1)$	$a(s_1,t_3)$
$c(s_1,u_2)$	$a(s_1,t_3)$		$c(s_1,u_2)$	$a(s_1,t_3)$
$c(s_1,u_3)$	$a(s_1,t_3)$		$c(s_1,u_3)$	$a(s_1,t_3)$
$c(s_1,u_4)$	$a(s_1,t_3)$		$c(s_1,u_4)$	$a(s_1,t_3)$
$c(s_1,u_5)$	$a(s_1,t_3)$		$c(s_1,u_5)$	$a(s_1,t_3)$
$c(s_1,u_1)$	$a(s_1,t_4)$		$c(s_1,u_1)$	$a(s_1,t_4)$
$c(s_1,u_2)$	$a(s_1,t_4)$		$c(s_1,u_2)$	$a(s_1,t_4)$
$c(s_1,u_3)$	$a(s_1,t_4)$		$c(s_1,u_3)$	$a(s_1,t_4)$
$c(s_1,u_4)$	$a(s_1,t_4)$		$c(s_1,u_4)$	$a(s_1,t_4)$
$c(s_1,u_5)$	$a(s_1,t_4)$		$c(s_1,u_5)$	$a(s_1,t_4)$

Table 2 shows the s_1-table, where identical ground atoms in the antecedence and consequence, respectively, are highlighted accordingly. Since the atoms in the antecedence and consequence of an atomic conditional must be of different predicates, the respective sets of ground atoms are always disjoint. So there are $4 = G_{A\backslash C}$ different antecedence ground atoms (*a-atoms*) and $5 = G_{C\backslash A}$ different consequence ground atoms (*c-atoms*) in the sub-table.

Numbers of Satisfied Ground Atoms. For some arbitrary world, let $satC$ and $satA$ denote the number of c-atoms and a-atoms, respectively, in a sub-table of an atomic conditional which are satisfied by that world. Then $satC \in N_C = \{0, 1, \ldots, G_{C\backslash A}\}$ and $satA \in N_A = \{0, 1, \ldots, G_{A\backslash C}\}$ holds, i.e. the numbers of satisfied c-atoms and a-atoms are from the respective range. On the other hand, for every such pair

$$(satC, satA) \in \mathcal{SP} := N_C \times N_A,$$

called *sat-pair* of an atomic conditional, there exists a world satisfying the respective number of c-atoms and a-atoms. We illustrate these ideas by considering the world

$$\omega' = \{c(s_1, u_1), c(s_1, u_3), c(s_1, u_4), a(s_1, t_1), a(s_1, t_2)\}.$$

In Tab. 3, the $satC' = 3$ and $satA' = 2$ atoms satisfied by ω' are highlighted. So $(satC', satA') = (3, 2)$ is the corresponding sat-pair. Changing our view back to the ground instances in Tab. 3, we easily see that $\text{app}(\omega') = G_{C \backslash A} \cdot satA' = 5 \cdot 2 = 10$ holds, i.e. 10 ground instances are applicable w.r.t. ω'. Furthermore, $\text{ver}(\omega') = satC' \cdot satA' = 3 \cdot 2 = 6$ holds, i.e. 6 of these ground instances are also verified by ω'. So we have $\text{va}_\Omega(\omega') = \langle \text{ver}(\omega'), \text{app}(\omega') \rangle = \langle 6, 10 \rangle \in \mathcal{VA}$. Next, we consider another world

$$\omega'' = \{c(s_1, u_2), c(s_1, u_4), c(s_1, u_5), a(s_1, t_1), a(s_1, t_4)\}.$$

Table 4 illustrates that ω'' satisfies some different ground atoms (compared to ω') and therefore also verifies some different ground instances. Nevertheless, ω' and ω'' coincide in the actual *numbers* of satisfied c-atoms and a-atoms, i.e. $(satC'', satA') = (satC'', satA'') = (3, 2)$ holds, and therefore both worlds have the same va-pair, i.e. $\text{va}_\Omega(\omega') = \text{va}_\Omega(\omega'') = \langle 6, 10 \rangle$. This example illustrates that if we are interested in possible va-pairs, then we do not necessarily have to consider worlds, but we can consider sat-pairs instead.

4   Computing WCI Using Combinatorics

Next, we show how the above consideration concerning just one sub-table can be extended to the complete ground-instance-table. So we consider the world

$$\begin{aligned}
\omega''' = \{&c(s_1, u_1), c(s_1, u_3), c(s_1, u_4), & &a(s_1, t_1), a(s_1, t_2) \\
&c(s_2, u_2), c(s_2, u_3), c(s_2, u_4), & &a(s_2, t_2), a(s_2, t_4) \\
&c(s_3, u_4), & &a(s_3, t_1), a(s_3, t_2), a(s_3, t_3), a(s_3, t_4)\}
\end{aligned}$$

Table 5 shows the complete ground-instance-table, where the atoms satisfied by ω''' are highlighted accordingly. With respect to the three sub-tables, we have the sat-pairs

$$(satC_1''', satA_1''') = (3, 2), \quad (satC_2''', satA_2''') = (3, 2), \quad (satC_3''', satA_3''') = (1, 4).$$

The overall number of applicable and verified ground instances can be determined by summing up the particular result of each sub-table:

$$\text{app}(\omega''') = G_{C \backslash A} \cdot satA_1''' + G_{C \backslash A} \cdot satA_2''' + G_{C \backslash A} \cdot satA_3''' = 5 \cdot 2 + 5 \cdot 2 + 5 \cdot 4 = 40$$
$$\text{ver}(\omega''') = satC_1''' \cdot satA_1''' + satC_2''' \cdot satA_2''' + satC_3''' \cdot satA_3''' = 3 \cdot 2 + 3 \cdot 2 + 1 \cdot 4 = 16$$

This yields $\text{va}_\Omega(\omega''') = \langle \text{ver}(\omega'''), \text{app}(\omega''') \rangle = \langle 16, 40 \rangle \in \mathcal{VA}$.

In these computations, the numbers resulting from the particular sat-pairs are just summed up, hence it does not actually matter from which concrete sub-table a sat-pair arises. Thus, when considering several sat-pairs, their particular order does not matter, and it is sufficient to consider unordered combinations of sat-pairs. Thus, the above combination of sat-pairs can be represented by the multiset (denoted by double braces):

$$CSP''' = \{\!\{(3, 2), (3, 2), (1, 4)\}\!\} \tag{10}$$

Table 5. Atoms satisfied by ω''' in the ground-instance-table

$c(s_1,Z) \mid a(s_1,Y)$	$c(s_2,Z) \mid a(s_2,Y)$	$c(s_3,Z) \mid a(s_3,Y)$
$c(s_1,u_1) \mid a(s_1,t_1)$	$c(s_2,u_1) \mid a(s_2,t_1)$	$c(s_3,u_1) \mid a(s_3,t_1)$
$c(s_1,u_2) \mid a(s_1,t_1)$	$c(s_2,u_2) \mid a(s_2,t_1)$	$c(s_3,u_2) \mid a(s_3,t_1)$
$c(s_1,u_3) \mid a(s_1,t_1)$	$c(s_2,u_3) \mid a(s_2,t_1)$	$c(s_3,u_3) \mid a(s_3,t_1)$
$c(s_1,u_4) \mid a(s_1,t_1)$	$c(s_2,u_4) \mid a(s_2,t_1)$	$c(s_3,u_4) \mid a(s_3,t_1)$
$c(s_1,u_5) \mid a(s_1,t_1)$	$c(s_2,u_5) \mid a(s_2,t_1)$	$c(s_3,u_5) \mid a(s_3,t_1)$
$c(s_1,u_1) \mid a(s_1,t_2)$	$c(s_2,u_1) \mid a(s_2,t_2)$	$c(s_3,u_1) \mid a(s_3,t_2)$
$c(s_1,u_2) \mid a(s_1,t_2)$	$c(s_2,u_2) \mid a(s_2,t_2)$	$c(s_3,u_2) \mid a(s_3,t_2)$
$c(s_1,u_3) \mid a(s_1,t_2)$	$c(s_2,u_3) \mid a(s_2,t_2)$	$c(s_3,u_3) \mid a(s_3,t_2)$
$c(s_1,u_4) \mid a(s_1,t_2)$	$c(s_2,u_4) \mid a(s_2,t_2)$	$c(s_3,u_4) \mid a(s_3,t_2)$
$c(s_1,u_5) \mid a(s_1,t_2)$	$c(s_2,u_5) \mid a(s_2,t_2)$	$c(s_3,u_5) \mid a(s_3,t_2)$
$c(s_1,u_1) \mid a(s_1,t_3)$	$c(s_2,u_1) \mid a(s_2,t_3)$	$c(s_3,u_1) \mid a(s_3,t_3)$
$c(s_1,u_2) \mid a(s_1,t_3)$	$c(s_2,u_2) \mid a(s_2,t_3)$	$c(s_3,u_2) \mid a(s_3,t_3)$
$c(s_1,u_3) \mid a(s_1,t_3)$	$c(s_2,u_3) \mid a(s_2,t_3)$	$c(s_3,u_3) \mid a(s_3,t_3)$
$c(s_1,u_4) \mid a(s_1,t_3)$	$c(s_2,u_4) \mid a(s_2,t_3)$	$c(s_3,u_4) \mid a(s_3,t_3)$
$c(s_1,u_5) \mid a(s_1,t_3)$	$c(s_2,u_5) \mid a(s_2,t_3)$	$c(s_3,u_5) \mid a(s_3,t_3)$
$c(s_1,u_1) \mid a(s_1,t_4)$	$c(s_2,u_1) \mid a(s_2,t_4)$	$c(s_3,u_1) \mid a(s_3,t_4)$
$c(s_1,u_2) \mid a(s_1,t_4)$	$c(s_2,u_2) \mid a(s_2,t_4)$	$c(s_3,u_2) \mid a(s_3,t_4)$
$c(s_1,u_3) \mid a(s_1,t_4)$	$c(s_2,u_3) \mid a(s_2,t_4)$	$c(s_3,u_3) \mid a(s_3,t_4)$
$c(s_1,u_4) \mid a(s_1,t_4)$	$c(s_2,u_4) \mid a(s_2,t_4)$	$c(s_3,u_4) \mid a(s_3,t_4)$
$c(s_1,u_5) \mid a(s_1,t_4)$	$c(s_2,u_5) \mid a(s_2,t_4)$	$c(s_3,u_5) \mid a(s_3,t_4)$

Computing $\mathcal{VA}$. We put the ideas above in a general form by introducing *combinations of sat-pairs* and a function on them leading directly to a va-pair.

Definition 5 ($\mathcal{CSP}$). *A multiset*

$$CSP = \{\!\!\{(satC_1, satA_1), \ldots, (satC_{G_{C\cap A}}, satA_{G_{C\cap A}})\}\!\!\}$$

consisting of $G_{C\cap A}$*-many sat-pairs* $(satC_i, satA_i) \in \mathcal{SP}$ *is called a* combination of sat-pairs *of* r. *The set*

$$\mathcal{CSP} := \{CSP \mid CSP \text{ is a combination of sat-pairs}\}$$

is the set of all possible combinations of sat-pairs *of* r.

Definition 6. *The* va-pair function $\mathrm{va}_C : \mathcal{CSP} \to \mathcal{VA}$ *on combinations of sat-pairs of* r *is defined by* $\mathrm{va}_C(CSP) := \langle v, a \rangle$ *with*

$$v = \sum_{(satC, satA) \in CSP} satC \cdot satA \quad and \quad a = G_{C\setminus A} \sum_{(satC, satA) \in CSP} satA$$

In contrast to the function va_Ω (Def. 1), the function va_C only considers combinations of sat-pairs instead of worlds.

Proposition 3. *Let r be an atomic conditional. Then we have*

$$\mathcal{VA} = \mathrm{va}_{\Omega}(\Omega) \qquad\qquad = \bigcup_{\omega \in \Omega} \{\mathrm{va}_{\Omega}(\omega)\} \qquad (11)$$

$$= \mathrm{va}_{\mathcal{C}}(\mathcal{CSP}) \qquad\qquad = \bigcup_{CSP \in \mathcal{CSP}} \{\mathrm{va}_{\mathcal{C}}(CSP)\} \qquad (12)$$

Proposition 3 states that the set $\mathcal{VA}$ can as well be determined via combinations of sat-pairs instead of considering worlds. In particular, (12) gives rise to an algorithm which computes $\mathcal{VA}$ by just running over the set $\mathcal{CSP}$, i. e. without taking into account the much larger set Ω at any point.

The size of $\mathcal{CSP}$ is determined by the well-known multiset coefficient $\left(\!\binom{n}{k}\!\right) = \binom{n+k-1}{k}$, which denotes number of multisets of cardinality k (here: $k = G_{C \cap A}$) with elements taken from a set of cardinality n (here: $n = |\mathcal{SP}|$):

Proposition 4. *The number of combinations of sat-pairs with respect to r is:*

$$|\mathcal{CSP}| = \left(\!\binom{|\mathcal{SP}|}{G_{C \cap A}}\!\right) = \binom{|\mathcal{SP}| + G_{C \cap A} - 1}{G_{C \cap A}} = \binom{G_{C \cap A} + G_{C \setminus A} + G_{A \setminus C} + G_{C \setminus A} \cdot G_{A \setminus C}}{G_{C \cap A}}$$

Example 4. In Ex. 3, we have $|\Omega| = 2^{|\mathcal{H}|} = 2^{G_{C \cap A} \cdot (G_{C \setminus A} + G_{A \setminus C})} = 2^{27} = 134{,}217{,}728$ worlds compared to just $|\mathcal{CSP}| = \binom{3+5+4+5 \cdot 4}{3} = \binom{32}{3} = 4{,}960$ combinations of sat-pairs of $r_{X_s Z_u | X_s Y_t}$. Both sets induce the $|\mathcal{VA}| = 348$ va-pairs of $r_{X_s Z_u | X_s Y_t}$ according to Prop. 3.

We get similar magnitudes of numbers by analyzing other examples involving atomic conditionals (e. g. as in Ex. 2), so we can state in general $|\Omega| \gg |\mathcal{CSP}|$.

Computing Weights of va-Pairs. Up to this point, we have achieved the first part of our goal: determining the WCI $(\mathcal{VA}, \mathrm{wgt})$ of an atomic conditional without any involvement of Ω. So we still have to show how the weight $\mathrm{wgt}(\langle v, a \rangle)$ of each va-pair can be determined also without considering Ω.

According to (8), the weight $\mathrm{wgt}(\langle v, a \rangle)$ of a va-pair corresponds to the number of worlds from Ω which induce $\langle v, a \rangle$. Thus, it seems hard to develop a closed-formed expression which directly provides the weight of a va-pair without considering Ω. However, Prop. 3 showed us that it is feasible to consider combinations of sat-pairs instead of worlds in a certain situation. Furthermore, in the previous examples we illustrated how worlds induce sat-pairs and combinations of sat-pairs, respectively. By employing basic techniques from the field of combinatorics, we indeed obtain a closed formula:

Proposition 5 (nw). *Let $CSP \in \mathcal{CSP}$ be a combination of sat-pairs of r. Let k be number of different sat-pairs contained in CSP and let $m_1, \ldots, m_k$ be the multiplicities of these sat-pairs. Then the function $\mathrm{nw} : \mathcal{CSP} \to \mathbb{N}$ with*

$$\mathrm{nw}(CSP) := \binom{G_{C \cap A}}{m_1, \ldots, m_k} \cdot \prod_{\substack{(satC, satA) \\ \in CSP}} \binom{G_{C \setminus A}}{satC} \cdot \binom{G_{A \setminus C}}{satA}$$

yields the number of worlds inducing a combination of sat-pairs.

Input: - a knowledge base $(\Sigma, \{r\})$ with r being an atomic condtional
Output: - the weighted conditional impacts $(\mathcal{VA}, \mathrm{wgt})$

1. $\mathcal{VA} := \emptyset$ // initialize set
2. for each $CSP \in \mathcal{CSP}$ // construct the next CSP systematically on demand
   (a) $\langle v, a \rangle := \mathrm{va}_\mathcal{C}(CSP)$ // compute the va-pair induced by CSP by eval. the
       //funct. $\mathrm{va}_\mathcal{C}$
   (b) if $\mathcal{VA} \cap \{\langle v, a \rangle\} = \emptyset$ // check if $\langle v, a \rangle$ appears for the first time
       then
          i. $\mathcal{VA} := \mathcal{VA} \cup \{\langle v, a \rangle\}$ // adjoin $\langle v, a \rangle$ to the set $\mathcal{VA}$
          ii. $\mathrm{wgt}(\langle v, a \rangle) := 0$ // initialize function value
   (c) // compute the number of worlds inducing CSP by evaluating the function
       //nw and
       // increase the weight of $\langle v, a \rangle$ by $\mathrm{nw}(CSP)$
       $\mathrm{wgt}(\langle v, a \rangle) := \mathrm{wgt}(\langle v, a \rangle) + \mathrm{nw}(CSP)$
   end loop

Fig. 1. Algorithm $\mathtt{WCI}_{\mathrm{at}}$ yielding $(\mathcal{VA}, \mathrm{wgt})$ of an atomic conditional in time $\mathcal{O}(|\mathcal{CSP}|)$

The above equation makes use of the well-known number of multiset permutations [1], which is defined as $\binom{G_{\mathsf{C} \cap \mathsf{A}}}{m_1, \ldots, m_k} = \frac{G_{\mathsf{C} \cap \mathsf{A}}!}{m_1! \cdot \ldots \cdot m_k!}$. For instance, by applying the function nw to the combination of sat-pairs CSP''' given in (10), where $G_{\mathsf{C} \cap \mathsf{A}} = 3$, we get:

$$\mathrm{nw}(CSP''') = \binom{3}{1, 2} \cdot \binom{5}{3} \cdot \binom{4}{2} \cdot \binom{5}{3} \cdot \binom{4}{2} \cdot \binom{5}{1} \cdot \binom{4}{4} = 54{,}000.$$

That is, besides the world ω''' from above, there is a total number of 54,000 worlds in Ω which induce CSP'''.

5   Practical Algorithm and Evaluation

Although the function nw in Prop. 5 does not provide the weight of a va-pair directly, it allows us develop an algorithm which successively computes all function values of wgt in parallel without considering Ω.

The algorithm $\mathtt{WCI}_{\mathrm{at}}$ depicted in Fig. 1 takes an atomic conditional r together with an appropriate signature Σ and computes $(\mathcal{VA}, \mathrm{wgt})$ by running over all elements from $\mathcal{CSP}$ once. In step (2), the main loop runs over each multiset $CSP \in \mathcal{CSP}$. Note that the next multiset CSP can be constructed systematically on demand each time, so that the algorithm does not have to store the set $\mathcal{CSP}$ at any point. Within the loop, the function $\mathrm{va}_\mathcal{C}$ (see Prop. 3) is employed for the current CSP to determine the corresponding va-pair $\mathrm{va}_\mathcal{C}(CSP)$. That way, the set $\mathcal{VA}$ is constructed successively in step (2(b)i). In step (2c), the number of worlds inducing CSP is determined by employing the function nw (see Prop. 5), and $\mathrm{nw}(CSP)$ is added to the current weight of the respective va-pair, i. e. the

Table 6. Results for computing the weighted conditional impacts $(\mathcal{VA}, \mathrm{wgt})$ for different atomic conditionals and numbers of constants; the numbers of constants for the sorted conditional $r_{X_s Z_u | X_s Y_t}$ refer to the sorts S, U, and T, respectively.

Atomic Conditional	$|Const|$	$|\Omega|$	$|\mathcal{CSP}|$	$|\mathcal{VA}|$	Runtime of Algorithm $\mathrm{WCI_{gen}}$	$\mathrm{WCI_{at}}$
$r_{X|X}$	10	2^{20}	286	66	3 sec	< 1 sec
	12	2^{24}	455	91	29 sec	< 1 sec
	15	2^{30}	816	136	30 min 32 sec	< 1 sec
	50	2^{100}	23,426	1,326	*unfeasible*	< 1 sec
$r_{X|XY}$	4	2^{20}	715	129	2 sec	< 1 sec
	5	2^{30}	4,368	301	56 min 38 sec	< 1 sec
	10	2^{100}	44,352,165	4,701	*unfeasible*	1 min 13 sec
	12	2^{156}	1,852,482,996	9,793	*unfeasible*	1 h 2 min
$r_{X_s Z_u | X_s Y_t}$	3+5+4	2^{27}	4,960	348	13 min 46 sec	< 1 sec
	3+6+5	2^{33}	13,244	644	$\approx$ 27 hours	< 1 sec
	3+10+10	2^{60}	302,621	4,215	*unfeasible*	< 1 sec
	4+10+10	2^{80}	9,381,251	7,685	*unfeasible*	11 sec
	5+10+10	2^{100}	234,531,275	12,155	*unfeasible*	5 min 22 sec
	6+10+10	2^{120}	4,925,156,775	17,625	*unfeasible*	1 h 53 min

va-pair which is induced by $\mathcal{CSP}$. That way, the correct weight $\mathrm{wgt}(\langle v, a \rangle)$ of each va-pair is computed incrementally.

Note that the set Ω is not considered in any step of the algorithm $\mathrm{WCI_{at}}$. In particular, the functions $\mathrm{va}_\mathcal{C}$ and nw employed by the algorithm are closed-form expressions which do not refer to Ω either. Thus, the overall runtime of the algorithm is determined by the size of the set $\mathcal{CSP}$, and the algorithm merely requires space $\mathcal{O}(|\mathcal{VA}|)$, which is no more than the size of the output. These observations yield:

Proposition 6. *The algorithm* $\mathrm{WCI_{at}}$ *in Fig. 1 computes the WCI* $(\mathcal{VA}, \mathrm{wgt})$ *of an atomic conditional in time* $\mathcal{O}(|\mathcal{CSP}|)$ *and space* $\mathcal{O}(|\mathcal{VA}|)$.

Table 6 shows some results for applying algorithm $\mathrm{WCI_{at}}$ to some conditionals from Ex. 2 and 3 together with various numbers of constants. For instance, for $r_{X_s Z_u | X_s Y_t}$ together with a set of 3, 10, and 10 constants of the respective sorts, the generic algorithm $\mathrm{WCI_{gen}}$ from [5], requiring time $\mathcal{O}(|\Omega|)$, must process $2^{60} \approx 10^{18}$ worlds which is already infeasible, whereas the algorithm $\mathrm{WCI_{at}}$ merely has to consider $|\mathcal{CSP}| = 302{,}621$ combinations of sat-pairs, taking less than one second to determine the weighted conditional impacts $(\mathcal{VA}, \mathrm{wgt})$. Thus, $\mathrm{WCI_{at}}$ allows to determine the actual set $\mathcal{VA}$ and its actual size in particular for an increasing number of constants; due to the obvious limitations of any generic algorithm working on Ω, such concrete numbers could not be computed before. The actual numbers for $|\mathcal{VA}|$ in Tab. 6 suggest that the number of va-pairs grows significantly slower than $|\mathcal{CSP}|$, i.e. we have:

$$|\Omega| \gg |\mathcal{CSP}| \gg |\mathcal{VA}|$$

Indeed, the size of $\mathcal{CSP}$, given by the binomial coefficient in Prop. 4, also grows rather fast in the number of constants. Nevertheless, it grows significantly slower than the size of Ω, which grows exponentially in a polynomial of the constants. So our novel algorithm $\mathtt{WCI_{at}}$ also serves as a proof of concept and illustrates that it is in fact possible to determine $(\mathcal{VA}, \mathrm{wgt})$ without considering the set Ω at all.

6 Conclusions and Future Work

The WCI of a relational probabilistic knowledge base are the essential ingredient for Maximum Entropy model computation. We presented a new approach allowing to compute the WCI of an atomic conditional based on combinatorics. The resulting algorithm fully abstracts from Ω, using the set $\mathcal{CSP}$ instead, and since $|\Omega| \gg |\mathcal{CSP}|$, it is much faster than a generic algorithm which has to run over Ω. In terms of a first proof of concept, we restricted our considerations to a single atomic conditional in this paper. In future work, we will investigate how the general concepts introduced here can be extended to more complex conditionals and to more than one conditional. For instance, a non-atomic conditional $(c(X) \mid a(X) \wedge b(Y))$ can be transformed into an atomic conditional $(c(X) \mid aAndb(X,Y))$ by introducing a new predicate $aAndb(X,Y)$ which captures the non-atomic formula in the antecedence. Furthermore, while the development of an incremental algorithm by extending the WCI appropriately when adding another conditional may not be feasible in all cases, the current concept can directly be extended to, e. g. a set of several atomic conditionals if we ensure that each conditional considers different predicates. We will also investigate to what extent techniques of lifted inference [3,9,16] can be adopted to our approach.

References

1. Brualdi, R.A.: Introductory Combinatorics (5th Edition). Pearson (2009)
2. Darroch, J.N., Ratcliff, D.: Generalized iterative scaling for log-linear models. Annals of Mathematical Statistics **43**(5), 1470–1480 (1972)
3. de Salvo Braz, R., Amir, E., Roth, D.: Lifted first-order probabilistic inference. In: IJCAI-05, pp. 1319–1325. Professional Book Center (2005)
4. Finthammer, M., Beierle, C.: Using equivalences of worlds for aggregation semantics of relational conditionals. In: Glimm, B., Krüger, A. (eds.) KI 2012. LNCS, vol. 7526, pp. 49–60. Springer, Heidelberg (2012)
5. Finthammer, M., Beierle, C.: A two-level approach to maximum entropy model computation for relational probabilistic logic based on weighted conditional impacts. In: Straccia, U., Calì, A. (eds.) SUM 2014. LNCS, vol. 8720, pp. 162–175. Springer, Heidelberg (2014)
6. Fischer, V., Schramm, M.: Tabl - a tool for efficient compilation of probabilistic constraints. Technical Report TUM-I9636, Technische Universität München (1996)
7. Getoor, L., Taskar, B. (eds.): Introduction to Statistical Relational Learning. MIT Press (2007)

8. Halpern, J.: Reasoning About Uncertainty. MIT Press (2005)
9. Kazemi, S.M., Buchman, D., Kersting, K., Natarajan, S., Poole, D.: Relational logistic regression. In: Proc. 14th International Conference on Principles of Knowledge Representation and Reasoning (KR-2014) (2014)
10. Kern-Isberner, G.: Conditionals in Nonmonotonic Reasoning and Belief Revision. LNCS, vol. 2087. Springer, Heidelberg (2001)
11. Kern-Isberner, G., Beierle, C., Finthammer, M., Thimm, M.: Comparing and evaluating approaches to probabilistic reasoning: Theory, implementation, and applications. Transactions on Large-Scale Data- and Knowledge-Centered Systems **6**, 31–75 (2012)
12. Kern-Isberner, G., Lukasiewicz, T.: Combining probabilistic logic programming with the power of maximum entropy. Artif. Intell. **157**(1–2), 139–202 (2004)
13. Kern-Isberner, G., Thimm, M.: Novel semantical approaches to relational probabilistic conditionals. In: Proc. KR-2010, pp. 382–391. AAAI Press, Menlo Park, CA (2010)
14. Kern-Isberner, G., Thimm, M.: A ranking semantics for first-order conditionals. In: ECAI-2012, pp. 456–461. IOS Press (2012)
15. Lukasiewicz, T.: Probabilistic logic programming with conditional constraints. ACM Trans. Comput. Logic **2**(3), 289–339 (2001)
16. Milch, B., Zettlemoyer, L., Kersting, K., Haimes, M., Kaelbling, L.P.: Lifted probabilistic inference with counting formulas. In: AAAI-2008, pp. 1062–1068. AAAI Press (2008)
17. Nilsson, N.: Probabilistic logic. Artificial Intelligence **28**, 71–87 (1986)
18. Paris, J.: The uncertain reasoner's companion - A mathematical perspective. University Press, Cambridge (1994)
19. Pearl, J.: Probabilistic Reasoning in Intelligent Systems. Morgan Kaufmann, San Mateo, Ca (1988)
20. Poole, D.: First-order probabilistic inference. In: Gottlob, G., Walsh, T. (ed.), Proceedings of the Eighteenth International Joint Conference on Artificial Intelligence (IJCAI-03), pp. 985–991. Morgan Kaufmann (2003)
21. Potyka, N., Beierle, C., Kern-Isberner, G.: A concept for the evolution of relational probabilistic belief states and the computation of their changes under optimum entropy semantics. Journal of Applied Logic (2015). (to appear)
22. Richardson, M., Domingos, P.: Markov logic networks. Machine Learning **62**(1–2), 107–136 (2006)
23. Shore, J., Johnson, R.: Axiomatic derivation of the principle of maximum entropy and the principle of minimum cross-entropy. IEEE Transactions on Information Theory, IT-26:26–37 (1980)

Assisting with Goal Formulation for Domain Independent Planning

Moritz Göbelbecker[✉]

Albert-Ludwigs-Universität Freiburg, Freiburg im Breisgau, Germany
goebelbe@informatik.uni-freiburg.de

Abstract. Domain independent planning systems have been used in an increasing number of applications, such as autonomous robots. However, most such systems either generate the planning goals with a domain specific goal component or they require the user to write fully fledged PDDL goal descriptions. In this paper we present a domain independent method based on referring expressions to implement a menu-driven interface to a planning system.

1 Introduction

One major reason to use domain independent planners to control the behaviour of autonomous systems is that they allow for more flexible behaviour in the face of unexpected situations than hardcoded decision making algorithms. Another reason is the added flexibility for the system designer to add new behaviours without having to make invasive changes to the system. Ideally, adding new capabilities only involves implementing them in a self-contained module and adding the appropriate actions to the planning domain. In practice, it is rarely that easy, but a number of frameworks exist that try to make the integration of low-level behaviour and planning as painless as possible, such as the ROS [12] integration of TFD-M [5].

Extended capabilities should often come with a greater range of achievable goals, but there are no automatic ways to communicate this extended range to users. Often, goals are either entirely or partially hardcoded so that users can only issue goals anticipated by the designer of the user interface. Other systems provide the maximum of flexibility by allowing arbitrary PDDL conditions as a goal, but this is hardly a suitable interface for most potential users and lacks discoverability even for experienced users.

In this paper, we first introduce a variant of referring expressions [4] based on a subset of first-order formulas that allow us to to incrementally build references to individual objects in a planning task. Then we use these references to create a menu-driven interface to a planner that only requires a minimal amount of domain specific adjustments to work, while still allowing users to select arbitrary goals.

© Springer International Publishing Switzerland 2015
S. Hölldobler et al. (Eds.): KI 2015, LNAI 9324, pp. 87–99, 2015.
DOI: 10.1007/978-3-319-24489-1_7

2   Background

As we are operating mostly on lifted planning problems, planning problems are given as a PDDL [10] domain and problem file. A *planning domain* is a tuple $\mathcal{D} = \langle \mathcal{T}, \mathcal{C}_d, \mathcal{P}, \mathcal{O} \rangle$, where

- $\mathcal{T} = \langle T, \prec \rangle$ is the *type system*, consisting of the set of types T along with a partial ordering $\prec$ describing sub-type relations,
- $\mathcal{C}_d$ is the set of typed *domain constant symbols*,
- $\mathcal{P}$ is the set of *predicate symbols* with associated arities and types, and
- $\mathcal{O}$ is the set of *planning operators* consisting of preconditions and effects.

As we are concerned with goal *generation*, we will omit the goal from the planning task description. A *planning task* is then a tuple $\Pi = \langle \mathcal{D}, \mathcal{C}_t, \mathcal{I} \rangle$, where

- $\mathcal{D}$ is a planning domain as defined above,
- $\mathcal{C}_t$ is a set of typed *task-dependent constant symbols* disjoint from $\mathcal{C}_d$, and
- $\mathcal{I}$ is the description of the *initial state*.

We will usually not distinguish between task and domain specific constants and will therefore refer to the union of both as the task's *objects* $\mathcal{C} = \mathcal{C}_d \cup \mathcal{C}_t$.

3   Building References

In order to specify a goal, a user must be able to refer to the elements of that goal: usually this includes at least the function or predicate that should be changed as well as the objects to which these apply. Figure 1 shows a problem in the *logistics* domain. We want to formulate the goal to deliver package p_1 to location L_4. In order to do so, we need to be able to refer to three elements: The `at` predicate, the `package` object p_1 and the goal `location` L_4. This is easy if we can specify each of those by name: "Set *at* of p_1 and L_4" or, as a PDDL goal, (at p₁ L₄). However, this is only possible if the user and the planner both agree on the meaning on the symbols p_1, L_4 and `at`. In many cases, however, there may be no such *shared reference* between the planner and the user. In our example, we will assume that the user has a correct understanding of the name *at*, but that they cannot relate to the identifiers p_1 and L_4: those are internal to the planning system with no way for the user to find out what they mean.

While this example uses an artificial benchmark domain, it often occurs in applications: in many robots that use planning systems, objects have internal IDs and can be identified to the user only via additional predicates (such as a *type* predicate) or they do not correspond to anything at all that the user can directly relate to (e.g. many systems use an arbitrary segmentation of space for navigation). Therefore, we have to refer to goal candidates with only those elements which are known to the user.

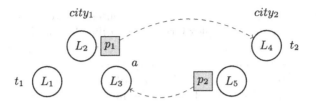

Fig. 1. A problem instance in the *logistics* domain, consisting of two cities, two trucks t_1 and t_2, two packages p_1, p_2 and one airplane a.

3.1 Referencing Objects

In the same way that we can construct (verbal) sentences that identify a concept without referring to it by name, we can create first-order sentences that identify an object. For example, the following first order sentence ϕ uniquely identifies L_4 in our example:

$$\phi(x) = location(x) \wedge \exists\, t\big(truck(t) \wedge at(t, x)\big)$$
$$\wedge \exists\, c, l_2\big(x \neq l_2 \wedge \forall\, l_3\ city(l_3, c) \leftrightarrow (l_3 = x \vee l_3 = l_2)\big)$$

Here x has to be a location at which there is at least one truck and x must be in a city that contains exactly two locations. This formula uniquely describes L_4, without referring to any object by name: L_1, L_2, L_3 are in a city consisting of three locations, there is no truck at L_5, and no other object is a location.

Definition 1. *Let $\phi(x)$ be an arbitrary, function-free first order formula with one free variable x, then $\phi(x)$ is a* reference *to an object o (or ϕ matches o) under an interpretation $\mathcal{I}$ iff $\mathcal{I} \models \phi(o)$.*

ϕ is a unique reference *iff also $\mathcal{I} \not\models \phi(o')$ for all $o' \neq o$. Otherwise, we call it a* partial reference.

This concept of references is closely linked to relational query languages [3], and for arbitrary, function-free first order formulas, checking whether there exists a matching object to a reference is precisely the query evaluation problem, which is PSPACE-complete [16]. So is checking whether a reference is unique:

Theorem 1. *Deciding whether a reference ϕ is unique is PSPACE-complete.*

Proof. Let $\phi(x)$ be an arbitrary reference, then the reference

$$\phi'(x) = \phi(x) \wedge \forall z\ \phi(z) \to z = x$$

is a reference to an object o iff ϕ is a unique reference to o which shows membership in PSPACE. Vice versa, given a reference $\psi(x)$ and a constant o,

$$\psi'(x) = (x = o) \wedge \exists x' \psi(x')$$

is a unique reference to o iff there exists an object that matches ψ. Thus the problem is PSPACE-complete.

Besides the complexity, arbitrary first order sentences have a number of drawbacks in our scenario: more complex formulas are difficult to understand for most humans, and are thus unsuitable as a means of user interaction. Also, we want to implement a menu-driven interface, and would thus prefer references that can be constructed incrementally. In particular, *monotonicity* is a desirable property: then, as we add elements to a reference, the number of matching objects will always decrease, so that the construction process will eventually terminate.

A query type that meets these requirements are *conjunctive queries* which consist only of existential quantifiers and conjunctions of atomic formulas.

Definition 2. *Given a set of predicate symbols $R_0, \ldots, R_n$, the formula $\phi(x)$ is a conjunctive (unique) reference to an object o if $\phi(x)$ is a (unique) reference to o and has the form*

$$\phi(x) = \exists x_1 \ldots x_n R_1(x_{11}, \ldots) \wedge \ldots \wedge R_m(x_{m1}, \ldots)$$

where each argument x_{ij} refers to one of the variables $x, x_1, \ldots, x_n$.

We will usually omit the quantifiers and simply write $\phi(x) = R_1(x_{11}, \ldots) \wedge \ldots \wedge R_m(x_{m1}, \ldots)$. Allowing only conjunctions makes sure that extending references never causes the number of matching objects to increase. (We will deal with the requirement that it *decreases* in the next section.) Allowing only existential quantifiers also helps us to avoid the complexities of quantifier nesting.

Deciding whether a conjunctive reference matches an object is NP-complete, as the query complexity of conjunctive queries is NP-complete [2]. The same is not true for testing uniqueness, which is complete for the complexity class $\mathsf{D^P}$, which is the class of decision problems that can be described by the intersection of an NP- and a co-NP-complete language. The SAT-UNSAT problem of deciding for two formulas θ and ψ whether θ is satisfiable and ψ is unsatisfiable is a complete problem for $\mathsf{D^P}$ [11].

Theorem 2. *Deciding whether a conjunctive reference ϕ is a unique reference to an object o is $\mathsf{D^P}$-complete.*

Proof. The problem is a member of $\mathsf{D^P}$ as we can guess an object x that satisfies ϕ, as well as two distinct objects x, x' as a counterexample if ϕ is not unique.

To show hardness, we reduce from SAT-UNSAT, with θ and ψ given in 3-clause CNF. Encoding the satisfiability of θ in a reference is simple, as for every clause $C_i^\theta = l_{i1} \vee l_{i2} \vee l_{i3}$ we can introduce a relation $R_i^\theta(y_{i1}, y_{i2}, y_{i3})$ which is true iff at least one of the satisfying literals l_{ik} is at the correct position.

To encode the unsatisfiability of ψ, we add for every clause C_i^ψ a relation $R_j^\psi(z_{j1}, z_{j2}, z_{j3}, x)$ which is true iff

1. one of the satisfying literals l_{jk} is at the correct position *and* x is equal to the constant o, or
2. all arguments z_{jk} are equal to $\perp$ and x is equal to the constant o'.

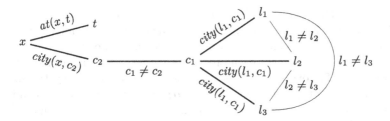

Fig. 2. A graph representing the dependencies of variables of a reference. Removing the inequalities results in a tree (bold lines) but renders the reference ambiguous.

The reference $\phi(x) = \bigwedge_{i=1}^{n} R_i^\theta(\ldots) \wedge \bigwedge_{j=1}^{m} R_j^\psi(\ldots, x)$ matches o' iff θ is satisfiable as the R_j^ψ are all satisfiable with $R_j^\psi(\bot, \bot, \bot, o')$. It matches o iff both θ and ψ are satisfiable. Therefore, ϕ is unique iff θ is satisfiable and ψ is unsatisfiable.

The complexity of evaluating conjunctive queries results from the many ways in which quantified variables can be combined. If we can decompose a reference into conjuncts which do not share quantified variables, we can evaluate every part separately and then compute the intersection of the partial results.

In the case of binary relations, these decompositions can be visualised as a graph, where every variable is a vertex and two variables are connected if they occur in the same relation. Figure 2 shows our reference to L_4 in this form. We can compute the matches for $location(x)$, $at(x,t) \wedge truck(t)$ and the *city*-subgraph separately, but the computation for c_1 cannot be decomposed further, as the free variables l_1, l_2 and l_3 all depend on each other due to the inequalities.

Removing cycles reduces the expressive power: in our example, we can no longer distinguish between cities 1 and 2 by counting the number of locations, as we cannot force three variables to be all different. However, computing the matches for a references becomes much easier, as we can simply collect results at the leaves of the dependency tree and propagate them to the root. With this simplification, we can add back negation: if M is the set of matching objects for a reference ϕ, then the matches for $\neg\phi$ are simply $\mathcal{C} \setminus M$. Allowing negation also means that we can always find a set of references that completely partition all objects which will be useful for our goal selection procedure.

Definition 3. *A simple reference is either*

- *An existentially quantified relation:* $\phi(x_0) = \exists x_1, \ldots, x_n R(x_0, \ldots, x_n)$
- *An existentially quantified conjunction of a relation and an arbitrary number of simple references* $\phi_0, \ldots, \phi_m$:

$$\phi(x_0) = \exists x_1, \ldots, x_n R(x_0, \ldots, x_n) \wedge \phi_0(x_{i_0}) \wedge \ldots \wedge \phi_m(x_{i_m})$$

- *A negation of a simple reference* ϕ': $\phi(x_0) = \neg\phi'(x_0)$

To apply this theory to planning problems, we have to identify the predicates which we can use to build more complex references to objects. For a planning problem Π we can create references from three types of relations:

- **Individual References**: These objects can be identified by name. The *city* objects in the logistic domain could be such a case, assuming the object names correspond to city names a human would understand. There is one relation $I_o(x) \Leftrightarrow o = x$ for each object $o \in C$ that can be identified by name.
- **Typename References**: These objects can be identified by the name of their type. The types *package, truck, airplane* and *location* are candidates for those. We also assume that the common *object* supertype can used to refer to any object. So for each type $t \in T$ there is one relation $t(x) \Leftrightarrow type(x) \preceq t$.
- **Relational References**: Objects can be referred to via predicates in which they occur as an argument. We used this in our examples in order to refer to locations by their *city* predicate, but we also could refer to a city by the locations it contains. So for every predicate $P \in \mathcal{P}$ there is a relation $R_P(x_1, \ldots, x_n) \Leftrightarrow P(x_1, \ldots, x_n) \in \mathcal{I}$.

3.2 Referencing Goals

A reference to a goal is not substantially different from a reference to an object. Using the references we built in the previous section, we can write the goal $at(p_1, L_4)$ as a formula[1] which we could then give directly to a planner which supports quantified conditions (e.g. the Fast Downward planner [7]):

$$\exists p, l, l_2, t : \ at_{goal}(p, l) \wedge package(p) \wedge at_{current}(p, l_2) \wedge city(l_2, city_1)$$
$$\wedge \ city(l, city_2) \wedge at_{current}(t, l) \wedge truck(t)$$

Note that we have introduced two copies of the *at* predicate. The copy at_{goal} is used to describe the desired goal and corresponds to the *at* predicate in the original task, whereas $at_{current}$ is immutable and always refers to the current state. If we had simply joined the formulas, we would have ended up with an unsolvable goal. If the reference is unique, we can instead resolve the reference manually and give the goal $at(p_1, L_4)$ directly to the planner. If there are multiple matching objects, it might be easier to let the planner do the work.

Goal References Via Actions. We also want to discuss an alternative way of referencing goals. Instead of using a predicate we can refer to a goal via an action. For example, the goal $at(p_1, L_4)$ could also be phrased as $\exists t \ \text{UNLOAD}(p_1, t, L_4)$.

```
(:action unload
    :parameters    (?o - obj ?t - truck ?loc - location)
    :precondition (and (at ?t ?loc) (at ?o ?t))
    :effect        (and (not (at ?o ?t)) (at (?o ?loc))))
```

One obvious situation, in which we would like to do this if we cannot use the goal predicate as a reference directly. Another reason is that it can be more

---

[1] To make the references simpler, we refer to the cities $city_1$ and $city_2$ as constants, not via individual references.

natural to state goals in terms of actions than in terms of states: one would rather say "Please bring me a cup of coffee" than "Please set the position of a cup of coffee to myself". Finally, there are cases where an action has several desired effects, so one does not have to specify all those goals separately. Conversely, however, it can be hard to distinguish the intended effect from side effects. Also, the user may have to specify action parameters that are not relevant to the goal. The UNLOAD action above demonstrates both issues and how they are related:

This action has two effects, (at ?o ?loc) and (not (at ?o ?t)). Usually we only care about the first effect (deliver a package to some place) but it is not impossible that one would use the second one (clear out this truck). In the first case, the $?t$ parameter is redundant, as we do not care which truck delivers our package. In the second case we do not care where the packages are dumped.

Thus, if we can remove side effects, we can go on to eliminate redundant parameters by simply removing the parameters that do not occur in the primary effect. If we cannot remove side effects we can try to exploit the fact that different effects use different parameters to split the action for the purpose of referencing goals. Instead of one action UNLOAD($?o, ?t, ?loc$) we could present the user with two actions: UNLOAD($?o, ?loc$) with the add effect and UNLOAD($?o, ?t$) with the delete effect.

4   Generating Goals

We use the ideas described in the previous section to implement a text-based prototype to assist users with goal selection. Figure 3 shows an example session in a robotics task. We use actions to refer to the goals, and objects can be referred by type (bottle, mug, etc.) or via some of their properties (content or location). We start out with the action selection, and choose the GIVE action. Arrows indicate that the goal selection can be narrowed down further. We can then continue down the menu, until we select the unique goal to bring the water bottle located in the living room to the user.

The input to the program consist of the planning domain and problem, as well as a domain specific (but problem independent) description of the available references: individually referrable constants, individually referrable types, types referrable by name and referrable predicates.

4.1   Generating References

In order to get to the desired goal as quickly as possible, we want to choose a reference that splits each set of goal candidates into partitions that allow the user to make a meaningful choice at every step. In the worst case, a poor partitioning would only split off one object at every step, leading to a degenerated tree. Algorithms for decision tree learning, such as the ID3 algorithm [13], solve this by choosing partitions that maximise its *information content*. For a partition P of $|P|$ objects with subsets P_k, the information $I(P) = \sum_k -\frac{|P|}{|P_k|} log_2 \frac{|P|}{|P_k|}$ is zero if P consists of only one cluster and maximal if P partitions each element into

1: → drop some object, some location
2: → give some object
3: → grasp some object
4: → go some location

$\phi_1 = object(x),\ I(P) = 10.3,\ C(\phi_1) = 1$

1: → give some bottle	$|P_1| = 4$	$\psi_1 = bottle(x)$
2: → give some mug	$|P_2| = 3$	$\psi_2 = mug(x)$
3: → give some plate	$|P_3| = 4$	$\psi_3 = plate(x)$
4: give an arbitrary object	$|P_4| = 1$	$\psi_4 = \top$

$\phi_2 = object(x) \wedge bottle(x),\ I(P) = 12.5,\ C(\phi_2) = 2$
1:   give some bottle with content = water and position = kitchen
2:   give the bottle with content = water and position = living-room
3:   give the bottle with content = apple-juice
4:   give all bottles
5:   give an arbitrary bottle

$\phi_3 = object(x) \wedge bottle(x)$
$\qquad \wedge contains(x, w) \wedge water(w) \wedge pos(x, r) \wedge l\text{-}room(r),\ \ I(P) = 0,\ C(\phi_3) = 6$

Fig. 3. An example session in a robotics scenario. Entries selected by the user are in bold. $I(P)$ denotes the information content of the current partition P, $C(\phi)$ the complexity of the current reference.

its own singleton set. Moreover, for a partition of a given size, its information is maximised if all entries contain the same number of elements. This method will prefer partitions with lots of small sets, which can lead to problems for the user if the number of sets becomes too large (e.g. so that the choices no longer fit on the screen). Therefore, we penalise partitions once their size reaches a threshold. Those being equal, we prefer partitions created by simpler references, where complexity is measured by the number of relations they contains.

The function SELECTREFERENCE that chooses the partitioning is shown in Algorithm 1. It is given an initial reference ϕ and a set of candidate objects O. If there is a unique matching object $M(\phi)$ among O, we return ϕ. Otherwise, we partition these objects according to a set of successor references, present the best of those to the user and then call the function recursively with the user-selected reference. The process is illustrated in the second menu in our example: after choosing the action, we have to select its argument which is of type *object* and is therefore initialised with $\phi_1 = object(x)$ as a starting reference. The partition with the best value ($I = 10.3$) contains three references, each referencing one type of objects (bottles, mugs and plates). Once the first partition has been selected, we continue this process with the new partition $\phi_2 = \phi_1 \wedge \psi_1$.

If the initial set of candidate objects O matches exactly the initial reference ϕ_1, carrying O through the function calls is merely a performance optimisation: this way we only have to check references against the currently active objects instead of against all objects in the planning problem.

Algorithm 1. SELECTREFERENCE

1: Input: reference ϕ, candidate objects O,
2: Output: reference ψ
3: **if** $|M(\phi) \cap O| \leq 1$ **then**
4:    **return** ϕ
5: $G \leftarrow$ SUCCESSORREFERENCES(ϕ)
6: $C \leftarrow \emptyset$
7: **for** $g = \{\psi_0, \ldots, \psi_n\} \in G$ **do**
8:    $P = \{\{o \in O : o \text{ matches } \psi_i\} : \psi_i \in g\}$
9:    $C \leftarrow (g, P)$
10: **if** all partitions in C are trivial **then**
11:    **return** ϕ
12: $g, P \leftarrow$ CHOOSEBESTPARTITION(C)
13: $i \leftarrow$ USERSELECTREFERENCE(g)
14: $\phi' \leftarrow \phi \wedge g[i]$
15: $O' \leftarrow P[i]$
16: **return** SELECTREFERENCE(ϕ', O')

By passing a smaller set of candidate objects to the initial call to SELECTREFERENCE, we can restrict the goals that can be constructed. There are three types of goal candidates that we want to remove: unreachable goals, goals that conflict with an existing goal and goals that are already true in the initial state. As deciding reachability of a goal candidate is computationally hard, we use the facts reachable in the *delete relaxation* of the problem to identify a majority of unreachable goals. For example, we do not allow the user to select the types of *person* or *robot* in step 2, as those cannot be given to anyone. To detect whether a goal conflicts with another, we use *mutex groups* that can be found via invariant synthesis [8]. Finally, we simply remove those goals that are already true in the initial state.

4.2 Finding Successor References

The selection procedure requires that a partition can be created from a set of *successor references*. A successor ϕ' of a reference ϕ can be created in two ways:

- If ψ is a reference, then $\phi' = \phi \wedge \psi$ is a successor of ϕ.
- If ϕ is a conjunction of references $\psi_1, \ldots, \psi_n$ and ψ'_i is the successor of ψ_i, then $\phi' = \psi_1 \wedge \ldots \wedge \psi'_i \wedge \ldots \wedge \psi_n$ is a successor of ϕ.

For our purpose, we also require that each successor reference is strictly narrower than its parent to make progress during the goal selection, and that the references in a candidate set are disjoint (so that they create partitions).

Some partitions are easy to obtain: The set of all individual references $I_o(x)$ can induce partitions which contain only singleton sets. Type references are also (mostly) simple: given a type reference $\phi(x) = t(x)$, the references created from its subtypes usually form a partition, as long as there is no multiple inheritance.

For arbitrary unquantified references, such as those induced by unary predicates, deciding whether a complete partition exists is the *Exact Cover* problem, and thus NP-complete. We use a simple greedy search algorithm to create candidate sets, which is sufficient for our purpose. Finally, if a set of references ϕ_i does not cover all objects, we can create the partition $\{\phi_1, \ldots, \phi_n, \bigwedge_{i=1}^{n} \neg \phi_i\}$, adding one partition for the remaining objects. All these partitions can be computed once and then reused during the selection procedure. Successor references created via these partitions are all of the first form, i.e. via conjunction.

For arbitrary references, such as the *content* reference in the third menu, we run into problems with this approach: the reference $\phi = \exists w\ content(x, w)$ by itself does not partition the *bottle* objects at all, as all of them contain something. It is only the successors such as $\exists w\ content(x, w) \wedge I_{water}(w)$ that form an improved partition. For this kind of references, we perform a depth-limited search through the successor space and only return the one that results in the best partition. We use a depth limit of 3, as references of that depth can already be hard to understand (the references in the example all have a depth of ≤ 1).

4.3 Beyond Atomic Goals

This approach can be easily extended to universally and existentially quantified goals. In some way, ambiguous goals are the rule, not the exception during the selection process: any reference that is not a leaf in the menu must by definition be ambiguous (but not vice versa: there may be leaves that are ambiguous if there are no more specific references). Simply using this ambiguous reference in a goal gives us existentially quantified goals.

In the second menu we can select the fourth option to keep the reference as $\phi = object(x)$. (We use the phrasing "an arbitrary object" instead of "some object" to distinguish existential goals from goals that can be refined further.) This would create the goal $\exists x\ position(x, user) \wedge object(x)$. In the same manner, we can quantify the first reference universally: $\forall x\ position(x, user) \wedge object(x)$. However, as the robot and the user are themselves *objects*, this goal is unsatisfiable and does not show up in the menu. The third menu shows an example where both universally and existentially quantified goals are displayed.

5   Evaluation

To test our system, we used existing planning problems and simulated the goal generation assistant on the original problems' goals: For every such *test goal* we simulated a traversal through the assistant's menu until we reached a leaf node, either because the menu node matched the goal exactly or because the reference could not be split any further.

We tested on a variety of IPC planning domains: *logistics*, *rovers* and *storage* plus the *tidyup* domain [9]. The last one was included as it models a service robot, an application that is similar to one of our intended use cases.

The behaviour of our system depends strongly on the number and type of relations that can be used to build up references. The higher the number of references (especially individual references to an object), the more likely it is that we can find an exact match for a given goal. To evaluate this impact, we created two configurations for every domain. In the minimal version (referred to in the results table as "*domain*-min") we allowed all relational references as well as type references, but no individual references. In a second configuration we added individual references to some object types:

Table 1. Results from the goal generation tests. The second column shows the number of problem instances, Acc^I and Acc^G are the individual and global accuracies of the references and the *-base* variants are the same for the baseline references. d_{avg} and d_{max} are the average and maximum depths of the goals and C the average complexity of the resulting references.

Domain	#	Acc^I	Acc^I_{base}	Acc^G	Acc^G_{base}	d_{avg}	d_{max}	C
logistics-min	28	23.4	118.9	7.2	15.0	3.4	5	5.7
logistics	28	4.1	118.9	3.3	15.0	4.3	5	8.3
rovers-min	30	1.9	11.6	1.5	2.9	5.0	13	25.9
rovers	30	1.3	8.6	1.1	3.1	4.2	12	15.2
storage-min	30	18.9	55.3	2.4	4.8	4.1	7	9.8
storage	30	5.6	55.3	1.8	4.8	4.6	7	10.0
tidyup-min	10	1.9	4.8	1.0	1.8	2.5	4	7.0
tidyup	10	1.5	4.8	1.0	1.8	2.5	4	8.9

- In *logistics*, these are all `city` objects.
- In the *rovers* domain, the camera `mode` as well as `rover` objects.
- In *storage* the `hoist` and `container` objects.
- And in the *tidyup* domain we allow references to individual `rooms`.

We were interested in three aspects: the precision of the references, their complexity and the quality of the splitting. Low precision will prevent users from choosing exactly the goal they want, more complex references are harder to understand and poor splitting can lead to very deep menus. To measure complexity, we used the number of relations that occur in a reference. To measure the quality of the splitting we used the maximal and average depths in which each goal was found – deep menus impact usability and are a sign of poor splitting.

To measure precision, we used the number of matching goals of each selected reference. For every test goal, we recorded which additional goals were matched by the best reference. From this, we computed two measures: the individual accuracy, Acc^I, represents the average number of goals that were matched by a single reference. In the best case, this has a value of 1. We can also evaluate all goals of a planning problem as a group by creating the union of all matching goals and dividing their number by the number of test goals. This measure, which we call the global accuracy, Acc^G, will usually be smaller than the individual accuracy, as multiple test goals may be encompassed by the same goal reference. To assess the quality of the references themselves, the individual measure is more useful, as the global accuracy depends strongly on the goals in the planning problem. However, we feel that it may give an indication on how well quantified references can cover typical goals in a given planning domain. We also compared both measures against a simple baseline, where we created a goal reference so that every argument is a reference with exactly one relation. This can be either an individual reference if possible or the most specific type reference that matches the goal's argument. E.g. the baseline reference for the goal $at(p_1, L_4)$ would be $at(p, l) \wedge package(p) \wedge location(l)$.

The results are shown in Table 1. We can see that (as expected) the accuracy improves if we allow more references, but the effect varies significantly between the different domains. *Logistics* and *storage* gain the most from adding additional references, as there is little structure in these domains that can be exploited by the reference generation. The opposite is true in the *rovers* domain. In *rovers* there are lots of heterogeneous relationships between objects as well as a number of unary predicates (such as `at_rock_sample`) that can be used to build references. The downside is the very high complexity of the generated references, which is indicated by the high number of relations and goal depth. In the minimal *rovers* domain, the reference generation will often chain references between many objects to refer to a goal. The result of this is that *rovers* is the only domain in which the reference complexity and tree depth decrease substantially when adding more references. In all other domains, the depth of the menu increases, which is a result of the improved precision of the goal selection.

The only domain where adding more relations has little effect is the *tidyup* domain. This is probably because there is a decent amount of structure in these problems while the problem instances are relatively small. The selection of goals may also play a role here, as goal are often replicated among all objects in the problem (such as wipe all tables). This is also the reason for the perfect global accuracy and the individual accuracy for the baseline method, which is still fair.

6   Related Work

Other research with similar goals is usually strongly linked to natural language processing and improving the understanding of language by relating it to a situated context [14,15]. However, there is nothing in our approach that is tied to verbal interfaces (even though our prototype is text-based, we are currently working on an graphical version). Our approach to referring objects is based on work on referring expressions [4]. Specifying goals in terms of actions is reminiscent of the way goals in hierarchical task networks (HTNs) [6] are given, though (compound) tasks in HTNs are also accompanied by decompositions which describe how to solve these tasks, which is not the case in our system, where choosing a goal via an action does not place any restrictions on the plan.

7   Conclusion and Future Work

In this paper, we have presented a concept of references to objects and planning goals. Using these, we have created a tool that allows users to formulate arbitrary goals and evaluated these methods on existing planning domains.

We plan to expand this work in several directions: we intend to investigate an extension to partially observable environments, in particular situations in which neither the planner nor the user know everything about the world. We would also like to extend the system to support (a subset) of LTL goals [1] to express, among others, consecutive and maintenance goals.

Acknowledgments. This work was supported by the DFG grant EXC1086 BrainLinks-BrainTools to the University of Freiburg, Germany.

References

1. Bacchus, F., Kabanza, F.: Planning for temporally extended goals. Ann. Math. Artif. Intell. **22**(1–2), 5–27 (1998)
2. Chandra, A.K., Merlin, P.M.: Optimal implementation of conjunctive queries in relational data bases. In: Proceedings of the Ninth Annual ACM Symposium on Theory of Computing, STOC 1977, pp. 77–90. ACM, New York (1977)
3. Codd, E.F.: Relational completeness of data base sublanguages. In: Database Systems, pp. 65–98. Prentice-Hall (1972)
4. Dale, R., Reiter, E.: Computational interpretations of the gricean maxims in the generation of referring expressions. CoRR cmp-lg/9504020 (1995)
5. Dornhege, C., Eyerich, P., Keller, T., Trüg, S., Brenner, M., Nebel, B.: Semantic attachments for domain-independent planning systems. In: Proceedings of the 19th International Conference on Automated Planning and Scheduling (ICAPS), pp. 114–121. AAAI Press (2009)
6. Erol, K., Hendler, J., Nau, D.S.: Semantics for hierarchical task-network planning. Technical report, University of Maryland at College Park, College Park, MD, USA (1994)
7. Helmert, M.: The fast downward planning system. J. Artif. Intell. Res. **26**, 191–246 (2006)
8. Helmert, M.: Concise finite-domain representations for PDDL planning tasks. Artif. Intell. **173**(5–6), 503–535 (2009)
9. Hertle, A., Dornhege, C., Keller, T., Mattmüller, R., Ortlieb, M., Nebel, B.: An experimental comparison of classical, FOND and probabilistic planning. In: Lutz, C., Thielscher, M. (eds.) KI 2014. LNCS, vol. 8736, pp. 297–308. Springer, Heidelberg (2014)
10. McDermott, D., Ghallab, M., Howe, A., Knoblock, C., Ram, A., Veloso, M., Weld, D., Wilkins, D.: PDDL - the planning domain definition language. Technical report TR-98-003, Yale Center for Computational Vision and Control (1998)
11. Papadimitriou, C.H., Yannakakis, M.: The complexity of facets (and some facets of complexity). In: Proceedings of the Fourteenth Annual ACM Symposium on Theory of Computing, STOC 1982, pp. 255–260. ACM, New York (1982)
12. Quigley, M., Conley, K., Gerkey, B., Faust, J., Foote, T.B., Leibs, J., Wheeler, R., Ng, A.Y.: ROS: an open-source robot operating system. In: ICRA Workshop on Open Source Software (2009)
13. Quinlan, J.R.: Induction of decision trees. Mach. Learn. **1**(1), 81–106 (1986)
14. Roy, D., Hsiao, K.Y., Mavridis, N.: Mental imagery for a conversational robot. Trans. Sys. Man Cyber. Part B **34**(3), 1374–1383 (2004)
15. Roy, D.: Semiotic schemas: a framework for grounding language in action and perception. Artif. Intell. **167**(1–2), 170–205 (2005)
16. Vardi, M.Y.: The complexity of relational query languages (extended abstract). In: Proceedings of the Fourteenth Annual ACM Symposium on Theory of Computing, STOC 1982, pp. 137–146. ACM, New York (1982)

Short-Term Wind Power Prediction with Combination of Speed and Power Time Series

Justin Heinermann[(✉)] and Oliver Kramer

Computational Intelligence Group, Department of Computing Science,
University of Oldenburg, Oldenburg, Germany
{justin.heinermann,oliver.kramer}@uni-oldenburg.de

Abstract. The integration of wind power generation into the power grid can only succeed with precise and reliable forecast methods. With different measurements available, machine learning algorithms can yield very good predictions for short-term forecast horizons. In this paper, we compare the use of wind power and wind speed time series as well as differences of subsequent measurements with Random Forests, Support Vector Regression and k-nearest neighbors. While both time series, wind power and speed, are well-suited to train a predictor, the best performance can be achieved by using both together. Further, we propose an ensemble approach combining RF and SVR with a cross-validated weighted average and show that the prediction performance can be substantially improved.

1 Introduction

For a successful integration of wind power into the power grid, precise prediction methods are needed. For short-term predictions of expected wind power output, it has been shown that machine learning techniques are well-suited [13]. With spatio-temporal information available, k-Nearest Neighbors (k-NN), Support Vector Regression (SVR), and Machine Learning Ensembles yield low prediction errors [8,12]. The question comes up for the choice of appropriate features for the wind power prediction problem. Most past work concentrates on univariate prediction models that map a single time series to target values. Our approach takes into account the features from neighboring turbines, but was in the past restricted to the use of power features. If available, it might be beneficial for the prediction to include the wind speed features as well. Many approaches compute a forecast of the speed and then transform it to a power value using a power curve (PC) model, see [13].

In this work, we analyze various regressors trained with patterns composed of different features, i.e., power output measurements, wind speed measurements, and differences of these. The algorithms we compare are k-NN, SVR, and Random Forests (RF) that turned out to be very successful in various applications, see [4]. Last, we combine the best combinations of regressors and their features to

© Springer International Publishing Switzerland 2015
S. Hölldobler et al. (Eds.): KI 2015, LNAI 9324, pp. 100–110, 2015.
DOI: 10.1007/978-3-319-24489-1_8

ensembles and show experimentally that these outperform their single predictor competitors.

This paper is structured as follows. In Section 2, an overview of related work is given. The spatio-temporal wind power prediction model and the used algorithms are described in Section 3. The experimental evaluation in Section 4 compares the use of the different feature spaces with the different regression algorithms. The combination of these predictors to an ensemble is analyzed in Section 5. Conclusions are drawn in Section 6.

2   Related Work

Kusiak, Zhang and Song [10] successfully apply different methods to short-term wind power prediction, one of which is the bagging trees algorithm. Fugon *et al.* [5] compare various algorithms for wind power forecasting and show that RF with and without random input selection yield a prediction performance similar to SVR, but recommend to prefer a linear model when the computation time grows too large. Salcedo *et al.* [12] use SVR for the reconstruction of wind speed values using neighboring turbines' measurements. Heinermann and Kramer [8] achieve good wind power prediction results using heterogeneous machine learning ensembles with a spatio-temporal model. In contrast to all prior work in the field of wind power prediction, we propose a new ensemble approach leveraging the information of different time series for the prediction.

In the field of numerical weather forecasts, it is quite common to use ensemble postprocessing. Gneiting *et al.* [6] found ensembles to reduce the prediction error by applying the ensemble model output statistics (EMOS) method to diverse weather forecasts. In contrast to machine learning ensembles, the predictor diversity is achieved by employing different initial values in the weather model. A similar domain to wind power prediction is time series prediction for solar power output. Chakraborty *et al.* [3] built up an ensemble of a weather forecast-driven Naïve Bayes Predictor as well as a kNN-based and a motif-based machine learning predictor. The results of the three predictors are combined with a Bayesian Model Averaging.

3   Wind Power Prediction with Machine Learning

3.1   Spatio-Temporal Regression Model

We treat short-term wind power prediction as a regression problem. In contrast to numerical weather predictions, machine learning methods usually only make use of the time series data itself. The history of measurements used to train the prediction model is called training data set $\mathbf{X} = \{(\mathbf{x}_1, y_1) \ldots, (\mathbf{x}_N, y_N)\} \subset \mathbb{R}^d \times \mathbb{R}$. When performing a forecast, the objective is to predict the measurement after a *forecast horizon* λ, e.g., in half an hour. The input patterns consist of μ past time steps, which we call the *feature window*. In this work, we use a spatio-temporal model based on the one proposed by Kramer *et al.* [9], who

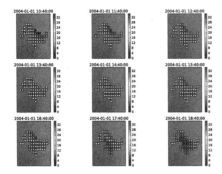

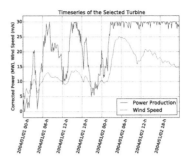

Fig. 1. Wind speed measurements for a wind park near Reno. The color denotes the wind speed, showing similar behavior for neighboring turbines.

Fig. 2. Example for speed and power time series for a wind park $(10 \times 3MW)$ near Tehachapi.

show the benefit of involving neighboring turbines to the input vector. Let $p_i(t)$ be the measurement of a turbine i at a time t, and $1 \leq i \leq m$ the indices of the m neighboring turbines. Then, for a target turbine with index j we define a pattern-label-pair $(\mathbf{x}, y)$ for a given time t_0 as

$$
\begin{pmatrix}
p_1(t_0 - \mu) & \dots & p_1(t_0) \\
\dots & \dots & \dots \\
p_m(t_0 - \mu) & \dots & p_m(t_0)
\end{pmatrix}
\rightarrow p_j(t_0 + \lambda) \tag{1}
$$

Figure 1 shows nine hourly wind speed measurements for a set of turbines near Reno. It can be seen that the wind speed time series of neighboring turbines show some correlation. Figure 2 shows both speed and power output time series for a wind turbine near Tehachapi. In former works, we mostly used the data of one time series to predict values of the same time series. Neighboring turbines show similar speeds at the same time and correlations between the turbines' speed time series exist. If one wants to give a power output prediction for a certain turbine based on its past time series measurements used as patterns, including the features of turbines in the vicinity of a few kilometers can significantly improve the prediction accuracy.

In our experiments, we use the *NREL Western Wind Resources Dataset*[1]. It consists of simulated wind power output for 32,043 wind turbines in the US, given in 10-minute time resolution for the years 2004 - 2006. For every turbine, there are 157,680 wind speed and power output measurements available, of which $\frac{1}{5}$ is used in this work. In our experiments, we use the power output data of ten wind parks[2] that consist of the target wind turbine and the 10 neighboring

---

[1] http://wind.nrel.gov/

[2] The IDs of the turbines in the NREL dataset are: Casper=23167, Cheyenne=17423, Hesperia=2028, Lancaster=2473, Las Vegas=6272, Palm Springs=1175, Reno=11637, Tehachapi=4155, Vantage=28981, Yucca Valley=1539.

turbines. The data from 01/2004 until 06/2005 is used as training data set and the data from 7/2005 until 12/2006 serves as test data set. We use a feature window $\mu = 6$ (1 hour) and providing a forecast for a horizon $\lambda = 3$ (30 minutes).

To measure the prediction accuracy, we employ the commonly used mean squared error (MSE). For a test set $\mathbf{X}' = \{(\mathbf{x}'_1, y'_1) \ldots, (\mathbf{x}'_N, y'_N)\} \subset \mathbb{R}^d \times \mathbb{R}$ and prediction model $f(\cdot)$, it is defined by:

$$E = \frac{1}{N} \sum_{i=1}^{N} (f(\mathbf{x}'_i) - y'_i)^2$$

The difference between the label y_i of a test instance and corresponding prediction $f(\mathbf{x}'_i)$ is squared in order to penalize larger differences. The mean of the squared prediction errors of the N test instances is computed as overall accuracy measure.

3.2 Nearest Neighbors Regression

A famous yet relatively simple approach for classification and regression is the k-NN model, see [7]. The prediction averages the label information of the k nearest neighbors, i.e., $f(\mathbf{x}) = \frac{1}{k} \sum_{i \in N_k(\mathbf{x})} y_i$, where N_k denotes the set of indices for the k nearest neighbors in T w.r.t. a distance metric, usually the Euclidean distance. While a naïve implementation takes $\mathcal{O}(|S| \cdot |T|)$ time for a training set T and a test set S, more efficient implementations with spatial data structures, e.g. k-d trees, are available [7] that offer logarithmic runtime for small dimensionalities $d \leq 15$.

3.3 Support Vector Regression

SVR is one of the state-of-the-art techniques for prediction tasks. It is based on Support Vector Machines (SVMs) that were proposed by Vapnik [14]. The basic idea of this algorithm is to map the input data into a higher dimension reproducing kernel Hilbert space $\mathcal{H} \subseteq \mathbb{R}^{\mathcal{X}} = \{f : \mathcal{X} \rightarrow \mathbb{R}\}$ induced by an associated *kernel function* $k : \mathcal{X} \times \mathcal{X} \rightarrow \mathbb{R}$. Subsequently, a linear regression is performed in this feature space that contains all considered models. For an SVR model, the optimization task equation can be formulated as:

$$\min_{f \in \mathcal{H}, b \in \mathbb{R}} \frac{1}{n} \sum_{i=1}^{n} L\big(y_i, f(\mathbf{X}_i + b)\big) + \lambda ||f||_{\mathcal{H}}^2,$$

where the first term specifies how well a model f fits to the data according to the definition of a particular function $L : \mathbb{R} \times \mathbb{R} \rightarrow [0, \infty)$. The term $||f||_{\mathcal{H}}^2$, used to measure the complexity of a particular function f, is the squared norm in the reproducing kernel Hilbert space. Ideally, one would like to generate models that represent the training data well and that are not too complex to avoid overfitting. The parameter λ is called regularization parameter and determines the trade-off between these two objectives.

3.4 Random Forest Regression

The idea of ensemble methods can be described as as building "a predictive model by integrating multiple models" [11]. One of the advantages is the possible improvement of prediction performance. Another reason for utilizing ensemble methods is the reduction of computational complexity, which can be helpful on very large data sets. A popular ensemble approach is the RF algorithm [1] that "uses a large number of individual, unpruned decision trees" [11]. Every decision tree is built with a subset sample from the training set, but only uses N of the available features of the patterns. One important factor for the success of ensembles is the concept of diversity. All the weak predictors should behave different if not uncorrelated to improve the prediction performance of the ensemble [2,11]. There are many ways to generate such diversity, like manipulating the used training sample, the employed features, and the weak predictors' parameters. Another possibility is the hybridization of multiple algorithms, which we call heterogeneous ensembles.

4 Comparison of Input Patterns

4.1 Comparing Speed and Power Features

When applying machine learning algorithms to real-world data, the choice of appropriate features is important for achieving good prediction results. For our wind prediction task, there are two time series available, i.e., wind speed and wind power measurements of every turbine. While former work often took only into account time series itself for prediction of future values, it could be beneficial to include all available data. In particular for wind, there is an important relation between the speed and the power values since the power output is a function of the actual wind speed.

For both available time series we also consider to preprocess the time series by including the differences of each measurement to the measurement before, thus including the slope as a feature. The use of these differences could contain a recent trend and helpful information to recognize recurring siuations appearing. We expect that different regression algorithms show different behaviors when running on other feature representations. It may be that one algorithm performs better on a particular feature set while another yields a lower prediction error for another feature set. Our objective is to compare the use of the two available time series and the preprocessed time series using RF, SVR, and k-NN regression methods. Because a choice of the right parameters is crucial for a good prediction result and the prevention of overfitting, we perform a grid search with 5-fold cross-validation (CV) on the training set with data from 01/2004 to 06/2005 to determine the optimal parameters for each turbine, the corresponding feature representation and the algorithm used. The trained predictor is then employed to make a prediction for a test set with data from 07/2005 to 12/2006. For RF, we vary the number of estimators chosen from $\{32, 64, 128, 256\}$. For the SVR,

Table 1. Comparison of MSE of RF, SVR, and k-NN using power output (P), speed (S), and differences (Δ) of the particular time series. For each target turbine, the best prediction error is printed in bold figures. The best prediction per algorithm and turbine is underlined.

(a) CV error

Turbine	RF				SVR				k-NN			
	P	P+Δ	S	S+Δ	P	P+Δ	S	S+Δ	P	P+Δ	S	S+Δ
Casper	10.54	**10.16**	11.41	10.69	10.31	<u>10.20</u>	11.17	10.89	11.91	<u>11.78</u>	13.63	13.05
Cheyenne	7.72	7.61	7.62	**7.27**	7.79	7.75	7.54	<u>7.34</u>	<u>8.48</u>	8.56	8.66	8.33
Hesperia	8.04	7.78	7.68	**7.16**	8.01	7.99	7.46	<u>7.30</u>	9.30	9.18	9.50	<u>9.13</u>
Lancaster	9.44	8.99	9.30	**8.28**	8.90	8.85	8.77	<u>8.66</u>	10.45	<u>10.36</u>	11.28	10.79
L.V.	9.92	9.49	10.12	<u>9.36</u>	9.36	**9.30**	9.96	9.66	11.03	<u>10.79</u>	11.88	11.42
P.S.	6.04	5.95	5.31	**4.90**	5.85	5.82	<u>5.05</u>	4.97	7.51	7.53	7.67	<u>7.41</u>
Reno	12.37	11.69	11.68	**<u>10.67</u>**	11.82	11.67	11.67	<u>11.29</u>	15.15	14.98	15.48	<u>14.84</u>
Tehachapi	7.65	<u>7.41</u>	8.35	7.89	7.44	**7.35**	8.04	7.98	9.02	<u>9.00</u>	9.86	9.49
Vantage	6.06	5.95	5.82	**<u>5.42</u>**	5.97	5.97	<u>5.59</u>	<u>5.59</u>	6.88	7.02	7.02	<u>6.81</u>
Y.V.	11.34	11.23	10.98	**<u>10.64</u>**	11.40	11.27	10.93	<u>10.76</u>	12.21	12.24	12.10	<u>11.77</u>

(b) Test error

Turbine	RF				SVR				k-NN			
	P	P+Δ	S	S+Δ	P	P+Δ	S	S+Δ	P	P+Δ	S	S+Δ
Casper	10.62	**<u>10.01</u>**	12.25	11.41	10.76	<u>10.43</u>	11.59	11.27	12.24	<u>12.05</u>	14.30	13.74
Cheyenne	7.29	7.21	7.12	<u>6.71</u>	7.17	7.10	6.75	**<u>6.70</u>**	7.93	7.99	7.87	<u>7.61</u>
Hesperia	7.69	7.50	7.39	**<u>6.91</u>**	7.62	7.70	7.21	<u>6.95</u>	8.76	8.59	8.92	<u>8.49</u>
Lancaster	8.19	8.05	7.66	**<u>7.06</u>**	8.01	7.88	7.43	<u>7.23</u>	9.15	9.01	9.34	<u>8.94</u>
L.V.	10.52	9.98	10.23	**<u>9.50</u>**	10.43	<u>10.32</u>	10.88	10.61	<u>11.85</u>	11.69	12.43	11.92
P.S.	5.84	5.80	5.23	**<u>4.78</u>**	5.94	5.86	4.95	<u>4.83</u>	7.11	7.06	7.25	<u>7.00</u>
Reno	13.94	13.39	14.04	**<u>12.78</u>**	13.66	<u>13.39</u>	14.23	13.68	16.65	<u>16.52</u>	17.58	16.88
Tehachapi	7.30	**<u>7.07</u>**	7.69	7.18	<u>7.23</u>	7.27	8.15	8.04	<u>8.45</u>	<u>8.45</u>	9.75	9.41
Vantage	6.81	6.69	6.51	**<u>6.11</u>**	6.64	6.60	6.34	<u>6.30</u>	<u>7.83</u>	7.84	8.17	7.92
Y.V.	9.14	9.18	8.72	**<u>8.51</u>**	9.05	9.00	8.66	**<u>8.51</u>**	9.73	9.84	9.57	<u>9.29</u>

the regularization parameter λ is chosen from $\{1, 10, 100, 1000\}$ using an RBF-kernel choosing its bandwidth σ from $\{0.0001, 0.001, 0.01, 0.1, 1.0\}$. For k-NN, k is chosen from $\{1, 5, 15, 20\}$.

The results of the comparison are presented in Table 1. For all three regression algorithms, it is a good choice to include differences of the used features for most of the turbines. For RF and SVR, using the speed time series for predicting the power output seems more promising than the power features . For the k-NN experiments, there is no clear answer whether the power or the speed features should better be preferred. We can observe that RF regression outperforms the other two regression algorithms for eight out of ten turbines w.r.t the CV error. The analysis of test errors shows that the CV-selected feature, parameter and algorithm choices perform similarly well on the test sets, too.

Table 2. Prediction error for combined patterns using power and speed measurements (a,b) without and (c,d) with differences included. The prediction errors lower than the ones using the same regression algorithm on the single time series presented in Table 1 are underlined. A lower error than the turbine optimum from Table 1 is printed in italics. The best value per turbine in each table is printed in bold figures.

(a) CV error

Turbine	RF	SVR	k-NN
Casper	_10.08_	**_9.98_**	11.91
Cheyenne	**7.51**	7.64	8.42
Hesperia	**7.26**	7.89	9.35
Lancaster	8.68	**8.61**	10.61
L.V.	9.57	**9.37**	11.21
P.S.	**5.36**	5.41	7.46
Reno	**11.08**	11.52	15.10
Tehachapi	**_6.85_**	7.42	9.00
Vantage	**5.80**	5.89	6.88
Y.V.	**10.93**	11.17	12.18

(b) Test error

Turbine	RF	SVR	k-NN
Casper	**_9.69_**	10.24	12.23
Cheyenne	7.09	**_6.99_**	7.89
Hesperia	**7.22**	7.38	8.70
Lancaster	7.59	**7.52**	9.20
L.V.	**9.78**	10.39	11.94
P.S.	**5.25**	5.29	7.08
Reno	**12.84**	13.34	16.55
Tehachapi	**_6.23_**	7.31	8.57
Vantage	**6.33**	6.48	7.92
Y.V.	**8.75**	8.89	9.60

(c) CV error with Δ

Turbine	RF	SVR	k-NN
Casper	**_9.28_**	_9.85_	11.74
Cheyenne	**7.15**	7.50	8.41
Hesperia	**_6.70_**	7.78	9.12
Lancaster	7.65	8.53	10.51
L.V.	**8.79**	9.18	10.97
P.S.	**_4.88_**	5.38	7.34
Reno	**10.14**	11.21	14.84
Tehachapi	**_6.29_**	7.25	8.91
Vantage	**5.47**	5.83	6.87
Y.V.	**_10.55_**	11.03	12.08

(d) Test error width Δ

Turbine	RF	SVR	k-NN
Casper	**_9.03_**	10.04	11.94
Cheyenne	**_6.66_**	6.80	7.87
Hesperia	**_6.59_**	7.21	8.52
Lancaster	**_6.87_**	7.48	8.99
L.V.	**_9.09_**	10.14	11.70
P.S.	**4.84**	5.20	6.88
Reno	**_11.58_**	12.80	16.32
Tehachapi	**5.78**	7.18	8.51
Vantage	**_5.88_**	6.36	7.85
Y.V.	**_8.50_**	8.78	9.66

4.2 Combining Speed and Power Features

In the following, we combine the features of both time series to one big pattern. Table 2 shows the experimental comparison for these composed features based on the power and speed (Tables 2 a and b) and also including the differences between the measurements (Tables 2 c and d). Because the patterns have different dimensionalities and different types of features, a parameter search is necessary for each experiment. Again, grid search with 5-fold CV is performed to find the best possible settings for each algorithm and target turbine. The main idea of the comparison is that the algorithms could behave differently when different features are used.

Tables 2 (a,b) show that without employing the feature differences, only for a few turbines the prediction can be improved for a particular algorithm. The optimal CV error and test error per turbine cannot be outperformed. However, when including the power and speed difference features to the pattern, a great improvement of CV error and test error can be observed for both RF and SVR, see Tables 2 (c,d). In nine out of ten cases, the optimal prediction error from Table 1 is outperformed. Therefore, we strongly recommend to consider the use of patterns consisting of the power measurements, the speed measurements, and their differences if available.

5   Ensemble Combination

5.1   Combination of Predictors Based on Different Time Series

One of the main reasons for the success of ensemble predictors is the diversity amongst the combined predictors, i.e., a different behavior or uncorrelated prediction errors. In Section 4, we showed that the use of different available time series features leads to an improvement of the prediction error. The question arises whether we can further decrease the prediction error by combining regressors based on the different time series features. First, we combine one predictor

Table 3. Comparison of MSE with combinations of predictors. Each combination consists of one prediction based on power time series and one prediction based on speed time series – using RF or SVR. For every park, the best value is printed in bold. Every value that outperforms the predictors from Table 1 for a given park is underlined. Every predictor that outperform the ones shown in Table 2 is printed in italics.

Turbine	RF+RF	RF+SVR	SVR+RF	SVR+SVR
Casper	9.69	**9.40**	9.67	9.64
Cheyenne	6.71	***6.60***	***6.60***	***6.60***
Hesperia	**6.71**	6.82	6.77	7.03
Lancaster	7.01	6.94	**6.88**	7.05
L.V.	**9.20**	9.59	9.28	9.93
P.S.	4.88	4.86	***4.83***	4.97
Reno	**11.87**	12.26	11.80	12.68
Tehachapi	**6.36**	6.58	6.44	6.87
Vantage	5.99	5.99	**5.94**	6.13
Y.V.	8.50	*8.47*	***8.36***	*8.49*

based on the power time series with one predictors based on the speed time series, each also using the differences between the particular time steps. The main idea is that the algorithms behave differently in different feature space and therefore give very diverse predictions for the same target time step. For both the power and speed time series patterns, each an RF and an SVR predictor are trained separately. To give a prediction, one predictor based on the power features and one predictor based on the speed features is selected and then combined by computing the mean of the two predictors' output values.

In Table 3, we can observe that a lower prediction error is possible compared to the regressors from Table 1, but in seven out of ten cases, the prediction is worse than the one based on the combined pattern shown in Tables 2 (c) and (d). With a weighted average, we could decrease the prediction error further, but still yielding no competitive results to the predictors using the combined patterns.

5.2   Combination of Predictors Based on All Available Features

As shown in Section 4, both RF and SVR yield very good prediction results when using combined patterns including power and speed measurements as well as differences. In this section, we combine the predictors to an ensemble. We only consider RF and SVR because of their superiority compared to k-NN. The two prediction values are combined by computing a weighted average with $\alpha \in (0,1)$:

$$f(\mathbf{x}) = \alpha \cdot f_{RF}(\mathbf{x}) + (1 - \alpha) \cdot f_{SVR}(\mathbf{x}) \qquad (2)$$

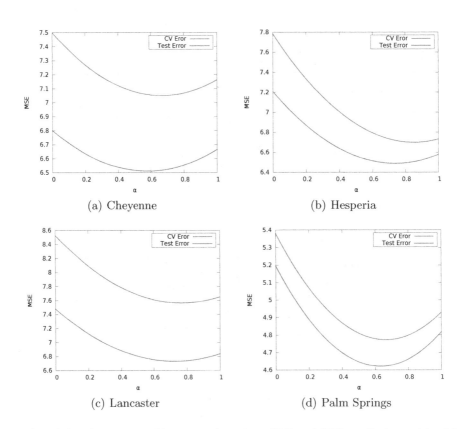

(a) Cheyenne

(b) Hesperia

(c) Lancaster

(d) Palm Springs

Fig. 3. CV and test error of linear combination of RF and SVR predictions with with all available features for varying coefficient α.

Figure 3 shows the experimental results for four selected turbines. From the plots, we can observe that the combination of the two predictors helps to improve the prediction error. While the special case $\alpha = 0.5$ is a good first guess, the best value varies from turbine to turbine. Finding a feasible α is a parameter tuning problem which we address with CV. The question arises, if an α value that performs best in CV on the training set, can also give a near-optimal solution for the prediction on the test set. The experimental results shown in Table 4 demonstrate the practical relevance of the proposed approach. In the CV, we optimize the setting for α w.r.t the lowest CV error. When using the optimal α found in the CV for the test set prediction, we observe a competetive test error. The achieved error and the found α are very close to the best possible α and test error for the test set, which can never be known in advance. The same behavior can be observed in Figure 3, where the plots of CV error and test error have very similar shapes and optima. With this type of ensemble combination, we get better predictions for eight out of ten turbines, compared to the use of single predictors form Section 4. Two exceptions are Tehachapi with $E = 5.78$ using RF on the combined pattern and $E = 5.84$ with the ensemble with CV optimal α and Las Vegas with $E = 9.09$ compared to $E = 9.12$. Summing up, we strongly recommend the combination of diverse predictors based on the combined patterns for wind power prediction.

Table 4. CV optimization of coefficient α. The CV error and test error with the found α are compared to the best possible α on the test set. The CV errors outperforming the single predictors shown in Table 2 (c) and the test errors outperforming the single predictors from Table 2 (d) are printed in italics.

Turbine	Best α (CV)	CV error	Test error	Best α (test)	Test error
Casper	0.67	*9.13*	*8.91*	0.73	8.90
Cheyenne	0.67	*7.05*	*6.52*	0.58	6.51
Hesperia	0.85	6.70	*6.50*	0.84	6.50
Lancaster	0.77	*7.56*	*6.74*	0.73	6.73
L.V.	0.62	*8.55*	9.12	0.84	9.04
P.S.	0.66	*4.77*	*4.62*	0.63	4.62
Reno	0.73	*9.92*	*11.35*	0.71	11.34
Tehachapi	0.78	*6.20*	5.84	1.0	5.76
Vantage	0.70	*5.40*	*5.80*	0.77	5.80
Y.V.	0.69	*10.43*	*8.34*	0.64	8.34

6   Conclusions

The integration of wind power generation into the smart grid can only succeed with precise and reliable forecast methods. With different measurements available, machine learning algorithms are able to achieve very good predictions for short-term horizons. In this paper, we compared the use of wind power and wind speed time series with RF, SVR, and k-NN regression. While both power and speed features contain an essential amount of information for the prediction task, we showed experimentally that both should be combined in order to improve the prediction error. It can be further increased by including the differences of the power and speed measurements, which allows important insights into the trend. Further, we proposed an ensemble method for wind power prediction employing one RF and one SVR regressor and combined both with a weighted average. A near-optimal weighting coefficient α can be determined by cross validation and the single predictors based on the different feature spaces are outperformed. In the future, we plan to integrate additional data like the weather condition and investigate time series preprocessing techniques.

References

1. Breiman, L.: Random forests. Mach. Learn. **45**(1), 5–32 (2001)
2. Brown, G., Wyatt, J., Harris, R., Yao, X.: Diversity creation methods: a survey and categorisation. Inf. Fusion **6**(1), 5–20 (2005)
3. Chakraborty, P., Marwah, M., Arlitt, M.F., Ramakrishnan, N.: Fine-grained photovoltaic output prediction using a bayesian ensemble. In: Proceedings of the AAAI Conference on Artificial Intelligence (AAAI) (2012)
4. Fernández-Delgado, M., Cernadas, E., Barro, S., Amorim, D.: Do we need hundreds of classifiers to solve real world classification problems? J. Mach. Learn. Res. **15**(1), 3133–3181 (2014)
5. Fugon, L., Juban, J., Kariniotakis, G., et al.: Data mining for wind power forecasting. In: Proceedings of the European Wind Energy Conference & Exhibition (EWEC) (2008)
6. Gneiting, T., Raftery, A.E., Westveld, A.H., Goldman, T.: Calibrated probabilistic forecasting using ensemble model output statistics and minimum CRPS estimation. Mon. Weather Rev. **133**(5), 1098–1118 (2005)
7. Hastie, T., Tibshirani, R., Friedman, J.: The Elements of Statistical Learning, 2nd edn. Springer, Heidelberg (2009)
8. Heinermann, J., Kramer, O.: On heterogeneous machine learning ensembles for wind power prediction. In: AAAI Workshops (2015)
9. Kramer, O., Gieseke, F., Satzger, B.: Wind energy prediction and monitoring with neural computation. Neurocomputing **109**, 84–93 (2013)
10. Kusiak, A., Zheng, H., Song, Z.: Short-term prediction of wind farm power: a data mining approach. IEEE Trans. Energy Convers. **24**(1), 125–136 (2009)
11. Rokach, L.: Ensemble-based classifiers. Artif. Intell. Rev. **33**(1–2), 1–39 (2010)
12. Salcedo-Sanz, S., Rojo-Álvarez, J., Martínez-Ramón, M., Camps-Valls, G.: Support vector machines in engineering: an overview. Wiley Interdisc. Rev. Data Min. Knowl. Discov. **4**(3), 234–267 (2014)
13. Soman, S.S., Zareipour, H., Malik, O., Mandal, P.: A review of wind power and wind speed forecasting methods with different time horizons. In: Proceedings of the North American Power Symposium (NAPS). IEEE (2010)
14. Vapnik, V.: The Nature of Statistical Learning Theory. Information Science and Statistics. Springer, Heidelberg (2000)

A Serendipity Model for News Recommendation

M. Jenders[(⊠)], T. Lindhauer, G. Kasneci, R. Krestel, and F. Naumann

Hasso Plattner Institute, Prof.-Dr.-Helmert-Str. 2-3, 14482 Potsdam, Germany
`maximilian.jenders@hpi.de`

Abstract. Recommendation algorithms typically work by suggesting items that are similar to the ones that a user likes, or items that similar users like. We propose a content-based recommendation technique with the focus on serendipity of news recommendations. Serendipitous recommendations have the characteristic of being unexpected yet fortunate and interesting to the user, and thus might yield higher user satisfaction. In our work, we explore the concept of serendipity in the area of news articles and propose a general framework that incorporates the benefits of serendipity- and similarity-based recommendation techniques. An evaluation against other baseline recommendation models is carried out in a user study.

1 Introduction

Popular recommendation algorithms employ similarity measures to generate their recommendation lists. Their abilities in predicting users' interest can be quantified using *accuracy*- and *relevance*-based measures. They can operate purely on item features or incorporate user profiles with preferences and ratings. While the resulting recommendations are often accurate, they tend to favor popular items or ones that users already know and therefore often miss opportunities to surprise users with items that are to some extent unrelated and unfamiliar, yet satisfactory.

In this paper, we aim to address this issue by focusing on serendipitous recommendations in the area of news articles. Serendipity refers to the event of stumbling upon something that is unexpected and yet useful. For example, when the task is to recommend news articles about "Turkey's EU membership", a traditional recommender would favor articles focusing on this very issue, which, while relevant, do not expand a reader's horizon beyond this topic. Meanwhile, a serendipitous recommendation might contain an article arguing that MTV Turkey already establishes stronger ties between Turkey and the West than an acceptance into the EU ever would. In fact, this notion of serendipity and its usefulness was confirmed in our user evaluation (Section 3.2).

Indeed, in cases such as the above, unexpected articles may complement similar ones, even if they do not show very high similarity (as an estimation of relevance) to known items. Algorithms that focus on both aspects (i.e., unexpectedness and similarity) can produce more useful recommendation lists by suggesting items that expand the user's horizon in addition to familiar items [8].

© Springer International Publishing Switzerland 2015
S. Hölldobler et al. (Eds.): KI 2015, LNAI 9324, pp. 111–123, 2015.
DOI: 10.1007/978-3-319-24489-1_9

Similar to a typical use case in practice, our approach does not assume user profiles to generate recommendations. Since serendipity is subject to general perception, we claim that serendipitous recommendations can be generated from content features alone with sufficient quality.

We conducted a survey to analyze the impact different features (e.g., named entities, the relationship between entities or between latent topics) on serendipity as perceived by humans[1]. We found that *unexpected combinations of latent topics* induce a strong and consistent signal upon which serendipity can be formalized. We used this insight to develop a purely content-based unexpectedness model in combination with a similarity model for pre-filtering (Section 2) and evaluated it against popular algorithms in a concluding user study (Section 3). All experiments were conducted on a subset of all news articles of the New York Times Corpus[2] published between 2005 and 2007.

We discovered two different facets of serendipity: On one hand, recommendations that display a high similarity to the original article (and could therefore be seen as discussing related and relevant subjects) were judged as surprising and interesting and could therefore be labeled serendipitous. On the other hand, the recommendations of our unexpectedness model were rated as decidedly less relevant with respect to the original article, nevertheless also highly surprising and interesting. In the above example, the aforementioned article about Turkey's MTV station exhibits a strong topic shift and is very unexpected. For the goal of recommending serendipitous articles, our unexpectedness model therefore is not a direct competitor to similarity-based recommendation, but focuses on a different facet of serendipity. We hence combined both models to yield the final serendipity-based recommendation algorithm that presents the best recommendations from both algorithms to the user.

2   A Serendipity Model

In this section, we discuss the creation of a recommendation model for newspaper articles based on serendipity, i.e., on unexpectedness and interestingness. Since the latter is highly user-dependent, we first focused on capturing the general unexpectedness of a document based on its contents alone without setting it in relation to specific other articles. Since the resulting model (Equation 3) does not compare documents, it can only be used to rank a corpus regarding *topical unexpectedness*. We then estimated the interestingness of documents through the similarity of the suggested article to the article currently being read, as it is the only available indication of user interest.

Our final serendipity model uses a non-linear combination of an unexpectedness and similarity model. It ranks recommendations separately for each model and then selects the most promising recommendations (for a given article) based on a boosting algorithm.

---

[1] This survey is not further described here due to space restrictions
[2] https://catalog.ldc.upenn.edu/LDC2008T19

2.1 Deriving an Unexpectedness Model

Bache et al. developed a model to quantify *document diversity* in the context of scientific papers [4]. The proposed model is given in Equation 1 and estimates the proportion of a topic z_i as its probability according to a latent Dirichlet allocation (LDA) model. $\delta(z_i, z_j)$ is the dissimilarity of two topics z_i, z_j and is estimated based on their co-occurrences across documents in the corpus. d denotes a document as a vector of term frequencies, while $div(d)$ expresses the topic diversity of a document.

$$div(d) = \sum_{i=1}^{k} \sum_{j=1}^{k} p(z_i|d) \cdot p(z_j|d) \cdot \delta(z_i, z_j) \tag{1}$$

The above model addresses the dissimilarity of topic pairs and considers their proportions in the documents. Hence, we base our model on this approach. We limit our model's calculations to the document's main topics $Z_{Main}(d)$ and use it to rank documents by their estimated *topical unexpectedness*:

$$u(d) = \sum_{\substack{z_i, z_j \in \\ Z_{Main}(d)}} sp(z_i, d) \cdot sp(z_j, d) \cdot dis(z_i, z_j) \cdot c(z_i, z_j, d) \tag{2}$$

$$u_{norm}(d) = u(d) \cdot norm(d, Z_{Main}(d)) \tag{3}$$

The model comprises four main components that are constructed with an information-theoretic background, which are detailed in Sections 2.2 through 2.5. The effects of the model's ratings on the corpus and the construction is described in Section 2.6.

2.2 Word Specificity Estimation: $sp(z_i, d)$

Instead of giving all words of a topic the same weight when estimating $p(z_i|d)$, we account for the words' ability to identify a topic by classifying words w by their posterior topic entropy $H[Z_w]$ with $Z_w \sim p(z|w)$ and their information content given the topic, defined as $-\log p(w|z)$. We transformed the entropy values to a linear scale by calculating $2^{H[Z_w]}$, which we have found to better discriminate the cases.

Words with low entropy are closely tied to only few topics and should therefore contribute more to their topic's proportions. We further discriminate them into *signal* and *specific* words through their information content. A *signal* word has low information content for a given topic and thus is likely to occur whenever the topic is present in a document. On the contrary, a *specific* word has a high information content and identifies very specific stories for a given topic, because it is rather uncommon for the topic.

We found that the main topics of an article often consist of both kinds of words while less prominent topics tend to contain many signal words. To decrease their influence, we use $sp(z_i, d)$ as defined in Equation 4 to estimate the proportion of topic z_i. In Equation 5, $\pi_{z_i}(d)$ denotes the projection of the document

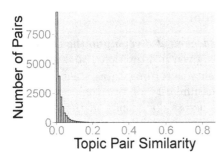
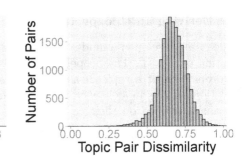

Fig. 1. Histogram of topic pair cosine similarity.

Fig. 2. Histogram of *dis* normalized to a $[0; 1]$ interval.

on the words assigned to topic z_i, while $freq(w_j)$ represents the frequency of the word w_j.

$$sp(z_i, \boldsymbol{d}) = \frac{specificity(z_i, \boldsymbol{d})}{\sum_{j=1}^{k} specificity(z_j, \boldsymbol{d})} \qquad (4)$$

$$specificity(z_i, \boldsymbol{d}) = \sum_{\substack{w_j \in \\ \pi_{z_i}(\boldsymbol{d})}} freq(w_j) \cdot \frac{-\log(p(w_j|z_i))}{2^{H[Z_{w_j}]}} \qquad (5)$$

2.3 Topic Dissimilarity Determination: $dis(z_i, z_j)$

Similar to [4], we found that topic similarity is best measured by topic co-occurrences across documents. Inspecting the cosine similarity for all topic pairs as depicted in Figure 1, we found that most pairs of topic vectors were almost orthogonal. When evaluating dissimilarity functions, we found that $dissim_{linear}(z_i, z_j) = 1 - sim(z_i, z_j)$ made a document's overall dissimilarity score highly dependent on its topic proportions, while $dissim_{inverse}(z_i, z_j) = 1/sim(z_i, z_j)$ was problematic with unimportant topics that have small proportions. As topics with small proportions were fairly common and highly dissimilar pairs among these might randomly occur, overall scores could become misleading.

Thus, we use *normalized pointwise mutual information* (NPMI), which measures how well two outcomes, here the two topics z_i and z_j, are determined by each other. It is defined in Equation 6, where $p(z_i, z_j) = \sum_{d \in D} p(z_i|\boldsymbol{d}) \cdot p(z_j|\boldsymbol{d}) \cdot p(\boldsymbol{d})$. To quantify dissimilarity, we construct $dis(z_i, z_j)$ as given in Equation 7. It interpolates the NPMI values to a scale of 0 to 1 to reflect the fact that the most similar topic pair does not contribute to the unexpectedness of an article.

$$npmi(z_i, z_j) = \log \frac{p(z_i, z_j)}{p(z_i) \cdot p(z_j)} / (-\log p(z_i, z_j)) \qquad (6)$$

$$dis(z_i, z_j) = \frac{npmi(z_i, z_j) - \min_{z_a, z_b \in Z} npmi(z_a, z_b)}{\max_{z_a, z_b \in Z} npmi(z_a, z_b) - \min_{z_a, z_b \in Z} npmi(z_a, z_b)} \qquad (7)$$

The resulting histogram when calculating $dis(z_i, z_j)$ on the corpus' topic pairs is depicted in Figure 2 and resembles a bell-shaped curve. Using this formulation, we experienced fewer problems with small topics while enjoying a sound information-theoretic foundation that better fits the probabilistic LDA model than a cosine-based formulation.

2.4   Limitation of Small Topics' Influence: $c(z_i, z_j, d)$

In the entire corpus, 80 percent of the the word-specific topic proportions in documents $sp(z_i, d)$ was determined by an average of 3.69 topics per document, while the remaining 20 percent consisted of 7.82 "Small topics", displaying moderate relative, but small absolute portions that influenced the model significantly.

Thus, we restrict the unexpectedness score calculation to the largest topics that make up 80 percent of a document, denoted as $Z_{Main}(d)$ and quantify our confidence whether a topic z_i in a document d can be recognized by a reader in shorter articles by $rec(z_i, d)$ as specified in Equation 8. $\pi_{z_i}(d)$ is the projection of the document on the words assigned to topic z_i. The logarithm ensures that the bias towards long document topics is less extreme. Finally, we define the confidence of a topic pair in a document $c(z_i, z_j, d)$ as the harmonic mean of their rec values as specified in Equation 9.

$$rec(z_i, d) = log(||\pi_{z_i}(d)||_1 + 1) \tag{8}$$

$$c(z_i, z_j, d) = \frac{2 * rec(z_i, d) * rec(z_j, d)}{rec(z_i, d) + rec(z_j, d)} \tag{9}$$

2.5   Topic Variety Normalization: $norm(d, Z_{Main}(d))$

According to our notion, serendipity occurs when at least one combination of unexpected topics is present. Thus, it is less important whether an article consists of more than two unexpected topics. However, by summing over all topic pairs, our model accounts for a document's topic variety, which is captured by the total number of subgroups of dissimilar topics. A larger set of main topics $Z_{Main}(d)$ implies a larger unexpectedness value when assuming similar topic proportions and equal dissimilarity values.

To account for this bias, we normalized a document by its set of main topics $Z_{Main}(d)$, i.e., $sp(z_i, d) = \frac{1}{|Z_{Main}(d)|}$ and defined the uniform Gini Index $gini_{uniform}$ as in Equation 10 and $norm$ accordingly in Equation 11. This formulation is indifferent of the true proportions in $Z_{Main}(d)$ and keeps the model's property to account for the topic balance.

$$gini_{uniform}(d, Z_{Main}(d)) = \sum_{\substack{z_i, z_j \in Z_{Main}(d) \\ z_i \neq z_j}} \left(\frac{1}{|Z_{Main}(d)|} \right)^2 \tag{10}$$

$$norm(d, Z_{Main}(d)) = \frac{1}{gini_{uniform}(d, Z_{Main}(d))} \tag{11}$$

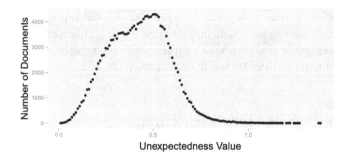

Fig. 3. Histogram of unexpectedness values for the 209,467 corpus documents. 31,968 articles with value 0 are omitted.

2.6 Corpus Exploration

We built our LDA model using the Mallet toolkit[3] and employ standard prepro-cessing techniques. The distribution of unexpectedness scores from Equation 3 for our corpus are shown in Fig 3. The scores are in $[0; 1.38]$ with median 0.38 when including the zero-valued articles, which consist of a single main topic, and 0.46 without. The *long tail* of highly unexpected articles in the range $[0.8; 1.38]$ accounts for 0.78 percent of the corpus.

3 Evaluation

In a recommendation context, suggestions have to be generated for a *source article* being read by a user who presumably shows interest in its topics. Our unexpectedness model can be used to rank documents in a corpus, but does not compare documents to a source article. As serendipity relies both on unexpected-ness and interestingness, we assume that recommendations have to demonstrate a certain similarity to a source article in order to ensure the reader could also be interested in them.

3.1 Ranking Algorithms

To identify an adequate combination of unexpectedness and interestingness for our serendipity model, we measured the individual influence of similarity and unexpectedness for the task of making serendipitous recommendations and added two baseline algorithms to evaluate the ranking strategies with respect to their induced serendipity. The ranking algorithms used were:

1. $rank_{unexp}$ ranked according to the score u of our unexpectedness model.
2. $rank_{cosine}$ ranked articles by their cosine similarity to the source article based on tf-idf document vectors.
3. $rank_{diversity}$ ranked articles by their diversity according to the model by Bache et al. [4] that we used as the basis of our work.
4. $rank_{dissimilarity}$ ranked articles by their topical dissimilarity with the source article, quantified by the Kullback Leibler divergence of the the two articles' topic distributions as given by the LDA model.

---

[3] http://mallet.cs.umass.edu/

5. $rank_{\text{serendipity}}$ employs a boosting algorithm to re-rank articles from $rank_{\text{unexp}}$ and $rank_{\text{cosine}}$. It is described in Section 3.4

As $rank_{\text{unexp}}$ and $rank_{\text{diversity}}$ do not consider the source article, many completely unrelated and thus probably very uninteresting articles were ranked prominently and would affect the evaluation. We therefore introduced a first step in which completely unrelated articles are excluded from the different rankings. We quantify the relatedness by calculating the cosine similarity to the source article with tf-idf document representations and select a similarity threshold of 0.2 to avoid irrelevant articles while keeping the set of retrieved articles large enough so that different re-ranking strategies could still be accurately discerned.

3.2 User Study

We evaluated the different re-ranking strategies in a user study. Six source articles were randomly selected, and for each article, the five highest ranked article recommendations from each re-ranking strategy were collected and presented to the participants in a random order. Due to articles being recommended by more than one strategy, these unions contained 14 to 19 recommendations.[4].

Each article was presented with its headline, publication date, and categorical classifiers provided with the corpus. To make the evaluation task less time-consuming, a short abstract was provided, along with the choice to display the entire article. As the corpus-supplied abstracts were only given for approximately one third of the data set, we applied the extractive summarization algorithm *KLSum* [9] that employs Kullback Leibler divergence to select sentences with the most similar word distributions to those of the original document. The resulting abstracts were manually inspected and found to have an overall similar summary quality except for one thread, where the articles recommended by $rank_{\text{unexp}}$ were substantially longer than the rest, resulting in a worse quality of the extracted summaries. We therefore removed this news thread from the evaluation.

As a response format, we used an integer scale ranging from 1 to 5 and displayed the options *Strongly Disagree* and *Strongly Agree* at the two extremes. In this way, two adjacent response options were equidistant and parametric statistics like means or variance could be calculated. For each article, we displayed the following two statements:

S1: This article is relevant regarding the source article.
S2: I am positively surprised by this article. I am glad I found it.

S1 regards the relevance of a recommended article with respect to the source article, while **S2** expresses the perceived serendipity when encountering an article. As the term *serendipity* represents a complex concept, we avoided the term and described it as *positive surprise*, expressing that the article is unexpected, but nevertheless useful to the reader.

---

[4] All data from the evaluation can be found at https://hpi.de/en/naumann/projects/knowledge-discovery-and-mining/serendipity.html

3.3 Results

Different participants tend to give ratings in different breadth and use different lower and upper bounds for bad and good recommendations. We thus employed *z-score normalization* [7], a common approach for normalizing ratings from different users to a common scale in a recommendation setting. Note that this normalization was carried out separately for each of the two statements, because they might display different rating behavior. The resulting normalized scores expressed by how many standard deviations the original scores deviated from the mean. Accordingly, a positive score indicated an above average answer.

To evaluate the serendipity of the algorithms, statement **S2** had to be assessed. The mean of the participant mean values expressed the average preference of an algorithm's serendipity by any participant. To compare the difference between two algorithms, the mean ratings of all participants were compared by a paired t-test at significance level 0.05. We were most interested in comparing $rank_{unexp}$ with the other three baseline approaches and thus Bonferroni-corrected the significance level to $\frac{0.05}{3} \approx 0.017$.

27 people took part in the study, resulting in 49 pairs of participants and source articles. All participants had a background in natural sciences and academia. The number of participants per source article ranged between 4 and 13, while most participants rated the recommendations for a single source article. However, three participants also rated the recommendations for five or six source articles.

We computed the box-plots of the mean surprise ratings (statement **S2**) across all participants for each of the algorithms in Figure 4 and could verify the high quality of the serendipity model. We also found that although $rank_{cosine}$ with a median value of 0.24 and mean value of 0.25 performed slightly better than $rank_{unexp}$ with mean and median value of 0.16, the difference was statistically not significant (p ¿ 0.1). Furthermore, the mean and median values of $rank_{unexp}$ were significantly higher than those of $rank_{diversity}$ and $rank_{dissimilarity}$ (p ¡ 0.01). We concluded that our unexpectedness function generates more surprising recommendations than these two algorithms. The comparison of $rank_{cosine}$ and $rank_{unexp}$ with $rank_{serendipity}$ is described in the next Section.

3.4 A Combined Serendipity Model

While $rank_{cosine}$ generated the most positively surprising and therefore potentially serendipitous articles compared to $rank_{unexp}$, the latter algorithm also generated better than average surprising recommendations. The mean Spearman's rank correlation between the recommendation rankings for all five source articles was 0.09, which means that rankings of both strategies were almost uncorrelated, indicating that serendipity occurs among articles that are highly similar as well as among articles that are less similar. This became obvious when we put the ratings for **S2**, capturing an article's serendipity, in relation to the ratings for **S1**, capturing an article's relevance to the source article, and obtained Figures 5a and 5b.

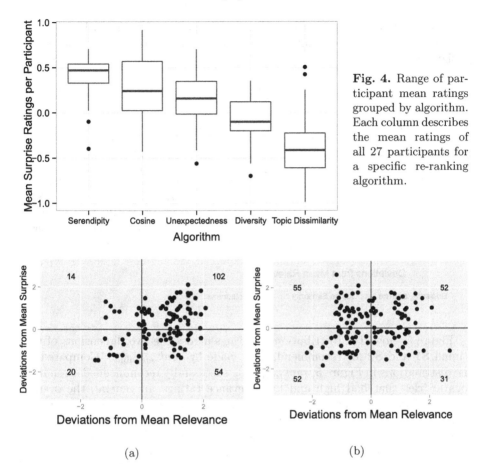

Fig. 4. Range of participant mean ratings grouped by algorithm. Each column describes the mean ratings of all 27 participants for a specific re-ranking algorithm.

(a)   (b)

Fig. 5. Comparison of the distribution of ratings in the two dimensions of relevance (statement **S1**) and positive surprise (statement **S2**) for $rank_{cosine}$ (a) and $rank_{unexp}$ (b). For each quadrant, the absolute number of ratings is given as some points overlap.

For $rank_{cosine}$, most of the positively surprising articles are concentrated in the similarity range $[0.4; 0.7]$, while they are in the range $[0.3; 0.4]$ for $rank_{unexp}$. Using this knowledge, we combined $rank_{unexp}$ and $rank_{cosine}$ to a joined serendipity ranking $rank_{serendipity}$ by constructing a boosting algorithm that estimates the likelihood that each article recommended by $rank_{unexp}$ or $rank_{cosine}$ will likely have a positive surprise rating, based on the ranking algorithm as well as on the similarity between recommended and source article.

We evaluated the five highest ranked recommendations from $rank_{serendipity}$ by ten-fold cross validation on the set of pairs of participants and chosen source articles. For the evaluation of those recommendations, the normalized surprise ratings were determined and aggregated per participant into a mean value. Over all participants' mean ratings, $rank_{serendipity}$ achieved a median surprise rating of 0.48 and mean surprise rating of 0.41. According to a paired t-test, this was significantly different from $rank_{unexp}$'s mean (p ¡ 0.01). A t-test with the mean of $rank_{cosine}$, 0.25 showed results in the range $[0.1; 0.05]$, which we did not regard as significant.

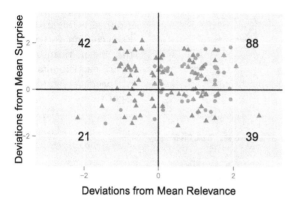

Fig. 6. Comparison of the rating distribution for the boosting algorithm $rank_{serendipity}$ in the two dimensions of relevance (according to statement **S1**) and serendipity (according to statement **S2**). For each quadrant, the absolute number of ratings is given.

Figure 5 shows the distribution of ratings across the two dimensions of the stimuli **S1** and **S2** for recommendations made by $rank_{serendipity}$. Compared to the distributions in Figure 5, $rank_{serendipity}$ successfully recommended serendipitous articles that had high and low relevance ratings. In general, the overall number of above-average serendipity ratings increased from 116 in Figure 5a and 107 in Figure 5b to 130. We furthermore noticed that the number of articles that were neither relevant nor serendipitous stayed on the level of $rank_{cosine}$. $rank_{serendipity}$ therefore successfully combines the benefits of both approaches. As $rank_{serendipity}$ was created based on the evaluation data, part of future work is to assess whether its validity holds for a different set of articles and participants.

This approach has to be taken with caution, because an algorithm shaped in retrospect to fit collected ratings easily overfits the data and does not generalize. Thus, the purpose of our considerations is to demonstrate that both algorithms can be synergistically combined and to outline a direction for future efforts that can be taken to develop a combined approach for the general case.

4 Related Work

Related work that aims to improve recommendations can be classified into *diversity*, *novelty*, and *serendipity*.

Diversity and Novelty. Diversity can be subdivided into two concepts: Firstly, *individual diversity* concerns the diversity of single recommendation lists. [16] target intra-list diversity using topical data and a greedy re-ranking procedure that focuses on items most dissimilar to previous items. Secondly, *aggregate diversity* concerns the diversity of all items a system recommends to its entire user base. [1] re-ranked recommendations from user-based collaborative filtering by their number of ratings to suggest less popular items.

The authors of [10] regard items that are dissimilar to the user's taste as novel and recommend diverse items, assuming that a diverse recommendation list also contains items that are novel to the user. In the field of music recommendation, the authors of [6] find that content-based systems are better at recommending novel items, as collaborative filtering systems are drawn to more popular items. However, these results do not imply that content-based systems are generally better suited to make novel recommendations.

Niche users are targeted by [14], who endeavor to make long tail recommendations that improve novelty, diversity, and serendipity.

Serendipity. Previous work on serendipity has focused on approaches that exploit a user's previous experiences with the system to induce serendipitous experiences and has been applied to various domains, such as artwork or music recommendation. For example, the authors of [5] used a lazy random walk algorithm on entities extracted from sources of user-generated content to generate serendipitous results. [3] focus on creating serendipitous recommendations by exploiting geo-spatial information of texts and evaluate it on a crowd-sourced news dataset.

A content-based recommender for artworks based on textual descriptions is built in [11] and uses a Naive Bayes classifier based on user feedback that models whether a user might like or dislike a document. Serendipitous documents are identified as those for which the classifier is most uncertain. Further, in the domain of music recommendation, the authors of [15] identify clusters of musicians that a user likes and try to recommend those musicians that belong to clusters yet unexplored by the user. A user-independent model for *general unexpectedness* of TV programmes based on word co-occurrence of their textual descriptions is presented in [2]. The serendipity model requires a clustering of items known by the user and is based on general unexpectedness as well as the distance of an item to the user-specific item clusters.

Many approaches use clustering to determine items users likely know; we also employ a soft clustering of news articles in form of topic modeling. In contrast to prior work, we propose a user-independent, content-based model that infers the unexpectedness of an article's topics from the item corpus instead of a user's preference ratings. While work on textual data of different domains exists, we address the problem for news articles.

Evaluating Serendipity. Little work exists on the evaluation of serendipity in user studies. A general survey framework for recommendation systems is developed by [12]. While it does not include serendipity, the authors note that the distinction of serendipity and novelty may be confusing for participants when evaluating both. In [13], different movie recommendation algorithms are evaluated regarding aspects like novelty and serendipity by a user study. The authors note the difficulty of evaluating serendipity due to its complex definition. In our work, we employ user studies for exploration as well as evaluation, because objective evaluation metrics that are universally applicable do not yet exist.

5   Conclusion

We presented a purely content-based algorithm that recommends serendipitous news articles based on an unexpectedness model of topic combinations in articles and a traditional cosine-based similarity model. By combining both models, we were able to incorporate the advantages of both and offer users a wide variety of serendipitous articles. The unexpectedness model currently focuses only on the dissimilarity of latent topics in documents. Incorporating further content-based features, e.g., named entities, authors, publication date, or even explicit user interest captured in user profiles could further increase the quality of recommendations and help offer even more serendipitous recommendations to users.

References

1. Adomavicius, G., Kwon, Y.: Improving aggregate recommendation diversity using ranking-based techniques. IEEE Trans. Knowl. Data Eng. **24**(5), 896–911 (2012)
2. Akiyama, T., Obara, K., Tanizaki, M.: Proposal and evaluation of serendipitous recommendation method using general unexpectedness. In: Workshop on the Practical Use of Recommender Systems, Algorithms and Technologies, p. 3 (2010)
3. Asikin, Y.A., Wörndl, W.: Stories around you: location-based serendipitous recommendation of news articles. In: Proceedings of the International Workshop on News Recommendation and Analytics (2014)
4. Bache, K., Newman, D., Smyth, P.: Text-based measures of document diversity. In: Proceedings of the International Conference on Knowledge Discovery and Data Mining, pp. 23–31. ACM (2013)
5. Bordino, I., Mejova, Y., Lalmas, M.: Penguins in sweaters, or serendipitous entity search on user-generated content. In: Proceedings of ACM International Conference on Information and Knowledge Management, CIKM, pp. 109–118 (2013)
6. Celma, O., Herrera, P.: A new approach to evaluating novel recommendations. In: Proceedings of the Conference on Recommender Systems, pp. 179–186. ACM (2008)
7. Desrosiers, C., Karypis, G.: A comprehensive survey of neighborhood-based recommendation methods. In: Ricci, F., Rokach, L., Shapira, B., Kantor, P.B. (eds.) Recommender Systems Handbook, pp. 107–144. Springer, Heidelberg (2011)
8. Ge, M., Delgado-Battenfeld, C., Jannach, D.: Beyond accuracy: evaluating recommender systems by coverage and serendipity. In: Proceedings of the Conference on Recommender Systems, pp. 257–260. ACM (2010)
9. Haghighi, A., Vanderwende, L.: Exploring content models for multi-document summarization. In: Proceedings of the Annual Conference of the North American Chapter of the Association for Computational Linguistics, pp. 362–370. ACL (2009)
10. Hurley, N., Zhang, M.: Novelty and diversity in top-n recommendation - analysis and evaluation. ACM Trans. Internet Technol. **10**(4), 14:1–14:30 (2011)
11. Iaquinta, L., De Gemmis, M., Lops, P., Semeraro, G., Filannino, M., Molino, P.: Introducing serendipity in a content-based recommender system. In: International Conference on Hybrid Intelligent Systems, pp. 168–173 (2008)
12. Pu, P., Chen, L., Hu, R.: A user-centric evaluation framework for recommender systems. In: Proceedings of the Conference on Recommender Systems, pp. 157–164. ACM (2011)

13. Said, A., Fields, B., Jain, B.J., Albayrak, S.: User-centric evaluation of a k-furthest neighbor collaborative filtering recommender algorithm. In: Proceedings of the Conference on Computer Supported Cooperative Work, pp. 1399–1408. ACM (2013)
14. Yin, H., Cui, B., Li, J., Yao, J., Chen, C.: Challenging the long tail recommendation. Proc. VLDB Endowment 5(9), 896–907 (2012)
15. Zhang, Y.C., Séaghdha, D.O., Quercia, D., Jambor, T.: Auralist: introducing serendipity into music recommendation. In: Proceedings of the International Conference on Web Search and Data Mining, pp. 13–22. ACM (2012)
16. Ziegler, C.-N., McNee, S.M., Konstan, J.A., Lausen, G.: Improving recommendation lists through topic diversification. In: Proceedings of the International Conference on World Wide Web, pp. 22–32. ACM (2005)

Axiomatization of General Concept Inclusions in Probabilistic Description Logics

Francesco Kriegel$^{(\boxtimes)}$

Institute for Theoretical Computer Science, TU Dresden, Dresden, Germany
francesco@tcs.inf.tu-dresden.de
http://lat.inf.tu-dresden.de/~francesco

Abstract. Probabilistic interpretations consist of a set of interpretations with a shared domain and a measure assigning a probability to each interpretation. Such structures can be obtained as results of repeated experiments, e.g., in biology, psychology, medicine, etc. A translation between probabilistic and crisp description logics is introduced and then utilized to reduce the construction of a base of general concept inclusions of a probabilistic interpretation to the crisp case for which a method for the axiomatization of a base of GCIs is well-known.

Keywords: Probabilistic description logics · Machine learning · Knowledge base · General concept inclusion

1 Introduction

This document proposes a method for axiomatizing a base of general concept inclusions for probabilistic interpretations. It is obtained by means of a translation between probabilistic description logics and crisp description logics, and well-known results for the construction of a base of GCIs for interpretations in crisp description logics. However, this approach does not add further complexity as the translations may be computed in polynomial time. There are several approaches for an integration of probabilities into description logics. This document follows the basic definitions of Lutz and Schröder in [12] where a probabilistic interpretation is defined as a family of standard interpretations over the same domain such that each interpretation has a specific probability. These structures naturally arise from experiments, e.g., in biology, psychology, or medicine, respectively, that are repeated several times. If for example the experiments may produce results with errors, or some effects may not always be observed, then repetition is advantageous. For all such sequences of interpretations over a shared domain the probability measure can easily be defined as a uniform discrete probability measure over all observed interpretations. We call such probabilistic interpretations (quasi-)uniform.

At first we introduce the probabilistic description logics $\mathbb{P}_{01}\mathcal{FLE}^{\perp}$ and $\mathbb{P}_{\geq}\mathcal{FLE}^{\perp}\mathcal{Q}^{\geq}$. Then we present a translation between $\mathbb{P}_{01}\mathcal{FLE}^{\perp}$ and $\mathcal{FLE}^{\perp}$ that satisfies certain consistency properties w.r.t. the underlying probabilistic interpretation. By means of the translation we utilize previous results for the construction of a base of general concept inclusions. In particular, the notion of a

© Springer International Publishing Switzerland 2015
S. Hölldobler et al. (Eds.): KI 2015, LNAI 9324, pp. 124–136, 2015.
DOI: 10.1007/978-3-319-24489-1_10

(canonical) base of GCIs is used here that has been found by Baader and Distel in [1,2,7] for the description logic $\mathcal{EL}^\perp$ w.r.t. greatest fixpoint semantics. Furthermore, it has been adapted by Borchmann, Distel, and Kriegel in [6] for $\mathcal{EL}^\perp$ w.r.t. role-depth bounds, and has been extended towards the more expressive description logic $\mathcal{ALEQR}^{\mathsf{Self}}$ in [11] (hence, may also be applied to the smaller description logics $\mathcal{FLE}^\perp$ and $\mathcal{FLE}^\perp \mathcal{Q}^\geq$). The construction of a base of probabilistic GCIs is also generalized towards the more expressive description logic $\mathbb{P}_{\geq}\mathcal{FLE}^\perp \mathcal{Q}^\geq$ but only in the case of quasi-uniform probabilistic interpretations.

Most-specific generalizations in probabilistic description logics have been subject of previous research. In [13–15] Peñaloza and Turhan investigated methods for the construction of most-specific concept description (w.r.t. a knowledge base) and least common subsumers in probabilistic $\mathcal{EL}$. Later, in [9,10] Ecke, Peñaloza, and Turhan, extended their results towards nominals and complex role inclusion axioms. This document also provides a method for the construction of probabilistic model-based most-specific concept descriptions (w.r.t. probabilistic interpretations).

2   The Description Logics $\mathbb{P}_{01}\mathcal{FLE}^\perp$ and $\mathbb{P}_{\geq}\mathcal{FLE}^\perp\mathcal{Q}^\geq$

At first, we introduce the probabilistic description logic $\mathbb{P}\mathcal{FLE}^\perp\mathcal{Q}^\geq$ that extends the well-known description logic $\mathcal{FLE}$. A *role description* is either a role name $r \in N_R$ or of the form $\mathbb{P}_{\bowtie p}\, r$ for a comparator $\bowtie \in \{ <, \leq, =, \geq, > \}$, a role name $r \in N_R$, and a probability threshold $p \in [0,1]$. Furthermore, *concept descriptions* may be inductively built according to the following syntax rule where s denotes a role description, $A \in N_C$ a concept name, $n \geq 2$ an integer, $\bowtie \in \{ <, \leq, =, \geq, > \}$, and $p \in [0,1]$:

$$C ::= \perp \mid \top \mid A \mid C \sqcap C \mid \exists s.\, C \mid \forall s.\, C \mid \geq n.\, s.\, C \mid \mathbb{P}_{\bowtie p}\, C$$

The description logic $\mathbb{P}_{01}\mathcal{FLE}^\perp$ does not allow for qualified $\geq$-restrictions $\geq n.\, s.\, C$, and only allows for probabilistic concept and role constructors $\mathbb{P}_{>0}$ and $\mathbb{P}_{=0}$. Furthermore, the description logic $\mathbb{P}_{\geq}\mathcal{FLE}^\perp\mathcal{Q}^\geq$ only allows for probabilistic constructors $\mathbb{P}_{\geq p}$.

A detailed overview on probabilistic extensions of the description logics $\mathcal{ALC}$ and $\mathcal{EL}$ and several complexity results for reasoning in probabilistic description logics have been given by Lutz and Schröder in [12].

A *probability measure* on a countable set W is a mapping $\mathbb{P}\colon 2^W \to [0,1]$ such that $\mathbb{P}(\emptyset) = 0$ and $\mathbb{P}(W) = 1$ hold, and furthermore for all countable pairwise disjoint sequences $(U_n)_{n \in \mathbb{N}}$ of subsets $U_n \subseteq W$ it is true that $\mathbb{P}(\biguplus_{n \in \mathbb{N}} U_n) = \sum_{n \in \mathbb{N}} \mathbb{P}(U_n)$, i.e., $\mathbb{P}$ is σ-*additive*. For a subset $U \subseteq W$ the value $\mathbb{P}(U)$ is the *probability* of U w.r.t. $\mathbb{P}$.

Let (N_C, N_R) be a signature. A *probabilistic interpretation* over (N_C, N_R) is a tuple $\mathcal{I} = (\Delta^{\mathcal{I}}, W, (\cdot^{\mathcal{I}_w})_{w \in W}, \mathbb{P})$ that consists of a set $\Delta^{\mathcal{I}}$, called *domain*, a countable set W of *worlds*, an *extension function* $\cdot^{\mathcal{I}_w}$ for each world $w \in W$, and a probability measure $\mathbb{P}$ on W. For each world $w \in W$ the tuple $(\Delta^{\mathcal{I}}, \cdot^{\mathcal{I}_w})$ is an interpretation over (N_C, N_R) that may be extended to all $\mathcal{FLE}^{\perp}\mathcal{Q}^{\geq}$-concept descriptions in the canonical way. Furthermore, for the probabilistic constructors $\mathbb{P}_{\bowtie p}$ with $\bowtie\ \in\ \{<, \leq, =, \geq, >\}$ and $p \in [0,1]$ their extensions are defined as follows:

$$(\mathbb{P}_{\bowtie p}\, C)^{\mathcal{I}_w} := \{\, d \in \Delta^{\mathcal{I}} \mid \mathbb{P}\{\, v \in W \mid d \in C^{\mathcal{I}_v}\,\} \bowtie p\,\},$$
$$(\mathbb{P}_{\bowtie p}\, r)^{\mathcal{I}_w} := \{\, (d, e) \in \Delta^{\mathcal{I}} \times \Delta^{\mathcal{I}} \mid \mathbb{P}\{\, v \in W \mid (d, e) \in r^{\mathcal{I}_v}\,\} \bowtie p\,\}.$$

Note that the extensions are independent of the world w, i.e., they coincide in all worlds of the probabilistic interpretation. An individual $d \in \Delta^{\mathcal{I}}$ is in the extension of $\mathbb{P}_{>0}\, C$ if and only if d is *possibly* in the extension of C, and is in the extension of $\mathbb{P}_{=1}\, C$ iff d is *almost surely* in the extension of C.

A world $w \in W$ is called *possible* if its probability is not 0, i.e., if $\mathbb{P}\{\, w\,\} > 0$ holds; otherwise we call w *impossible*. For a probabilistic interpretation we denote the set of all possible worlds by W_ε, and the set of all impossible worlds by W_0. Of course, $W_\varepsilon \uplus W_0$ is a partition of W, and $\mathbb{P}(W_\varepsilon) = 1$ and $\mathbb{P}(W_0) = 0$ hold.

A *general concept inclusion (GCI)* is of the form $C \sqsubseteq D$ where C and D are concept descriptions. It holds in a probabilistic interpretation $\mathcal{I}$ if and only if $C^{\mathcal{I}_w} \subseteq D^{\mathcal{I}_w}$ is satisfied for all worlds $w \in W$, and we shall denote this by $\mathcal{I} \models C \sqsubseteq D$.

Let $\mathcal{I}$ be a probabilistic interpretation. Then a TBox $\mathcal{B}$ is called *base of GCIs* for $\mathcal{I}$ if $\mathcal{I}$ models all GCIs in $\mathcal{B}$, i.e., $\mathcal{B}$ is *sound*, and whenever a GCI holds in $\mathcal{I}$ then it follows from $\mathcal{B}$, i.e., $\mathcal{B}$ is *complete*.

3   Translation between $\mathbb{P}_{01}\mathcal{FLE}^{\perp}$ and $\mathcal{FLE}^{\perp}$

It is readily verified that $d \in (\mathbb{P}_{>0}\, C)^{\mathcal{I}_w}$ holds if and only if there is a possible world $v \in W_\varepsilon$ such that $d \in C^{\mathcal{I}_v}$ hold. Analogously, $d \in (\mathbb{P}_{=1}\, C)^{\mathcal{I}_w}$ is equivalent to the statement that $d \in C^{\mathcal{I}_v}$ is true for all possible worlds $v \in W_\varepsilon$. Similar statements hold for the probabilistic role constructors $\mathbb{P}_{>0}\, r$ and $\mathbb{P}_{=1}\, r$. Hence, it is possible to translate $\mathbb{P}_{01}\mathcal{FLE}^{\perp}$-concept descriptions into $\mathcal{FLE}^{\perp}$-concept descriptions and vice versa.

For this purpose a new role name $\omega_{\mathbb{P}}$, and role names $r_{>0}, r_{=1}$ for each existing role name $r \in N_R$, are introduced into the signature, and we shall denote the extended signature by

$$(N_C, N_R)^{\mathbb{P}}_{01} := (N_C, N_R \uplus \{\, \omega_{\mathbb{P}}\,\} \uplus \{\, r_{>0}, r_{=1} \mid r \in N_R\,\}).$$

Then the translation function $\tau \colon \mathbb{P}_{01}\mathcal{FLE}^{\perp}(N_C, N_R) \to \mathcal{FLE}^{\perp}(N_C, N_R)^{\mathbb{P}}_{01}$ and its inverse τ^{-1} are inductively defined as follows:

$$\tau(r) := r \qquad\qquad\qquad \tau^{-1}(r) := r$$
$$\tau(\mathbb{P}_{>0}\, r) := r_{>0} \qquad\qquad \tau^{-1}(r_{>0}) := \mathbb{P}_{>0}\, r$$
$$\tau(\mathbb{P}_{=1}\, r) := r_{=1} \qquad\qquad \tau^{-1}(r_{=1}) := \mathbb{P}_{=1}\, r$$
$$\tau(A) := A \qquad\qquad\qquad \tau^{-1}(A) := A$$

$$\tau(C \sqcap D) := \tau(C) \sqcap \tau(D)$$
$$\tau(\exists s. C) := \exists \tau(s). \tau(C)$$
$$\tau(\forall s. C) := \forall \tau(s). \tau(C)$$
$$\tau(\mathbb{P}_{>0} C) := \exists \omega_{\mathbb{P}}. \tau(C)$$
$$\tau(\mathbb{P}_{=1} C) := \forall \omega_{\mathbb{P}}. \tau(C)$$

$$\tau^{-1}(C \sqcap D) := \tau^{-1}(C) \sqcap \tau^{-1}(D)$$
$$\tau^{-1}(\exists s. C) := \exists \tau^{-1}(s). \tau^{-1}(C)$$
$$\tau^{-1}(\forall s. C) := \forall \tau^{-1}(s). \tau^{-1}(C)$$
$$\tau^{-1}(\exists \omega_{\mathbb{P}}. C) := \mathbb{P}_{>0} \tau^{-1}(C)$$
$$\tau^{-1}(\forall \omega_{\mathbb{P}}. C) := \mathbb{P}_{=1} \tau^{-1}(C)$$

For each probabilistic interpretation $\mathcal{I} = (\Delta^{\mathcal{I}}, W, (\cdot^{\mathcal{I}_w})_{w \in W}, \mathbb{P})$ over (N_C, N_R) we define the interpretation $\mathcal{I}^{\times} := (\Delta^{\mathcal{I}} \times W, \cdot^{\mathcal{I}^{\times}})$ over $(N_C, N_R)_{01}^{\mathbb{P}}$ whose extension function is given as follows:

$$A^{\mathcal{I}^{\times}} := \{ (d, w) \mid d \in A^{\mathcal{I}_w} \} \qquad (A \in N_C)$$
$$r^{\mathcal{I}^{\times}} := \{ ((d, w), (e, w)) \mid (d, e) \in r^{\mathcal{I}_w} \} \qquad (r \in N_R)$$
$$\omega_{\mathbb{P}}^{\mathcal{I}^{\times}} := \{ ((d, v), (d, w)) \mid \mathbb{P} \{ w \} > 0 \}$$
$$r_{>0}^{\mathcal{I}^{\times}} := \{ ((d, w), (e, w)) \mid (d, e) \in (\mathbb{P}_{>0} r)^{\mathcal{I}_w} \}$$
$$r_{=1}^{\mathcal{I}^{\times}} := \{ ((d, w), (e, w)) \mid (d, e) \in (\mathbb{P}_{=1} r)^{\mathcal{I}_w} \}$$

The special role $\omega_{\mathbb{P}}$ connects each individual d in an arbitrary world to itself in a possible world. Then the following lemma shows the connection between the given translation functions.

Lemma 1. *Let $\mathcal{I} = (\Delta^{\mathcal{I}}, W, (\cdot^{\mathcal{I}_w})_{w \in W}, \mathbb{P})$ be a probabilistic interpretation, $d \in \Delta^{\mathcal{I}}$ an individual, $w \in W$ a world, and C a $\mathbb{P}_{01}\mathcal{FLE}^{\perp}$-concept description. Then the following equivalence holds:*

$$d \in C^{\mathcal{I}_w} \text{ if and only if } (d, w) \in \tau(C)^{\mathcal{I}^{\times}}.$$

Proof. by structural induction on C.

induction base: $C = A$
Of course, it holds that $\tau(A) = A$. Thus, the equivalence follows by definition of $\mathcal{I}^{\times}$.
inductive step: $C = D \sqcap E$

$$d \in (D \sqcap E)^{\mathcal{I}_w} \Leftrightarrow d \in D^{\mathcal{I}_w} \text{ and } d \in E^{\mathcal{I}_w}$$
$$\overset{\text{I.H.}}{\Leftrightarrow} (d, w) \in \tau(D)^{\mathcal{I}^{\times}} \text{ and } (d, w) \in \tau(E)^{\mathcal{I}^{\times}}$$
$$\Leftrightarrow (d, w) \in (\tau(D) \sqcap \tau(E))^{\mathcal{I}^{\times}} = \tau(D \sqcap E)^{\mathcal{I}^{\times}}$$

inductive step: $C = \exists r. D$

$$d \in (\exists r. D)^{\mathcal{I}_w} \Leftrightarrow \exists e \in \Delta^{\mathcal{I}} : (d, e) \in r^{\mathcal{I}_w} \text{ and } e \in D^{\mathcal{I}_w}$$
$$\overset{\text{I.H.}}{\Leftrightarrow} \exists e \in \Delta^{\mathcal{I}} : ((d, w), (e, w)) \in \tau(r)^{\mathcal{I}^{\times}} \text{ and } (e, w) \in \tau(D)^{\mathcal{I}^{\times}}$$
$$\Leftrightarrow (d, w) \in (\exists r. \tau(D))^{\mathcal{I}^{\times}} = \tau(\exists r. D)^{\mathcal{I}^{\times}}$$

The equivalences are also satisfied for probabilistic roles $\mathbb{P}_{>0}\, r$, since

$$(d, e) \in (\mathbb{P}_{>0}\, r)^{\mathcal{I}_w} \Leftrightarrow ((d, w), (e, w)) \in r_{>0}^{\mathcal{I}^\times}$$

and $\tau(\mathbb{P}_{>0}\, r) = r_{>0}$ hold by definition. Analogously for $\mathbb{P}_{=1}\, r$.
inductive step: $C = \forall r.\, D$

$$d \in (\forall r.\, D)^{\mathcal{I}_w} \Leftrightarrow \forall e \in \Delta^{\mathcal{I}} : (d, e) \in r^{\mathcal{I}_w} \text{ implies } e \in D^{\mathcal{I}_w}$$

$$\overset{\text{I.H.}}{\Leftrightarrow} \forall e \in \Delta^{\mathcal{I}} : ((d, w), (e, w)) \in \tau(r)^{\mathcal{I}^\times} \text{ implies } (e, w) \in \tau(D)^{\mathcal{I}^\times}$$

$$\Leftrightarrow (d, w) \in (\forall r.\, \tau(D))^{\mathcal{I}^\times} = \tau(\forall r.\, D)^{\mathcal{I}^\times}$$

With the same arguments as for existential restrictions, the statements also hold for probabilistic roles.
inductive step: $C = \mathbb{P}_{>0}\, D$

$$d \in (\mathbb{P}_{>0}\, C)^{\mathcal{I}_w} \Leftrightarrow \exists v \in W : \mathbb{P}\{\, v\,\} > 0 \text{ and } d \in C^{\mathcal{I}_v}$$

$$\overset{\text{I.H.}}{\Leftrightarrow} \exists v \in W : ((d, w), (d, v)) \in \omega_{\mathbb{P}}^{\mathcal{I}^\times} \text{ and } (d, v) \in \tau(C)^{\mathcal{I}^\times}$$

$$\Leftrightarrow (d, w) \in (\exists \omega_{\mathbb{P}}.\, \tau(C))^{\mathcal{I}^\times} = \tau(\mathbb{P}_{>0}\, C)^{\mathcal{I}^\times}$$

inductive step: $C = \mathbb{P}_{=1}\, D$

$$d \in (\mathbb{P}_{=1}\, C)^{\mathcal{I}_w} \Leftrightarrow \forall v \in W : \mathbb{P}\{\, v\,\} > 0 \text{ implies } d \in C^{\mathcal{I}_v}$$

$$\overset{\text{I.H.}}{\Leftrightarrow} \forall v \in W : ((d, w), (d, v)) \in \omega_{\mathbb{P}}^{\mathcal{I}^\times} \text{ implies } (d, v) \in \tau(C)^{\mathcal{I}^\times}$$

$$\Leftrightarrow (d, w) \in (\forall \omega_{\mathbb{P}}.\, \tau(C))^{\mathcal{I}^\times} = \tau(\mathbb{P}_{=1}\, C)^{\mathcal{I}^\times} \qquad \square$$

As a corollary it follows that $C^{\mathcal{I}_w} \times \{\, w\,\} = \tau(C)^{\mathcal{I}^\times} \cap (\Delta^{\mathcal{I}} \times \{\, w\,\})$ and hence also

$$\tau(C)^{\mathcal{I}^\times} = \biguplus_{w \in W} C^{\mathcal{I}_w} \times \{\, w\,\}$$

hold for all $\mathbb{P}_{01}\mathcal{FLE}^\perp$-concept descriptions C and all probabilistic interpretations $\mathcal{I}$.

4   Construction of a Base of GCIs in $\mathbb{P}_{01}\mathcal{FLE}^\perp$

The translation τ can additionally be used to translate valid general concept inclusions of $\mathcal{I}$ into valid general concept inclusions of $\mathcal{I}^\times$. Since τ has an inverse we may also translate GCIs in the opposite direction. A more sophisticated characterization is given in the next lemma.

Lemma 2. *Let $\mathcal{I}$ be a probabilistic interpretation and C, D be $\mathbb{P}_{01}\mathcal{FLE}^\perp$-concept descriptions. Then the general concept inclusion $C \sqsubseteq D$ holds in $\mathcal{I}$ if and only if the translated GCI $\tau(C) \sqsubseteq \tau(D)$ holds in $\mathcal{I}^\times$.*

Proof. Consider an arbitrary individual $d \in \Delta^{\mathcal{I}}$ and an arbitrary world $w \in W$. Then the following equivalences hold:

$$\mathcal{I} \models C \sqsubseteq D \Leftrightarrow \forall w \in W \; \forall d \in \Delta^{\mathcal{I}} : d \in C^{\mathcal{I}_w} \Rightarrow d \in D^{\mathcal{I}_w}$$

$$\overset{\text{Lem.1}}{\Leftrightarrow} \forall (d, w) \in \Delta^{\mathcal{I}} \times W : (d, w) \in \tau(C)^{\mathcal{I}^{\times}} \Rightarrow (d, w) \in \tau(D)^{\mathcal{I}^{\times}}$$

$$\Leftrightarrow \mathcal{I}^{\times} \models \tau(C) \sqsubseteq \tau(D).$$

$\square$

Having all necessary notions and lemmata at hand, we are now ready to formulate the main proposition for the construction of a base of GCIs in $\mathbb{P}_{01}\mathcal{FLE}^{\perp}$. We have seen that we may translate between valid GCIs of $\mathcal{I}$ and $\mathcal{I}^{\times}$, and the following proposition shows that it is possible to translate a base for $\mathcal{I}^{\times}$ into a base for $\mathcal{I}$.

Proposition 3. *Let $\mathcal{I}$ be a probabilistic interpretation. Every base of GCIs for the interpretation $\mathcal{I}^{\times}$ can be translated into a base of GCIs for $\mathcal{I}$; in particular, if $\mathcal{B}$ is a base of GCIs for $\mathcal{I}^{\times}$, then the set $\tau^{-1}(\mathcal{B}) := \{ \tau^{-1}(C) \sqsubseteq \tau^{-1}(D) \mid C \sqsubseteq D \in \mathcal{B} \}$ is a base of GCIs for $\mathcal{I}$.*

Proof. Firstly, we show soundness of the translation $\tau^{-1}(\mathcal{B})$. For this purpose consider a GCI $C \sqsubseteq D \in \mathcal{B}$. Since $\mathcal{B}$ is a base for $\mathcal{I}^{\times}$, it follows that $C \sqsubseteq D$ holds in $\mathcal{I}^{\times}$. By Lemma 7, we may conclude that $\tau^{-1}(C) \sqsubseteq \tau^{-1}(D)$ holds in $\mathcal{I}$.

Secondly, we prove completeness of $\tau^{-1}(\mathcal{B})$. Let $C \sqsubseteq D$ be a GCI holding in $\mathcal{I}$. Lemma 7 then states that $\tau(C) \sqsubseteq \tau(D)$ holds in $\mathcal{I}^{\times}$, and thus follows from $\mathcal{B}$. It remains to show that $\tau^{-1}(\mathcal{B})$ entails $C \sqsubseteq D$. Consider an arbitrary model $\mathcal{J}$ of the translation $\tau^{-1}(\mathcal{B})$. Using Lemma 7 it follows that $\mathcal{J}^{\times}$ must be a model of $\mathcal{B}$. By completeness of $\mathcal{B}$, we conclude that $\mathcal{J}^{\times} \models \tau(C) \sqsubseteq \tau(D)$, and finally Lemma 7 yields that $\mathcal{J} \models C \sqsubseteq D$. Consequently, $\tau^{-1}(\mathcal{B})$ is complete for $\mathcal{I}$. $\square$

However, the converse direction cannot be shown, as not every interpretation over $(N_C, N_R)_{01}^{\mathbb{P}}$ is induced by a probabilistic interpretation, and hence may have different extensions for the additional role names. Thus, we are not able to prove that minimality of the base is preserved. In particular, it is only possible to conclude $C \sqsubseteq D$ if $\tau(C) \sqsubseteq \tau(D)$, but not vice versa.

Lemma 4. *Let C and D be two $\mathbb{P}_{01}\mathcal{FLE}^{\perp}$-concept descriptions. If $\tau(C) \sqsubseteq \tau(D)$, then also $C \sqsubseteq D$ is satisfied.*

Proof. Let $\mathcal{I}$ be an arbitrary probabilistic interpretation over (N_C, N_R), and consider its induced interpretation $\mathcal{I}^{\times}$ over $(N_C, N_R)_{01}^{\mathbb{P}}$. By presumption, it follows that $\tau(C)^{\mathcal{I}^{\times}} \subseteq \tau(D)^{\mathcal{I}^{\times}}$. Now consider an arbitrary world $w \in W$ and an individual $d \in \Delta^{\mathcal{I}}$. Using the previous Lemma 1 we get the following:

$$d \in C^{\mathcal{I}_w} \Leftrightarrow (d, w) \in \tau(C)^{\mathcal{I}^{\times}}$$

$$\Rightarrow (d, w) \in \tau(D)^{\mathcal{I}^{\times}}$$

$$\Leftrightarrow d \in D^{\mathcal{I}_w}.$$

As a consequence, we have $C \sqsubseteq D$. $\square$

5 Translation between $\mathbb{P}_{\geq}\mathcal{FLE}^{\perp}\mathcal{Q}^{\geq}$ and $\mathcal{FLE}^{\perp}\mathcal{Q}^{\geq}$

A probabilistic interpretation $\mathcal{I}$ is called *quasi-uniform* if all possible worlds have the same probability, i.e., if $\mathbb{P}\{v\} = \mathbb{P}\{w\}$ holds for all $v, w \in W_{\varepsilon}$. Then $\mathbb{P}\{w\} = \varepsilon$ holds for all possible worlds $w \in W_{\varepsilon}$ where $\varepsilon := \frac{1}{|W_{\varepsilon}|}$, and in particular it follows that only finitely many possible worlds exist. A quasi-uniform probabilistic interpretation is *uniform* if it does not contain impossible worlds.

In this section we only consider quasi-uniform probabilistic interpretations. Hence, let $\mathcal{I}$ be quasi-uniform with probability ε for each possible world. We will extend the translation function τ as introduced in the previous section to a translation τ_{ε} from $\mathbb{P}_{\geq}\mathcal{FLE}^{\perp}\mathcal{Q}^{\geq}$ to $\mathcal{FLE}^{\perp}\mathcal{Q}^{\geq}$. For this purpose we have to extend the signature (N_C, N_R) by adding new roles $r_{\geq k}$ for each role name $r \in N_R$. In particular, we define

$$(N_C, N_R)_{\geq}^{\mathbb{P}} := (N_C, N_R \uplus \{\omega_{\mathbb{P}}\} \uplus \{r_{\geq k} \mid k \in \{1, \ldots, |W_{\varepsilon}|\}\}).$$

Then the mapping τ_{ε} extends τ as follows:

$$\tau_{\varepsilon}(\mathbb{P}_{\geq p} r) := r_{\geq \lceil \frac{p}{\varepsilon} \rceil} \qquad\qquad \tau_{\varepsilon}^{-1}(r_{\geq k}) := \mathbb{P}_{\geq k \cdot \varepsilon} r$$

$$\tau_{\varepsilon}(\mathbb{P}_{\geq p} C) := \exists \omega_{\mathbb{P}}.\, \tau_{\varepsilon}(C) \quad (p \in (0, \varepsilon]) \qquad \tau_{\varepsilon}^{-1}(\exists \omega_{\mathbb{P}}.\, C) := \mathbb{P}_{\geq \varepsilon}\, \tau_{\varepsilon}^{-1}(C)$$

$$\tau_{\varepsilon}(\mathbb{P}_{\geq p} C) := \,\geq \lceil \tfrac{p}{\varepsilon} \rceil.\, \omega_{\mathbb{P}}.\, \tau_{\varepsilon}(C) \quad (p \in (\varepsilon, 1)) \qquad \tau_{\varepsilon}^{-1}(\geq n.\, \omega_{\mathbb{P}}.\, C) := \mathbb{P}_{\geq n \cdot \varepsilon}\, \tau_{\varepsilon}^{-1}(C)$$

$$\tau_{\varepsilon}(\mathbb{P}_{\geq 1} C) := \forall \omega_{\mathbb{P}}.\, \tau_{\varepsilon}(C) \qquad\qquad \tau_{\varepsilon}^{-1}(\forall \omega_{\mathbb{P}}.\, C) := \mathbb{P}_{\geq 1}\, \tau_{\varepsilon}^{-1}(C)$$

Of course, the induced interpretation $\mathcal{I}^{\times}$ must also interpret the new role names $r_{\geq k}$. Hence, we define the following extensions for them:

$$r_{\geq k}^{\mathcal{I}^{\times}} := \{((d, w), (e, w)) \mid (d, e) \in (\mathbb{P}_{\geq k \cdot \varepsilon}\, r)^{\mathcal{I}_w}\}$$
$$= \{((d, w), (e, w)) \mid \mathbb{P}\{w \in W \mid (d, e) \in r^{\mathcal{I}_w}\} \geq k \cdot \varepsilon\},$$

i.e., $((d, w), (e, w)) \in r_{\geq k}^{\mathcal{I}^{\times}}$ holds iff there are k possible worlds w that satisfy $(d, e) \in r^{\mathcal{I}_w}$.

Unfortunately, the mappings τ_{ε} and τ_{ε}^{-1} are not mutually inverse. For arbitrary concept descriptions C it only holds that $\tau_{\varepsilon}(\tau_{\varepsilon}^{-1}(C)) = C$. For the concept description $C = \mathbb{P}_{\geq p} A$ we have $\tau_{\varepsilon}(\mathbb{P}_{\geq p} A) = \,\geq \lceil \tfrac{p}{\varepsilon} \rceil.\, \omega_{\mathbb{P}}.\, A$, and hence $\tau_{\varepsilon}^{-1}(\tau_{\varepsilon}(\mathbb{P}_{\geq p} A)) = \mathbb{P}_{\geq \varepsilon \cdot \lceil \frac{p}{\varepsilon} \rceil} A$. Obviously, if p is not of the form $k \cdot \varepsilon$ for a $k \in \mathbb{N}$, then the concept descriptions are not equal. However, we may show that the concept descriptions $\tau_{\varepsilon}^{-1}(\tau_{\varepsilon}(C))$ and C have the same extensions w.r.t. the interpretation $\mathcal{I}$.

Lemma 5. *Let $\mathcal{I}$ be a quasi-uniform probabilistic interpretation with $\frac{1}{\varepsilon}$ possible worlds, i.e., the probability of each possible world is ε. Then for each $\mathbb{P}_{\geq}\mathcal{FLE}^{\perp}\mathcal{Q}^{\geq}$-concept description C and all worlds $w \in W$ the following equation holds:*

$$C^{\mathcal{I}_w} = (\tau_{\varepsilon}^{-1}(\tau_{\varepsilon}(C)))^{\mathcal{I}_w}.$$

Proof. by structural induction on C.

(induction base) Let $C = A$ be a concept name. Then it holds that $\tau_\varepsilon^{-1}(\tau_\varepsilon(A)) = A$, and hence the claim is trivial.

(induction step) At first consider a probabilistic concept description $C = \mathbb{P}_{\geq p} D$. Then we have the following equivalences:

$$d \in (\mathbb{P}_{\geq p} D)^{\mathcal{I}_w} \Leftrightarrow \mathbb{P}\{\, v \in W \mid d \in D^{\mathcal{I}_v} \,\} \geq p$$
$$\overset{*}{\Leftrightarrow} \mathbb{P}\{\, v \in W \mid d \in D^{\mathcal{I}_v} \,\} \geq \varepsilon \cdot \lceil \tfrac{p}{\varepsilon} \rceil$$
$$\overset{\text{I.H.}}{\Leftrightarrow} \mathbb{P}\{\, v \in W \mid d \in (\tau_\varepsilon^{-1}(\tau_\varepsilon(D)))^{\mathcal{I}_v} \,\} \geq \varepsilon \cdot \lceil \tfrac{p}{\varepsilon} \rceil$$
$$\Leftrightarrow d \in (\mathbb{P}_{\geq \varepsilon \cdot \lceil \frac{p}{\varepsilon} \rceil} \tau_\varepsilon^{-1}(\tau_\varepsilon(D)))^{\mathcal{I}_w}$$
$$\Leftrightarrow d \in (\tau_\varepsilon^{-1}(\tau_\varepsilon(\mathbb{P}_{\geq p} D)))^{\mathcal{I}_w}.$$

For the equivalence $*$ note that $p \leq \varepsilon \cdot \lceil \tfrac{p}{\varepsilon} \rceil$ always holds. The other direction follows from the fact that for each individual d which satisfies $\mathbb{P}\{\, v \in W \mid d \in D^{\mathcal{I}_v} \,\} \geq p$ there must be at least $\lceil \tfrac{p}{\varepsilon} \rceil$ possible worlds v with $d \in D^{\mathcal{I}_v}$ since all possible worlds have probability ε. Hence, it suffices to enforce a probability $\geq \varepsilon \cdot \lceil \tfrac{p}{\varepsilon} \rceil$.

Analogously, we can prove that $s^{\mathcal{I}_w} = (\tau_\varepsilon^{-1}(\tau_\varepsilon(s)))^{\mathcal{I}_w}$ holds for all (probabilistic) roles s.

Consider a conjunction $C = D \sqcap E$. Then we infer the following equations:

$$(D \sqcap E)^{\mathcal{I}_w} = D^{\mathcal{I}_w} \cap E^{\mathcal{I}_w}$$
$$\overset{\text{I.H.}}{=} (\tau_\varepsilon^{-1}(\tau_\varepsilon(D)))^{\mathcal{I}_w} \cap (\tau_\varepsilon^{-1}(\tau_\varepsilon(E)))^{\mathcal{I}_w}$$
$$= (\tau_\varepsilon^{-1}(\tau_\varepsilon(D)) \sqcap \tau_\varepsilon^{-1}(\tau_\varepsilon(E)))^{\mathcal{I}_w}$$
$$= (\tau_\varepsilon^{-1}(\tau_\varepsilon(D \sqcap E)))^{\mathcal{I}_w}.$$

Finally, let $C = \exists s. D$ be an existential restriction. Then we can make the following observations:

$$d \in (\exists s. D)^{\mathcal{I}_w} \Leftrightarrow \exists e \in \Delta^{\mathcal{I}}: (d, e) \in s^{\mathcal{I}_w} \text{ and } e \in D^{\mathcal{I}_w}$$
$$\overset{\text{I.H.}}{\Leftrightarrow} \exists e \in \Delta^{\mathcal{I}}: (d, e) \in (\tau_\varepsilon^{-1}(\tau_\varepsilon(s)))^{\mathcal{I}_w} \text{ and } e \in (\tau_\varepsilon^{-1}(\tau_\varepsilon(D)))^{\mathcal{I}_w}$$
$$\Leftrightarrow d \in (\exists \tau_\varepsilon^{-1}(\tau_\varepsilon(s)). \tau_\varepsilon^{-1}(\tau_\varepsilon(D)))^{\mathcal{I}_w}$$
$$\Leftrightarrow d \in (\tau_\varepsilon^{-1}(\tau_\varepsilon(\exists s. D)))^{\mathcal{I}_w}.$$

The case of C being a value restriction or a qualified $\geq$-restriction can be treated analogously. $\qquad\square$

Lemma 6. *Let $\mathcal{I}$ be a quasi-uniform probabilistic interpretation with $\tfrac{1}{\varepsilon}$ possible worlds. Then for all individuals $d \in \Delta^{\mathcal{I}}$, all worlds $w \in W$, and all $\mathbb{P}_{\geq}\mathcal{FLE}^{\perp}\mathcal{Q}^{\geq}$-concept descriptions C, the following equivalence holds:*

$$d \in C^{\mathcal{I}_w} \Leftrightarrow (d, w) \in \tau_\varepsilon(C)^{\mathcal{I}^\times}.$$

Proof. analogously to Lemma 1. We only show the induction step for a concept description $\mathbb{P}_{\geq p} C$ where $p \in (\varepsilon, 1)$. According to the definition of τ_ε, we have that $\tau_\varepsilon(\mathbb{P}_{\geq p} C) = \geq \lceil \frac{p}{\varepsilon} \rceil . \omega_\mathbb{P} . \tau_\varepsilon(C)$. Furthermore, the following equivalences hold:

$$d \in (\mathbb{P}_{\geq p} C)^{\mathcal{I}_w} \Leftrightarrow \mathbb{P}\{ v \in W \mid d \in C^{\mathcal{I}_v} \} \geq p$$

$$\Leftrightarrow \exists^{\geq \lceil \frac{p}{\varepsilon} \rceil} v \in W_\varepsilon : d \in C^{\mathcal{I}_v}$$

$$\overset{\text{I.H.}}{\Leftrightarrow} \exists^{\geq \lceil \frac{p}{\varepsilon} \rceil} v \in W : ((d, w), (d, v)) \in \omega_\mathbb{P}^{\mathcal{I}^\times} \text{ and } (d, v) \in \tau_\varepsilon(C)^{\mathcal{I}^\times}$$

$$\Leftrightarrow (d, w) \in (\geq \lceil \frac{p}{\varepsilon} \rceil . \omega_\mathbb{P} . \tau_\varepsilon(C))^{\mathcal{I}^\times} . \qquad \Box$$

6   Construction of a Base of GCIs in $\mathbb{P}_{\geq} \mathcal{FLE}^\perp \mathcal{Q}^{\geq}$

In the previous section 4 we have seen how a base of $\mathbb{P}_{01} \mathcal{FLE}^\perp$-GCIs holding in a probabilistic interpretation $\mathcal{I}$ can be constructed by means of a base of $\mathcal{FLE}^\perp$-GCIs holding in the induced interpretation $\mathcal{I}^\times$ over the extended signature $(N_C, N_R)_{01}^\mathbb{P}$. Similar results can be obtained in the case of a uniform probabilistic interpretation in the description logic $\mathbb{P}_{\geq} \mathcal{FLE}^\perp \mathcal{Q}^{\geq}$. A more sophisticated answer is given below.

Lemma 7. *Let $\mathcal{I}$ be a quasi-uniform probabilistic interpretation with $\frac{1}{\varepsilon}$ possible worlds, and C, D let be $\mathbb{P}_{\geq} \mathcal{FLE}^\perp \mathcal{Q}^{\geq}$-concept descriptions. Then the general concept inclusion $C \sqsubseteq D$ is valid in $\mathcal{I}$ if and only if the translated GCI $\tau_\varepsilon(C) \sqsubseteq \tau_\varepsilon(D)$ is valid in $\mathcal{I}^\times$.*

Proof. analogously to Lemma 2. $\Box$

Proposition 8. *Let $\mathcal{I}$ be a quasi-uniform probabilistic interpretation with $\frac{1}{\varepsilon}$ possible worlds. If $\mathcal{B}$ is a base of $\mathcal{FLE}^\perp \mathcal{Q}^{\geq}$-GCIs for the induced interpretation $\mathcal{I}^\times$, then the translation*

$$\tau_\varepsilon^{-1}(\mathcal{B}) := \{ \tau_\varepsilon^{-1}(C) \sqsubseteq \tau_\varepsilon^{-1}(D) \mid C \sqsubseteq D \in \mathcal{B} \}$$

is a base of $\mathbb{P}_{\geq} \mathcal{FLE}^\perp \mathcal{Q}^{\geq}$-GCIs for $\mathcal{I}$.

Proof. analogously to Proposition 3. $\Box$

7   Probabilistic Model-Based Most-Specific Concept Descriptions

Model-based most-specific concept descriptions (w.r.t. interpretations) have been introduced by Baader and Distel in [1,2] as an adaption of the well-known notion of most-specific concept descriptions (w.r.t. knowledge bases). Ecke, Peñaloza, and Turhan, investigated those most-specific concept descriptions and also least common subsumers in probabilistic extensions of the light-weight description logic $\mathcal{EL}$, cf. [9,10,13–15]. However, they gave constructions for those generalizations w.r.t. knowledge bases (w.r.t. open-world assumption). In the following text the notion of a probabilistic mmsc w.r.t. interpretations (w.r.t. closed-world assumption) is introduced. Furthermore, we present a proposition that reduces their computation to crisp description logics.

Definition 9. *Let $\mathcal{I} = (\Delta^{\mathcal{I}}, W, (\cdot^{\mathcal{I}_w})_{w \in W}, \mathbb{P})$ be a probabilistic interpretation and $X \subseteq \Delta^{\mathcal{I}}$ a set of individuals. Then a $\mathbb{P}_{01}\mathcal{FLE}^{\perp}$-concept description C is called* probabilistic model-based most-specific concept description (pmmsc) *of X in $\mathcal{I}$ if it satisfies the following conditions:*

(PM1) For all worlds $w \in W$ it holds that $X \subseteq C^{\mathcal{I}_w}$.
(PM2) If D is a $\mathbb{P}_{01}\mathcal{FLE}^{\perp}$-concept description such that $X \subseteq \bigcap_{w \in W} D^{\mathcal{I}_w}$, then $C \sqsubseteq D$.

In the same way we may define the pmmsc in $\mathbb{P}_{\geq}\mathcal{FLE}^{\perp}\mathcal{Q}^{\geq}$.

All pmmscs for a subset X in $\mathcal{I}$ are equivalent, and hence we shall denote the pmmsc by $X^{\mathcal{I}}$.

Proposition 10. *Let $\mathcal{I}$ be a probabilistic interpretation and $X \subseteq \Delta^{\mathcal{I}}$ a set of individuals. Then the following statements hold:*

1. *The $\mathbb{P}_{01}\mathcal{FLE}^{\perp}$-mmsc $X^{\mathcal{I}}$ is equivalent to the translation $\tau^{-1}((X \times W)^{\mathcal{I}^{\times}})$.*
2. *If $\mathcal{I}$ is quasi-uniform with $\frac{1}{\varepsilon}$ possible worlds, then the $\mathbb{P}_{\geq}\mathcal{FLE}^{\perp}\mathcal{Q}^{\geq}$-mmsc $X^{\mathcal{I}}$ is equivalent to the translation $\tau_{\varepsilon}^{-1}((X \times W)^{\mathcal{I}^{\times}})$.*

Proof. Both statements can be proven analogously. We show the two conditions of a pmmsc according to Definition 9.

Firstly, the definition of the mmsc in the default setting yields that $X \times W \subseteq (X \times W)^{\mathcal{I}^{\times}\mathcal{I}^{\times}}$. From Lemmata 1 and 6 it follows that $X \subseteq (\tau^{-1}((X \times W)^{\mathcal{I}^{\times}}))^{\mathcal{I}_w}$ for all worlds $w \in W$, i.e., $\tau^{-1}((X \times W)^{\mathcal{I}^{\times}})$ satisfies (PM1).

Secondly, consider a concept description D such that $X \subseteq D^{\mathcal{I}_w}$ for all worlds $w \in W$. Consequently, by Lemmata 1 and 6 it follows that $X \times \{w\} \subseteq \tau(D)^{\mathcal{I}^{\times}}$ for all $w \in W$, i.e., $X \times W \subseteq \tau(D)^{\mathcal{I}^{\times}}$ is true. By definition of mmscs, we conclude that $(X \times W)^{\mathcal{I}^{\times}} \sqsubseteq \tau(D)$. Then Lemmata 2 and 7 yield that $\tau^{-1}(X \times W)^{\mathcal{I}^{\times}} \sqsubseteq D$, and hence $\tau^{-1}(X \times W)^{\mathcal{I}^{\times}}$ satisfies (PM2). $\square$

8 Choice of Semantics

Upon translation of the probabilistic interpretation $\mathcal{I}$ to the crisp interpretation $\mathcal{I}^{\times}$, we have to introduce the additional role $\omega_{\mathbb{P}}$ to encode the possibility of worlds. However, this leads to cyclic interpretations as then every pair (p, w) is connected to all pairs (p, v) where $v \in W_{\varepsilon}$ is a possible world. Of course, $\mathcal{I}$ must contain at least one possible world to ensure that $\mathbb{P}(W_{\varepsilon}) = 1$ holds. However, in cyclic interpretations like $\mathcal{I}^{\times}$ all model-based most-specific concept descriptions only exist w.r.t. a role-depth bound, cf. [6], or in gfp-semantics, cf. [7]. The limitation of the role-depth is a practical means to ensure the existence of mmscs and is used here.

Usually, mmscs are computed from description graphs induced by interpretations. It turns out that in the case of interpretations constructed from probabilistic interpretations we do not have to consider all paths in the graph. In particular, the following lemma shows that we may ignore paths with two subsequent $Q\,\omega_{\mathbb{P}}$-edges where Q is one of the quantifiers $\exists$, $\forall$, or $\geq n$.

Lemma 11. *For arbitrary* $\mathbb{P}_{\geq}\mathcal{FLE}^{\perp}\mathcal{Q}^{\geq}$*-concept descriptions* C, D *and probability thresholds* $p, q \in [0, 1]$ *the following equivalence holds:*

$$\mathbb{P}_{\geq p}\,(C \sqcap \mathbb{P}_{\geq q}\,D) \equiv \mathbb{P}_{\geq p}\,C \sqcap \mathbb{P}_{\geq q}\,D.$$

Proof. The statement easily follows from the following observations:

$$d \in (\mathbb{P}_{\geq p}\,(C \sqcap \mathbb{P}_{\geq q}\,D))^{\mathcal{I}_w}$$
$$\Leftrightarrow \mathbb{P}\{\,v \in W \mid d \in C^{\mathcal{I}_v}\text{ and }\mathbb{P}\{\,u \in W \mid d \in D^{\mathcal{I}_u}\,\} \geq q\,\} \geq p$$
$$\Leftrightarrow \mathbb{P}\{\,v \in W \mid d \in C^{\mathcal{I}_v}\,\} \geq p \text{ and } \mathbb{P}\{\,u \in W \mid d \in D^{\mathcal{I}_u}\,\} \geq q$$
$$\Leftrightarrow d \in (\mathbb{P}_{\geq p}\,C \sqcap \mathbb{P}_{\geq q}\,D)^{\mathcal{I}_w}.$$

As the equivalences hold for arbitrary probabilistic interpretations $\mathcal{I}$ and worlds $w \in W$, the concept equivalence is true in general. $\qquad\square$

The lemma above yields (after translation w.r.t. τ, or τ_ε, respectively) that in order to compute model-based most-specific concept descriptions we do not have to consider any paths in the description graph of $\mathcal{I}^{\times}$ that have two subsequent $Q\,\omega_{\mathbb{P}}$-edges.

However, we cannot interchange $\exists r$ and $\mathbb{P}_{\geq p}$ restrictions as even in the simplest case the concept descriptions $\exists r.\,\mathbb{P}_{\geq \frac{1}{2}}\,A$ and $\mathbb{P}_{\geq \frac{1}{2}}\,\exists r.\,A$ may have different extensions in a probabilistic interpretation. Consider for example the uniform probabilistic interpretation $\mathcal{I} = (\{\,d, e\,\}, \{\,v, w\,\}, {}^{\mathcal{I}_v}, {}^{\mathcal{I}_w}, \{\{\,v\,\} \mapsto \frac{1}{2}, \{\,w\,\} \mapsto \frac{1}{2}\,\})$. The extension functions are given by the two graphs below:

Then it holds that $(\exists r.\,\mathbb{P}_{\geq \frac{1}{2}}\,A)^{\mathcal{I}_{w_1}} = \{\,d\,\}$, but $(\mathbb{P}_{\geq \frac{1}{2}}\,\exists r.\,A)^{\mathcal{I}_{w_1}} = \emptyset$.

For the computation of the induced interpretation $\mathcal{I}^{\times}$ all vertices in the two graphs above are equipped with $\omega_{\mathbb{P}}$-loops and furthermore there are $\omega_{\mathbb{P}}$-edges between vertices for the same individual in different worlds. Then the following mmscs can be obtained:

$$(d, w_1)^{\mathcal{I}^{\times}} = \exists r.\,\mathbb{P}_{>0}\,A \sqcap \mathbb{P}_{>0}\,\exists r.\,\mathbb{P}_{>0}\,A$$
$$(d, w_2)^{\mathcal{I}^{\times}} = \mathbb{P}_{>0}\,\exists r.\,\mathbb{P}_{>0}\,A$$
$$(e, w_1)^{\mathcal{I}^{\times}} = \mathbb{P}_{>0}\,A$$
$$(e, w_2)^{\mathcal{I}^{\times}} = A \sqcap \mathbb{P}_{>0}\,A$$
$$(\Delta^{\mathcal{I}} \times W)^{\mathcal{I}^{\times}} = \top$$

If $\mathcal{I}$ is a probabilistic interpretation such that all mmscs exist in the interpretations $\mathcal{I}_w$ for all worlds $w \in W$, then also all mmscs exist in the induced interpretation $\mathcal{I}^{\times}$. They can be computed by means of restricted unravellings as follows: Consider the description graph $\mathcal{G}_{\mathcal{I}^{\times}}^{(d,w)}$ of $\mathcal{I}^{\times}$ that is rooted at (d, w).

Then we consider the *restricted unravelling* $\mathcal{G}_{\mathcal{I}^\times}^{(d,w)} \upharpoonright_\infty^{\omega_\mathbb{P}}$ such that only paths in $\mathcal{G}_{\mathcal{I}^\times}^{(d,w)}$ that do not have two subsequent $\omega_\mathbb{P}$-edges are allowed as vertices in the restricted unravelling. Since the mmscs in all interpretations $\mathcal{I}_w$ exist, there are no infinite paths from each (e, v). As a consequence, we obtain that all model-based most-specific concept descriptions exist in $\mathcal{I}^\times$.

9   Complexity of Base Construction

In both probabilistic description logics $\mathbb{P}_{01}\mathcal{FLE}^\perp$ and $\mathbb{P}_{\geq}\mathcal{FLE}^\perp\mathcal{Q}^\geq$ the complexity of the construction of a base of GCIs can be double-exponential in the size of the input interpretation. The translation of the probabilistic interpretation $\mathcal{I}$ to the crisp interpretation $\mathcal{I}^\times$ can be obtained in polynomial time. The same holds for the translation of concept descriptions, i.e., they may be translated in polynomial time. Furthermore, the computation of a base of GCIs for a crisp interpretation has double-exponential time complexity in the worst case. This is due to the fact that the necessary induced context $\mathbb{K}_\mathcal{I}$ of an interpretation may have exponential size in $\mathcal{I}$ (since there may be exponentially many model-based most-specific concept descriptions for $\mathcal{I}$), and furthermore the canonical implicational base of a formal context may have an exponential size w.r.t. the size of the formal context. Hence, the construction of bases of GCIs for probabilistic interpretations also has a double-exponential time complexity in the worst case.

10   Conclusion

We have defined translations between probabilistic description logics and crisp description logics that preserve entailment of general concept inclusions. They have been used to reduce the problem of construction of a base of GCIs for a probabilistic interpretation to the same problem in crisp description logics for which a well-known and practical solution exists. For this purpose we used the description $\mathcal{FLE}^\perp\mathcal{Q}^\geq$ that was equipped with probabilistic role and concept constructors, in the first case only allowing probabilities > 0 and $= 1$ to express *possibility* and *certainty almost everywhere*, and in the other case only allowing for lower-bound probabilities $\geq p$ where $p \in (0, 1]$.

Furthermore, we have shown how most-specific concept descriptions can be constructed for probabilistic interpretations – again by a reduction to the crisp case.

References

1. Baader, F., Distel, F.: A finite basis for the set of $\mathcal{EL}$-implications holding in a finite model. Tech. rep. 07–02. Dresden, Germany: Inst. für Theoretische Informatik, TU Dresden (2007)
2. Baader, F., Distel, F.: A finite basis for the set of $\mathcal{EL}$-implications holding in a finite model. In: Medina, R., Obiedkov, S. (eds.) ICFCA 2008. LNCS (LNAI), vol. 4933, pp. 46–61. Springer, Heidelberg (2008)

3. Baader, F., et al. (eds.): The Description Logic Handbook: Theory, Implementation, and Applications. Cambridge University Press, New York (2003). ISBN 0-521-78176-0
4. Borchmann, D.: Learning Terminological Knowledge with High Confidence from Erroneous Data. Ph.D. thesis. Dresden, Germany: Dresden University of Technology (2014)
5. Borchmann, D.: Towards an error-tolerant construction of $\mathcal{EL}^{\perp}$-ontologies from data using formal concept analysis. In: Cellier, P., Distel, F., Ganter, B. (eds.) ICFCA 2013. LNCS, vol. 7880, pp. 60–75. Springer, Heidelberg (2013)
6. Borchmann, D., Distel, F., Kriegel, F.: Axiomatization of General Concept Inclusions from Finite Interpretations. LTCS-Report 15–13. Dresden, Germany: Chair for Automata Theory, Institute for Theoretical Computer Science, Technische Universität Dresden (2015)
7. Distel, F.: Learning Description Logic Knowledge Bases from Data using Methods from Formal Concept Analysis. Ph.D. thesis. Dresden, Germany: Dresden University of Technology (2011)
8. Distel, F.: Model-based Most Specific Concepts in Description Logics with Value Restrictions. Tech. rep. 08–04. Dresden, Germany: Institute for theoretical computer science, TU Dresden (2008)
9. Ecke, A., Peñaloza, R., Turhan, A.-Y.: Completion-based Generalization Inferences for the Description Logic $\mathcal{ELOR}$ with Subjective Probabilities. International Journal of Approximate Reasoning 55(9), 1939–1970 (2014)
10. Ecke, A., Peñaloza, R., Turhan, A.-Y.: Role-depth bounded least common subsumer in prob-$\mathcal{EL}$ with nominals. In: Eiter, T., et al. (eds.) Proceedings of the 26th International Workshop on Description Logics (DL-2013), vol. 1014. CEUR-WS. Ulm, Germany, pp. 670–688 (2013)
11. Kriegel, F.: Extracting ALEQR(Self)-knowledge bases from graphs. In: Proceedings of the International Workshop on Social Network Analysis Using Formal Concept Analysis (SNAFCA-2015). CEUR Workshop Proceedings. CEUR-WS.org (2015)
12. Lutz, C., Schröder, L.: Probabilistic description logics for subjective uncertainty. In: Principles of Knowledge Representation and Reasoning: Proceedings of the Twelfth International Conference, KR 2010, Toronto, Ontario, Canada, May 9–13, 2010
13. Peñaloza, R., Turhan, A.-Y.: Instance-based non-standard inferences in $\mathcal{EL}$ with subjective probabilities. In: Bobillo, F., Costa, P.C.G., d'Amato, C., Fanizzi, N., Laskey, K.B., Laskey, K.J., Lukasiewicz, T., Nickles, M., Pool, M. (eds.) URSW 2008-2010/UniDL 2010. LNCS, vol. 7123, pp. 80–98. Springer, Heidelberg (2013)
14. Peñaloza, R., Turhan, A.-Y.: Role-depth bounded least common subsumers by completion for $\mathcal{EL}$- and prob-$\mathcal{EL}$-TBoxes. In: Haarslev, V., Toman, D., Weddell, G. (eds.) Proc. of the 2010 Description Logic Workshop (DL 2010), vol. 573. CEUR-WS (2010)
15. Peñaloza, R., Turhan, A.-Y.: Towards approximative most specific concepts by completion for $\mathcal{EL}$ with subjective probabilities. In: Lukasiewicz, T., Peñaloza, R., Turhan, A.-Y. (eds.) Proceedings of the First International Workshop on Uncertainty in Description Logics (UniDL 2010), vol. 613. CEUR-WS (2010)

Kernel Feature Maps from Arbitrary Distance Metrics

Markus Schneider[1,2]([⊠]), Wolfgang Ertel[2], and Günther Palm[1]

[1] Institute of Neural Information Processing, University of Ulm, Ulm, Germany
mschneider@linkdot.org
[2] Institute for Artificial Intelligence, Ravensburg-Weingarten University of Applied Sciences, Weingarten, Germany

Abstract. The approximation of kernel functions using explicit feature maps gained a lot of attention in recent years due to the tremendous speed up in training and learning time of kernel-based algorithms, making them applicable to very large-scale problems. For example, approximations based on random Fourier features are an efficient way to create feature maps for a certain class of scale invariant kernel functions. However, there are still many kernels for which there exists no algorithm to derive such maps. In this work we propose an efficient method to create approximate feature maps from an *arbitrary distance metric* using pseudo line projections called *Distance-Based Feature Map* (DBFM). We show that our approximation does not depend on the input dataset size or the dimension of the input space. We experimentally evaluate our approach on two real datasets using two metric and one non-metric distance function.

1 Introduction

Kernel methods such as the Support Vector Machine (SVM) are among the most effective tools in machine learning. They can be applied in various applications, for example in classification [21], anomaly detection [19], clustering [4], dimensionality reduction [7,20] and regression [16,23]. The strength of these methods is the transformation of the original input space $\mathcal{X}$ into a high dimensional feature space $\mathcal{H}$ where simple, linear methods can be applied to gain a similar predictive power as non-linear algorithms. The idea is that kernel methods do not work with the embedding $\phi\colon \mathcal{X} \to \mathcal{H}$ directly, but with the inner product $\langle \phi(x), \phi(y) \rangle = k(x, y)$ implicitly defined by the kernel function k. A key is the observation that as long as one has access to the kernel k it is not necessary to represent $\phi(x)$ explicitly. For example the linear approximation of a function f in $\mathcal{H}$ can be represented as

$$f(x) = \langle w, \phi(x) \rangle = \left\langle \sum_{i=1}^{n} \alpha_i \phi(x_i), \phi(x) \right\rangle = \sum_{i=1}^{n} \alpha_i k(x_i, x), \qquad (1)$$

where $\alpha_i \in \mathbb{R}$ for all $1 \leq i \leq n$. The Representer Theorem [9] guarantees the existence of such an expansion under fairly reasonable conditions.

© Springer International Publishing Switzerland 2015
S. Hölldobler et al. (Eds.): KI 2015, LNAI 9324, pp. 137–150, 2015.
DOI: 10.1007/978-3-319-24489-1_11

Kernel methods are also preferred since it is often easier to define the similarity between two objects than to choose meaningful features. For example if a distance function $\tau \colon \mathcal{X} \times \mathcal{X} \to \mathbb{R}$ obeys certain properties[1], then

$$k(x, y) = \exp\left(-\gamma\tau(x, y)\right) \tag{2}$$

is a positive semidefinite kernel for all $\gamma \geq 0$ and can be seen as the similarity between x and y as shown in [3].

Unfortunately most kernel methods do not scale with the size of the training data set. For example algorithms operating on the kernel matrix exhibit a training time quadratic in the number of samples. Also a representation as in Eq. (1) can become problematic in situations where predictions have to be made in high frequency as [25] showed that the number of support vectors can grow linearly with the size of the training set. This cost can be prohibitive in many large-scale problems.

To overcome this problem, efforts are made to explicitly use the feature map ϕ. For example the *linear* Support Vector Machine can be efficiently trained and evaluate the decision boundary, both in constant time and memory [22]. However, the feature map ϕ can rarely be calculated in practice as the feature space $\mathcal{H}$ is usually infinite dimensional. But it is often possible to derive a finite dimensional approximation $\hat{\phi}\colon \mathcal{X} \to \mathbb{R}^r$ such that

$$k(x, y) \approx \langle\hat{\phi}(x), \hat{\phi}(y)\rangle. \tag{3}$$

Up to now, such an approximation can only be calculated for certain types of kernel function which we will review in the next section.

In this work we present an explicit feature map for kernels defined as in Eq. (2). More formally we solve the following problem:

Problem 1. Given a metric space $(\mathcal{X}, \tau)$, where $\mathcal{X}$ is a set and τ a metric on $\mathcal{X}$. Derive a feature function $\hat{\phi}$ such that

$$\exp\left(-\gamma\tau(x, y)\right) \approx \langle\hat{\phi}(x), \hat{\phi}(y)\rangle \tag{4}$$

for all $x, y \in \mathcal{X}$ and some $\gamma \in \mathbb{R}$.

Solving this problem has far-reaching implications since every positive definite kernel k induces a distance function by

$$\tau(x, y)^2 = k(x, x) + k(y, y) - 2k(x, y) \tag{5}$$

and hence we can define feature maps based on arbitrary kernels.

Our contribution is an approach, called *Distance-Based Feature Map* (DBFM), to efficiently tackle Problem 1 with computational complexity independent of the dataset size and the dimension of the input space, hence making it applicable to very large-scale applications. Today, this is the only technique to derive explicit feature maps from arbitrary distance metrics.

---

[1] τ needs to be a kernel of conditionally negative type. See [3]

The remainder of the paper is structured as follows: We begin with the formal definition of a kernel and feature function in terms of a reproducing kernel Hilbert space. Then we will review among other feature map approximations the Random Kitchen Sink approach which we will utilize in the subsequent section. We show the FastMap projection can be used to derive our Distance-Based Feature Map approach. In the last section we experimentally evaluate our approach on two real datasets using two metric distances and show that even with non-metric distance functions we can achieve a reasonable performance.

2 Related Work

Subsequently we will use $\mathcal{S}$ to denote the training dataset $\mathcal{S} = \{x_1, \ldots, x_n\} \subset \mathcal{X}$ with n samples.

Following [26] a Hilbert space $(\mathcal{H}, \langle \cdot, \cdot \rangle)$ of functions $f : \mathcal{X} \to \mathbb{R}$ is said to be a *reproducing kernel Hilbert space* (RKHS) if the evaluation functional $\delta_x : \mathcal{H} \to \mathbb{R}$, $\delta_x : f \mapsto f(x)$ is continuous. The function $k : \mathcal{X} \times \mathcal{X} \to \mathbb{R}$ which satisfies the reproducing property

$$\langle f(\cdot), k(x, \cdot) \rangle = f(x) \quad \text{and in particular} \tag{6}$$

$$\langle k(x, \cdot), k(y, \cdot) \rangle = k(x, y). \tag{7}$$

is called the *reproducing kernel* of $\mathcal{H}$, where $\langle \cdot, \cdot \rangle$ denotes the inner product. We call a function $\phi : \mathcal{X} \to \mathcal{H}$ *feature map* if

$$k(x, y) = \langle \phi(x), \phi(y) \rangle \tag{8}$$

and we will use the notation $\phi(x) = k(x, \cdot)$.

2.1 Kernel Approximations

The key idea behind Random Kitchen Sinks (RKS) introduced in [14,15] is to approximate a given kernel by a function $\hat{\phi}$ such that

$$k(x, y) \approx \langle \hat{\phi}(x), \hat{\phi}(y) \rangle. \tag{9}$$

This approximation is based on Bochner's theorem for translation invariant kernels (such as the Gaussian RBF, Laplace, Matérn covariance, etc.) which states that such a kernel can be represented as

$$k(x, y) = \int_z \phi_z^\star(x) \phi_z(y) \lambda(z) \text{ with } \phi_z(x) = e^{i\langle z, x \rangle}, \tag{10}$$

where $\phi^\star$ is the complex conjugate of ϕ. If the measure λ is normalized to be a probability measure, the expression above represents an expectation and can be estimated as

$$k(x, y) \approx \frac{1}{r} \sum_{i=1}^{r} \phi_{z_i}^\star(x) \phi_{z_i}(y) \tag{11}$$

using r samples from λ. The sum above can then be reformulated as an inner product yielding $k(x,y) \approx \langle \hat{\phi}(x), \hat{\phi}(y) \rangle$. Often λ is found by applying the inverse Fourier Transform to the kernel as in the next example.

For the Gaussian RBF kernel

$$k(x,y) = \exp\left(-\frac{\|x-y\|^2}{2\sigma^2} \right), \tag{12}$$

λ is the normal distribution with variance σ^2. Hence an approximation can be generated as

$$Z \in \mathbb{R}^{r \times d} \text{ with } Z_{ij} \sim \mathcal{N}(0, \sigma^2) \tag{13}$$

$$\hat{\phi}(x) = \frac{1}{\sqrt{r}} \exp(iZx), \tag{14}$$

where d is the input space dimension and r is the number of basis function expansions. Recently [10] proposed an approximation to Z such that the product Zx can be calculated in $\mathcal{O}(r \log d)$ while requiring $\mathcal{O}(r)$ storage. Theoretical bounds of the RKHS approximation can be found in [15]. In general, the approximate accuracy increases with the number of samples r.

This idea gained a lot of attention and was further developed in several ways: Still based on Bochner's theorem, the Random Kitchen Sink approach was further generalized to the class of histogram-based kernels in [11]. Approximate feature maps for additive homogeneous kernels of the form

$$k(x,y) = \sum_{i=1}^{n} k_i(x_i, y_i) \tag{15}$$

had been introduced by [28]. The authors of [8] presented an approximation for positive definite dot product kernels of the form $k(x,y) = f(\langle x,y \rangle)$.

2.2 Nyström's Feature Map

An alternative to the random feature map approximation are Nyström methods [29] which use only a random subset of the training data. It projects the data into a subspace spanned by r vectors $\phi(x_1), \ldots, \phi(x_r)$ calculated from the kernel matrix

$$K \in \mathbb{R}^{n \times n} \tag{16}$$

$$K_{i,j} = k(x_i, x_j). \tag{17}$$

For $i = 1, \ldots, n$ let λ_i, v_i be the eigenvalues and eigenvectors respectively. The Nyström feature map $\hat{\phi}$ is then given by

$$\hat{\phi}(x) = D^{-\frac{1}{2}} V^T [k(x, x_1), \ldots, k(x, x_r)]^T \tag{18}$$

where D is the diagonal matrix containing the first r eigenvalues and $V = (v_1, \ldots, v_r)$.

3   Distance Based Feature Maps

The approach we propose represents the distance function τ in a way such that kernel approximations like the Random Kitchen Sink method can be applied to create an explicit features map $\hat{\xi}$ with the property

$$\langle \hat{\xi}(x), \hat{\xi}(y) \rangle \approx \exp\left(-\gamma \tau(x, y)\right). \tag{19}$$

In the first step we project the elements from $\mathcal{X}$ into an Euclidean space $\mathbb{R}^t$, $t \in \mathbb{N}$ such that distances are preserved. This can be achieved with random line projections called *FastMap* as introduced in [6]. It was originally proposed as an approach to map points onto a low-dimensional manifold such that dissimilarities are approximately preserved, when only a distance function is provided. FastMap can also be used as an alternative to Multi-Dimensional Scaling (MDS) [27] for visualization purposes or to tackle the problem of approximate nearest neighbor retrieval [2].

The basic idea of FastMap to define a t-dimensional embedding is to project an object $x \in \mathcal{X}$ onto a line defined by two *pivot points* $p, q \in \mathcal{X}$. This projection can be derived from the cosine law and is given by

$$L_{p,q}(x) = \frac{\tau(x, p)^2 + \tau(p, q)^2 - \tau(x, q)^2}{2\tau(p, q)} \tag{20}$$

as illustrated in Fig. 1. The points are r times iteratively projected to the hyperplanes perpendicular to an orthogonal set of previous hyperplanes. The pivot points are chosen in a way such that p and q are the most dissimilar objects: First q is randomly selected from the set of all data points. The point that is farthest apart from q is selected as p. In the last step q is updated to be point farthest apart from p. Thus, the complexity of FastMap is $\mathcal{O}(tn)$ while requiring $\mathcal{O}(td)$ storage for the pivots.

We propose an approach based on the FastMap embedding with some modifications. Notice that for large datasets it is not feasible to iterate t times over all n data points to find the pivot elements. For example the linear Support Vector

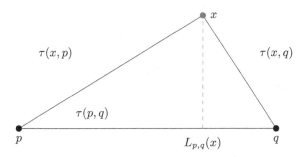

Fig. 1. The pseudo line projection from Eq. (20). x is the point to project with p and q as pivot points.

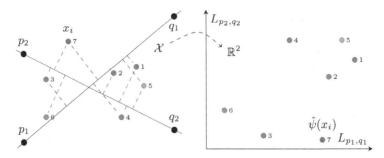

Fig. 2. A sketch of Distance Based Random Features. The points x_i are projected onto the lines spanned by (p_1, q_1) and (p_2, q_2). The position on these lines (calculated with $L_{p_1,q_1}(x)$ and $L_{p_2,q_2}(x)$) define their coordinates in the new space on the right.

Machine can find a separating hyperplane using only a subset of the training data. Hence it would be impractical to have a computational complexity linear in n to calculate the feature function.

Therefore, we suggest to sample t pivot pairs from the training dataset $\mathcal{S}$

$$\mathcal{P} = \{(p_1, q_1), \ldots, (p_t, q_t)\} \subset \mathcal{S} \times \mathcal{S} \tag{21}$$

$$\text{with } p_i \neq q_i \quad 1 \leq i \leq t \tag{22}$$

and use these to calculate t line projections[2] reducing the computational complexity to $\mathcal{O}(t)$. Based on the FastMap projections we form the mapping

$$\hat{\psi} \colon \mathcal{X} \to \mathbb{R}^t \tag{23}$$

$$\hat{\psi}(x) = \left(L_{p_1,q_1}(x), \ldots, L_{p_t,q_t}(x)\right)^T \tag{24}$$

which we will refer to as the *projection map*. The projection map takes an element $x \in \mathcal{X}$, applies all t line projections with pivot elements from $\mathcal{P}$ and collects the result in a vector as sketched in Fig. 2. Since FastMap attempts to preserve dissimilarities we have that $\|\hat{\psi}(x) - \hat{\psi}(y)\|$ is approximately proportional to $\tau(x, y)$. Hence we can find an $\alpha \geq 0$ which depends on γ to approximate the kernel function from Eq. (2) in terms of the projection map as

$$\exp\left(-\alpha \|\hat{\psi}(x) - \hat{\psi}(y)\|\right) \approx \exp\left(-\gamma \tau(x, y)\right). \tag{25}$$

This is an important reformulation in which we replaced the distance function by a norm. The vectors $\psi(x)$ and $\psi(y)$ are both elements of $\mathbb{R}^t$ with dimension independent of the input space dimension.

---

[2] It is also possible to run the original pivot choosing algorithm on the reduced set $\mathcal{P}$ in $\mathcal{O}(t^2)$, however, this did (experimentally) not yield better results as random pivots.

The approximation from Eq. (25) now allows the applications of the Random Kitchen Sink approach to create explicit feature maps $\hat{\xi}$ as

$$\hat{\xi}(x) = \hat{\phi}(\psi(x)) = \frac{1}{\sqrt{r}} \exp\left(iZ\hat{\psi}(x)\right) \text{ where} \tag{26}$$

$$Z \in \mathbb{R}^{r \times t} \text{ with } Z_{ij} \sim \mathcal{N}(0, \alpha^{-2}) \tag{27}$$

resulting in the final approximation

$$\langle \hat{\xi}(x), \hat{\xi}(y) \rangle \approx \exp\left(-\gamma\tau(x, y)\right) \tag{28}$$

forming an explicit feature map which is the final result of our work. The overall complexity for the feature map calculation itself is $\mathcal{O}(t + r \log t)$ while requiring $\mathcal{O}(r + td)$ storage. Both t and r influence the approximation accuracy and do not depend on the dimension of the data or the number of samples in the training dataset which makes our approach applicable to very large-scale applications. However, the computational complexity of our proposed approach depends on the computational complexity of the distance function through $L_{p,q}$ in Eq. (20). If the distance function can not be evaluated efficiently the approximation will be accordingly slower.

Remarks

Alternatively to an exponential kernel as in Eq. (28) we can also use $\hat{\psi}$ to create another kernel based on τ as:

$$s(x, y) = -\frac{1}{2}\|\hat{\psi}(x) - \hat{\psi}(y)\|^2 + \frac{1}{2}\|\hat{\psi}(x) - \hat{\psi}(x_0)\|^2 + \frac{1}{2}\|\hat{\psi}(y) - \hat{\psi}(x_0)\|^2$$

$$= \langle \hat{\psi}(x), \hat{\psi}(y) \rangle + \langle \hat{\psi}(x_0), \hat{\psi}(x_0) \rangle - \langle \hat{\psi}(x), \hat{\psi}(x_0) \rangle - \langle \hat{\psi}(y), \hat{\psi}(x_0) \rangle$$

where x_0 is an arbitrary point in $\mathcal{X}$ (see also [18]). It is not hart to see that the sum in the last equation can be written as a single inner product

$$\langle \hat{\psi}(x) - \hat{\psi}(x_0), \hat{\psi}(y) - \hat{\psi}(x_0) \rangle$$

and is therefore a feature map of $s(x, y)$.

The proposed approach depends on several parameters γ, r and t. The parameter γ is common for the squared exponential (or Gaussian RBF) kernel. This parameter is typically found by means of cross-validation.

The parameters r and t control the accuracy for the Random Kitchen Sink and Distance Based Random Feature approximations respectively. It is a trade-off between speed and precision. r is typically between 5.000 and 20.000, where t strongly depends on the distance function. In our experiments we achieved a reasonable performance with r between 100 to 200. The higher these parameters, the better is the feature map approximation.

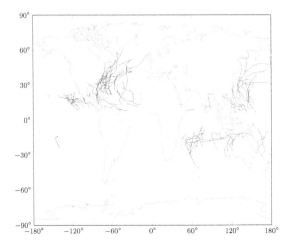

Fig. 3. Random samples from the hurricane dataset.

4   Experimental Results

In this section we use three different distance functions to create explicit feature maps using the approach presented in this work which is based on random line projections.

We compare the left and the right hand side of Eq. (28) which are the proposed approximate feature map and the kernel created by a given distance function, respectively. We will compare the values of $\langle \hat{\xi}(x), \hat{\xi}(y) \rangle$ and $\exp\left(-\gamma \tau(x, y)\right)$ graphically in a scatter plot where ideally all points lie on the diagonal line. For a quantitative comparison we use *Spearman's rank correlation coefficient* (Spearman's rho) [24] which measures the statistical dependence between two variables. A perfect Spearman correlation of +1 occurs when both variables are monotonically related, even if their relationship is not linear.

For the Random Kitchen Sink approximation we used $r = 10,000$ kernel expansions in all our experiments. The number of random projections t (pivot pairs) is varied and the effects on the approximation quality as well as the runtime are evaluated. Each experiment was repeated 10 times and we present these raw result without averaging.

In the following we empirically evaluate three different distance measures on two different datasets. The first experiment is conducted on the discrete Fréchet distance.

4.1   Discrete Fréchet Distance

The Fréchet distance between two curves in a metric space can be used as a measure between them. The work of [5] presents a discrete variation of this measure. An intuitive definition of the Fréchet distance is the minimal distance required to connect points on two curves. It is often illustrated as a dog on one curve and its handler on another curve. Both are connected through a leash and can only go forward, but vary their speed. The Fréchet distance is minimal length of any leash necessary such that both, the dog and its handler can move the curves from the starting points to the endpoints.

In this experiment we build an explicit feature map using the discrete Fréchet distance and evaluate in empirically on the *hurricane dataset*.

The hurricane dataset contains 7057 records of hurricane tracks collected by the National Oceanic and Atmospheric Administration[3] (NOAA). We use only the longitude and latitude coordinates which describe the track of each hurricane. The tracks are not necessarily of the same length (as illustrated in Fig. 3) which makes it impossible for example to apply the Euclidean distance.

The results of this experiment are illustrated in Fig. 5. In the plot on the left we see the dependence of Spearman's coefficient on the random projections. We report the result of each of the 10 repetitions and indicate their mean by the solid line. Obviously, the more pivot points are used, the better gets the approximation. Since the pivot pairs are chosen at random there is more variance if fever pairs are used.

Fig. 5b shows the time needed to calculate the kernel value between all pairs of 50 random points. This confirms the linear dependence on the number of pivot pairs as evident from Eq. (20).

The difference between the approximation $\langle \hat{\xi}(x), \hat{\xi}(y) \rangle$ and the target kernel value $\exp(-\gamma \tau(x, y))$ is illustrated in the scatter plot in Fig. 5c, where we used 1000 random samples from the hurricane dataset. Even though there is not a perfect linear dependence, both functions assign a similar rank to the inputs which reflects the impression we got from Spearman's correlation coefficient.

4.2   Hellinger Distance

The Hellinger distance is used as a measure for the similarity between two distributions. It is closely related to the Bhattacharyya distance which we will review in the next experiment. We look at the Hellinger distance first, since unlike the Bhattacharyya distance, it does obey the triangle inequality and is a proper metric.

For two probability distributions P and Q the Bhattacharyya coefficient is defined as

$$BC(P, Q) = \int \sqrt{P(x)Q(x)}\, \mathrm{d}x \qquad (29)$$

for continuous probability distributions and

$$BC(P, Q) = \sum_x \sqrt{P(x)Q(x)} \qquad (30)$$

if P and Q are discrete. The Hellinger distance is then defined as

$$\tau(P, Q) = \sqrt{1 - BC(P, Q)}. \qquad (31)$$

---

[3] http://www.ncdc.noaa.gov/ibtracs/

Fig. 4. Random samples from the 8 Scene Categories dataset.

We apply this distance measure on the *8 Scene Categories* dataset[4] which contains 8 outdoor scene categories: coast, mountain, forest, open country, street, inside city, tall buildings and highways. There are a total of 2600 RGB color images with 256 × 256 pixels. A small subset is shown in Fig. 4. As image features we use color histograms and local binary pattern histograms [12] which are then used as arguments for the Hellinger distance.

The experimental results are shown in Fig. 6. Even for a small number of random samples we get a nearly perfect Spearman correlation coefficient between 0.9990 and 0.9996 and negligible variance. Also the computation time exhibits a lower variance than the one in the previous experiment. This is due to the fact that the histogram features which serve as inputs for the Hellinger distance are all of the same size, whereas the hurricane trajectories vary in length. For the latter, the time for each random projection therefore depends on the chosen pivots. The high Spearman's rho value is also reflected in the scatter plot, where all points are very close to on the diagonal. Notice that the faster computation time is due to the slow evaluation of the discrete Fréchet distance.

4.3   Bhattacharyya Distance

In this experiment we investigate the implications of a non-metric distance measure. We require $(\mathcal{X}, \tau)$ to be a metric space since then the pseudo line projections are theoretically justified and we want to show the effects if this requirement is violated. Experimentally we observed also reasonable results with distance functions which do not obey the triangle inequality such as the Bhattacharyya distance. Other research also supports the usefulness of FastMap embedding for non-metric spaces [1,17].

The Bhattacharyya distance is used to measure the similarity of two probability distributions and is closely related to Hellinger's distance. For two probability

---

[4] http://people.csail.mit.edu/torralba/code/spatialenvelope/

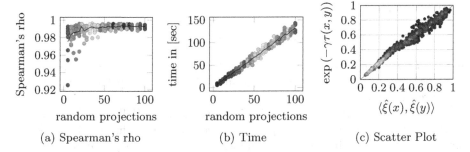

(a) Spearman's rho

(b) Time

(c) Scatter Plot

Fig. 5. Experimental results for the discrete *Fréchet distance*. In (a) we show the effect of the number of pivots on the Spearman's rank correlation coefficient. In (b) we see that time to calculate the feature maps increases linear with the number of pivots. We repeated each experiment 10 times represented by the marker in the plot. The solid black line is the mean and the color indicates the variance. The last figure (c) shows a scatter plot between the approximation and the true kernel value for 1000 random samples from the dataset, where the color is proportional to the density.

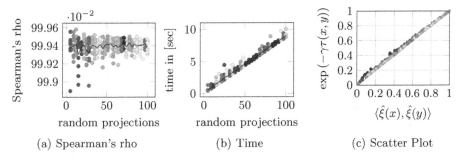

(a) Spearman's rho

(b) Time

(c) Scatter Plot

Fig. 6. Experimental results for the *Hellinger distance*. The plots show the same information as the ones in Fig. 5. The approximation of the Hellinger distance is very accurate in terms of Spearman's rho with a value between 0.9990 and 0.9996 (we rescaled the y-axis for better visualization). This is also reflected in the nearly perfect scatter plot in (c).

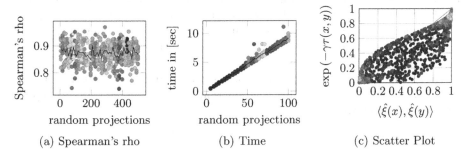

(a) Spearman's rho

(b) Time

(c) Scatter Plot

Fig. 7. Experiments using the *Bhattacharyya distance* exhibit a larger variance for Spearman's correlation coefficient. Also the scatter plot reflects the effect of a non-metric distance measure.

distributions P and Q it is defined as

$$\tau(P, Q) = -\ln\left(BC(P, Q)\right) \tag{32}$$

and used for example in [13] to calculate distances between images. As in the previous experiment we use color histograms and local binary pattern histograms as image features.

The results are illustrated in Fig. 7. In contrast to Hellinger distance we observe a very high variance of Spearman's correlation coefficient. This means the choice of pivot pairs has a high influence on the accuracy. We also do not observe a decrease in variance as in the other experiments when more random projections are used[5]. We assume that this is an effect of the missing triangle inequality since the pseudo line projections as in Fig. 1 are harder to justify.

Nevertheless a rank correlation coefficient above 0.75 can still be useful, but demonstrates some disadvantaged as illustrated the respective scatter plot. However, as mentioned at the beginning we suggest to use the proposed approach solely in metric spaces and only fall back to non-metric distance measures if this is not possible.

5   Conclusion

Explicit representations of kernels as inner product of feature maps results in an enormous speedup in training and prediction time for Support Vector Machines and other kernel-based algorithms and are therefore of central importance. Up to now, one can only derive approximate feature maps for certain types of kernel functions. In this work we presented a methodology which enables us to create explicit feature maps from an *arbitrary* distance metric. In other words we can derive approximate feature maps for *every* kernel of the form $\exp\left(-\gamma\tau(x, y)\right)$ with metric τ. Hence we significantly extended the set of kernels for which approximate feature maps can be calculated.

Furthermore we showed that this feature map can be computed in loglinear time $\mathcal{O}(t + r\log t)$ and $\mathcal{O}(r + td)$ storage, both independent of the size of the training dataset n. This makes our approach applicable to algorithms working on very large-scale applications and datasets. The proposed technique only require two parameters which are easy and intuitively to specify since they only determine the approximation quality. They can be interpreted as a trade-off between speed and precision.

We empirically evaluated our proposed feature map on two metric distance measures and one non-metric distance function. All datasets used in our experiment are publicly available.

---

[5] As shown Fig. 7a we used up to 500 random projections (5 times more than in the other experiments) without a decrease of variance.

References

1. Athitsos, V., Alon, J., Sclaroff, S., Kollios, G.: Learning Embeddings for Fast Approximate Nearest Neighbor Retrieval. Nearest-neighbor Methods in Learning and Vision: Theory and Practice, p. 143 (2005)
2. Athitsos, V., Potamias, M., Papapetrou, P., Kollios, G.: Nearest neighbor retrieval using distance-based hashing. In: IEEE 24th International Conference on Data Engineering, ICDE 2008, pp. 327–336. IEEE (2008)
3. Bekka, B., de La Harpe, P., Valette, A.: Kazhdan's property (T). Cambridge University Press (2008)
4. Dhillon, I.S., Guan, Y., Kulis, B.: Kernel k-means: spectral clustering and normalized cuts. In: Proceedings of the Tenth ACM SIGKDD International Conference on Knowledge Discovery and Data Mining, pp. 551–556. ACM (2004)
5. Eiter, T., Mannila, H.: Computing discrete Fréchet distance. Rapport technique num. CD-TR **94**, 64 (1994)
6. Faloutsos, C., Lin, K.I.: FastMap: A fast algorithm for indexing, data-mining and visualization of traditional and multimedia datasets. In: Proceedings of the 1995 ACM SIGMOD International Conference on Management of Data, vol. 24(2), pp. 163–174 (1995)
7. Fukumizu, K., Bach, F.R., Jordan, M.I.: Dimensionality reduction for supervised learning with reproducing kernel Hilbert spaces. The Journal of Machine Learning Research **5**, 73–99 (2004)
8. Kar, P., Karnick, H.: Random feature maps for dot product kernels. In: International Conference on Artificial Intelligence and Statistics, pp. 583–591 (2012)
9. Kimeldorf, G.S., Wahba, G.: A correspondence between Bayesian estimation on stochastic processes and smoothing by splines. The Annals of Mathematical Statistics, 495–502 (1970)
10. Le, Q., Sarlós, T., Smola, A.: Fastfood: approximating kernel expansions in loglinear time. In: Proceedings of the International Conference on Machine Learning (2013)
11. Li, F., Ionescu, C., Sminchisescu, C.: Random fourier approximations for skewed multiplicative histogram kernels. In: Goesele, M., Roth, S., Kuijper, A., Schiele, B., Schindler, K. (eds.) Pattern Recognition. LNCS, vol. 6376, pp. 262–271. Springer, Heidelberg (2010)
12. Ojala, T., Pietikainen, M., Maenpaa, T.: Multiresolution gray-scale and rotation invariant texture classification with local binary patterns. IEEE Transactions on Pattern Analysis and Machine Intelligence **24**(7), 971–987 (2002)
13. Ott, L., Pang, L., Ramos, F., Howe, D., Chawla, S.: Integer Programming Relaxations for Integrated Clustering and Outlier Detection. arXiv preprint arXiv:1403.1329 (2014)
14. Rahimi, A., Recht, B.: Random features for large-scale kernel machines. In: Advances in Neural Information Processing Systems, pp. 1177–1184 (2007)
15. Rahimi, A., Recht, B.: Weighted sums of random kitchen sinks: Replacing minimization with randomization in learning. In: Advances in Neural Information Processing Systems, pp. 1313–1320 (2008)
16. Rasmussen, C.E., Williams, C.K.I.: Gaussian Processes for Machine Learning (Adaptive Computation and Machine Learning). The MIT Press (2005)
17. Schnitzer, D., Flexer, A., Widmer, G.: A fast audio similarity retrieval method for millions of music tracks. Multimedia Tools and Applications **58**(1), 23–40 (2012)

18. Schölkopf, B.: The kernel trick for distances. In: Proceedings of the 2000 Conference on Advances in Neural Information Processing Systems 13, vol. 13, p. 301. MIT Press (2001)
19. Schölkopf, B., Platt, J.C., Shawe-Taylor, J., Smola, A.J., Williamson, R.C., Sch, B.: Estimating the support of a high-dimensional distribution. Neural Computation **13**(7), 1443–1471 (2001)
20. Schölkopf, B., Smola, A., Müller, K.-R.: Kernel principal component analysis. In: Gerstner, W., Hasler, M., Germond, A., Nicoud, J.-D. (eds.) ICANN 1997. LNCS, vol. 1327, pp. 583–588. Springer, Heidelberg (1997)
21. Schölkopf, B., Smola, A.J.: Learning with kernels: support vector machines, regularization, optimization, and beyond. MIT press (2001)
22. Shalev-Shwartz, S., Singer, Y., Srebro, N.: Pegasos: Primal estimated sub-gradient solver for svm. In: Mathematical Programming (2007)
23. Smola, A.J., Schölkopf, B.: A tutorial on support vector regression. Statistics and Computing **14**(3), 199–222 (2004)
24. Spearman, C.: The proof and measurement of association between two things. The American Journal of Psychology **15**(1), 72–101 (1904)
25. Steinwart, I.: Sparseness of support vector machines. The Journal of Machine Learning Research **4**, 1071–1105 (2003)
26. Steinwart, I., Christmann, A.: Support vector machines. Springer (2008)
27. Torgerson, W.S.: Multidimensional scaling: I. Theory and method. Psychometrika **17**(4), 401–419 (1952)
28. Vedaldi, A., Zisserman, A.: Efficient Additive Kernels via Explicit Feature Maps. IEEE Transactions on Pattern Analysis and Machine Intelligence **34**(3), 480–492 (2012)
29. Williams, C., Seeger, M.: Using the Nyström method to speed up kernel machines. In: Proceedings of the 14th Annual Conference on Neural Information Processing Systems, pp. 682–688. No. EPFL-CONF-161322 (2001)

A Doppelkopf Player Based on UCT

Silvan Sievers[✉] and Malte Helmert

University of Basel, Basel, Switzerland
{silvan.sievers,malte.helmert}@unibas.ch

Abstract. We propose doppelkopf, a trick-taking card game with similarities to skat, as a benchmark problem for AI research. While skat has been extensively studied by the AI community in recent years, this is not true for doppelkopf. However, it has a substantially larger state space than skat and a unique key feature which distinguishes it from skat and other card games: players usually do not know with whom they play at the start of a game, figuring out the parties only in the process of playing.

Since its introduction in 2006, the UCT algorithm has been the dominating approach for solving games in AI research. It has notably achieved a playing strength comparable to good human players at playing go, but it has also shown good performance in card games like Klondike solitaire and skat. In this work, we adapt UCT to play doppelkopf and present an algorithm that generates random card assignments, used by the UCT algorithm for sampling. In our experiments, we discuss and evaluate different variants of the UCT algorithm, and we show that players based on UCT improve over simple baseline players and exhibit good card play behavior also when competing with a human player.

1 Introduction

Doppelkopf (literally "double head") is a trick-taking card game for four players. It is mostly played in Germany, with a popularity only slightly lower than that of *skat*, which has been well-studied by the AI community in recent years [5,10,11,14,16,17]. However, to the best of our knowledge, doppelkopf has not been subject to AI research yet, although it has a much larger state space than skat and a unique feature which potentially makes it harder for computers playing it due to increasing uncertainty: at the start of a game, the parties are usually not known to the players until specific cards have been revealed, and hence collaboration at the beginning is difficult and subject to assumptions and inference. This work aims at introducing doppelkopf as a research topic and providing a baseline against which future work can compare.

Upper Confidence Bounds applied to Trees (UCT) [15] is a *Monte Carlo* tree search algorithm which has experienced a lot of success since its first application to the game of go [12]: It has successfully been used for (complete information) General Game Playing [9], and for many scenarios of acting under uncertainty, including the Canadian Traveler's Problem [8], probabilistic planning [13], Klondike solitaire [4], and multi-player games like hearts, spades, Chinese

© Springer International Publishing Switzerland 2015
S. Hölldobler et al. (Eds.): KI 2015, LNAI 9324, pp. 151–165, 2015.
DOI: 10.1007/978-3-319-24489-1_12

checkers [23], and skat [19]. Hence, it seems natural to use UCT to establish a baseline computer player for doppelkopf. To be able to use UCT on a full game state space in contrast to the actual belief state space the doppelkopf players are confronted with, we present an algorithm that computes random card assignments consistent with the game history, which can then be used by the UCT algorithm for game simulations. In our experiments, we evaluate different variants of UCT in different settings, showing that players based on UCT improve over baseline players and show good card play behavior also when playing with a human.

2   Doppelkopf

In this section, we present doppelkopf in a short form, discussing only the basic rules. Official rules have only been defined after the foundation of the Deutscher Doppelkopf Verband (German Doppelkopf Association; DDV) in 1982 [1]. Consequently, there is a large pool of house rules used by hobby players. In this work, we exclusively consider the official rules which are used for tournament play. For an exhaustive description of the game, we refer to the first author's Master's thesis [22] or the DDV [1].

2.1   Game Play

Doppelkopf is a trick-taking card game for four players. The deck consists of a double shortened French deck, with a total of 48 cards (the 2s to 8s are removed). This means there are the regular four suits clubs (♣), spades (♠), hearts (♡) and diamonds (♢), each consisting of two aces (A), two tens (10), two kings (K), two queens (Q), two jacks (J) and two nines (9). The card point values are the same as in skat, i.e. an ace is worth 11 points, a ten 10, a king 4, a queen 3, a jack 2, and a nine 0 points, which sums up to a total of 240 card points in a doppelkopf deck. In every game, the *re* party competes against the *kontra* party, (usually) aiming at collecting at least 121 card points.

A game starts by dealing every player 12 cards, the so-called *hand*, which must be hidden from and not communicated to the other players. Before the actual *card play phase* can start, players need to settle the type of the current game in the *game type determination phase*. While there are various *solo game* types where one player forms the re party and plays against the three other players of the kontra party, the most common and default game type is the so-called *normal game*, where two players play against the two others. The chosen game type also dictates how the cards are divided into *suits* and what *rank* each card has in its suit. For the remainder of this section, we will focus on normal games and again refer to the literature for more details about other game types [1,22].

In a normal game, there is a *trump suit*, consisting of the following cards in descending order: ♡10, ♣Q, ♠Q, ♡Q, ♢Q, ♣J, ♠J, ♡J, ♢J, ♢A, ♢10, ♢K, ♢9. The remaining suits (♣, ♠, ♡) each form a separate non-trump suit, sorted as follows: A, 10, K, 9 (with the exception of $\heartsuit$, where the tens are part of the trump suit). The parties are as follows: the players holding a $\clubsuit$Q form the re party, opposing the other players forming the kontra party, and hence the parties are not known to the players at the beginning of a game. If a player p has both $\clubsuit$Q, p has the option to play a solo or to play a *marriage*, where one of the other three players, according to specific rules, joins the marriage player p to form the re party. As soon as the parties are settled in the case of a marriage, the game continues like a normal game.

The card play rules are independent of the chosen game type and exactly the same as in skat. In short, one player starts by playing any card, thereby settling the suit to be played in this *trick*, which everybody has to follow if possible. The player who played the highest card of that suit (or of the *trump suit*) *wins* the trick, adding its summed card point value to their account, and starts the next trick by playing any card. After completing twelve tricks, the game ends, the winning party and the *game value* are determined (see below), and the next game can start.

In the card play phase (during the first few tricks), independently of the game type, players can make *announcements* to increase the game value. The "basic" announcements (in German: "Ansagen", literally "to announce") are *re* and *kontra*, depending on the announcing player's party. They do not increase the threshold for winning the game, but reveal the announcing player's party to the others. Further announcements (in German: "Absagen", literally "to reject") are *no 90* (*no 60*, *no 30*), which claims that the other party will not manage to win 90 (60, 30) card points, and *schwarz* (literally "black"), which claims that the other party will not win a single trick. If the other party reaches the "rejected goal" nevertheless, the announcing party loses the game. The official rules precisely specify the latest time point in terms of number of cards a player is still holding up to which the player is allowed to make (further) announcements.

2.2 Game Evaluation

The game value is determined in terms of *score points* (not to be confused with card points): +1 for winning the game; +2 if re (kontra) was announced; +1 if the losing party has less than 90 (60, 30) card points or won no trick; +1 if no 90 (no 60, no 30, schwarz) was announced; +1 if the winning party achieved at least 120 (90, 60, 30) card points against an announcement of no 90 (no 60, no 30, schwarz) of the other party. The players of the winning party are rewarded with the positive game value, the others with the negative game value (zero-sum notation). In case of solo games, the game value is multiplied by 3 for the soloist.

In normal games, there are additional extra score points rewarded as follows: +1 for *winning against the elders*, i.e. the kontra party wins; +1 for the party *catching a fox*, i.e. winning a trick where an opponent played an $\diamondsuit$A; +1 for the party *making a doppelkopf*, i.e. winning a trick worth at least 40 card points; +1 for the party winning the last trick if the highest card played in this trick is a *charlie*, i.e. a $\clubsuit$J.

2.3   Discussion

With 48 cards, there are $\binom{48}{12} \cdot \binom{36}{12} \cdot \binom{24}{12} \cdot \binom{12}{12} \approx 2.4 \cdot 10^{26}$ possible card deals. For a fixed deal, the number of possible game states only in terms of cards that have (not) been played is $\sum_{i=0}^{48} 4 \cdot \binom{12}{\lfloor (i+3)/4 \rfloor} \cdot \binom{12}{\lfloor (i+2)/4 \rfloor} \cdot \binom{12}{\lfloor (i+1)/4 \rfloor} \cdot \binom{12}{\lfloor i/4 \rfloor} \approx 2.4 \cdot 10^{13}$. Multiplying the two numbers gives $5.6 \cdot 10^{39}$, which is only a rough upper bound on the size of the card state space, because game states can be consistent with many different card deals. However, this does not consider the various game types, the moves players make in the game determination phase of the game, or the announcement moves. We think that the large state space of doppelkopf, its uncertainty of knowledge about parties and its strategic depth make doppelkopf an interesting benchmark problem for AI research.

3   The UCT Algorithm

In this section, we present the UCT algorithm [15], a state-of-the-art algorithm for many problems of acting under uncertainty, adapted to doppelkopf. We start with a high-level description of the algorithm. While we ideally would like to determine the move which maximizes the expected outcome of the game for the moving player in a given game state, computing all possible card deals consistent with the game history and computing all possible outcomes of a game under a given card assignment is usually infeasible. The UCT algorithm avoids this problem by relying on sampling. More precisely, UCT is a Monte Carlo tree search algorithm which repeatedly simulates the game starting in the current state until a terminal game state is reached, also called performing a *rollout*. To perform such a rollout of the game, the UCT algorithm needs to assume a fixed card deal, i.e. a fixed card assignment of the remaining cards to all other players. We discuss how to compute such a card assignment in more detail in the next section and assume a fixed card assignment for the moment. At the end of a rollout, the outcome of the game is used to compute *UCT rewards* for all players. This information is stored in a *tree* of game states which is incrementally built over the course of performing rollouts and which serves to bias future computations of rollouts. At *any time*, the algorithm can be terminated and the move leading to the successor state with the highest average UCT reward can be returned.

3.1   UCT for Doppelkopf

We now describe the computation of one UCT rollout under a fixed card assignment. Let s_0 denote the current game state for which UCT is queried, let $V^k(s_i)$ denote the *number of rollouts* among the first k rollouts of the UCT algorithm in which state s_i was reached, and let $R_j^k(s_i)$ denote the *average UCT reward* (defined below) obtained by player j in the first k rollouts when completing a rollout from state s_i. Both $V^k(s_i)$ and $R_j^k(s_i)$ are stored in the UCT tree. Each rollout, given the fixed card assignment, starts in state s_0 and iteratively chooses a successor state until a terminal game state is reached. Let s_i be the current state reached in the $(k+1)$st rollout, with n possible successor states $s'_1, \ldots, s'_n$, and let p be the player to move in s_i. UCT favors selecting successors that have led to high UCT rewards for p in previous rollouts (where $R^k_p(s'_j)$ is high) and that have been rarely tried in previous rollouts (where $V^k(s'_j)$ is low). Balancing those two criteria is commonly called the *exploration-exploitation* dilemma, which UCT attempts to solve by treating the decision corresponding to successor selection at state s_i as a *multi-armed bandit problem* and applying the *UCT formula*, which is based on the UCB1 formula introduced by Auer et al. [2] in the context of such multi-armed bandit problems. UCT chooses the successor s'_j which maximizes the UCT formula

$$R^k(s'_j) + C\sqrt{\frac{\log(V^k(s_i))}{V^k(s'_j)}},$$

where C is a bias parameter to guide the amount of exploration. If $V^k(s'_j) = 0$, the value of the *exploration term* (the second term) is considered to be ∞, leading to every successor s'_j being chosen at least once, if s_i is reached at least n times. In our experiments, we use a random successor state from the set of unvisited ones, leading to a variant of UCT which is sometimes called *blind* UCT. After the completion of a rollout, the V and R values of states visited during the rollout are updated.

When reaching a terminal game state, the algorithm has to compute the UCT reward for all players, based on their achieved game score points. This is done by multiplying the game score points with 500 and adding to it, as a bias towards achieving more card points, the card points achieved by the party.[1] We choose 500 to ensure that the card points bias serves a pure tie breaker only, because the maximum of 240 card points can never exceed 500, which is obtained if assuming the smallest possible game value of 1.

UCT comes with theoretical guarantees about convergence and regret bounds: Kocsis and Szepesv?ri [15] prove that every state is visited infinitely many times, given enough rollouts, and that states which have been unpromising previously are chosen less and less frequently over time, proving that the algorithm eventually converges to a stable policy. Furthermore, they prove that the average UCT reward of every state lies in the interval of its expectation plus minus the exploration term, which grows logarithmically in the number of visits of the state, i.e. the regret of the policy UCT converges to is bounded from the optimal policy logarithmically in the number of rollouts.

3.2 Variants

Recent work in the area of General Game Playing discusses modeling the belief state space of incomplete information games and using classical complete infor-

---

[1] We also experimented using the card points achieved only by the player and obtained results with no significant difference.

mation algorithms such as Minimax or UCT on the actual states corresponding to a belief state [7,20,21]. While we stick to the approach of instantiating belief states into full game states and then using UCT on the complete information state space — which proved to be very successful in various applications [4,8,13,19,23]— we propose two *versions* of the UCT algorithm to vary the number of card assignments used. The first version, called *ensemble-UCT*, performs several regular UCT computations, each with a different card assignment, fixed over all rollouts of that computation. Hence, it constructs a different tree for every such UCT computation and in the end chooses the action which leads to the state maximizing the average UCT reward, averaged over all UCT computations. The second version, called *single-UCT*, computes a new card assignment for every rollout. As a consequence, the constructed tree can contain states which are not consistent across different rollouts. In a given rollout, only successors consistent with the current card assignment are considered for selection. This leads to fewer parts of the tree being reusable over different rollouts, but avoids the potential problem of computing only a few different card assignments as in the ensemble-UCT version.

Furthermore, we consider two variants of constructing the tree over the course of performing rollouts that differ in how previously unseen states are handled. The first variant adds a node for *every* new state encountered during a rollout to the tree. The second variant only adds the *first* new state encountered and continues the remainder of the rollout as a so-called *Monte Carlo simulation*, which consists of random successor selection until a terminal game state is reached. Note that this behavior does not differ from the first variant, which also chooses random successors when encountering a state with previously unseen successors. The difference only lies in the amount of statistics recorded for states encountered during rollouts. With the first variant, the constructed tree grows quickly, including many nodes in the tree that will potentially not be visited again, especially if they led to "bad" results in the rollout they were encountered. Still, the more information available, the more quickly the UCT algorithm converges. With the second variant, the tree grows more slowly, only including information about states that have a high probability of being revisited in future rollouts. We suspect that not performing a Monte Carlo simulation should be beneficial particularly with the ensemble-UCT version, because it uses the same card assignment over many rollouts and is hence expected to obtain similar results in different rollouts for the same state. With the single-UCT version, different rollouts may lead to very different outcomes even for the same state.

4   The Card Assignment Problem

We now consider the *card assignment problem* (CAP): in a game state s with player p to move, assign all remaining cards to all other players such that the card assignment is *consistent* with the game history. A card assignment is consistent if it respects all information about the other players' hands available to p. Our goal when solving the CAP is to compute a solution uniformly at random to avoid generating any bias towards specific card assignments in the computation of the UCT algorithm.

In state s, the following information about other players' hands is available to p: if a player p' is playing a marriage[2] and did not play one or both of their ♣Q yet, p' still needs to have both or one; re players not having played their ♣Q yet must still hold it and kontra players cannot hold a ♣Q, where in both cases many scenarios can lead to knowing a player's party; all players who could not follow suit at some point in the game cannot have any card of that suit.

To assign cards uniformly at random, we have to be able to compute the exact number of possible consistent card assignments for arbitrary states. Then, taking into account the number of consistent card assignments before and after hypothetically assigning a card to player, we can compute the exact probability for this specific assignment. However, computing the number of solutions for the CAP, i.e. computing the number of consistent card assignments, is #P-hard:[3] the CAP can be formulated as a *matching problem* in graph theory (see e.g. [6]), where solving the CAP corresponds to finding a perfect bipartite matching, or more generally as a *CSP* (see e.g. [18]). Computing the number of perfect matchings in a bipartite graph (#PBM) is #P-complete, because it is closely connected to the #P-complete problem of computing the permanent of 0-1-matrices [24], and counting the solutions of a CSP (#CSP) is a straightforward generalization of #PBM. For #PBM, there exists a fully polynomial time randomized approximation scheme [3]. However, using this approximation seems to demand an infeasible amount of computation, considering that we would need to solve the CAP up to four times for every remaining card to be assigned, and that we would need to compute a new assignment of all remaining cards for every rollout if using the single-UCT version. We hence propose our own algorithm to approximate a uniformly random card assignment in the following.

The algorithm first computes the set of cards that every player can potentially have without violating consistency. It then performs the following steps, every time starting over again after successfully assigning one or more cards to a player: if there is a card that can only be assigned to one player, assign it to that player; if there is a player that needs exactly as many cards assigned as there are possible cards it can have, assign all those cards to that player; if there is a player that needs one ♣Q, assign one to that player; otherwise assign an arbitrary of the remaining cards to an arbitrary player that can have it.

It is easy to see that the algorithm can only generate consistent card assignments, because it never assigns a card to player that is not allowed to have it in a consistent card assignment. We further argue that there exists a possible card-to-player assignment of all remaining cards in every iteration of the algorithm: if a card cannot be assigned to any player, then there must have been an earlier iteration in which that card could only have been assigned to one player and the

---

[2] In specific situations in the game type determination phase, it is also possible to *infer* that a player wanted to play a marriage.

[3] Informally, #P is the class of counting problems associated with decision problems in NP.

algorithm would have chosen that assignment. Because the algorithm assigns at least one card in every iteration, it terminates after at most as many iterations as there are cards left to be assigned initially.

Our algorithm does not generate consistent card assignments uniformly at random for several reasons: first, the algorithm does not consider the number of possible card assignments when randomly choosing a card and a player to assign to. Second, it does not consider the number of card slots of the player, hence treating assigning a card to a player with one open slot as likely as assigning it to a player with many open slots. Third, prioritizing the assignment of a ♣Q to a player does not consider the probability of that player getting a ♣Q without enforcing it.

5   Experiments

In this section, we report results for several variants of the UCT algorithm for doppelkopf. While there are many commercial doppelkopf programs and the open source program FreeDoko[4] which comes with various types of configurable computer players (e.g. using simulations, search trees, or heuristics), it is a technically challenging task to evaluate these different programs together with our algorithm due to the lack of a common framework. We hence evaluate the UCT players in competition against each other and fill up empty player spots with random players. Random players do not take part in the game determination phase, do not make announcements and play random cards in every trick. They can be seen as "dummy players" which do not influence the game.

Our general experimental setup is as follows: we compare two different UCT players by letting them play together with two identical random players, playing 1000 games with random card deals. We repeat those 1000 games in *every possible permutation* of player positions, so that every player plays every hand on every position once. The UCT algorithm generally computes 10000 rollouts every time it is queried for a game state, independent of the UCT version used. We evaluate a player's performance as the average score points per game in the 95% confidence interval. We report the results achieved by each UCT player and, in parenthesis, by both random players. The best result of every comparison is highlighted in bold. Note that with overlapping confidence intervals, the results are not always statistically significant. More precise results could be obtained by increasing the number of games played.[5]

5.1   Exploration in the UCT Algorithm

In a first series of experiments, we investigate the influence of exploration in both the ensemble-UCT and the single-UCT versions. Simultaneously, we test

---

[4] http://free-doko.sourceforge.net/en/FreeDoko.html

[5] Computing a set of 1000 games with two UCT players using the ensemble-UCT version takes roughly 19.5h in average to complete. With the single-UCT version, the average is roughly 46h, due to the high number of card assignments which need to be computed.

different combinations of the number of performed UCT computations X and
the number of rollouts Y performed in each such computation for the ensemble-
UCT version (denoted X/Y in the following). We disable performing Monte
Carlo simulations and discuss their influence below.

Table 1. Comparison of different values for the exploration bias C for different configurations of the ensemble-UCT version.

ensemble-UCT (5/2000)	
$C = 6000$ vs. $C = 8000$	1.48 ± 0.07 vs. $\mathbf{1.90 \pm 0.08}$ (vs. -1.69 ± 0.05)
$C = 8000$ vs. $C = 12000$	1.42 ± 0.08 vs. $\mathbf{2.07 \pm 0.10}$ (vs. -1.74 ± 0.05)
$C = 12000$ vs. $C = 16000$	1.65 ± 0.10 vs. $\mathbf{1.83 \pm 0.12}$ (vs. -1.74 ± 0.05)
$C = 16000$ vs. $C = 24000$	$\mathbf{1.63 \pm 0.12}$ vs. 1.41 ± 0.13 (vs. -1.52 ± 0.06)
$C = 24000$ vs. $C = 32000$	$\mathbf{1.35 \pm 0.13}$ vs. 1.20 ± 0.13 (vs. -1.27 ± 0.06)

ensemble-UCT (10/1000)	
$C = 6000$ vs. $C = 8000$	1.49 ± 0.06 vs. $\mathbf{1.94 \pm 0.07}$ (vs. -1.72 ± 0.05)
$C = 8000$ vs. $C = 12000$	1.49 ± 0.07 vs. $\mathbf{2.16 \pm 0.09}$ (vs. -1.83 ± 0.05)
$C = 12000$ vs. $C = 16000$	1.82 ± 0.10 vs. $\mathbf{2.01 \pm 0.11}$ (vs. -1.92 ± 0.05)
$C = 16000$ vs. $C = 24000$	$\mathbf{1.92 \pm 0.11}$ vs. 1.79 ± 0.12 (vs. -1.86 ± 0.05)
$C = 24000$ vs. $C = 32000$	$\mathbf{1.86 \pm 0.12}$ vs. 1.66 ± 0.12 (vs. -1.76 ± 0.06)

ensemble-UCT (20/500)	
$C = 6000$ vs. $C = 8000$	1.52 ± 0.06 vs. $\mathbf{1.95 \pm 0.07}$ (vs. -1.73 ± 0.05)
$C = 8000$ vs. $C = 12000$	1.65 ± 0.07 vs. $\mathbf{2.08 \pm 0.09}$ (vs. -1.86 ± 0.05)
$C = 12000$ vs. $C = 16000$	1.88 ± 0.09 vs. $\mathbf{1.91 \pm 0.10}$ (vs. -1.90 ± 0.05)
$C = 16000$ vs. $C = 24000$	$\mathbf{1.93 \pm 0.10}$ vs. 1.75 ± 0.10 (vs. -1.84 ± 0.05)
$C = 24000$ vs. $C = 32000$	$\mathbf{1.93 \pm 0.10}$ vs. 1.59 ± 0.10 (vs. -1.76 ± 0.05)

Table 1 shows the results of the ensemble-UCT version. On a pairwise basis,
we compare using different values for the exploration bias C, each for the three
combinations 5/2000 (first block), 10/1000 (second block), and 20/500 (third
block). The first observation is that the results are consistent across all configurations: With increasing C, performance first increases up to a sweet-spot
approximately around $C = 16000$ and then decreases. Considering that the
UCT reward can theoretically range from -16740 to $+16740$ (assuming a solo
game with the highest possible value of 11, not including irrational counter-
announcements), and most often will range from -2000 to $+2000$ (assuming an
average game value of 4), a value of $C = 16000$, multiplied with the square root
term of the UCT formula (ranging between 0 and 1), seems to be appropriate
to strongly favor exploration at the beginning, reducing exploration more and
more as the number of rollouts increases.

Next, we compare the three combinations with a fixed C against each other.
Table 2 shows that the combination 10/1000 achieves the best performance.
Apparently, there is a trade-off between the number of different card assignments
considered and the number of rollouts performed with a fixed card assignment.
Both using too few different card assignments and performing too few rollouts
with each card assignment hurts the quality of the UCT computation.

We now turn our attention to results of the single-UCT version displayed
in Table 3. We observe a similar trend for changing values of approximately

Table 2. Comparison of different combinations of the number of UCT computations and rollouts for the ensemble-UCT version.

ensemble-UCT (C=16000)	
5/2000 vs. 10/1000	1.67 ± 0.12 vs. $\mathbf{1.83 \pm 0.11}$ (vs. -1.75 ± 0.05)
10/1000 vs. 20/500	$\mathbf{2.10 \pm 0.11}$ vs. 1.70 ± 0.10 (vs. -1.90 ± 0.05)

C, however the best performance is achieved with a lower value of $C = 8000$. Furthermore, the performance of the players using the single-UCT version compared to the baseline players is weaker than with the ensemble-UCT version. This lower absolute performance also explains why choosing a lower value for C is better with the single-UCT version. We will compare the two UCT versions directly against each other below.

Table 3. Comparison of different values for the exploration bias C for the single-UCT version.

single-UCT	
$C = 2000$ vs. $C = 4000$	0.26 ± 0.06 vs. $\mathbf{1.18 \pm 0.08}$ (vs. -0.72 ± 0.05)
$C = 4000$ vs. $C = 6000$	0.37 ± 0.07 vs. $\mathbf{1.32 \pm 0.09}$ (vs. -0.85 ± 0.05)
$C = 6000$ vs. $C = 8000$	0.53 ± 0.07 vs. $\mathbf{0.85 \pm 0.09}$ (vs. -0.69 ± 0.05)
$C = 8000$ vs. $C = 10000$	$\mathbf{0.52 \pm 0.08}$ vs. 0.47 ± 0.09 (vs. -0.50 ± 0.05)
$C = 10000$ vs. $C = 12000$	$\mathbf{0.33 \pm 0.08}$ vs. 0.33 ± 0.09 (vs. -0.33 ± 0.04)
$C = 12000$ vs. $C = 14000$	$\mathbf{0.30 \pm 0.09}$ vs. 0.05 ± 0.09 (vs. -0.18 ± 0.05)

For the remainder of this section, we choose the combination 10/1000 and $C = 16000$ for the ensemble-UCT version and $C = 8000$ for the single-UCT version.

5.2   Influence of Announcements and Monte Carlo Simulations

In the following, we discuss the influence of two other parameters. We start by investigating the influence of making announcements by comparing a UCT player who is allowed to make announcements against one who is not. Table 4 shows the comparison for both UCT versions. We observe that for both UCT versions, UCT players clearly profit from being allowed to make announcements. This means that on average, they win more games than they lose if they make an announcement. Finding the right amount of announcement making is a very important way of increasing the score points gained on average. Also on a human level of playing, this is crucial for top performance.

Second, we investigate the influence of performing a Monte Carlo simulation when reaching a new state, adding only one new state rather than all states encountered during rollouts to the tree. Table 5 shows the comparison for both UCT versions. We observe that for the ensemble-UCT version, not performing

Table 4. Comparison of allowed and forbidden announcing for both UCT versions.

ensemble-UCT (10/1000, C=16000)
Announcing vs. no announcing|**1.70 $\pm$ 0.07** vs. 0.79 $\pm$ 0.05 (vs. -1.25 ± 0.04)

single-UCT (C=8000)
Announcing vs. no announcing|**0.48 $\pm$ 0.06** vs. 0.19 $\pm$ 0.05 (vs. -0.33 ± 0.04)

a Monte Carlo simulation achieves a significantly better result than performing a simulation, while the opposite is true for the single-UCT version. This confirms our assumption that the ensemble-UCT version, due to the fixed card assignment for every single UCT computation, particularly profits from not performing a simulation but recording all information gained during rollouts. Using the single-UCT version, information gained in previous rollouts may be misleading in rollouts with different card assignments, hence storing and reusing all information can be harmful.

Table 5. Comparison of using and not using a Monte Carlo simulation for both UCT versions.

ensemble-UCT (10/1000, C=16000)
No MC simulation vs. MC simulation|**2.15 $\pm$ 0.11** vs.   1.73 $\pm$ 0.09 (vs. -1.94 ± 0.05)

single-UCT (C=8000)
No MC simulation vs. MC simulation| 0.34 $\pm$ 0.08 vs. **0.85 $\pm$ 0.08** (vs. -0.59 ± 0.05)

5.3   Ensemble-UCT versus Single-UCT

Our next experiment compares the two UCT versions in their best configuration (en-semble-UCT: 10/1000, $C = 16000$, no Monte Carlo simulation; single-UCT: $C = 8000$, Monte Carlo simulation) directly against each other. The ensemble-UCT version achieves a score points average of 4.52 ± 0.11, the single-UCT version -1.25 ± 0.08, and the random players -1.63 ± 0.05. Hence our previous observation is not only confirmed, but the performance of the single-UCT version drops even below 0, and remains only slightly above the baseline players' performance. We conclude that using a new card assignment for every rollout leads to less informed UCT trees, probably caused by the fact that rollouts may be incompatible to each other, frequently preventing reusing all information across rollouts.

5.4   Game Analysis Against a Human

Finally, we evaluate the ensemble-UCT version in a setup with a human and two random players, playing two tournaments consisting of 24 games each. Note that we cannot repeat these games in all permutations because a human cannot easily forget previously played hands. Furthermore, playing 24 games is a very low amount to draw conclusions from. Hence the results are not significant, but the games still serve as a basis for investigating the playing behavior of the UCT player in the following. The results of the first (second) tournament are as follows: the human player achieves 43 (15) score points, the UCT player -9 (7), and the random players -15 (-35) and -19 (13), respectively.

We observe several trends in the playing behavior of the UCT player p: first, p plays many solo games: 7 (9) in the first (second) tournament, winning only 4 (5) of them. While the absolute value of score points achieved in those games is positive ($+3$ and $+15$), it is a lower average per game than what p (probably) could have achieved by playing a normal game. Analyzing the hands p decided to play a solo with for their use in a game with four humans, we think that 4 (4) hands have no chances of being won in the first (second) tournament, 2 (3) have borderline chances (e.g. depend on p being the starting player and on a "good" card distribution to other players), and 1 (2) have a good chance of being won or are clear solo hands. In nearly all of the cases, the hands are excellent for a normal game, and especially with such hands, playing a solo only makes sense if there is a very high chance of winning.

Second, in normal games, p never makes an announcement unless the opposing party already made an announcement. All of the games with such a "counter-announcement" are lost for p, leading to a loss of 10 score points in each of the tournaments. However, p always announces re when playing a solo, which is reasonable.

Third, we observe that p plays the stronger the earlier it knows the parties (e.g. in all marriage games) – which should not be surprising, as this usually reduces the amount of reasonable card moves drastically. Also generally, p's playing strength increases over the course of a game, with fewer remaining options to play. For example, it won the last trick with a charlie several times, scoring an extra score point. This increasing playing strength also (partly) explains the less informed decisions about solo playing and the (missing) announcement making, both taking place at the beginning of a game.

5.5   Discussion

Our experiments show that using an ensemble of UCT computations has clear benefits over only performing a single UCT computation which uses different instantiations of the current belief state in every rollout. While a player based on the ensemble-UCT version shows good card play performance, the ability to correctly evaluate a hand for solo play and to decide whether to make an announcement or not is less developed. A possibility of enhancing the performance of such players with respect to hand evaluation would be to use a separate algorithm for this purpose, as it has e.g. been done in skat [14]. An algorithm for hand evaluation could profit from analyzing all cards simultaneously, in the context of a given game type, rather than ranking every possible move by estimating the outcome of the game when making this particular move next.

More generally, there are other possibilities of improving our current UCT players. First, analyzing the bias of the card assignment algorithm could help in improving the algorithm to come closer to uniformly at random generating card assignments, which in turn could have a positive impact on the performance of UCT. Second, and this seems to be very important, domain specific knowledge could help in the simulation phase of a rollout: rather than randomly choosing a successor, using a heuristic approach such as a rule based successor selection could greatly improve the quality of rollouts, especially of the first few hundred rollouts of a UCT computation, where little or no information from previous rollouts is available. In particular, this would accelerate the convergence of the UCT algorithm. Third, the computation of UCT rollouts currently underlies the assumption that the other players act similar to the UCT player itself, i.e. the decision making for other players is the same. This assumption could be dropped and decision making for other players could be replaced by heuristic based or even random successor selection. Fourth, a UCT player could keep relevant parts of the tree(s) constructed in previous UCT computations for the next move it will be queried for, thus starting the new UCT computation with an already initialized tree. This would potentially accelerate the convergence of the UCT computation.

6   Conclusion

We introduced doppelkopf as a benchmark problem for AI research. Although the game play is similar as in skat, a well-established game in the AI community, doppelkopf has a much larger state space and more strategical playing depth. As a baseline for future research, we adapted the UCT algorithm, a state-of-the-art approach for many other scenarios of acting under uncertainty. We discussed the problem of uniformly at random generating consistent card assignments, which are required to compute UCT rollouts under full information. Because this computation is inherently hard, we presented our own algorithm to approximate the uniformly-at-random computation. We experimented with several variants of the UCT algorithm and obtained good results against baseline players. While hand evaluation, required for solo play decisions and announcement making, tends to be overly optimistic, UCT based players showed good card play skills.

We presented several ideas for improving our current UCT players in future work. Apart from those improvements, we would like to compare our UCT players against computer players of other types. A first step towards this end could be to replace the random players by rule based or other heuristic players. Second, more importantly, our implementation of UCT players could be integrated with other existing doppelkopf systems such as the open source FreeDoko program.

References

1. Deutscher Doppelkopf Verband. http://www.doko-verband.de (Online; in German; accessed April 28, 2015)
2. Auer, P., Cesa-Bianchi, N., Fischer, P.: Finite-time analysis of the multiarmed bandit problem. Machine Learning **47**, 235–256 (2002)
3. Bezáková, I., Štefankovič, D., Vazirani, V.V., Vigoda, E.: Accelerating simulated annealing for the permanent and combinatorial counting problems. In: Proceedings of the Seventeenth Annual ACM-SIAM Symposium on Discrete Algorithms, pp. 900–907. SODA 2006. ACM (2006)
4. Bjarnason, R., Fern, A., Tadepalli, P.: Lower bounding Klondike solitaire with Monte-Carlo planning. In: Gerevini, A., Howe, A., Cesta, A., Refanidis, I. (eds.) Proceedings of the Nineteenth International Conference on Automated Planning and Scheduling, ICAPS 2009, pp. 26–33. AAAI Press (2009)
5. Buro, M., Long, J.R., Furtak, T., Sturtevant, N.: Improving state evaluation, inference, and search in trick-based card games. In: Boutilier, C. (ed.) Proceedings of the 21st International Joint Conference on Artificial Intelligence (IJCAI 2009), pp. 1407–1413 (2009)
6. Cormen, T.H., Leiserson, C.E., Rivest, R.L.: Introduction to Algorithms. The MIT Press (1990)
7. Edelkamp, S., Federholzner, T., Kissmann, P.: Searching with partial belief states in general games with incomplete information. In: Glimm, B., Krüger, A. (eds.) KI 2012. LNCS, vol. 7526, pp. 25–36. Springer, Heidelberg (2012)
8. Eyerich, P., Keller, T., Helmert, M.: High-quality policies for the Canadian traveler's problem. In: Fox, M., Poole, D. (eds.) Proceedings of the Twenty-Fourth AAAI Conference on Artificial Intelligence, AAAI 2010, pp. 51–58. AAAI Press (2010)
9. Finnsson, H., Björnsson, Y.: Simulation-based approach to general game playing. In: Proceedings of the Twenty-Third AAAI Conference on Artificial Intelligence, AAAI 2008, pp. 259–264. AAAI Press (2008)
10. Furtak, T., Buro, M.: Using payoff-similarity to speed up search. In: Walsh [25], pp. 534–539
11. Furtak, T., Buro, M.: Recursive Monte Carlo search for imperfect information games. In: 2013 IEEE Conference on Computational Intelligence in Games (CIG), Niagara Falls, ON, Canada, August 11–13, pp. 1–8. IEEE (2013)
12. Gelly, S., Wang, Y., Munos, R., Teytaud, O.: Modification of UCT with Patterns in Monte-Carlo Go. Tech. Rep. 6062, INRIA (November 2006)
13. Keller, T., Eyerich, P.: PROST: Probabilistic planning based on UCT. In: McCluskey, L., Williams, B., Silva, J.R., Bonet, B. (eds.) Proceedings of the Twenty-Second International Conference on Automated Planning and Scheduling (ICAPS 2012), pp. 119–127. AAAI Press (2012)
14. Keller, T., Kupferschmid, S.: Automatic bidding for the game of skat. In: Dengel, A.R., Berns, K., Breuel, T.M., Bomarius, F., Roth-Berghofer, T.R. (eds.) KI 2008. LNCS (LNAI), vol. 5243, pp. 95–102. Springer, Heidelberg (2008)
15. Kocsis, L., Szepesvári, C.: Bandit based Monte-Carlo planning. In: Fürnkranz, J., Scheffer, T., Spiliopoulou, M. (eds.) ECML 2006. LNCS (LNAI), vol. 4212, pp. 282–293. Springer, Heidelberg (2006)
16. Kupferschmid, S., Helmert, M.: A Skat player based on Monte Carlo simulation. In: Proceedings of the Fifth International Conference on Computers and Games, CG 2006, pp. 135–147 (2006)

17. Long, J.R., Buro, M.: Real-time opponent modeling in trick-taking card games. In: Walsh [25], pp. 617–622
18. Russell, S., Norvig, P.: Artificial Intelligence – A Modern Approach. Prentice Hall (2003)
19. Schäfer, J.: The UCT Algorithm Applied to Games with Imperfect Information. Master's thesis, Otto-von-Guericke-Universität Magdeburg (July 2008)
20. Schofield, M.J., Cerexhe, T.J., Thielscher, M.: Hyperplay: A solution to general game playing with imperfect information. In: Hoffmann, J., Selman, B. (eds.) Proceedings of the Twenty-Sixth AAAI Conference on Artificial Intelligence, AAAI 2012, pp. 1606–1612. AAAI Press (2012)
21. Schofield, M.J., Thielscher, M.: Lifting model sampling for general game playing to incomplete-information models. In: Proceedings of the Twenty-Ninth AAAI Conference on Artificial Intelligence, AAAI 2015, pp. 3585–3591. AAAI Press (2015)
22. Sievers, S.: Implementation of the UCT Algorithm for Doppelkopf. Master's thesis, University of Freiburg, Germany (April 2012)
23. Sturtevant, N.R.: An analysis of UCT in multi-player games. In: van den Herik, H.J., Xu, X., Ma, Z., Winands, M.H.M. (eds.) CG 2008. LNCS, vol. 5131, pp. 37–49. Springer, Heidelberg (2008)
24. Valiant, L.G.: The complexity of computing the permanent. Theoretical Computer Science 8, 189–201 (1979)

An Empirical Case Study on Symmetry Handling in Cost-Optimal Planning as Heuristic Search

Silvan Sievers[1]([✉]), Martin Wehrle[1], Malte Helmert[1], and Michael Katz[2]

[1] University of Basel, Basel, Switzerland
{silvan.sievers,martin.wehrle,malte.helmert}@unibas.ch
[2] IBM Research, Haifa, Israel
katzm@il.ibm.com

Abstract. Symmetries provide the basis for well-established approaches to tackle the state explosion problem in state space search and in AI planning. However, although by now there are various symmetry-based techniques available, these techniques have not yet been empirically evaluated and compared to each other in a common setting. In particular, it is unclear which of them should be preferably applied, and whether there are techniques with stronger performance than others. In this paper, we shed light on this issue by providing an empirical case study. We combine and evaluate several symmetry-based techniques for cost-optimal planning as heuristic search. For our evaluation, we use state-of-the-art abstraction heuristics on a large set of benchmarks from the international planning competitions.

1 Introduction

Common tasks in heuristic search and classical planning face the state explosion problem, meaning that the task's state space grows exponentially in the size of a compact description. As a consequence, the ability to effectively tackle the state explosion problem is crucial in order to scale to large problem sizes. A well-established approach for this purpose is based on the detection and exploitation of *problem symmetries*. Originating in the area of computer aided verification [14], symmetries have also been successfully applied in the heuristic search and planning communities [4,5,8–10,18,19,21,24,25]. Search techniques based on symmetries traditionally take into account that "symmetrical" states can be treated in an analogous way as the "original" state, thereby attempting to reduce the size of the task's reachable search space. For example, for a robot that has to carry a blue and a red ball to a destination location, it does not matter in which hand it actually carries the blue and the red ball, rendering the corresponding states symmetrical.

Symmetries have been studied in several variations. *Symmetrical lookups*, introduced in the context of pattern database heuristics for the sliding tile puzzle [3], maximize heuristic values over symmetrical states. Similarly, *dual lookups*

S. Hölldobler et al. (Eds.): KI 2015, LNAI 9324, pp. 166–180, 2015.
DOI: 10.1007/978-3-319-24489-1_13

can be considered as an instantiation of symmetry exploitation for permutation problems. In a nutshell, dual lookups compute two heuristic values per state, one for the actual state and one for the "dual" state which is known to have the same goal distance. Hence, maximizing the estimations over these states preserves admissibility [8,25]. For classical planning as heuristic search, symmetries have been applied to prune symmetrical states explicitly [4,18]. In addition, Sievers et al. [24] recently studied symmetries on a factored level for computing abstraction heuristics based on the merge-and-shrink framework [13]. Apparently, each of these techniques has shown to be useful in a particular context, but from a more global point of view, it is unclear which technique should be applied in which setting, if there are techniques that perform stronger than others, and if they can be combined to increase performance even further.

In this paper, we provide an empirical evaluation of these symmetry techniques. As the planning community offers a large and diverse benchmark set from the international planning competitions, we perform our study in the context of domain-independent planning. Our evaluation includes symmetries for cutting the search space as well as for computing merge-and-shrink heuristics. Furthermore, we adapt the concept of symmetrical and dual lookups to planning. While Shleyfman et al. [21] have shown that several planning heuristics are invariant under symmetries, this is presumably not the case for abstraction heuristics like merge-and-shrink, which are subject to our study.

2 Background

A SAS$^+$ planning task [2], augmented with operator costs, is defined as a tuple $\Pi = \langle \mathcal{V}, \mathcal{O}, s_0, s_\star, cost \rangle$ consisting of a finite set $\mathcal{V}$ of finite-domain state variables, a finite set of operators $\mathcal{O}$, an initial state s_0, a goal $s_\star$, and an operator cost function $cost$. States are defined by mappings from the variables in $\mathcal{V}$ to corresponding values in their domains. The goal description is specified as a conjunction of variable/value pairs (also called *facts*). An operator consists of a precondition and an effect which are both represented as conjunctions of facts. An operator o is applicable in a state s if o's precondition complies with s, and applying o in s yields the successor state $s(o)$ by setting o's effect variables in s accordingly. A plan is a sequence of operators that is sequentially applicable in s_0 and leads to a state that complies with the goal $s_\star$. The cost of a plan π is the sum of the costs of operators in the plan. A plan π is called optimal if its cost is minimal among all plans. A planning task Π induces a state transition graph $\mathcal{T}_\Pi$, where $\mathcal{T}_\Pi$'s vertices are Π's states, and there is an edge between states s and s' if there is an operator o that is applicable in s and $s' := s(o)$.

We will provide a short introduction to techniques that exploit symmetries for different purposes. We refer to the literature for details and more formal descriptions.

2.1   Structural Symmetries and Orbit Space Search

We base on the notion of *structural symmetries* (called symmetries for short in the following) which have recently been introduced by Shleyfman et al. [21]. Such symmetries map facts to facts and operators to operators in a way that forces the induced mapping on the state transition graph $\mathcal{T}_\Pi$ to be an automorphism of $\mathcal{T}_\Pi$ that maps goal nodes to goal nodes. Symmetries induce equivalence relations on $\mathcal{T}_\Pi$'s nodes, i.e. on the set of Π's states. Two states s and s' are in the same equivalence class if there is a symmetry σ such that $\sigma(s) = s'$.

In general, finding the coarsest equivalence relation is NP-hard [16]. Hence, in practice, an equivalence between two states s and s' is established via a *procedural* mapping $\mathcal{C} : \mathcal{S} \rightarrow \mathcal{S}$ from states to states in their equivalence class which induces an over-approximation of the coarsest equivalence relation. Two states s and s' are said to be equivalent if they are mapped to the same state by $\mathcal{C}$. The equivalence classes induced by $\mathcal{C}$ are called *orbits*. Pruning algorithms based on symmetry elimination only consider the orbits instead of all states. In the following, we consider symmetry elimination based on *orbit space search* [6]. Orbit space search performs the search directly on the space induced by the orbits of all states: For all encountered states s, a symmetrical representative of the orbit of s is computed and used for the further search.

2.2   Factored Symmetries and Merge-and-Shrink

Symmetries have also been studied on a factored level [24] for computing merge-and-shrink (M&S) heuristics [13]. Merge-and-shrink heuristics represent a popular class of abstraction heuristics. Starting from the "atomic" abstractions that represent the projection on single variables, the merge-and-shrink computation iterativeley selects two elements from the current set of abstractions, possibly unifies abstract states in one or both abstractions so that the product of their sizes respects a given size limit (the so-called *shrink* step), and then computes the synchronized product of the two abstractions (the so-called *merge* step). The resulting synchronized product replaces the two abstractions, and the process repeats until one abstraction is left.

In this framework, for a given set of abstractions Θ during the computation of merge-and-shrink, *factored symmetries* capture *locally* symmetrical aspects of (some of) the abstractions in Θ. Such symmetries can be used for lossless shrinking and to devise merging strategies for computing merge-and-shrink abstractions by preferably merging those abstractions that are affected by common factored symmetries.

2.3   Symmetrical Lookups

The concept of symmetrical lookups has been successfully proposed in the area of search, but has not been evaluated in the planning area so far. We have adapted symmetrical lookups for planning as follows: For a given heuristic h and state s, we define the heuristic value $\bar{h}(s)$ for s as the maximum of

$\{h(s), h(s^1), \ldots, h(s^m)\}$, where s^i for $i \in \{1, \ldots, m\}$ are states located in the same orbit as s (i.e. states symmetrical to state s). From a theoretical point of view, there is no further restriction on the set $S = \{s^1, \ldots, s^m\}$ of symmetrical states. At the extreme ends of the spectrum, S could be empty (i.e. no symmetrical lookups are performed), or could contain the whole set of states from the orbit of s (which is presumably expensive to compute in practice). From a practical point of view, several strategies to compute S are possible, and it remains an experimental question to find the sweet-spot of the tradeoff to increase the heuristic values as much as possible, while still being efficiently computable.

While the use of symmetrical lookups preserves the admissibility of a given heuristic h, it generally renders h to be *inconsistent*, which means that the resulting heuristic $\bar{h}$ does no longer satisfy the equality $\bar{h}(s) \leq \bar{h}(s') + cost(o)$, where s' is the successor state of s when operator o is applied. To alleviate this problem, *bidirectional pathmax (BPMX)* has been proposed and successfully applied in the heuristic search community [7]. Informally speaking, BPMX "repairs" inconsistent jumps in the heuristic values for s and successor state $s(o)$ (and vice versa) by adapting the values accordingly. Like symmetrical lookups, BPMX has not been applied in the planning context. Because symmetrical lookups as we adapted them to planning face the same problem of rendering heuristic values inconsistent, we also adapt BPMX to planning: whenever a node is expanded, the heuristic values of its successors are recursively updated up to a given recursion depth.

3   Experimental Study

We evaluate the previously discussed symmetry techniques for classical planning using A* search or orbit space search in combination with several abstraction heuristics from the planning literature. All techniques are implemented in the Fast Downward planner [12]. We use the optimal benchmarks from the International Planning Competition (IPC) up to IPC2011 with language features supported by the investigated heuristics (44 domains with a total of 1396 tasks). All experiments are performed on computers with Intel Xeon E5-2660 CPUs running at 2.2 GHz and with a time bound of 30 minutes and a memory bound of 2 GB, as common in IPCs. We compute both structural symmetries and factored symmetries with the graph automorphism tool *Bliss* [15].

3.1   Symmetries in Common Planning Benchmarks

In a first experiment, we investigate the occurrence of symmetries in the set of considered planning benchmarks. To the best of our knowledge, despite the success of symmetry handling in planning, no previous work has *quantitatively* analyzed the occurrence of symmetries in commonly used planning benchmarks so far. In the following, we report the number of tasks of every domain in which we discovered at least one non-trivial symmetry generator, the sum and the median of such generators aggregated over all tasks of every domain, as well as the number of discovered symmetry generators of different *orders*.[1] Table 1 lists the data.

The first and general observation we make (columns 2 and 3) is that there are lots of symmetries in this standard set of planning benchmarks, even more than one might have expected. In particular, only 3 domains (Blocksworld and the two Parcprinter domains) do not expose a symmetry in any task, and in 1103 tasks symmetries do occur. Furthermore, in 38 out of 44 domains, more than half of the tasks contain symmetries, and in most of these 38 domains, almost all the tasks are symmetrical. This huge number of symmetries is remarkable as the domains stem from quite different areas, covering both academic and real-world scenarios. It shows that symmetries are a quite general concept that often occurs in practice. Obviously, the large number of symmetries particularly explains the recent success of the symmetry techniques evaluated in planning. In addition, it suggests that further improvements based on symmetry-exploiting techniques are achievable—we will come back to this point below.

Furthermore, we observe that there is a remarkable difference in the number of generators found in the different domains, both with respect to the sum and with respect to the median (columns 4 and 5), which shows that the domains are structured quite differently in this respect. Interestingly, considering the generators' order for every task, we observe that the vast majority of generators has the simplest possible order of two. In rare cases, however, there also exist more complex generators of higher order. We should note that even having all generators being of order 2 does not ensure that all elements of the group will be of that order. An example can be seen in Gripper domain, where generators found by Bliss represent either (a) symmetries between two grippers, or (b) symmetries between ball i and ball $i + 1$, for all $1 \leq i < n$. All generators are of order 2, but there are elements of all orders up to n that can be composed out of those generators. Note also that other tools for finding automorphisms of coloured graphs might have found a different set of generators. Lastly, note that group or generator orders are only some of the features describing group structure and knowing a group structure could result in better exploitation of the found symmetries. Apparently, as we will see in the next sections, the existing methods already yield powerful symmetry elimination techniques for planning. It remains an open question *why* so many of the generators discovered by Bliss have this particular order. We suspect that the generators' order depends on the *representation* of the considered planning task. Currently, we have used the SAS$^+$ representation generated by the Fast Downward planner. It will be interesting to investigate if there are more suitable SAS$^+$ representations that are more amenable to finding generators of higher order, and if the available symmetry-techniques can profit from them.

---

[1] The order of a generator σ is defined as the smallest number of function compositions with itself that yields the identity function, i.e. $order(\sigma) = n$ if n is the smallest number with $\underbrace{\sigma \circ \cdots \circ \sigma}_{n} = id$.

Table 1. Properties of IPC domains: total number of tasks (total), number of tasks with at least one symmetry (symm), and number of generators for every domain (sum and median over all tasks), histogram of generators' order.

	# tasks		# generators		# generators of order			
	total	symm	sum	median	2	3	4	5
airport	50	42	205	4	205	-	-	-
barman-11	20	20	73	4	73	-	-	-
blocks	35	0	0	0	0	-	-	-
depot	22	22	118	4	118	-	-	-
driverlog	20	20	85	3	85	-	-	-
elevators-08	30	20	38	1	38	-	-	-
elevators-11	20	13	23	1	23	-	-	-
floortile-11	20	20	48	2	48	-	-	-
freecell	80	1	1	0	1	-	-	-
grid	5	5	27	5	27	-	-	-
gripper	20	20	460	23	460	-	-	-
logistics00	28	28	116	3.5	116	-	-	-
logistics98	35	35	2757	51	2756	1	-	-
miconic	150	141	1893	13	1892	1	-	-
mprime	35	35	649	15	649	-	-	-
mystery	30	28	471	10.5	471	-	-	-
nomystery-11	20	20	54	2.5	54	-	-	-
openstacks-08	30	30	221	7	221	-	-	-
openstacks-11	20	20	149	7	149	-	-	-
openstacks	30	11	20	0	19	-	-	1
parcprinter-08	30	0	0	0	0	-	-	-
parcprinter-11	20	0	0	0	0	-	-	-
parking-11	20	20	150	7.5	150	-	-	-
pathways-noneg	30	29	210	7	210	-	-	-
pegsol-08	30	30	58	2	58	-	-	-
pegsol-11	20	20	40	2	40	-	-	-
pipesworld-notankage	50	50	470	8	470	-	-	-
pipesworld-tankage	50	50	1547	22.5	1547	-	-	-
psr-small	50	32	73	1	73	-	-	-
rovers	40	32	381	4	381	-	-	-
satellite	36	36	12115	92	12115	-	-	-
scanalyzer-08	30	26	201	6	200	1	-	-
scanalyzer-11	20	18	142	6.5	142	-	-	-
sokoban-08	30	27	114	3	113	-	1	-
sokoban-11	20	19	66	3	65	-	1	-
tidybot-11	20	7	13	0	13	-	-	-
tpp	30	29	197	6	197	-	-	-
transport-08	30	30	76	2	76	-	-	-
transport-11	20	20	50	2	50	-	-	-
trucks	30	29	96	3	96	-	-	-
visitall-11	20	11	16	1	16	-	-	-
woodworking-08	30	22	244	5	244	-	-	-
woodworking-11	20	16	150	5	150	-	-	-
zenotravel	20	19	199	6	199	-	-	-
Total	1396	1103	24016	4	24010	3	2	1

3.2 Setup of the Study

Our evaluation focuses on abstraction heuristics because they represent a popular class of planning heuristics used for cost-optimal planning that are presumably not invariant under symmetries. In more detail, we evaluate heuristics based on merge-and-shrink [13], iPDB [11] in the implementation by Sievers, Ortlieb and Helmert [22], and CEGAR [20].

To use symmetrical lookups and orbit space search in combination with merge-and-shrink heuristics, we need to make sure that the heuristics yield admissible values for all symmetrical states. While this might seem obvious at first glance, admissibility is no longer guaranteed for regular merge-and-shrink heuristics within a straight-forward combination: in Fast Downward, abstract states in intermediate abstractions are pruned if they are unreachable from the initial state of the task. However, as the applied symmetries do not stabilize the initial state, admissibility can be violated because a non dead-end state could have a symmetrical state which corresponds to such a pruned abstract state. To address this issue, we simply disable this pruning within the computation of merge-and-shrink in all configurations that combine merge-and-shrink with orbit search. (The alternative of only using symmetries that additionally stabilize the initial state yields fewer symmetries and performs worse.) For the combinations of merge-and-shrink with symmetrical lookups and without orbit space search, we address this problem by ignoring symmetrical states with values of infinity if the original state is not evaluated to infinity. (The alternatives of only using symmetries that also stabilize the initial state again performs worse, and disabling the pruning of unreachable states within merge-and-shank is slightly worse in this setting.)

In the following, we focus on merge-and-shrink heuristics because all symmetry techniques (including factored symmetries) are applicable. Results for iPDB and CEGAR are discussed at the end of the section.

3.3   Symmetrical Lookups and BPMX

We investigate the following questions: First, how much can symmetrical lookups reduce the number of expansions and increase the coverage (i.e. the number of solved problems)? Second, what is the influence of the number of considered symmetrical states? Third, can these techniques improve the total runtime? Fourth, how important is BPMX in this setting? We report results for the best available merge-and-shrink configuration in Fast Downward, which uses the merging strategy DFP [23] and the shrinking strategy based on bisimulation [17] with size limit 50000.

We address the first three questions (i.e. no use of BPMX yet) in a first experiment, reported in Table 2. We compare the baseline, i.e. A* with merge-and-shrink (base), to merge-and-shrink with the inclusion of symmetrical lookups for 1 symmetrical state found by a short random walk in the orbit (slone), and for 5, 10 or all symmetrical states found by a breadth first search in the orbit (slsub5, slsub10, slall). We observe the following trends. Symmetrical lookups generally help in increasing the coverage and reducing the number of expansions,[2] both with respect to the sum over all commonly solved tasks as well as with respect

---

[2] Note that we generally report the number of expansions excluding the last f layer to avoid the (arbitrary) tie-breaking effects in the last f layer.

Table 2. M&S (base) vs. M&S with symmetrical lookups: one symmetrical state computed via a short random walk (slone), a subset of symmetrical states of size 5/10 (slsub5/10), all symmetrical states (slall).

	base	slone	slsub5	slsub10	slall
Coverage	652	656	**658**	**658**	**658**
Expansions sum	607602428	501671723	493848579	**471769190**	493848579
Expansions median	1263	1059	**811**	**811**	**811**

to the median over all tasks solved by at least one configuration (where unsolved tasks are counted as infinity). While the extreme ends of the spectrum (considering one vs all symmetrical states) does not hit the sweet spot of the tradeoff to be as informative and efficient as possible, considering *some* symmetrical states can considerably decrease the number of expansions while still being efficiently computable. In the following, when referring to symmetrical lookups, we always mean the best configuration where the h value is maximized over 10 additional symmetrical states (and call it "sl" from here on).

Next, we compare the baseline against the best configuration with symmetrical lookups in more details on a per-task base. Figure 1 shows results as scatterplots of expansions and total time for this comparison. The plot for expansions (left) shows that using symmetrical lookups improves the heuristic quality in quite a lot of problems (reduced number of expansions). Considering the runtime (right plot), we see that computing symmetrical states as expected incurs a computational overhead that results in a general increase of runtime. Still, the coverage increases as previously shown in Table 3, and hence the heuristic quality improvement in this comparison outweighs the increase in runtime.

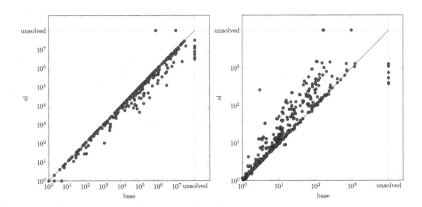

Fig. 1. M&S (base) vs. M&S with symmetrical lookups (sl): expansions (left) and total time (right)

Table 3. M&S (base) vs. M&S with symmetrical lookups (sl) with and without BPMX of varying depth X (-bpX).

	base	sl	sl-bp1	sl-bp2	sl-bp10
Coverage	652	**658**	**658**	**658**	**658**
Expansions sum	607602428	**471769190**	471769292	471769236	471769236
Expansions median	1260	**751**	**751**	**751**	**751**

Finally, we investigate to which extent BPMX can help in combination with symmetrical lookups, which generally render heuristics to be inconsistent. We evaluate three variants: the most simple variant that only updates h values of successor states (bp1), a variant that updates the h values recursively up to a depth of 2 (i.e. for successor states of successor states, including the parents if there exist invertible operators, which corresponds to BPMX in the sense of Felner et al. [7]) (bp2), and a variant that performs up to 10 recursive updates of h values of previously visited states (bp10). Table 3 shows the results.

We observe that, in contrast to results reported in the heuristic search community, BPMX does not help when applied for planning problems. The reduction in expansions compared to using symmetrical lookups without BPMX is very small, in a range not visible when comparing the median over tasks, and there is no coverage gain. As one would expect based on these numbers, a comparison of symmetrical lookups with BPMX (with recursive updates up to depth 10) against the baseline yields scatterplots that look the same as the plots in Fig. 1. Also a direct comparison of using symmetrical lookups with and without BPMX shows that the number of expansions remains the same for nearly all tasks, and the runtime slightly increases for some tasks. A more detailed analysis reveals that heuristic value corrections due to BPMX only occur in 13 domains, in approximately 2% of all tasks for which the merge-and-shrink abstraction was successfully computed, which shows that in most cases, merge-and-shrink with symmetrical lookups still remains a consistent heuristic.

We conclude that symmetrical lookups with not too much overhead, i.e. for a limited number of additional symmetrical states evaluations in every state, can yield performance improvements for planning. Using BPMX may improve the heuristic quality in very few cases, but the computational overhead never pays off (but it also does not hurt in terms of coverage in the tested configurations). In the following, we hence stick to using symmetrical lookups without BPMX.

3.4   Results for Merge-and-Shrink Heuristic

In our final experiments for merge-and-shrink, we compare all techniques. We again use A* with merge-and-shrink as baseline (base), and combine merge-and-shrink with symmetrical lookups (sl) as before, with orbit space search (oss), and with factored symmetries in the configuration "symm" reported by Sievers et al. [24] (fs). Table 4 shows domain-wise coverage and the number of expansions as

Table 4. Domain-wise coverage and aggregated expansions (sum and median) for M&S with all symmetry combinations. Abbreviations: base: A*, oss: orbit space search, sl: symmetrical lookups, fs: factored symmetries; X-Y: combination of X and Y; all: combination of oss, sl and fs.

	base	oss	sl	fs	oss-sl	oss-fs	sl-fs	all
airport (50)	18	18	18	18	18	18	18	18
barman-11 (20)	4	8	4	4	7	8	4	7
blocks (35)	27	27	27	26	27	27	26	26
depot (22)	6	8	7	7	8	9	7	9
driverlog (20)	12	13	12	12	13	13	12	13
elevators-08 (30)	16	19	17	16	19	18	17	18
elevators-11 (20)	13	16	14	13	16	15	14	15
floortile-11 (20)	5	5	5	2	5	3	2	3
freecell (80)	20	20	20	20	20	20	20	20
grid (5)	2	2	2	2	2	2	2	2
gripper (20)	19	20	19	18	20	20	18	20
logistics00 (28)	20	20	20	20	20	20	20	20
logistics98 (35)	5	5	5	4	5	5	4	5
miconic (150)	72	76	73	77	75	78	76	78
mprime (35)	23	22	23	23	22	23	23	23
mystery (30)	16	16	16	16	15	17	16	16
nomystery-11 (20)	18	18	20	16	20	18	16	18
openstacks-08 (30)	20	24	19	20	23	24	19	23
openstacks-11 (20)	15	19	14	15	18	19	14	18
openstacks (30)	7	7	7	7	7	7	7	7
parcprinter-08 (30)	14	13	14	14	13	13	14	13
parcprinter-11 (20)	10	9	10	10	9	9	10	9
parking-11 (20)	2	2	2	7	2	7	7	7
pathways-noneg (30)	4	4	4	4	4	4	4	4
pegsol-08 (30)	29	29	29	27	29	28	27	28
pegsol-11 (20)	19	19	19	17	19	18	17	18
pipesworld-nt (50)	16	18	15	16	16	18	16	16
pipesworld-t (50)	14	17	14	15	17	17	15	17
psr-small (50)	50	50	50	50	50	50	50	50
rovers (40)	8	8	8	8	8	8	8	8
satellite (36)	6	7	6	6	6	7	6	7
scanalyzer-08 (30)	13	18	13	12	18	17	12	17
scanalyzer-11 (20)	10	14	10	9	14	13	9	13
sokoban-08 (30)	26	29	27	30	29	30	30	30
sokoban-11 (20)	20	20	20	20	20	20	20	20
tidybot-11 (20)	1	1	1	1	1	1	1	1
tpp (30)	6	7	7	6	8	7	6	7
transport-08 (30)	11	11	11	11	11	11	11	11
transport-11 (20)	6	7	7	6	7	7	7	7
trucks (30)	7	8	7	8	8	9	8	9
visitall-11 (20)	9	9	9	10	9	10	10	10
woodworking-08 (30)	13	13	13	13	13	12	13	12
woodworking-11 (20)	8	8	8	8	8	7	8	7
zenotravel (20)	12	12	12	10	12	11	11	12
Coverage sum (1396)	652	696	658	654	691	**698**	655	692
Expansions sum	5.16e+8	2.68e+8	4.01e+8	3.65e+8	2.54e+8	2.39e+8	3.44e+8	**2.32e+8**
Expansions median	5077	4292	4481	7432	2814	5499	6216	4593

the sum over commonly solved tasks and as the median over all tasks solved by at least one configuration.

Comparing the individual techniques to the baseline (columns 2–5), we observe that all symmetry techniques help, both in terms of coverage and expansions. For the domains with no symmetries (Blocksworld and both Parcprinter domains), there is a slight reduction in coverage for some configurations due to the overhead of searching for symmetries without finding any. For all other domains, orbit space search and symmetrical lookups only reduce coverage in a very few cases, whereas factored symmetries perform worse in a few more cases. Generally, orbit space search yields by far the strongest performance improvement (both in terms of coverage and expansions), compared to symmetrical lookups and factored symmetries that increase the coverage rather modestly, but also reduce expansions.

When combining the individual techniques (columns 6–9), we again observe that orbit space search increases the coverage for all configurations, i.e. it is always beneficial to include it with either of the other two techniques, compared to only using one of the other techniques (with one exception in the domain nomystery). The combination of factored symmetries with orbit space search is particularly beneficial, achieving the overall highest coverage, improving over both using only factored symmetries or only using orbit space search. The opposite holds for the combination of symmetrical lookups with orbit space search: coverage decreases compared to only using orbit space search. We generally observe that adding symmetrical lookups to a configuration decreases the number of expansions as expected, but does not increase performance in terms of coverage, due to the computational overhead.

3.5   Results for iPDB and CEGAR Heuristics

We investigate orbit space search and symmetrical lookups with iPDB and with the CEGAR heuristic in its best configuration using the landmarks and goals decomposition [20]. Again, we report results for computing 10 symmetrical states when using symmetrical lookups, and leave out BPMX as its benefit is negligible also in this context. Table 5 shows a domain-wise overview of coverage and summarized expansions (summed over commonly solved tasks and the median over all tasks solved by at least one configuration of the heuristic) for A^* with the corresponding heuristic (base), and for the corresponding heuristic combined with orbit space search (oss), symmetrical lookups (sl), and the combination thereof (oss-sl).

For CEGAR, we observe that orbit space search is again, as for merge-and-shrink, the most improving symmetry-based technique. However, the are also several domains in which coverage decreases and the median of expansions is even higher than with the baseline. Presumably, due to the way they are constructed, CEGAR abstractions are especially well-informed along a path from the initial state to the goal, but not necessarily on a symmetrical path (because our symmetries do not stabilize the initial stated). Furthermore, due to the CEGAR computation starting the refinement near goal states, CEGAR abstractions yield well-informed heuristics close to the goal, which often results in fewer expansions on the last f layer than with other heuristics. Indeed, computing the median of expansions including the last f layer, the number for CEGAR with orbit space search is smaller than for the baseline. The second observation

Table 5. CEGAR and iPDB with A* (base), with orbit space search (oss), with A* and symmetrical lookups (sl), and with a combination of oss and sl (oss-sl).

	CEGAR				iPDB			
	base	oss	sl	oss-sl	base	oss	sl	oss-sl
airport (50)	**32**	24	30	28	**23**	**23**	**23**	23
barman-11 (20)	4	**8**	4	6	4	**8**	4	7
blocks (35)	18	18	18	18	28	28	28	28
depot (22)	6	**7**	6	**7**	8	10	7	**11**
driverlog (20)	10	11	10	**12**	13	13	13	13
elevators-08 (30)	18	**19**	**19**	**19**	20	**21**	20	**21**
elevators-11 (20)	15	**16**	**16**	**16**	16	**17**	16	**17**
floortile-11 (20)	2	2	2	2	2	**3**	2	**3**
freecell (80)	52	**53**	**53**	52	20	20	20	
grid (5)	2	2	2	2	3	3	3	3
gripper (20)	7	**20**	7	**20**	7	**20**	7	**20**
logistics00 (28)	**20**	15	**20**	16	21	20	**21**	20
logistics98 (35)	**9**	5	8	6	5	5	5	5
miconic (150)	71	**75**	66	73	55	**60**	55	58
mprime (35)	26	24	**27**	23	**23**	**23**	**23**	**23**
mystery (30)	**17**	16	**17**	15	16	**17**	16	**17**
nomystery-11 (20)	**14**	13	**14**	**14**	18	**20**	19	**20**
openstacks-08 (30)	20	**24**	19	23	20	**24**	19	23
openstacks-11 (20)	15	**19**	14	18	15	**19**	14	18
openstacks (30)	7	7	7	7	7	7	7	7
parcprinter-08 (30)	22	22	22	22	13	13	13	13
parcprinter-11 (20)	17	17	17	17	9	9	9	9
parking-11 (20)	0	0	0	0	7	7	7	7
pathways-noneg (30)	4	4	4	4	4	4	4	4
pegsol-08 (30)	28	28	28	28	28	**29**	27	28
pegsol-11 (20)	18	18	18	18	19	**20**	18	19
pipesworld-notankage (50)	17	**20**	17	18	21	**24**	20	22
pipesworld-tankage (50)	13	**18**	13	17	16	**20**	16	19
psr-small (50)	49	**50**	49	**50**	49	**50**	49	**50**
rovers (40)	7	7	7	7	8	8	8	8
satellite (36)	6	**7**	6	6	6	6	6	6
scanalyzer-08 (30)	12	**16**	12	15	13	**18**	13	**18**
scanalyzer-11 (20)	9	**12**	9	11	10	**14**	10	**14**
sokoban-08 (30)	22	**27**	20	26	29	**30**	29	**30**
sokoban-11 (20)	19	**20**	17	**20**	20	20	20	20
tidybot-11 (20)	**14**	10	**14**	**14**	14	14	14	14
tpp (30)	7	**8**	7	**8**	6	**7**	6	**7**
transport-08 (30)	11	11	11	11	11	11	11	11
transport-11 (20)	6	6	6	6	6	**7**	6	**7**
trucks (30)	12	12	12	12	8	**10**	9	**10**
visitall-11 (20)	9	9	9	9	16	16	16	16
woodworking-08 (30)	12	12	12	12	9	9	9	9
woodworking-11 (20)	7	7	7	7	4	4	4	4
zenotravel (20)	12	12	**13**	**13**	11	**12**	11	11
Sum (1396)	698	**731**	689	728	661	**723**	657	713
Expansions sum	50.8e+8	29.2e+8	44.5e+8	**19.1e+8**	33.2e+8	15.0e+8	31.4e+8	**13.3e+8**
Expansions median	5118	7285	5799	**2906**	6931	2440	6339	**1952**

for CEGAR is that adding symmetrical lookups reduces the summed number of expansions as for merge-and-shrink, but also decreases coverage due to the computational overhead both compared to the baseline and orbit space search.

Considering iPDB, we observe a behavior more similar to merge-and-shrink than CEGAR: orbit space search is the best performer in terms of coverage in 42 out of 44 domains, and expansions are greatly decreased. However, including symmetrical lookups is again only beneficial in terms of expansions, but not for coverage.

4 Discussion

Our case study shows that symmetries frequently occur in various planning tasks, and confirms that currently available symmetry-techniques can significantly help for planning with state-of-the-art abstraction heuristics. Most notably, this is the case for orbit space search, where the number of solved problems usually increases considerably for all of the considered heuristics. For the other techniques, i.e. symmetrical lookups and factored symmetries, the improvement in coverage is often rather modest (and in some cases, coverage can even decrease). We furthermore observe that BPMX does not perform equally strong for planning as for search.

Despite the improvement obtained with existing symmetry-techniques, one can argue that there is even room for further improvement because there are several domains (e.g., Airport or Rovers) where symmetries do occur, but the number of solved tasks could not be increased nevertheless. Even in the domain with the highest number of discovered symmetries (Satellite), the coverage increase is rather modest (one more solved task with merge-and-shrink and the CEGAR heuristic, no improvement for iPDB). Exploiting these symmetries more accurately can potentially yield even stronger symmetry-techniques. Additionally, it will be interesting to investigate the impact of the SAS^+ representation on the occurrence of symmetries.

Acknowledgments. This work was supported by the Swiss National Science Foundation (SNSF) as part of the project "Automated Reformulation and Pruning in Factored State Spaces (ARAP)".

References

1. Proceedings of the Twenty-Ninth AAAI Conference on Artificial Intelligence, AAAI 2015. AAAI Press (2015)
2. Bäckström, C., Nebel, B.: Complexity results for SAS^+ planning. Computational Intelligence **11**(4), 625–655 (1995)
3. Culberson, J.C., Schaeffer, J.: Pattern databases. Computational Intelligence **14**(3), 318–334 (1998)
4. Domshlak, C., Katz, M., Shleyfman, A.: Enhanced symmetry breaking in cost-optimal planning as forward search. In: McCluskey, L., Williams, B., Silva, J.R., Bonet, B. (eds.) Proceedings of the Twenty-Second International Conference on Automated Planning and Scheduling, ICAPS 2012. AAAI Press (2012)

5. Domshlak, C., Katz, M., Shleyfman, A.: Symmetry breaking: Satisficing planning and landmark heuristics. In: Borrajo, D., Kambhampati, S., Oddi, A., Fratini, S. (eds.) Proceedings of the Twenty-Third International Conference on Automated Planning and Scheduling, ICAPS 2013, pp. 298–302. AAAI Press (2013)
6. Domshlak, C., Katz, M., Shleyfman, A.: Symmetry breaking in deterministic planning as forward search: Orbit space search algorithm. Tech. Rep. IS/IE-2015-03, Technion, Haifa (2015)
7. Felner, A., Zahavi, U., Holte, R., Schaeffer, J., Sturtevant, N., Zhang, Z.: Inconsistent heuristics in theory and practice. Artificial Intelligence **175**, 1570–1603 (2011)
8. Felner, A., Zahavi, U., Schaeffer, J., Holte, R.C.: Dual lookups in pattern databases. In: Kaelbling, L.P., Saffiotti, A. (eds.) Proceedings of the 19th International Joint Conference on Artificial Intelligence, IJCAI 2005, pp. 103–108. Professional Book Center (2005)
9. Fox, M., Long, D.: The detection and exploitation of symmetry in planning problems. In: Dean, T. (ed.) Proceedings of the Sixteenth International Joint Conference on Artificial Intelligence, IJCAI 1999, pp. 956–961. Morgan Kaufmann (1999)
10. Fox, M., Long, D.: Extending the exploitation of symmetries in planning. In: Ghallab, M., Hertzberg, J., Traverso, P. (eds.) Proceedings of the Sixth International Conference on Artificial Intelligence Planning and Scheduling, AIPS 2002, pp. 83–91. AAAI Press (2002)
11. Haslum, P., Botea, A., Helmert, M., Bonet, B., Koenig, S.: Domain-independent construction of pattern database heuristics for cost-optimal planning. In: Proceedings of the Twenty-Second AAAI Conference on Artificial Intelligence, AAAI 2007, pp. 1007–1012. AAAI Press (2007)
12. Helmert, M.: The Fast Downward planning system. Journal of Artificial Intelligence Research **26**, 191–246 (2006)
13. Helmert, M., Haslum, P., Hoffmann, J., Nissim, R.: Merge-and-shrink abstraction: A method for generating lower bounds in factored state spaces. Journal of the ACM **61**(3), 16:1–63 (2014)
14. Ip, C.N., Dill, D.L.: Better verification through symmetry. Formal Methods in System Design **9**(1–2), 41–75 (1996)
15. Junttila, T., Kaski, P.: Engineering an efficient canonical labeling tool for large and sparse graphs. In: Proceedings of the Ninth Workshop on Algorithm Engineering and Experiments, ALENEX 2007, pp. 135–149. SIAM (2007)
16. Luks, E.M.: Permutation groups and polynomial-time computation. In: Groups and Computation, DIMACS Series in Discrete Mathematics and Theoretical Computer Science, vol. 11, pp. 139–175 (1993)
17. Nissim, R., Hoffmann, J., Helmert, M.: Computing perfect heuristics in polynomial time: On bisimulation and merge-and-shrink abstraction in optimal planning. In: Walsh, T. (ed.) Proceedings of the 22nd International Joint Conference on Artificial Intelligence, IJCAI 2011, pp. 1983–1990 (2011)
18. Pochter, N., Zohar, A., Rosenschein, J.S.: Exploiting problem symmetries in state-based planners. In: Burgard, W., Roth, D. (eds.) Proceedings of the Twenty-Fifth AAAI Conference on Artificial Intelligence, AAAI 2011, pp. 1004–1009. AAAI Press (2011)
19. Rintanen, J.: Symmetry reduction for SAT representations of transition systems. In: Giunchiglia, E., Muscettola, N., Nau, D. (eds.) Proceedings of the Thirteenth International Conference on Automated Planning and Scheduling, ICAPS 2003, pp. 32–40. AAAI Press (2003)

20. Seipp, J., Helmert, M.: Diverse and additive Cartesian abstraction heuristics. In: Proceedings of the Twenty-Fourth International Conference on Automated Planning and Scheduling, ICAPS 2014, pp. 289–297. AAAI Press (2014)
21. Shleyfman, A., Katz, M., Helmert, M., Sievers, S., Wehrle, M.: Heuristics and symmetries in classical planning. In: Proceedings of the Twenty-Ninth AAAI Conference on Artificial Intelligence, AAAI 2015 [1], pp. 3371–3377 (2015)
22. Sievers, S., Ortlieb, M., Helmert, M.: Efficient implementation of pattern database heuristics for classical planning. In: Borrajo, D., Felner, A., Korf, R., Likhachev, M., Linares López, C., Ruml, W., Sturtevant, N. (eds.) Proceedings of the Fifth Annual Symposium on Combinatorial Search, SoCS 2012, pp. 105–111. AAAI Press (2012)
23. Sievers, S., Wehrle, M., Helmert, M.: Generalized label reduction for merge-and-shrink heuristics. In: Proceedings of the Twenty-Eighth AAAI Conference on Artificial Intelligence, AAAI 2014, pp. 2358–2366. AAAI Press (2014)
24. Sievers, S., Wehrle, M., Helmert, M., Shleyfman, A., Katz, M.: Factored symmetries for merge-and-shrink abstractions. In: Proceedings of the Twenty-Ninth AAAI Conference on Artificial Intelligence, AAAI 2015 [1], pp. 3378–3385 (2015)
25. Zahavi, U., Felner, A., Holte, R.C., Schaeffer, J.: Duality in permutation state spaces and the dual search algorithm. Artificial Intelligence **172**(4–5), 514–540 (2008)

Necessary Observations in Nondeterministic Planning

David Speck[(✉)], Manuela Ortlieb, and Robert Mattmüller

Research Group Foundations of AI, University of Freiburg,
Freiburg Im Breisgau, Germany
{speckd,ortlieb,mattmuel}@informatik.uni-freiburg.de

Abstract. An agent that interacts with a nondeterministic environment can often only partially observe the surroundings. This necessitates observations via sensors rendering more information about the current world state. Sensors can be expensive in many regards therefore it can be essential to minimize the amount of sensors an agents requires to solve given tasks. A limitation for sensor minimization is given by essential sensors which are always required to solve particular problems. In this paper we present an efficient algorithm which determines a set of necessary observation variables. More specifically, we develop a bottom-up algorithm which computes a set of variables which are always necessary to observe, in order to always reach a goal state. Our experimental results show that the knowledge about necessary observation variables can be used to minimize the number of sensors of an agent.

Keywords: AI planning · Nondeterministic planning · Partial observability · Observation actions

1 Introduction

An agent that interacts with a nondeterministic environment can often only partially observe the surroundings. Acting in such an environment with uncertainty necessitates observations of the current world state via sensors to obtain more information for reaching a goal state. Such sensors can be expensive with regards to battery, money, weight, maintenance, and time. Therefore it can be useful or even essential to minimize the amount of sensors necessary to solve a particular planning task. More precisely, we consider the sensors an agent needs to be fitted with. In this paper, we discuss the problem of minimizing a set of necessary sensors and *not* the problem of minimizing the amount of sensor observations. For example, in a specific robotic application, an RGB-D camera can handle all the observations a laser scanner would be used for, thus obviating the latter. Regarding an extraterrestrial mission such a sensor reduction can be essential to minimize the weight. We represent the uncertainty of a current world state as a set of world states denoted as belief state. Applying and selecting actions and observations via sensors for belief states (decision points) in such an environment is called offline partially observable nondeterministic planning. Similar to

© Springer International Publishing Switzerland 2015
S. Hölldobler et al. (Eds.): KI 2015, LNAI 9324, pp. 181–193, 2015.
DOI: 10.1007/978-3-319-24489-1_14

Mattmüller et al. [1] we reduce the problem of sensor minimization by assuming that a sensor and its measured data are represented by a state variable which can be observed. This simplification induces a search for a minimal set of variables $\mathcal{O}$ where only the variables contained in $\mathcal{O}$ can be observed and still every planning task of the underlying planning domain is solvable. After the removal of a variable o from the set of observable variables $\mathcal{O}$ we call o reduced. In addition, we reduce the problem of finding such a set of variables from the planning domain level to the planning task level. As Mattmüller et al. [1] mentioned, it is possible to generalise the results if such a planning task is reasonably chosen with regard to the underlying planning domain. Clearly, necessary observation variables of a planning task Π can never be reduced without losing power with regard to solving problems because if such a necessary observation variable is not observable, at least planning task Π is not solvable anymore. Furthermore, a necessary observation variable o is an element of every minimal set of variables $\mathcal{O}$ which is still sufficient to solve every planning task of the underlying planning domain if only the variables of $\mathcal{O}$ are observable. Considering the previous example, if an RGB-D camera is necessary to track the localization of a robot, this camera can never be reduced particularly with regard to localization problems. Such a knowledge about necessary sensors can improve the runtime of a sensor reduction procedure depending on its construction. To our knowledge, three recent studies on observation minimization have been published. Two of them developed by Huang et al. [2,3] deal with observation minimization for a fixed plan in different settings. Firstly, they presented an algorithm which calculates an approximately minimal set of observations for a given set of variables $\mathcal{V}$ and a fixed strong plan π where all variables $\mathcal{V}$ are possibly observable. The algorithm identifies all state pairs which need to be distinguished in plan π and always chooses the observation variable which distinguishes the most remaining not distinguished state pairs [2]. Secondly, Huang et al. [3] extended their results/algorithm and presented an attempt to solve the problem of observation reduction for general plans with contexts. The work of Mattmüller et al. [1] is closely connected to this work in regard to the same problem setting. They worked on a top-down approach which greedily removes observation variables by the trial and error method still sufficient to solve a particular planning task. This greedy top-down algorithm returns an inclusion minimal set of observation variables. While here, a bottom-up procedure is presented which collects stepwise necessary observation variables, i.e. variables which always have to be observed to solve a particular planning task.

2   Preliminaries

We formally define partially observable nondeterministic (POND) planning similar to the definition of Mattmüller et al. [1] using a *finite-domain representation* for the state variables. A *POND planning task skeleton* is a 5-tuple $\Pi = \langle \mathcal{V}, B_0, B_*, \mathcal{A}, \mathcal{W} \rangle$, where $\mathcal{V}$ is a finite set of *state variables*, B_0 is an *initial belief state*, B_* is a *goal description*, $\mathcal{A}$ is a finite set of *nondeterministic actions*, and

$\mathcal{W} \subseteq \mathcal{V}$ is a set of possible observable variables. Every state variable v in $\mathcal{V}$ has a finite *domain* $\mathcal{D}_v$ and an *extended domain* $\mathcal{D}_v^+$, where $\bot$ denotes the *undefined/don't-care* value. A function s, where $s(v) \in \mathcal{D}_v^+$ for all $v \in \mathcal{V}$ is called a *partial state*. Partial state s is defined for a variable v if $s(v) \neq \bot$. The *scope* of a partial state s is the set of all variables v which are defined in s, i.e. $scope(s) = \{v \in \mathcal{V} \mid s(v) \neq \bot\}$. We call a partial state s a *state* if s is defined for all variables of $\mathcal{V}$ which means $scope(s) = \mathcal{V}$. A variable-value pair is called a fact and denoted by (v, d) or $v = d$, where $v \in \mathcal{V}$ and $d \in \mathcal{D}_v$. The set $\mathcal{S}$ represents all states over $\mathcal{V}$ and the set $\mathcal{B}$ represents all *belief states* over $\mathcal{V}$, where $\mathcal{B} = 2^{\mathcal{S}}$. We call a belief state B a *goal belief state* iff $B \subseteq B_*$. A partial state s_p can be used as a *condition* or as an *update* on a state s. We say a condition s_p is *satisfied* in a state s iff s agrees with all defined variables of s_p. An update s_p on a state s leads to a new state s' that agrees with s_p on all defined variables and with s on all other variables. An action $a \in \mathcal{A}$ is of the form $a = \langle Pre, Eff \rangle$ where the two components are a partial state *Pre* called *precondition* and a finite set *Eff* of partial states *eff* called *effect*. We call the partial states *eff* $\in$ *Eff* of an action a the *nondeterministic outcomes* of a. We denote the set of all facts as precondition *Pre* or effect *Eff* of an action $a = \langle Pre, Eff \rangle$ by $pre(a)$ and $eff(a)$, where $eff(a)$ is the union over all facts of every nondeterministic outcome *eff* $\in$ *Eff*. The union over a set of actions A is analogously defined as $pre(A)$ and $eff(A)$, i.e. $pre(A) = \bigcup_{a \in A} pre(a)$ and $eff(A) = \bigcup_{a \in A} eff(a)$. *Applications* in POND planning are defined as follows: The application of a nondeterministic outcome *eff* to a state s is a state $app(eff, s)$ resulting from an update of s with *eff*. The application of an effect *Eff* to a state s results in a set of states $app(Eff, s) = \{app(eff, s) \mid eff \in Eff\}$. An action $a = \langle Pre, Eff \rangle$ is applicable in a state s if its precondition *Pre* is satisfied in s. An action $a = \langle Pre, Eff \rangle$ is applicable in a belief state B if its precondition *Pre* is satisfied in all states s, where $s \in B$. The application of an action $a = \langle Pre, Eff \rangle$ in a belief state B is a belief state $app(a, B) = \{app(eff, s) \mid eff \in Eff, s \in B\}$ if a is applicable in B and undefined otherwise. To complete the definition of partially observable nondeterministic planning we define an *observation variable* or in short *observation* as a variable $o \in \mathcal{W}$. The result of an *observation application* to a belief state B is a belief state $app(o, B) = \{\{s \in B \mid s(o) = d\} \mid d \in \mathcal{D}_o\} \backslash \{\emptyset\}$ where $app(o, B)$ is a non-empty subset of B and contains only states according to the possible values of o.

A POND *planning task* $\Pi[\mathcal{O}] = \langle \Pi, \mathcal{O} \rangle$ is a tuple, where Π is a POND planning task skeleton, and $\mathcal{O} \in \mathcal{W}$ is a finite set of observations. Actions and observations have positive unit costs for applications. In the following sections we will denote a planning task $\Pi[\mathcal{O}] = \langle \Pi, \mathcal{O} \rangle$ also as Π if it is clearly understandable from the context. We call a partial mapping π from belief states to applicable actions or observations a *plan* for a given POND planning task. A plan π is *closed* if every belief state B reachable from the initial belief state B_0 following π is a goal belief state or plan π is defined for B. If from every belief state B reachable from initial belief state B_0 following π at least one goal state $B' \subseteq B_*$ is reachable following π, we call π *proper*. A plan π is a *strong cyclic plan* for a POND planning task if π is closed and proper. We denote by

$\mathcal{B}_\pi$ the set of all belief states which are non-goal states and reachable from the initial belief state B_0 following π, including B_0. An action or observation *occurs* in a plan π if there exists a belief state $B \in \mathcal{B}_\pi$, where $\pi(B) = a$ or $\pi(B) = o$ [1,4]. Let $a = \langle Pre, Eff \rangle$, with $Eff = \{eff_1, \ldots, eff_n\}$ be an action. The *strong outcome*

$$eff_i^s(v) = \begin{cases} eff_i(v) & \text{if } v \in scope(eff_i) \\ Pre(v) & \text{otherwise} \end{cases}$$

contains all facts which are always true after applying action a with a resulting outcome of eff_i. The *strong effect* $Eff^s = \{eff_1^s, \ldots, eff_n^s\}$ contains all corresponding strong outcomes of Eff.

Applying and selecting actions in deterministic environments where an initial world state is fully known is called classical planning. We define classical planning as a special case of POND planning. A *classical planning task* using *finite-domain representation* for the state variables is a 4-tuple $\Pi_{det} = \langle \mathcal{V}, \mathcal{A}_{det}, s_o, B_* \rangle$, where $\mathcal{V}$ is a finite set of state variables, s_o is an *initial world state* over $\mathcal{V}$, $\mathcal{A}_{det}$ is a finite set of *deterministic actions* over $\mathcal{V}$, and B_* is a goal description. An action $a \in \mathcal{A}_{det}$ in classical planning is a nondeterministic action a with the restriction that effect Eff contains only one nondeterministic outcome eff, i.e $|Eff| = 1$. We call such an action a a *deterministic action*. In classical planning actions are applied in world states and result in world states. A deterministic action $a = \langle Pre, Eff \rangle$ is applicable in a world state s if its precondition Pre is satisfied in s. The *application* of an action $a = \langle Pre, Eff \rangle$ to a world state s is the world state $app(a, s) = app(eff, s)$, where $\{eff\} = Eff$ if a is applicable in s and undefined otherwise. Hereafter, if we talk about preconditions and effects in classical planning we only mention facts, i.e. we ignore undefined variables. A (classical) *plan* π_{det} for a planning task $\Pi_{det} = \langle \mathcal{V}, \mathcal{A}_{det}, s_o, B_* \rangle$ is a sequence of applicable actions $a_0, \ldots, a_n$ with a world state sequence $s_0, \ldots, s_{n+1}$ where $app(a_i, s_i) = s_{i+1}$ and $s_{n+1} \in B_*$ is a goal world state. An action $a \in \mathcal{A}_{det}$ *occurs* in a plan π_{det} if it is contained in the application sequence of π_{det}. The *determinization* of a nondeterministic action $a = \langle Pre, Eff \rangle$, with $Eff = \{eff_1, \ldots, eff_n\}$, is a set of n actions $a^i = \langle Pre, \{eff_i\} \rangle$ generated by the function $\mathcal{A}_{det}(a)$.[1] Such an action $a^i = \langle Pre, \{eff_i\} \rangle$ is a deterministic action. Every POND planning task $\Pi = \langle \mathcal{V}, B_0, B_*, \mathcal{A}, \mathcal{W} \rangle$ has $|B_0|$ unique classical (deterministic) planning tasks $\Pi_{det} = \langle \mathcal{V}, \mathcal{A}_{det}, s_0, B_* \rangle$ where $\mathcal{A}_{det} = \bigcup_{a \in \mathcal{A}} \mathcal{A}_{det}(a)$ and $s_0 \in B_0$. The function $n(a^i) : \mathcal{A}_{det} \to \mathcal{A}$ maps a determinized action $a^i \in \mathcal{A}_{det}$ back to its original nondeterministic action $a \in \mathcal{A}$. A *disjunctive action landmark* or in short *landmark* of a classical planning task Π_{det} is a set of actions L such that at least one action of L occurs in every plan for Π_{det}. Originally the landmark cut procedure by Helmert and Domshlak [5] is used as a heuristic function by calculating disjunctive landmarks of a classical planning task. We will slightly modify the procedure by returning the disjunctive landmarks of a classical planning task Π_{det} instead of the heuristic value and denote the resulting landmarks by $LM\text{-}cut(\Pi_{det})$.

---

[1] For simplification we assume that every determinized action has a particular unique ID which may lead to duplications of actions.

3   Necessary Observations

Targeting observation reduction regarding a POND planning task we can search for observations that can never be reduced, i.e. observations that are always necessary for every strong cyclic plan. We call such an observation a necessary observation and define it as follows.

Definition 1 (Necessary Observation). *A necessary observation of a POND planning task Π is an observation o such that it occurs at least once in every strong cyclic plan for Π. We call a set of necessary observations o a necessary observation set $\mathcal{N}$.*

For example, we assume a nondeterministic BLOCKSWORLD with two blocks A and B. Initially, block A is located on block B. The goal is variable *B-clear* which means that no block is on B. There exists only one action *pick-up-A-B* with two outcomes: either block A is picked up or nothing happens and block A remains on block B. Furthermore, we assume that it is only possible to observe if any block is located on block X by observation *X-clear*. Obviously, action *pick-up-A-B* has to be applied until block A is picked up for reaching the goal state. The only possibility for verifying that block A is picked up is to observe *B-clear* which is why observation *B-clear* occurs in every strong cyclic plan for the problem. Thus in this setting *B-clear* is a necessary observation and additionally the only one. However, not always necessary observations exist. We assume that the previous example contains also an observation *X-picked* which encodes if block X is picked up. Now we can construct two different strong cyclic plans – one with observation *B-clear* and one with *A-picked* because observations *B-clear* and *A-picked* verify whether *B-clear* is satisfied after applying action *pick-up-A-B*. Therefore none of these observations occurs in every strong cyclic plan and consequently no necessary observation exists. Interestingly, the reduction of an unnecessary observation can lead to additional necessary observations. Regarding the previous example, by reducing observation *B-clear* observation *A-picked* becomes necessary and vice versa. This property will be topic of upcoming research.

Necessary observation sets and cardinality or inclusion minimal observation sets sufficient to solve a POND planning task are closely connected. To formalize this connection, we need a theorem formulated by Mattmüller et al. [1].

Theorem 1 (Mattmüller et al., 2014 [1]). *Given a POND planning task skeleton Π the problem of finding a cardinality (OBSERVECARDMIN) or an inclusion minimal set of observations (OBSERVEINCLMIN) $\mathcal{O} \subseteq \mathcal{W}$ for Π such that there exists a strong cyclic plan for $\Pi[\mathcal{O}]$, or returning NONE if no such set $\mathcal{O}$ exists, is 2-EXPTIME-complete.*   □

Clearly, every cardinality minimal solution is also inclusion minimal, but not vice versa. Therefore, the following results regarding the OBSERVECARDMIN problem hold also for the OBSERVEINCLMIN problem.

Theorem 2. *A necessary observation set is a subset of all solutions for the* OBSERVECARDMIN *problem.*

Proof. A solution $\mathcal{O}$ for the OBSERVECARDMIN problem is a cardinality minimal set such that there exists a strong cyclic plan π. By Definition 1 a necessary observation set $\mathcal{N}$ contains only necessary observation o such that o occurs in every strong cyclic plan π for Π. Therefore, a strong cyclic plan π for Π can only exist if all elements of a necessary observation set $\mathcal{N}$ are contained in $\mathcal{O}$, i.e. $\mathcal{N} \subseteq \mathcal{O}$. $\square$

Next we proof that every planning task has a unique and well-defined maximal necessary observation set $\mathcal{N}^*$. The latter property is the main idea of the following bottom-up procedure which computes iteratively necessary observation sets and combines all corresponding necessary observations to one resulting necessary observation set.

Theorem 3. *The maximal necessary observation set $\mathcal{N}^*$ of a planning task Π is unique and well-defined.*

Proof. Every planning task Π has at least one maximal necessary observation set $\mathcal{N}^*$ (Definition 1). We assume that $\mathcal{N}_1^*$ and $\mathcal{N}_2^*$ are two maximal necessary observation sets of a planning task Π with $\mathcal{N}_1^* \neq \mathcal{N}_2^*$. Thus, there exists at least one necessary observation o which is an element of the symmetric difference $\mathcal{N}_1^* \triangle \mathcal{N}_2^*$, i.e. $o \in \mathcal{N}_1^* \triangle \mathcal{N}_2^*$. By definition, a maximal necessary observation set $\mathcal{N}^*$ contains all necessary observations which leads to a contradiction. Therefore exactly one necessary observation set $\mathcal{N}^*$ exists for a planning task Π (uniqueness). From the uniqueness of $\mathcal{N}^*$ follows that $\mathcal{N}^*$ is well-defined. $\square$

3.1 Bottom-Up Search

We present an algorithm called NOS which computes a necessary observation set for a given POND planning task Π. The NOS algorithm is divided in two parts. First, we present a calculation of necessarily needed nondeterministic actions using determinized planning tasks Π_{det} and landmarks computed by the landmark cut procedure $LM\text{-}cut(\Pi_{det})$. The second part is about getting a necessary observation set from a set of landmarks $\mathcal{L}$. In this part we search for differences between desired outcomes contained in the landmarks, i.e. outcomes which lead further to a goal state, and outcomes which are undesired as they belong to the same original nondeterministic action. Figure 1 provides an overview of the different steps of the NOS algorithm.

Part 1: Given a POND planning task Π we use the landmark cut procedure to generate landmarks for a corresponding determinized (classical) planning task Π_{det}. The application of a deterministic action, i.e. an action with only one outcome, of a POND planning task can never be a reason for an observation. The uncertainty of a world state presented in a belief state is evoked by an earlier

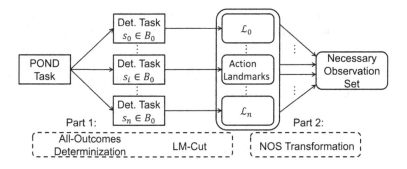

Fig. 1. Overview of the different steps of the Nos algorithm.

nondeterministic action or the uncertainty of the initial state. Therefore, we are only interested in nondeterministic actions with more than one outcome. Thus we modify a determinized (classical) planning task Π_{det} by the cost function

$$c_{det}(a) = \begin{cases} 1 & \text{if } |\textit{Eff}| > 1 \text{ where } n(a) = \langle \textit{Pre}, \textit{Eff} \rangle \\ 0 & \text{otherwise} \end{cases} \tag{1}$$

which maps all actions $a \in \mathcal{A}_{det}$ with more than one outcome (nondeterministic) in Π to cost 1 and all other actions $a' \in \mathcal{A}_{det}$ with only one outcome in Π to cost 0 (deterministic). A planning task Π_{det} with cost function c_{det} is denoted as Π_{det}^c. We compute a set of landmarks for a determinized (classical) planning task Π_{det} as

$$\mathcal{L} = \textit{LM-cut}(\Pi_{det}^c) \ . \tag{2}$$

Every landmark of Π_{det}^c contains only outcomes of nondeterministic actions. Finally, given a POND planning task Π we compute families of landmarks for a sampled number of determinized planning task Π_{det} and collect all landmarks $\textit{LM-cut}(\Pi_{det}^c)$ as one final set of landmarks $\mathcal{L}$.

Part 2: Computing a necessary observation set out of a computed set of landmarks $\mathcal{L}$ is the second step of the Nos algorithm. As mentioned before we search for differences between desired outcomes and undesired outcomes of a nondeterministic action. For that reason we group outcomes of the same original action contained in a landmark. Such a group of outcomes is called a *parallel outcome* $P \subseteq \mathcal{A}_{det}$, where each action $a \in P$ has the same original action in the corresponding POND planning task Π, i.e. $\forall a, a' \in P : n(a) = n(a')$. Using parallel outcomes we can define grouped landmarks as follows.

Definition 2 (Grouped Landmarks). *We call $L^G = \{\mathcal{P}_L^a \mid a \in L\}$ a grouped landmark where $\mathcal{P}_L^a = \{a' \in L \mid n(a) = n(a')\}$ forms disjoint equivalence classes with nondeterministic actions of the same original actions as representatives.*

Concluding, we define undesired outcomes of a parallel outcome as $\overline{P}$ and call it *complement* of a parallel outcome set P which contains all actions $a \notin P$, where

$n(a) = n(P)$. Attached with the latter concept it becomes possible to compute necessary observations given a set of landmarks $\mathcal{L}$ (Part 1) using functions (1) and (2) and the following six functions.[2]

Function $symDiffs(\mathcal{P})$ collects all sets of facts (symmetric differences) which can be chosen to distinguish the outcomes of a parallel outcome $\mathcal{P}$ (desired) from an outcome of its complement $\overline{\mathcal{P}}$ (undesired).

$$symDiffs(\mathcal{P}) = \{ eff^s(\mathcal{P}) \,\triangle\, eff^s(\{a\}) \mid a \in \overline{\mathcal{P}} \} \tag{3}$$

Transform all facts to observation variables.

$$obsVars(\mathcal{P}) = \bigcup_{D \in symDiffs(\mathcal{P})} \{\{ v \in \mathcal{W} \mid \exists d \neq \bot : (v,d) \in D \}\} \tag{4}$$

Collect all variables which are necessary to distinguish the outcomes of parallel outcome $\mathcal{P}$ from the outcomes of its complement $\overline{\mathcal{P}}$.

$$singleVars(\mathcal{P}) = \{ v \in D \mid D \in obsVar(\mathcal{P}) \wedge |D| = 1 \} \tag{5}$$

Compute a necessary observation set for a given landmark. Remove parallel outcomes which have an empty observation choice and therefore cannot be completely distinguished.

$$nos(L) = \bigcap_{\mathcal{P} \in L^G \,:\, \emptyset \notin obsVars(\mathcal{P})} singleVars(\mathcal{P}) \tag{6}$$

Remove all landmarks from a set of landmarks which contain a parallel outcome $\mathcal{P}$ with an empty complement $\overline{\mathcal{P}}$ and therefore never lead to an uncertainty by applying the original action.

$$pruneL(\mathcal{L}) = \{ L \in \mathcal{L} \mid \forall \mathcal{P} \in L^G : \overline{\mathcal{P}} \neq \emptyset \} \tag{7}$$

Collect all necessary observation sets computed for every landmark individually.

$$nos(\mathcal{L}) = \bigcup_{L \in pruneL(\mathcal{L})} nos(L) \tag{8}$$

As in previous examples we assume a nondeterministic BLOCKSWORLD but with three blocks A, B, and C instead of only two blocks. There exist exactly two actions *put-on-block-B-C* and *put-tower-on-block-A-B-C* which are visualized in Figure 2. Action *put-on-block-B-C* has an effect where either block B drops down to the table (0) or block B is stacked on block C (1), and action *put-tower-on-block-A-B-C* has an effect where either tower A-B drops down to the table (0) or tower A-B is stacked on block C (1). Furthermore, it is only possible to observe if any block is located on block X by observation X-*clear*. We assume $L = \{put\text{-}on\text{-}block\text{-}B\text{-}C^1, put\text{-}tower\text{-}on\text{-}block\text{-}A\text{-}B\text{-}C^1\}$ to be a land-

---

[2] Notice that at least one outcome of every landmark occurs in every plan for Π_{det} and that a strong cyclic plan for the corresponding POND planning task Π always contains such outcomes which additionally need to be verified by observations.

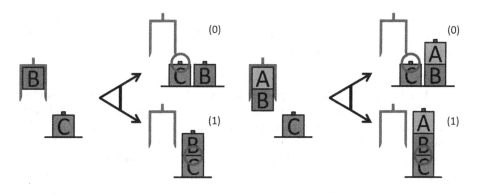

Fig. 2. Actions *put-on-block-B-C* (left) and *put-tower-on-block-A-B-C* (right) with there corresponding possible outcomes.

mark. Thus the goal is to apply an action such that any block is located on block C afterwards, i.e. $\overline{C\text{-}clear}$. The corresponding grouped landmark of L is $L^G = \{\{put\text{-}on\text{-}block\text{-}B\text{-}C^1\}, \{put\text{-}tower\text{-}on\text{-}block\text{-}A\text{-}B\text{-}C^1\}\}$. The symmetric differences of observable facts which distinguishes the desired outcomes (1) of both actions contained in L^G from their corresponding undesired outcome (0) is $C\text{-}clear$ (Figure 2). Therefore to ensure that at least one outcome of L occurs observation $C\text{-}clear$ has to be applied and the resulting necessary observation set is $\mathcal{N} = \{C\text{-}clear\}$.

NOS Algorithm: Using Part 1 and Part 2 it becomes possible to calculate a necessary observation set for a given POND planing task Π and a number of considered initial states k. Algorithm NOS (Algorithm 1) computes a necessary observation set $\mathcal{N}$ which is a subset of a maximal necessary observation set $\mathcal{N}^*$. Every variable $o \in \mathcal{N}$ is observed at least once in any strong cyclic plan π for Π. Algorithm 1 iterates over a number k of determinized planning tasks with different initial states and first collects the corresponding landmarks and then computes necessary observations using the landmarks.

Algorithm 1. NOS(Π, k)

Require: $\Pi = \langle \mathcal{V}, B_0, B_*, \mathcal{A}, \mathcal{W} \rangle, k \in \mathbb{N}$
1: $\mathcal{N} = \emptyset;\ \mathcal{L} = \emptyset;$
2: **for** $\{s_0, \ldots, s_k\} \subseteq B_0$ **do**
3:    $\Pi_{det} = \langle \mathcal{V}, \mathcal{A}_{det}, s_i, B_* \rangle$
4:    $\mathcal{L} = \mathcal{L} \cup LM\text{-}cut(\Pi_{det}^c)$
5: $\mathcal{N} = nos(\mathcal{L})$
6: **return** $\mathcal{N}$

In the following we show the runtime of Algorithm 1 and proof its correctness.

Theorem 4. *The runtime complexity of Algorithm 1 is bounded by $\mathcal{O}(\|\Pi\|^4 * k)$ where $\Pi = \langle \mathcal{V}, B_0, B_*, \mathcal{A}, \mathcal{W} \rangle$ is an input POND planning task, and k is the number of considered initial states.*

Proof. The landmark cut procedure is bounded in runtime by $\mathcal{O}(\|\Pi_{det}\|^2)$ [6] and Algorithm 1 contains k of such procedures, which leads to a runtime bounded by $\mathcal{O}(\|\Pi_{det}\|^2 * k)$. The size of a set of landmarks $\mathcal{L}$ computed by the landmark cut procedure for one determinzed planning task Π_{det} is bounded by $\mathcal{O}(\|\Pi_{det}\|)$. Overall we have k landmark cut procedures wherefore the amount of landmarks is bounded by $\mathcal{O}(\|\Pi_{det}\| * k)$. Function $nos(L)$ (6) is bounded in runtime by $\mathcal{O}(\|\Pi_{det}\|)$. Thus, function $nos(\mathcal{L})$ (8) is bounded by $\mathcal{O}(\|\Pi_{det}\|^2 * k)$. The determinization of a planning task Π_{det} can be bounded by $\mathcal{O}(\|\Pi\|^2)$ resulting in an upper bound complexity of $\mathcal{O}(\|\Pi\|^4 * k)$.

Theorem 5. *Algorithm NOS (Algorithm 1) returns a necessary observation set for a given POND planning task Π, i.e. Algorithm 1 is correct.*

Proof. Reducing the cost of an action has no side effects for other actions which is why a landmark for Π_{det}^c is also a landmark for Π_{det}. A strong cyclic plan π for Π is a composition of plans π_{det} for Π_{det}. At least one action of every landmark computed by $LM\text{-}cut(\Pi_{det}^c)$ occurs in every plan π_{det}. To verify that one of the outcomes contained in a landmark happened, an observation is necessary. Such an observation is always contained in the symmetric difference of the strong effect of an outcome contained in a landmark and an outcome which is not contained in the landmark belonging to the same original nondeterministic action. Therefore collecting observations which are always required to distinguish all outcomes of a landmark from outcomes not contained in the landmark of the same original action results in a necessary observation set.

3.2 Observation Minimization

A necessary observation set can be used to improve the runtime of the GREEDY algorithm by Mattmüller et al. [1]. The GREEDY algorithm is a top-down approach which greedily removes observation variables by the trial-and-error method until a solution $\mathcal{O}$ for the OBSERVEINCLMIN problem remains. The authors mentioned that a useful extension for the GREEDY algorithm is a heuristic which orders the candidate variables of removal. A precomputed necessary observation set does not order but rather eliminate such candidates. For every candidate variable of removal which is part of a necessary observation set, one removal iteration of the GREEDY algorithm is eliminated. Therefore, we get the following Algorithm 2 in pseudo code. Clearly, if no necessary observation is found or if the input size of the planning task is small, there is no runtime improvement. Nevertheless, for every reduced candidate variable of removal one planning procedure is eliminated. Such a planning procedure is (even with plan reuse) 2-EXPTIME-complete [7]. Our results show that Algorithm 2 outperforms the original GREEDY algorithm.

Algorithm 2. PRUNEDGREEDY(Π, k)

Require: $\Pi = \langle \mathcal{V}, B_0, B_*, \mathcal{A}, \mathcal{W} \rangle, k \in \mathbb{N}$
1: $\mathcal{N} = \text{NOS}(\Pi, k)$
2: set candidates of removal $\mathcal{O}$ to $\mathcal{O} \setminus \mathcal{N}$
3: $\mathcal{O} = \text{GREEDY}(\Pi)$
4: **return** $\mathcal{O}$

---

4 Experiments

We implemented Algorithm 1 and the GREEDY algorithm returning a solution for the OBSERVEINCLMIN problem using the MYND planner [1]. The overall 172 analysed POND planning tasks belong to the BLOCKSWORLDSENSE (only block clear observations), TIDYUP or FIRSTRESPONDERS domain. Every planning task belonging to the BLOCKSWORLDSENSE domain and FIRSTRESPONDERS domain has only one initial state ($|B_0| = 1$) and therefore only one determinized planning task. Whereas the planning tasks of the TIDYUP domain have an initial belief state containing up to 10^9 initial states. We used a memory limit of 4 GB. Table 1 summarizes our experimental results analysing Algorithm 1. The runtime of Algorithm 1 considering one and ten initial states was around 1 second whereas the runtime considering all initial states $s_0 \in B_0$ was up to one hour. Interestingly, for almost every task of the TIDYUP domain, there is no difference between the necessary observation set $\mathcal{N}B_0$ calculated by considering all initial states B_0 and the necessary observation set $\mathcal{N}S_1$ considering only 1 initial state. Therefore, we can argue that at least for planning tasks belonging to the TIDYUP domain, sampling over a number of initial states (e.g. 1) still leads to good results in practice. This is due to the fact that deterministic plans for different initial states of a planning task usually have similar subgoals and therefore similar landmarks.

Table 1. Cardinality of observation sets (variables). Legend: B_0 = initial belief state, $\mathcal{W}$ = possible observations, $\mathcal{N}$ = necessary observation set computed by the NOS algorithm (B_0 = considering all initial states, S_k = considering k sampled initial states).

Domain (#Tasks)	$\varnothing|B_0|$	$\varnothing|\mathcal{W}|$	$\varnothing|\mathcal{N}B_0|$	$\varnothing|\mathcal{N}S_1|$	$\varnothing|\mathcal{N}S_{10}|$
BWSENSE(30)	1.00	10.00	6.53	-	-
FRPONDERS(75)	1.00	10.36	2.61	-	-
TIDYUP(67)	$\approx 2 * 10^4$	23.30	5.61	5.61	5.61
All(172)	$\approx 8 * 10^3$	15.34	4.46	4.46	5.61

Concluding Figure 3 visualizes our experimental results analysing the runtime improvement of Algorithm 2 with respect to the original GREEDY algorithm [1]. We consider only instances which are solved by both algorithms and aborted the calculation after one hour using a memory limit of 4 GB. Furthermore, we display planning tasks where at least one of the two algorithms was able to solve that task in time. Overall, Algorithm 2 solves *eight* more planning tasks within one hour computation time. A few instances have a shorter runtime using the original GREEDY algorithm. This can be either traced back to a small state space (ID: 7), where the additional computation of a necessary observation set takes more time then it saves; or it can be due to nondeterministic decisions of the MYND planner (ID: 39). The latter also causes that one planning task (ID: 43) was only solved by the original GREEDY algorithm and was not solved in time by the extended version. Finally, considering the runtime of unsolved instances as (at least) 60 minutes, Algorithm 2 (PRUNEDGREEDY) was on average 526 seconds (over 8.5 minutes) faster then the original GREEDY Algorithm [1].

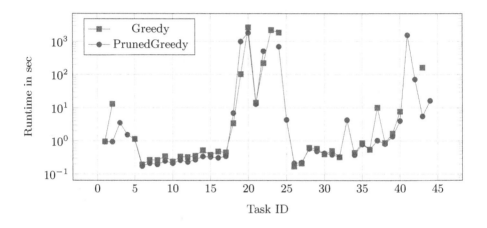

Fig. 3. Overall runtime of the GREEDY Algorithm [1] and Algorithm 2 (PRUNED-GREEDY). Legend: 1-5 = BLOCKSWORLDSENSE, 6-25 = FIRSTRESPONDERS, 26-44 = TIDYUP.

5   Conclusion and Future Work

We introduced the concept of necessary observations and discussed its connection to the recent results of observation minimization. Additionally, we presented an efficient bottom-up algorithm (NOS) for finding a set of necessary observations of a given POND planning task with polynomial runtime in size of the input size of the planning task and considered initial states. Furthermore, we extended the top-down GREEDY algorithm of Mattmüller et al. [1] with the NOS Algorithm which leads to a smaller set of candidates for removal by precomputing a necessary observation set. Our experiments show that the NOS algorithm is a useful extension for the GREEDY algorithm and is superior in terms of runtime.

For future work we plan to compute necessary observation sets in every iteration step of the GREEDY algorithm. In addition, we want to use necessary observations computed by the presented algorithm as a heuristic value for planning which possibly leads to plans with less observations.

References

1. Mattmüller, R., Ortlieb, M., Wacker, E.: Minimizing necessary observations for nondeterministic planning. In: Lutz, C., Thielscher, M. (eds.) KI 2014. LNCS, vol. 8736, pp. 309–320. Springer, Heidelberg (2014)
2. Huang, W., Wen, Z., Jiang, Y., Wu, L.: Observation reduction for strong plans. In: Proc. 20th International Joint Conference on Artificial Intelligence (IJCAI 2007), pp. 1930–1935 (2007)
3. Huang, W., Wen, Z., Jiang, Y., Peng., H.: Structured plans and observation reduction for plans with contexts. In: Proc. 21st International Joint Conference on Artificial Intelligence (IJCAI 2009), pp. 1721–1727 (2009)
4. Cimatti, A., Pistore, M., Roveri, M., Traverso, P.: Weak, strong, and strong cyclic planning via symbolic model checking. Artificial Intelligence $147(1-2)$, 35–84 (2003)
5. Helmert, M., Domshlak, C.: LM-cut: Optimal planning with the landmark-cut heuristic. In: Seventh International Planning Competition (IPC 2011), pp. 103–105 (2011)
6. Helmert, M., Domshlak, C.: Landmarks, critical paths and abstraction: what's the difference anyway? In: Proc. 21st International Joint Conference on Artificial Intelligence (IJCAI 2009), pp. 162–169 (2009)
7. Rintanen, J.: Complexity of planning with partial observability. In: Proc. 14th International Conference on Automated Planning and Scheduling (ICAPS 2004), pp. 345–354 (2004)

Analogical Representation of RCC-8 for Neighborhood-Based Qualitative Spatial Reasoning

Diedrich Wolter[1]([✉]) and Arne Kreutzmann[2]

[1] Smart Environments, University of Bamberg, Bamberg, Germany
diedrich.wolter@uni-bamberg.de
[2] University of Bremen, Bremen, Germany
arne@sfbtr8.uni-bremen.de

Abstract. Qualitative representations of spatial knowledge aim to capture the essential properties and relations of the underlying spatial domain. In addition, conceptual neighborhood has been introduced to describe how qualitative spatial relations may change over time. Current qualitative representations mainly use symbolic constraint-based languages that are detached from the underlying domain with the downside that a well-formed sentence is not necessarily consistent. This makes it difficult to design efficient knowledge manipulation techniques that consistently advance a representation with respect to conceptual neighborhood. In this paper we argue for *analogical spatial representations* that inherently obey domain restrictions and, as a result, are consistent per se. We develop a graph-based analogical representation for RCC-8, the construction of which is based on neighborhood transitions realized by efficient graph transformations. The main benefit of the developed representation is an improved efficiency for neighborhood-based reasoning tasks that need to manipulate spatial knowledge under the side condition of consistency, such as planning or constraint relaxation.

1 Introduction

Qualitative Spatial and Temporal Representation and Reasoning (QSTR) [2] aims at capturing human-level concepts of space and time using finite sets of relations over a particular spatial or temporal domain. Existing qualitative representation approaches define symbolic constraint-based languages to encode spatio-temporal knowledge using the relations from a particular so-called qualitative calculus as constraints. An important reasoning problem is that of deciding consistency, i.e., deciding whether a set of constraints can be realized in the given domain.

Aside from reasoning about consistency, there exists another class of reasoning tasks, which is concerned with the evolution of qualitative spatial configurations over time, e.g., qualitative planning or simulation tasks as well as retrieval or relaxation problems based on a notion of similarity of spatial configurations. Given qualitative descriptions of start and end configurations S and E,

© Springer International Publishing Switzerland 2015
S. Hölldobler et al. (Eds.): KI 2015, LNAI 9324, pp. 194–207, 2015.
DOI: 10.1007/978-3-319-24489-1_15

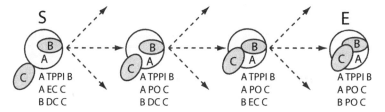

Fig. 1. A simple qualitative planning problem: finding a sequence of qualitative scenarios (here illustrated by concrete example depictions) that connects S and E.

a question could for example be "What is the simplest way to get from S to E?" which calls for an as-short-as-possible sequence of configurations such that consecutive configurations are connected only by elementary changes of the spatial relations. See Fig. 1 for an example using the well-known RCC-8 calculus [14] for topological relations. Answering this question can provide helpful information for planning manipulation tasks in robotic applications [17]. To describe spatial change on a qualitative level, the concept of *conceptual neighborhood* between spatial relations has been introduced [6] and later been extended from individual relations to complex spatial configurations [13]. Difficulties of handling neighborhoods in complex configurations arise from the fact that several relations may constrain one another. For example, consider situation E in Fig. 1: there is no way to detach region C from A by continuous movement without either affecting the relation holding between C and B or B and A. Neighborhood-based reasoning tasks require the modification of a qualitative spatial representation under the side condition of consistency, i.e., to respect such interdependent relation changeovers. In context of the aforementioned planning task, maintaining consistency ensures that the individual steps are valid sub-goals for motion planning. Further neighborhood-based reasoning tasks are discussed in [5,9].

Algorithmically, existing approaches to neighborhood-based reasoning either ignore interdependent relation changeovers [5] (which is acceptable in context of qualitative similarity assessment but yields an upper approximation) or employ a generate-and-filter approach [3]. The latter employs tree search to identify a sequence of changes that transforms one representation into another, using consistency checking to filter out nodes that represent inconsistent representations. As a result the search space grows exponentially with respect to the number of relations that need to be changed. Already identifying a conceptually neighbored configuration gives rise to this problem if multiple relations need to be changed at once. It may indeed be necessary to alter several relations between one object and all other objects at once, for example in configurations in which the spatial extent of all n objects are equal, $n - 1$ relations change in the next neighborhood transition. As a consequence, $O(n)$ levels of the search tree involving $O(2^n)$ nodes would have to be explored. This triggers the following research question: Is there a more efficient way of determining conceptual neighborhood among spatial configurations?

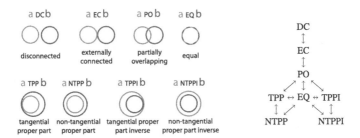

Fig. 2. Left: The eight base relations of the RCC-8 calculus. Right: The RCC-8 conceptual neighborhood graph if size persistency is not enforced.

The contribution of this paper is to show that identifying and performing neighborhood transitions is possible in polynomial time. Our approach is based on the idea of employing a data structure that is *analogical* in the sense of [12], i.e., a representation that retains important domain structures. Our graph-based representation of RCC-8 scenarios retains topological structure to the level of detail captured by RCC-8 relations, not allowing consistency among RCC-8 relations to be violated. Neighborhood transitions, including construction of the representation, are then realized as polynomial time graph transformations. We show that our representation provides a model for the RCC-8 theory and give algorithms that operationalize the formal approach to RCC-8 presented in [10,16] by integrating it with the concept of conceptual neighborhoods.

The paper is structured as follows. Sect. 2 contains background information on qualitative spatial representations. In Sect. 3, we present our analogical representation for RCC-8 as well as neighborhood transition and construction procedures. In Sect. 4, we discuss the algorithmic realization and analyze the computational properties of our approach.

2   Qualitative Representation of Space

Qualitative representations define a set $\mathcal{R}$ of spatial relations over a domain of objects D. For every pair of objects from the domain, exactly one relation $R \in \mathcal{R}$ holds, i.e., the set of relations (also called *base relations* or *atomic relations*) is jointly exhaustive and pairwise disjoint (JEPD). This approach generalizes to higher arity relations, but this paper is only concerned with the set of binary relations defined in the RCC-8 calculus, which are shown in Fig. 2.

A qualitative representation is a set of constraints expressed in a quantifier-free constraint language based on a set of relations. Technically speaking, we have a *constraint network* $N = (X, D, C)$ with variables $X = \{X_1, X_2, \ldots, X_n\}$ over the domain D whose valuations are constrained by binary relations given in the constraint matrix C.

Using the set-based semantics of relations and classical set-operations $\{\cup, \cap, \cdot^C\}$, one obtains a Boolean set algebra over the set of so-called *general relations*, the set of all possible unions of base relations. By employing unions of relations as constraint relations, one can express uncertainty. The constraints in a qualitative constraint network are written in the form $\{X_1\ c_{12}\ X_2, X_1\ c_{13}\ X_3, \ldots\}$ with $c_{11}, c_{12}, \ldots, c_{nn} \in 2^{\mathcal{R}}$ representing unions of base relations. Constraint networks defined by qualitative relations are assumed to be complete in the sense that there exists a constraint between every pair of variables. This is no limitation since the union of all base relations can serve as a non-restrictive constraint. A constraint network in which all constraints are atomic relations is called a *scenario*.

A qualitative constraint network is *consistent* if there exists a valuation of variables with objects from the domain that satisfies all constraints. A prominent approach in qualitative spatial reasoning is based on a symbolic method that builds on relation-algebraic operations defined on the set of general relations. For this approach, operations for *composition* and *converse* of relations are required. The structure comprising base relations, converse, and composition is known as a *qualitative calculus* [4,11]. Using these operations the so-called algebraic closure algorithm enforces a local consistency called algebraic closure or path-consistency in $O(n^3)$ time, which already decides consistency of RCC-8 scenarios [1]. The class of RCC-8 constraint networks that can be handled with this method has later been extended, but deciding consistency of arbitrary RCC-8 constraint networks remains NP-complete [15].

Neighborhood-based reasoning tasks are based on the notion of *conceptual neighborhood* by Freksa [6]: A base relation is said to be a *conceptual neighbor* of a second base relation if there exists a continuous transformation that brings two objects from the second relation to the first with no other relation holding in between. Galton [7] defines conceptual neighborhood similar, but allows the relation to be reflexive while Freksa considers it as being irreflexive – here, this difference does not matter though. Conceptual neighborhoods have been used to describe how qualitative relations evolve over time when the objects in the domain are subject to continuous transformations such as movement or deformation. Depending on which kind of transformations are considered, the neighborhood relation may be symmetric if transformations are reversible. We write $R \rightsquigarrow R'$ to denote that R' is a conceptual neighbor of R and we use $\leftrightsquigarrow$ to denote symmetric neighborhood relations. The conceptual neighborhood relation is commonly visualized in a so-called conceptual neighborhood graph as shown in Fig. 2 for RCC-8, assuming that regions can move, deform, grow, or shrink [8].

As most neighborhood-based reasoning tasks such as planning involve more than just two objects, one needs to generalize the notion of conceptual neighborhood from a relation between two objects to an entire scenario, i.e., a matrix of atomic constraints. This can be done in a straightforward way, saying that two scenarios are neighbored if a continuous transformation changes one scenario into another with no other scenario holding in between. Changing one relation in a qualitative constraint network may lead to an inconsistent network or, put differently, one change can entail other, simultaneous changes. To this end, [13] have introduced generalized (n, l)-neighborhoods to aggregate individual neighborhood transitions, where n determines the total number of variables considered and l is the number of objects that can be transformed simultaneously. They however assume this structure to be computed beforehand. In our work we investigate generalized $(n, 1)$-neighborhoods for arbitrarily many variables n and we aim to compute all direct neighborhood transitions together with their implications. Depending on the context in which our representation is used, different approaches to measure the degree of change may be useful, e.g., whether to count implications as separate changes or not. Our approach provides the basis to define such measures, but this is not further addressed in this paper.

3   Analogical Representation for RCC-8

RCC-8 describes the connectivity among regions, differentiating between connectivity of interiors (e.g., relation PO) and connectivity of closures of a region (e.g., relation EC). Thus, our analogical representation identifies the parts required to describe a given scenario and links them by containment information. Our representation constitutes the decisive finite fragment of a model for the RCC-8 calculus (a strict model in the sense of [16]). Roughly speaking, the analogical representation is the directed graph of region nestings from now on called the *inclusion graph* (see Fig. 3 for an example) and later defined formally. We employ the approach to RCC-8 based on Boolean connection algebras introduced in [16] to show that our representation is a model for RCC-8. Our inclusion graph can be interpreted as a partially ordered set which, equipped with a notion of connectivity, constitutes a Boolean connection algebra as noted in [10].

Definition 1. *A Boolean connection algebra is a Boolean algebra* $< A, \perp, \top, \check{\ }, \vee, \wedge >$ *equipped with a connection relation* C *that satisfies four axioms:*

1. *C is symmetric and reflexive on* $A \setminus \{\perp\}$
2. *$\forall x \in A$: $x \neq \top \rightarrow C(x, x^{\check{\ }})$*
3. *$\forall x, y, z \in A \setminus \{\perp\}$: $C(x, y \vee z)$ iff $C(x, y)$ or $C(x, z)$*
4. *$\forall x \in A \setminus \{\top\}$: $\exists y \in A \setminus \{\perp\}$: $\neg C(x, y)$*

Our definition of inclusion graphs is similar to that of *maptrees* which have been proposed as topological representations by considering embeddings of connected graphs in closed surfaces [18,19]. We proceed differently since maptrees aim at a more fine-grained topological representation than captured by RCC-8. Using maptrees would complicate defining transition on the (coarser) level of RCC-8 relations and possibly affect efficiency of computing transitions.

Let us assume we are given an RCC-8 scenario with variables $X = \{X_1, X_2, \ldots, X_n\}$. Our task is to define the inclusion graph as a directed graph $G = (V, E)$ whose vertices stand for distinct open and closed regions of the topological space in the given scenario. The set of vertices includes three special elements, the universe vertex $\{\mathcal{U}\}$ (the universe being a special region containing all other regions), the void $\emptyset$ not containing any region, and an outside o

	A	B	C
A	EQ	PO	NTPPI
B	PO	EQ	NTPPI
C	NTPP	NTPP	EQ

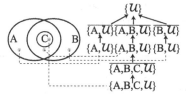

Fig. 3. RCC-8 scenario and a possible visualization with its corresponding inclusion graph.

contained in $\mathcal{U}$ and not containing any other regions. All other elements of V are sets $\{X_{i_1}, X_{i_2}, \ldots, X_{i_k}, \mathcal{U}\}$ or $\overline{\{X_{i_1}, X_{i_2}, \ldots, X_{i_k}, \mathcal{U}\}}$ representing parts of the topological space. The idea is to interpret elements of V by means of set intersection and to use $\overline{\phi}$ to denote closure of an open region ϕ. Thus, the intersection of regions A and B would be represented by a vertex $\{A, B, \mathcal{U}\}$ (see Fig. 3), while $\overline{\{A, B, \mathcal{U}\}}$ represents the closure $\text{CL}(A \cap B)$. To ease the notation, we say that $\overline{A} \in \overline{\{A, B, \mathcal{U}\}}$. The edges of the inclusion graph represent proper containment relations, i.e., $(v, v') \in E$ implies a subset relation between the parts represented by v and v'.

In order to obtain RCC-8 semantics for our graph we define regions (sets of vertices) $r : X \to 2^V$, their closures CL, and connectivity $\mathbf{C}$, as this allows us to apply the standard specification of RCC-8 [1]. The definition, adapted to our notation, is summarized in Tab. 1. The open region represented by variable X is written as $r(X)$, its closure $\text{CL}(X)$ respectively. Given a set of variables $X = \{X_1, X_2, \ldots, X_n\}$ and an inclusion graph $G = (V, E)$, we define the RCC-8 interpretation of G as follows:

$$r(X_i) := \{v \in V | X_i \in v\} \tag{1}$$

$$\text{CL}(X_i) := r(X_i) \cup \{v \in V | \overline{X_i} \in v\} \tag{2}$$

$$\widetilde{V'} := V' \cup \{v \in V | \overline{v} \in V'\} \cup \{\overline{v} \in V | v \in V'\} \tag{3}$$

$$\mathbf{C}(V', V'') \leftrightarrow \widetilde{V'} \cap \widetilde{V''} \neq \emptyset \tag{4}$$

The definition of $\mathbf{C}$ uses an auxiliary function $\sim$ to address connectedness of open and closed regions: closed regions are connected to any open region they are contained in, which is achieved by growing the closed region prior to testing for overlap. Note that we distinguish vertices $v \in V$ representing open regions from $\overline{v} \in V$ representing closures. Now we are ready to give the definition of an inclusion graph:

Definition 2 (inclusion graph). *Let $X = \{X_1, X_2, \ldots, X_n\}$ be a set of variables referring to spatial regions. Then we call directed graph $G = (V, E)$ an inclusion graph of X if V is a two-sorted set with elements of type v and $\overline{v}$, $V \subseteq 2^{X \cup \{o, \mathcal{U}, \emptyset\}} \cup 2^{\overline{X \cup \{o, \mathcal{U}, \emptyset\}}}$ and the following properties are satisfied:*

Table 1. Formal specification of RCC-8 relations, omitting model constraints $\mathbf{C}(r(A), r(A))$ and $\mathbf{C}(r(B), r(B))$ which ensure that regions $r(A)$ and $r(B)$ are non-empty.

Relation	Clauses
A DC B	$\neg\mathbf{C}(\mathrm{CL}(A), \mathrm{CL}(B))$
A EC B	$\mathbf{C}(\mathrm{CL}(A), \mathrm{CL}(B)), \neg\mathbf{C}(r(A), r(B))$
A PO B	$\mathbf{C}(r(A), r(B)), \mathbf{C}(r(A), \mathrm{CL}(B)^C), \mathbf{C}(\mathrm{CL}(A)^C, r(B))$
A EQ B	$\mathbf{C}(r(A), r(B)), \quad \mathbf{C}(\mathrm{CL}(A), \mathrm{CL}(B)), \quad \neg\mathbf{C}(r(A), \mathrm{CL}(B)^C),$
	$\neg\mathbf{C}(\mathrm{CL}(A)^C, r(B))$
A TPP B	$\mathbf{C}(r(A), r(B)), \quad \mathbf{C}(\mathrm{CL}(A)^C, r(B)), \quad \neg\mathbf{C}(\mathrm{CL}(A), \mathrm{CL}(B)^C),$
	$C(\mathrm{CL}(A), r(B)^C)$
A TPPI B	clauses for TPP(B,A)
A NTPP B	$\mathbf{C}(r(A), r(B)), \neg\mathbf{C}(\mathrm{CL}(A), r(B)^C),$
A NTPPI B	clauses for NTPP(B,A)

$$\forall v \in V : (\{\mathcal{U}\}, v) \notin E \wedge (\overline{v}, v) \notin E \tag{5}$$

$$\forall v \in V : v \neq \{\mathcal{U}\} \rightarrow (\overline{v} \in V \wedge (v, \overline{v}) \in E) \tag{6}$$

$$\forall v \in V : \forall (v', v) \in E : X_i \in v \rightarrow X_i \in v' \tag{7}$$

$$\forall X_i : \forall v \in \mathrm{CL}(X_i), v' \in r(X_i) : (v, v') \in E \tag{8}$$

$$\forall \overline{v} \in V : \exists v' \in V : (\overline{v}, v') \in E \tag{9}$$

$$\forall v \in V : (v, \{o\}) \notin E \tag{10}$$

We now show that the properties required for inclusion graphs to hold reflect the semantics of RCC-8 relations according to Equations 1–4 and Tab. 1. As shorthand notation we write $\mathrm{rcc}_{V,E}(X_i, X_j)$ to denote the RCC-8 relation between variables X_i and X_j indicated by inclusion graph (V, E).

Theorem 1. *The inclusion graph $G = (V, E)$ of a set of variables $\{X_1, \ldots, X_n\}$ is a model of RCC-8.*

Proof. According to [16, Theorems 4 and 5] it suffices to show that our inclusion graph constitutes a Boolean connection algebra (see Def. 1). Since our graph vertices V are sets, $< 2^V, \emptyset, V, {}^C, \cup, \cap >$ is a Boolean (set) algebra with more than two elements (we have at least 3 special vertices), i.e., we have $\top = V$, $\bot = \emptyset$, $\check{} = {}^C$ (set complement in V), $\vee = \cup$, and $\wedge = \cap$. We now show that our definition of $\mathbf{C}$ satisfies the axioms. Symmetry of $\mathbf{C}$ is obvious and $\mathbf{C}$ is also reflexive since $V' \cap V' \neq \emptyset$ for any $V' \neq \emptyset$. With respect to Axiom 2, observe that in $\mathbf{C}(V', V'^C)$ from $V' \neq \top$ and connectivity of our graph V' contains a vertex but not its successor and predecessor. By Eq. 3, $\widetilde{V'}$ and $\widetilde{V'^C}$ share the common successor or predecessor and, hence, are connected. Axiom 3 directly follows from $\vee = \cup$ and Eq. 4. Axiom 4 states that there is a non-empty region which is not connected to any region $V' \subset V$. Intuitively, the complement of any open set contains another open region. With respect to all sets $r(X_i)$ the outlier vertices $\overline{\{o\}}, \{o\} \in V$ already satisfy the condition due to property Eq. 10.

The inclusion graph involves outlier vertices solely to apply existing theorems in the proof of Theorem 1. In a practical implementation, these vertices are not necessary.

3.1 Conceptual Neighborhood Transitions

We now define conceptual neighborhood transformations that consistently modify inclusion graphs. In addition to the neighborhood transitions shown in Fig. 2, we include an additional transition that allows us to grow a new region. In the following, we will use (V, E) to denote the inclusion graph and $\{X_1, \ldots, X_n\}$ is the set of region variables from which the graph has been constructed. To ease readability we use ϕA as a shorthand notation for an arbitrary vertex $\{A\} \cup \phi$ with $A \notin \phi$. To save space, we omit transformations that are purely symmetrical, e.g., A PO $B \rightsquigarrow A$ TPPI B which can be easily obtained from B PO $A \rightsquigarrow B$ TPP A.

Definition 3. *A graph transformation is called* admissible *if it preserves Properties 5–10 of inclusion graphs.*

Admissibility of transformation is important as these transformations consistently modify the RCC-8 interpretation since no model properties are violated. In the pictorial representation we add a special edge $\perp$ to indicate if no edge is allowed to end at a node.

Birth Add a new region which is DC to all existing regions (here shown twice).

$$\mathcal{U} \quad \xdashrightarrow{\text{add } A} \quad \mathcal{U} \quad \xdashrightarrow{\text{add } B} \quad \mathcal{U}$$

Lemma 1. *Birth is admissible.*

Proof. It is straightforward to check that the newly introduced vertices agree with the invariances, in particular that Properties 7 and 9 are satisfied.

$DC \rightsquigarrow EC$ If two closures share a common direct ancestor and are currently not connected, then they can be externally connected by inserting a new part which stands for the common closure of the two regions. If two closures share a common *direct* ancestor, their closure is connected exactly once, and their inner regions are not connected, then the connecting closure can be removed.

$$\phi \quad \xleftrightarrow{A \text{ DC } B \rightsquigarrow A \text{ EC } B} \quad \phi$$

Lemma 2. *Transition* $DC \leftrightsquigarrow EC$ *is admissible.*

Proof. Property 9 gives us that the common direct ancestor ϕ is an open region and, with respect to EC $\rightsquigarrow$ DC, the preconditions that A and B are not connected other than by $\overline{\phi AB}$ ensures that there can be no ϕAB which we could disconnect violating Property 9. Direction DC $\rightsquigarrow$ EC only affects Property 7, respecting the inclusion relation.

$EC \leftrightsquigarrow PO$ Any closure $\overline{AB}$ without inner region can be extended by an inner region AB. The added AB is part of any interior of $r(A)$ and $r(B)$; thus, edges $(\phi AB, v)$ for all $v \in r(A) \cup r(B)$ must be added.

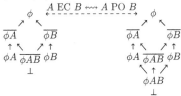

Lemma 3. *The transition* $EC \leftrightsquigarrow PO$ *is admissible.*

Proof. Only Properties 6 and 9 are affected by this transition but it is straightforward to see that they are not violated.

$PO \leftrightsquigarrow TPP$ For A PO $B \rightsquigarrow A$ TPP B the parts of A overlapping $\mathrm{CL}(B)^C$ need to be removed; thus, as a precondition for PO $\rightsquigarrow$ TPP, there must not be another vertex v with $(v, \overline{\phi A}) \in E$ or $(v, \phi A) \in E$. The other direction is admissible since we grow a region within another open region.

Lemma 4. *The transition* $PO \leftrightsquigarrow TPP$ *is admissible.*

Proof. While TPP $\rightsquigarrow$ PO is admissible as the inserted subgraph suits the properties, direction PO $\rightsquigarrow$ TPP is secured by the precondition of having no region within A or $\overline{A}$.

$TPP \leftrightsquigarrow EQ$ For A TPP $B \rightsquigarrow A$ EQ B, we remove the part only belonging to B which must not contain other parts.

Lemma 5. *The transition TPP ↭ EQ is admissible.*

Proof. EQ ⤳ TPP is admissible since we simply grow a new region within an open one. EQ ⤳ TPP is admissible since the precondition ensures that $\not\exists(v, B) \in E$ with $v \neq AB$.

PO ↭ EQ As a precondition for PO ⤳ EQ, there must be no part contained in either A or B, i.e., $\forall(v, v') \in E : (v' = \phi A \lor v' = \phi B) \to v = \phi AB$.

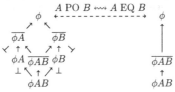

Lemma 6. *PO ↭ EQ is admissible.*

Proof. While EQ ⤳ PO is admissible because we can grow a region within an open region. The other direction can, by precondition, only be performed such that one cannot violate Property 6 or Property 9.

TPP ↭ NTPP As a precondition for TPP ⤳ NTPP, there must not be another $\overline{\psi A} \in V$ with $\psi \neq \phi$.

$$\phi \quad \underset{\longleftarrow{\scriptstyle A\ \text{TPP}\ B\ ↭\ A\ \text{NTPP}\ B}\longrightarrow}{} \quad \phi$$

Lemma 7. *TPP ↭ NTPP is admissible.*

Proof. Only the direction TPP ⤳ NTPP bears danger of violating a property as it detaches the closure of A from the closure of B. The precondition ensures that $\overline{AB}$ is not connected to any other region and, hence, not breaking Property 6.

NTPP ↭ EQ As precondition for NTPP ⤳ EQ, there must not be any other part of B, i.e., $\not\exists(v, v') \in E$ with $v \neq \phi AB \land v' = \psi B$.

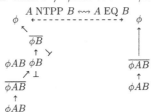

Algorithm 1. Constructing the inclusion graph

1: **function** CONSTRUCT$(({X_1, X_2, \ldots, X_n}, C = {c_{ij}}))$
2:     $V \leftarrow {{U}, \emptyset, \overline{{o}}, {o}}$
3:     $E \leftarrow {(({o}, \overline{{o}}), ({o}, {\mathcal{U}}))}$
4:     **for** $i = 1, 2, \ldots, n$ **do**
5:         $V \leftarrow V \cup {{X_i}, \overline{{X_i}}}$ ▷ birth of X_i
6:         $E \leftarrow E \cup {(({X_i}, {\mathcal{U}}), ({X_i}, \overline{{X_i}}))}$
7:         **while** $\exists i > j : \mathrm{rcc}_{V,E}(X_i, X_j) \neq c_{ij}$ **do**
8:             perform sequence of transitions that moves X_i to its goal relation c_{ij}
    with X_j
9:         **end while**
10:     **end for**
11:     **return** (V, E)
12: **end function**

Lemma 8. *The transition NTPP $\leadsto$ EQ is admissible.*

Proof. Follows analogously to TPP $\leadsto$ EQ.

These graph transformations are neighborhood transitions that consistently modify the RCC-8 interpretation as shown in the lemmata. The transitions have the desired effect of altering one relation according to the conceptual neighborhood of RCC-8 by construction according to Properties 1–4. Implicit changes of relations involving either object A or B may occur, but the transformations do not affect connectivity between any two regions other than A and B specified in the rules.

3.2   Constructing the Representation

A special feature of our approach is that conceptual neighborhood transitions are employed to construct the representation. We use the transformation *birth* to iteratively create a new region disconnected to all other regions and then move it to its goal position. By doing so, correctness of the algorithm follows from admissibility of the transitions. The complete construction is shown in Algorithm 1.

Theorem 2. *Algorithm 1 computes an inclusion graph G from a consistent RCC-8 scenario S such that the RCC-8 interpretation of the graph is S.*

Proof. (sketch) Correctness of the algorithm directly follows from the fact that only admissible neighborhood transitions are performed. The condition of the "while" loop implies that the algorithm can only terminate with a graph G whose RCC-8 interpretation is identical to C. It remains to be shown that the algorithm terminates. Before a region has reached its goal position, there exists at least one other region to which the region must be connected and which is not contained in any other region. Thus, one can connect these regions and move the current one, if needed, further inside. In other words, we only need to move regions further inside which can only be happening finitely many times.

4 Algorithmic Realization

In this section, we discuss the algorithmic realization of our approach and analyze the computational costs of constructing the representations and performing neighborhood transitions. To facilitate an efficient implementation, we supplement the inclusion graph with a vector indexed by the variables X_i involved in a given RCC-8 scenario. The vector grants access to all vertices in $\text{CL}(X_i)$.

Theorem 3. *For a given RCC-8 scenario with n variables, the corresponding inclusion graph comprises $O(n^2)$ vertices and can be constructed in $O(n^4)$ time.*

Proof. No transformation rule introduces more than two new vertices and every rule needs to be applied at most once for every pair of variables (cp. proof of Theorem 2). Since we have $O(n^2)$ relations to satisfy, no more than $O(n^2)$ vertices can be generated. With respect to time complexity, n regions are processed. In each step of the main loop, $O(n)$ relations need to be satisfied and it takes a constant set of relation transformations to satisfy one relation (the longest path in the conceptual neighborhood graph is 4 steps). Checking applicability of a transformation rule might require to consider all $O(n^2)$ vertices, which results in a total time complexity of $O(n \cdot n \cdot n^2) = O(n^4)$.

Theorem 4. *Given an inclusion graph that involves n variables, all possible neighborhood transitions can be enumerated in $O(n^4)$ time.*

Proof. For checking the applicability of a neighborhood transformation, we need to consider at most all $O(n^2)$ vertices for every pair of variables which yields $O(n^4)$ for checking all possible transitions.

4.1 Experimental Evaluation

We implemented the proposed method to study the average computational cost. For our evaluation we generated random consistent RCC-8 scenarios from 3 to 150 variables by performing random neighborhood transitions. We recorded the

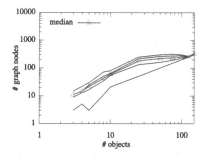
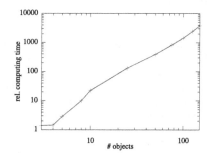

Fig. 4. Left: Size of inclusions graphs in vertices per object. Right: Average relative computation time for performing neighborhood transitions.

number of vertices of the inclusion graph, the distribution of which is presented in Fig. 4 left, separated into quartiles. Also, we recorded the average computing time for performing a neighborhood transition. Fig. 4 right shows the development relative to the time required for networks with $n = 3$ variables. While both results accord with the theoretical results, we observe that the distribution of numbers of vertices is concentrated around the median and the coefficient of quadratic growth (slope of the 'line' in log/log-scale) is small.

5   Conclusions

We proposed analogical spatial representations as a novel approach to neighborhood-based reasoning with qualitative spatial representations. The advantage of our approach is that a consistent state of the representation is maintained at any time. While the general idea is applicable to a variety of spatial and temporal representations, this paper is concerned with an analogical representation for the RCC-8 calculus. RCC-8 is of particular interest as it is widely used and since an analogical representation for arbitrary topological spaces is challenging. Our representation is based on the characterization of RCC-8 using on Boolean connection algebras [16]. We operationalize the theoretic foundations in terms of algorithms to construct and to modify the representation. The result is a set of operators that allows us to consistently generate conceptual neighborhoods for a complete scenario in polynomial time, including entailed simultaneous transitions. Our analysis demonstrates that this novel approach is computationally efficient. Thus, analogical spatial representations provide an excellent basis for performing neighborhood-based spatial reasoning.

While this paper focuses on RCC-8, other qualitative calculi could similarly benefit from an analogical representation to speed up neighborhood-based reasoning tasks – investigating such representations is subject to future work.

Acknowledgments. This work has been partially funded by the Deutsche Forschungsgemeinschaft (DFG) for the SFB/TR 8 Spatial Cognition, project R3-[Q-Shape]. Financial support is gratefully acknowledged.

References

1. Bennett, B.: Logical Representations for Automated Reasoning about Spatial Relationships. Ph.D. thesis, School of Computer Studies, The University of Leeds (1997)
2. Cohn, A.G., Renz, J.: Qualitative spatial representation and reasoning. In: van Harmelen, F., Lifschitz, V., Porter, B. (eds.) Handbook of Knowledge Representation, pp. 551–596. Elsevier (2007)
3. Condotta, J.F., Kaci, S., Schwind, N.: A framework for merging qualitative constraints networks. In: Wilson, D., Lane, H.C. (eds.) Proceedings of the Twenty-First International Florida Artificial Intelligence Research Society Conference, pp. 586–591. AAAI Press (2008)
4. Dylla, F., Mossakowski, T., Schneider, T., Wolter, D.: Algebraic properties of qualitative spatio-temporal calculi. In: Tenbrink, T., Stell, J., Galton, A., Wood, Z. (eds.) COSIT 2013. LNCS, vol. 8116, pp. 516–536. Springer, Heidelberg (2013)

5. Dylla, F., Wallgrün, J.O.: Qualitative spatial reasoning with conceptual neighborhoods for agent control. Journal of Intelligent and Robotic Systems **48**(1), 55–78 (2007)
6. Freksa, C.: Conceptual neighborhood and its role in temporal and spatial reasoning. In: Singh, M., Travé-Massuyès, L. (eds.) Decision Support Systems and Qualitative Reasoning, North Holland, pp. 181–187 (1991)
7. Galton, A.: Qualitative Spatial Change. Spatial Information Systems. Oxford University Press (2000)
8. Gerevini, A., Nebel, B.: Qualitative spatio-temporal reasoning with RCC-8 and allen's interval calculus: computational complexity. In: Proceedings of ECAI 2002, pp. 312–316. IOS Press (2002)
9. Condotta, J.-F., Kaci, S., Marquis, P., Schwind, N.: Merging qualitative constraints networks using propositional logic. In: Sossai, C., Chemello, G. (eds.) ECSQARU 2009. LNCS, vol. 5590, pp. 347–358. Springer, Heidelberg (2009)
10. Li, S., Ying, M.: Generalized region connection calculus. Artificial Intelligence **160**(1), 1–34 (2004)
11. Ligozat, G., Renz, J.: What is a qualitative calculus? a general framework. In: Zhang, C., W. Guesgen, H., Yeap, W.-K. (eds.) PRICAI 2004. LNCS (LNAI), vol. 3157, pp. 53–64. Springer, Heidelberg (2004)
12. Palmer, S.: Fundamental aspects of cognitive representation. In: Rosch, E., Lloyd, B. (eds.) Cognition and Categorization, pp. 259–303. Erlbaum (1978)
13. Ragni, M., Wölfl, S.: Temporalizing spatial calculi: on generalized neighborhood graphs. In: Furbach, U. (ed.) KI 2005. LNCS (LNAI), vol. 3698, pp. 64–78. Springer, Heidelberg (2005)
14. Randell, D.A., Cui, Z., Cohn, A.: A spatial logic based on regions and connection. In: Principles of Knowledge Representation and Reasoning, pp. 165–176. Morgan Kaufmann (1992)
15. Renz, J.: Maximal tractable fragments of the region connection calculus: a complete analysis. In: Proceedings of the Internatoinal Joint Conference on Artificial Intelligence (IJCAI). Morgan Kaufmann (1999)
16. Stell, J.G.: Boolean connection algebras: A new approach to the Region-Connection Calculus. Artificial Intelligence **122**(1), 111–136 (2000)
17. Westphal, M., Dornhege, C., Wölfl, S., Gissler, M., Nebel, B.: Guiding the generation of manipulation plans by qualitative spatial reasoning. Spatial Cognition and Computation: An Interdisciplinary Journal **11**(1), 75–102 (2011)
18. Worboys, M.: The maptree: a fine-grained formal representation of space. In: Xiao, N., Kwan, M.-P., Goodchild, M.F., Shekhar, S. (eds.) GIScience 2012. LNCS, vol. 7478, pp. 298–310. Springer, Heidelberg (2012)
19. Worboys, M.: Using maptrees to characterize topological change. In: Tenbrink, T., Stell, J., Galton, A., Wood, Z. (eds.) COSIT 2013. LNCS, vol. 8116, pp. 74–90. Springer, Heidelberg (2013)

Grid-Based Angle-Constrained Path Planning

Konstantin Yakovlev$^{(\boxtimes)}$, Egor Baskin, and Ivan Hramoin

Institute for Systems Analysis of Russian Academy of Sciences, Moscow, Russia
{yakovlev,baskin,hramoin}@isa.ru

Abstract. Square grids are commonly used in robotics and game development as spatial models and well known in AI community heuristic search algorithms (such as A*, JPS, Theta* etc.) are widely used for path planning on grids. A lot of research is concentrated on finding the shortest (in geometrical sense) paths while in many applications finding smooth paths (rather than the shortest ones but containing sharp turns) is preferable. In this paper we study the problem of generating smooth paths and concentrate on angle constrained path planning. We put angle-constrained path planning problem formally and present a new algorithm tailored to solve it – LIAN. We examine LIAN both theoretically and empirically. We show that it is sound and complete (under some restrictions). We also show that LIAN outperforms the analogues when solving numerous path planning tasks within urban outdoor navigation scenarios.

Keywords: Path planning · Path finding · Heuristic search · Grids · Grid worlds · Angle constrained paths · A* · Theta* · LIAN

1 Introduction

Path planning is one of the key abilities for an intelligent agent (robot, unmanned vehicle, computer game character etc.) to autonomously operate in either real or virtual world. Typically, in Artificial Intelligence, agent's environment is modeled with weighted graph which vertices correspond to locations the agent can occupy and edges correspond to trajectories the agent can traverse (line segments, curves of predefined shape etc.). Each edge is assigned a non-negative real number (weight, cost) by a weighting function which is used to quantitatively express characteristics of the corresponding trajectory (length, potential risk of traversing, etc.). Thus to solve a path planning problem one needs *a)* to construct a graph (given the description of the environment) and *b)* to find a path (preferably – the shortest one) on this graph.

Among the most commonly used graph models one can name visibility graphs [1], Voronoi diagrams [2], navigation meshes [3], regular grids [4]. The latter are the most widespread for several reasons. First, they appear naturally in many virtual environments (computer games are the most obvious example [5]) and even in real world scenarios, say in robotics, it is the grids that are commonly used as spatial models [6]. Second, even if the environment is described in some other way it is likely that forming a grid out of this description will be less burdensome than constructing other abovementioned models due to grid's "primitive" structure.

© Springer International Publishing Switzerland 2015
S. Hölldobler et al. (Eds.): KI 2015, LNAI 9324, pp. 208–221, 2015.
DOI: 10.1007/978-3-319-24489-1_16

After the graph is constructed the search for a path on it can be carried out by the well known Dijkstra's algorithm [7] or A* algorithm [8] (which is the heuristic modification of Dijkstra) or many of their derivatives: ARA* [9], HPA* [10], R* [11], Theta* [12], JPS [13] to name a few. Some of these algorithms are tailored to grid path finding (JPS, Theta*, HPA*), others are suitable for any graph models (with A* and Dijkstra being the most universal ones). Many of them, in fact – almost all of them, overcome their predecessors in terms of computational efficiency (at least for a large class of tasks). Some algorithms are tailored to single-shot path planning while others demonstrate their supremacy on solving bunches of tasks. But only a few of them are taking the shape of the resultant path into account although it can be quite useful in many applications. For example, a wheeled robot or an unmanned aerial vehicle simply can not follow a path with sharp turns due to their dynamic constraints. The most common way to incorporate these constraints into path planning process is to extend the search space with the agent's control laws encodings – see [14] for example. This leads to significant growth of the search space and path finding becomes computationally burdensome. So it can be beneficial to stay within grid-based world model and spatial-only search space and focus on finding the smooth paths (rather than the short ones) and thus indirectly guarantee the feasibility of that paths against the agent's dynamic constraints.

We find the idea of generating smooth paths very appealing and address the following angle constrained path planning problem. Given a square grid the task is to find a path as a sequence of grid sections (ordered pairs of grid elements) such that an angle of alteration between each two consecutive sections is less or equal than some predefined threshold. We present novel heuristic search algorithm – LIAN (from "limited angle") – of solving it. We examine LIAN both theoretically, showing that it is sound and complete (under some constraints), and experimentally, testing LIAN's applicability in urban outdoor navigation scenarios.

To the best of our knowledge, no direct competitors to LIAN are present nowadays, although there exists one or more implicit analogues – path planning methods that can be attributed to as taking the shape of the path into account. For example A*-PS [10] runs A*-search on a grid and after it is finished performs a preprocessing step to eliminate intermediate path elements. Thus the resultant path starts looking more realistic and at the same time it becomes shorter. Theta* (or more precise – Basic Theta*) [12] uses the same idea – intermediate grid elements skipping – but it performs the smoothing procedure online, e.g. on each step of the algorithm. In [15] a modification of Basic Theta* (also applicable to A*-PS) algorithm is presented which uses special angle-based heuristic to focus the search in order to construct more straightforward paths to the goal. In [16] another modification of Basic Theta* – weighted angular rate constrained Theta* (wARC-Theta*) - is described. wARC-Theta* uses special techniques to take into account agent's angular rate (and other) constraints staying within grid model e.g. without extending the spatial model with agent's orientation (heading) information but rather performing the corresponding calculations online. wARC-Theta* with some minor adaptations can be used to solve the angle constrained path planning problem we are interested in. Unfortunately, the algorithm is incomplete, e.g. it fails to solve a wide range of path planning tasks although the solutions to these tasks do exist. With some modifications, explained further in the paper, the performance of wARC-Theta* can be improved and the number of successfully solved tasks can be increased. This improved version of wARC-Theta* is seen to be the only direct analogue of the proposed algorithm so we use it to perform the comparative experimental analysis. Obtained results show that the newly proposed algorithm – LIAN – significantly outperforms wARC-Theta*: LIAN solves much more tasks and uses significantly less computational resources (processor time and memory).

The latter of the paper is organized as follows. In section 2 we express the angle constrained path planning problem formally. In section 3 the new algorithm of solving it – LIAN – is present, as well as modified wARC-Theta* algorithm is described. In section 4 the results of the comparative experimental study are given.

2   Angle Constrained Path Planning Problem on Square Grid

Two alternative types of square grid notations are widespread nowadays: center-based, when agent's locations are tied to the centers of grid cells, and corner-based, when agent's locations are tied to the corners, respectively (see figure 1).

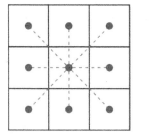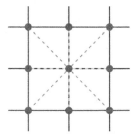

Fig. 1. Square grids: center-based (left) and corner-based (right).

We adopt the center-based notation and consider a grid to be a finite set of cells A that can be represented as a matrix $A_{M \times N} = \{a_{ij}\}$, where i, j – are cell position indexes (coordinates) and M, N – are grid dimensions. Each cell is labeled either traversable or un-traversable and the set of all traversable cells is denoted as A^+. In case cell coordinates can be omitted, lower case Latin characters will be used: a, b, c etc.

A line-of-sight function, $los: A^+ \times A^+ \rightarrow \{true, false\}$, is given and an agent is allowed to move from one traversable cell to the other if los returns true on them (or, saying in other words, if there exist a line-of-sight between them). In our work, as in many others, we use well-known in computer graphics Bresenham algorithm [17] to detect if line-of-sight between two cells exist or not. This algorithms draws a "discrete line section" (see figure 2) and if it contains only traversable cells than los is supposed to return true (otherwise los returns false).

A metric function, $dist: A^+ \times A^+ \rightarrow \Re$, is given to measure the distance between any two traversable cells. We use Euclid distance, e.g $dist(a_{ij}, a_{lk}) = \sqrt{(l-i)^2 + (k-j)^2}$ as metric function.

An ordered pair of grid cells is a section: $e=\langle a_{ij}, a_{lk}\rangle$, and it is traversable *iff los*(a_{ij}, a_{lk})=*true*. The length of a section $\langle a_{ij}, a_{lk}\rangle$ equals *dist*(a_{ij}, a_{lk}). Two sections that have exactly a middle cell in common, e.g. $e_1=\langle a_{ij}, a_{lk}\rangle$, $e_2=\langle a_{lk}, a_{vw}\rangle$, are called adjacent.

Δ-section is such a section $e=\langle a_{ij}, a_{lk}\rangle$ that it's endpoint, a_{lk}, belongs to *CIRCLE*(a_{ij}, Δ), where *CIRCLE* is a set of cells identified by the well-known in computer graphics Midpoint algorithm [18] (which is a modification of the abovementioned Brezenham's algorithm for drawing "discrete circumferences") – see figure 2.

A path between two distinct traversable cells s (start cell) and g (goal cell) is a sequence of traversable adjacent sections such that the first section starts with s and the last ends with g: $\pi(s, g)=\pi=\{e_1, ..., e_v\}$, $e_1=\langle s, a\rangle$, $e_v=\langle b, g\rangle$. The length of the path $len(\pi)$ is the sum of the lengths of the sections forming that path.

Given two adjacent sections $e_1=\langle a_{ij}, a_{lk}\rangle$, $e_2=\langle a_{lk}, a_{vw}\rangle$ an angle of alteration is the angle between the vectors $\overrightarrow{a_{ij}a_{lk}}$ and $\overrightarrow{a_{lk}a_{vw}}$, which coordinates are $(l - i, k - j)$ and $(v - l, w - k)$ respectively (see figure 2). This angle is denoted as $\alpha(e_1, e_2)$ and it's value is denoted as $|\alpha(e_1, e_2)|$.

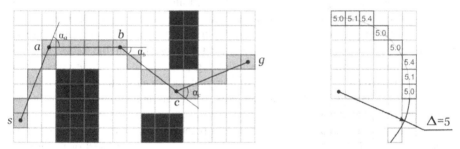

Fig. 2. Main concepts of the angle constrained path planning problem. On the left: traversable sections are depicted as solid lines; cells identified by the Bresenham algorithm are shaded grey; angles of alterations are denoted as $\alpha_a, \alpha_b, \alpha_c$; the path being depicted is a Δ-path, Δ=5. On the right: *CIRCLE* set – cells identified by the Midpoint algorithm, Δ=5.

Given a path $\pi=\{e_1, ..., e_v\}$ we will call the value $\alpha_m(\pi)=\alpha_m=\max\{|\alpha(e_1, e_2)|, |\alpha(e_2, e_3)|, ..., |\alpha(e_{v-1}, e_v)|\}$ the maximum angle of alteration of the path.

Now we are interested in solving angle constrained path planning problem which is formulated as following. Given two distinct traversable cells s (start cell) and g (goal cell) and the value α_m: $0<\alpha_m<180$, find a path $\pi(s, g)$ such that $\alpha_m(\pi)\leq\alpha_m$ (angle constrained path).

Shortest angle constrained path is considered to be the optimal solution. For the reasons explained further in the paper, we are also interested in a special class of solutions of the problem, so called Δ-solutions. Δ-solution is an angle constrained path each section of which, except maybe the last one, is the Δ-section (the path depicted on the figure 2 is a Δ-path, Δ=5).

3   Algorithms for the Angle Constrained Path Planning

3.1   wTheta*-LA

In [13] H. Kim *et al.* present a modification of Basic Theta* [9] algorithm tailored to solve grid path planning problem for an agent with angular rate constraints. Authors do not consider the maximum angle of alteration constraint – as described above – directly. Instead, they investigate the case when the speed and the turning radius of an agent are given and calculate angle constraint online, taking into account the length of the path sections involved. But if one replaces the original procedure of angle constraint calculation with the one which always returns a_m, their algorithm becomes applicable to the angle constrained path problem we are interested in. We call such an algorithm Theta*-LA (LA stands for "limited angle").

Theta*-LA is a pretty straightforward modification of Theta*. The only difference is that when Theta* tries to connect a cell to it's grandparent (in order to skip the intermediate element, e.g. parent, from the path) it validates only the line-of-sight constraint (e.g. if line-of-sight exists between the cell and it's grandparent the former is being connected to the latter), while Theta*-LA validates also angle constraint, and if an angle between the sections defined by the trio: grandparent-parent-cell is greater than the predefined threshold a_m, than parent cell is kept in the sequence. This straightforward technique leads to the following problem: if the angle constraint is less than 45° (which is likely to be a common, realistic scenario) the algorithm fails to circumnavigate large obstacles and thus fails to find an angle constrained path - see figure 3 for detailed explanation.

The main reason Theta*-LA fails to find a path in many cases is that it does not store the intermediate path elements but rather tries to make path sections as long as possible. In the original paper [13] H.Kim *et. al* give a hint how this problem can be partially solved but do not describe it in details – they suggest weighting the grid, e.g. assigning each grid cell a non-negative weight value and taking cells' weights into account while calculating the length of the section. Using weights to penalize the cells residing close to the obstacles in such way that Theta*-LA first prefers processing cells residing at some distance of the obstacles potentially leads to another grandparent-parent-cell sequences and improves the overall performance of the algorithm.

We have implemented the grid weighting procedure that makes cells lying close to the obstacles less attractive to the algorithm and call such an algorithm wTheta*-LA. We use the following strategy: given two parameters – radius r and max weighting penalty p – discrete circumferences of radius r with the centers in the cells a lying on the boundaries of the obstacles are constructed (by the referred in section 1 Midpoint algorithm). Than the rays connecting a and each cell forming the circumference are traced and each ray cell, say a', is assigned the weight as follows: $w(a')=p\cdot(1 + (1 - dist(a, a'))/r)$ - see figure 3. During the search, a modified length calculation formula is used, e.g. $len(\langle a, b\rangle)=dist(a, b)\cdot(1+avgW)$, where $avgW$ – is the average weight of the cells lying on Bresenham line in between a and b.

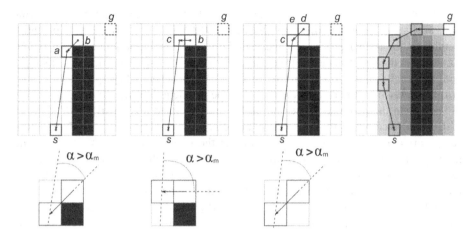

Fig. 3. Theta*-LA and wTheta*-LA circumnavigating the obstacle. Left: when expanding cell a, b is discarded due to the violation of the maximum angle alteration constraint, the search continues to c; b is discarded again for the same reason; d is also discarded so the search would continue to e, which is a dead end. Right: weighting the grid alters the direction of the search and the obstacle can be successfully circumnavigated.

Experimental analysis (see section 4) shows that weighting significantly improves algorithm's performance, but still vast variety of path planning tasks remains unsolved. One can suggest playing further with the weighting parameters values or modifying the weighting procedure itself, but we prefer to design a new algorithm that a) does not require any grid preprocessing at all and b) theoretically guarantees completeness (at least for a defined class of tasks). Such an algorithm is described further.

3.2   LIAN

LIAN (from "limited angle") is a heuristic search algorithm tailored to solve angle constrained path planning problem on square grids. LIAN relies on A* [5] search strategy of the state-space, uses line-of-sight checks as Theta* [9] and exploits the idea of multiple parents as R* [8].

As well as A* our algorithm explores the grid cells and calculates so called g-values, where g-value of a cell a, $g(a)$, is the length of the path (angle constrained path) from start cell s to a found so far. Along with the g-value each cell is obligatory characterized by the parent pointer (like Theta* but unlike A* where parent pointers are commonly used but are not obligatory) – $bp(a)$, which points to the grid cell which is a predecessor of a. Any grid cell can have *multiple* parents (this makes LIAN similar to R*). Thus when we are talking about the search space of LIAN we are talking about the space consisting of nodes which are the triples: cell, g-value, parent pointer (which actually points to the node, not the cell). Nodes will be denoted as [**a**], and [**a**]=[a, g([**a**]), bp([**a**])]. So, [**a**] is a node and a is a corresponding cell. bp([**a**]) is a node (e.g. bp([**a**])=[**a'**]) and $bp(a)$ is a corresponding cell ($bp(a)=a'$).

As well as any other A*-like search algorithm LIAN maintains and stores in memory two lists of nodes: *OPEN* and *CLOSED*. *OPEN* is the set of nodes – potential candidates for further processing and it initially contains the only element $[s, 0, \varnothing]$. *CLOSED* is the set of nodes that have already been processed. On each step node [a] with minimal f-value, $f([a])$,is retrieved from *OPEN*, where $f([a])=g([a])+h(a)$, and $h(a)$ is a heuristic estimate (e.g. $dist(a, g)$) of the path length from a to the goal cell (as in A*). Then the potential successors of [a] are generated $SUCC([a])=SUCC$. In A* *SUCC* is formed out of the cells which are adjacent to a. Unlikely, in LIAN potential successors correspond to the cells residing at the fixed distance $\Delta \in N$ (which is the input parameter of the algorithm) from a. To identify such cells Midpoint algorithm (described in section 1) is invoked: a discrete circumference of radius Δ is drawn and the nodes corresponding to the cells forming this circumference are added to *SUCC*. If the distance from a to g is less than Δ, then the goal node is also added to the *SUCC* list. To distinguish between the potential successor nodes and the corresponding cells we will use the record [**succ**$_i$] to denote the former and $succ_i$ to denote the latter.

After the set of potential successors is constructed it's pruning is done. First nodes corresponding to un-traversable cells are eliminated. Second, the nodes that violate line-of-sight constraint are pruned. Third, the nodes that correspond to the cells that violate maximum angle of alteration constraints are discarded, e.g. the nodes [**succ**$_i$] that correspond to such cells $succ_i$: $|\alpha(\langle bp(a), a\rangle, \langle a, succ_i\rangle)|>\alpha_m$ (*NB*: if the start node is processed the angle constraints are ignored). Forth, the cells that have been visited before are pruned, e.g. if the *CLOSED* list contains a node with the same cell and parent pointer then such potential successor is discarded.

1. **LIAN**(*start, goal*, Δ, α_m)
2. | $bp([start]) := \varnothing$; $g([start]) := 0$;
3. | *OPEN*.push([**start**]); *CLOSED* := $\varnothing$;
4. | **while** *OPEN*.size > 0
5. | [a] := argmin$_{[a] \in OPEN}$ $f([a])$;
6. | *OPEN*.remove([a]);
7. | **if** $a = goal$
8. | *getPathFromParentPointers*([a]);
9. | return "path found";
10. | *CLOSED*.push([a]);
11. | *Expand*([a], Δ, α_m);
12. | return "no path found"
13. **end**

14. **Expand**([a], Δ, α_m)
15. | $SUCC$ = *getCircleSuccessors*([a], Δ);
16. | **if** $dist(a, goal) < \Delta$
17. | *SUCC*.push([**goal**]);
18. | **for each** [a'] $\in$ *SUCC*
19. | **if** a' is un-traversable
20. | continue;
21. | **if** $|\alpha(\langle bp(a), a\rangle, \langle a, a'\rangle)| > \alpha_m$
22. | continue;
23. | **for each** [a''] $\in$ *CLOSED*
24. | **if** $a'=a''$ **and** $bp(a')=bp(a'')$
25. | continue;
26. | **if** *LineOfSight*(a, a') = false
27. | continue;
28. | $g([a']) := g([a]) + dist(a, a')$;
29. | *OPEN*.push([a']);
30. **end**

Fig. 4. LIAN Algorithm

After fixing the *SUCC* set, g-values of the successors are calculated: $g([\textbf{\textit{succ}}_i])=g([\textbf{a}])+d(a,\ succ_i)$ and corresponding nodes are added to *OPEN*. [a] is added to *CLOSED*.

Algorithm's stop criterion is the same as used in A*: LIAN stops when a node corresponding to the goal cell is retrieved from *OPEN* (in that case the path can be reconstructed using parent pointers). If the *OPEN* list becomes empty during the search algorithm reports *failure* to found a path.

The proposed algorithm has the following properties.

Property 1. LIAN always terminates.

Sketch of Proof. Algorithm is performing the search until the *OPEN* list is empty (or until the goal node is retrieved from it). *OPEN* contains only elements that refer to the grid cells the total number of which is finite. The number of potential parents of the cell is also finite. At the same time when a new node is generated LIAN checks whether this node (the node defined by the same cell and the same parent) has been processed before already (lines 24-26). And in case the answer is 'yes' it is pruned and not added to *OPEN*. Thus, the total number of nodes potentially addable to *OPEN* is finite. Given the fact that on each step of the algorithm an element is removed from *OPEN* (line 6) one can infer that sooner or later this list will contain no elements, or the goal node will be retrieved. In both cases (lines 4, 7) algorithm terminates.

Property 2. If only Δ-solutions are under investigation then LIAN is sound and complete, e.g. if Δ-solution to the angle constrained path planning task exists LIAN finds it, if no Δ-solution exist, LIAN reports *failure*.

Sketch of Proof. LIAN's parameter Δ well defines the set of potential successors for any node as the set of nodes corresponding to the cells residing at the Δ-distance. All successors that correspond to the traversable cells and satisfy the maximum angle of alteration and line-of-sight constraints are added to *OPEN* (except those that have been examined before). Thus, sooner or later *all* paths compromised of the Δ-sections (except, maybe, the last section – lines 16-17) will be constructed and evaluated and the sought path, if it exist, will be found. By construction this path is a Δ-solution of the given task. If LIAN reports *failure* it means that *all* the potential paths – candidates for the Δ-solution have been examined (otherwise *OPEN* list still contains some elements and LIAN continues the search), which in turn means no Δ-solution exists.

Property 3. If different Δ-solutions to the angle constrained path planning task exist LIAN returns the shortest one.

Sketch of Proof. LIAN uses the same *OPEN* prioritization strategy as A* which guarantees finding the shortest path if the admissible heuristic is used. LIAN uses Euclidian distance function *dist*, which is admissible (and consistent as well) heuristic. Thus LIAN returns the shortest Δ-solution possible.

We would like to notice further that just like A* LIAN allows heuristic weighting, e.g. calculating f-values in the following way – $f[\textbf{a}]=g([\textbf{a}])+w{\cdot}h(a)$, where $w>1$. Weighting the heuristic commonly makes it inadmissible thus the optimality of the solution can not be guaranteed any more. But at the same time, it's known that in many practical applications, grid path planning inclusively, heuristic weighting radically improves algorithm's performance while the quality of the solution decreases insignificantly. So we would also like to use LIAN with weighted heuristic as practically-wise we are interested in finding the solution as quickly as possible.

3.3   D-LIAN

Necessity to initialize LIAN with fixed Δ leads to the obvious problem: which exact value to choose? In cluttered spaces setting Δ too high will likely make LIAN report *failure* because line-of-sight constraints will be continuingly violated resulting in exhausting of *OPEN* list (there simply will be no candidates to fill it up). At the same time setting Δ too low leads to the reduction of potential successors set – *SUCC* – for any node under expansion (the lower the value Δ is the fewer cells form the discrete circumference of radius Δ) and thus *OPEN* list is likely to exhaust again.

To address this problem and make LIAN behavior more flexible and adaptable we suggest dynamically change Δ while performing the search. The modification of LIAN that uses this technique will be referred to as D-LIAN.

D-LIAN works exactly the same as LIAN but uses a bit modified *Expand*() procedure: it refines the *SUCC* set in 2 phases. Traversability check, maximum angle of alteration check and *CLOSED* list check (lines 19-26) are separated from the line-of-sight check (line 27). Namely, when some [**succ**$_i$] passes checks encoded in lines 19-26 it is added to *SUCC2* and iteration over *SUCC* set continues. Thus phase 1 ends with forming *SUCC2* – set of traversable nodes not processed before and not violating maximum angle of alteration constraint. Then all elements of *SUCC2* are checked against line-of-sight constraint and elements that successfully pass this check are added to *OPEN* (just as before). The difference is when *all* the line-of-sights checks on *SUCC2* elements fail. In that case Δ value is half decreased and *Expand*() procedure is invoked again (while usual LIAN just finishes node's expansion and no successors are added to *OPEN*). D-LIAN consequently repeats the *Expand*() procedure (and each time half-decreased value of Δ is used) until some valid successor(s) is generated or until value of Δ reaches some predefined threshold – Δ_{min} (set by the user). In the latter case D-LIAN stops node expansion and no successors are added to *OPEN*.

If, at some step of node [**a**] expansion process, valid successors are generated, Δ-value is remembered and then the search from [**a**] continues using that exact value of Δ (we will refer to it as to $\Delta([\mathbf{a}])$). If next n successive expansions of [**a**] are all characterized by successful successors generation and decreasing of $\Delta([\mathbf{a}])$ was not used to generate them then $\Delta([\mathbf{a}])$ is half increased. The upper limit on Δ value – Δ_{max} – is also set by the user. Thus while performing the search D-LIAN dynamically adjusts Δ in order to generate as many successors of each node as it is needed to solve the task.

One of the features of D-LIAN is that multiple Δ values are potentially used during the search. Technically this is achieved by storage of Δ-value referenced to a node. Thus D-LIAN node becomes a quadruple: $[a, g(a), bp([\mathbf{a}]), \Delta([\mathbf{a}])]$. Input parameters of D-LIAN are: Δ_{init} – initial value of Δ, Δ_{min} – the lower threshold, Δ_{max} – the upper threshold, n – the number of steps after which Δ is half-increased. In the experiments we used the following bindings: $n=2$, $\Delta_{min}=\Delta_{init}/2$, $\Delta_{max}=\Delta_{init}$.

4   Experimental Analysis

The experimental setup for the comparative study of the algorithms considered in the paper – LIAN, D-LIAN, Theta*-LA, wTheta*-LA – was the Windows7-operated PC, iCore2 quad 2.5GHz, 2Gb RAM. All the algorithms were coded in C++ using the same data structures and programming techniques.

Urban outdoor navigation scenario was targeted and path finding for small unmanned aerial vehicle (UAV) performing nap-of-the-earth flight was addressed.

Each grid involved in the tests was constructed using OpenStreetMaps (OSM) data [19]. To generate a grid a 1347m x 1347m fragment of actual city environment was retrieved from OSM and discretized to 501 x 501 grid so one cell refers to (approx.) 2,7m x 2,7m area. Cells corresponding to the areas occupied by buildings were marked un-traversable. 80 different city environments were used and 5 different start-goal locations were chosen for each environment fragment residing more than 1350m one from the other (so $dist(start, goal) \geq 500$). Thus, in total, testbed consisted of the 400 various path planning tasks. Targeted angle constraints were: 20°, 25° and 30° (these figures were advised by the peers involved in UAV controllers design).

The following indicators were used to compare the algorithms:

sr – success rate – number of the successfully accomplished angle constrained path planning tasks divided by the number of all tasks;

t – time (in seconds) – time needed for an algorithm to produce solution;

m – memory (in nodes) – number of elements stored in OPEN$\cup$CLOSED (the memory consumption of the algorithm);

pl – path length (in meters) – the length of the resulting angle-constrained path.

Preliminary tests had been conducted to roughly assess the performance of the algorithms. The following observations were made. First, LIAN under some parameterizations terminates minutes after it was invoked. So a 60-seconds time limit was suggested for further testing, e.g. if any algorithm did not terminate within 60 seconds the result of the test was considered to be *failure*. Second, using weighted heuristic radically improves LIAN's computational performance while path length reduces insignificantly (around 1-2%). So if further tests LIAN was run with the heuristic weight equal to 2. Third, "the best" parameters for wTheta*-LA ($p=0.1$, $r=12$) were identified and these parameters were used further on.

The main series of tests involved the following algorithms: 4 instances of LIAN, each using it's own Δ: 3, 5, 10, 20, referred, further as LIAN-3, LIAN-5, LIAN-10, LIAN-20; Theta*-LA and wTheta*-LA. Thus, 7*400=2800 experiments in total were conducted. Obtained results are shown on figure 5.

Figures shown in the table (except sr and *PAR-10* indicators) are the averaged values with *failures* not considered while averaging. Namely, for each algorithm t, m, pl values were averaged taking into account only it's respective positive results. *PAR-10* is the penalized average runtime – metrics that averages the runtime but takes *failures* into account [20]: if an algorithm fails to solve a task, t is set (penalized) for that run to be 10*cut-of-$time$ (where cut-off-$time$ equals 60) and in the end all the obtained t values are averaged. Thus PAR-10 can be seen as an integral indicator of algorithm's ability to solve various path planning tasks as quick as possible.

	$\alpha_m = 20$					$\alpha_m = 25$					$\alpha_m = 30$				
	sr	PAR-10	t	m*	pl	sr	PAR-10	t	m*	pl	sr	PAR-10	t	m*	pl
LIAN-3	31%	417	1,1	40,1	1503	31%	417	1,1	40,1	1503	99%	3	0,4	6,5	1619
LIAN-5	93%	41	0,6	8,7	1634	98%	12	0,5	6,3	1617	98%	11	0,5	6,1	1611
LIAN-10	86%	86	1,1	10,3	1632	90%	65	1,1	7,8	1619	92%	52	0,9	6,3	1610
LIAN-20	66%	209	2,7	12,7	1627	72%	171	1,4	7,8	1625	79%	130	1,6	7,8	1628
Theta*-LA	4%	581	0,8	16,1	1454	12%	536	2,1	37,5	1574	31%	421	2,2	47,4	1580
wTheta*-LA	14%	522	2,1	35,9	1504	55%	277	2,76	58,3	1598	73%	165	2,7	61,0	1567

*m is expressed in kilonodes, 1 kilonode = 1 000 nodes

Fig. 5. LIAN, Theta*-LA and wTheta*-LA results.

As one can see Theta*-LA is totally inapplicable to angle-constrained path planning when angle constraint is set to 20°-30°. In that case it fails to solve two thirds (or more) of tasks. Weighting a grid, e.g. using wTheta*-LA, significantly (up to several times) improves the performance. But still, wTheta*-LA successfully handles only 14%-55%-73% of the tasks (for angle constraints 20°, 25°, 30° respectively), while the worst LIAN result, e.g. the result of LIAN-20 is 66%-72%-79% respectively. So, one can say, that in general even the "worst" LIAN is 1,5 times better (in terms of the number of successfully handled tasks) than "the best" wTheta*-LA.

Worth mentioning are the results of LIAN-3. While it solves 99% of tasks when angle limit is 30°, in case the latter is 20°-25° only one third of tasks is solved. It indirectly confirms the hypothesis (see section 3.3) that lower values of Δ should be avoided in general. Setting Δ too high – 20 in our case – also degrades the algorithm performance.

If we now take a closer look at the results of best LIAN instances, e.g LIAN-5 and LIAN-10, and compare them to the best results achieved by limited angle Theta*, e.g. to wTheta*-LA results, and use normalization, we'll get the following picture – see figure 6.

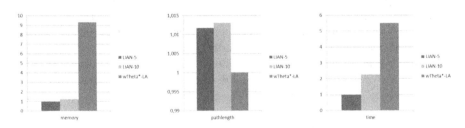

Fig. 6. Normalized LIAN-5, LIAN-10, wTheta*-LA results.

As one can see LIAN-5 and LIAN-10 both significantly (up to 5-10 times) outperform wTheta*-LA in terms of time and memory usage. At the same time, path produces by them are only 1% longer that wTheta*-LA paths.

When the best algorithms of LIAN family (e.g. LIAN-5 and LIAN-10) were identified we conducted another experiment, tailored to answer the following question – can their performance be further improved by using dynamic Δ adjustment technique as described in section 3.3? So we repeated 400 tests but now only LIAN-5, LIAN-10 and their dynamic modifications D-LIAN-5, D-LIAN-10 were used (the latter were parameterized as it was suggested in section 3.3). The results are shown in figure 7.

| | $\alpha_m = 20$ | | | | | $\alpha_m = 25$ | | | | | $\alpha_m = 30$ | | | | |
	sr	PAR-10	t	m*	pl	sr	PAR-10	t	m*	pl	sr	PAR-10	t	m*	pl
DLIAN-5	95%	34	0,8	8,9	1632	98%	12	0,5	6,1	1616	99%	8	0,4	6,7	1614
LIAN-5	93%	41	0,6	8,7	1634	98%	12	0,5	6,3	1617	98%	11	0,5	6,1	1611
DLIAN-10	86%	86	1,0	8,9	1628	90%	59	0,8	6	1624	93%	43	1,0	5,9	1615
LIAN-10	86%	86	1,1	10,3	1632	89%	65	1,1	7,8	1619	92%	52	0,9	6,3	1610

*m is expressed in kilonodes, 1 kilonode = 1 000 nodes

Fig. 7. LIAN and D-LIAN results.

As one can see dynamic adjustment of Δ increases the chances of finding a solution. It also decreases running time and memory usage in some cases (for example, when $\Delta=10$, dynamic adjustment reduces the memory consumption on notable 10-15%). So D-LIAN proves to be a worthwhile modification of LIAN.

Summing up all the results one can claim that LIAN (especially with dynamic Δ adjustment, and initial Δ values set to 5 or 10) is an effective algorithm to solve angle constrained path planning problems on square grids and it significantly outperforms it's direct competitors, e.g. wTheta*-LA, in terms of computational efficiency and the ability to accomplish path finding tasks (at least when the urban outdoor navigation scenarios are under consideration).

5   Conclusions and Future Work

We have investigated the angle constrained path planning problem for square grids and presented a new parameterized algorithm – LIAN (and it's variation D-LIAN) – for solving it. We have proved that LIAN is sound and complete (with the respect to it's input parameter – Δ). We have studied LIAN experimentally in various modeled outdoor navigation scenarios and showed that it significantly outperforms existing analogues: it solves more angle constrained path planning tasks than the competitors while using less memory and processing time.

In future we intend to develop more advanced techniques of dynamic Δ adjustment, aimed at further improvement of LIAN performance. Another appealing direction of research is evaluating LIAN in real environments, e.g. implementing LIAN as part of the intelligent control system that automates navigation of a mobile robot or unmanned aerial vehicle in real world.

Acknowledgements. This work was partially supported by RFBR, research project No. 15-07-07483.

References

1. Lozano-Pérez, T., Wesley, M.A.: An algorithm for planning collision-free paths among polyhedral obstacles. Communications of the ACM **22**(10), 560–570 (1979)
2. Bhattacharya, P., Gavrilova, M.L.: Roadmap-based path planning-Using the Voronoi diagram for a clearance-based shortest path. IEEE Robotics & Automation Magazine **15**(2), 58–66 (2008)
3. Kallmann, M.: Navigation queries from triangular meshes. In: Boulic, R., Chrysanthou, Y., Komura, T. (eds.) MIG 2010. LNCS, vol. 6459, pp. 230–241. Springer, Heidelberg (2010)
4. Yap, P.: Grid-Based Path-Finding. In: Cohen, R., Spencer, B. (eds.) Canadian AI 2002. LNCS (LNAI), vol. 2338, pp. 44–55. Springer, Heidelberg (2002)
5. Sturtevant, N.R.: Benchmarks for grid-based pathfinding. IEEE Transactions on Computational Intelligence and AI in Games **4**(2), 144–148 (2012)
6. Elfes, A.: Using occupancy grids for mobile robot perception and navigation. Computer **22**(6), 46–57 (1989)
7. Dijkstra, E.W.: A note on two problems in connexion with graphs. Numerische Mathematik **1**(1), 269–271 (1959)
8. Hart, P.E., Nilsson, N.J., Raphael, B.: A formal basis for the heuristic determination of minimum cost paths. IEEE Transactions on Systems Science and Cybernetics **4**(2), 100–107 (1968)
9. Likhachev, M., Gordon, G., Thrun, S.: ARA*: Anytime A* with Provable Bounds on Sub-Optimality, Advances in Neural Information Processing Systems 16 (NIPS). MIT Press, Cambridge (2004)
10. Botea, A., Muller, M., Schaeffer, J.: Near optimal hierarchical path finding. Journal of Game Development **1**(1), 7–28 (2004)
11. Likhachev, M., Stentz, A.: R* Search. In: Proceedings of the Twenty-Third AAAI Conference on Artificial Intelligence. AAAI press, Menlo Park (2008)
12. Nash, A., Daniel, K., Koenig, S., Felner, A.: Theta*: any-angle path planning on grids. In: Proceedings of the National Conference on Artificial Intelligence, vol. 22, No. 2, p. 1177. AAAI Press, Menlo Park (2007)
13. Harabor, D., Grastien, A.: Online graph pruning for pathfinding on grid maps. In: AAAI 2011 (2011)
14. Kuwata, Y., Karaman, S., Teo, J., Frazzoli, E., How, J.P., Fiore, G.: Real-time motion planning with applications to autonomous urban driving. IEEE Transactions on Control Systems Technology **17**(5), 1105–1118 (2009)
15. Munoz, P., Rodriguez-Moreno, M.: Improving efficiency in any-angle path-planning algorithms. In: 2012 6th IEEE International Conference Intelligent Systems (IS), pp. 213–218. IEEE (2012)

16. Kim, H., Kim, D., Shin, J.U., Kim, H., Myung, H.: Angular rate-constrained path planning algorithm for unmanned surface vehicles. Ocean Engineering **84**, 37–44 (2014)
17. Bresenham, J.E.: Algorithm for computer control of a digital plotter. IBM Systems Journal **4**(1), 25–30 (1965)
18. Pitteway, M.L.V.: Algorithms of conic generation. In: Fundamental Algorithms for Computer Graphics, pp. 219–237. Springer, Heidelberg
19. http://wiki.openstreetmap.org/wiki/Database
20. Hutter, F., Hoos, H.H., Leyton-Brown, K., Stützle, T.: ParamILS: an automatic algorithm configuration framework. Journal of Artificial Intelligence Research **36**(1), 267–306 (2009)

Technical Communications

Efficient Axiom Pinpointing with EL2MCS

M. Fareed Arif[1]([✉]), Carlos Mencía[1], and Joao Marques-Silva[1,2]

[1] CASL, University College Dublin, Dublin, Ireland
farif@ucdconnect.ie, {carlos.mencia,jpms}@ucd.ie
[2] INESC-ID, IST, ULisboa, Lisbon, Portugal

Abstract. Axiom pinpointing consists in computing a set-wise minimal set of axioms that explains the reason for a subsumption relation in an ontology. Recently, an encoding of the classification of an $\mathcal{EL}^+$ ontology to a polynomial-size Horn propositional formula has been devised. This enables the development of a method for axiom pinpointing based on the analysis of unsatisfiable propositional formulas. Building on this earlier work, we propose a computation method, termed EL2MCS, that exploits an important relationship between minimal axiom sets and minimal unsatisfiable subformulas in the propositional domain. Experimental evaluation shows that EL2MCS achieves substantial performance gains over existing axiom pinpointing approaches for lightweight description logics.

1 Introduction

Axiom pinpointing consists in identifying a minimal set of axioms (MinA) that explains a given subsumption relation in an ontology. This problem is useful for debugging ontologies, and finds several application domains, including medical informatics [15,20,32]. Earlier axiom pinpointing algorithms [5,6] in lightweight Description Logics (i.e., $\mathcal{EL}$ and $\mathcal{EL}^+$) generate a (worst-case exponential-size) propositional formula and compute the MinAs by finding its minimal models, which is an NP-hard problem. More recently, a polynomial-size encoding is devised in [33,34] that encodes the classification of an $\mathcal{EL}^+$ ontology into a Horn propositional formula (i.e. it can be exponentially more compact than earlier work [5,6]). This encoding is exploited by the axiom pinpointing algorithm EL$^+$SAT [33,34], based on SAT methods [25] and SMT-like techniques [17]. Although effective at computing MinAs, these dedicated algorithms often fail to enumerate MinAs to completion, or to prove that no additional MinA exists.

Building on this previous work, we present a new approach for axiom pinpointing in $\mathcal{EL}^+$ DLs, termed EL2MCS. It is based on a relationship between MinAs and minimal unsatisfiable subformulas (MUSes) of the Horn formula encoding [33,34]. The relationship between MUSes and MinAs makes it possible to benefit from the large recent body of work on extracting MUSes [8,9,14, 16,24,29], but also minimal correction subsets (MCSes), as well as their minimal hitting set relationship [7,18,31], which for the propositional case allows for exploiting the performance of modern SAT solvers. The relationship between

© Springer International Publishing Switzerland 2015
S. Hölldobler et al. (Eds.): KI 2015, LNAI 9324, pp. 225–233, 2015.
DOI: 10.1007/978-3-319-24489-1_17

axiom pinpointing and MUS enumeration was also studied elsewhere independently [22], where the proposed approach iteratively computes implicants [12,24] instead of exploiting hitting set dualization.

Experimental results, considering instances from medical ontologies, show that EL2MCS significantly outperforms existing approaches [4,19,22,34].

The remainder of the paper is structured as follows. Section 2 introduces basic definitions and notation. Section 3 describes the propositional Horn encoding and our proposed axiom pinpointing approach. The experimental results are reported in Section 4 and Section 5 concludes the paper.

2   Preliminaries

2.1   Lightweight Description Logics

The standard definitions of $\mathcal{EL}^+$ are assumed [3,6,33]. Starting from a set $\mathsf{N_C}$ of *concept names* and a set $\mathsf{N_R}$ of *role names*, every concept name in $\mathsf{N_C}$ is an $\mathcal{EL}^+$ concept description that also uses $\top$, $\sqcap$, and $\exists r.C$ constructs to define concept descriptions and role chains $r_1 \circ \cdots \circ r_n$ from roles in $\mathsf{N_R}$. A TBox is a finite set of *general concept inclusion (GCI)* of form $C \sqsubseteq D$ and *role inclusion* (RI) axioms of form $r_1 \circ \cdots \circ r_n \sqsubseteq s$. For a TBox $\mathcal{T}$, $\mathsf{PC}_\mathcal{T}$ denotes the set of *primitive concepts* of $\mathcal{T}$, representing the smallest set of concepts that contains the top concept $\top$, and all the concept names in $\mathcal{T}$. $\mathsf{PR}_\mathcal{T}$ denotes the set of *primitive roles* of $\mathcal{T}$, representing all role names in $\mathcal{T}$. The main inference problem for $\mathcal{EL}^+$ is concept subsumption [3,6]:

Definition 1 (Concept Subsumption). *Let C, D represent two $\mathcal{EL}^+$ concept descriptions and let $\mathcal{T}$ represent an $\mathcal{EL}^+$ TBox. C is subsumed by D w.r.t. $\mathcal{T}$ (denoted $C \sqsubseteq_\mathcal{T} D$) iff $C^\mathcal{I} \subseteq D^\mathcal{I}$ in every model $\mathcal{I}$ of $\mathcal{T}$.*

Finding an explanation, termed *axiom pinpointing*, consists of computing a minimal axiom subset *(MinA)* that explains the subsumption relation.

Definition 2 (MinA). *Let $\mathcal{T}$ be an $\mathcal{EL}^+$ TBox, and let $C, D \in \mathsf{PC}_\mathcal{T}$ be primitive concept names, with $C \sqsubseteq_\mathcal{T} D$. Let $\mathcal{S} \subseteq \mathcal{T}$ be such that $C \sqsubseteq_\mathcal{S} D$. If $\mathcal{S}$ is such that $C \sqsubseteq_\mathcal{S} D$ and $C \not\sqsubseteq_{\mathcal{S}'} D$ for $\mathcal{S}' \subsetneq \mathcal{S}$, then $\mathcal{S}$ is a minimal axiom set (MinA) w.r.t. $C \sqsubseteq_\mathcal{T} D$.*

2.2   Propositional Satisfiability

Standard propositional satisfiability (SAT) definitions are assumed [10]. We consider propositional CNF formulas and use a clause-set based representation of such formulas. Formulas are represented by $\mathcal{F}$, $\mathcal{M}$, $\mathcal{M}'$, $\mathcal{C}$ and $\mathcal{C}'$, but also by φ and ϕ. Horn formulas are such that every clause contains at most one positive literal. In this paper, we explore both MUSes and MCSes of CNF formulas.

Definition 3 (MUS). *$\mathcal{M} \subseteq \mathcal{F}$ is a Minimal Unsatisfiable Subformula (MUS) of $\mathcal{F}$ iff $\mathcal{M}$ is unsatisfiable and $\forall_{\mathcal{M}' \subsetneq \mathcal{M}} \mathcal{M}'$ is satisfiable.*

Definition 4 (MCS). $\mathcal{C} \subseteq \mathcal{F}$ is a Minimal Correction Subformula *(MCS) of* $\mathcal{F}$ *iff* $\mathcal{F} \setminus \mathcal{C}$ *is satisfiable and* $\forall_{\mathcal{C}' \subsetneq \mathcal{C}} \, \mathcal{F} \setminus \mathcal{C}'$ *is unsatisfiable.*

A well-known result, which will be used in the paper is the minimal hitting set relationship between MUSes and MCSes of an unsatisfiable formula $\mathcal{F}$ [7,11,18,31].

Theorem 1. *Let* $\mathcal{F}$ *be unsatisfiable. Then, each MCS of* $\mathcal{F}$ *is a minimal hitting set of the MUSes of* $\mathcal{F}$ *and each MUS of* $\mathcal{F}$ *is a minimal hitting set of the MCSes of* $\mathcal{F}$.

A *partial MaxSAT*, formula φ is that partitioned into a set of hard (φ_H) and soft (φ_S) clauses, i.e. $\varphi = \{\varphi_H, \varphi_S\}$. Hard clauses must be satisfied while soft clauses can be relaxed. We have used partial MaxSAT encoding and enumeration of MUSes [7,18] using minimal hitting set duals [7,11,18,31] in our proposed solution.

3   Computation Technique and Tool Overview (EL2MCS)

This section introduces the main organization of our approach. It works over the propositional Horn encoding used in EL$^+$SAT [33,34], and exploits a close relationship between MinAs and MUSes.

3.1   Horn Formula Encoding

In EL$^+$SAT, the Horn formula $\phi^{all}_{\mathcal{T}(po)}$ mimics the classification of TBox $\mathcal{T}$ and is constructed as follows [33,34]:

1. For every axiom (concretely ax_i), create an axiom selector propositional variable $s_{[ax_i]}$. For trivial GCI of the form $C \sqsubseteq C$ or $C \sqsubseteq \top$, $s_{[ax_i]}$ is constant true.

2. During the execution of the classification algorithm [3,6], for every application of a rule (concretely r) generating some assertion (concretely a_i), add to $\phi^{all}_{\mathcal{T}(po)}$ a clause of the form,

$$\left(\bigwedge_{a_j \in \text{ant}(r)} s_{[a_j]} \right) \rightarrow s_{[a_i]}$$

where $s_{[a_i]}$ is the selector variable for a_i and $\text{ant}(r)$ are the antecedents of a_i with respect to a completion rule r.

For axiom pinpointing the SAT-based algorithms [33,34], exploiting the ideas from early work on SAT solving [25] and AllSMT [17], compute MinAs for any subsumption relation (i.e., $C_i \sqsubseteq D_i$) using the list of assumption variables $\{\neg s_{[C_i \sqsubseteq D_i]}\} \cup \{s_{[ax_i]} \mid ax_i \in \mathcal{T}\}$. The following theorem is fundamental for this work [33,34], and is extended in the next section to relate MinAs with MUSes of propositional formulas.

Theorem 2 (Theorem 3 in [34]). *Given an* $\mathcal{EL}^+$ *TBox* $\mathcal{T}$, *for every* $\mathcal{S} \subseteq \mathcal{T}$ *and for every pair of concept names* $C, D \in \text{PC}_{\mathcal{T}}$, $C \sqsubseteq_{\mathcal{S}} D$ *if and only if the Horn propositional formula* $\phi^{all}_{\mathcal{T}(po)} \wedge (\neg s_{[C \sqsubseteq D]}) \wedge_{ax_i \in \mathcal{S}} (s_{[ax_i]})$ *is unsatisfiable.*

3.2 MinAs as MUSes

Although not explicitly stated, the relation between axiom pinpointing and MUS extraction has been apparent in earlier work [6,33,34].

Theorem 3 ([1]). *Given an $\mathcal{EL}^+$ TBox $\mathcal{T}$, for every $\mathcal{S} \subseteq \mathcal{T}$ and for every pair of concept names $C, D \in \mathsf{PC}_\mathcal{T}$, $\mathcal{S}$ is a **MinA** of $C \sqsubseteq_\mathcal{S} D$ if and only if the Horn propositional formula $\phi^{\text{all}}_{\mathcal{T}(\text{po})} \wedge (\neg s_{[C \sqsubseteq D]}) \wedge_{ax_i \in \mathcal{S}} (s_{[ax_i]})$ is **minimally unsatisfiable**.*

Based on Theorem 3 and the MUS enumeration approach in [18], we can now outline our axiom pinpointing approach.

3.3 Axiom Pinpointing Using MaxSAT

As described earlier, the axiom pinpointing algorithm [33,34] explicitly enumerates the selection variables (i.e., $s_{[ax_i]}$) in an AllSMT-inspired approach [17]. In contrast, our approach is to model the problem as partial maximum satisfiability (MaxSAT), and enumerate over the MUSes of the MaxSAT problem formulation. Therefore, all clauses in $\phi^{\text{all}}_{\mathcal{T}(\text{po})}$ are declared as hard clauses. Observe that, by construction, $\phi^{\text{all}}_{\mathcal{T}(\text{po})}$ is satisfiable. In addition, the constraint $C \sqsubseteq_\mathcal{T} D$ is encoded with another hard clause, namely $(\neg s_{[C \sqsubseteq_\mathcal{T} D]})$. Finally, the variable $s_{[ax_i]}$ associated with each axiom ax_i denotes a *unit soft clause*. The intuitive justification is that the goal is to include as many axioms as possible, leaving out a minimal set which, if included, would cause the complete formula to be unsatisfiable. Thus, each of these sets represents an MCS of the MaxSAT problem formulation, but also a minimal set of axioms that needs to be dropped for the subsumption relation not to hold (i.e. a *diagnosis* [20]). MCS enumeration can be implemented with a MaxSAT solver [18,27] or with a dedicated algorithm [23]. It is well-known (e.g. see Theorem 1) that MCSes are minimal hitting sets of MUSes, and MUSes are minimal hitting sets of MCSes [7,11,18,31]. Thus, we use explicit minimal hitting set duality to obtain the MUSes we are looking for, starting from the previously computed MCSes.

3.4 EL2MCS Tool

The organization of the EL2MCS tool is shown in Figure 1. The first step is similar to EL$^+$SAT [33,34] in that a propositional Horn formula is generated. The next step, however, exploits the ideas in Section 3.3, and generates a partial MaxSAT encoding. We can now enumerate the MCSes of the partial MaxSAT formula using the CAMUS2 tool [23][1]. The final step is to exploit minimal hitting set duality for computing all the MUSes given the set of MCSes [18]. This is achieved with the CAMUS tool[2]. The hypergraph traversal computation tools, shd [28] and MTminer [13], could be used instead in this phase. It

---

[1] Available from http://logos.ucd.ie/web/doku.php?id=mcsls
[2] Available from http://sun.iwu.edu/~mliffito/camus/

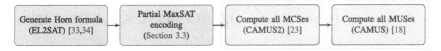

Fig. 1. The EL2MCS tool

should be observed that, although MCS enumeration uses CAMUS2 (a modern implementation of the MCS enumerator in CAMUS [18], capable of handling partial MaxSAT formulae), alternative MCS enumeration approaches were considered [23] but found not to be as efficient.

4   Experimental Evaluation

This section presents an empirical evaluation of EL2MCS[3], which is compared to the state-of-the-art tools EL$^+$SAT [34], JUST [19], CEL [4] and SATPin [22]. EL$^+$SAT and SATPin are SAT-based approaches, whereas CEL and JUST use dedicated reasoners.

The medical ontologies used in the experiments are GALEN [30] (two variants: FULL-GALEN and NOT-GALEN), Gene [2], NCI [35] and SNOMED-CT [36]. As in earlier work [34], for each ontology 100 subsumption query instances were considered. So, there are 500 instances. In addition, for the SAT-based tools, including EL2MCS, the instances were simplified with the *cone-of-influence* (COI) reduction technique. CEL and JUST use their own similar simplification techniques. The comparison with CEL and JUST imposes additional constraints. CEL reports at most 10 MinAs, so only 397 instances with up to 10 MinAs were considered in the comparison with CEL. JUST is only able to handle a subset of $\mathcal{EL}^+$, so the comparison with JUST only considers 292 instances it can return correct results. The experiments were performed on a Linux Cluster (2GHz), with a time limit of 3600s.

By the time limit, out of the 500 instances, EL$^+$SAT solves 241, SATPin solves 458 and EL2MCS solves 470. For the few instances EL2MCS does not solve, it computes thousands of MCSes by the time limit without reporting any MinA. In these cases, EL$^+$SAT and SATPin are able to return some MinAs, although not achieving complete enumeration. Regarding the comparison with CEL, out of 397 instances, CEL solves 394 and EL2MCS solves all of them. Compared with JUST, out of the 292 instances considered, JUST solves 242 and EL2MCS solves 264. It is worth mentioning that there is no instance some tool is able to solve and EL2MCS is not. Table 1 compares EL2MCS with the other tools in terms of the number of instances it performed better and worse (wins/losses). Unsolved instances where some method computed some MinAs and EL2MCS did not, are counted as losses. As we can observe, in most cases, EL2MCS performs better than any other tool. Figure 2 shows four scatter plots with a pairwise comparison of EL2MCS and each other tool in terms of their

---

[3] Available from http://logos.ucd.ie/web/doku.php?id=el2mcs

Table 1. Summary of results comparing EL2MCS with EL$^+$SAT, SATPin, CEL and JUST.

	vs EL$^+$SAT	vs SATPin	vs CEL	vs JUST
#Wins / #Losses	359 / 106	353 / 114	379 / 18	236 / 28
%Wins / %Losses	71.8% / 21.2%	70.6% / 22.8%	96.2% / 4.5%	80.8% / 9.6%

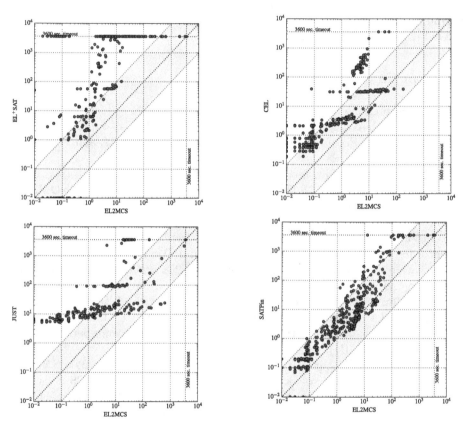

Fig. 2. Plots comparing EL2MCS with EL$^+$SAT, CEL, JUST and SATPin (runtimes in secs).

running times. They reveal very significant differences in favor of EL2MCS in all cases. EL2MCS is remarkably faster than any other tool for most instances, in many cases with performance gaps of more than one order of magnitude. The greatest advantages are over EL$^+$SAT, CEL and JUST. On a few instances, JUST is faster than EL2MCS. However, note that JUST is only able to handle a subset of $\mathcal{EL}^+$, and so it is expected to be very efficient on this kind of instances. SATPin performs better than other alternatives, solving a few instances less than EL2MCS, but still EL2MCS outperforms it consistently in terms of running time.

5   Conclusions and Future Work

This paper presents the EL2MCS tool for axiom pinpointing of $\mathcal{EL}^+$ ontologies. Building on previous work [33,34], EL2MCS exploits a close relationship between MinAs and MUSes of propositional formulas, and instruments an efficient algorithm that relies on explicit minimal hitting set dualization of MCSes and MUSes of unsatisfiable formulas. Experimental results over well-known benchmarks from medical ontologies reveal that EL2MCS significantly outperforms the state of the art, thus constituting a very effective alternative for this problem. A natural research direction is to attempt to improve EL2MCS by substituting some of its parts by other advanced novel alternatives (e.g. MCS extraction and enumeration [21,26]).

Acknowledgment. We thank R. Sebastiani and M. Vescovi, for authorizing the use of EL$^+$SAT [34]. We thank N. Manthey and R. Peñaloza, for bringing SAT-Pin [22] to our attention, and for allowing us to use their tool. This work is partially supported by SFI PI grant BEACON (09/IN.1/I2618), by FCT grant POLARIS (PTDC/EIA-CCO/123051/2010), and by national funds through FCT with reference UID/CEC/50021/2013.

References

1. Arif, M.F., Marques-Silva, J.: Towards efficient axiom pinpointing of $\mathcal{EL}^+$ ontologies. CoRR, abs/1503.08454 (2015). http://arxiv.org/abs/1503.08454
2. Ashburner, M., Ball, C.A., Blake, J.A., Botstein, D., Heather Butler, J., Cherry, M., Davis, A.P., Dolinski, K., Dwight, S.S., Eppig, J.T., et al.: Gene ontology: tool for the unification of biology. Nature Genetics **25**(1), 25–29 (2000)
3. Baader, F., Brandt, S., Lutz, C.: Pushing the $\mathcal{EL}$ envelope. In: IJCAI, pp. 364–369 (2005)
4. Baader, F., Lutz, C., Suntisrivaraporn, B.: CEL — a polynomial-time reasoner for life science ontologies. In: Furbach, U., Shankar, N. (eds.) IJCAR 2006. LNCS (LNAI), vol. 4130, pp. 287–291. Springer, Heidelberg (2006)
5. Baader, F., Peñaloza, R., Suntisrivaraporn, B.: Pinpointing in the description logic $\mathcal{EL}$. In: DL (2007)
6. Baader, F., Peñaloza, R., Suntisrivaraporn, B.: Pinpointing in the description logic $\mathcal{EL}^+$. In: Hertzberg, J., Beetz, M., Englert, R. (eds.) KI 2007. LNCS (LNAI), vol. 4667, pp. 52–67. Springer, Heidelberg (2007)
7. Bailey, J., Stuckey, P.J.: Discovery of minimal unsatisfiable subsets of constraints using hitting set dualization. In: Hermenegildo, M.V., Cabeza, D. (eds.) PADL 2004. LNCS, vol. 3350, pp. 174–186. Springer, Heidelberg (2005)
8. Belov, A., Heule, M.J.H., Marques-Silva, J.: MUS extraction using clausal proofs. In: Sinz, C., Egly, U. (eds.) SAT 2014. LNCS, vol. 8561, pp. 48–57. Springer, Heidelberg (2014)
9. Belov, A., Lynce, I., Marques-Silva, J.: Towards efficient MUS extraction. AI Commun. **25**(2), 97–116 (2012)
10. Biere, A., Heule, M., van Maaren, H., Walsh, T. (eds.): Handbook of Satisfiability, vol. 185 (2009)

11. Birnbaum, E., Lozinskii, E.L.: Consistent subsets of inconsistent systems: structure and behaviour. J. Exp. Theor. Artif. Intell. **15**(1), 25–46 (2003)
12. Bradley, A.R., Manna, Z.: Checking safety by inductive generalization of counterexamples to induction. In: FMCAD, pp. 173–180 (2007)
13. Hébert, C., Bretto, A., Crémilleux, B.: A data mining formalization to improve hypergraph minimal transversal computation. Fundammenta Informaticae **80**(4), 415–433 (2007)
14. Junker, U.: QuickXplain: preferred explanations and relaxations for over-constrained problems. In: AAAI, pp. 167–172 (2004)
15. Kalyanpur, A., Parsia, B., Sirin, E., Cuenca-Grau, B.: Repairing unsatisfiable concepts in OWL ontologies. In: Sure, Y., Domingue, J. (eds.) ESWC 2006. LNCS, vol. 4011, pp. 170–184. Springer, Heidelberg (2006)
16. Lagniez, J.-M., Biere, A.: Factoring out assumptions to speed up MUS extraction. In: Järvisalo, M., Van Gelder, A. (eds.) SAT 2013. LNCS, vol. 7962, pp. 276–292. Springer, Heidelberg (2013)
17. Lahiri, S.K., Nieuwenhuis, R., Oliveras, A.: SMT techniques for fast predicate abstraction. In: Ball, T., Jones, R.B. (eds.) CAV 2006. LNCS, vol. 4144, pp. 424–437. Springer, Heidelberg (2006)
18. Liffiton, M.H., Sakallah, K.A.: Algorithms for computing minimal unsatisfiable subsets of constraints. J. Autom. Reasoning **40**(1), 1–33 (2008)
19. Ludwig, M.: Just: a tool for computing justifications w.r.t. EL ontologies. In: ORE 2014, vol. 1207, pp. 1–7 (2014)
20. Ludwig, M., Peñaloza, R.: Error-tolerant reasoning in the description logic $\mathcal{EL}$. In: Fermé, E., Leite, J. (eds.) JELIA 2014. LNCS, vol. 8761, pp. 107–121. Springer, Heidelberg (2014)
21. Malitsky, Y., O'Sullivan, B., Previti, A., Marques-Silva, J.: Timeout-sensitive portfolio approach to enumerating minimal correction subsets for satisfiability problems. In: ECAI, pp. 1065–1066 (2014)
22. Manthey, N., Peñaloza, R.: Exploiting SAT technology for axiom pinpointing. Technical Report LTCS 15–05, Chair of Automata Theory, Institute of Theoretical Computer Science, Technische Universität Dresden, April 2015. https://ddll.inf.tu-dresden.de/web/Techreport3010
23. Marques-Silva, J., Heras, F., Janota, M., Previti, A., Belov, A.: On computing minimal correction subsets. In: IJCAI (2013)
24. Marques-Silva, J., Janota, M., Belov, A.: Minimal sets over monotone predicates in boolean formulae. In: Sharygina, N., Veith, H. (eds.) CAV 2013. LNCS, vol. 8044, pp. 592–607. Springer, Heidelberg (2013)
25. Marques-Silva, J., Lynce, I., Malik, S.: Conflict-driven clause learning SAT solvers. In: Biere, et al. (eds.) [10], pp. 131–153
26. Mencía, C., Previti, A., Marques-Silva, J.: Literal-based MCS extraction. In: IJCAI (2015)
27. Morgado, A., Liffiton, M., Marques-Silva, J.: MaxSAT-based MCS enumeration. In: Biere, A., Nahir, A., Vos, T. (eds.) HVC. LNCS, vol. 7857, pp. 86–101. Springer, Heidelberg (2013)
28. Murakami, K., Uno, T.: Efficient algorithms for dualizing large-scale hypergraphs. CoRR, abs/1102.3813 (2011)
29. Nadel, A., Ryvchin, V., Strichman, O.: Efficient MUS extraction with resolution. In: FMCAD, pp. 197–200 (2013)
30. Rector, A.L., Horrocks, I.R.: Experience building a large, re-usable medical ontology using a description logic with transitivity and concept inclusions. In: Workshop on Ontological Engineering, pp. 414–418 (1997)

31. Reiter, R.: A theory of diagnosis from first principles. Artif. Intell. **32**(1), 57–95 (1987)
32. Schlobach, S., Huang, Z., Cornet, R., van Harmelen, F.: Debugging incoherent terminologies. J. Autom. Reasoning **39**(3), 317–349 (2007)
33. Sebastiani, R., Vescovi, M.: Axiom pinpointing in lightweight description logics via horn-SAT encoding and conflict analysis. In: Schmidt, R.A. (ed.) CADE-22. LNCS, vol. 5663, pp. 84–99. Springer, Heidelberg (2009)
34. Sebastiani, R., Vescovi, M.: Axiom pinpointing in large $\mathcal{EL}^+$ ontologies via SAT and SMT techniques. Technical Report DISI-15-010, DISI, University of Trento, Italy, April 2015. http://disi.unitn.it/rseba/elsat/elsat_techrep.pdf
35. Sioutos, N., de Coronado, S., Haber, M.W., Hartel, F.W., Shaiu, W.-L., Wright, L.W.: NCI thesaurus: A semantic model integrating cancer-related clinical and molecular information. Journal of Biomedical Informatics **40**(1), 30–43 (2007)
36. Spackman, K.A., Campbell, K.E., Côté, R.A.: SNOMED RT: a reference terminology for health care. In: AMIA (1997)

Abducing Hypotheses About Past Events from Observed Environment Changes

Ann-Katrin Becker[1]([✉]), Jochen Sprickerhof[1],
Martin Günther[1,2], and Joachim Hertzberg[1,2]

[1] Knowledge Based Systems Group, Osnabrück University,
Albrechtstr. 28, 49076 Osnabrück, Germany
{ann_katrin.becker,jochen.sprickerhof}@uni-osnabrueck.de
http://www.informatik-uni-osnabrueck.de/kbs/
[2] DFKI Robotics Innovation Center, Osnabrück Branch,
Albert-Einstein-Straße 1, 49076 Osnabrück, Germany
martin.guenther@dfki.de, joachim.hertzberg@uni-osnabrueck.de

Abstract. Humans perform abductive reasoning routinely. We hypothesize about what happened in the past to explain an observation made in the present. This is frequently needed to model the present, too.

In this paper we describe an approach to equip robots with the capability to abduce hypotheses triggered by unexpected observations from sensor data. This is realized on the basis of KnowRob, which provides general knowledge about objects and actions. First we analyze the types of environment changes that a robot may encounter. Thereafter we define new reasoning methods allowing to abduce past events from observed changes. By projecting the effects of these hypothetical previous events, the robot gains knowledge about consequences likely to expect in its present. The applicability of our reasoning methods is demonstrated in a virtual setting as well as in a real-world scenario. In these, our robot was able to abduce highly probable information not directly accessible from its sensor data.

1 Motivation

Imagine Calvin the delivery robot tasked with delivering a set of packages. When it passes by Martin's office door early in the morning, it notices that the door is still closed, so it continues on its round without stopping to check whether Martin is inside. Half an hour later, Calvin observes from the end of the corridor that the door is now open, so it concludes that Martin is in his office, and the package can be delivered (see Figure 1).

This paper considers the question of how we can enable a robot to draw this kind of conclusion automatically in a wide variety of situations, based on abductive reasoning on its internal knowledge base.

In order to do so, we build upon the KnowRob Knowledge Processing Framework [9]. This provides a large amount of basic knowledge of objects and actions, as well as methods to reason about their effects. In the past, it has been shown

© Springer International Publishing Switzerland 2015
S. Hölldobler et al. (Eds.): KI 2015, LNAI 9324, pp. 234–240, 2015.
DOI: 10.1007/978-3-319-24489-1_18

Fig. 1. Via abductive reasoning our robot is able to hypothesize that Martin is in his office by observing the open office door only.

that this framework may be utilized for planning [8]. That is, knowing the current and provided a desirable future environment state, the robot is able to derive a sequence of actions that it must perform to invoke the desired state.

Yet, reasoning about past events, which are not explicitly recorded in the knowledge base, has not been a topic of robotics research so far, although this is desirable in a variety of situations. In the above example the robot may open the office door to check if Martin is present, but explicitly checking such facts is usually expensive and sometimes even impossible. Instead, abducing a plausible sequence of events that explain the open door (e.g., Martin, who has the key, opened the door) is much faster and suggests the fact of Martin's presence, too. In general reasoning about observed environment changes or in other words hypothesizing about events that caused them, poses additional hypotheses about the current state of the environment. Thus reasoning about the past helps a robot to keep its knowledge base up to date and as complete as possible.

In the following section we present the techniques used to enable our robot to perform abductive reasoning about past events responsible for certain environment changes. The applicability of our methods is demonstrated in the delivery scenario described above as well as in a real world experiment. Afterwards we compare our approach to the literature and discuss open questions to be tackled in future research on this topic.

2 Abducing the Cause of Environment Changes

At first we need to examine the changes that a robot may encounter in its surroundings. Usually, these result from actions performed by other individuals sharing the environment, while the robot only observes their effects. Classifying

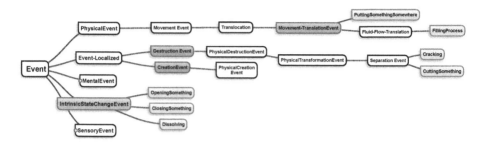

Fig. 2. Excerpt of KnowRob's basic ontology illustrating different types of events [9].

the different actions recorded in KnowRob's basic ontology (for an excerpt refer to Figure 2) by these effects, we identified five categories.

First, there are the so-called State Change Events, which change one or more properties of a known object instance; this is an instance that has been encountered by the robot previously, such as a specific office door. Second and third are Creation and Destruction Events. The former leads to the appearance of a new object instance, while the latter results in an object disappearing from the location that it previously occupied. These categories comprise events such as *CuttingSomething*, which leads to the appearance of at least one additional instance of a certain object, but also several *MovementTranslationEvents*, for example, *PuttingSomethingSomewhere*. This is modeled as from an external, decoupled view of an observer who did not perform the movement himself nor observed its execution: a new object instance and one that was moved from somewhere are not distinguishable. The last two categories we call Partial Creation and Destruction Events. These add or remove some part of a known object instance such as a *FillingProcess* that adds some new fluid to a known container object. Note that these categories are not pairwise disjoint. *CrackingAnEgg*, for instance, is a Destruction as well as a Creation Event, as during its conduction an egg gets destroyed, but instances of egg yolk and egg white are created.

This categorization allowed us to specify the input for our abductive reasoning mechanisms. Remember that our goal is to abduce a set of actions that could be responsible for an observed environment change. As in KnowRob reasoning is performed via Prolog [7], we defined Prolog predicates for each category of events. All information available on the observed change is provided as input. For example, if the state of a known object instance has changed, the instance the property of which changed, and the previous and current property values are provided. If, on the other hand, a new object has appeared, only this is passed to the corresponding predicate.

Upon reasoning depending on the method, all actions acting on a certain object or producing a specific output are tested for their effects. This means, we check if applied to the previous world state executing an action results in the current world state. If this is the case, the action is added to the result set, which contains all actions that could be responsible for the observed changes. Note that if the object acted upon is not specified via the input parameters, such as for an observed state change, the result set is comprised of pairs of action and object acted-on.

In the introductory example the delivery robot may send the following query to the knowledge base upon observing the changed state of Martin's office door:

```
?- find_cause_of_stateChange(Door-1', stateOfObject, ObjectStateLocked',
                             ObjectStateOpen', ?ResultSet).
ResultSet = [OpeningALockedDoor'].
```

This results in the conclusion that the door must have been unlocked previously. The knowledge base additionally tells us that Martin is the only one possessing a key. Thus, the robot now hypothesizes that Martin is inside his office, as entering the office is an further effect of the *OpeningALockedDoor* action, and consequently proceeds delivering the package to him.

3   Real World Experiment

One of the real-world scenarios to test our reasoning methods on-line using real sensor data was generating hypotheses about the contents of a drinking glass. These hypotheses could not have been retrieved by mere visual perception of the filled glass. This shows the ability of our abductive reasoning techniques to generate additional hidden knowledge.

For the experiment we placed a robot that monitors its surroundings via a Kinect-like depth sensor in front of a table. This contained an empty drinking glass and several juice Tetra Paks, whose labels were not readable from the robot's point of view. At this point whenever asked for the contents of the visible drinking glass the robot correctly identified it as empty. Now we took one of the Tetra Paks, let us call it *TetraPak-1*, and poured juice into the glass until it was completely filled, see Figure 3. Our robot correctly identified the performed *FillingProcess* and recorded it in its knowledge base. After this, asking the robot for the content of the drinking glass resulted in the following feedback.

First, it correctly identified the juice color as yellow, for example. As it knows that in general drinking glasses contain drinks, in case of a yellowish color the glass may either be filled with mango or orange juice. These were the only yellow drinks recorded in the knowledge base. As a next step, the system reasoned to identify which actions might have influenced the content of the glass. This can only be achieved by a filling process acting on a container containing mango or orange juice. The last filling process performed on the glass instance was a *FillingProcess* featuring *TetraPak-1* as a source, which as a general Tetra Pak instance may contain one of the juices. Thus, the robot correctly informs the user that to its knowledge the content of the glass is the same as the content of *TetraPak-1*. This hypothesis could not have been generated by mere visual perception of the filled glass. Now in case the robot is asked to serve a glass of orange juice, this hypothesis may be utilized to identify the contents of the glass by inspecting the label of *TetraPak-1*.

Note that if presented several filling processes, the robot only regarded the last one as relevant for the contents of the glass. If the last filling process involved

Fig. 3. Illustration of the different steps of a filling process as observed from our robot's camera.

a Tetra Pak known to contain cranberry juice, but the glass contained a yellow liquid, the filling process was correctly estimated as outdated. Furthermore, with slight changes it is possible to apply the system for the reverse reasoning process. If the specific contents of the glass is known and a filling process from a general Tetra Pak instance has been observed, the system can conclude the contents of the Tetra Pak to be the same as the contents of the glass. Afterwards, in case there are other glasses on the table recorded to have been filled from the same Tetra Pak, the type of their contents is known, too.

Our code, a readme with installation and running instructions, as well as rosbags of this experiment are available online[1].

4   Related Work

Obviously the introductory delivery problem could be solved in many different ways. First of all we could handcraft a probabilistic model that predicts the occupancy of a persons office [10], based on factors such as the door status and day time. This might be even more accurate sometimes, yet a model would be necessary not only for each person but for every other scenario as well. Our method generalizes to all actions and effects recorded in the underlying knowledge base.

Other approaches could include default reasoning [6] and non-monotonic reasoning techniques such as preferential reasoning [1]. However, so far none of these have been utilized in a practical approach comparable with our work, to our knowledge. In the robotic community similar contributions are rare, too. Mason [2,3] utilizes environment change, in particular the appearance or disappearance of groups of features, to classify these as objects rather than stationary background. Nitti et al. [4,5] use Statistical Relational Learning to infer hidden parameters such as magnetism like we do, but do not reason about past actions.

---

[1] http://kos.informatik.uos.de/infer_hidden_params

Especially when performing abductive reasoning online, new challenges arise. The main issue is how to limit abduction, so that our robot is still able to operate effectively, rather than busy generating hypotheses about its surroundings, most of which are irrelevant. We tackle this by applying our abductive reasoning methods only in accordance with the robot's current task. The robot monitors changes in the environment continuously via its sensors. However, only if we need to deliver a package to Martin, we analyze the cause of the status change of his office door. Similarly, only if we are interested in the content of a specific drinking glass, we abduce its source. This way, we keep our knowledge base compact and prevent the robot from being occupied with permanently abducing new hypotheses.

5   Conclusion and Future Work

We enabled a robot to perform abductive reasoning about past events to explain and generate hypotheses about hidden features of the current world state. The robot was able to perform this reasoning on-line on the basis of the available KnowRob Knowledge Processing Framework. The hypothesis generation shown in the examples in this paper is mundane and essentially simple; yet, they were beyond the reasoning capabilities of state-of-the-art robots. Our reasoning approach is added to an existing knowledge representation framework in use for robots, KnowRob, which gives us the flexibility to apply this approach to a variety of situations. Additionally we propose to apply abductive reasoning only if relevant for the currently pursued task, rather than generating all possible conclusions directly, which would be resource-consuming.

In future work we aim at applying our reasoning methods in further and more complex online scenarios. One of these scenarios could include tracking the ownership of certain objects. Imagine a breakfast table at which all persons have their own drinking glasses, yet these are not distinguishable by their looks. The people at this table keep their drinking glasses throughout the day, but they might change their positions, for instance, from the table to the lounge and take their glasses with them. Now if Martin's glass has disappeared from the table and a new glass appeared in the lounge, we can hypothesize that this belongs to Martin. Further we intend to use the presented reasoning methods to facilitate object recognition via preselection. In the drink scenario, based on the coloring of the drinking glass contents, the robot hypothesizes that a certain Tetra Pak instance contains either mango or orange juice. Thus, it is able to take this information into account upon identifying the exact label of the Tetra Pak.

References

1. Lehmann, D., Magidor, M.: Preferential logics: the predicate calculus case. In: Proc. 3rd. Theoretical Aspects of Reasoning about Knowledge, pp. 57–72 (1980)
2. Mason, J., Marthi, B.: An object-based semantic world model for long-term change detection and semantic querying. In: Proc. IROS, pp. 3851–3858 (2012)

3. Mason, J., Marthi, B., Parr, R.: Object disappearance for object discovery. In: Proc. IROS, pp. 2836–2843 (2012)
4. Nitti, D., Laet, T.D., Raedt, L.D.: A particle filter for hybrid relational domains. In: Proc. IROS, pp. 2764–2771 (2013)
5. Nitti, D., Laet, T.D., Raedt, L.D.: Relational object tracking and learning. In: Proc. IROS (2014)
6. Reiter, R.: A logic for default reasoning. Artificial Intelligence **13**(1), 81–132 (1980)
7. Sterling, L., Shapiro, E.: The Art of Prolog: Advanced Programming Techniques. MIT Press (1994)
8. Tenorth, M., Beetz, M.: A unified representation for reasoning about robot actions, processes, and their effects on objects. In: Proc. IROS (2012)
9. Tenorth, M., Beetz, M.: KnowRob: A knowledge processing infrastructure for cognition-enabled robots. Int. J. of Robotics Research **32** (2013)
10. Wang, D., Federspiel, C.C., Rubinstein, F.: Modeling occupancy in single person offices. Energy and Buildings **37**(2), 121–126 (2005)

A Software System Using a SAT Solver for Reasoning Under Complete, Stable, Preferred, and Grounded Argumentation Semantics

Christoph Beierle$^{(\boxtimes)}$, Florian Brons, and Nico Potyka

Department of Computer Science, University of Hagen, 58084 Hagen, Germany
beierle@fernuni-hagen.de

Abstract. LabSAT is a software system that for a giving abstract argumentation system AF can determine some or all extensions, and can decide whether an argument is credulously or sceptically accepted. These tasks are solved for complete, stable, preferred, and grounded semantics. LabSAT's implementation employs recent results on the connection between argumentation and Boolean satisfiability and uses the SAT solver Lingeling. In this paper, we give an overview of LabSAT and its capabilities and compare its performance to two other computational argumentation systems.

1 Introduction

For the field of knowledge representation and reasoning, argumentation, historically being a discipline within philosophy, has gained increasing importance since it is one of the most fundamental types of commonsense reasoning. Such types of every-day inferences are relevant both for the modelling of real-world scenarios and for man-machine interactions, and furthermore, argumentation supports nonmonotonic inferences [13]. In order to be able to compare different approaches to the formalization of argumentation, a common framework is useful. Such a framework is provided by abstract argumentation systems, introduced by Dung [9]. For an abstract argumentation system, a semantics is given by a set of extensions, and for each semantics, different computational problems like the determination of some or of all extensions arise.

The purpose of this paper is to present the software system LabSAT [5] (available at https://github.com/fbrns/LabSATSolver) that solves several essential problems for four different standard semantics. LabSAT uses Caminada's labeling approach [6,7] and the computational problems are reduced to Boolean satisfiability problems [2]. To solve the resulting satisfiability problems, the SAT solver Lingeling [3,4] is used. We give an overview of LabSAT's capabilities, evaluate it with respect to different test sets, and compare its performance to the systems Aspartix and Cegartix.

© Springer International Publishing Switzerland 2015
S. Hölldobler et al. (Eds.): KI 2015, LNAI 9324, pp. 241–248, 2015.
DOI: 10.1007/978-3-319-24489-1_19

2 Background: Abstract Argumentation Systems and Labelings

We briefly recall the background of abstract argumentation systems and the SAT encoding of labelings. In this paper, we only consider finite sets of arguments.

Definition 1 (Abstract argumentation system). *An abstract argumentation system is a pair $AF = (\mathcal{A}, \hookrightarrow)$ with a finite set of arguments $\mathcal{A}$ and a binary relation $\hookrightarrow \subseteq \mathcal{A} \times \mathcal{A}$ where $A \hookrightarrow B$ reads as A* attacks B. *A set $\mathcal{S} \subseteq \mathcal{A}$* attacks *$A \in \mathcal{A}$, denoted $\mathcal{S} \hookrightarrow A$, if there is an argument $B \in \mathcal{S}$ such that $B \hookrightarrow A$. For an argument $A \in \mathcal{A}$, the set $A^+ = \{B \in \mathcal{A} \mid A \hookrightarrow B\}$ is the set of arguments attacked by A, $A^- = \{B \in \mathcal{A} \mid B \hookrightarrow A\}$ is the set of attackers of A, and $\mathcal{S}^+ = \{B \in \mathcal{A} \mid \mathcal{S} \hookrightarrow B\}$ for a set $\mathcal{S} \subseteq \mathcal{A}$.*

Definition 2 (Conflict-free, defense). *Let $(\mathcal{A}, \hookrightarrow)$ be an abstract argumentation system. A set $\mathcal{S} \subseteq \mathcal{A}$ is* conflict-free *if there are no arguments $A, B \in \mathcal{S}$ with $A \hookrightarrow B$. $\mathcal{S}$* defends *an argument $A \in \mathcal{A}$ iff every argument $B \in A^-$ is attacked by $\mathcal{S}$.*

Thus, a set $\mathcal{S}$ is conflict-free iff $\mathcal{S} \cap \mathcal{S}^+ = \emptyset$. The notion of defending an argument is the base for the characteristic function of an argumentation system that can be used to specify when a set of arguments is admissible or satisfies further desirable properties.

Definition 3 (Complete, preferred, stable, grounded extension). *Let $(\mathcal{A}, \hookrightarrow)$ be an argumentation system. The* characteristic function *$\mathbf{F} : 2^{\mathcal{A}} \to 2^{\mathcal{A}}$ of $(\mathcal{A}, \hookrightarrow)$ is defined by $\mathbf{F}(\mathcal{S}) = \{A \in \mathcal{A} \mid \mathcal{S}$ defends $A\}$. Let $\mathcal{S} \subseteq \mathcal{A}$ be a conflict-free set.*

- *$\mathcal{S}$ is an* admissible extension *iff $\mathcal{S}$ defends every element in $\mathcal{S}$, i.e., iff $\mathcal{S} \subseteq \mathbf{F}(\mathcal{S})$.*
- *$\mathcal{S}$ is a* complete extension *iff $\mathcal{S}$ is admissible and every argument defended by $\mathcal{S}$ also belongs to $\mathcal{S}$, i.e., iff $\mathcal{S} = \mathbf{F}(\mathcal{S})$.*
- *$\mathcal{S}$ is a* preferred extension *iff $\mathcal{S}$ is admissible and maximal with respect to set inclusion, i.e., iff for every admissible extension $\mathcal{S}'$ with $\mathcal{S} \subseteq \mathcal{S}'$ we have $\mathcal{S} = \mathcal{S}'$.*
- *$\mathcal{S}$ is a* stable extension *iff it attacks every argument in $\mathcal{A} \setminus \mathcal{S}$, i.e, iff $\mathcal{S}^+ = \mathcal{A} \setminus \mathcal{S}$.*
- *The* grounded extension *of $(\mathcal{A}, \hookrightarrow)$ is the least fixpoint of $\mathbf{F}$.*

Extensions can be characterized by labeling functions that assign one of the labels *in*, *out*, *undec* to each argument. The following definition precisely characterizes complete extensions, corresponding to the set of all arguments labeled *in* [6].

Definition 4. *For a given $AF = (\mathcal{A}, \hookrightarrow)$, a function $\ell : \mathcal{A} \to \{in, out, undec\}$ is a* complete labeling *iff for all $A \in \mathcal{A}$:*

$\ell(A) = out$ *iff $\ell(B) = in$ for some $B \in A^-$.*
$\ell(A) = in$ *iff $\ell(B) = out$ for all $B \in A^-$.*
$\ell(A) = undec$ *iff $\ell(B) \neq in$ for all $B \in A^-$, and $\ell(C) = undec$ for some $C \in A^-$.*

Labelings can be expressed as solutions of a Boolean satisfiability problem. While different encodings have been proposed, we will employ the encoding used in [8] where for each argument $A_i \in \mathcal{A}$, three Boolean variables I_i, O_i, U_i are introduced. Exactly one of the variables I_i, O_i, U_i must be true, indicating that the label of A is *in*, *out*, or *undec*, respectively. One of several possible encodings of complete labelings [8] is:

Definition 5 (SAT encoding $SAT_{co}(\mathbf{AF})$ of complete labeling ([8, Prop. 4,C_2])). *For* $AF = (\mathcal{A}, \hookrightarrow)$ *and an index function* $\phi : \{1, \ldots, |\mathcal{A}|\} \to \mathcal{A}$, *the SAT encoding* $SAT_{co}(AF)$ *of complete labelings for* AF *is the conjunction of the following formulas:*

$$\bigwedge_{i \in \{1, \ldots, |\mathcal{A}|\}} ((I_i \vee O_i \vee U_i) \wedge (\neg I_i \vee \neg O_i) \wedge (\neg I_i \vee \neg U_i) \wedge (\neg O_i \vee \neg U_i)) \quad (1)$$

$$\bigwedge_{\{i | \phi(i)^- = \emptyset\}} (I_i \wedge \neg O_i \wedge \neg U_i) \quad (2)$$

$$\bigwedge_{\{i | \phi(i)^- \neq \emptyset\}} \left(\bigwedge_{\{j | \phi(j) \hookrightarrow \phi(i)\}} \neg I_i \vee O_j \right) \quad (3)$$

$$\bigwedge_{\{i | \phi(i)^- \neq \emptyset\}} \left(\neg O_i \vee \left(\bigvee_{\{j | \phi(j) \hookrightarrow \phi(i)\}} I_j \right) \right) \quad (4)$$

$$\bigwedge_{\{i | \phi(i)^- \neq \emptyset\}} \left(\left(\bigwedge_{\{j | \phi(j) \hookrightarrow \phi(i)\}} (\neg U_i \vee \neg I_j) \right) \wedge \left(\neg U_i \vee \left(\bigvee_{\{j | \phi(j) \hookrightarrow \phi(i)\}} U_j \right) \right) \right) \quad (5)$$

Each argument must be exactly one of *in*, *out*, *undec* (1), and if it has has no attackers, it must be *in* (2). If it has attackers and it is *in*, all of its attackers must be out (3), if it is *out*, at least one attacker must be *in* (4), and if it is *undec*, none of its attackers may be *in* and at least one must be *undec* (5).

3 Overview of the LabSAT System

The four semantics given in Def. 3 will be denoted by CO (complete), PR (preferred), ST (stable), and GR (grounded). Given an abstract argumentation system $AF = (\mathcal{A}, \hookrightarrow)$, $A \in \mathcal{A}$, and a semantics XX $\in \{$CO, PR, ST, GR$\}$, we consider the following problems:

ES-XX : determine some XX extension
EE-XX: determine all XX extensions
DC-XX: decide whether A is in some XX extension (A is accepted credulously)
DS-XX: decide whether A is in all XX extensions (A is accepted sceptically)

The 16 resulting problems are covered by the *First International Competition on Computational Models of Argumentation*[1], and the purpose of LabSAT is to solve all 16 problems. To do so, LabSAT employs the SAT encoding of labelings and uses the SAT solver Lingeling [3,4] for solving the resulting satisfiability problems.

Complete Semantics. To determine all complete extensions, LabSAT uses $SAT_{co}(AF)$ and iterates over all existing extensions and, after displaying the set of arguments that was retrieved, excludes the solution that resulted in satisfiable. Some extension is found by using the same mechanism, in this case the iterator is only called once. The problem of deciding an argument A credulously is solved by adding the clause $I_{\phi^{-1}(A)}$ to the SAT problem. If some extension exists, the argument is credulously inferred. To prove that an argument is in every complete extension, LabSAT uses the grounded extension. If A is in the minimal extension w.r.t. set inclusion, the argument is skeptically inferred.

Stable Semantics. Since stable extensions are complete extensions with no argument having label *undec*, the conjunction $\neg U_1 \wedge \ldots \wedge \neg U_{|\mathcal{A}|}$ is added to $SAT_{co}(AF)$. The problems ES-ST, EE-ST, and DS-ST are then computed in the same way as for the complete extensions. For DC-ST, the iterator is called repeatedly until a set without the argument A is found; otherwise, the argument is skeptically inferred.

Preferred Semantics. For preferred extensions, a maximization w.r.t. set inclusion is required. For this, LabSAT provides an implementation of the algorithm PrefSat given in [8]. The algorithm is initialized with $SAT_{co}(AF)$, and complete extensions are maximized by trying to add arguments. LabSAT then handles ES-PR, EE-PR, and DS-PR in the same way as for complete semantics, and DC-PR as for stable semantics.

Grounded Semantics. The grounded extension is computed without the use of a SAT solver. Instead, LabSAT implements the algorithm for the grounded extension provided in [12]. Since the grounded extension is unique, the problems ES-GR and EE-GR are the same problem and also DC-GR and DS-GR coincide. LabSAT computes the grounded extension directly and displays it or checks for the argument A, respectively.

LabSAT Implementation. For the implementation of LabSAT, Java 7 is used. The connection to the SAT solver Lingeling [3,4] which is implemented in C, is realized with the Java Native Interface (JNI). Every reasoning task is a combination of two core types, the type `Problem` and the type `Reasoner`. The abstract class `Reasoner` contains the encoding for the complete extensions. The encoding is adjusted or replaced by concrete classes, which extends the abstract class `Reasoner`. In addition, the abstract class `Reasoner` implements the interface `Iterator`, which allows iterative calls of the SAT solver. Concrete classes, which extend the abstract class `Problem`, use the `Iterator` and handle the

---

[1] ICCMA'15 – http://argumentationcompetition.org/2015

results with regard to the given problem, which may be any of the 16 problems described above.

4   Evaluation

For evaluating LabSAT, argumentation graphs were generated randomly, given a number of arguments and given a probability that an argument attacks another one. For every $n = 1, \ldots, 10$, the test set $T_{0.2}$ contains 10 graphs with $n \times 30$ nodes and with an attack probability of 0.2. Correspondingly, for every $n = 1, \ldots, 10$, $T_{0.4}$ contains 10 graphs with $n \times 50$ nodes and with an attack probability of 0.4. All results shown for solving a graph with k nodes refer to the average of the solution times for the corresponding 10 graphs having k nodes, thus avoiding any peculiar effects that might arise in a randomly generated graph. Problems not solved within a time limit of 10 minutes are classified as unsolved. The evaluation was carried out on an AMD Phenom II X4 840 processor (3,2 GHz) with 4 GB RAM, using Ubuntu Linux 14.10. The performance of LabSAT is compared to two systems that also both use a reduction-based approach. For Aspartix[2] [11], we used a configuration where the resulting answer set programs (ASP) are computed with Gringo (Version 3.0.5) and Clasp(D) with metasp (Version 3.0.6, 1.1)[3]. The second system used for comparison is Cegartix (version 0.3)[4] [10] that employs the SAT solver MiniSAT.

Figure 1 (a) - (b) shows the evaluation results of the two test sets $T_{0.2}$ and $T_{0.4}$ for EE-CO for Aspartix and LabSAT. For $T_{0.2}$, both systems exhibit a performance drop at 210 nodes; LabSAT can not compute graphs with more than 240 nodes, Aspartix not with more than 270 nodes. For $T_{0.4}$, both can solve graphs up to 450 nodes, with very similar computation times.

For stable semantics, $T_{0.2}$ yields similar results as for EE-CO (Figure 1 (c)). The performance is almost identical for Aspartix and LabSAT, and slightly better than for EE-CO since all literals U_i are false. For $T_{0.4}$, Figure 1 (d) shows a performance edge for LabSAT which can also compute all graphs with 500 nodes.

Computing EE-PR is more expensive (Figure 1 (e) - (f)). For $T_{0.2}$, Aspartix solves all graphs with 210 nodes, LabSAT all graphs with 240 nodes. Here, LabSAT's implementation of PrefSat using Lingeling is faster than Aspartix. This also holds for $T_{0.4}$ where Aspartix solves graphs with up to 300 nodes and LabSAT solves graphs with up to 400 nodes.

Cegartix addresses reasoning under different semantics. For preferred semantics, sceptical reasoning is implemented. For this decision problem DS-PR, Cegartix is slower than LabSAT which can also compute much larger graphs (Figure 2).

---

[2] http://www.dbai.tuwien.ac.at/research/project/argumentation/systempage
[3] http://potassco.sourceforge.net
[4] http://www.dbai.tuwien.ac.at/research/project/argumentation/cegartix

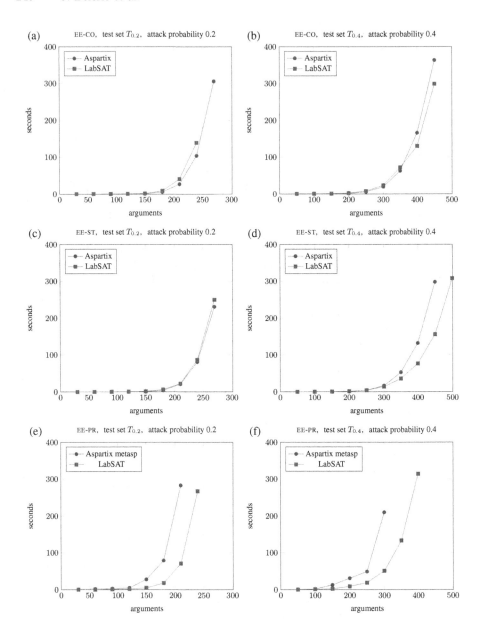

Fig. 1. Enumerating all complete ((a) - (b)), stable ((c) - (d)), and preferred ((e) - (f)) extensions

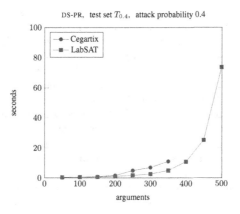

Fig. 2. Comparison Cegartix – LabSAT for DS-PR

5 Conclusions and Future Work

LabSAT allows solving several computational problems for abstract argumentation systems under complete, stable, preferred, and grounded semantics: It can determine some or all extensions and can decide whether an argument is in some or in all extensions. LabSAT employs the SAT encoding of Caminada's labeling approach and the PrefSat algorithm from [8] and uses the SAT solver Lingeling [3,4]. Based on a first evaluation with two test sets, its performance is comparable to Aspartix for complete and stable semantics, while for preferred semantics, it has a leading edge over Aspartix and Cegartix both in computation time as well as in the size of problems that can be handled. For a more thorough assessment of LabSAT, the effect of using the performant SAT solver Lingeling as back-end should be investigated, and a more elaborate evaluation is needed. LabSAT has been submitted to ICCMA'15 (cf. Section 3); within this competition, more than 15 software systems will be evaluated and compared with respect to a large array of different argumentation problems. Furthermore, the successive extension of an argumentation system by adding new arguments without having to compute the semantics from scratch should be investigated, cf. [1].

References

1. Baumann, R., Brewka, G., Wong, R.: Splitting argumentation frameworks: an empirical evaluation. In: Modgil, S., Oren, N., Toni, F. (eds.) TAFA 2011. LNCS, vol. 7132, pp. 17–31. Springer, Heidelberg (2012)
2. Besnard, P., Doutre, S.: Checking the acceptability of a set of arguments. In: Delgrande, J.P., Schaub, T. (eds.) Proc. of the 10th International Workshop on Non-Monotonic Reasoning (NMR 2004), pp. 59–64 (2004)

3. Biere, A.: Lingeling, Plingeling and Treengeling entering the SAT competition 2013. In: Balint, A., Belov, A., Heule, M., Järvisalo, M. (eds.) Proceedings of SAT Competition 2013. Department of Computer Science Series of Publications B, vol. B-2013-1, pp. 51–52. University of Helsinki (2013)

4. Biere, A.: Yet another local search solver and Lingeling and friends entering the sat competition 2014. In: Balint, A., Belov, A., Heule, M., Järvisalo, M. (eds.) Proceedings of SAT Competition 2014. Department of Computer Science Series of Publications B, vol. B-2014-2, pp. 39–40. University of Helsinki (2014)

5. Brons, F.: Verwendung des Labelling-Ansatzes nach Caminada als aussagenlogisches Erfüllbarkeitsproblem für die Berechnung der Semantik abstrakter Argumentationssysteme. M.Sc. Thesis, Dept. of Computer Science, University of Hagen, Germany (2015). (in German)

6. Caminada, M.: On the issue of reinstatement in argumentation. In: Fisher, M., van der Hoek, W., Konev, B., Lisitsa, A. (eds.) JELIA 2006. LNCS (LNAI), vol. 4160, pp. 111–123. Springer, Heidelberg (2006)

7. Caminada, M., Gabbay, D.: A logical account of formal argumentation. Studia Logica **93**(2–3), 109–145 (2009)

8. Cerutti, F., Dunne, P.E., Giacomin, M., Vallati, M.: Computing preferred extensions in abstract argumentation: a SAT-based approach. In: Black, E., Modgil, S., Oren, N. (eds.) TAFA 2013. LNCS, vol. 8306, pp. 176–193. Springer, Heidelberg (2014). (extended version as technical report)

9. Dung, P.: On the acceptability of arguments and its fundamental role in nonmonotonic reasoning, logic programming and n-person games. Artificial Intelligence **77**, 321–357 (1995)

10. Dvořák, W., Järvisalo, M., Wallner, J.P., Woltran, S.: Complexity-sensitive decision procedures for abstract argumentation. Artif. Intell. **206**, 53–78 (2014)

11. Egly, U., Gaggl, S., Woltran, S.: Answer set programming encodings for argumentation frameworks. Argument and Computation **1**(2), 147–177 (2010)

12. Modgil, S., Caminada, M.: Proof theories and algorithms for abstract argumentation frameworks. In: Simari, G., Rahwan, I. (eds.) Argumentation in Artificial Intelligence, pp. 105–129. Springer (2009)

13. Prakken, H., Vreeswijk, G.: Logics for defeasible argumentation. In: Gabbay, D., Guenthner, F. (eds.) Handbook of Philosophical Logic, vol. 4, pp. 219–318. Springer, Netherlands (2002)

On the KL Divergence of Probability Mixtures for Belief Contraction

Kinzang Chhogyal[1,2]([✉]), Abhaya Nayak[2], and Abdul Sattar[1]

[1] Griffith University, Brisbane, Australia
kin.chhogyal@mq.edu.au, a.sattar@griffith.edu.au
[2] Macquarie University, Sydney, Australia
abhaya.nayak@mq.edu.au

Abstract. Probabilistic belief change is an operation that takes a probability distribution representing a belief state along with an input sentence representing some information to be accommodated or removed, and maps it to a new probability distribution. In order to choose from many such mappings possible, techniques from information theory such as the *principle of minimum cross-entropy* have previously been used. Central to this principle is the *Kullback-Leibler (KL) divergence*. In this short study, we focus on the *contraction* of a belief state P by a belief a, which is the process of turning the belief a into a non-belief. The contracted belief state P_a^- can be represented as a mixture of two states: the original belief state P, and the resultant state $P_{\neg a}^*$ of revising P by $\neg a$. Crucial to this mixture is the mixing factor ϵ which determines the proportion of P and $P_{\neg a}^*$ that are to be used in this process. We show that once ϵ is determined, the KL divergence of P_a^- from P is given by a function whose only argument is ϵ. We suggest that ϵ is not only a mixing factor but also captures relevant aspects of P and $P_{\neg a}^*$ required for computing the KL divergence.

1 Introduction

Cognitive agents use new information to form beliefs, and change, or even discard, existing beliefs. In AI, the field of *belief change* Alchourrón et al. [1985] studies how a rational agent's set of beliefs, represented as sentences, may change when a piece of new information is acquired. It is convenient to view beliefs probabilistically when a finer grain of uncertainty is desired. The *belief state* of an agent is then represented by a probability distribution. The two main operations that are employed to represent change in a belief state are *contraction* and *revision*. Contraction removes sentences that are beliefs whereas revision accommodates information that is possibly inconsistent with existing beliefs. The results of both these operations are (usually) new belief states. One of the main guiding principles in belief change is that of *minimal information loss* which

---

We thank the referees for valuable comments. We also acknowledge the help of the Australian Research Council (ARC) for partially funding this research via ARC grant DP150104133.

S. Hölldobler et al. (Eds.): KI 2015, LNAI 9324, pp. 249–255, 2015.
DOI: 10.1007/978-3-319-24489-1_20

says that in the process of belief change the loss of information should be minimised. As belief states are probability distributions, researchers have resorted to the *principle of minimum cross-entropy* from information theory which is a technique that minimizes relative information loss and thus provides a way of selecting new belief states. The principle of minimum cross-entropy is based on the *Kullback-Leibler* divergence which measures the similarity between two probability distributions. In this paper, we study the Kullback-Leibler divergence of the belief state obtained after the contraction of a belief from the original belief state. Following Gärdenfors [1988], we represent the contracted belief state P_a^- as the ϵ-mixture of two states: the original belief state P, and the resultant state $P_{\neg a}^*$ of revising P by $\neg a$. The factor ϵ determines the proportion of P and $P_{\neg a}^*$ to be used in this process. Our main contribution is a simple but somewhat surprising result that the value of Kullback-Leibler divergence can be solely determined by ϵ. We conclude the paper with a brief discussion of the implication of this result.

2   Background

Consider a finite set of propositional variables from which a language $\mathcal{L}$ is generated. The set of all possible worlds (interpretations) of $\mathcal{L}$ is Ω. Lower case Roman letters $a, b, \ldots$ are sentences in $\mathcal{L}$ and, ω with or without subscript represents worlds in Ω. An agent's belief state can be represented as a single sentence by the special symbol k or as a set of sentences K. Given a probability distribution P, the belief set K is the *top* of P, i.e., the set of sentences that have a probability of 1. Henceforth, P will be referred to as the belief state. Given P, the probability of a sentence a is given by $P(a) = \sum_\omega P(\omega)$, where $\omega \models a$. If $P(a) = 1$, we say a is *belief*. If $P(a) = 0$, a is a *disbelief*, i.e. $\neg a$ is a belief. For all other cases, a is called a *non-belief*. The two belief change operations we are interested in are *probabilistic belief revision* and *probabilistic belief contraction*. Belief revision provides a mechanism for accommodating belief contravening information while retaining consistency if the new information is self-consistent. Thus, a belief becomes a *disbelief* as a result. Let P be the current belief state of an agent. Upon receiving word that a is false, the agent *revises* P by $\neg a$ to transform P to a new belief state represented by $P_{\neg a}^*$ where a is a disbelief. Thus, $P(a) = 1$ and $P_{\neg a}^*(a) = 0$. Similarly, in the case of belief contraction, an existing belief is discarded/suspended and thus its status is reduced to that of a *non-belief*. The contraction of P by a is represented by the new belief state P_a^-. Thus, $P(a) = 1$ but $0 < P_a^-(a) < 1$. The semantics of revision and contraction of probabilistic belief states is given by the movement of probabilities between the worlds in Ω. When revising P by $\neg a$, we must ensure that all a-worlds have zero probability mass, i.e. $\sum_\omega P_{\neg a}^*(\omega) = 0$, where $\omega \models a$. This way $P_{\neg a}^*(a) = 0$ as required. On the other hand, in contracting P by a, some models of a must have non-zero probability mass but the sum of these masses should not equal 1, i.e. $0 < \sum_\omega P_a^-(\omega) < 1$, where $\omega \models a$. Revision and contraction are functions that map belief states and input sentences to belief states. Thus, given the set of all belief states $\mathbb{P}$, $* : \mathbb{P} \times \mathcal{L} \to \mathbb{P}$ and $- : \mathbb{P} \times \mathcal{L} \to \mathbb{P}$. These functions must of course be subject to some conditions. For instance, as we mentioned earlier, $P^*_{\neg a}(a) = 0$ for revision and $0 < P^-_a(a) < 1$ for contraction. The former constitutes the so called *revision postulates*, $P^*1 - P^*5$, where as the latter constitutes *contraction postulates*, $P^-1 - P^-5$ Gärdenfors [1988]. In this work, rather than looking at contraction directly, we assume that a revision function satisfying $P^*1 - P^*5$ is already available and take contraction to be defined via revision revision as follows:

Definition 1. *Gärdenfors [1988] Given P with $P(a) = 1$, for all $x \in \mathcal{L}$ and some ϵ, $0 \leq \epsilon < 1$:*

$$P^-_a(x) = \epsilon \cdot P(x) + (1 - \epsilon) \cdot P^*_{\neg a}(x).$$

Thus, P^-_a is a *mixture* of P and $P^*_{\neg a}$, and is often also written as $P\epsilon P^*_{\neg a}$. It is understood that in the trivial case when a is *not* a belief, i.e. $P(a) < 1$, the contraction is vacuously trivial, and this is achieved by setting $\epsilon = 1$. The following theorem guarantees that probabilistic contraction functions obtained via Definition 1 satisfy the contraction postulates.

Theorem 1. *Gärdenfors [1988] If a revision function satisfies $P^*1 - P^*5$, then the contraction function generated by Definition 1 satisfies $P^-1 - P^-5$, where $P^*1 - P^*5$ are probabilistic revision postulates.*

3   Information Theory and Probabilistic Belief Contraction

The requirement that any contraction function must satisfy postulates $P^-1 - P^-5$ constrains the probabilistic contraction functions rather weakly, and plausible methods to help further narrow down potential candidates are required. One of the ways that researchers have approached the probabilistic belief change problem is from the perspective of information theory. In Kern-Isberner [2008] the author studies the problem of updating probabilistic conditional knowledge bases based on a propositional language. This is further extended to deal with relational languages in Potyka et al. [2013] where as in Ramachandran et al. [2012], the problem of probabilistic belief contraction in a setting similar to ours is considered. The common theme in all these works is the use of two important ideas from information theory, namely the *principle of maximum entropy* Jaynes [1957] and the *principle of minimum cross-entropy* (**PME**) Kullback and Leibler [1951]. In this work, we consider the Kullback-Leibler divergence on which **PME** is based.

Definition 2. *Given two discrete probability distributions P and Q over the set of worlds Ω, the Kullback-Leibler (KL) divergence of Q from P is defined as:*

$$D_{KL}(P \parallel Q) = \sum_{\omega \in \Omega} P(\omega) \ln \left(\frac{P(\omega)}{Q(\omega)} \right)$$

Intuitively, the KL divergence measures the difference between two probability distributions. If P is the real distribution then it measures how good an approximation Q is of P or alternatively how close Q is to P. It can also be viewed as measuring how much information is lost in moving from P to Q. The following are some important properties of the KL divergence: **1)** $D_{KL}(P \parallel Q) \geq 0$, **2)** $D_{KL}(P \parallel Q) = 0$ iff $P(\omega) = Q(\omega)$ for all $\omega \in \Omega$, and **3)** $D_{KL}(P \parallel Q) \neq D_{KL}(Q \parallel P)$. The first property says that the KL divergence is always non-negative. The second property says that the KL divergence between two distributions is 0 if and only if the distributions are equal. The third property says that in general the KL divergence is not symmetric. We will also adopt the convention that $0/0 = 0$.

So, the question arises of how and why **PME** (KL divergence) is used in the context of probabilistic contraction. The agent's belief state is to be changed from P to P_a^-. While undergoing this change to turn a from a belief into a non-belief, the agent should try and keep as much of its old information as possible. In other words, it must try to minimize information loss and this is where **PME** comes in. In selecting a probability distribution for the new belief state P_a^-, the agent should choose a distribution that is as similar to P as possible. Since the KL divergence measures the difference between probability distributions, the probability distribution with the minimum KL divergence should be the one chosen for P_a^-, which in simple words is what the **PME** says. Given its importance, we next explore the KL divergence of P_a^-.

4 ϵ and KL Divergence

Recall from Defintion 1 that $P_a^-(x) = \epsilon \cdot P(x) + (1-\epsilon) \cdot P_{\neg a}^*(x)$. What is intriguing about this equation is the role of ϵ. Gärdenfors [1988] interprets P_a^- in the definition above as "*a compromise between the states of belief represented by P and $P_{\neg a}^*$, where ϵ is a measure of degree of closeness to the beliefs in P.*" This view of ϵ raises the question of whether it has any relation to the KL divergence since both ϵ and the KL divergence deal with the notion of closeness between belief states (probability distributions). In the following, we investigate the role that ϵ plays in determining the KL divergence. Observe from Defintion 1 that P_a^- is a function of the P, ϵ and $P_{\neg a}^*$. Prima facie, this suggests that the KL divergence of P_a^- from P will itself be a function of P, ϵ and $P_{\neg a}^*$. However, assuming we are given the old belief state P, the crucial factors really are ϵ and $P_{\neg a}^*$. The best combination of the two should be chosen in order to minimize the KL divergence. We have the following result about the KL divergence of P_a^- from P:

Theorem 2. *Let Ω be the set of all worlds and P and $P_{\neg a}^*$ be probability distributions over Ω where a is accepted as a belief in state P and $P_{\neg a}^*$ is obtained after the revision of P by $\neg a$. Let $P_a^- = P\epsilon P_{\neg a}^*$. Then, $DL_{KL}(P \parallel P_a^-) = ln(\frac{1}{\epsilon})$.*

Proof. We know from Definition 2

$$D_{KL}(P \parallel P_a^-) = \sum_{\omega \in \Omega} P(\omega) \ln \left(\frac{P(\omega)}{P_a^-(\omega)} \right)$$

Using Definition 1:

$$D_{KL}(P \parallel P_a^-) = \sum_{\omega \in \Omega} P(\omega) \ln \left(\frac{P(\omega)}{\epsilon \cdot P(\omega) + (1 - \epsilon) \cdot P_{\neg a}^*(\omega)} \right)$$

Since for any $\omega \in \Omega$, either $\omega \models a$ or $\omega \models \neg a$ but not both, we can break the summation into two parts. Let $\Omega = \{\omega_1, \ldots, \omega_{i-1}, \omega_i, \ldots, \omega_n\}$ where $\omega \models a$ for $\omega \in \{\omega_1, \ldots, \omega_{i-1}\}$ and $\omega \models \neg a$ for $\omega \in \{\omega_i, \ldots, \omega_n\}$. We get:

$$D_{KL}(P \parallel P_a^-) = D'_{KL}(P \parallel P_a^-) + D''_{KL}(P \parallel P_a^-)$$

where $D'_{KL}(P \parallel P_a^-)$ and $D''_{KL}(P \parallel P_a^-)$ is the KL divergence applied to sets $\{\omega_1, \ldots, \omega_{i-1}\}$ and $\{\omega_i, \ldots, \omega_n\}$ respectively.

Case A: Consider $D'_{KL}(P \parallel P_a^-)$ first. We know that for each $\omega \in \{\omega_1, \ldots, \omega_{i-1}\}$, $P_{\neg a}^*(\omega) = 0$, since $\omega \models a$, and $\sum_{\omega \in \{\omega_1, \ldots, \omega_{i-1}\}} P(\omega) = 1$. Thus,

$$D'_{KL}(P \parallel P_a^-) = \sum_{\omega \in \{\omega_1, \ldots, \omega_{i-1}\}} P(\omega) \ln \left(\frac{P(\omega)}{\epsilon \cdot P(\omega) + (1 - \epsilon) \cdot 0} \right)$$

$$= \sum_{\omega \in \{\omega_1, \ldots, \omega_{i-1}\}} P(\omega) \ln \left(\frac{1}{\epsilon} \right)$$

$$= \ln \left(\frac{1}{\epsilon} \right) \sum_{\omega \in \{\omega_1, \ldots, \omega_{i-1}\}} P(\omega)$$

$$= \ln \left(\frac{1}{\epsilon} \right).$$

Case B: Now consider $D''_{KL}(P \parallel P_a^-)$. In this case, for any $\omega \in \{\omega_i, \ldots, \omega_n\}$, $P(\omega) = 0$ since $\omega \not\models a$. So we get,

$$D''_{KL}(P \parallel P_a^-) = \sum_{\omega \in \{\omega_i, \ldots, \omega_n\}} P(\omega) \ln \left(\frac{P(\omega)}{\epsilon \cdot P(\omega) + (1 - \epsilon) \cdot P_{\neg a}^*(\omega)} \right)$$

$$= \sum_{\omega \in \{\omega_i, \ldots, \omega_n\}} 0 \cdot \ln \left(\frac{0}{\epsilon \cdot 0 + (1 - \epsilon) \cdot P_{\neg a}^*(\omega)} \right)$$

$$= \sum_{\omega \in \{\omega_i, \ldots, \omega_n\}} 0 \cdot \ln(0)$$

$$= 0.$$

Therefore,

$$D_{KL}(P \parallel P_a^-) = D'_{KL}(P \parallel P_a^-) + D''_{KL}(P \parallel P_a^-)$$

$$= \ln\left(\frac{1}{\epsilon}\right) + 0$$

$$= \ln\left(\frac{1}{\epsilon}\right) \qquad \square.$$

Theorem 2 offers a quick way of computing the KL divergence once one knows what ϵ is. Note that if $\epsilon = 1$, then P and P_a^- are the same and there should be no divergence between them. This is exactly what we get from Theorem 2 as $\ln(\frac{1}{1}) = 0$. At the other extreme, if $\epsilon = 0$, $\ln(\frac{1}{0})$ is infinitely big or in other words, P and P_a^- maximally divergent. This is the case when $P_a^- = P_{\neg a}^*$ and there is no common world that both P and P_a^- assign non-zero probability mass to.

This result may indeed look a little baffling. One would think that the divergence of P_a^- from P would depend on both P_a^- and P. Since P_a^- is defined in terms of P, ϵ and $P_{\neg a}^*$, it would follow that it would definitely depend on both ϵ and $P_{\neg a}^*$, and possibly also on P. But as Theorem 2 shows, the divergence of P_a^- from P is fully determined by ϵ alone. This is illustrated in the Example 1 below.

Example 1. Let the language $\mathcal{L}$ and the corresponding set of possible worlds Ω be generated from the atoms c, d and e. Let P be a probabilistic belief state such that $[k] = \{\omega \in \Omega \mid P(\omega) \neq 0\} = \{\bar{c}de, c\bar{d}e, cde\}$ (see the Table 1 below). Thus $k \equiv (c \vee d) \wedge e$. Let $a \equiv (c \wedge \neg d) \vee (d \wedge e)$, whereby $k \models a$. Let $*_1$ and $*_2$ be two distinct probabilistic revision functions and $\neg a$ a belief in both $P_{\neg a}^{*1}$ and $P_{\neg a}^{*2}$. Let $\epsilon = 0.1$, and P_a^{-1} and P_a^{-2} be obtained from Definition 1 using P, and $P_{\neg a}^{*1}$ and $P_{\neg a}^{*2}$ respectively. Using Definition 2, we get $D'_{KL}(P \parallel P_a^{-1}) = D'_{KL}(P \parallel P_a^{-2}) = 2.3026$. This is exactly equal to $\ln(\frac{1}{\epsilon}) = 2.3026$ which we previously derived.

Table 1. Check marks under k and a show their models. Refer to Example 1 for details.

ω	k	a	P	$P_{\neg a}^{*1}$	P_a^{-1}	$P_{\neg a}^{*2}$	P_a^{-2}
$\bar{c}\bar{d}\bar{e}$			0	0.35	0.315	0	0
$\bar{c}\bar{d}e$			0	0	0	0.1	0.09
$\bar{c}d\bar{e}$			0	0.5	0.45	0.2	0.18
$\bar{c}de$	✓	✓	0.25	0	0.025	0	0.025
$c\bar{d}\bar{e}$		✓	0	0	0	0	0
$c\bar{d}e$	✓	✓	0.4	0	0.04	0	0.04
$cd\bar{e}$			0	0.15	0.135	0.7	0.63
cde	✓	✓	0.35	0	0.035	0	0.035

One way of explaining this clash of Theorem 2 against our intuition is to assume that ϵ somehow captures the features of P and $P_{\neg a}^*$ that are critical for computing the KL divergence. Indeed, in our earlier work, Chhogyal et al. [2015], we provided a way of computing the value of ϵ using features of both P and $P^*_{\neg a}$ in an argumentation framework. Nonetheless, perhaps there is more to the proper understanding of the mixing factor ϵ than that meets the eye.

5 Conclusion

In this short study, we examined the relation between ϵ and the KL divergence of P^-_a from P, where the contracted belief state P^-_a is given by the ϵ-mixture of two states P and $P^*_{\neg a}$. We showed that the KL divergence of P^-_a from P can simply be computed as $\ln(\frac{1}{\epsilon})$. Since P and $P^*_{\neg a}$ do not play any direct role in the determination of the divergence of P^-_a from P, we have suggested that the mixing factor ϵ itself captures all the required aspects of P and $P^*_{\neg a}$. We suspect ϵ plays a bigger role than just being a mixing factor, and we intend to take a closer look at it in our future work.

References

Alchourrón, C.E., Gärdenfors, P., Makinson, D.: On the logic of theory change: Partial meet contraction and revision functions. J. Symb. Log. **50**(2), 510–530 (1985)

Chhogyal, K., Nayak, A.C., Zhuang, Z., Sattar, A.: Probabilistic belief contraction using argumentation. In: Proceedings of the Twenty-Fourth International Joint Conference on Artificial Intelligence, IJCAI 2015, Buenos Aires, Argentina, pp. 2854–2860, July 25–31, 2015

Gärdenfors, P.: Knowledge in Flux. Modelling the Dymanics of Epistemic States. MIT Press (1988)

Jaynes, E.T.: Information theory and statistical mechanics. Physical Review **106**(4), 620 (1957)

Kern-Isberner, G.: Linking iterated belief change operations to nonmonotonic reasoning. In: Principles of Knowledge Representation and Reasoning: Proceedings of the Eleventh International Conference, KR 2008, pp. 166–176 (2008)

Kullback, S., Leibler, R.A.: On information and sufficiency. The Annals of Mathematical Statistics, 79–86 (1951)

Potyka, N., Beierle, C., Kern-Isberner, G.: Changes of relational probabilistic belief states and their computation under optimum entropy semantics. In: Timm, I.J., Thimm, M. (eds.) KI 2013. LNCS, vol. 8077, pp. 176–187. Springer, Heidelberg (2013)

Ramachandran, R., Ramer, A., Nayak, A.C.: Probabilistic belief contraction. Minds and Machines **22**(4), 325–351 (2012)

A Critical Review on the Symbol Grounding Problem as an Issue of Autonomous Agents

Richard Cubek[1]([⊠]), Wolfgang Ertel[1], and Günther Palm[2]

[1] Institute for Artificial Intelligence,
Ravensburg-Weingarten University of Applied Sciences, Weingarten, Germany
richard.cubek@hs-weingarten.de
http://iki.hs-weingarten.de
[2] Institute of Neural Information Processing, Ulm University, Ulm, Germany

Abstract. Many recent papers claim, that the symbol grounding problem (SGP) remains unsolved. Most AI researchers ignore that and the autonomous agents (or robots) they design indeed do not seem to have any "problem". Anyway, these claims should be taken rationally, since nearly all these papers make "robots" a subject of the discussion - leaving some kind of impression that what many roboticists do in the long run has to fail because of the SGP not yet being solved. Starting from Searle's chinese room argument (CRA) and Harnad's reformulation of the problem, we take a look on proposed solutions and the concretization of the problem by Taddeo's and Floridi's "Z condition". We then refer to two works, which have recently shown that the Z-conditioned SGP is unsolvable. We conclude, that the original, hard SGP is not relevant in the context of designing goal-directed autonomous agents.

1 From Searle's CRA to Harnad's SGP

With the CRA [29], Searle started a famous discussion among philosophers and AI researchers. Roughly summarized, he outlined a person (not knowing chinese) in a room, who receives questions in written chinese and answers them (again in written chinese) simply by manipulating chinese symbols according to a set of rules. Since the person in the room is a metaphor for a programmable machine, Searle's core argument is, that such a machine always only operates on *meaningless* symbols, it would thus never have *understanding* and always lack *intentionality*. He formulates the question:

"*But could something think, understand, and so on solely in virtue of being a computer with the right sort of program?*" - And argues why the answer is "*no*": "*Because the formal symbol manipulations by themselves don't have any intentionality; they are quite meaningless; they aren't even symbol manipulations, since the symbols don't symbolize anything.*"

Searle does *not* neglect the possibility, that an artificial machine might have understanding or even consciousness (he even gives arguments for it), but he says that a machine based only on the manipulation of symbols (*"any Turing machine simulation of human mental phenomena"*) will not do so.

© Springer International Publishing Switzerland 2015
S. Hölldobler et al. (Eds.): KI 2015, LNAI 9324, pp. 256–263, 2015.
DOI: 10.1007/978-3-319-24489-1_21

There is no need to discuss his argument, because there is already a huge amount of literature about critical replies on the CRA, e.g. [10,18,23]. Even if the CRA (or some aspects of it) are often defended, e.g [4,21,24], Damper claimed that there is a broad agreement in the AI community that the CRA is "somehow wrong" [13]. He shows, that the discourse continues because there is a disagreement on what is wrong with the CRA, which again is a result of the fact that the thought experiment leaves too many details to be filled by the audience. He concludes that therefore the discussion will never end (and it seems he was right). One critical point about the CRA is the meaning of *meaning* or *meaningless symbols*. This again is a difficult topic on its own [26,27] and there seems to be no general consensus on it. This is very important, as it might depend on the definition of meaning, whether the CRA is a strong argument (and thus whether the SGP can be solved).

Consequently, from the CRA Harnad derived the SGP, concentrating on Searle's "meaningless" symbols as they seem to be the core of the problem [17]:

"How can the meanings of the meaningless symbol tokens, manipulated solely on the basis of their (arbitrary) shapes, be grounded in anything but other meaningless symbols?".

He outlines a solvable SGP as analogous to learning chinese as a second language from a chinese/chinese dictionary. The argument that cryptologists of ancient languages seem to be able to solve such a task is, that their efforts are grounded in a first language, namely real world experience. Shortly summarized, his argument is that symbols must be grounded bottom-up from sensory inputs in order to have meaning. He introduces *categorical representations* which are reductions of sensory inputs to features, which are invariant to certain categories of inputs. Thus, an agent must be able to identify sensory inputs representing members of certain categories (and to discriminate them from members of other categories). This ability must be learned from experience. The categories again can be named by symbols. These symbols are then intrinsic to the system, as they evolved from categories of sensory inputs from the real world and thus have meaning, or as stated by Harnad:

"The symbol meanings are accordingly not just parasitic on the meanings in the head of the interpreter, but intrinsic to the dedicated symbol system itself."

Naturally, Harnad's solution does not satisfy Searle, who even denies that symbol grounding is the problem [30]:

"The problem for cognitive science is not symbol grounding, but symbol meaning and symbol content in general."

For the sake of completeness, we should mention the well-known position of Brooks, who claims that we do not need meaningful symbols at all [5,6]. According to him, a purely connectionist system (as neural networks) implicitly models representation (without reason) in form of activation patterns among the units. The activation patterns of course could be bound to symbols, but he argues there is no reason to do so, since processes being analog to symbol manipulation and reasoning are handled by the dynamics of the interacting units on their own.

Anyway, most AI researchers agree, that symbolic languages are very helpful in the design of autonomous agents, as they enable knowledge by representation and the achievement of long-term goals by planning in a relatively simple way. Thus, the SGP is still a discussed topic. Many recent papers claim that it remains unsolved and the discussion lasts to this day, e.g. [1,3,16,20,25,36].

2   A Solution: Adaptive Language Games

Independent from Searle's opinion (symbol grounding not being the problem), many researchers proposed a possible solution to Harnad's SGP, e.g. [14,22,28,35]. A very often cited solution was demonstrated in the well-known adaptive language games from Steels [32–34], an implementation derived from Wittgenstein's language games [40]. Steels criticizes the solutions being proposed so far, as learning is supervised (examples and counterexamples are selected by humans) and the symbol systems are derived from an existing human language. As he claims, the semantics are thus still coming from humans.

In the most basic version of a language game, the color guessing game [33], a robot (*speaker*) tries to draw the intention of another robot (*listener*) to a certain, randomly chosen color. The speaker builds a category of it distinguishing it from other colors and names it by randomly combining syllables into a word (e.g. "wabado" or "bolima"). The listener tries to guess the color. Based on success or failure, both agents adapt categorization and naming. After a while, their perceptually grounded categorizations become increasingly similar, finally sharing a vocabulary for colors. Successful experiments with groups of more complex embodied agents, more objects and even representations with grammatical structure followed. According to the results, Steels finally concludes in [31]:

"I argue that these experiments show that we have an effective solution to the symbol grounding problem, if there is ever going to be one: we have identified the right mechanisms and interaction patterns so that the agents autonomously generate meaning, autonomously ground meaning in the world through a sensorimotor embodiment and perceptually grounded categorization methods, and autonomously introduce and negotiate symbols for invoking these meanings. [...] There is no human prior design to supply the symbols or their semantics, neither by direct programming nor by supervised learning."

3   Concretizing the Problem: The Z Condition

As required by Harnad, the goal of Steels was that embodied agents generate intrinsic meaning by autonomous sensorimotor interaction with the environment. Anyway, Taddeo and Floridi [36] criticize the color guessing game. They claim that according to Peirce's view of the semiotic triangle, the symbols referring to objects are only meaningful if they are interpreted by an autonomous agent that already has semantics for the vocabulary. But as they conclude, the agent cannot be the interpreter without begging the question. Otherwise, if the agent is semantically committed, it cannot provide a solution to the SGP (since intrinsic meaning according to Harnad has to be generated autonomously).

They conclude, that any valid solution of the SGP in an agent must be free of *innatism* (no presupposed semantic resources) and *externalism* (no semantic resources added from outside). This is called the *zero semantic commitment condition* (or *Z condition*). The Z condition as a concretization of the SGP indeed seems correct. They proceed identifying three types of symbol grounding approaches being proposed so far (representational, semi-representational and non-representational). All of them try to ground the symbols through sensorimotor capacities, but all are shown to violate the Z condition [36].

Consequently, they present their own solution [37]. It is based on so-called *action-based semantics* where meanings of symbols are generated as internal states of agents, which are correlated to performed actions. A purpose of an action has no direct influence on the generation of meaning. A more detailed explanation would go beyond the scope of this paper, especially as the solution has been claimed not to satisfy their own Z condition [1] and the symbols in the solution even to remain useless at all [1, 25]. But more important, there are principal problems with the Z condition itself [16, 25].

4   Core Problems of the Z Condition

Müller [25] replied on the Z condition paper, uncovering several problems of it. The most important one is the necessary goal orientation (directedness) as a minimal requirement of any autonomous agent - otherwise such an agent obviously has no reason for existence (as it is also mentioned in [7,34]). Müller claims that directedness has semantics as a necessary condition, thus the agent cannot be born with directedness (violating innatism) nor can directedness be supplied from an external source (violating externalism). At least, any goal-oriented agent needs some mechanism that makes certain data stand out with respect to other, marking success. This mechanism is either built-in (innate) or supplied externally. He concludes the dilemma of the Z condition:

"Without goals, there is no 'trying', nothing is 'better', and there is no 'success'. Either the system really is an agent [...], which implies having goals, or it is just a system that interacts with its environment - without goals."

Fields [16] goes a step further. He shows that under reasonable physical conditions, the (Z-conditioned) SGP is equivalent to the quantum system identification problem. This is the problem of determining which quantum system a given experimental outcome characterizes (i.e. relating observational outcomes to specific collections of physical degrees of freedom). It is shown to be unsolvable, which as he claims, renders the (Z-conditioned) SGP unsolvable. Fields concludes:

"The in-principle referential ambiguity of all symbols referring to physical systems demonstrated here vindicates the model-theoretic view of semantics as fundamentally stipulative. It shows, in particular, that the semantics of a symbol cannot be "intrinsic" to either the symbol or the symbol system in which it is

embedded as desired by Harnad or Searle. The apparently intrinsic semantics of human symbol systems can only, on this reasoning, be an artifact of how their use is experienced".

Fields also gives a comment which is similar to Müller's argument. Regarding agents learning purely from environmental feedback, he states the question, how far such approaches satisfy the Z condition, since evaluation of feedback from the environment embodies implicit semantic assumptions. Vice-versa, Müller finally argues similar to Fields' artifact of *experienced intrinsic semantics*, as he finally concludes that the Z condition tackles the problem of real instrinsic meaning, i.e. felt experience - which as he concludes at the end can be delegated to Chalmer's well-known hard problem of consciousness [8], the question of why felt experience (qualia) exists at all. Following Müller and Fields, Harnad's SGP, as correctly concretized by the Z condition, is not solvable.

5   Consciousness at the Root of the Matter

Let us summarize the positions on the SGP in chronological order:

1. Intrinsic meaning of symbols cannot arise in computers (Searle).
2. Unaided bottom-up symbol grounding causes intrinsic meaning (Harnad).
3. Symbol grounding problem is solved (Steels).
4. Symbol grounding solution must satisfy Z condition (Taddeo & Floridi).
5. Z-conditioned symbol grounding is unsolvable (Müller, Fields).

We can see that there is a clear causal chain. Searle started the discussion, arguing that a computer-based agent would never have understanding, as it always manipulates meaningless symbols. It would thus always lack intentionality. Harnad formulated the SGP after explaining the CRA, based directly on the terms used by Searle - concentrating on "meaning". He also formulates, for which case the meaning would be intrinsic to the system. Several solutions have then been proposed, a very promising one by Steels. Claiming, that none of these really solved Harnad's problem, Taddeo and Floridi introduced the Z condition - concretizing the SGP. Finally, Müller and Fields show, that it is unsolvable, and that it can be delegated to the hard problem of consciousness.

Interestingly, what was shown by Müller and Fields at the end of the causal chain, has already been postulated by Chalmers [8] regarding its beginning:

"In the original version, Searle directs the argument against machine intentionality rather than machine consciousness, arguing that it is 'understanding' that the chinese room lacks. All the same, it is fairly clear, that consciousness is at the root of the matter. What the core of the argument establishes directly, if it succeeds, is that Chinese room system lacks conscious states, such as the conscious experience of understanding chinese."

We want to support the conclusions of Chalmers, Müller and Fields, giving some additional thoughts. In the original paper, Searle avoids the term *consciousness*, writing about *intentionality* (and *meaning*) instead. Anyway, the terms are closely related, e.g. in one of the most influental works of psychology

[2], Brentano describes intentionality as *"characteristic of all acts of conscious-ness"*. Even if we exclude consciousness, intentionality exhibits reason. But from a purely objective view of the world, there are just meaningless physical states, there is no reason and hence no intentionality. There was no reason to design a living being, it is only a remaining result of random biochemical processes, planless evolution. There is no metabolism for the reason to survive, but survival appears only as a result of metabolism. Similarly, there is no reason or meaning in neural activation patterns, they are just physical states as a result of previous physical processes. Consequently, intentionality (as requested by Searle) can always only be a concept of felt experience, which is not yet explainable.

On the other Hand, Harnad's SGP can be treated as solved (at least to a certain degree) by Steels language games. But it is again Müller [25] who shows that Steels recapitulation of Searle's original question is clearly wrong. This confusion is symptomatic for the whole discussion about the SGP. If it was motivated by the CRA, but the original Author (Searle) describes it as not relevant in this regard, its further investigations remain questionable. Especially, as its correct concretization by the Z condition is shown to be unsolvable. Finally, if humans have innate directedness (genetics) and receive external semantics since birth (culture), why should then robots fulfill the Z condition?

6 Conclusion

Many papers, especially in robotics, refer to Harnad's SGP, e.g. [9,11,12,15,38,39]. What they do is symbol grounding in the sense of finding some kind of association between symbols and percepts. Harnad explicitly mentioned, that this kind of solution trivializes the SGP. The grounding, as it is often implemented, is not restricted to bottom-up (as required in the original problem) but often also top-down. And they probably all violate the Z condition due to many (good) reasons (e.g. pre-programmed innate behavior, predefined symbols and knowledge, learning from human demonstration etc.). These solutions all work fine, but in fact they do not offer solutions to the original SGP, which is shown to be a hard, under correct conditions even unsolvable problem. But the roboticists do well, since there is obviously no reason to tackle the problem. The goal should be the design of robots (or autonomous agents in general), that have intelligent, goal-directed behavior - independently from understanding or feeling. Thus, we conclude that the original, Z-conditioned SGP is not relevant for the design of goal-directed autonomous agents. What is relevant is the research and engineering about methods, that bridge the gap between symbolic and sub-symbolic representations (which should not be called a "problem").

Müller summarizes it by his question: *"What symbol grounding problem should we try to solve?"*. He identifies the *hard* SGP, unnecassarily tackling consciousness, and the *easy* SGP. The latter one is the question of how to explain and reproduce *behavioral ability* and *function* of meaning, which is the one he claims we should go for. Finally, it is Harnad himself who states, that we should not think about *feeling*, as long as *function* is not solved [19].

References

1. Bielecka, K.: Why taddeo and floridi did not solve the symbol grounding problem. Journal of Experimental & Theoretical Artificial Intelligence, 1–15 (2014)
2. Brentano, F.: Psychology from an Empirical Standpoint (Psychologie vom empirischen Standpunkt). Linda L. McAlister. Trans. Antos C. Rancurello, DB Terrell, and Linda L. McAlister. Repr. New York: Routledge & Kegan Paul (1874)
3. Bringsjord, S.: The symbol grounding problem remains unsolved. Journal of Experimental & Theoretical Artificial Intelligence, 1–10 (2014)
4. Bringsjord, S., Noel, R.: Real robots and the missing thought experiment in the chinese room dialectic (2002)
5. Brooks, R.A.: Elephants don't play chess. Robotics and Autonomous Systems **6**(1), 3–15 (1990)
6. Brooks, R.A.: Intelligence without representation. Artificial Intelligence **47**(1), 139–159 (1991)
7. Cangelosi, A., Greco, A., Harnad, S.: Symbol grounding and the symbolic theft hypothesis. In: Simulating the Evolution of Language, pp. 191–210. Springer (2002)
8. Chalmers, D.J.: The conscious mind: In search of a fundamental theory. Oxford University Press (1997)
9. Chella, A., Coradeschi, S., Frixione, M., Saffiotti, A.: Perceptual anchoring via conceptual spaces. In: Proceedings of the AAAI-04 Workshop on Anchoring Symbols to Sensor Data, AAAI. AAAI Press (2004)
10. Cole, D.: Thought and thought experiments. Philosophical Studies **45**(3), 431–444 (1984)
11. Coradeschi, S., Saffiotti, A.: An introduction to the anchoring problem. Robotics and Autonomous Systems **43**(2–3), 85–96 (2003)
12. Cubek, R., Ertel, W., Palm, G.: High-level learning from demonstration with conceptual spaces and subspace clustering. In: Proceedings of the IEEE Int. Conference on Robotics and Automation (ICRA) (2015)
13. Damper, R.: The chinese room argumentdead but not yet buried. Journal of Consciousness Studies **11**(5–6), 159–169 (2004)
14. Davidsson, P.: Toward a general solution to the symbol grounding problem: combining machine learning and computer vision. In: AAAI Fall Symposium Series, Machine Learning in Computer Vision: What, Why and How, pp. 157–161 (1993)
15. Fichtner, M.: Anchoring symbols to percepts in the fluent calculus. KI-Künstliche Intelligenz **25**(1), 77–80 (2011)
16. Fields, C.: Equivalence of the symbol grounding and quantum system identification problems. Information **5**(1), 172–189 (2014)
17. Harnad, S.: The symbol grounding problem. Physica D: Nonlinear Phenomena **42**, 335–346 (1990)
18. Harnad, S.: Mind, machines and searle ii: What's wrong and right about searle's chinese room argument? (2001)
19. Harnad, S., Scherzer, P.: First, scale up to the robotic turing test, then worry about feeling. Artificial Intelligence in Medicine **44**(2), 83–89 (2008)
20. van Hateren, J.: How the symbol grounding of living organisms can be realized in artificial agents. arXiv preprint arXiv:1503.04941 (2015)
21. Jahren, N.: Can semantics be syntactic? In: Epistemology and Cognition, pp. 155–174. Springer (1991)
22. Mayo, M.J.: Symbol grounding and its implications for artificial intelligence. In: Proceedings of the 26th Australasian Computer Science Conference, vol. 16, pp. 55–60. Australian Computer Society, Inc. (2003)

23. Melnyk, A.: Searle's abstract argument against strong ai. Synthese **108**(3), 391–419 (1996)
24. Moor, J.H.: The pseudorealization fallacy and the chinese room argument. In: Aspects of Artificial Intelligence, pp. 35–53. Springer (1988)
25. Müller, V.C.: Which symbol grounding problem should we try to solve? Journal of Experimental & Theoretical Artificial Intelligence (ahead-of-print), 1–6 (2014)
26. Ogden, C.K., Richards, I.A., Malinowski, B., Crookshank, F.G.: The meaning of meaning. Harcourt, Brace & World New York (1946)
27. Putnam, H.: Meaning and reference. The Journal of Philosophy, 699–711 (1973)
28. Rosenstein, M.T., Cohen, P.R.: Continuous categories for a mobile robot. In: AAAI/IAAI, pp. 634–640 (1999)
29. Searle, J.R.: Minds, brains, and programs. Behavioral and Brain Sciences **3**(03), 417–424 (1980)
30. Searle, J.R.: The failures of computationalism. Think (Tilburg, The Netherlands: Tilburg University Institute for Language Technology and Artificial Intelligence) **2**, 68–71 (1993)
31. Steels, L.: The symbol grounding problem has been solved. so whats next. Symbols and embodiment: Debates on meaning and cognition, pp. 223–244 (2008)
32. Steels, L., Belpaeme, T., et al.: Coordinating perceptually grounded categories through language: A case study for colour. Behavioral and Brain Sciences **28**(4), 469–488 (2005)
33. Steels, L., Kaplan, F.: Situated grounded word semantics. In: IJCAI, pp. 862–867 (1999)
34. Steels, L., Vogt, P.: Grounding adaptive language games in robotic agents. In: Proceedings of the Fourth European Conference on Artificial Life, vol. 97 (1997)
35. Sun, R.: Symbol grounding: a new look at an old idea. Philosophical Psychology **13**(2), 149–172 (2000)
36. Taddeo, M., Floridi, L.: Solving the symbol grounding problem: a critical review of fifteen years of research. Journal of Experimental & Theoretical Artificial Intelligence **17**(4), 419–445 (2005)
37. Taddeo, M., Floridi, L.: A praxical solution of the symbol grounding problem. Minds and Machines **17**(4), 369–389 (2007)
38. Tellex, S., Kollar, T., Dickerson, S., Walter, M.R., Banerjee, A.G., Teller, S., Roy, N.: Approaching the symbol grounding problem with probabilistic graphical models. AI Magazine **32**(4), 64–76 (2011)
39. Tenorth, M., Beetz, M.: Knowrob - knowledge processing for autonomous personal robots. In: IEEE/RSJ International Conference on Intelligent Robots and Systems, IROS 2009, pp. 4261–4266. IEEE (2009)
40. Wittgenstein, L., Anscombe, G.E.M.: Philosophische Untersuchungen - Philosophical Investigations. Blackwell Oxford (1953)

Accurate Online Social Network User Profiling

Raïssa Yapan Dougnon[1], Philippe Fournier-Viger[1(✉)],
Jerry Chun-Wei Lin[2], and Roger Nkambou[3]

[1] Department of Computer Science, Université de Moncton, Moncton, Canada
{eyd2562,philippe.fournier-viger}@umoncton.ca
[2] School of Computer Science and Technology,
Harbin Institute of Technology Shenzhen Graduate School, Shenzhen, China
jerrylin@ieee.org
[3] Department of Computer Science,
Université du Quebec à Montréal, Montreal, Canada
nkambou.roger@uqam.ca

Abstract. We present PGPI+ (Partial Graph Profile Inference+) an improved algorithm for user profiling in online social networks. PGPI+ infers user profiles under the constraint of a partial social graph using rich information about users (e.g. group memberships, views and likes) and handles nominal and numeric attributes. Experimental results with 20,000 user profiles from the Pokec social network shows that PGPI+ predicts user profiles with considerably more accuracy and by accessing a smaller part of the social graph than five state-of-the-art algorithms.

Keywords: Social networks · Inference · User profiles · Partial graph

1 Introduction

Various approaches have been proposed to infer detailed user profiles on social networks using publicly disclosed information such as relational Naïve Bayes classifiers [8], label propagation [6], majority voting [3], linear regression [7], Latent-Dirichlet Allocation [1] and community detection [9]. It was shown that these approaches can accurately predict hidden attributes of user profiles in many cases. However, all these approaches assume that the full or a large part of the social graph is available for training (e.g. [6]). However, in real-life, it is generally unavailable or may be very costly to obtain or update [4]. A few approaches do not assume a full social graph such as majority-voting [3]. However, they do not let the user control the trade-off between the number of nodes accessed and prediction accuracy, which may lead to low accuracy. Furthermore, several algorithms do not consider the rich information that is available on social networks (e.g. group memberships, "likes" and "views") [3,6,8,9]. Besides, many approaches treat numeric attributes (e.g. age) as nominal attributes [3], which may decrease inference accuracy. To address these limitations, we present the PGPI+ (Partial Graph Profile Inference) algorithm, which extends our previous work PGPI [4]. PGPI+ lets the user select how many nodes of the social

© Springer International Publishing Switzerland 2015
S. Hölldobler et al. (Eds.): KI 2015, LNAI 9324, pp. 264–270, 2015.
DOI: 10.1007/978-3-319-24489-1_22

graph can be accessed to infer a user profile, can use not only information about friendship links and profiles but also about group memberships, likes and views, when available. Moreover, it can predict values of numeric attributes.

2   Problem Definition

The problem of user profiling is commonly defined as follows [2,6,8,9]. A *social graph* $\mathcal{G}$ is a quadruplet $\mathcal{G} = \{N, L, V, A\}$. N is the set of nodes in $\mathcal{G}$. $L \subseteq N \times N$ is a binary relation representing the links (edges) between nodes. Let be m attributes to describe users of the social network such that $V = \{V_1, V_2, ...V_m\}$ contains for each attribute i, the set of possible attribute values V_i. Finally, $A = \{A_1, A_2, ...A_m\}$ contains for each attribute i a relation assigning an attribute value to nodes, that is $A_i \subseteq N \times V_i$. The problem of inferring the user profile of a node $n \in N$ in a social graph $\mathcal{G}$ is to guess the attribute values of n using the other information provided in $\mathcal{G}$.

The problem definition can be extended to consider additional information from social networks such as Facebook (views, likes and group memberships).An *extended social graph* $\mathcal{E}$ is a tuple $\mathcal{E} = \{N, L, V, A, G, NG, P, PG, LP, VP\}$ where N, L, V, A are defined as previously. G is a set of groups that a user can be a member of. The relation $NG \subseteq N \times G$ indicates the membership of users to groups. P is a set of publications such as pictures, texts, videos that are posted in groups. PG is a relation $PG \subseteq P \times G$, which associates a publication to the group(s) where it was posted. LP is a relation $LP \subseteq N \times P$ indicating publication(s) liked by each user (e.g. "likes" on Facebook). VP is a relation $VP \subseteq N \times P$ indicating publication(s) viewed by each user (e.g. "views" on Facebook), such that $LP \subseteq VP$.Let $maxFacts \in \mathbf{N}^+$ be a parameter set by the user. The problem of inferring the user profile of a node $n \in N$ using a partial (extended) social graph $\mathcal{E}$ is to accurately predict the attribute values of n by accessing no more than $maxFacts$ facts from the social graph. A *fact* is a node, group or publication from N, G or P (excluding n). Lastly, the above definition can be extended for numeric attributes. For those attributes, instead of aiming at predicting an exact attribute value, the goal is to predict a value that is as close as possible to the real value.

3   The Proposed PGPI+ Algorithm

The proposed PGPI+ algorithm extends PGPI [4] (Algorithm 1) to improve its prediction accuracy and coverage, and to handle numerical attributes. PGPI [4] is a lazy algorithm designed to perform predictions under the constraint of a partial social graph. PGPI takes as parameter a node n_i, an attribute k to be predicted, the $maxFacts$ parameter, a parameter named $maxDistance$, and an (extended) social graph $\mathcal{E}$. PGPI outputs a predicted value v for attribute k of node n_i. To predict the value of an attribute k, PGPI relies on a map M. This map stores pairs of the form (v, f), where v is a possible value v for attribute k, and f is positive real number called the *weight* of v. PGPI automatically calculates the weights by applying two procedures named PGPI-G and PGPI-N. These latter respectively update weights by considering the (1) views, likes and group memberships of n_i, and (2) its friendship links. After applying these procedures, PGPI returns the value v associated to the highest weight in M as the prediction. In PGPI, half of the $maxFacts$ facts that can be used to make a prediction are used by PGPI-G and the other half by PGPI-N. If globally the $maxFacts$ limit is reached, PGPI does not perform a prediction. PGPI-N or PGPI-G can be deactivated. If PGPI-N is deactivated, only views, likes and group memberships are considered to make a prediction. If PGPI-G is deactivated, only friendship links are considered. In the following, we respectively refer to these versions of PGPI as PGPI-N and PGPI-G (and as PGPI-N+/PGPI-G+ for PGPI+).

PGPI-N works as follows. To predict an attribute value of a node n_i, it explores the neighborhood of n_i restricted by the parameter $maxDistance$ using a breadth-first search. It first initializes a queue Q and pushes n_i in the queue. Then, while Q is not empty and the number of accessed facts is less than $maxFacts$, the first node n_j in Q is popped. Then, $F_{i,j} = W_{i,j}/dist(n_i, n_j)$ is calculated. $W_{i,j} = C_{i,j}/C_i$, where $C_{i,j}$ is the number of attribute values common to n_i and n_j, and C_i is the number of known attribute values for node n_i. $dist(x, y)$ is the number of edges in the shortest path between n_i and n_j. Then, $F_{i,j}$ is added to the weight of the attribute value of n_j for attribute k, in map M. Then, if $dist(x, y) \le maxDistance$, each unvisited node n_h linked to n_j is pushed in Q and marked as visited. PGPI-G is similar to PGPI-N. It is also a lazy algorithm. But it uses a majority voting approach to update weights based on group and publication information (views and likes). Due to space limitation, we do not describe it. The reader may refer to [4] for more details.

Algorithm 1. The PGPI algorithm

    input : n_i: a node, k: the attribute to be predicted, $maxFacts$: a user-defined threshold, $\mathcal{E}$: an extended social graph
    output: the predicted attribute value v

1 $M = \{(v, 0)|v \in V_k\}$;
2 // Apply PGPI-G and PGPI-N
3 Initialize a queue Q and add n_i to Q;
4 **while** Q is not empty and $|accessedFacts| < maxFacts$ **do**
5      $n_j = Q.pop()$; $F_{i,j} \leftarrow W_{i,j}/dist(n_i, n_j)$;
6   Update (v, f) as $(v, f + F_{i,j})$ in M, where $(n_j, v) \in A_k$;
7   **if** $dist(n_i, n_j) \le maxDistance$ **then for each** node $n_h \ne n_i$ such that $(n_h, n_j) \in L$ and n_h is unvisited, push n_h in Q and mark n_h as visited ;
8 **end**
9 **return** a value v such that $(v, z) \in M \wedge \nexists(v', z') \in M|z' > z$;

Optimizations to Improve Accuracy and Coverage. In PGPI+, we redefine the formula $F_{i,j}$ used by PGPI-N by adding three optimizations. The new formula is $F_{i,j} = W_{i,j} \times (T_{i,j} + 1)/newdist(n_i, n_j) \times R$. The first optimization is to add the term $T_{i,j} + 1$, where $T_{i,j}$ is the number of common friends between n_i and n_j, divided by the number of friends of n_i. This term is added to consider that two persons having common friends (forming a triad) are more likely to have similar attribute values. The constant 1 is used so that if n_i and n_j have no common friends, $F_{i,j}$ is not zero.

The second optimization is based on the observation that the term $dist(n_i, n_j)$ makes $F_{i,j}$ decrease too rapidly. Thus, nodes that are not immediate neighbors but were still close in the social graph had a negligible influence on their respective profile inference. To address this issue, $dist(n_i, n_j)$ is replaced by $newdist(n_i, n_j) = 3 - (0.2 \times dist(n_i, n_j))$, where it is assumed that $maxDistance < 15$. It was empirically found that this formula provides higher accuracy.

The third optimization is based on the observation that PGPI-G had too much influence on predictions compared to PGPI-N. To address this issue, we multiply the weights calculated using the formula $F_{i,j}$ by a new constant R. This thus increases the influence of PGPI-N+ on the choice of predicted values. In our experiments, we have found that setting R to 10 provides the best accuracy.

Furthermore, a fourth optimization is integrated in the main procedure of PGPI+. PGPI does not make a prediction when it reaches the $maxFacts$ limit. However, it may have collected enough information to make an accurate prediction. In PGPI+, a prediction is always performed.

Extension to Handle Numerical Attributes. In PGPI+, to handle numeric attributes, we first modified how the predicted value is chosen. Recall that the value predicted by PGPI for nominal attributes is the one having the highest weight in M (line 12). However, for numeric attribute, this approach provides poor accuracy because few users have exactly the same attribute value. To address this issue, PGPI+ calculates the predicted values for numeric attributes as the weighed sum of all values in M.

Second, we adapted the weighted sum so that it ignores outliers because if unusually large values are in M, the weighted sum provides inaccurate predictions. For example, if a young user has friendship links to a few 20 years old friends but also a link to his 90 years old grandmother, the prediction may be inaccurate. Our solution to this problem is to ignore values in M that have a weight more than one standard deviation away from the mean. In our experiment, it greatly improves prediction accuracy for numeric attributes.

Third, we change how $W_{i,j}$ is calculated. Recall that in PGPI, $W_{i,j} = C_{i,j}/C_i$, where $C_{i,j}$ is the number of attribute values common to n_i and n_j, and C_i is the number of known attribute values for node n_i. This definition does not work well for numeric attributes because numeric attributes rarely have the same value. To consider that numeric values may not be equal but still be close, $C_{i,j}$ is redefined as follows in PGPI+. The value $C_{i,j}$ is the number of values common to n_i and n_j for nominal attributes, plus a value $CN_{i,j,k}$ for each numeric attribute k. The value $CN_{i,j,k}$ is calculated as $(v_i - v_j)/\alpha_k$ if $(v_i - v_j) < \alpha_k$, and is otherwise 0, where α_k is a user-defined constant. Because $CN_{i,j,k}$ is a value in [0,1], numeric attributes may not have more influence than nominal attributes on $W_{i,j}$.

4   Experimental Evaluation

We compared the accuracy of PGPI+, PGPI-N+ and PGPI-G+ algorithms with PGPI, PGPI-N and PGPI-G, and three Naïve Bayes classifiers [5]: (1) Naïve Bayes (NB) infer user profiles based on correlation between attribute values, (2) Relational Naïve Bayes (RNB) consider the probability of having friends with specific attribute values, and (3) Collective Naïve Bayes (CNB) combines NB and RNB. Those three latter algorithms are adapted to work with a partial graph by training them with $maxFacts$ users chosen randomly of the full social graph. We used a dataset of 20,000 user profiles from the Pokec social network obtained at https://snap.stanford.edu/data/. We used 10 attributes, including three numeric attributes. Synthetic data about groups was generated as in [4].

Fig. 1 shows the influence of the number of accessed facts on accuracy for each algorithm when the $maxFacts$ parameter is varied, for nominal attributes. The *accuracy* is the number of correctly predicted values, divided by the number of prediction opportunities. PGPI algorithms are not shown in this figure due to lack of space. It can be observed that PGPI+/PGPI-N+/PGPI-G+ provides the best results. No results are provided for PGPI-N+ for more than 6 facts because the dataset do not contains enough links. It is interesting to note that PGPI-N+ only uses real data (contrarily to PGPI+/PGPI-G+) and still performs better than all other algorithms.

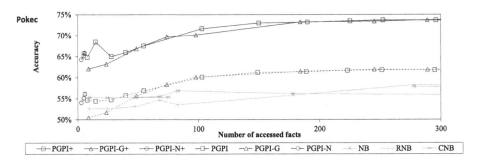

Fig. 1. Accuracy w.r.t. number of accessed facts for nominal attributes

Table 1 shows the best results in terms of accuracy for each attribute and algorithm. The last row of each table indicates the number of accessed facts to obtain these results. The best accuracy was in general achieved by PGPI+ algorithms for all attributes.

Table 2 compares the best accuracy of PGPI/PGPI+ algorithms for numeric attributes in terms of average error and standard deviation of predicted values from the real values. PGPI+ performs the best on overall. Other algorithms could not be compared because they are designed for nominal attributes.

Table 3 shows the best accuracy for each algorithm. The proposed PGPI+ algorithms provide an accuracy that is considerably higher than the accuracy of the compared algorithms.

Table 1. Best accuracy results for nominal attributes

attribute	PGPI+	PGPI-N+	PGPI-G+	NB	RNB	CNB
Gender	95.60%	61.40%	**95.77%**	52.80%	53.80%	53.60%
English	**76.35%**	63.79%	76.00%	69.74%	69.74%	69.74%
French	**87.46%**	84.48%	87.42%	86.91%	85.60%	86.87%
German	62.39%	54.31%	**62.85%**	47.83%	48.12%	47.83%
Italian	94.87%	94.25%	94.85%	94.65%	95.38%	**95.41%**
Spanish	**95.15%**	94.54%	95.14%	94.38%	95.08%	94.29%
Smoker	65.21%	62.34%	**65.42%**	63.43%	63.43%	63.12%
Drink	**71.65%**	63.36%	71.47%	70.41%	70.41%	70.41%
Marital status	**76.57%**	70.86%	76.40%	76.11%	76.02%	76.07%
Region	18.60%	10.20%	**18.71%**	6.20%	6.20%	6.20%
$|facts|$	334	6	347	375	378	278

Table 2. Average error and standard deviation for numerical attributes

algorithm	age	weight	height
PGPI+	2.94 (4.55)	**9.83 (10.32)**	**7.70 (11.75)**
PGPI-N+	3.92 (4.56)	14.60 (12.56)	10.32 (12.55)
PGPI-G+	2.89 **(4.45)**	9.83 (10.37)	7.71 (11.76)
PGPI	2.55 (4.80)	11.67 (11.53)	8.75 (12.43)
PGPI-N	4.35 (5.11)	17.28 (15.61)	14.0 (36.52)
PGPI-G	**2.20** (4.78)	10.75 (10.86)	8.35 (12.45)

Table 3. Best accuracy for nominal attributes using the full social graph

algorithm	accuracy	algorithm	accuracy
PGPI+	73.8	PGPI-G	56.2
PGPI-N+	**73.9**	NB	57.48
PGPI-G+	65.9	RNB	56.37
PGPI	62.0	CNB	56.40
PGPI-N	62.1	LP	47.31

5 Conclusion

We proposed an algorithm named PGPI+ for user profiling in online social networks under the constraint of a partial social graph and using rich information. PGPI+ improves PGPI's prediction accuracy/coverage and handle numerical attributes. Experimental results show that PGPI+ predicts user profiles with much more accuracy and by accessing a smaller part of the social graph than five state-of-the-art algorithms. Moreover, an interesting result is that profile attributes such as gender can be predicted with more than 95% accuracy using PGPI+.

References

1. Chaabane, A., Acs, G., Kaafar, M.A.: You are what you like! information leakage through users interests. In: Proc. of the 19th Annual Network and Distributed System Security Symposium. The Internet Society (2012)
2. Chaudhari, G., Avadhanula, V., Sarawagi, S.: A few good predictions: selective node labeling in a social network. In: Proc. of the 7th ACM International Conference on Web Search and Data Mining, pp. 353–362. ACM (2014)
3. Davis Jr, C.A., et al.: Inferring the location of twitter messages based on user relationships. Transactions in GIS **15**(6), 735–751 (2011)
4. Dougnon, R.Y., Fournier-Viger, P., Nkambou, R.: Inferring user profiles in online social networks using a partial social graph. In: Barbosa, D., Milios, E. (eds.) Canadian AI 2015. LNCS (LNAI), vol. 9091, pp. 84–99. Springer, Heidelberg (2015)
5. Heatherly, R., Kantarcioglu, M., Thuraisingham, B.: Preventing private information inference attacks on social networks. IEEE Transactions on Knowledge and Data Engineering **25**(8), 1849–1862 (2013)
6. Jurgens, D.: Thats what friends are for: inferring location in online social media platforms based on social relationships. In: Proc. of the 7th International AAAI Conference on Weblogs and Social Media, pp. 273–282. AAAI Press (2013)
7. Kosinski, M., Stillwell, D., Graepel, T.: Private traits and attributes are predictable from digital records of human behavior. National Academy of Sciences **110**(15), 5802–5805 (2013)
8. Lindamood, J., Heatherly, R., Kantarcioglu, M., Thuraisingham, B.: Inferring private information using social network data. In: Proc. of the 18th International Conference on World Wide Web, pp. 1145–1146. ACM (2009)
9. Mislove, A., Viswanath, B., Gummadi, K.P., Druschel, P.: You are who you know: inferring user profiles in online social networks. In: Proc. of the 3rd ACM International Conference on Web Search and Data Mining, pp. 251–260. ACM (2010)

LewiSpace: An Educational Puzzle Game Combined with a Multimodal Machine Learning Environment

Ramla Ghali[✉], Sébastien Ouellet, and Claude Frasson

Université de Montréal, 2920 Chemin de la Tour, Montréal, Canada
{ghaliram,frasson}@iro.umontreal.ca, sebouel@gmail.com

Abstract. In this paper, we will present an educational game that we developed in order to teach a chemistry lesson, namely drawing a Lewis diagram. We also conducted an experiment to gather data about the cognitive and emotional states of the learners as well as their behaviour throughout our game by using three types of sensors (electroencephalography, eye tracking, and facial expression recognition with an optical camera). Primary results show that a machine learning model (logistic regression) can predict with some success whether the learner will give a correct or a wrong answer to a task presented in the game, and paves the way for an adaptive version of the game. This latter will challenge or assist learners based on some features extracted from our data in order to provide real-time adaptation specific to the user.

Keywords: Educational game · Electroencephalogram · Eye tracking · Facial expression recognition · Logistic regression model

1 Introduction

Today, the use of video games as an educational tool is widespread. Educational video games, also known as Serious Games (SG), are mainly characterized by their ability to combine two fundamental aspects [1]: (1) an educational aspect and (2) a playful aspect. Some researchers believe that educational games are effective tools because they include more adequate learning strategies [19]. However, other researchers believe that educational video games are more effective because they include *Game Based Features* and allow learners to use certain mental states improving learning processes. Specifically, they increase motivation and engagement [13, 15]. Nevertheless, most existing educational games present some downfalls [17]. For example, many works focus on the playful aspect which increases motivation and pleasure but not necessarily contributes to improving the learning process that depends on the pedagogical content.

In order to achieve an adequate balance between entertainment and educational aspects, we propose a first version of a 3D puzzle game called **LewiSpace**. We hypothesize that this game emphasizes learning how to draw Lewis diagrams rather than playful features. Our goal with the study described in the current paper is to investigate whether it is possible to predict a learner's success and his desired level of help based on information

© Springer International Publishing Switzerland 2015
S. Hölldobler et al. (Eds.): KI 2015, LNAI 9324, pp. 271–278, 2015.
DOI: 10.1007/978-3-319-24489-1_23

gathered through different types of data: electroencephalography, eye tracking, facial expression recognition and a self-report Big Five personality questionnaire. Since this is part of a larger project that aims to develop a game that will be able to adapt in real-time to learners, we first studied in this paper the importance of each sensor used and how it improves the prediction of a learner's success or failure in each mission encountered in our game.

The organization of the paper is as follows: the first section reports previous works in similar fields. The second section describes our SG *LewiSpace*. In the third section, we describe the experimental procedure. Finally, the fourth section discusses the importance of each type of sensor and suggests a machine learning model applicable to a future version of the game.

2   Related Work

The use of educational games instead of Intelligent Tutoring Systems (ITS) is becoming of a great importance due to its benefits (attractive environment, motivational aspect, educational content, incitation, rewards, etc.). Therefore, new researchers are moving towards using this tool as a new learning environment in the Human Computer Interaction field. Among these educational games, we cite as examples: *PrimeClimb* [4], *iStart-me* [10] and *Crystal Island* [18].

The main problem with these tools is that they do not integrate a sufficient degree of feedback specific to the current learners. In order to solve this problem, recent researchers focused on the possibility of integrating AI techniques in this type of environment by incorporating machine learning algorithms and non-intrusive sensors.

Among the existing intelligent educational games, we describe as an example *Crystal Island* [12]. In [12], Lester and colleagues reviewed the possibility of giving SG the intelligence criterion by focusing on four key issues: (1) the planning the narrative aspects tutorial, (2) the recognition of emotions of the learner, (3) the modeling of learner knowledge and (4) the recognition of goals of the learner. The authors developed an automatic dynamic *framework* integrated into the game for each issue.

On the other hand, some works are focused on the recognition of cognitive states during the interaction with e-learning environments. For instance, D'Mello and his team [6] have used *eye tracking* data to dynamically detect emotions of boredom and disengagement. Dynamic tracking of eye movements was integrated into a tutor that identifies when a learner is bored. In the case of student disengagement, the tutor tries to speak and attract the learner's attention. Recently, Jacques and colleagues [11] also used gaze data features in order to predict two main emotions: boredom and curiosity in Meta tutor system [2].

In our work, rather than produce a system that detects specific states, we combine predictions from existing packages and use them as features for our machine learning model. The packages are *FaceReader 6.0* tool, that we use this sensor to extract seven basic emotions in addition to the valence and arousal of each emotion [14], the

Affectiv Suite provided by *Emotiv EEG* sensor [9], and the *Tobii Tx300* sensor to predict workload through pupil diameter measurements [3].

3   LewiSpace: An Educational Puzzle Game

LewiSpace is an educational game aiming to teach learners how to represent chemical compounds using Lewis diagrams. The game is designed to be explored by college students who have no knowledge about how to build Lewis diagrams. It has an exploratory environment (3D) developed with *Unity 4.5*, in which we integrated EEG and eye tracking sensors data with the *Emotiv* SDK v2.0.0.20 LITE and the *Tobii* SDK 3.0.

The player is introduced as an astronaut, led by a non-player character (Commander Arnold), who survives a mishap while surveying a planet. The player is told to explore an underground structure until he gets back to the surface, where he encounters obstacles solved by producing compounds described by Lewis diagrams.

Five different missions exist: (1) produce water (H_2O (figure 1)), (2) produce a methane gas to light a torch (CH_4), (3) dissolve debris using sulfuric acid (H_2SO_4), (4) craft a refrigerant (C_2F_3Cl) and (5) fill up a fuel cell using ethanol (C_2H_6O). The missions are constructed in ascending order of difficulty according to the complexity of the representations and the player can't progress to the next mission before completing the latest one. By exploring our educational game, the player accumulates a certain number of atoms that he adds to his inventory and uses to craft chemical compounds, to unlock paths and to move to another stage of the game.

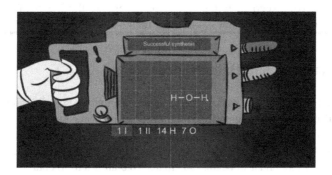

Fig. 1. Using a Lewis diagram tool to produce H_2O molecule

As mentioned before, the diagrams are constructed according some given rules between the first and third mission (Table 1) and the periodic table of the atoms.

Table 1. Instructions and rules presented in LewiSpace

Missions	Instructions
M1	- Hydrogen atoms can only bond once. This is because a single covalent bond involves one pair of electrons, and hydrogen needs 2 electrons to be full. This is an exception, as other atoms need 8 electrons. This is known as the octet rule, atoms tend to combine to satisfy it.
M2	- Double covalent bonds involve 2 pairs of electrons. You can figure out if single or double bonds are needed with the octet rule and with the number of valence electrons the atoms have. - Open your Periodic Table by pressing I. Each column (except the pink-colored ones) group atoms by their number of valence electrons. For example, hydrogen has 1, calcium (Ca) has 2, aluminum (Al) has 3, fluorine (F) has 7. - When crafting a compound, each single bond you add represents 2 electrons, shared between two atoms. If an atom doesn't have 8 electrons after you sum up its lone electrons and those shared through bonds, you might have to add double bonds or to redraw the structure.
M3	- It's often important to consider formal charges when drawing structures. You can calculate each atom's formal charge by substracting each bond (1 for a single, 2 for a double one) and each lone electron from its initial number of valence electrons. - If the formal charge is not zero, you might be able to reconfigure the diagram (change the shape or the type of bonds). The octet rule can be violated in some cases. - Also, keep in mind that elements in the third row of the Periodic Table can sometimes hold more than 8 electrons

4   Experiment and Data Preprocessing

We conducted an experiment where 40 participants (including 25 males) from **University of Montreal** participated voluntarily in the experimental process (figure 2). During the experiment, EEG data was recorded with the *Emotiv* headset (sample rate of 128 Hz), eye tracking was performed with the *Tobii Tx300*, and facial expression recognition was done with *FaceReader 6.0* and a webcam. *FaceReader 6.0* allows us to obtain a real-time classification of seven basic emotions defined by Ekman [7]: happy, sad, angry, surprised, scared, disgusted, and neutral, as well as measures of valence and arousal [14].

Given the data's sequential nature, the data stream was divided in individual sequences according to the learners' trials recorded by the game. Each **sequence** was then reduced to a **feature vector** consisting of the **4** metrics, **median**, **standard deviation**, **maximum**, and **minimum** values for each feature gathered during the game session: short-term excitement, long-term excitement, meditation, frustration, boredom from the *Affectiv* suite from *Emotiv*, pupil diameter from the *eye tracking* sensors to measure learner's workload [3], arousal, valence and the seven emotions

Fig. 2. The experimental process

mentioned above from *FaceReader* (15 features at total). A total of 633 sequences (across 33 participants) were used to produce 60-dimensional feature vectors. 7 participants were ignored for analysis as technical errors corrupted data segments essential for a correct synchronisation of all data streams. The Python Library, *Scikit-learn* [19], was used to manipulate data and train machine learning (ML) models.

5   Results

Support vector machine with a Radial Basis Function (RBF) kernel and logistic regression models were tested with a grid search on values of gamma (for SVMs) and C to produce the highest balanced accuracy with a **leave-one-participant-out scheme**. This scheme was used in order to promote the selection of a model that can generalize well for a new participant from previous participants. Both algorithms performed similarly. A more relevant comparison is the **importance of the features** gathered by the sensors throughout the game session. Table 2 describes the difference in accuracies, and Table 3 presents a confusion matrix for the best model. Balanced accuracy is determined by the mean of correct classifications for each class while according both classes the same weight. Overall accuracy is the mean number of correct classifications with weighting for the number of samples (therefore giving more weight to the "failure" class), and the mean participant accuracy is the mean of the number of correct classifications per participant, ignoring whether or not a participant produced more or less samples in the dataset, similarly to the balanced accuracy.

Table 2. Feature selection through classification accuracies

	All features (3 sensors)	Ignores pupil diameter	Ignores Emotiv	Ignores facial expression recognition	Adding Big Five Questionnaire
Balanced accuracy	0.564	0.564	0.501	0.564	0.584
Overall accuracy	0.603	0.603	0.256	0.603	0.564
Mean participant accuracy	0.593	0.593	0.312	0.593	0.549

Table 3 shows that ignoring the *Emotiv* has the **highest impact** on performance, whereas the other features do not seem to change the accuracies when ignored. Adding five features from the self-reported Big Five Questionnaire (5 measures), we note that the balanced accuracy is highest, but at the cost of the overall accuracy, which means that the classifier predicts more often that a task will be successful but mispredicts more sequences in total. Ideally, the model should be balanced between those two measures of accuracy. A model that measures only the features from the *Emotiv* **headset** was therefore tested and produces the **best results** so far but still very similar to one which uses all features, with a balanced accuracy of **0.570**, an overall accuracy of **0.635** and a mean participant accuracy of **0.609**. However, this indicates that other features are not useful and might even add noise to the dataset. Table 3 shows its confusion matrix, where predicted values are shown vertically, and true values horizontally.

Table 3. Confusion matrix for a logistic regression model with *Emotiv* headset features

	Failure	Success	Total number
Failure	0.665	0.335	532
Success	0.525	0.475	101
Total number	407	226	633

Finally, we present the ROC curves (see figure 3) for each participant compared with the random baseline using our best model, a logistic regression (C value of 0.1). Differences between participants suggest that we should more closely investigate individually trained models.

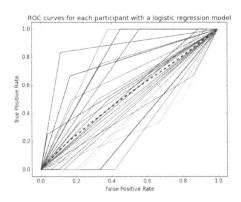

Fig. 3. Receiver operating characteristic curves for the 33 participants

6   Conclusions and Future Work

In the current paper, we presented our educational game aimed at teaching players how to draw Lewis diagrams as well as our study designed to investigate the use of physiological data (electroencephalography, eye tracking, and facial expression recognition) in order to detect the performance of the learner using ML models. Our findings shows that a logistic regression model trained with EEG features is most suitable for detecting when learners will experience failures and need more help and examples to understand the educational content. Future work will involve developing a version of the game that reacts in real-time to the players' physiological data in order to help or challenge them accordingly.

References

1. Alvarez, J., Michaud, L.: Serious Games: Advergaming, edugaming, training and more IDATE (2008)
2. Azevedo, R., Johnson, A., Chauncey, A., Burkett, C.: Self-regulated learning with Meta-Tutor: Advancing the science of learning with metacognitive tools. In: New Science of Learning, pp. 225–247 (2010)
3. Bartels, M., Marshall, S.P.: Measuring cognitive workload across different eye tracking hardware plateforms. In: ETRA 2012, Santa Barbara, CA (2012)
4. Conati, C., Jaques, N., Muir, M.: Understanding Attention to Adaptive Hints in Education-al Games: An Eye-Tracking Study. International Journal of Artificial Intelligence in Education 23(1–4), 136–161 (2013)
5. D'Mello, S., Olney, A., Williams, C., Hays, P.: Gaze tutor: A gaze-reactive intelligent tutoring system. International Journal of Human-Computer Studies 70(5), 377–398 (2012)
6. Ekman, P.: Universal facial expressions of emotion. California Mental Health Research Digest 8, 151–158 (1970)
7. Elliot, A.J., Pekrun, R.: Emotion in the Hierarchical Model of Approach-Avoidance Achievement Motivation. Emotion in Education, 57–74 (2007)
8. Gherguluscu, I., Muntean, C.H.: A Novel Sensor-Based Methodology for Learner's Moti-vation Analysis in Game-Based Learning. Interactive with Computers 26(4) (2014)
9. Jackson, G.T., Dempsey, K.B., McNamara, D.S.: Game-based Practice in a Reading Strat-egy Tutoring System: Showdown in iSTART-ME. Computer Games, 115–138 (2012)
10. Jaques, N., Conati, C., Harley, J., Azevedo, R.: Predicting Affect from Gaze Data During Interaction with an Intelligent Tutoring System (2014)
11. Lester, J.C., Ha, E.H., Lee, S.Y., Mott, B.W., Rowe, J.P., Sabourin, J.L.: Serious Games Get Smart: Intelligent Game-Based Learning Environments. AI Magazine 34(4) (2013)
12. Lester, J., Spires, H., Nietfeld, J., Minogue, J., Mott, W., Lobene, E.: Designing game-based learning environments for elementary science education: A narrative-centered learn-ing perspective. Information Sciences 264, 4–18 (2014)
13. Lewinski, P., den Uyl, T.M., Butler, C.: Automated facial coding: validation of basic emo-tions and facs aus in FaceReader. Journal of Neuroscience, Psychology, and Economics 7(4), 227–236 (2014)
14. McNamara, D.S., Jackson, G.T., Graesser, A.: Intelligent Tutoring and Games (ITaG). Ch3, Gaming for Classroom-Based Learning: Digital Role: Playing as a Motivator of Study (2010)
15. Oliver, P.J., Srivastava, S.: The Big-Five Trait Taxonomy: History, Measurement, and Theoretical Perspectives dans L. Pervin et O.P. John (eds.) Handbook of Personality: Theory and Research, 2nd edn (1999)

16. Prensky, M.: Digital Game Based Learning. McGraw-Hill, New York (2001)
17. Rowe, J., Mott, B., McQuiggan, S., Robison, J., Lee, S., Lester, J.: Crystal island: A narrative-centered learning environment for eighth grade microbiology. In: Workshop on Intelligent Educational Games at the 14th International Conference on Artificial Intelligence in Education, Brighton, UK, pp. 11–20 (2009)
18. Woolf, B.P.: Building Intelligent Interactive Tutors: Student-centered strategies for revolutionizing e-learning. Morgan Kaufmann Publishers Inc. (2007)
19. Pedregosa, et al.: Scikit-learn: Machine learning in Python. JMLR **12**, 2825–2830 (2011)

Event Detection in Marine Time Series Data

Stefan Oehmcke[1,2]([✉]), Oliver Zielinski[2], and Oliver Kramer[1]

[1] Computational Intelligence Group, Department of Computing Science,
University Oldenburg, Oldenburg, Germany
{stefan.oehmcke,oliver.zielinski,oliver.kramer}@uni-oldenburg.de
[2] Institute for Chemistry and Biology of the Marine Environment,
University Oldenburg, Oldenburg, Germany

Abstract. Automatic detection of special events in large data is often more interesting for data analysis than regular patterns. In particular, the processes in multivariate time series data can be better understood, if a deviation from the normal behavior is found. In this work, we apply a machine learning event detection method to a new application in the marine domain. The marine long-term data from the stationary platform at Spiekeroog, called Time Series Station, are a challenge, because noise, sensor drifts and missing data complicate analysis of the data. We acquire labels for evaluation with help of experts and test different approaches, which include time context into patterns. The used event detection method is local outlier factor (LOF). To improve results, we apply dimensionality reduction to the data. The analysis of the results shows, that the machine learning techniques can find special events, which are of interest to experts in the field.

Keywords: Event detection · Anomaly detection · LOF · Time series · Marine systems · Wadden sea

1 Introduction

The growing infrastructures of information and sensor systems in the marine domain lead to an increased demand of data mining solutions. Marine sensors collect time series data for water measurements, including water salinity, pressure, or temperature and meteorological measurements, like wind speed, direction, and air temperature. An important task is the automatic detection of anomalies or special event to support the human decision makers. Special events are in some way different from the regular data. Even experts often disagree on the definition of such events, which complicates to capture them in mathematical form.

The marine data is collected by a stationary platform called Time Series Station Spiekeroog (TSS), which is located between the islands of Langeoog and Spiekeroog (53°45′1.0″ N, 7°40′16.3″ E) in the North Sea (German Bight) [2,13], see Figure 1. Because of its position in a tidal channel, the currents are very

© Springer International Publishing Switzerland 2015
S. Hölldobler et al. (Eds.): KI 2015, LNAI 9324, pp. 279–286, 2015.
DOI: 10.1007/978-3-319-24489-1_24

strong, which challenges the station's hardware, but offers interesting data. The difficulties in acquiring this real-world data result in high noise, sensor drifts, and missing data. Since 2002, the long-term data collected by the TSS are used for study of marine processes. One of the research interests is to find extreme events in the past, like storm surges or unusual sensor value movements [16]. An automatic detection helps to focus on the analysis of these events and possibly reveal previously unseen events. Our approach introduced in this paper allows the automatic detection of anomalous events that supports the expert's decision process. The evaluation is based on label information collected in a small expert survey. At first, a general definition of time series events is given in Section 2. Section 3 discusses related work. The experiments with marine data from the Time Series Station will be shown in Section 4. Conclusions are presented in Section 5.

 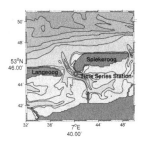

Fig. 1. The Time Series Station Spiekeroog and it's position in the Wadden Sea.

2   Time Series Event Definition

In literature, the terms extreme event, outlier, novelty, or anomaly haven often similar meanings depending on the application [5]. For our marine application the term event is best suited, which is why this paper will mainly use this term. In its simplest form event detection for time series data can be described as a binary classification problem: $f(\mathbf{x}_t) = y$ with $y \in \mathcal{Y} = \{normal, event\}$. To get label y for a pattern $\mathbf{x}_t \in \mathcal{X} : \{\mathbf{x}_1, \ldots, \mathbf{x}_n\}$ we need to approximate function $f : \mathcal{X} \to \mathcal{Y}$. A pattern $\mathbf{x}_t$ is a vector of d features x_i, with $i \in \{1, \ldots, d\}$. Set $\mathcal{X}$ is linear ordered by time with index t. Generally $f(\mathbf{x}_t) = event$ will be true if: $o_{score}(\mathcal{A}(t, \delta), B(t, \delta)) > \gamma$, where o_{score} is an outlier score function, $\mathcal{A}$ is the reference set, B is the tested set with $\mathbf{x}_t \in B$, and δ is a time span. Another representation of the problem just uses the outlier score $o_{score}(\mathcal{A}(t, \delta), B(t, \delta)) = y, y \in [0, 1]$, where a higher score represents a higher "outlierness". Events are anomalous in relation to a family of sequential sets $\mathcal{A}$ of the data $\mathcal{X}$. Set $\mathcal{A}$ is subset of the power set:

$$\mathcal{A}(t, \delta) \subseteq \mathcal{P}(\mathcal{X}) = \{A(t_j, \delta) | A(t_j, \delta) \subseteq \mathcal{X}\}, t_j \in \{1, \cdots, n\}. \tag{1}$$

with time span δ and start time $t_j = [1, n - \delta]$. The reference set may also contain unknown events. In set $B(t, \delta)$ an event is suspected. It has a duration, which is defined by its time span δ and time $t = [\frac{\delta}{2}, n - \frac{\delta}{2}]$.

It is the objective of event detection to find the optimal settings for parameters $\mathcal{A}$, B, δ and γ for an outlier function o_{score}. Usually, some of these parameters are known through domain knowledge. Because of the vague definition of event detection, the optimal parameters vary, depending on the application domain and dataset. Most interesting are events that are *multivariate*. Multivariate events can only be found by analyzing multiple feature sources simultaneously, which are a subset of the d feature sources. If a set $B(t, \delta) \subseteq \mathcal{X}$ has a time span $\delta > 1$, the pattern is extended by δ additional time steps: $B(t, \delta) := \mathcal{X}_{t - \frac{\delta}{2} : t + \frac{\delta}{2}} = (x_1^{t - \frac{\delta}{2}}, \cdots, x_d^{t - \frac{\delta}{2}}, \cdots, x_1^{t + \frac{\delta}{2}}, \cdots, x_d^{t + \frac{\delta}{2}})^T$. This way a patterns gains in previous and following features, which enables access to the time context.

The outlier score o_{score} defines how much the sets in $\mathcal{A}$ differ from B and what this difference is. Because of the lack of labels, we use an unsupervised outlier score. Local outlier factor (LOF) by Breuning et al. [4] is one of the standard methods for event detection. Here the outlier score for pattern $\mathbf{x}$ is calculated by comparing to the local density of it k-nearest neighbors $N_k(\mathbf{x})$:

$$LOF_k(\mathbf{x}) := \frac{1}{|N_k(\mathbf{x})|} \cdot \sum_{\mathbf{x}' \in N_k(\mathbf{x})} \frac{\sum\limits_{\hat{\mathbf{x}} \in N_k(\mathbf{x})} rd_k(\mathbf{x}, \hat{\mathbf{x}})}{\sum\limits_{\bar{\mathbf{x}} \in N_k(\mathbf{x}')} rd_k(\mathbf{x}', \bar{\mathbf{x}})}. \tag{2}$$

To get the reachability-distance rd_k of two points $\mathbf{x}$ and $\mathbf{x}'$, either the distance between them, or the k-distance $dst_k(\mathbf{x}')$ is used, depending on which value is higher. The k-distance $dst_k(\mathbf{x}')$ is defined as distance of $\mathbf{x}$ to its k-th neighbor. Often the Euclidean distance is used as distance metric.

An alternative to finding an appropriate threshold γ, is to use a top-k method, where only the k patterns with the highest outlier score are marked as outlier [8]. For time series data there can be multiple high outlier scores around an event, which mark the same event several time. To minimize this, we extended the top-k method with a temporal border around the highest local outlier score, so no pattern within the border can be chosen. Thereafter the next highest score not within the border is chosen and so on. This adaption is called top-k-time.

3 Related Work

Although many event detection methods have been proposed, only a few applications can be found in the marine domain. For a state-of-the-art overview of temporal outlier detection approaches, we recommend the survey of Gupta et al. [7]. Modenesi et al. [12] compare several methods for detecting novelties in synthetic time series data.

In the maritime domain, outlier detection is used by Auslander et al. [1] to analyze video data. They compare global to local algorithms and report the conditions under which these algorithms perform well. Another maritime application is the detection of anomalies in vessel movement. There, the general objective is to find suspicious movements. Li et al. [10] use a rule- and motif-based framework, which is able to learn at different granularity levels. A framework of Riveiro et al. [14] is proposed, which combines a SOMS-method for event detection and a user interface for easy usage.

4   Experimental Analysis

The minute-wise time series dataset is unlabeled and covers the time from October 10, 2014 until April 13, 2015. This period lies in the storm season, which guarantees that at least extreme value events are included. We calculated the centered rolling median of 15 minutes to clean the data of noise, like in [3]. In addition, only every 15th data point is used to reduce the size of the dataset without much loss of information. This results in 17,856 of originally 267,840 patterns. 5,285 (~30%) are missing due to maintenance or connection issues. Pattern are interpolated by piecewise cubic Hermite interpolation polynomial [6], whenever less or equal than ten points in a row are missing. Of the available patterns, 5,627 are interpolated values. Experts recommend a selection of sensors for our event detection as feature input. This selection contains water salinity, pressure and temperature as well as air temperature, wind direction and speed measurements. Overall, a pattern consists of 16 sensor values and nine time features, which amounts to a total of 25 features.

4.1   Acquiring Labels For Evaluation

In order to evaluate any event detection method, it is necessary to have labeled patterns. Those labeled patterns were acquired by letting five experts decide, if a pattern is special. Every expert is asked to evaluate the same set of 60 patterns with an easy-to-use web-based survey that displays the different sensors as time series plots. The selection of these 60 patterns is done with the top-20-time results of three different methods for feature handling: The first method just uses the raw pattern with its 25 features. Further, the squared difference of each sensor value to the centered rolling mean of time span δ is added to the raw pattern as second method. This method emphasizes deviations, like extreme values or shift of values. The last one builds a window of features around every pattern's time index t with all pattern in a time span δ. As observed time span δ the tidal cycle of about 14 hours is chosen, to have enough margin to the average cycle of 12 hours and 25 minutes. This time span is logical, because the TSS's is in a tidal inlet, which creates most special events in this period. The o_{score} is averaged over 30 runs and computed with LOF using a neighborhood size of 75.

To visualize this experiment we reduce the time series data to four dimensions. The dimensionality reduction is employed by isometric mapping [15] (ISOMAP) with 156 neighbors and the results are shown in Figure 2. ISOMAP is a nonlinear dimensionality reduction method, which is capable of finding a low-dimensional embedding for high-dimensional data with help of a neighborhood graph. Further, we also added the last dimension as height of the plot.

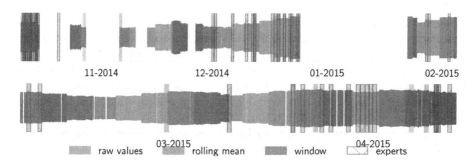

Fig. 2. Reduced time series to four dimensions and marked top-k-outliers and the experts' evaluation. Every found event by an expert must also be marked by the method, because only method results are shown to the experts.

Colorized areas are events identified by the three methods and the areas marked with hatches are confirmed by experts.

4.2 Results and Further Improvement

Of all expert-evaluated patterns 50 (83.33%) are marked by the experts as events at least once. Not once all experts agree completely on the label of a pattern, while over half of the experts agree on seven labels. Because of the different opinions on the events that come with different expertise, we do not average the expert's results, but use every event that is marked by the experts as event. This way, methods that encourage the finding of events for every expert are preferred. For each method the F_1-score is calculated and results are shown in Figure 3. The calculation accounts for different settings for k, by labeling the k highest scores as events and the rest as normal data. Interestingly, the F_1-score for small k is low, but rises with larger k. The reason is probably the high positive rate in the test set. With a k of 20 the first method, with the raw features, performs best and the others are only good while the k is small. The first method find false-positives with their highest scored events, while the other methods have a higher recall with small k.

To further analyze and improve our results, the methods need to be evaluated on all labeled patterns. Here, the average precision score is best suited, because it considers the ranking of the scores and represents the area under the precision-recall-curve. Probability values are needed for the average precision score, which is why the outlier scores of each method are normalized with Gaussian normalization like in [9]. In addition, different setups are tested on this test set: First, the smoothing of data is done via centered rolling median of 15 minutes and 60 minutes, but we retain the tumbling of every 15th data point to keep the current dataset size. Second, dimensionality reduction from 25 features to four and 10 features is done with ISOMAP that uses a neighborhood size of 156. Through this, the amount of features in the window method can be reduced from 1,400 ($= 25 \cdot 56$) to 224 ($= 4 \cdot 56$) or 560 ($= 10 \cdot 56$) features per pattern, while the observed 14 hours are 56 parts with length of 15 minutes. Table 1 summarizes the results. Additionally, the precision-recall-curve of the highest scores per method are shown in Figure 3. Surprisingly the method with raw features performs well, although it contains just one point in time. The highest average precision scores are achieved with dimensional reduction. Responsible is the high dimensionality that is introduced by the sliding window method and the doubling of features by the rolling mean method. With applied ISOMAP, the dimensionality is small enough for LOF to escape the curse-of-dimensionality and use the potential time context information to detect events.

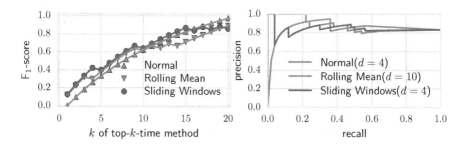

Fig. 3. On the left side we show the change of F_1-score with increasing k for the feature handling methods used for label acquisition. On the right side the precision-recall-curve of best runs of each method is presented.

Table 1. Comparison of feature handling methods. The highest scores of each method are highlighted with bold fonts and the *-symbol shows the highest overall score.

Methods	Average Precision Score					
	$T = 15$	$T = 60$	$(T = 15\ d = 4)$	$(T = 60\ d = 4)$	$(T = 15\ d = 10)$	$(T = 60\ d = 10)$
Raw Values	.821	.803	.841	.807	.761	**.850**
Roll. Mean	.855	.877	.830	.885	**.901**	.850
Window	.800	.801	.846	**.938***	.809	.801

It should be noted that these first results could be prone to overfitting and will be tested in further research with other periods of the TSS. The setting $k = 20$ for the top-k-time events is chosen to not overburden the experts and it is unknown if a higher k setting for the top-k-time events would yield significantly more events. Further experiments should also consider optimization of parameters, like the neighborhood size of LOF or ISOMAP.

5   Conclusion

In this paper, we employ machine learning event detection to time series data in the marine domain. Our data is based on marine sensors from the TSS, which collects long-term data in a tidal inlet of the Wadden Sea. For the experimental evaluation labels for potential events, chosen by machine learning methods, were acquired from experts. About 83.34% of the detected events were confirmed to be true-positives. Dimensionality reduction preprocessing with ISOMAP led to higher average precision scores. Further, ISOMAP was used to visualize the high-dimensional time series with four features. The resulting plot is suited to visually detect outliers.

In the future we will get more labels from experts and use semi-supervised learning to further improve the results. In addition, other outlier score functions could be used, like Isolation Forest [11].

Acknowledgments. We thank the ministry of science and culture of Lower Saxony for supporting us with the graduate school *Safe Automation of Maritime Systems (SAMS)*. Our gratitude goes to the experts of the Time Series Station at Spiekeroog for their support: Thomas Badewien, Axel Braun, Daniela Meier, Anne-Christin Schulz, and Lars Holinde.

References

1. Auslander, B., Gupta, K.M., Aha, D.W.: A comparative evaluation of anomaly detection algorithms for maritime video surveillance. In: SPIE Defense, Security, and Sensing, pp. 801907–801907. International Society for Optics and Photonics (2011)
2. Badewien, T.H., Zimmer, E., Bartholomä, A., Reuter, R.: Towards continuous long-term measurements of suspended particulate matter (SPM) in turbid coastal waters. Ocean Dynamics **59**(2), 227–238 (2009)
3. Basu, S., Meckesheimer, M.: Automatic outlier detection for time series: an application to sensor data. Knowledge and Information Systems **11**(2), 137–154 (2007)
4. Breunig, M.M., Kriegel, H.P., Ng, R.T., Sander, J.: Lof: identifying density-based local outliers. In: Proceedings of the 2000 ACM SIGMOD International Conference on Management of Data, SIGMOD 2000, pp. 93–104. ACM (2000)
5. Chandola, V., Banerjee, A., Kumar, V.: Anomaly detection: A survey. ACM Computing Surveys (CSUR) **41**(3), 15 (2009)
6. Fritsch, F.N., Carlson, R.E.: Monotone piecewise cubic interpolation. SIAM Journal on Numerical Analysis **17**(2), 238–246 (1980)
7. Gupta, M., Gao, J., Aggarwal, C., Han, J.: Outlier detection for temporal data. Synthesis Lectures on Data Mining and Knowledge Discovery **5**(1), 1–129 (2014)
8. Jin, W., Tung, A.K., Han, J.: Mining top-n local outliers in large databases. In: Proceedings of the Seventh ACM SIGKDD International Conference on Knowledge Discovery and Data Mining, pp. 293–298. ACM (2001)
9. Kriegel, H.P., Kröger, P., Schubert, E., Zimek, A.: Interpreting and unifying outlier scores. In: SDM, pp. 13–24. SIAM (2011)
10. Li, X., Han, J., Kim, S., Gonzalez, H.: Roam: rule-and motif-based anomaly detection in massive moving object data sets. In: SDM, vol. 7, pp. 273–284. SIAM (2007)
11. Liu, F.T., Ting, K.M., Zhou, Z.H.: Isolation forest. In: Eighth IEEE International Conference on Data Mining, ICDM 2008, pp. 413–422. IEEE (2008)
12. Modenesi, A.P., Braga, A.P.: Analysis of time series novelty detection strategies for synthetic and real data. Neural Processing Letters **30**(1), 1–17 (2009)

13. Reuter, R., Badewien, T.H., Bartholomä, A., Braun, A., Lübben, A., Rullkötter, J.: A hydrographic time series station in the wadden sea (southern north sea). Ocean Dynamics **59**(2), 195–211 (2009)
14. Riveiro, M., Falkman, G., Ziemke, T.: Improving maritime anomaly detection and situation awareness through interactive visualization. In: 2008 11th International Conference on Information Fusion, pp. 1–8. IEEE (2008)
15. Tenenbaum, J.B., De Silva, V., Langford, J.C.: A global geometric framework for nonlinear dimensionality reduction. Science **290**(5500), 2319–2323 (2000)
16. Zielinski, O., Busch, J.A., Cembella, A.D., Daly, K.L., Engelbrektsson, J., Hannides, A.K., Schmidt, H.: Detecting marine hazardous substances and organisms: sensors for pollutants, toxins, and pathogens. Ocean Science **5**(3), 329–349 (2009)

A Componentwise Simulated Annealing EM Algorithm for Mixtures

Affan Pervez[(✉)] and Dongheui Lee

Technische Universität München, Munich, Germany
{affan.pervez,dhlee}@tum.de

Abstract. This paper addresses the problem of fitting finite Gaussian Mixture Model (GMM) with unknown number of components to the univariate and multivariate data. The typical method for fitting a GMM is Expectation Maximization (EM) in which many challenges are involved i.e. how to initialize the GMM, how to restrict the covariance matrix of a component from becoming singular and setting the number of components in advance. This paper presents a simulated annealing EM algorithm along with a systematic initialization procedure by using the principals of stochastic exploration. The experiments have demonstrated the robustness of our approach on different datasets.

1 Introduction

Finite mixture models provide a probabilistic tool for modeling arbitrarily complex probability density functions and have been used in a variety of different applications [9], [12,13]. The usual approach for fitting a GMM is EM, which provides the maximum likelihood (ML) parameter estimate of the model. K-means can be used for initializing EM. During EM the estimate may converge to the boundary of the parameter space (singular covariance matrix), causing likelihood to approach infinity. When this occurs, EM should be aborted and restarted with different initialization of the parameters. *Deterministic Annealing EM* (DAEM) algorithm [21] has been proposed for avoiding the estimate to converge at the boundary of the parameter estimate but it can get trapped at saddle points [21].

Broadly speaking there are three main approaches for estimating the number of components [7]: EM based methods [6], [16], Variational Bayesian methods [23] and stochastic methods by using Markov Chain Monte Carlo (MCMC) sampling [2], [19]. Variational Bayesian methods avoid overfitting but only provide an approximate solution while Stochastic methods are computationally very expensive. Moreover there are two types of EM based methods in which the number of components need not to be fixed in advance: Firstly *divisive* where the estimate starts from a single component which split into multiple components as the algorithm proceeds [3,4], [25] and secondly *agglomerative* where the estimate starts from a large number of components which are decreased as the algorithm proceeds [7,8]. A variety of ways have been proposed for splitting or merging GMM components [3], [14], [22], [24,25].

© Springer International Publishing Switzerland 2015
S. Hölldobler et al. (Eds.): KI 2015, LNAI 9324, pp. 287–294, 2015.
DOI: 10.1007/978-3-319-24489-1_25

2   Overview of EM Algorithm

A GMM with k components is parameterized by $\boldsymbol{\Theta}_{(k)} = \{\pi_m, \boldsymbol{\mu}_m, \boldsymbol{\Sigma}_m\}_{m=1}^{k}$ where $\pi_1, \ldots, \pi_k$ are mixing coefficients / priors with constraints $0 < \pi_m < 1$ and $\sum_{m=1}^{k} \pi_m = 1$, $\boldsymbol{\mu}_1, \ldots, \boldsymbol{\mu}_k$ are means and $\boldsymbol{\Sigma}_1, \ldots, \boldsymbol{\Sigma}_k$ are covariance matrices. The log-likelihood of a dataset $\mathbf{y}_{\mathrm{obs}} = \{\mathbf{y}^{(1)}, \cdots, \mathbf{y}^{(n)}\}$ for a GMM is defined as:

$$\mathcal{L}(\boldsymbol{\Theta}_{(k)}, \mathbf{y}_{\mathrm{obs}}) = \sum_{i=1}^{n} log \sum_{m=1}^{k} \pi_m \mathcal{N}(\mathbf{y}^{(i)}; \boldsymbol{\mu}_m, \boldsymbol{\Sigma}_m) \tag{1}$$

The parameters are updated by cycling through the E-step and the M-step [6]. In the E-step, the expected value of complete data log-likelihood is calculated using the old parameters estimate, which is used for maximization in the M-step. It is a common practice to add a small regularization term $\lambda \mathbf{I}$ in all covariance matrics of the GMM at each update cycle. The EM is terminated when the increase in log-likelihood becomes very small i.e. $\frac{\mathcal{L}^{t+1}}{\mathcal{L}^{t}} - 1 < \epsilon$.

3   Stochastic Exploration Initialization Approach

Many nature inspired algorithms exist for solving discrete optimization problems [11]. It is a well known fact that humans by nature are social animals. A person who is alone will tend to find other people and will stay in a community, if possible. Not only humans but animals also exhibit such behavior [10]. Given this, now consider a scenario where an individual is alone at a location. Seeking someone is important due to the above mentioned reasons. If there is no heuristic about the surrounding then with equal probability it will start to look in any direction. Suppose that there are many individuals like this at a place, what will happen when one comes in interaction with someone else? Most probably its search pace will decrease, since living in a group provides more stability. Now they also have a heuristic about the search direction.

Surprisingly it is not difficult to import the proposed approach for initializing a GMM. Now each observation will act like an individual so we will place a Gaussian at each observation. In the begining the covariance matrix is diagonal, with small equal positive value δ in the diagonal. The prior value of each component is $\frac{1}{n}$ at this stage where n is the total number of observations. After this the next step is exploration phase. The exploration is done by slightly expanding each component and then testing that whether it has sufficient overlap with one of its neighbouring Gaussians. The rate of expansion of each Gaussian is inversely propotional to its prior value. For expanding a Gaussian, we add exploration terms in the standard deviation (σ) of each eigenvector of its covariance matrix. The magnitude of each exploration term is proportional to its corresponding σ.

Once two Gaussians have sufficient overlap we can merge them. For detecting overlap between two components we define the coefficient $\mathbf{C}$. When two Gaussians are multiplied then the resulting density is again a Gaussian but multiplied with this coefficient [17] i.e. $\mathcal{N}(\boldsymbol{\mu}_Q, \boldsymbol{\Sigma}_Q) \times \mathcal{N}(\boldsymbol{\mu}_R, \boldsymbol{\Sigma}_R) = \mathbf{C}_{QR} \mathcal{N}(\boldsymbol{\mu}_S, \boldsymbol{\Sigma}_S)$ where $\mathbf{C}_{QR} = \mathcal{N}(\boldsymbol{\mu}_Q; \boldsymbol{\mu}_R, \boldsymbol{\Sigma}_Q + \boldsymbol{\Sigma}_R)$. The $\mathbf{C}$ has a property that as we expand the

Gaussians via exploration, it keeps on increasing and then at a certain point it starts to decrease. As the C passes its peak value, which is detected as its value decreases in the next iteration, we merge the two Gaussians as in [25].

The exploration and merging cycles continue until the component count reaches a predifined value k_{max} where $k_{max} \gg k_{optimal}$. Since in the begining of the algorithm $k = n$, this can pose significant computation load. An elegant way to bound the computational load is to sample (without replacement) k_{start} observations from the dataset and use them for initialization where $k_{start} < n$. So now for the Stochastic Exploration initialization approach the algorithmic complexity will be $\mathcal{O}(k_{start}^2)$ instead of $\mathcal{O}(n^2)$.

4   Component-Wise Simulated Annealing EM for Mixtures

The proposed CSAEM^2 algorithm is the combination of Component-Wise EM for Mixtures (CEM^2) and simulated annealing algorithm. As mentioned by [5] that CEM^2 is a serial decomposition of optimization problem with a coordinate-wise maximization. It goes through E-step and then applies M-step to update only one component at a time. For simulated annealing we have a temperature parameter τ which is gradually decreased to zero. The temperature value defines the probability of taking annealing step. The initial value of temperature is set to a small value as higher value of temperature can completly disturb the discovered GMM. During annealing iterations the responsibility (contribution of the component q, for generating the data point i) is calculated as:

$$\gamma_{q,i} = \frac{\left(\pi_q \mathcal{N}(y_i; \mu_q, \Sigma_q)\right)^{\Phi_q}}{\sum\limits_{l=1, l \neq q}^{k} \pi_l \mathcal{N}(y_i; \mu_l, \Sigma_l) + \left(\pi_q \mathcal{N}(y_i; \mu_q, \Sigma_q)\right)^{\Phi_q}}$$

where $0 \leq \Phi_q \leq 1$. The amount of annealing Φ_q is inversely proportional to the weight of a component q and is calculated as $\Phi_q = \frac{\pi_q}{\max(\pi)}$. The annealing induces the fuzziness in the membership of the components with no annealing $(\max(\Phi) = 1)$ for the component with highest weight and highest annealing $(\min(\Phi))$ for the component with lowest weight.

When CSAEM^2 converges (after annealing iterations) then we generate all the possible $(k-1)$ component GMMs and switch to the one which yield highest likelihood value. CSAEM^2 and components merging are repeatedly applied until the components count k reaches k_{min} (usually one). The parameters $\hat{\Theta}_{(k)}$ of all the models generated after applying CSAEM^2 are stored as candidate GMMs.

We remove a component m if $n\pi_m < \alpha(d+1)$ with $\alpha = 2$. As mentioned by [16], a component requires the support of at least $d + 1$ observations for avoiding the covariance matrix to become singular i.e. $n\pi_m \geq (d+1)$. For a large value for k_{max}, many or all components can get removed simultaneously with general EM [8]. With the CEM^2, if a component dies, its weight is immediately distributed among other components, thus increasing the survival probability of the other components.

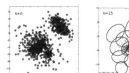

Fig. 1. Initialization results of sythetic datasets with stochastic exploration approach

For model selection we have used *Mixture Minimum Discription Length* (MMDL) criterion [7]. It is similar to the *Bayesian Information Criterion* (BIC) [20] but it has an additional term for representing skewness. It is defined as:

$$\mathcal{C}_{\text{MMDL}}\left(\hat{\boldsymbol{\Theta}}_{(k)}, k\right) = -\mathcal{L}(\hat{\boldsymbol{\Theta}}_{(k)}, \mathbf{y}) + \frac{N(k)}{2}\log n + \frac{N(1)}{2}\sum_{m=1}^{k}\log(\pi_m)$$

where $N(k)$ is the number of free parameters in a k component GMM.

5 Experiments

We used following parameter values: $k_{start} = 150$ ($k_{start} = 250$ for Sythetic Dataset 2) , $k_{max} = 15, k_{min} = 1$, Annealing Iterations$= 400, \tau = 0.05, \epsilon = 10^{-5}, \lambda = max(10^{-4}, min(D > 0))$ where D is a $n \times n$ matrix with $D(Q, R) = \|\mathbf{y}^{(Q)} - \mathbf{y}^{(R)}\|^2$.

5.1 Results of Stochastic Exploration Initialization Approach

Figure 1 shows the results of stochastic exploration approach on the synthetic dataset (section 5.2 : Dataset 1). The first column contains the highly overfitted $k = n$ component GMM while the second column contains the simplified $k = k_{max}$ component GMM obtained by stochastic exploration. The third column contains the MMDL value for the GMMs formed during transition from the $k = n$ component GMM to the $k = k_{max}$ component GMM. The initialization approach consistently decreases the MMDL value and thus improves the model representation while decreasing the number of components. The same behaviour can be observed in the last column which contains the MMDL value for the GMMs formed during transition from the $k = k_{start}$ component GMM to the $k = k_{max}$ component GMM.

5.2 Results of CSAEM²

Experiment with Synthetic Dataset
Dataset 1: 1000 samples were drawn from the four component bivariate GMM with

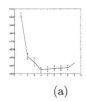 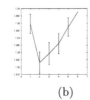 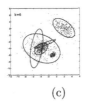 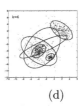

(a)	(b)	(c)	(d)

Fig. 2. (a) Result of 50 Monte Carlo simulations on synthetic Dataset 1 showing mean MMDL value (of 50 experiments) for components, with vertical bars depicting standard deviation in each value. (b) Same as (a) but for Dataset 2. GMM just before (c) and after (d) annealing step.

$$\pi_1 = \pi_2 = \pi_3 = 0.3, \pi_4 = 0.1, \boldsymbol{\mu}_1 = \boldsymbol{\mu}_2 = \begin{bmatrix} -4 \\ -4 \end{bmatrix} \boldsymbol{\mu}_3 = \begin{bmatrix} 2 \\ 2 \end{bmatrix}, \boldsymbol{\mu}_4 = \begin{bmatrix} -1 \\ -6 \end{bmatrix}$$

$$\boldsymbol{\Sigma}_1 = \begin{bmatrix} 1 & 0.5 \\ 0.5 & 1 \end{bmatrix}, \boldsymbol{\Sigma}_2 = \begin{bmatrix} 6 & -2 \\ -2 & 6 \end{bmatrix}, \boldsymbol{\Sigma}_3 = \begin{bmatrix} 2 & -1 \\ -1 & 2 \end{bmatrix} \boldsymbol{\Sigma}_4 = \begin{bmatrix} 0.125 & 0 \\ 0 & 0.125 \end{bmatrix}$$

This GMM has also been used by [8], [24] and [14]. It provides a challenging scenario of overlaping components with two components having a common mean. We performed a Monte Carlo (MC) simulation of 50 experiments. The results are shown in Figure 2a. In all experiments our algorithm identified the right four component GMM.

Dataset 2: 800 samples were drawn from the two component 10 dimensional GMM with $\pi_1 = \pi_2 = 0.5, \boldsymbol{\mu}_1 = [0, \ldots, 0]^\top, \boldsymbol{\mu}_2 = [2, \ldots, 2]^\top, \boldsymbol{\Sigma}_1 = \boldsymbol{\Sigma}_2 = \mathbf{I}$. The GMM contain high dimensional fused components. Figure 2b contain the result of 50 MC experiments and every time our approach correctly identified the two component GMM.

Effect of Annealing: The effect of annealing during CSAEM[2] can be observed in Figure 2(c-d). The annealing increases the coverage and thus the survival probability of the weak components while the components with high prior values are unaffected by annealing. Another interesting property of annealing is depicted in Figure 3. The maximum value of $f = \sum_{i=1}^{k} \log(\pi_i)$ is attained when $\pi_i = \frac{1}{k}$. Similarly the minimum value of $g = \sum_{i=1}^{k} (\frac{1}{k} - \pi_i)^2$ is attained when $\pi_i = \frac{1}{k}$. It can be observed in Figure 3 that there is a sharp decrease in the value of g and a sharp increase in the value of f after annealing cycles (Dataset 1). Thus annealing has a tendency of redistributing the values of π more equally.

Experiment with Real Datasets

Now we consider Acidity and Enzyme datasets having skewed gaussians. They have been extensively studied by [18] and their optimal number of components are three and four respectively [15,18]. We performed a Monte Carlo simulation of 50 experiments and in all the experiments CSAEM[2] detected the same three and four component GMMs as shown in Figure 4(a-b). Then we also considered a well known relatively higher (four) dimensional Iris dataset [1]. The dataset

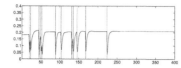 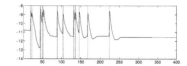

Fig. 3. The value of $\sum_{i=1}^{k} (\frac{1}{k} - \pi_i)^2$ (left) and $\sum_{i=1}^{k} \log(\pi_i)$ (right) during the annealing iterations of CSAEM^2. Vertical dashed lines depict the instances when annealing was applied.

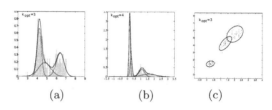

(a)   (b)   (c)

Fig. 4. Results of CSAEM^2 on (a) Acidity, (b) Enzyme and (c) Iris datasets. In (a-b), data is encoded in histograms while (c) contains the projection of data on the two axis with highest variances

contains three classes with 50 samples for each class. Again we performed a Monte Carlo simulation of 50 experiments and with hundred percent success rate detected the three component GMM as shown in Figure 4(c).

Comparison with Similar EM Approaches: [7,8] has presented similar EM based approaches where the components count starts from k_{max} and are brought down to k_{min}. These algorithms explicitly target the components with low prior values for switching to a $(k-1)$ component GMM and thus often fail when there is a component with very low prior value. Our approach increases the survival probability of the weak components and hence overcomes this problem. Now we performed a Monte Carlo simulation of 50 experiments. 710 samples were drawn from the four component bivariate GMM:

$$\pi_1 = \frac{10}{71}, \pi_2 = \frac{20}{71}, \pi_3 = \frac{40}{71}, \pi_4 = \frac{1}{71}, \boldsymbol{\mu}_1 = \begin{bmatrix} 1 \\ 0 \end{bmatrix}, \boldsymbol{\mu}_2 = \begin{bmatrix} 3 \\ 4 \end{bmatrix}, \boldsymbol{\mu}_3 = \begin{bmatrix} 3 \\ -3 \end{bmatrix}$$

$$\boldsymbol{\mu}_4 = \begin{bmatrix} 8 \\ 8 \end{bmatrix}, \boldsymbol{\Sigma}_1 = \boldsymbol{\Sigma}_4 = \mathbf{I}, \boldsymbol{\Sigma}_3 = \begin{bmatrix} 2 & 1.9 \\ 1.9 & 2 \end{bmatrix}, \boldsymbol{\Sigma}_2 = \begin{bmatrix} 2 & -1.5 \\ -1.5 & 2 \end{bmatrix}$$

All algorithms used same $k_{max}, k_{min}, \epsilon$ and λ values. Although the components are quite well separated from each other, the approaches presented in [7,8] performed very poorly while our algorithm outperformed these methods as can be seen in Table 1.

Robustness against k_{max}: Choosing $k_{max} \gg k_{optimal}$ provides robustness against initialization issues but it can be underestimated. Now we test the per-

Table 1. Percentage frequency of choosing k clusters for 50 experiments by our approach and the approaches presented by Figueiredo et al. (1999,2002).

k	Our method	Figueiredo et al. (2002)	Figueiredo et al. (1999)
3	0	0	1
4	47	1	17
5	3	13	16
6	0	14	7
7	0	10	4
8	0	8	2
9	0	2	2
10	0	2	1

Table 2. Percentage frequency of choosing $k_{opt} = 4$ clusters for 100 experiments by our approach with random initialization and stochastic exploration initialization.

k_{max}	Random initialization	Our initialization
6	62	88
7	84	93
8	91	95
9	93	97

formance of our approach with relatively smaller values of k_{max} for the simulated dataset with a weak component. For comparison, the initial k_{max} component GMM is obtained with two methods: the random initialization procedure presented in Figueiredo et al. (2002) and our initialization procedure. The results are summarized in Table 2. We can see that our initialization has high frequency of detecting right number of components, even when starting with relatively smaller k_{max}.

6   Conclusion

We have proposed a novel nature inspired initialization approach for fitting a GMM. It utilizes search strategy where each component looks for its nearby component. Two components are merged when they have high overlap. CSAEM^2 is applied when the components count reaches k_{max}. A component is annihilated if it becomes too weak. $(k-1)$ components GMM is obtained by selecting the one which yields highest likelihood value. MMDL criterion is used to select the optimal model complexity. Our approach has shown promising results on challenging simulated and real datasets.

References

1. Anderson, E.: The irises of the gaspe peninsula. Bulletin of the American Iris society **59**, 2–5 (1935)
2. Bensmail, H., Celeux, G., Raftery, A.E., Robert, C.P.: Inference in model-based cluster analysis. Statistics and Computing **7**(1), 1–10 (1997)
3. Blekas, K., Lagaris, I.E.: Split–merge incremental Learning (SMILE) of mixture models. In: de Sá, J.M., Alexandre, L.A., Duch, W., Mandic, D.P. (eds.) ICANN 2007. LNCS, vol. 4669, pp. 291–300. Springer, Heidelberg (2007)
4. Calinon, S., Pervez, A., Caldwell, D.G.: Multi-optima exploration with adaptive gaussian mixture model. In: IEEE International Conference on Development and Learning and Epigenetic Robotics (ICDL), pp. 1–6 (2012)

5. Celeux, G., Chrétien, S., Forbes, F., Mkhadri, A.: A component-wise EM algorithm for mixtures. Journal of Computational and Graphical Statistics (2012)
6. Dempster, A.P., Laird, N.M., Rubin, D.B., et al.: Maximum likelihood from incomplete data via the em algorithm. Journal of the Royal Statistical Society **39**(1), 1–38 (1977)
7. Figueiredo, M.A.T., Leitão, J.M.N., Jain, A.K.: On fitting mixture models. In: Hancock, E.R., Pelillo, M. (eds.) EMMCVPR 1999. LNCS, vol. 1654, pp. 54–69. Springer, Heidelberg (1999)
8. Figueiredo, M.A., Jain, A.K.: Unsupervised learning of finite mixture models. IEEE Transactions on Pattern Analysis and Machine Intelligence **24**(3), 381–396 (2002)
9. Koo, S., Lee, D., Kwon, D.S.: Incremental object learning and robust tracking of multiple objects from RGB-D point set data. Journal of Visual Communication and Image Representation **25**(1), 108–121 (2014)
10. Krause, J., Ruxton, G.D.: Living in groups. Oxford University Press (2002)
11. Krause, J., Cordeiro, J., Parpinelli, R.S., Lopes, H.S.: A survey of swarm algorithms applied to discrete optimization problems. Swarm Intelligence and Bio-inspired Computation: Theory and Applications. Elsevier Science & Technology Books, 169–191 (2013)
12. Lee, D., Nakamura, Y.: Mimesis model from partial observations for a humanoid robot. The International Journal of Robotics Research **29**(1), 60–80 (2010)
13. Lee, D., Ott, C., Nakamura, Y.: Mimetic communication with impedance control for physical human-robot interaction. In: IEEE International Conference on Robotics and Automation, ICRA 2009, pp. 1535–1542. IEEE (2009)
14. Luo, B., Wei, S., et al.: Estimation for the number of components in a mixture model using stepwise split-and-merge em algorithm. Pattern Recognition Letters **25**(16), 1799–1809 (2004)
15. McGrory, C.A., Titterington, D.: Variational approximations in bayesian model selection for finite mixture distributions. Computational Statistics & Data Analysis **51**(11), 5352–5367 (2007)
16. McLachlan, G., Peel, D.: Finite mixture models. John Wiley & Sons (2004)
17. Petersen, K.B., Pedersen, M.S.: The matrix cookbook. Technical University of Denmark, pp. 7–15 (2008)
18. Richardson, S., Green, P.J.: On bayesian analysis of mixtures with an unknown number of components (with discussion). Journal of the Royal Statistical Society: Series B (Statistical Methodology) **59**(4), 731–792 (1997)
19. Roeder, K., Wasserman, L.: Practical bayesian density estimation using mixtures of normals. Journal of the American Statistical Association **92**(439), 894–902 (1997)
20. Schwarz, G., et al.: Estimating the dimension of a model. The Annals of Statistics **6**(2), 461–464 (1978)
21. Ueda, N., Nakano, R.: Deterministic annealing em algorithm. Neural Networks **11**(2), 271–282 (1998)
22. Ueda, N., Nakano, R., Ghahramani, Z., Hinton, G.E.: Smem algorithm for mixture models. Neural Computation **12**(9), 2109–2128 (2000)
23. Valente, F., Wellekens, C., et al.: Variational bayesian gmm for speech recognition
24. Zhang, B., Zhang, C., Yi, X.: Competitive em algorithm for finite mixture models. Pattern Recognition **37**(1), 131–144 (2004)
25. Zhang, Z., Chen, C., Sun, J., Luk Chan, K.: Em algorithms for gaussian mixtures with split-and-merge operation. Pattern Recognition **36**(9), 1973–1983 (2003)

The Polylingual Labeled Topic Model

Lisa Posch[1,2]([✉]), Arnim Bleier[1], Philipp Schaer[1], and Markus Strohmaier[1,2]

[1] GESIS – Leibniz Institute for the Social Sciences, Cologne, Germany
{lisa.posch,arnim.bleier,philipp.schaer,markus.strohmaier}@gesis.org
[2] Institute for Web Science and Technologies,
University of Koblenz-Landau, Mainz, Germany

Abstract. In this paper, we present the *Polylingual Labeled Topic Model*, a model which combines the characteristics of the existing *Polylingual Topic Model* and *Labeled LDA*. The model accounts for multiple languages with separate topic distributions for each language while restricting the permitted topics of a document to a set of predefined labels. We explore the properties of the model in a two-language setting on a dataset from the social science domain. Our experiments show that our model outperforms LDA and Labeled LDA in terms of their held-out perplexity and that it produces semantically coherent topics which are well interpretable by human subjects.

Keywords: Thesauri · Classification · Probabilistic linking · Topic models

1 Introduction

Topic models are a popular and widely used method for the analysis of textual corpora. *Latent Dirichlet Allocation (LDA)* [2], one of the most popular topic models, has been adapted to a multitude of different problem settings, such as modeling labeled documents with *Labeled LDA (L-LDA)* [9] or modeling multilingual documents with *Polylingual Topic Models (PLTM)* [7]. Textual corpora often exhibit both of these characteristics, containing documents in multiple languages which are also annotated with a classification system. However, there is currently no topic model which possesses the ability to process multiple languages while simultaneously incorporating the documents' labels.

To close this gap, this paper introduces the *Polylingual Labeled Topic Model (PLL-TM)*, a model which combines the characteristics of PLTM and L-LDA. PLL-TM models multilingual labeled documents by generating separate distributions over the vocabulary of each language, while restricting the permitted topics of a document to a set of predefined labels. We explore the characteristics of our model in a two-language setting, with German natural language text as the first language and the controlled *SKOS* vocabulary of a thesaurus as the second language. The labels of the documents, in our setting, are classes from the classification system with which our corpus is annotated.

© Springer International Publishing Switzerland 2015
S. Hölldobler et al. (Eds.): KI 2015, LNAI 9324, pp. 295–301, 2015.
DOI: 10.1007/978-3-319-24489-1_26

Contributions. The main contribution of this paper is the presentation of the PLL-TM. We present the model's generative storyline as well as an easy-to-implement inference strategy based on Gibbs sampling. For evaluation, we compute the held-out perplexity and conduct a word intrusion task with human subjects using a dataset from the social science domain. On this dataset, the PLL-TM outperforms LDA and L-LDA in terms of its predictive performance and generates semantically coherent topics. To the best of our knowledge, PLL-TM is the first model which accounts for multiple vocabularies and, at the same time, possesses the ability to restrict the topics of a document to its labels.

2   Related Work

Topic models are generative probabilistic models for discovering latent topics in documents and other discrete data. One of the most popular topic models, LDA, is a generative Bayesian model which was introduced by Blei et al. [2]. In this section, we review LDA, as well as the two other topic models whose characteristics we are going to integrate into PLL-TM.

LDA. Beginning with LDA [2], we follow the common notation of a document d being a vector of N_d words, $\boldsymbol{w}_d$, where each word w_{di} is chosen from a vocabulary of V terms. A collection of documents is defined by $\mathcal{D} = \{\boldsymbol{w}_1,...,\boldsymbol{w}_D\}$. LDA's generative storyline can be described by the following steps.

1. For each document $d \in \{1,...,D\}$, a distribution θ_d over topics is drawn from a symmetric K-dimensional Dirichlet prior parametrized by α:

$$\theta_d \sim Dir(\alpha) \ . \tag{1}$$

2. Then, for each topic $k = \{1,...,K\}$, a distribution ϕ_k over the vocabulary is drawn form a V-dimensional Dirichlet distribution parametrized by β:

$$\phi_k \sim Dir(\beta) \ . \tag{2}$$

3. In the final step, the ith word in document d is generated by first drawing a topic index z_{di} and subsequently, a word w_{di} from the topic indexed by z_{di}:

$$w_{di} \sim Cat(\phi_{z_{di}}) \ , \qquad\qquad z_{di} \sim Cat(\theta_d) \ . \tag{3}$$

Labeled LDA. Ramage et al. [9] introduced L-LDA, a supervised version of LDA. In L-LDA, a document d's topic distribution θ_d is restricted to a subset of all possible topics $\Lambda_d \subseteq \{1,..,K\}$. Here, collection of documents is defined by $\mathcal{D} = \{(\boldsymbol{w}_1,\Lambda_1),...,(\boldsymbol{w}_D,\Lambda_D)\}$. The first step in L-LDA's generative storyline draws the distribution of topics θ_d for each document $d \in \{1,...,D\}$

$$\theta_d \sim Dir(\alpha\boldsymbol{\mu}_d) \ , \tag{4}$$

where α is a continuous positive valued scalar and $\boldsymbol{\mu}_d$ is a K-dimensional vector

$$\mu_{dk} = \begin{cases} 1 & \text{if } k \in \Lambda_d \\ 0 & \text{otherwise} \ , \end{cases} \tag{5}$$

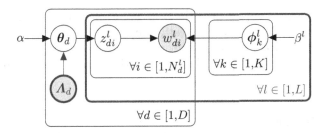

Fig. 1. The PLL-TM in plate notation. Random variables are represented by nodes. Shaded nodes denote the observed words and labels, bare symbols indicate the fixed priors α and β^l. Directed edges between the nodes then define conditional probabilities, where the child node is conditioned on its parents. The rectangular plates indicate replication over data-points and parameters. Colors indicate the parts which are inherited from L-LDA (blue) and PLTM (green). Black is used for the LDA base.

indicating which topics are permitted. Once these label-restricted topic distributions are drawn, the process of generating documents continues identically to the generative process of LDA. In the case of $\Lambda_d = \{1,..,K\}$ for all documents, no restrictions are active and L-LDA is reduced to LDA.

Polylingual Topic Model. Ni et al. [8] extended the generative view of LDA to multilingual documents. Mimno et al. [7] elaborated on this concept, introducing the *Polylingual Topic Model* (PLTM). PLTM assumes that the documents are available in L languages. A document d is represented by $[\boldsymbol{w}_d^1,...,\boldsymbol{w}_d^L]$, where for each language $l \in 1,...,L$, the vector $\boldsymbol{w}_d^l$ consists of N_d^l words which are chosen from a language specific vocabulary with V^l terms. A collection of documents is then defined by $\mathcal{D} = \{[\boldsymbol{w}_1^1,...,\boldsymbol{w}_1^L],...,[\boldsymbol{w}_D^1,...,\boldsymbol{w}_D^L]\}$. The generative storyline is equivalent to LDA's except that steps 2 and 3 are repeated for each language. Hence, for each topic $k = \{1,...,K\}$ in each language $l \in \{1,...,L\}$, a language specific topic distribution ϕ_k^l over the vocabulary of length V^l is drawn:

$$\phi_k^l \sim Dir(\beta^l) . \tag{6}$$

Then, the ith word of language l in document d is generated by drawing a topic index z_{di}^l and subsequently, a word w_{di}^l from a language specific topic distribution indexed by z_{di}^l:

$$w_{di}^l \sim Cat(\phi_{z_{di}^l}^l) , \qquad\qquad z_{di}^l \sim Cat(\theta_d) . \tag{7}$$

Note that in the special case of just one language, i.e. $L = 1$, PLTM is reduced to LDA.

3 The Polylingual Labeled Topic Model

In this section, we introduce the *Polylingual Labeled Topic Model (PLL-TM)*, which integrates the characteristics of the models described in the previous section into a single model. Figure 1 depicts the PLL-TM in plate notation. Here, a collection of documents is defined by $\mathcal{D} = \{[\boldsymbol{w}_1^1,...,\boldsymbol{w}_1^L],\boldsymbol{\Lambda}_1)),...,[\boldsymbol{w}_D^1,...,\boldsymbol{w}_D^L],\boldsymbol{\Lambda}_D)\}$.

The generative process follows three main steps:

1. For each document $d \in \{1,...,D\}$, we draw the distribution of topics

$$\theta_d \sim Dir(\alpha\boldsymbol{\mu}_d) , \tag{8}$$

where $\boldsymbol{\mu}_d$ is computed according to Equation 5.

2. For each topic $k \in \{1,...,K\}$ in each language $l \in \{1,...,L\}$, we draw a distribution over the vocabulary of size V^l:

$$\phi_k^l \sim Dir(\beta^l) , \tag{9}$$

3. Next, for each word in each language l of document d, we draw a topic

$$w_{di}^l \sim Cat(\phi_{z_{di}^l}^l) , \qquad\qquad z_{di}^l \sim Cat(\theta_d) . \tag{10}$$

Note that PLL-TM contains both PLTM and L-LDA as special cases.

For inference, we use collapsed Gibbs sampling [6] for the indicator variables $\boldsymbol{z}$, with all other variables integrated out. The full conditional probability for a topic k is given by

$$P(z_{di}^l = k \mid w_{di}^l = t,...) \propto \frac{n_{dk}^{\neg di} + \alpha}{n_{d.}^{\neg di} + K\alpha} \times \frac{n_{kt}^{l\neg di} + \beta^l}{n_{k.}^{l\neg di} + V^l\beta^l} , \tag{11}$$

where n_{dk} is the number of tokens allocated to topic k in document d, and n_{kt}^l is the number of tokens of word $w_{di}^l = t$ which are assigned to topic k in language l. Furthermore, $\cdot$ is used in place of a variable to indicate that the sum over its values (i.e. $n_{d.} = \sum_k n_{dk}$) is taken and $\neg di$ to mark the current token as excluded. While the full conditional posterior distribution is reminiscent of the one used in PLTM, the assumptions of the L-LDA model restrict the probability $P(z_{di}^l = k)$ to those $k \in \boldsymbol{\Lambda}_d$ with which document d is labeled.

Table 1. This table shows the five most probable terms for two classes in the CSS, generated by PLL-TM, in two languages: *TheSoz* (TS) and German natural language words with their translation (AB).

Population Studies, Sociology of Population:
TS: population development, demographic aging, population, demographic factors, demography
AB: wandel, demografischen, bevlkerung, deutschland, entwicklung
(change, demographic, population, germany, development)

Developmental Psychology:
TS: child, developmental psychology, adolescent, personality development, socialization research
AB: entwicklung, sozialisation, kinder, kindern, identitt
(development, socialization, children, children, identity)

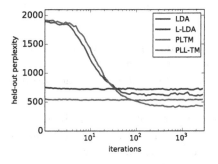 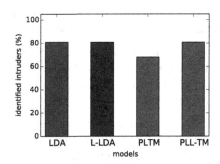

(a) Comparison of the held-out perplexity (lower values are better) as a function of iterations.

(b) Comparison of the semantic coherence (word intrusion) of the generated topics.

Fig. 2. Evaluation of the PLL-TM. These figures show that on the SOLIS dataset, PLL-TM outperforms LDA and L-LDA in terms of its predictive performance and produces topics with a higher semantic coherence than PLTM.

4   Evaluation

For our evaluation, we use documents from the *Social Science Literature Information System (SOLIS)*. The documents are manually indexed with the SKOS *Thesaurus for the Social Sciences (TheSoz)* [10] and manually classified with the *Classification for the Social Sciences (CSS)* by human domain experts. For our experiments, we used all SOLIS documents which were published in the years 2008 to 2013, resulting in a corpus of about 60.000 documents.

We explore the characteristics of our model in a two-language setting, with German natural language text as the first language (*AbstractWords*) and the controlled *SKOS* vocabulary of a thesaurus as the second language (*TheSoz*). The labels of the documents, in our setting, are classes from the CSS. After applying standard preprocessing to remove rare words and stopwords, *TheSoz* consisted of 802.764 tokens over a vocabulary of 7.406 distinct terms, and *AbstractWords* consisted of 5.417.779 tokens over a vocabulary of about 43.000 distinct terms. In our corpus, each document is labeled with an average of 2.14 classes.

We compare four different topic models: LDA, L-LDA, PLTM and PLL-TM. The unilingual models (i.e. LDA and L-LDA) were trained on language *TheSoz*; the polylingual models (i.e. PLTM and PLL-TM) were trained on *TheSoz* and *AbstractWords*. The documents in our corpus were labeled with a total of 131 different classes from the CSS and we trained the unlabeled models with an equal number of topics. α and β^l were specified with 0.1 and 0.01, respectively. Table 1 shows the topics generated by PLL-TM for two classes of the CSS, reporting the five most probable terms for the languages *TheSoz* and *AbstractWords*.

Language Model Evaluation. For an evaluation of the predictive performance, we computed the held-out perplexity for all models. We held out 1.000

documents as test set $\mathcal{D}_{test}$ and, with the remaining data $\mathcal{D}_{train}$, we trained the four models. We split each test document in the following way:

- x_{d1}: All words of language *AbstractWords* and a randomly selected 50% of the words in language *TheSoz* which occur in document d.
- x_{d2}: The remaining 50% of the words in language *TheSoz* which occur in document d.

The test documents for the unilingual models were split analogously, with x_{d1} consisting of 50% percent of the words in language *TheSoz* which occur in document d. For each document d, we computed the perplexity of x_{d2}.

Figure 2a shows the results of this evaluation. One can see that the labeled models both start out with a lower perplexity and need less iterations to achieve a good performance, which is due to the fact that the labels provide additional information to the model. In contrast, the unlabeled models need almost 100 iterations to achieve a comparable performance. On our corpus, PLL-TM outperformed LDA and L-LDA, and even though PLL-TM had a higher perplexity than PLTM, it is important to keep in mind that PLTM does not possess the ability to produce topics which correspond to the classes of the CSS.

Human Evaluation of the Topics. Chang et al. [4] proposed a formal setting in which humans evaluate the latent space of a topic model. For evaluating the topics' semantic coherence, they proposed a *word intrusion* task: Crowdworkers were shown six terms, five of which were highly probable terms in a topic and one was an "intruder" – an improbable term for this topic which had a high probability in some other topic.

We conducted the word intrusion task for the four topic models on Crowd-Flower [1], with ten distinct workers for each topic in each model. Figure 2b shows the results of this evaluation for the different models. For each model, the figure depicts the percentage of topics for which the ten workers collectively detected the correct intruder. The collective decision was based on CrowdFlower's *confidence score*, i.e. the level of agreement between workers weighted by each worker's percentage of correctly answered test questions. The results show that PLL-TM produces topics which are equally coherent as unilingual models, and more coherent than the topics produced by PLTM.

5   Discussion and Conclusions

In this paper, we presented PLL-TM, a joint model for multilingual labeled documents. The results of our evaluation showed that PLL-TM was the only model which produced both highly interpretable topics and achieved a good predictive performance. Compared to L-LDA, the only other model capable of incorporating label information, our model produced equally well interpretable topics while achieving a better predictive performance. Compared to PLTM, the only other model capable of dealing with multiple languages, PLL-TM had a lower predictive performance, but produced topics with a higher semantic coherence. For future work, we plan an evaluation of the model in a label prediction task and an application of the model in a setting with more than two natural languages. Furthermore, we plan an evaluation on a larger dataset using a more memory-friendly inference strategy such as *Stochastic Collapsed Variational Bayesian Inference* [5], which has been shown to be applicable outside of its original LDA application [3].

References

1. Biewald, L.: Massive multiplayer human computation for fun, money, and survival. In: Harth, A., Koch, N. (eds.) ICWE 2011. LNCS, vol. 7059, pp. 171–176. Springer, Heidelberg (2012)
2. Blei, D.M., Ng, A.Y., Jordan, M.I.: Latent dirichlet allocation. Journal of Machine Learning Research **3**, 993–1022 (2003)
3. Bleier, A.: Practical collapsed stochastic variational inference for the hdp. In: NIPS Workshop on Topic Models: Computation, Application, and Evaluation (2013)
4. Chang, J., Boyd-Graber, J.L., Gerrish, S., Wang, C., Blei, D.M.: Reading tea leaves: how humans interpret topic models. In: Advances in Neural Information Processing Systems 22: 23rd Annual Conference on Neural Information Processing Systems 2009. Proceedings of a meeting held December 7–10, 2009, Vancouver, British Columbia, Canada, pp. 288–296 (2009)
5. Foulds, J.R., Boyles, L., DuBois, C., Smyth, P., Welling, M.: Stochastic collapsed variational bayesian inference for latent dirichlet allocation. In: The 19th ACM SIGKDD International Conference on Knowledge Discovery and Data Mining, KDD 2013, Chicago, IL, USA, pp. 446–454, August 11–14, 2013
6. Griffiths, T.L., Steyvers, M.: Finding scientific topics. In: Proceedings of the National Academy of Sciences (2004)
7. Mimno, D.M., Wallach, H.M., Naradowsky, J., Smith, D.A., McCallum, A.: Polylingual topic models. In: Proceedings of the 2009 Conference on Empirical Methods in Natural Language Processing, EMNLP 2009, August 6–7, 2009, Singapore, A meeting of SIGDAT, a Special Interest Group of the ACL, pp. 880–889 (2009)
8. Ni, X., Sun, J., Hu, J., Chen, Z.: Mining multilingual topics from wikipedia. In: Proceedings of the 18th International Conference on World Wide Web, WWW 2009, Madrid, Spain, pp. 1155–1156, April 20–24, 2009
9. Ramage, D., Hall, D.L.W., Nallapati, R., Manning, C.D.: Labeled LDA: a supervised topic model for credit attribution in multi-labeled corpora. In: Proceedings of the 2009 Conference on Empirical Methods in Natural Language Processing, EMNLP 2009, August 6–7, 2009, Singapore, A meeting of SIGDAT, a Special Interest Group of the ACL, pp. 248–256 (2009)
10. Zapilko, B., Schaible, J., Mayr, P., Mathiak, B.: Thesoz: A SKOS representation of the thesaurus for the social sciences. Semantic Web **4**(3), 257–263 (2013)

Improving Heuristics On-the-fly
for Effective Search in Plan Space

Shashank Shekhar$^{(\boxtimes)}$ and Deepak Khemani

Department of Computer Science and Engineering,
Indian Institute of Technology, Chennai, India
{sshekhar,khemani}@cse.iitm.ac.in

Abstract. The design of domain independent heuristic functions often
brings up experimental evidence that different heuristics perform well
in different domains. A promising approach is to monitor and reduce
the error associated with a given heuristic function even as the planner
solves a problem. We extend this single-step-error adaptation to heuristic
functions from Partial Order Causal Link (POCL) planning. The goal
is to allow a partial order planner to observe the effective average-step-
error during search. The preliminary evaluation shows that our approach
improves the informativeness of the state-of-the-art heuristics. Our planner solves more problems by using the improved heuristics as compared
to when it uses current heuristics in the selected domains.

1 Introduction

The performance of a domain independent planner is critically influenced by
the design of the heuristic function. The study of heuristics in classical state
space planning has received significant interest in the past. There are many good
heuristic evaluation functions with varying performances on different domains.
This is often due to the nature of the planning problem characterized by the
degree and nature of interaction between subgoals. One approach to finding
better heuristic functions is to learn from a set of solved examples in each
domain [1,9,16]. However such methods have considerable overheads in terms of
collecting training data and learning from it. Another approach is to examine the
single-step-error associated with the different heuristic functions on-the-fly. The
single-step-error also varies for individual domains. The last decade has also seen
a resurgence in use of heuristics derived from state space approaches [2,3,14] to
POCL planning [11,15]. We adapt and modify a procedure for monitoring single-
step-error associated with some state-of-the-art heuristic functions [19].

A partial plan is quite complex structurally and developing a well informed
heuristic function is comparatively a harder task [20]. The basic idea behind this
error monitoring approach is to avoid a heuristic function taking a similar view
of the problems in different domains, by measuring and trying to correct the
error in the heuristic value on-the-fly. We discuss the pros and cons of capturing
the single-step-error during search and empirically show that the performance
of a planner which is built on top of Versatile Heuristic Partial Order Planner

S. Hölldobler et al. (Eds.): KI 2015, LNAI 9324, pp. 302–308, 2015.
DOI: 10.1007/978-3-319-24489-1_27

(VHPOP) [22] that uses fully grounded actions, can be improved. The preliminary evaluations have shown very promising results over some domains with different degree and nature of interactions between the subgoals and actions. The evaluations also show that our approach results in more informed decision during search, even being competitive on the time required as well. For a few problem instances in these domains we find shorter plan lengths too, more specifically for larger instances over the domains.

In the background section we give a brief overview of POCL planning along with the heuristic functions employed. Following to this we describe our adapted procedure for minimizing single-step-error associated with a heuristic function. Finally we briefly present our preliminary evaluations and the future work.

2 Background

POCL planning dissociates the task of finding actions that form a plan and the placement of those actions in the plan. The search algorithm operates in a space of partial plans, starting with a null plan. Actions are added to the plan to achieve some objective, characterized as removing *flaws* in the partial plan. Following [14,21,22] we work with fully grounded actions *in lieu* of partially instantiated operators, trading delayed commitment for speed.

A partial plan is a tuple $\Pi = (A, O, L, B)$, where A is a set of actions (with two dummy actions a_0 and a_∞), O is a set of ordering constraints among actions, L is a set of causal links (CL) among actions and B is a set of binding constraints. A CL between two actions a_i and a_j can be represented as $a_i \xrightarrow{p} a_j$ which signifies that the action a_i produces a proposition p which is consumed, as a precondition, by the action a_j. An ordering constraint between actions $(a_i \prec a_j)$ signifies that a_i is scheduled before a_j in the plan. An open condition (OC), $\xrightarrow{p} a_j$ in POCL planning is a proposition p that is a precondition for the action a_j and for which the supporting causal link is absent. An unsafe link (UL) (also called a threat) is a causal link $a_i \xrightarrow{p} a_j$ that can *potentially* be broken by an action a_k if it were to be scheduled in between a_i and a_j and a negative effect of a_k unifies with p. The set F of *flaws* for a partial plan π is, $F(\pi) = \text{OC}(\pi) \cup \text{UL}(\pi)$. The threat (mentioned above) can be resolved by (a) *promotion* that is adding an ordering constraint $(a_k \prec a_i)$ or (b) *demotion* that is adding an ordering constraint $(a_j \prec a_k)$. Here separation is not applicable as we use grounded actions.

A solution plan is a partial plan that has no flaws. Each possible linearization of such a partial plan is a valid plan. A detailed algorithm of POCL planning can be found in [22]. The POCL planning is a two stage process, the first - select the most promising partial plan, and the second - select a flaw (if any) in the chosen plan and resolve it. The process terminates when a partial plan without a flaw is selected. For the early accomplishment of this two stage process, we need good heuristic functions at both the stages. Following the literature [14,15,21,22] we investigate an approach to enhance the informativeness of the state-of-the-art (non-temporal) heuristics, employed in the first stage of POCL planning. In the next subsection, we give a brief description of the state-of-the-art heuristics for POCL planning.

2.1   Heuristics for POCL Planning

A good heuristic reduces search (flaw resolutions) by making appropriate choices during the planning process [18]. A good strategy in the second stage is to select the most demanding flaw and a refinement that leaves minimum refinements to be done subsequently. This enables to search to backtrack early from wrong choices. We use the following flaw selection heuristics from literature - Most-Cost (MC), Most-Cost-Local (MC-Loc), Most-Work (MW) and Most-Work-Local (MW-Loc) [22]. A criterion for selecting a partial plan from the *set* of candidates is the number of actions needed to resolve all the open conditions in it [14]. Two powerful heuristics for POCL planning based on *means ends analysis* are, (a) the relax heuristic h_{relax} [14] and (b) the additive heuristic (with and without actions reuse) h^r_{add} [22]. These non-temporal heuristics are the best ones for POCL planning, but they overlook the associated negative interactions between the actions in partial plans. Often these heuristic functions produce large overestimating or underestimating values.

Some improvements have been shown in [3] where heuristics computing using state space approaches have been used in POCL planning. In this work, we enhance heuristics directly in POCL planning. Therefore, we do not give any direct comparison of our approach to the approach mentioned in [3]. We consider the definition of $h^*(\pi)$ from [14] which says,

Definition 1. *For given a partial plan π, $h^*(\pi)$ gives the minimum number of new actions required to convert a partial plan to a solution plan* [14].

A heuristic function should produce an estimate close to h^*. This is often difficult due to the varying nature of interactions between subgoals in different planning domains. We describe two state-of-the-art heuristic functions. The references cited provide for more details.

Relax Heuristic - $h_{relax}(\pi)$: A simple approach is to count the number of open goals (OC) in the partial plan [10,17,18]. Various techniques have been proposed to cater to positive as well as negative subgoal interactions [5,8,12,13]. Reviving Partial Order Planning (RePOP) [14] addresses positive subgoal interactions using a serial planning graph for the subgoal reachability analysis. The heuristic $h_{relax}(\pi)$ (a variant of FF heuristic [8]) proposed by Nguyen et al. [14] uses Graphplan [4].

Accounting for Positive Interaction - $h^r_{add}(\pi)$: Younes et al. [22] address the positive interactions between subgoals while ignoring the negative interactions. This technique is used (as a variant of h_{add} [7]) for ranking the partial plans for the first time by Younes et al. [22]. Here $h^r_{add}(\pi)$ is a substitute for

$h_{\mathrm{add}}(\pi)$ as the latter has no provision for reusing actions. Younes et al. [22] define $h_{\mathrm{add}}(\pi)$ as well that is an adaption of additive heuristic. The additive heuristic h_{add} adds up the steps required by each open goal [5–7].

3   Improved Heuristics for POCL Planning

Adapting the concept introduced by Thayer et al. [19] of capturing the *single-step-error*, we define the minimum number of refinements needed for a partial plan (π_i) as the sum of the cost of its current best possible refined partial plan (π_{i+1}) and the corresponding refinement R_i. That is, $h^*(\pi_i) = cost(R_i) + h^*(\pi_{i+1})$. Estimating $h^*(\pi_i)$ during search is a tedious task and therefore we approximate it as, $h(\pi_i) = cost(R_i) + h(\pi_{i+1})$.

Theorem 1 is adapted from [19] for POCL planning. We refer to [19] for the proof of Theorem 1 and also for the additional details.

Theorem 1. *For given a heuristic function h and a partial plan π_i that leads to a solution plan after some refinement steps, the improved heuristic function h^{a} is,*

$$h^{\mathrm{a}}(\pi_i) \;=\; h(\pi_i) \;+\; \sum_{\substack{\pi^* \text{ from} \\ \pi_i \rightsquigarrow \text{ solution plan}}} \epsilon_{h(\pi^*)} \tag{1}$$

where $\pi_i \rightsquigarrow$ solution plan, captures a set of partial plans along the path between π_i and the solution plan that includes π_i and excludes the solution plan, and the term ϵ is single-step-error associated with h.

3.1   Improvement Heuristic

The improved heuristic estimate based on a given inadmissible heuristic h is, $h^{\mathrm{a}}(\pi_i) = h(\pi_i)\big/(1 - \epsilon_h^{\mathrm{avg}})$. The term $\epsilon_h^{\mathrm{avg}}$ is an average of the step errors, defined later in this section. Here h^{a} is an inadmissible heuristic as well but it is close to h^*. This is just an assumption as we do not give any theoretical bound for h^a to h^*. We capture the single-step-error associated with h as, $\epsilon_{h(\pi_i)} = \big(cost(R_i) + h(\pi_{i+1}) - h(\pi_i)\big)$. Here ϵ_h is either positive or negative since h is an inadmissible and one cannot expect the property of monotonicity to be satisfied. We refer to [19] for further explanation where we consider a node as a partial plan π everywhere. By following Theorem 1, we approximate the total effort required in resolving all the flaws of a partial plan π as,

$$h^{\mathrm{a}}(\pi_i) \;=\; h(\pi_i) \;+\; \sum_{\substack{\pi^* \text{ from} \\ \pi_i \rightsquigarrow \text{ solution plan}}} \epsilon_{h(\pi^*)} \tag{2}$$

The term $\epsilon_h^{\mathrm{avg}}$ used earlier is an average-step-error associated with h which is,

$$\epsilon_h^{\mathrm{avg}} \;=\; \sum_{\substack{\pi^* \text{ from} \\ \pi_i \rightsquigarrow \text{ solution plan}}} \epsilon_{h(\pi^*)} \;\Big/\; h^{\mathrm{a}}(\pi_i) \tag{3}$$

Table 1. Performance comparison in Gripper domain from IPC-1. MW-Loc is used for flaw selection in both parts of this table.

Instance	h_{add}^{r} with *effort*						$h_{add}^{r\text{-}a}$ with *effort*					
	Algo	Gen	Vis	PL	CPU	DE	Algo	Gen	Vis	PL	CPU	DE
gripper-06	IDA	–	–	–	–	–	**IDA**	**1.5K**	**880**	**15**	**12**	**183**
gripper-08	wA	–	–	–	–	–	**wA**	**1.8K**	**1K**	**15**	**20**	**208**
Instance	h_{add} with *effort*						h_{add}^{a} with *effort*					
gripper-08	IDA	1.1K	605	21	12	153	IDA	640	274	21	4	54
gripper-12	IDA	3.4K	2.0K	43	40	612	**IDA**	**1.9K**	**767**	**33**	**24**	**195**
gripper-20	IDA	20K	11K	79	365	3.7K	**IDA**	**8.7K**	**3.3K**	**59**	**168**	**1K**

Table 2. Performance comparison in Logistics domain from IPC-2. MC-Loc and MW-Loc are used for flaw selection in the top half and bottom half respectively. Instances are also used for evaluating the performance of VHPOP in [22].

Instance	h_{add}^{r} with *effort*						$h_{add}^{r\text{-}a}$ with *effort*					
	Algo	Gen	Vis	PL	CPU	DE	Algo	Gen	Vis	PL	CPU	DE
logistics-a	IDA	317	174	51	76	13	IDA	308	169	51	76	13
logistics-b	HC	244	127	42	88	8	HC	243	130	42	88	8
logistics-c	IDA	307	158	50	116	9	IDA	309	159	50	116	9
logistics-d	IDA	1.4K	678	73	420	68	**IDA**	**654**	**338**	**70**	**412**	**42**
Instance	h_{add}^{r} without *effort*						$h_{add}^{r\text{-}a}$ without *effort*					
logistics-a	IDA	1.8K	1.4K	59	108	172	**IDA**	**634**	**463**	**51**	**72**	**61**
logistics-b	IDA	1.4K	904	48	104	113	**A**	**826**	**467**	**43**	**100**	**71**
logistics-c	IDA	1.7K	1.1K	57	260	138	**IDA**	**1.0K**	**764**	**52**	**136**	**108**
logistics-d	wA	–	–	–	–	–	**wA**	**3.5K**	**1.9K**	**70**	**484**	**367**

Using the above derivation, we can improve a heuristic h' just by replacing h with h'. For example, after improvement, h_{add}^{r} will become $h_{add}^{r\text{-}a}$. In a similar way, we use Eq. 2 to improve h_{add} and h_{add}^{r} with their variants in the evaluation.

4   Empirical Evaluation

All the experiments have been performed on Intel dual-core PC with 4Gb of RAM. These experimental results on planning domains from different international planning competitions (IPC) are the basis for claims made in this paper. The preliminary evaluations are performed in some domains that are Gripper, Logistics and Rovers. We consider only non-temporal STRIPS problem instances in these domains. We use an upper limit of **1,000,000** on the number of partial plans generated, apart from a time limit of **900** seconds.

Table 3. Performance comparison in Rovers domain from IPC-5. MW-Loc is used for flaw selection.

Instance	h_{add} with *effort*						h_{add}^a with *effort*					
	Algo	Gen	Vis	PL	CPU	DE	Algo	Gen	Vis	PL	CPU	DE
problem-15	wA	1.1K	702	44	12	44	wA	1.3K	826	43	20	45
problem-30	wA	84K	57K	162	8K	20K	wA	16K	9.5K	130	632	920
problem-35	wA	447K	351K	466	210K	102K	wA	186K	118K	377	38K	17K
problem-40	wA	-	-	-	-	-	wA	93K	66K	325	9.5K	1.8K

4.1 Experimentation

The evaluation demonstrates that the planner becomes more informed as search progresses. We employed four well known search algorithms that are A* (A), wA* (wA), Iterative Deepening A* (IDA), Hill Climbing (HC). We consider four heuristics that are h_{add} and h_{add}^r with their respective improvements h_{add}^a and h_{add}^{r-a}. They are evaluated with *effort* and without *effort* [22]. Results mentioned in the tables are very promising. In the tables, *Algo* indicates best of A, wA, IDA and HC. *Gen* is nodes (partial plan) generated, *Vis* is nodes visited, *PL* is plan length, *CPU* is execution time in milliseconds, *DE* is dead-ends. Best results are shown in **bold**. Dash indicates no solution was found within the specified limits.

Table 1 to 3 contain different sized planning problems and the effort required by the planner to find the plans. Table-1 shows that for larger problems the heuristic gets more opportunity to see the overall global average-step-error. The second half of Table-1 shows that on instances from gripper-10 to gripper-20 (only gripper-12 and gripper-20 are shown), the improved heuristic comprehensively outperforms h_{add}. Currently we ignore some possible comparisons, for example, current and improved versions of h_{add}^r without *effort etc* due to lack of space. In the second half of Table-2, the improved heuristic gives shorter plan lengths, while also being competitive on the other standards. Table-3 shows the evaluations performed in the rovers domain from IPC-5. We could solve **3** more instances with improved heuristics out of **40** instances. We observe that the proposed improvement for POCL planning consistently performs better in all of the domains compared to current version of the heuristics.

5 Future Work

Considering the initial success of our approach, we intend to extend this work in future to test the informativeness of the improved heuristics in other domains from different IPCs. We also aim to exploit some other aspects of POCL planning to achieve more accurate estimates. Recent literature [1,9,19] talks about the usage of machine learning techniques to enhance performance of a planner. We plan to incorporate some learning aspects into our approach, for example to learn relations among features associated with a planning domain. This will allow us to reap the benefit of both offline learning and online error correction.

References

1. Arfaee, S.J., Zilles, S., Holte, R.C.: Learning heuristic functions for large state spaces. Artificial Intelligence **175**(16), 2075–2098 (2011)
2. Bercher, P., Biundo, S.: Encoding partial plans for heuristic search. In: Proceedings of the 4th Workshop on Knowledge Engineering for Planning and Scheduling (KEPS 2013), pp. 11–15. Citeseer (2013)
3. Bercher, P., Geier, T., Biundo, S.: Using state-based planning heuristics for partial-order causal-link planning. In: Timm, I.J., Thimm, M. (eds.) KI 2013. LNCS, vol. 8077, pp. 1–12. Springer, Heidelberg (2013)
4. Blum, A.L., Furst, M.L.: Fast planning through planning graph analysis. Artificial Intelligence **90**(1), 281–300 (1997)
5. Bonet, B., Geffner, H.: Planning as heuristic search. Artificial Intelligence **129**(1), 5–33 (2001)
6. Bonet, B., Loerincs, G., Geffner, H.: A robust and fast action selection mechanism for planning. In: AAAI/IAAI. pp. 714–719 (1997)
7. Haslum, P., Geffner, H.: Admissible heuristics for optimal planning. In: AIPS, pp. 140–149. Citeseer (2000)
8. Hoffmann, J.: FF: The fast-forward planning system. AI Magazine **22**(3), 57 (2001)
9. Jesús Virseda, J., Borrajo, D., Alcázar, V.: Learning heuristic functions for cost-based planning. Planning and Learning, 6 (2013)
10. Joslin, D., Pollack, M.E.: Least-cost flaw repair: A plan refinement strategy for partial-order planning (1994)
11. McAllester, D., Rosenblatt, D.: Systematic nonlinear planning (1991)
12. McDermott, D.: Using regression-match graphs to control search in planning. Artificial Intelligence **109**(1), 111–159 (1999)
13. Nguyen, X., Kambhampati, S.: Extracting effective and admissible state space heuristics from the planning graph. In: AAAI/IAAI, pp. 798–805 (2000)
14. Nguyen, X., Kambhampati, S.: Reviving partial order planning. In: IJCAI, vol. 1, pp. 459–464 (2001)
15. Penberthy, J.S., Weld, D.S.: UCPOP: A sound, complete, partial order planner for ADL, pp. 103–114. Morgan Kaufmann (1992)
16. Samadi, M., Felner, A., Schaeffer, J.: Learning from multiple heuristics. In: AAAI, pp. 357–362 (2008)
17. Schattenberg, B.: Hybrid Planning And Scheduling. Ph.D. thesis, Ulm University, Institute of Artificial Intelligence (2009). URN: urn:nbn:de:bsz:289-vts-68953
18. Schubert, L., Gerevini, A.: Accelerating partial order planners by improving plan and goal choices. In: Proceedings of the Seventh International Conference on Tools with Artificial Intelligence, pp. 442–450. IEEE (1995)
19. Thayer, J.T., Dionne, A.J., Ruml, W.: Learning inadmissible heuristics during search. In: ICAPS (2011)
20. Weld, D.S.: AAAI-10 classic paper award: Systematic nonlinear planning a commentary. AI Magazine **32**(1), 101 (2011)
21. Younes, H.L., Simmons, R.G.: On the role of ground actions in refinement planning. In: AIPS, pp. 54–62 (2002)
22. Younes, H.L., Simmons, R.G.: Versatile Heuristic Partial Order Planner. J. Artif. Intell. Res. (JAIR) **20**, 405–430 (2003)

Hierarchical Hybrid Planning
in a Mobile Service Robot

Sebastian Stock[1,2]([⊠]), Masoumeh Mansouri[3],
Federico Pecora[3], and Joachim Hertzberg[1,2]

[1] DFKI-RIC Osnabrück Branch, 49069 Osnabrück, Germany
sebastian.stock@dfki.de
[2] Osnabrück University, 49069 Osnabrück, Germany
[3] Örebro University, 70182 Örebro, Sweden

Abstract. Planning with diverse knowledge, i.e., hybrid planning, is essential for robotic applications. However, powerful heuristics are needed to reason efficiently in the resulting large search spaces. HTN planning provides a means to reduce the search space; furthermore, meta-CSP search has shown promise in hybrid domains, both wrt. search and online plan adaptation. In this paper we combine the two approaches by implementing HTN-style task decomposition as a meta-constraint in a meta-CSP search, resulting in an HTN planner able to handle very rich domain knowledge. The planner produces partial-order plans and if several goal tasks are given, subtasks can be shared, leading to shorter plans. We demonstrate the straightforward integration of different kinds of knowledge for causal, temporal and resource knowledge as well as knowledge provided by an external path planner. The resulting online planner, CHIMP, is integrated in a plan-based robot control system and is demonstrated to physically guide a PR2 robot.

Keywords: Robot planning · Hierarchical task networks · Cognitive robotics

1 Introduction

Robot task planning has to be hybrid, i.e., span over temporal, spatial, and resource reasoning, in addition to task sequence and condition achievement. Consider a waiter robot as used as the demo example throughout the paper (Fig. 1). To serve sugar and a hot coffee, it must reason about the consequences of each action's duration (reasoning about time), explore alternative ways of bringing coffee and sugar considering available resources (reasoning about method decomposition and resources), and obtain a kinematically feasible path (reasoning about space). A solution to each subproblem has to take into account the solutions of the others. In fact, any feasible plan fulfilling the high-level requirements

This work was supported by the EC Seventh Framework Program theme FP7-ICT-2011-7, grant agreement no. 287752.

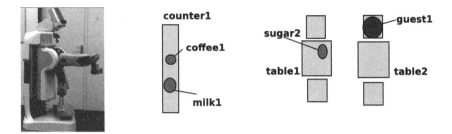

Fig. 1. Demo scenario. Photo: PR2 carrying milk pot and coffee jug. Sketch: Part of the fake restaurant layout and initial situation. Another counter2 is located far away.

(e.g., serve a "hot" coffee) is a solution in the cross-product of the individual search spaces. Note that many of these search spaces correspond to domain-dependent knowledge that varies among different robot platforms. Therefore, as proposed by [8], the different sub-spaces should be integrated in a general way to avoid designing a new integrated algorithm for each new application.

In response to this challenge, we use a meta-CSP approach [8] for achieving hybrid problem solvers. It is based on principles of constraint reasoning and the notion of abstraction through meta-constraints, which represent high-level requirements. However, as casting hybrid robot planning as a meta-CSP means searching for a plan in the cross-product of the different representation sub-spaces (time, space, resources, etc.), a powerful means for guiding the search is needed to keep this feasible. In this paper, we propose to use HTN planning [4] as this means. It focuses dramatically the search through the cross-product search space by its decomposition rules. We show how to integrate HTN planning in a straightforward way in the disguise of a meta-constraint in the meta-CSP; this is done in our new planner CHIMP ("Conflict-driven Hierarchical Meta-CSP Planner"). The resulting plans are hybrid owing to the meta-CSP representation, and they are hierarchical owing to the HTN decomposition structure, which keeps being visible in the final plan representation.

2   Related Work

Integrating HTN planning with other forms of reasoning has been attempted in several ways. ANML [10] is an expressive planning language supporting temporal relations, resource usage, and HTN methods. The first planner to integrate most of ANML, including HTN task decomposition, is the recently introduced planner FAPE [3]. It interleaves deliberative acting, plan repair and re-planning.

Attaching a theory procedurally to a set of symbols (e.g., a task or state) is common practice in combining task and motion planning, and is essential for online planning. Predicates act as interfaces between the discrete space of high-level specification and the continuous space of robot configuration. Many application systems use HTN planning as a means of high-level domain modeling for task planning. [9] interleave geometric planning and HTN-based task planning.

Predicates are shared between the two planners, allowing them to backtrack to a certain level in the joint search space. [5] integrate task and motion planning with a hierarchical planner. It uses the hierarchy not only as a heuristic, but commits to choices at an abstract level and starts to execute parts of the hierarchy without creating a full plan. This assumes that actions are reversible, which is not required by our approach, and it does not include temporal and resource reasoning, and it creates only total-order plans. [6] verifies kinematic feasibility of choices made by HTN planning through geometric backtracking.

While the mentioned approaches aim at integrating specific forms of knowledge, we argue that the problem should be solved in a more general way. Therefore, we extend the work by [8], which casts the problem of reasoning about action into a meta-constraint. Although capable of combining task planning with other forms of reasoning, it does not leverage sophisticated planning heuristics, nor does it provide hierarchical decomposition capabilities in its domain specification language, an issue we address explicitly in this paper.

3   Approach

A meta-CSP [8] is a high-level CSP representing a hybrid problem in different levels of abstraction. Meta-constraints impose high-level requirements on a common constraint network that is called a *ground-CSP*. Parts of this constraint network that do not adhere to these requirements are called *meta-variables*. Meta-variables represent flaws, the resolution of which are *meta-values*, i.e., different ways of resolving a flaw. Meta-constraints and their meta-variables define a *meta-CSP*, i.e., a constraint network at a higher abstraction level.

Therefore, our planner CHIMP uses a constraint-based representation for its state and tasks. This allows CHIMP to impose requirements by adding constraints or variables. Its variables in the ground-CSP are *fluents* that consist of a predicate symbol, a set of symbolic variables, a flexible temporal interval, within which the predicate evaluates to **true**, and a function that indicates the fluent's use of reusable resources. We distinguish state fluents and task fluents. They can be bound by three types of constraints: temporal, binding and causal constraints. We use convex relations in Allen's Interval Algebra (IA) [1,7] as temporal constraints. Binding constraints restrict the domain of symbolic variables of fluents. They are used to ground methods and operators. Causal constraints represent the causal relations of the resulting plan. For details we refer to [11].

To do HTN planning in the meta-CSP approach, we represent standard HTN task decomposition as a meta-constraint. Its meta-variables are the set of unplanned task fluents with no unplanned predecessors. These conflicts get resolved either by applying an operator or method to the unplanned task, or by unifying the unplanned task to a previously planned task fluent. In both cases additional constraints or variables are added to the ground-CSP. As usual in the meta-CSP approach, propagation in the underlying constraint networks is applied. If this leads to an inconsistency in one of those constraint networks, we backtrack.

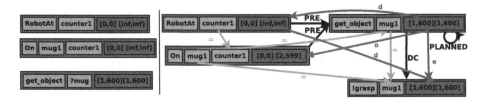

Fig. 2. Left: Constraint network of the initial situation. Predicates and variables of a fluent are green, time intervals are red. Right: Result of applying a method. Causal constraints are black, binding constraints are green and temporal constraints are red.

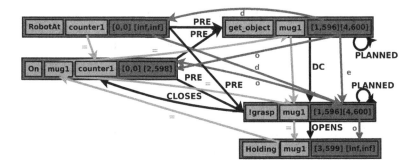

Fig. 3. Result of applying a method and an operator.

Fig. 2, left, shows an example. The constraint network consists of two fluents representing the initial situation (the robot is at counter 1 and mug 1 is on counter 1) and a fluent for the task of getting some mug. Applying a method to get_object results in the right constraint network of Fig. 2. The method connects the RobotAt and On fluents as preconditions to the task fluent. This adds binding and temporal constraints, too, by which the symbolic variables of the get_object fluent are ground. Furthermore, the new task fluent !grasp is created and connected to get_object with a decomposition relation (dc) and temporal and binding constraints. As the robot is already at counter 1, the task get_object is decomposed to the single subtask !grasp. If the robot were at a different position, another method that involves driving would be used.

Next, we can apply an operator to the fluent !grasp (cf. Fig. 3). Analogously to the previous method, it adds constraints for the preconditions. The fluent On is a negative effect of grasping. Therefore, the causal relation closes is added. As a positive effect the robot is now Holding mug 1. The finish times of both effects are updated according to the temporal relations they have with the operator.

Fig. 4 gives an example for unifying a task to a task that was already planned. There are two goal tasks for getting mugs: one for mug 1 and another for mug 2. Initially, the conflict is the second task for driving, which is unplanned. This can be resolved by adding a unification constraint to the other driving tasks that has already been planned. This way the second drive need not be decomposed.

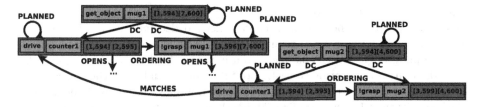

Fig. 4. Constraint network after unifying the tasks for driving. The Binding and temporal constraints and preconditions and effects are omitted for simplicity.

Whereas the HTN approach as such provides a very powerful means to reduce the search space, choosing appropriate value-ordering heuristics is important. The value-ordering heuristic used in our scenario favors, first, unification of tasks; second, a low number of subtasks; and third, binding preconditions to fluents with a late starting time. Details of this are out of the scope of this paper.

An advantage of the meta-CSP approach is that we can enforce other kinds of high-level requirements by adding further meta-constraints. In our demonstration scenario it is important for the robot to estimate the time it takes to drive from one area to another to make sure that tasks that have a deadline will not take too long. This depends on the restaurant layout itself but also objects like unforeseen chairs that block the robot's path. An appropriate source for this kind of knowledge is the robot's path planner. Therefore, a meta-constraint is created whose meta-variables are tasks of type !move_base for which no duration was assigned. Such a conflict is resolved by setting its expected duration based on a the distance between the start and goal poses calculated by the robot's path planner by way of procedural attachment.

Resource reasoning becomes crucial when generating partial-order plans. To ensure resource feasibility a meta-constraint is added like in [8], who use a precedence constraint posting method as proposed by [2].

4   Performance Example

We demonstrate our approach in the restaurant scenario shown in Fig. 1. Our robot gets the goal task of serving a coffee to guest 1, The latest finish time is set to 600 sec. to make sure that the coffee is served hot. Serving a coffee implies that a sugar pot and a milk jug have to be on the table, too. We model this requirement as subtasks in the method for serving coffee.

The initial situation has two sugar pots, one on counter 2 and one on table 1. The only milk jug is on counter 1. Standard HTN planning could create a plan that involves driving to counter 2 in the kitchen to get the sugar. This is causally feasible, but the guest would get served cold coffee. As CHIMP is aware of time, it notices that this plan takes too long, i.e., is temporally infeasible. Therefore, it tries alternative HTN methods that lead to using the other sugar from table 2.

An estimate of the expected duration of driving is added to the constraint network as a meta-value posted by the meta-constraint encapsulating the path planner (see previous section). This duration accounts for the actual restaurant layout and provokes the search to choose method decompositions that do not conflict with the temporal requirement. This is but one example of other kinds of external knowledge that the planner can use, thanks to the meta-CSP approach.

A domain representation consisting of 11 operators and 28 methods was used. After sending the goal to the robot, it generated a plan containing 39 operators, of which Listing 4.1 shows the first 8 with their predicates and flexible temporal intervals in milliseconds. The time points indicate that the plan is partially ordered, e.g., !move_torso and !tuck_arms have the same earliest start time, and both arms may be moved to the side in parallel. By using resource constraints we made sure that it can only manipulate one object at a time, as the robot has to look at the object. Therefore, it picks up coffee 1 after picking up milk 1. In the remainder of the plan the robot completes the goal task, using sugar 2 from table 1. Note that the domain contained no methods for moving multiple objects. The planner used its partial-order planning capability and the task unification to already planned tasks for interleaving the tasks of moving the coffee and the milk. As a result of its limited holding capacity it was planned to bring the sugar after the first two objects.

The complete plan-based execution cycle was run on a physical PR2 robot. CHIMP's planning time was 20.5 seconds. For plan execution, a time-line based dispatching approach was employed. The constraint network is permanently updated as the time proceeds and actions are finished. An action is dispatched as soon as its earliest start time is less than the robot's time. For details about the integration on the real robot and an evaluation of the runtime for various demo problems we refer to [11], which also describes how plans for additional goal tasks can be merged online into an existing plan that is being executed.

```
!move_base(preMAreaECnt1)         [12,   464970], [30012, 494970]
!move_torso(TorsoUpPosture)       [30013, 498972], [34013, 502972]
!tuck_arms(UnTucked UnTucked)     [30013, 494971], [34013, 498971]
!move_arm_to_side(lArm1)          [34014, 498972], [38014, 502972]
!move_arm_to_side(rArm1)          [34014, 498972], [38014, 502972]
!move_straight(mAreaEastCnt1)     [38015, 502973], [42015, 506973]
!pick_up_object(milk1 rArm1)      [42016, 506974], [46016, 510974]
!pick_up_object(coffee1 lArm1)    [46016, 510974], [50016, 514974]
```

Listing 4.1. First 8 operators of the plan for serving a hot coffee with milk and sugar.

5   Conclusion and Outlook

We have presented the hierarchical hybrid planner CHIMP that combines the advantages of HTN planning and meta-CSP reasoning; and have integrated it on a physical PR2 robot. With HTN task decomposition as a meta-Constraint it employs a powerful tool to restrict the huge hybrid search space – a part that was lacking in the meta-CSP approach. It produces partial-order plans with actions that can be executed in parallel. This and the sharing of subtasks may lead to shorter plans without the need of modeling further HTN methods.

More kinds of knowledge may be introduced by attaching further meta-Constraints. We demonstrated this by example of an external path planner; we will extend it with spatial knowledge as done in [8]. In other future work we will investigate means for repairing parts of the plan and we will explore value ordering heuristics for meta-values in more detail.

References

1. Allen, J.: Towards a general theory of action and time. Artif. Intell. **23**(2), 123–154 (1984)
2. Cesta, A., Oddi, A., Smith, S.F.: A constraint-based method for project scheduling with time windows. Journal of Heuristics **8**(1), 109–136 (2002)
3. Dvorak, F., Bit-Monnot, A., Ingrand, F., Ghallab, M.: A flexible ANML actor and planner in robotics. In: Proc. of Planning and Robotics Workshop at ICAPS (2014)
4. Erol, K., Hendler, J., Nau, D.: HTN Planning: complexity and expressivity. In: Proc. AAAI, pp. 1123–1128 (1994)
5. Kaelbling, L.P., Lozano-Pérez, T.: Hierarchical planning in the now. In: IEEE Conference on Robotics and Automation (ICRA) (2011)
6. Lagriffoul, F., Dimitrov, D., Saffiotti, A., Karlsson, L.: Constraint propagation on interval bounds for dealing with geometric backtracking. In: Proc. of IEEE/RSJ Int'l Conf. on Intelligent Robots and Systems (2012)
7. Ligozat, G.: A new proof of tractability for ORD-Horn relations. In: AAAI Workshop on Spatial and Temporal Reasoning (1996)
8. Mansouri, M., Pecora, F.: More knowledge on the table: Planning with space, time and resources for robots. In: IEEE International Conference on Robotics and Automation (ICRA) (2014)
9. de Silva, L., Pandey, A.K., Alami, R.: An interface for interleaved symbolic-geometric planning and backtracking. In: IROS. IEEE (2013)
10. Smith, D.E., Cushing, W.: The ANML language. In: Proc. of the Scheduling and Planning Applications Workshop at ICAPS (2008)
11. Stock, S., Mansouri, M., Pecora, F., Hertzberg, J.: Online task merging with a hierarchical hybrid task planner for mobile service robots. In: Proc. IEEE/RSJ Int'l Conf. on Intelligent Robots and Systems (IROS) (2015) (in press)

Towards Episodic Memory Support for Dementia Patients by Recognizing Objects, Faces and Text in Eye Gaze

Takumi Toyama[✉] and Daniel Sonntag

DFKI GmbH, Saarbrücken, Germany
takumi.toyama@dfki.de

Abstract. Humans forget events or certain types of information sometimes even when the information is important. There are patients who suffer from diseases such as dementia that result in memory loss. Using an eye tracker and image analysis modules, we develop a system that recognizes everyday objects, faces and text that the user looks at. This system can be effectively used to support an individual user's memory by logging certain types of everyday information that the user perceives and tries to organize in his or her memory. We present a technical implementation of an episodic memory support.

1 Introduction

Worldwide, there are more than 24 million people living with some form of dementia that results in memory loss, such as Alzheimer's disease [8]. For these people, it is hard to recall a certain type of information, e.g., names of family members, what they have had for breakfast, etc. These types of memory disorder result in loss of *episodic memory* [15], in particular, which accounts for our memory of specific events and experiences that can be associated with contextual information. Towards compensating such mental disorder, our goal is to provide the user with episodic memory augmentations by using AI technologies.

Autobiographical events (times, places, associated emotions, and other contextual who, what, when, where, why knowledge) that can be explicitly stated constitute information fragments for which a prosthetic memory organization would be needed. A major question concerns the recall of only useful information along the thought process of the individual (and not to slow it down).

For everyday memory support, we aim to develop a system that can recognize everyday visual content that the user gazes at and construct an episodic memory database entry of the event[1]. The episodic memory database is used to save and retrieve the user's personal episodic memory events. As an initial step for such a system, we present a method for recognition of everyday objects, faces, and text that the user looks at. For this, we combine a wearable eye tracking system with image analysis modules. More specifically, we prioritize the eye gaze information

---

[1] https://vimeo.com/132704158

© Springer International Publishing Switzerland 2015
S. Hölldobler et al. (Eds.): KI 2015, LNAI 9324, pp. 316–323, 2015.
DOI: 10.1007/978-3-319-24489-1_29

extracted from the eye tracker in order to recognize the visual contents in the video. By applying multiple recognition modules in parallel, we recognize the visual content of different categories (objects, faces, and text). The recognition result is stored in the database, which is later used to be retrieved by the user (or the system).

2 Related Work

Several systems were presented towards everyday memory aid. For example, a video diary system was presented by Kawamura et al. [7] in which they provided a framework for retrieving the user's location and object from his or her egocentric view. Lee and Dey have shown the potential of life-logging systems for providing memory cues for episodic memory impairment [9]. Orlosky et al. presented a system that can help the user for context recognition and recall in a reading scenario by using an eye tracker and a head-mounted display (HMD) [12]. A system for augmenting facial memory was presented by Iwamura et al. [6].

For human-computer interaction (HCI), eye gaze input is often used to infer where in a scene the user's region-of-interest exists. This information can be effectively used to recognize the object that the user gives attention to [14,18]. Recently, there has also been considerable interest in the potential of eye gaze for sensing people's everyday activities, see for example [2,5]. Furthermore, eye gaze in Intelligent User Interfaces opens the way to design novel attention-based intelligent user interfaces. Attention and salience are of particular interest to generalize the identification of key objects in special activities. A new interesting direction is the combination with bio-inspired vision systems [20].

Towards HCI and memory compensation, to support older adults and help them cope with the changes of aging, in particular with cognitive decline, and automation as caregiver, see the work of [4,13,16] as well as opportunities and challenges for human factors engineering according to the dramatic changes that are taking place in the demographic structure [3].

3 Approach

Eye Tracking Apparatus. To apply the memory aid system to everyday various situations, we need to have a wearable eye tracking device. Recently, wearable eye trackers have become very light-weight and robust. In Figure 1, we show examples of wearable eye tracking devices (SMI Eye Tracking Glasses (ETG) and PupilLabs Eyetracker). Using this type of eye tracker, we extract the user's gaze position and the scene image, which are later used to recognize the visual content that the user gazes at.

Local Gaze Region Cropping. In order to remove irrelevant information in the scene image and to recognize only the content that is currently being focused by the user, we crop a local gaze region from the entire scene image. In the bottom of Figure 1, an example of the cropping process is shown. As shown in this example,

Fig. 1. Wearable eye trackers. Left) PupilLabs Eyetracker, Right) SMI ETG with Brother AirScouter (HMD), Middle) Scene camera image, and Bottom) Cropped local gaze region.

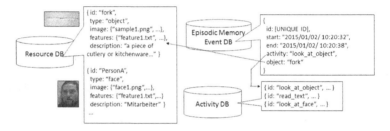

Fig. 2. Three databases.

background (irrelevant) objects and faces are excluded from recognition. We crop a local gaze region with a fixed window size ($l_{width} \times l_{height}$). Based on initial recognition test and previous work by [18], we tune the window size for individual image analysis modules, i.e., 320×240 for object recognition, 640×480 for face recognition, and 320×160 for text recognition, which give a good balance for system recall and precision.

Databases. We use three different databases for our episodic memory support system as shown in Figure 2. In the *resource database*, we store the information of resources (objects and faces) including IDs (e.g., "object:fork", "face:PersonA", etc.), descriptions, and image features. The *activity database* stores the information about everyday activities. From this activity database, the system retrieves how to describe an event for each recognized visual content. For example, the type of event that the user reads textual descriptions of a pill case can be represented by "read_text". We would extend this activity database for storing more complex episodic events in the future; however, we only use three primitive activities ("look_at_faces", "look_at_object", and "read_text") in this paper for the sake of simplicity. Finally, we have the *episodic memory event database* which stores

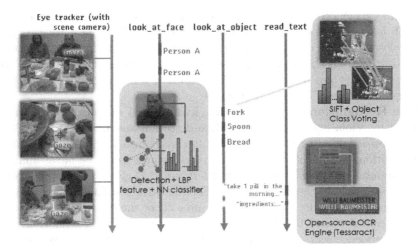

Fig. 3. The recognition modules.

all the recognized events. When any visual content is recognized by the system, the event information is added in the event database; the event entry consists of the beginning and end time, resource ID, and activity ID: e.g., [2015/01/02 10:20:32:345, 2015/01/02 10:20:38:706, "object:fork", "look_at_object"].

For retrieval of previous events, our current investigations include case-based reasoning: CBR is used for detecting scenarios where a patient would need help or the scenarios where the patient has to be reminded of some important activity, such as taking medicines [11]. All the scenarios are modeled as event sequences and stored as cases in CBR. The user would be able to see real life events that he or she has forgotten as something that was really experienced - either video sequences or pictures from the individual memory can be projected into the user's field of view [12].

Recognition of Objects, Faces, and Text. We recognize everyday visual content that the user gaze at by running three different recognition modules in parallel as shown in Figure 3. The three modules are: local feature-based object recognition, face recognition, and text recognition. The recognition modules used here have already shown the feasibilities in combination with a mobile eye tracker in individual recognition scenarios such as [18] and [17]. They respectively correspond to the activity entries: "look_at_object", "look_at_face", and "read_text". Each recognition module calculates the confidence score of the recognition, which is used to reject less confident recognition results, i.e., if the confidence score is less than a threshold value, the result is rejected.

- **Local Feature-based Object Recognition**: We use Scale-invariant features transform (SIFT) [10] for object recognition. First, from the images in the resource database, we extract SIFT features for individual objects. When a new local gaze region image (query image) is provided from the eye tracker, the system extracts SIFT features from the query image and retrieve the closest SIFT feature vector (using the Euclidean distance) in the database. Then, the closest feature cast a vote for the recognition result. The one collects the majority votes is the final recognition result. To calculate the confidence score c_{obj}, the votes are normalized to have norm 1 and the highest value is the confidence score of recognition result.

- **Face Recognition**: We use Haar-like features and cascaded AdaBoost proposed by Viola and Jones [19] for face detection and LBP features [1] with a nearest-neighbour (NN) method for face recognition. Similar to the object recognition, we first save the LBP image features from the facial images in the resource database. Then, a new query image is given, the system extracts the closest face to the gaze position. For the extracted facial image, we compute the LBP feature vector. The resource ID of the closest (in terms of the Euclidean distance) facial LBP vector is returned as the recognition result. The confidence score c_{fac} is calculated by the inverse value of the Euclidean distance to the closest LBP feature vector.

- **Text Recognition**: For text recognition, we use an open-source library called *Tesseract*[2]. The cropped local gaze region image is directly sent to the Tesseract recognition engine. Because the center of the local image is the gaze position, we take the word which is the closest to the center as the gazed text. To filter out noisy recognition results, we search for the recognized word in a *word dictionary*. In this work, we used an English dictionary which contains 10,000 everyday words. The Levenshtein distance is used to calculate the similarity between the recognized word and words in the dictionary (standard approach). The closest word in terms of the Levenshtein distance is returned as the recognition result. The confidence score c_{tex} is given by multiplication of the confidence score provided by the Tesseract and the Levenshtein distance.

4   Preliminary Experiment

We conduct an experiment to evaluate the performance of the proposed recognition system to understand the principles that should control the way information is stored and retrieved from the episodic memory database. For the evaluation, we recorded gaze data with scene image videos in a particular everyday scenario, which we call a 'breakfast' scenario. To evaluate the proposed recognition system in an everyday scenario, we recorded gaze and scene image videos where the wearer had breakfast with four other participants.

Setup. We prepared a breakfast table where we placed objects of 21 different categories as shown in Figure 4. One participant wore the SMI ETG and sat at the table. Other two participants sat at the other side and the other two participants sat at the left side of the table. To record natural eye gaze data and the video images, we only asked the participants to enjoy the breakfast as they normally do. During the recording, they talked naturally and the wearer

---

[2] https://code.google.com/p/tesseract-ocr/

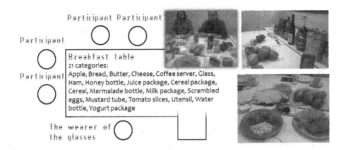

Fig. 4. The setup for the breakfast scenario.

of the glasses was allowed to eat and drink whatever he wants. We recorded an 8 minute video with eye gaze data and applied the recognition of objects and faces. To test the text recognition as well, we recorded additional video sequences (after having breakfast) where the users read labels written on a pill box (intake management after meal).

Results. To distinguish the objects and faces that the wearer actually gazed at from those that the user only glanced at, we set that 10 frames was the minimum duration for labeling, i.e., we labeled the objects and faces that the wearer looked at more than 10 frames. The goal of recognition was to recognize those actually gazed objects and faces.

The wearer gazed at the faces of participants 46 times in total. The recall and the precision of the face recognition was 90.9% and 91.5%, respectively. Overall, the face recognition performed quite well because we always had similar distances to the faces and viewing perspectives. On the other hand, we found that the object recognition failed for some objects such as cheese, utensils, and glass where we cannot extract many SIFT features (For these objects, the number of extracted features within a local region was normally less than 20). With the best case (among different threshold values), we had 37.1% of recall and 70.2% of precision. We also tested the text recognition when the wearer read labels on a pill case. If the letter size in the image is too small (less than 30 pixels), it could not recognize the text at all. If the size is large enough (approx. more than 40 pixels), it could recognize the text relatively good (79.7% accuracy). Thus, though it is not feasible to recognize small characters, it would be sufficient for large text such as one written on a poster.

5   Conclusion

Towards constructing episodic memory event database of the user, we developed a method for recognition of the visual content that the user gazes at in an everyday scenario. Though the face recognition showed robustness, we still have to improve object recognition in natural environments. In future work, we will use an HMD (as shown in Figure 1) to present the information of previous events or recognized objects to the user to further evaluate the presented technical implementation of episodic memory along the thought-process of the user.

References

1. Ahonen, T., Hadid, A., Pietikainen, M.: Face Description with Local Binary Patterns: Application to Face Recognition. IEEE Transactions on Pattern Analysis and Machine Intelligence **28**, 2037–2041 (2006)
2. Bulling, A., Roggen, D., Tröster, G.: Wearable EOG goggles: Seamless sensing and context-awareness in everyday environments. Journal of Ambient Intelligence and Smart Environments **1**, 157–171 (2009)
3. Czaja, S.J., Sharit, J.: The aging of the population: Opportunities and challenges for human factors engineering. The Bridge: Linking Engineering and Society **39**(1), 34–40 (2009)
4. Haigh, K.Z., Yanco, H.: Automation as caregiver: a survey of issues and technologies. In: AAAI-02 Workshop on Automation as Caregiver: The Role of Intelligent Technology in Elder Care, pp. 39–53 (2002)
5. Ishiguro, Y., Mujibiya, A., Miyaki, T., Rekimoto, J.: Aided eyes: eye activity sensing for daily life. In: The 1st Augmented Human International Conference (AH 2010), pp. 1–7 (2010)
6. Iwamura, M., Kunze, K., Kato, Y., Utsumi, Y., Kise, K.: Haven't we met before? A realistic memory assistance system to remind you of the person in front of you. In: Proceedings of the 5th Augmented Human International Conference (AH 2014) (2014)
7. Kawamura, T., Kono, Y., Kidode, M.: Wearable interfaces for a video diary: towards memory retrieval, exchange, and transportation. In: Proceedings of the Sixth International Symposium on Wearable Computers, (ISWC 2002), pp. 31–38 (2002)
8. Label, L.: Dementia Facts and Statistics (2009). http://www.disabled-world.com/health/aging/dementia/statistics.php
9. Lee, M.L., Dey, A.K.: Lifelogging memory appliance for people with episodic memory impairment. In: Proceedings of the 10th International Conference on Ubiquitous Computing - UbiComp 2008, vol. 344, p. 44 (2008)
10. Lowe, D.: Object recognition from local scale-invariant features. In: Proceedings of the Seventh IEEE International Conference on Computer Vision, vol. 2 (1999)
11. Marling, C., Whitehouse, P.: Case-based reasoning in the care of alzheimers disease patients. In: Case-Based Reasoning Research and Development, vol. 208, pp. 702–715 (2001)
12. Orlosky, J., Toyama, T., Sonntag, D., Kiyokawa, K.: Using eye-gaze and visualization to augment memory. In: Streitz, N., Markopoulos, P. (eds.) DAPI 2014. LNCS, vol. 8530, pp. 282–291. Springer, Heidelberg (2014)
13. Pollack, M.E.: Intelligent Technology for an Aging Population: The Use of AI to Assist Elders with Cognitive Impairment. Ai Magazine **26**, 9–24 (2005)
14. Qvarfordt, P., Zhai, S.: Conversing with the user based on eye-gaze patterns. In: Proceedings of the SIGCHI Conference on Human Factors in Computing Systems - CHI 2005, p. 221 (2005)
15. Simons, J.S., Graham, K.S., Galton, C.J., Patterson, K., Hodges, J.R.: Semantic knowledge and episodic memory for faces in semantic dementia. Neuropsychology **15**(1), 101–114 (2001)

16. Sonntag, D.: Collaborative multimodality. KI-Künstliche Intelligenz **26**(2), 161–168 (2012)
17. Sonntag, D., Toyama, T.: On-body IE: a head-mounted multimodal augmented reality system for learning and recalling faces. In: Proceedings of the 9th International Conference on Intelligent Environments (IE 2013), pp. 151–156. IEEE, Atgens (2013)
18. Toyama, T., Kieninger, T., Shafait, F., Dengel, A.: Gaze guided object recognition using a head-mounted eye tracker. In: Proceedings of the Symposium on Eye Tracking Research and Applications - ETRA 2012, pp. 91–98 (2012)
19. Viola, P., Jones, M.: Robust Real-Time Face Detection. International Journal of Computer Vision **57**, 137–154 (2004)
20. Zillich, M., Krüger, N.: Special issue on bio-inspired vision systems. KI **29**(1), 5–7 (2015)

Deriving a Primal Form for the Quadratic Power Kernel

Tim vor der Brück$^{(\boxtimes)}$ and Steffen Eger$^{(\boxtimes)}$

Text Technology Lab, Goethe Universität Frankfurt am Main, Frankfurt, Germany
{vorderbr,steeger}@em.uni-frankfurt.de

Abstract. Support vector machines (SVMs) have become a very popular machine learning method for text classification. One reason for their popularity is the possibility of using different types of kernels, which makes them very flexible and allows for dividing data sets that are not linearly separable. This paper shows a method how the primal form of the quadratic power kernel can be derived by using complex numbers. The paper also describes an application of this kernel to text categorization following the Dewey Document Classification (DDC) scheme. In our evaluation, the power kernel (PK) led to a competitive f-measure to those of the compared kernels and was faster to compute than all but the linear kernel.

1 Introduction

SVMs have become a very popular machine learning method for text classification. One reason for their popularity is the possibility of using different types of kernels. This paper derives a decomposition of the quadratic PK with complex numbers and describes an application for this kernel for document classification. In our evaluation, the PK led to a similar f-measure as those of the compared kernels and was faster to compute than all but the linear kernel. The application part of the paper is related to text classification employing the Dewey Document Classification scheme [5].

The decision function of an SVM [10] is given by $dc : \mathbb{R}^n \to \{1, 0, -1\}$, which assigns a given vector to the predicted class: $dc(\mathbf{x}) := \text{sgn}(\langle \mathbf{w}, \mathbf{x} \rangle + b)$ where sgn : $\mathbb{R} \to \{1, 0, -1\}$ is the signum function and the vector $\mathbf{w}$ as well as the constant b are determined by the SV optimization.

The decision function above is specified in the so-called primal form. It can be converted into the equivalent dual form: $dc(\mathbf{x}) = \text{sgn}(\sum_{j=1}^{m} y_j \alpha_j \langle \mathbf{x}, \mathbf{x}_j \rangle + b)$ where α_j and b are constants determined by the SV optimization and m is the number of SVs, since the previously unseen vector (the vector to classify) must only be compared with the SVs $\mathbf{x}_j$. The vectors that are located on the wrong side of the hyperplane, i.e., the vectors which prevent a perfect fit of the SV optimization, are also considered as SVs. Thus, the number of SVs can be quite large. The scalar product, which is used to estimate a similarity value between feature vectors, can be generalized to a kernel function. A kernel function K is a similarity function between two vectors or datasets where the matrix of kernel

© Springer International Publishing Switzerland 2015
S. Hölldobler et al. (Eds.): KI 2015, LNAI 9324, pp. 324–330, 2015.
DOI: 10.1007/978-3-319-24489-1_30

values is symmetric and positive semidefinite. The decision function for a kernel-based SVM is given in the dual form by: $dc(\mathbf{x}) := \text{sgn}(\sum_{j=1}^{m} y_j \alpha_j K(\mathbf{x}, \mathbf{x}_j) + b)$. Let $\Phi : \mathbb{R}^n \to \mathbb{R}^l$ be a function that transforms a vector into another vector space (often higher dimensional) and chosen in such a way that the kernel function can be represented by: $K(\mathbf{x}_1, \mathbf{x}_2) = \langle \Phi(\mathbf{x}_1), \Phi(\mathbf{x}_2) \rangle$. With that, the decision function in the primal form is given by: $dc(\mathbf{x}) := \text{sgn}(\langle \mathbf{w}, \Phi(\mathbf{x}) \rangle + b)$.

Note that the function Φ might convert the data into very high dimensional space. In this case, the dual form should be used for the optimization process as well as for the classification of previously unseen data. One might think that the primal form is not needed. However, the primal form has one important advantage. If the normal vector of the hyperplane is known, the classification of a previously unseen vector can be accomplished just by applying the signum function, the function Φ and one scalar multiplication. This is often much faster than computing the kernel function for the previously unseen vector and each SV, which is required for classifying a previously unseen vector with the dual form. The most popular kernel is the scalar product, also called the linear kernel. In this case, the transformation function Φ is the identity: $K_{lin}(\mathbf{x}_1, \mathbf{x}_2) := \langle \mathbf{x}_1, \mathbf{x}_2 \rangle$. A further popular kernel function is the RBF, given by: $K_r(\mathbf{x}_1, \mathbf{x}_2) := e^{-\gamma ||\mathbf{x}_1 - \mathbf{x}_2||^2}$ where $\gamma \in \mathbb{R}$, $\gamma > 0$ is a constant that has to be manually specified. In the primal form, this kernel function can be represented by a function Φ_r that transforms the argument vector into infinite dimensional space [8, p.47].

2 The Power Kernel

The PK is a conditionally positive definite kernel and is given by $K_s(\mathbf{x}_1, \mathbf{x}_2) := -||\mathbf{x}_1 - \mathbf{x}_2||^p$ for some $p \in \mathbb{R}$ [2, 6, 9]. A kernel is called conditionally positive-definite if it is symmetric and satisfies [8]

$$\sum_{j,k=1}^{n} c_i \overline{c_j} K(\mathbf{x}_j, \mathbf{x}_k) \geq 0 \; \forall c_i \in \mathbb{K} \text{ with } \sum_{i=1}^{m} c_i = 0 \tag{1}$$

and $\overline{c_j}$ is the complex-conjugate of c_j. We consider here a generalized form of the PK for $p := 2$ with $K_{pow}(\mathbf{x}_1, \mathbf{x}_2) := -a||\mathbf{x}_1 - \mathbf{x}_2||^2 + c$ with $a, c \in \mathbb{R}$ and $a > 0$. The expression $-a||\mathbf{x}_1 - \mathbf{x}_2||^2 + c$ can also be written as: $-a\langle (\mathbf{x}_1 - \mathbf{x}_2), (\mathbf{x}_1 - \mathbf{x}_2) \rangle + c = -a(\langle \mathbf{x}_1, \mathbf{x}_1 \rangle - 2\langle \mathbf{x}_1, \mathbf{x}_2 \rangle + \langle \mathbf{x}_2, \mathbf{x}_2 \rangle) + c$. For deciding which class a previously unseen vector belongs to we can use the decision function in the dual form:

$$dc(\mathbf{x}) := \text{sgn}(\sum_{j=1}^{m} y_j \alpha_j K_{pow}(\mathbf{x}, \mathbf{x}_j) + b) = \text{sgn}(\sum_{j=1}^{m} y_j \alpha_j (-a||\mathbf{x} - \mathbf{x_j}||^2 + c) + b)$$

$$\tag{2}$$

The decision function shown in formula (2) has the drawback that the previously unseen vector has to be compared with each SV, which can be quite time consuming. This can be avoided, if we reformulate formula (2) to:

$$dc(\mathbf{x}) = \text{sgn}(\sum_{j=1}^{m} y_j\alpha_j(-a\langle\mathbf{x},\mathbf{x}\rangle + 2a\langle\mathbf{x},\mathbf{x}_j\rangle - a\langle\mathbf{x}_j,\mathbf{x}_j\rangle + c) + b)$$

$$= \text{sgn}(-a\langle\mathbf{x},\mathbf{x}\rangle \sum_{j=1}^{m} y_j\alpha_j + 2\langle\mathbf{x}, a\sum_{j=1}^{m} y_j\alpha_j\mathbf{x}_j\rangle \tag{3}$$

$$-a\sum_{j=1}^{m} y_j\alpha_j\langle\mathbf{x}_j,\mathbf{x}_j\rangle + c\sum_{i=1}^{m} y_j\alpha_j + b)$$

With $\mathbf{z} := a\sum_{j=1}^{m} y_j\alpha_j\mathbf{x}_j$, $\mathbf{u} := a\sum_{j=1}^{m} y_j\alpha_j\langle\mathbf{x}_j,\mathbf{x}_j\rangle$ and $c' = c\sum_{i=1}^{m} y_j\alpha_j$, formula (3) can be rewritten as:

$dc(\mathbf{x}) = \text{sgn}(-a\langle\mathbf{x},\mathbf{x}\rangle \sum_{i=1}^{m} y_j\alpha_j + 2\langle\mathbf{x},\mathbf{z}\rangle - \mathbf{u} + c' + b)$. The expressions $\mathbf{u}$, $\mathbf{z}$, $(\sum_{i=1}^{m} y_j\alpha_j)$, and c' are identical for every vector $\mathbf{x}$ and can be precomputed. Note that there exists no primal form for the PK based on real number vectors which is stated by the following proposition.

Proposition 1. Let $a,c \in \mathbb{R}$ with $a > 0$ and $n, l \in \mathbb{N}$. Then there is no function $\Phi_{re} : \mathbb{R}^n \to \mathbb{R}^l$ (re indicates that Φ_{re} operates on real numbers) with $\langle\Phi_{re}(\mathbf{x}_1), \Phi_{re}(\mathbf{x}_2)\rangle = -a||\mathbf{x}_1 - \mathbf{x}_2||^2 + c$ ($\forall\mathbf{x}_1, \mathbf{x}_2 \in \mathbb{R}^n$).

Proof. If such a function existed, then, for all $\mathbf{x} \in \mathbb{R}^n$,

$$||\Phi_{re}(\mathbf{x})||^2 = \langle\Phi_{re}(\mathbf{x}), \Phi_{re}(\mathbf{x})\rangle = -a \cdot 0 + c = c$$

which requires that $c \geq 0$ since the square of a real number cannot be negative. Now, consider $\mathbf{x}, \mathbf{y} \in \mathbb{R}^n$ with $||\mathbf{x} - \mathbf{y}||^2 > \frac{2c}{a} \geq 0$. On the one hand, we have, by the Cauchy-Schwartz inequality,

$$|\langle\Phi_{re}(\mathbf{x}), \Phi_{re}(\mathbf{y})\rangle| \leq ||\Phi_{re}(\mathbf{x})|| \cdot ||\Phi_{re}(\mathbf{y})|| = \sqrt{c} \cdot \sqrt{c} = c.$$

On the other hand, it holds that

$$|\langle\Phi_{re}(\mathbf{x}), \Phi_{re}(\mathbf{y})\rangle| = |-a||\mathbf{x} - \mathbf{y}||^2 + c| = |a|\,||\mathbf{x} - \mathbf{y}||^2 - c| > 2c - c = c,$$

a contradiction. ∎

Although no primal form and therefore no function Φ_{re} exists for real number vectors, such a function can be given if complex number vectors are used instead. In this case, the function Φ_c is defined with a real domain and a complex codomain: $\Phi_c : \mathbb{R}^n \to \mathbb{C}^{4n+1}$ and

$$\Phi_c(\mathbf{x}) := (\sqrt{a}(x_1^2 - 1), \sqrt{a}i, \sqrt{2a}x_1, \sqrt{a}ix_1^2, \dots,$$
$$\sqrt{a}(x_n^2 - 1), \sqrt{a}i, \sqrt{2a}x_n, \sqrt{a}ix_n^2, \sqrt{c})^\top. \tag{4}$$

Note that no scalar product can be defined for complex numbers that fulfills the usual conditions of bilinearity and positive-definiteness simultaneously[1]. Thus, the bilinearity condition is dropped for the official definition and only sesquilinearity is required. The standard scalar product is defined as the sum of the products of the vector components with the associated complex conjugated vector components of the other vector. Let $\mathbf{x}_1, \mathbf{x}_2 \in \mathbb{C}^n$, then the scalar product is given by [1]: $\langle \mathbf{x}_1, \mathbf{x}_2 \rangle := \sum_{k=1}^{n} x_{1k}\overline{x_{2k}}$. In contrast, we use a modified scalar product (marked by a "*") where, analogously to the real vector definition, the products of the vector components are summated: $\langle^* \mathbf{x}_1, \mathbf{x}_2 \rangle := \sum_{k=1}^{n} x_{1k}x_{2k}$. This product (not a scalar product in strict mathematical sense) is a bilinear form but no longer positive definite. For real number vectors this modified scalar product is identical to the usual definition. With this modified scalar product we get

$$\langle^* \Phi_c(\mathbf{x}_1), \Phi_c(\mathbf{x}_2) \rangle = -ax_{11}^2 - ax_{21}^2 + 2ax_{11}x_{21} - \cdots - ax_{1n}^2$$
$$-ax_{2n}^2 + 2ax_{1n}x_{2n} + c = -a||\mathbf{x}_1 - \mathbf{x}_2||^2 + c \tag{5}$$

which is just the result of the PK. The SVM model can be determined using the dual form. Thus, no complex number optimization is necessary. For the decision on the class to which a data vector should be assigned we switch to the primal form. The vector $\mathbf{w} \in \mathbb{C}^{4n+1}$ is calculated by: $\mathbf{w} := \sum_{j=1}^{m} \alpha_j y_j \Phi_c(\mathbf{x}_j)$ for all SVs $\mathbf{x}_j \in \mathbb{R}^n$. The decision function is then given by: $dc(\mathbf{x}) := \text{sgn}(\langle^* \mathbf{w}, \Phi_c(\mathbf{x}) \rangle + b)$. Note that the modified scalar product $\langle^* \mathbf{w}, \Phi_c(\mathbf{x}) \rangle$ must be a real number. This is stated in the following proposition.

Proposition 2. Let $\mathbf{w} = \sum_{j=1}^{m} \alpha_j y_j \Phi_c(\mathbf{x}_j)$ with $\mathbf{x}_j \in \mathbb{R}^n$, $\alpha_j \in \mathbb{R}$, $y_j \in \{-1, 1\}$, $j = 1, \cdots, m$, Φ_c as defined in formula (4) and $\mathbf{x} \in \mathbb{R}^n$. Then $\langle^* \mathbf{w}, \Phi_c(\mathbf{x}) \rangle$ is a real number.

Proof. $\langle^* \mathbf{w}, \Phi_c(\mathbf{x}) \rangle$ is given by:

$$\langle^* \mathbf{w}, \Phi_c(\mathbf{x}) \rangle = \langle^* \sum_{j=1}^{m} \alpha_j y_j \Phi_c(\mathbf{x}_j), \Phi_c(\mathbf{x}) \rangle$$

$$= \sum_{j=1}^{m} \langle^* \alpha_j y_j \Phi_c(\mathbf{x}_j), \Phi_c(\mathbf{x}) \rangle \quad (\langle^*.\rangle \text{ is bilinear})$$

$$= \sum_{j=1}^{m} \alpha_j y_j \langle^* \Phi_c(\mathbf{x}_j), \Phi_c(\mathbf{x}) \rangle \tag{6}$$

$$= \sum_{j=1}^{m} \alpha_j y_j (-a||\mathbf{x}_j - \mathbf{x}||^2 + c) \quad (\text{see formula (5)})$$

which is clearly a real number.   ∎

---

[1] This can be verified by a simple calculation: Consider some vector $\mathbf{x} \neq \mathbf{0}$ and $\mathbf{x} \in \mathbb{C}^n$. Since $\langle .,. \rangle$ is positive definite: $\langle \mathbf{x}, \mathbf{x} \rangle > 0$, by bilinearity: $\langle \sqrt{-i}\mathbf{x}, \sqrt{-i}\mathbf{x} \rangle = -i\langle \mathbf{x}, \mathbf{x} \rangle \not> 0$).

The PK is related to the polynomial kernel (PyK) since it can also be represented by a polynomial. However, it has the advantage over the PyK that it is faster to compute and that the number of dimensions in the target space grows only linearly and not exponentially with the number of dimensions in the original space [2,9]. It remains to show that the decision functions following the primal and dual form are also equivalent for the modified form of the scalar product. This is stated in the follow proposition:

Proposition 3. Let $\mathbf{x}, \mathbf{x}_1, \cdots, \mathbf{x}_m \in \mathbb{R}^n$, $\alpha \in \mathbb{R}^m$, $y \in \{-1,1\}^m$, $\mathbf{w} := \sum_{j=1}^m \alpha_j y_j \Phi_c(\mathbf{x}_j)$ and $\langle {}^*\Phi_c(\mathbf{z}_1), \Phi_c(\mathbf{z}_2) \rangle = K(\mathbf{z}_1, \mathbf{z}_2) \; \forall \mathbf{z}_1, \mathbf{z}_2 \in \mathbb{R}^n$. Then $\mathrm{sgn}(\langle {}^*\mathbf{w}, \Phi_c(\mathbf{x}) \rangle + b) = \mathrm{sgn}(\sum_{j=1}^m \alpha_j y_j K(\mathbf{x}, \mathbf{x}_j) + b)$.

$$Proof. \;\; \mathrm{sgn}(\langle {}^*\mathbf{w}, \Phi_c(\mathbf{x}) \rangle + b) = \mathrm{sgn}(\langle {}^*\sum_{j=1}^m \alpha_j y_j \Phi_c(\mathbf{x}_j), \Phi_c(\mathbf{x}) \rangle + b)$$

$$= \mathrm{sgn}(\sum_{j=1}^m \langle {}^*\alpha_j y_j \Phi_c(\mathbf{x}_j), \Phi_c(\mathbf{x}) \rangle + b) \quad (\langle {}^*. \rangle \text{ is bilinear})$$

$$= \mathrm{sgn}(\sum_{j=1}^m \alpha_j y_j \langle {}^*\Phi_c(\mathbf{x}_j), \Phi_c(\mathbf{x}) \rangle + b) = \mathrm{sgn}(\sum_{j=1}^m \alpha_j y_j K(\mathbf{x}_j, \mathbf{x}) + b)$$

$$= \mathrm{sgn}(\sum_{j=1}^m \alpha_j y_j K(\mathbf{x}, \mathbf{x}_j) + b) \qquad (K \text{ is symmetric})$$

(7)

∎

We use the PK for text classification where a text is automatically labeled with its main topics (called categories). The classification scheme we employ is the so-called DDC (Dewey Document Classification), which is the leading classification scheme in libraries [5]. It consists of a three digit number and one decimal position. We classify documents into their appropriate 10 DDC top level categories. For that, a training set is given, where the DDC categories are already annotated. A set of features is then extracted from this training set and these features are afterwards employed by an SVM (here *libsvm* [3]) to assign one or more DDC categories to previously unseen examples. The features of one instance (document) are the geometric means of the tfidf-values of the terms occurring in this document and their GSS coefficients [4,7].

3 Evaluation and Discussion

The evaluation and training was done with 4 000 German documents, containing in total 114 887 606 words and 9 643 022 sentences, requiring a storage space of 823.51MiB. There are 400 documents of each toplevel DDC category. 2 000 of the texts were used for training, 2 000 for evaluation. The corpus originates from the OAI (Open Archive Initiative) and was collected by the Bielefeld University

Library. We tested the correctness of the category assignments for the first DDC level (10 categories). Each document is assigned at least one DDC category. Multiple assignments are also possible. First, precision, recall and f-measure were computed for each OAI category for the PK, the square, the cubic, the RBF kernel and the linear kernel (see Table 1). The free parameters of the square, the cubic and the RBF kernel are determined by a grid search on an independent data set containing 2 000 texts. On the same held-out dataset, we adjusted the SVM-threshold parameter b to optimize the f-measure. Second, the time (on an Intel Core i7) was determined required to obtain the classifications for the PK (primal and dual form), the RBF, square, and linear kernel (see Table 1). The time needed for building the model was not counted, since this time is only required once and therefore irrelevant for the practical document classification task. The f-measure for the PK is higher than the f-measures of all other kernels and is faster to compute than all kernels except the linear (naturally, the classification with the primal form of the linear kernel is faster than the classification with the PK). Furthermore, the complex decomposition of the PK leads to a considerable acceleration of the classification process in comparison with the dual form.

In this paper we derived a primal form for the power kernel with complex numbers. By using complex numbers we can obtain a much simpler and nicer representation than the modified dual form. Although the primary focus of this paper is to contribute to the theory, the obtained results can also be useful in practice. We demonstrated that the primal form and the modified dual form can both speed up the classification process considerably, since it is no longer necessary to compare the vector to be classified with every SV. Finally, the evaluation shows that the f-measure of the PK is competitive to the other evaluated kernels and its runtime superior to that of the PyK (exponent 2 and 3) and the RBF kernel.

Table 1. F-measures and runtime for different kernels evaluated on the OAI corpus.

| C. | F-Measure | | | | | Runtime | | | | | |
	Power	Square	Cubic	RBF	Linear	Power Primal	Power Dual	Square Dual	Cubic Dual	RBF Dual	Lin. Dual
0	**0.810**	0.800	0.803	0.793	0.796	**6 426**	46 200	50 256	50 979	47 246	44 322
1	**0.753**	0.746	0.723	0.726	0.735	**9 339**	98 289	115 992	132 845	122 751	93 550
2	0.869	**0.877**	0.757	0.874	0.875	**5 822**	48 359	57 603	67 200	65 508	46 786
3	0.603	0.594	0.577	**0.621**	0.589	23 774	134 636	165 604	177 211	159 897	111 516
4	**0.653**	0.219	0.057	0.537	0.625	10 103	118 322	77 634	93 613	111 153	103 548
5	0.740	0.700	0.742	0.700	**0.743**	32 501	104 865	72 772	135 820	138 107	96 637
6	0.683	0.685	0.661	0.668	**0.692**	24 375	105 614	116 892	120 919	126 498	95 423
7	**0.710**	0.709	0.652	0.663	0.668	19 206	113 971	122 128	143 562	120 371	100 640
8	0.687	0.674	0.569	0.671	**0.692**	11 236	99 288	106 215	118 378	105 942	84 381
9	**0.726**	0.699	0.478	0.675	0.695	20 822	125 358	139 004	168 837	138 395	111 245
All	**0.723**	0.670	0.602	0.693	0.711	**16 361**	99 490	102 410	120 936	113 587	88 805

Acknowledgments. We thank Vincent Esche, Tom Kollmar and Alexander Mehler for valuable remarks and discussions.

References

1. Beutelsbacher, A.: Lineare Algebra. Vieweg, Braunschweig (2010)
2. Boolchandani, S.D., Sahula, V.: Exploring efficient kernel functions for support vector machine based feasability models for analog circuits. International Journal of Design Analysis and Tools for Circuits and Systems 1(1), 1–8 (2011)
3. Chang, C.-C., Lin, C.-J.: LIBSVM: a library for support vector machines (2001)
4. Joachims, T.: The Maximum Margin Approach to Learning Text Classifiers: Methods, Theory, and Algorithms. Ph.D. thesis, Universität Dortmund, Informatik, LS VIII (2000)
5. OCLC. Dewey decimal classification summaries. a brief introduction to the dewey decimal classification (2012). http://www.oclc.org/dewey/resources/summaries/default.htm (last access August 17, 2012)
6. Sahbi, H., Fleuret, F.: Scale-invariance of support vector machines based on the triangular kernel. Technical Report 4601, Institut National de Recherche en Informatique et an Automatique (2002)
7. Salton, G., Buckley, C.: Term-weighting approaches in automatic text retrieval. Information Processing & Management 25(5), 513–523 (1998)
8. Schölkopf, B., Smola, A.J.: Learning with Kernels - Support Vector Machines, Regularization, Optimization and Beyond. MIT Press, Cambridge (2002)
9. Souza, C.: Kernel functions for machine learning applications (2010). http://crsouza.blogspot.de/2010/03/kernel-functions-for-machine-learning.html
10. Vapnik, V.: Statistical Learning Theory. John Wiley & Sons, New York (1998)

Doctoral Consortium Contributions

Towards an Expert System
for the Field of Neurology Based on Fuzzy Logic

Mirco Josefiok[⊠] and Jürgen Sauer

Carl von Ossietzky Universität Oldenburg,
Ammerländer Heerstraße 114-118, 26129 Oldenburg, Germany
{mirco.josefiok,juergen.sauer}@uni-oldenburg.de
http://www.uni-oldenburg.de/sao

Abstract. Differential diagnoses in the field of neurology are very complex whereas a fast and precise treatment is absolutely necessary for a positive outcome for patients. Support through expert systems has shown to improve practitioners performance in certain areas. In this paper an approach for an expert system for the field of neurology based on fuzzy logic is presented. The client and server side applications, as well as the knowledge base are explained. Furthermore an overview of remaining challenges and issues is given.

Keywords: Expert system · Fuzzy logic · Health care · Neurology

1 Introduction

Finding a valid diagnosis and a subsequent treatment is a very complex process. Especially in that case when multiple differential diagnoses need to be taken into consideration. Finding the right diagnosis is most of the time a lengthy process. In the field of neurology practitioners often need to deal with varying and unclear symptoms and indications, which are sometimes not directly related to the disease being diagnosed. A fast treatment is absolutely necessary and improves a patients outcome significantly.

Whilst it has been shown that support by expert systems could improve performance of practitioners in certain areas, they are usually not used in health care. Reasons for this are for example: lack of transparency of the results, a large and unmaintainable knowledge base, lack of usability and the reliance on crisp rules [2,9].

In this paper we present an approach for an expert system for the field of neurology based on fuzzy logic. The paper is structured as follows. An introduction and motivation is given in Section 1, in Section 2 the related work is presented, the approach for the expert system is presented Section 3 and the paper concludes with a summary in Section 4.

© Springer International Publishing Switzerland 2015
S. Hölldobler et al. (Eds.): KI 2015, LNAI 9324, pp. 333–340, 2015.
DOI: 10.1007/978-3-319-24489-1_31

2   Related Work

In a recent survey we searched PubMed, Mendeley and Google Scholar with the terms *neurology, expert systems, diagnosis support systems, decision support systems* and *healthcare* in various combinations. The survey has been conducted in accordance to the PRISMA (Preferred Reporting Items for Systematic Reviews and Meta-Analyses) statement [16]. We identified more than 15,000 references. After further filtering only seven full text references, actually dealing with diagnosis support systems in neurology, remained [14].

Bunke et al. [6] discuss two different approaches for expert systems in neurology. Their main intention is to compare a rule-based approach with a database approach. Two prototypes have been developed and compared. The authors decide to only implement their expert systems focusing on diagnoses related to the median nerve. They create the necessary rules by using statements like *if condition then conclusion* and using a commercial expert system shell called EXSYS. The authors implement 163 rules and 17 possible diagnoses. The database is created in a similar fashion but using relations. Subsequently the two approaches are compared regarding their response time and accuracy. No details are given on how the knowledge base is created or its validation. Bickel and Grunewald [3] present an expert system for the field of neurology developed on top of the commercial program Filemaker-7.0. They added about 400 diagnoses with their corresponding symptoms. The authors evaluated their approach in two steps. First, the performance was tested with 15 predefined cases. The test persons had minor neurological experience. In that case the program was able to find the correct diagnosis in every time. Second, real cases were used. With real cases a correct diagnosis was found in approximately 80% of the trials. The authors are both practicing physicians and therefore derived the data necessary for the expert system from their daily work and corresponding specialized literature. Vaghefi and Isfahani [18] present an expert system named Roses, developed with the objective to support the diagnostic process of six neurological diseases of children. The knowledge base is modeled by using the Java Expert System Shell (JESS) [10]. In its last incarnation the system suffers from low reliability. Only about 65% correct diagnoses can be made. Another major issue identified during testing, is the need for a graphical user interface, enabling the modification of the knowledge base by users. Reimers and Bitsch [17] develop and distribute an expert system which aims at supporting medical staff in finding a correct diagnosis to a hypothesis. The authors create a comprehensive knowledge base by evaluating specialized literature. Neither information on how the knowledge base is represented nor validation results are given. Borgohain and Sanyal [4,5] present two expert systems which share the same approach but a different knowledge base. Both systems have been created using JESS and therefore do not contain any fuzzy information. The main source for creating the knowledge base for the systems are interviews with doctors and postgraduate students of a nearby hospital. The knowledge base is thereafter extended by using specialized literature and internet research. The systems is evaluated by testing its rule base against a few test cases which have not been further specified. Both systems provide accurate diagnoses when the symptoms were fully given. However, the authors described no practical application experiences or tests with real cases. Ghahazi et al. [11] present an approach for an expert system based on fuzzy logic for diagnosing Multiple Sclerosis. They perform the diagnosis on base of basic patient data, symptoms and signs. They work with crisp inputs which lead to uncertain results. For storing their data they use a spreadsheet. The system is evaluated with multiple test cases from specialized literature and performs well. The integration of a spreadsheet based solution in the daily work flow of medical staff is perceived as problematic.

No references which show or hint at a routine application of any expert system were found for the approaches discovered with our survey. This supports our previous findings [19]. In all cases no considerations regarding user interface, comprehensibility of suggestions, expandability and customizability of knowledge are published. For practitioners in healthcare it is crucial that the results of the expert systems are comprehensible.

3   NeuroRec Approach

The framework conditions for our approach are determined by a theoretical concept and a corresponding business process. Both were developed in close cooperation with experts from the health care domain. The process formalizes how practitioners can be supported by an expert system in their daily routine. Multiple sub-processes specify how case data, meta data and patient data are prepared and provided. The concept is formalized using the Business Process Modelling and Notion (BPMN) [19].

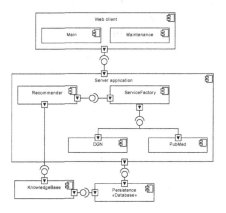

Based on this concept the development of the NeuroRec approach began. The approach itself consists of a knowledge base, a processing component and a metadata provider which fetches additional information in form of literature references etc. from third party services. NeuroRec is implemented as a client–server solution. Figure 1 shows a simplified architecture of the prototypical implementation. The knowledge base, as well as additional data (e.g user information) are stored in a relational database. The implementation is described in more

Fig. 1. NeuroRec Architecture

detail in Section 3.2 and the creation of the knowledge base is described in Section 3.1.

3.1   NeuroRec Knowledge Base

A main requirement derived from various expert interviews is that the rule base should be expandable and maintainable by domain experts. Another very important requirement is that results from the system should transparent and comprehensible [12]. Moreover it is necessary to transform the expert knowledge and knowledge derived from specialist literature into a meaningful knowledge base which can be utilized for an expert system. During the process of defining linguistic variables and basic rules it became obvious that crisp rules are not sufficient for a medical context. Many information can be interpreted in different ways and often there are soft transitions in the classification of symptoms. For example body temperature can be classified as hypothermia, normal, fever, hyperthermia or hyperpyrexia. The exact classification depends on where the temperature has been measured (e.g. anus, oral, arm or ear). Based on these findings we decided to adopt an approach based on fuzzy language. We chose to use Fuzzy Control Language (FCL) as a representation for the knowledge base. FCL was standardized by IEC 61131-7 and different Java implementations exist, eg. jFuzzyLogic [7]. This allows for using the knowledge base in different applications.

The foundation for finding linguistic variables and specifying rules are the guidelines and pathways provided by the DGN. The guidelines are very comprehensive, are constantly extended and reworked and can, in some parts, be interpreted in different ways. But, in cooperation with medical specialists from a local hospital, we are continually expanding the knowledge base.

Listing 1.1 shows a set of rules for the diagnosis of vestibular neuritis. The underlying fuzzy controller takes the symptoms vertigo, tendency to fall, nystagmus, Unterberger test and their classifications as an input. The rules shown in listing 1.1 are derived from these inputs. According to which symptoms and classifications have been determined a quantifiable value, according to the defuzzification method, is calculated. This can be mapped to a linguistic variable which represents a certain probability for a certain diagnosis is given.

```
RULE 1 : IF Drehschwindel IS  ploetzlich AND Fallneigung IS links AND Spontannystagmus IS rechts AND
         Unterbergerversuch IS links THEN Neuritis_vestibularis IS wahrscheinlich;
RULE 2 : IF Drehschwindel IS  ploetzlich AND Fallneigung IS rechts AND Spontannystagmus IS links AND
         Unterbergerversuch IS rechts THEN Neuritis_vestibularis IS wahrscheinlich;
RULE 3 : IF Drehschwindel IS  dauernd AND Fallneigung IS rechts AND Spontannystagmus IS links AND
         Unterbergerversuch IS rechts THEN Neuritis_vestibularis IS moeglich;
RULE 4 : IF Drehschwindel IS  ploetzlich AND Fallneigung IS rechts AND Spontannystagmus IS links THEN
         VestibulaeresSyndrom IS moeglich;
RULE 5 : IF Drehschwindel IS  dauernd AND Fallneigung IS rechts AND Spontannystagmus IS links THEN
         Neuritis_vestibularis IS kaum_moeglich;
```

Listing 1.1. FCL Example for Vestibular neuritis

Usually multiple fuzzy controllers with diagnoses with similar symptoms are used to obtain multiple differential diagnoses. It is then up to the specialists to use the provided metadata and the given differential diagnoses to chose the most reliable diagnosis and a subsequent treatment.

3.2   NeuroRec Software

The NeuroRec software is in ongoing development [15]. It consits of a Web client and a server side application. The implementation of the client emphasizes self-service and the usage of metadata for supporting practitioners [13].

For developing the server side part of the prototype, we chose JAVA as a programming language and some lightweight frameworks (e.g. Spark). The prototype does not require a dedicated application server but only a Java Virtual Machine. Moreover, it relies on a relational database for storing data. The application is organized in loosely coupled components. We implemented a structure conforming to the Representational State Transfer (REST) software architecture style. Corresponding Web services for data exchange between client and server are implemented. This allows for a multi-client approach in further iterations. For different functionality individual components were developed. The recommender component, as can be seen in Figure 1, handles the processing of the knowledge base.

In addition, meaningful metadata is provided through the integration of third-party services. Domain specific knowledge is fetched, regarding diagnoses, symptoms and clinical pathways, from the "Deutsche Gesellschaft f?r Neurologie (DGN)" [8]. Also PubMed is searched for supplementary literature to the recommendations produced by the corresponding component.

Our prototypical Web client uses the Web services of the server side prototype. It is developed using HTML5/JavaScript, especially AngularJS [1]. Maintaining the knowledge base is critical for experts. They must be able to modify the individual function blocks without the need of dealing with the details of fuzzy logic and FCL. We developed a set of GUI elements to support experts in doing so abstracting the FCL into form fields. Figure 2 shows part of a dialog with which users can create FCL function blocks. Prior to this they can add diagnoses and related symptoms with similar dialogues. We are still improving the user interface and there will be more help assistance for creating function blocks.

Figure 3 shows a screenshot of the main view where users can actually work with the created data. ① shows a selected patient. Basic information about the patient is provided (e.g. name, address etc.). Possible other fields to display would be age, sex etc. Information about medication, planned treatments etc can be seen at ②. ③ shows a fever curve and other related information is displayed. To this date patient data is only sample data. ④ shows the selected symptoms with a short description. Possible diagnoses with additional information can be seen at ⑤. For selecting symptoms a dedicated dialog is available. Metadata in form of literature references is provided at ⑥.

4   Summary and Further Procedure

As stated in Section 3.2 the system is still in active development. Whilst the feedback from practitioners and other stakeholders from the health care domain was very positive, further formalizing the guidelines will take more time. When all parts of the system are reasonable mature we strive for making them accessible to the public. This will hopefully lead to increased feedback and therefore to an improved expert system.

What we have to focus later on are legal issues. This is because offering computer based diagnosis support solution, which offers potential diagnoses as

Fig. 2. Fuzzy Control Language Function Block Creation

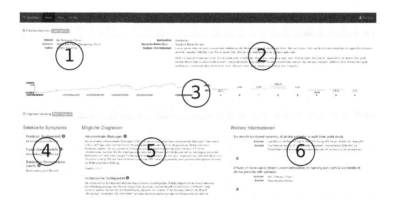

Fig. 3. Client Prototype

a result, is, from a legal point of view, quite complicated. We are well aware of those issues which is why, for the moment, we see the main use case for such a system as teaching platform and support platform for assistant doctors or students.

Various concepts and parts of the approach were evaluated through expert interviews [12,15,19]. In addition, the knowledge base is constantly discussed with experts and evaluated with cases from specialized literature. We work in close cooperation with different experts from local hospitals and public health researchers to improve NeuroRec. At the end of the year we plan to have completed a fully working prototype. It is planned to start with user tests afterwards.

References

1. AngularJS Team: AngularJS - HTML enhanced for web apps! (2015). https://angularjs.org/ (last visited May 22, 2015)
2. Berner, E.: Clinical decision support systems: state of the art. AHRQ Publication (09) (2009)
3. Bickel, A., Grunewald, M.: Ein Expertensystem für das Fachgebiet Neurologie-Möglichkeiten und Grenzen. Fortschritte der Neurologie, 723–731 (2006)
4. Borgohain, R., Sanyal, S.: Rule Based Expert System for Cerebral Palsy Diagnosis, pp. 1–4 (2012a). arXiv preprint arXiv:1207.0117, http://arxiv.org/abs/1207.0117
5. Borgohain, R., Sanyal, S.: Rule Based Expert System for Diagnosis of Neuromuscular Disorders, pp. 1–5 (2012b). arXiv preprint arXiv:1207.2104, http://arxiv.org/abs/1207.2104
6. Bunke, H., Flückiger, F., Ludin, H.P., Conti, F.: Diagnostic expert systems in neurology - a comparison between a rule based prototype and a database oriented approach. In: Rienhoff, O., Piccolo, U., Schneider, B. (eds.) Expert Systems and Decision Support in Medicine. LNCS, vol. 36, pp. 209–212. Springer, Heildelberg (1988)
7. Cingolani, P., Alcala-Fdez, J.: jfuzzylogic: a robust and flexible fuzzy-logic inference system language implementation. In: FUZZ-IEEE, pp. 1–8. Citeseer (2012)
8. Deutsche Gesellschaft für Neurologie e.V.: Deutsche Gesellschaft für Neurologie e.V. (2015). http://www.dgn.org (last visited January 22, 2015)
9. Dinevski, D., Bele, U., Šarenac, T., Rajkovič, U., Šušteršič, O.: Clinical decision support systems. Studies in health technology and informatics, pp. 217–238, December 2013
10. Friedman-Hill, E.: JESS in Action. Manning Greenwich, CT (2003)
11. Ghahazi, M.A., Fazel Zarandi, M.H., Harirchian, M.H., Damirchi-Darasi, S.R.: Fuzzy rule based expert system for diagnosis of multiple sclerosis. In: 2014 IEEE Conference on Norbert Wiener in the 21st Century (21CW), pp. 1–5. IEEE (2014)
12. Josefiok, M.: Measuring and monitoring the rehabilitation of patients on monitoring stations via the analyses of poly-structured data. In: Jahrestagung der Gesellschaft für Informatik e.V. (GI) Informatik 2014, vol. 44. LNI, GI (2014)
13. Josefiok, M., Korfkamp, D., Witt, J.: An approach for a web-based analysis solution with MUSTANG. In: The Seventh International Conferences on Advanced Service Computing. IARIA XPS Press (2015a)
14. Josefiok, M., Krahn, T., Sauer, J.: A survey on expert systems for diagnosis support in the field of neurology. In: Howlett, R.J., Jain, L.C. (eds.) Intelligent Decision Technologies - Proceedings of the 4th International Conference on Intelligent Decision Technologies (IDT 2015). Springer (2015b)
15. Josefiok, M., Norkus, O., Sauer, J.: An approach for a web-based diagnosis cockpit for the field of neurology. In: The Third International Conference on Building and Exploring Web Based Environments. IARIA XPS Press (2015c)
16. Moher, D., Liberati, A., Tetzlaff, J., Altman, D.G., Group, T.P.: Preferred Reporting Items for Systematic Reviews and Meta-Analyses: The PRISMA Statement. PLoS Med. 6(7), e1000097 (2009). http://dx.doi.org/10.1371/journal.pmed.1000097

17. Reimers, C.D., Bitsch, A.: Differenzialdiagnose Neurologie. Kohlhammer, Stuttgart (2008)
18. Vaghefi, S.Y.M., Isfahani, T.M.: Roses: an expert system for diagnosing six neurologic diseases in children title. In: Int. Conf. Intelligent Systems & Agents, pp. 259–260 (2009)
19. Weiß, J.P., Josefiok, M., Krahn, T., Appelrath, H.J.: Entwicklung eines fachkonzepts für die klinische entscheidungsunterstützung durch analytische informationssysteme. In: Proceedings of the 12th International Conference on Wirtschaftsinformatik (WI2015) (2015)

Dynamics of Belief:
Horn Knowledge Base and Database Updates

Radhakrishnan Delhibabu$^{(\boxtimes)}$

Knowledge-Based Systems Group, Kazan Federal University, Kazan, Russia
rdelhibabu@it.kfu.ru

Abstract. The dynamics of belief and knowledge is one of the major components of any autonomous system that should be able to incorporate new pieces of information. In order to apply the rationality result of belief dynamics theory to various practical problems, it should be generalized in two respects: first it should allow a certain part of belief to be declared as immutable; and second, the belief state need not be deductively closed. Such a generalization of belief dynamics, referred to as base dynamics, is presented in this paper, along with the concept of a generalized revision algorithm for knowledge bases (Horn or Horn logic with stratified negation). We show that knowledge base dynamics has an interesting connection with kernel change via hitting set and abduction. In this paper, we show how techniques from disjunctive logic programming can be used for efficient (deductive) database updates. The key idea is to transform the given database together with the update request into a disjunctive (datalog) logic program and apply disjunctive techniques (such as minimal model reasoning) to solve the original update problem. The approach extends and integrates standard techniques for efficient query answering and integrity checking. The generation of a hitting set is carried out through a hyper tableaux calculus and magic set that is focused on the goal of minimality. The present paper provides a comparative study of view update algorithms in rational approach. For, understand the basic concepts with abduction, we provide an abductive framework for knowledge base dynamics. Finally, we demonstrate how belief base dynamics can provide an axiomatic characterization for insertion a view atom to the database. We give a quick overview of the main operators for belief change, in particular, belief updates versus database updates.

Keywords: AGM · Belief revision · Belief update · Horn knowledge base dynamics · Kernel change · Abduction · Hyber tableaux · Magic set · View update · Update propagation

1 Introduction

We live in a constantly changing world, and consequently our beliefs have to be revised whenever there is new information. When we encounter a new piece of information that contradicts our current beliefs, we revise our beliefs *rationally*.

Thesis consists of following publications [8],[9],[10],[11],[12] and [13].

© Springer International Publishing Switzerland 2015
S. Hölldobler et al. (Eds.): KI 2015, LNAI 9324, pp. 341–348, 2015.
DOI: 10.1007/978-3-319-24489-1_32

In the last three decades, the field of computer science has grown substantially beyond mere number crunching, and aspires to imitate rational thinking of human beings. A separate branch of study, *artificial intelligence* (AI) has evolved, with a number of researchers attempting to represent and manipulate knowledge in a computer system. Much work has been devoted to study the statics of the knowledge, i.e. representing and deducting from fixed knowledge, resulting in the development of expert systems. The field of logic programming, conceived in last seventies, has proved to be an important tool for handling static knowledge. However, such fixed Horn knowledge based systems can not imitate human thinking, unless they are accomplish revising their knowledge in the light of new information. As mentioned before, this revision has to take place rationally. This has led to a completely new line of research, the **dynamics of belief**.

Studies in dynamics of belief are twofold: What does it mean to *rationally* revise a belief state? How can a belief state be represented in a computer and revised? The first question is more philosophical theory, and a lot of works have been carried out from epistemological perspective to formalize belief dynamics. The second question is computation oriented, and has been addressed differently from various perspectives of application. For example, a lot of algorithms have been proposed in logic programming to revise a Horn knowledge base or a database represented as a logic program; number of algorithms are there to carry out a view update in a rational database; algorithm to carry out diagnosis; algorithm for abduction reasoning and so on. We need the concept of "change" in some form or other and thus need some axiomatic characterization to ensure that the algorithms are rational. Unfortunately, till this date, these two tracks remain separate, with minimal sharing of concepts and results. The primary purpose of the paper is to study these two developments and integrate them.

When a new piece of information is added to a Horn knowledge base [14,15,25], it may become inconsistent. Revision means modifying the Horn knowledge base in order to maintain consistency, by keeping the new information and removing the least possible previous information. In our case, update means revision and contraction, that is insertion and deletion in database perspective. Previous works [3,4] have explained connections between contraction and knowledge base dynamics. Our Horn knowledge base dynamics is defined in two parts: an immutable part (Horn formulae) and updatable part (literals) (for definition and properties see the works of [17,19,27,30]. Knowledge bases have a set of integrity constraints. In the case of finite knowledge bases, it is sometimes hard to see how the update relations should be modified to accomplish certain Horn knowledge base updates. .

2   Motivation

In the general case of arbitrary formulae, the revision problem for knowledge bases is hard to solve. So we restrict the revision problem to *Horn formulae*. The connection between belief change and database change is an interesting one since so far the two communities have independently considered two problems that are very similar, and our aim is to bring out this connection.

We aim to bridge the gap between philosophical and database theory. In such a case, Hansson's [18] kernel change is related to the abductive method. Aliseda's [2] book on abductive reasoning is one of our key motivation. Wrobel's [31] definition of first-order theory revision was helpful to frame our algorithm. On the other hand, we are dealing with the view update problem. Keller and Minker's (Keller 1985 and Minker 1996) work is one the motivation for the view update problem. In Figure 1 understand the concept of view update problem in rational way. Figure show that foundation form Belief Revision theory, intermediate step handle to Horn knowledge base, this step very impairment that agent have background knowledge and he/she made decision with postulate may require to process next step. Target of the application is connect database updates via Horn knowledge base with abduction reasoning. All clear procedure shown in each section.

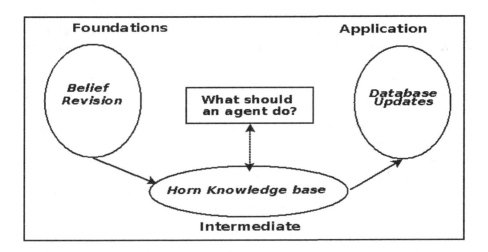

Fig. 1. Layout of the paper

Following example illustrates the motivation of the paper:

Example 1. Consider a database with an (immutable) rule that a staff member is a person who is currently working in a research group under a chair. Additional (updatable) facts are that matthias and gerhard are group chairs, and delhibabu and aravindan are staff members in group infor1. Our first integrity constraint (IC) is that each research group has only one chair ie. $\forall x, y, z$ $(y=z) \leftarrow$ group_chair(x,y) $\wedge$ group_chair(x,z). Second integrity constraint is that a person can be a chair for only one research group ie. $\forall x, y, z$ $(y=z) \leftarrow$ group_chair(y,x) $\wedge$ group_chair(z,x).

Immutable part: staff_chair(x,y)← staff_group(x,z),group_chair(z,y).

Updatable part: group_chair(infor1,matthias)←
group_chair(infor2,gerhard)←
staff_group(delhibabu,infor1)←
staff_group(aravindan,infor1)←

Suppose we want to update this database with the information, staff_chair (aravindan,gerhard); From the immutable part, we can deduce that this can be achieved by asserting staff_group(<u>aravindan</u>,z) $\bigwedge$ group_chair(z,<u>gerhard</u>)

If we are restricted to definite clauses, there are three plausible ways to do this: first case is, aravindan and gerhard belong to infor1, i.e, staff_group(<u>aravind-an</u>,infor1) $\bigwedge$ group_chair(infol,<u>gerhard</u>). We need to delete both base facts group_chair(infor1,matthias)← and group_chair(infor2,gerhard)←, because our first IC as well as second IC would be violated otherwise. In order to change the view, we need to insert group_chair(infor1,gerhard)← as a base fact. Assume that we have an algorithm that deletes the base facts staff_group(delhibabu,-infor1)← from the database. But, no rational person will agree with such an algorithm, because the fact staff_group(delhibabu,infor1)← is not "relevant" to the view atom.

Second case, aravindan and gerhard belong to infor2, that is staff_group (<u>aravindan</u>,infor2) $\bigwedge$ group_chair(infor2,gerhard). Simply, insert the new fact staff_group(aravindan,infor2)← to change the view. Suppose an algorithm deletes the base facts staff_group(aravindan,infor1)← from the database, then it can not be "rational" since these facts are not "relevant" to the view atom.

Third case, aravindan and gerhard belong to infor3 (free assignment of the group value), that is staff_group(<u>aravindan</u>,infor3) $\bigwedge$ group_chair(info3,<u>gerhard</u>). Suppose, we insert new base fact group_chair(infor3,gerhard) ←, our second IC does not follow. Suppose an algorithm inserts the new base fact staff_group(aravindan,infor2)← or staff_group(aravindan,infor1)← is deleted, then it can not be "rational".

The above example highlights the need for some kind of "relevance policy" to be adopted when a view atom is to be inserted to a deductive database. How many such axioms and policies do we need to characterize a "good" view update? When are we sure that our algorithm for view update is "rational"? Clearly, there is a need for an axiomatic characterization of view updates. By axiomatic characterization, we mean explicitly listing all the rationality axioms that are to be satisfied by any algorithm for view update.

The basic idea in [5,6] is to employ the model generation property of hyper tableaux and magic set to generate models, and read off diagnosis from them. One specific feature of this diagnosis algorithm is the use of semantics (by transforming the system description and the observation using an initial model of the correctly working system) in guiding the search for a diagnosis. This semantical guidance by program transformation turns out to be useful for database updates as well. More specifically we use a (least) Herbrand model of the given database to transform it along with the update request into a logic program in such a way that the models of this transformed program stand for possible updates.

We discuss two ways of transforming the given database together with the view update (insert and delete) request into a logic program resulting in two variants of view update algorithms. In the first variant, a simple and straightforward transformation is employed. Unfortunately, not all models of the transformed program represent a rational update using this approach. The second variant of the algorithm uses the least Herbrand model of the given database for the transformation. In fact what we referred to as offline preprocessing before is exactly this computation of the least Herbrand model. This variant is very meaningful in applications where views are materialized for efficient query answering. The advantage of using the least Herbrand model for the transformation is that all models of the transformed logic program (not just the minimal ones) stand for a rational update.

When dealing with the revision of a Horn knowledge base (both insertions and deletions), there are other ways to change a Horn knowledge base and it has to be performed automatically also [16] and [28]. Considering the information, change is precious and must be preserved as much as possible. The *principle of minimal change* [7,17,20,29] can provide a reasonable strategy. On the other hand, practical implementations have to handle contradictory, uncertain, or imprecise information, so several problems can arise: how to define efficient change in the style of Carlos Alchourrón, Peter Gärdenfors, and David Makinson (AGM) [1]; what result has to be chosen [22,23,26]; and finally, according to a practical point of view, what computational model to explore for the Horn knowledge base revision has to be provided?

The significance of our work can be summarized in the following:

- To define a new kind of revision operator on Horn knowledge base and obtain axiomatic characterization for it.
- To propose new generalized revision algorithm for Horn knowledge base dynamics, and study its connections with kernel change and abduction procedure.
- To develop a new view insertion algorithm for databases.
- To design a new view update algorithm for stratifiable Deductive Database (DDB), using an axiomatic method based on Hyper tableaux and magic sets.
- To study an abductive framework for Horn knowledge base dynamics.
- To present a comparative study of view update algorithms and integrity constraint.
- Finally, to shown connection between belief update versus database update.

3   Conclusion

The main contribution of this research is to provide a link between theory of belief dynamics and concrete applications such as view updates in databases. We argued for generalization of belief dynamics theory in two respects: to handle certain part of knowledge as immutable; and dropping the requirement that belief state be deductively closed. The intended generalization was achieved by introducing the concept of Horn knowledge base dynamics and generalized revision for the same. Further, we studied the relationship between Horn knowledge base dynamics and abduction resulting in a generalized algorithm for revision based on abductive procedures. The successfully demonstrated how Horn knowledge base dynamics provide an axiomatic characterization for update an literals to a stratifiable (definite) deductive database.

In bridging the gap between belief dynamics and view updates, we observe that a balance has to be achieved between computational efficiency and rationality. While rationally attractive notions of generalized revision prove to be computationally inefficient, the rationality behind efficient algorithms based on incomplete trees is not clear at all. From the belief dynamics point of view, we may have to sacrifice some postulates, vacuity, to gain computational efficiency. Further weakening of relevance has to be explored, to provide declarative semantics for algorithms based on incomplete trees.

On the other hand, from the database side, we should explore various ways of optimizing the algorithms that would comply with the proposed declarative semantics. We believe that partial deduction and loop detection techniques, will play an important role in optimizing algorithms. Note that, loop detection could be carried out during partial deduction, and complete SLD-trees can be effectively constructed wrt a partial deduction (with loop check) of a database, rather than wrt database itself. Moreover, we would anyway need a partial deduction for optimization of query evaluation.

We have presented two variants of an algorithm for update a view atom from a definite database. The key idea of this approach is to transform the given database into a logic program in such a way that updates can be read off from the models of this transformed program. We have also shown that this algorithm is rational in the sense that it satisfies the rationality postulates that are justified from philosophical angle. In the second variant, where materialized view is used for the transformation, after generating a hitting set and removing corresponding EDB atoms, we easily move to the new materialized view. An obvious way is to recompute the view from scratch using the new EDB (i.e., compute the Least Herbrand Model of the new updated database from scratch) but it is certainly interesting to look for more efficient methods.

Acknowledgments. I would like to thanks Gerhard Lakemeyer and Chandrabose Aravindan both my Germany and Indian PhD supervisor, give encourage to write the paper. I owe my deepest gratitude to Ramaswamy Ramanujam from Institute of Mathematical Sciences and Ulrich Furbach from University Koblenz-Landau for my PhD thesis member. I thank to my PhD thesis examiner's Eduardo Fermé from University of Madeira, Mohua Banerjee from Indian Institute of Technology Kanpur and Arindama Singh form Indian Institute of Technology Madras. The author acknowledges the support of SSN College of Engineering research funds and RWTH Aachen, where he is visiting scholar with an Erasmus Mundus External Cooperation Window India4EU by the European Commission. This work was also funded by the subsidy of the Russian Government Program of Competitive Growth of Kazan Federal University.

References

1. Alchourron, C.E., Gärdenfors, P., Makinson, D.: On the logic of theory change: Partial meet contraction and revision functions. Journal of Symbolic Logic **50**, 510–530 (1985)
2. Aliseda, A.: Abductive Resoning Logic Investigations into Discovery and Explanation. Springer, vol. 330 (2006)
3. Aravindan, C., Dung, P.M.: Belief dynamics, abduction, and database. In: MacNish, C., Moniz Pereira, L., Pearce, D.J. (eds.) JELIA 1994. LNCS, vol. 838, pp. 65–85. Springer, Heidelberg (1994)
4. Aravindan, C.: Dynamics of Belief: Epistmology, Abduction and Database Updat. Ph.D. Thesis, AIT (1995)
5. Aravindan, C., Baumgartner, P.: A rational and efficient algorithm for view deletion in databases. In: Logic Programming proceedng International Symposium, pp. 165–179 (1997)
6. Behrend, A., Manthey, R.: A transformation-based approach to view updating in stratifiable deductive databases. In: Hartmann, S., Kern-Isberner, G. (eds.) FoIKS 2008. LNCS, vol. 4932, pp. 253–271. Springer, Heidelberg (2008)
7. Dalal, M.: Investigations into a theory of base revision: preliminary report. In: Seventh National Converence on Artificial Intelligence (AAAI), pp. 475–479. St. Paul (1988)
8. Delhibabu, R., Lakemeyer, G.: A Rational and Efficient Algorithm for View Revision in Databases. Applied Mathematics & Information Sciences **7**(3), 843–856 (2013)
9. Delhibabu, R.: An Abductive Framework for Horn Knowledge Base Dynamics. Applied Mathematics & Information Sciences **9**(2), 571–582 (2014)
10. Delhibabu, R., Behrend, A.: A New Rational Algorithm for View Updating in Relational Databases. Applied Intelligence **42**(3), 466–480 (2014)
11. Delhibabu, R.: Comparative Study of View Update Algorithms in Rational Choice Theory. Applied Intelligence **42**(3), 447–465 (2014)
12. Delhibabu, R.: A Better Understanding of the Dynamics of Belief Update VS Database Update. Studia Logica - Submitted (2014)
13. Delhibabu, R.: Dynamics of Belief: Horn Knowledge Base And Database Updates. Springer Briefs - Submitted (2015)
14. Delgrande, J.P.: Horn Clause Belief Change: Contraction Functions, pp. 156–165. KR (2008)
15. Delgrande, J.P., Peppas, P.: Revising horn theories. In: Proceedings of the Twenty-Second International Joint Conference on Artificial Intelligence, vol. 2, pp. 839–844 (2011)
16. Fermé, E.L.: Actualizacion de Bases de Conocimiento usando Teorias de Cambio de Creenica. lberamia, pp. 419–436 (1992)
17. Fermé, E.L., Hansson, S.O.: Shielded contraction. In: Frontiers in Belief Revision, Applied Logic Series, pp. 85–107. Kluwer Academic Publishers (2001)
17. Gärdenfors, P.: Knowledge in flux. MIT Press, Cambridge (1998)
18. Hansson, S.O.: A Textbook of Belief Dynamics. Kluwer Academic Publishers, Dordrecht (1997)
19. Hansson, S.O., Fermé, E.L., Cantwell, J., Falappa, M.: Credibility-Limited Revision. Journal of Symbolic Logic **66**(4), 1581–1596 (2001)
20. Herzig, A., Rifi, O.: Propositional Belief Base Update and Minimal Change. Artificial Intelligence **115**(1), 107–138 (1999)

21. Keller, A.: Updating Relational Databases Through Views. Stanford University, Ph.D. Thesis (1985)
22. Lakemeyer, G.: A Logical Account of Relevance. International Joint Conference on AI **1**, 53–861 (1995)
23. Lobo, J., Trajcevski, G.: Minimal and Consistent Evolution of Knowledge Bases. Journal of Applied Non-Classical Logics **7**(1), 117–146 (1997)
24. Minker, J.: Logic and databases: a 20 year retrospective. In: Pedreschi, D., Zaniolo, C. (eds.) LID 1996. LNCS, vol. 1154, pp. 1–57. Springer, Heidelberg (1996)
25. Papini, O.: Knowledge-base revision. The Knowledge Engineering Review **15**(4), 339–370 (2000)
26. Nayak, A.C.: Is revision a special kind of update? In: Wang, D., Reynolds, M. (eds.) AI 2011. LNCS, vol. 7106, pp. 432–441. Springer, Heidelberg (2011)
27. Nebel, B.: How hard is it to revise a belief base?. In: Handbook of Defeasible Reasoning and Uncertainty Management Systems, pp. 77–145 (1998)
28. Rodrigues, O., Benevidas, M.: Belief revision in pseudo-definite sets. In: Proceeding of the 11th Brazilian Symposium on AI (1994)
29. Schulte, O.: Minimal belief change and pareto-optimality. In: Australian Joint Conference on Artificial Intelligence, pp. 144–155 (1999)
30. Segerberg, K.: Irrevocable Belief Revision in Dynamic Doxastic Logic. Notre Dame Journal of Formal Logic **39**(3), 287–306 (1998)
31. Wrobel, S.: First order Theory Refinement. IOS Frontier in AI and Application Series, Advances in ILP, ed. Raedt, LD. IOS Press, Amsterdam (1995)

Rock, Paper, Scissors
What Can I Use in Place of a Hammer?
(Extended Abstract)

Madhura Thosar[✉]

Faculty of Computer Science, Institute of Knowledge and Language Engineering,
Otto-von-Guericke-Universität Magdeburg,
Universitätsplatz 2, 39106 Magdeburg, Germany
madhura.thosar@iws.cs.uni-magdeburg.de
http://theo.cs.uni-magdeburg.de/

1 Motivation

Humans have become extremely sophisticated in their use of tools compare to their animal counterparts. It is not just the dexterity but also the diversity in tool use that makes humans alpha-males of tool-use. Consider the following typical scenarios:

Scenario 1: George's 2 years old son, James, could not reach the water tab of the wash basin. Since George was already using the stool, George quickly grabbed a *suitable* plastic container box and settled it by the front side of the wash basin. Now James could easily reach the basin by standing over the box.

Scenario 2: Fred wanted to hammer a nail into a wall for hanging a painting he bought recently. Since he lost his hammer the other day, he grabbed an *suitable* shoe and hammered the nail into the wall using the heel of the shoe.

In both the scenarios, a substitute was chosen from the existing objects and was maneuvered in a similar way to the original tool when the original tool was not available. Moreover, it is worth noting in the above scenarios that neither Georg nor Fred interacted physically with every single object present in the environment to determine a substitute. In situations like these, humans seem to know what *kind* of object is appropriate as a substitute. This skill is significant because it allows humans to adapt to unforeseen situations when performing tasks. Similar to above scenarios, when a robot is operating in a dynamic environment, it can not be assumed that a tool required to solve a given task will always be available. For instance, a service robot is asked to serve drinks on a tray, but the tray is broken; such mishaps in day-to-day activities are common. In situations like these, an effective way for a robot would be to adapt like humans, for example, by using a substitute, like an eating plate for serving. However the question is how to enable a robot to find a substitute without interacting with the objects.

In my doctoral research, I would like to address this problem using the techniques from the area of knowledge representation and reasoning in the context of

© Springer International Publishing Switzerland 2015
S. Hölldobler et al. (Eds.): KI 2015, LNAI 9324, pp. 349–355, 2015.
DOI: 10.1007/978-3-319-24489-1_33

a service robot. The primary goal of the research is to propose a representation to express the knowledge about objects and develop a reasoner based on the proposed representation to determine a possible substitute. Such a system would be helpful since, when a tool is found to be unavailable during the task execution, finding the substitute in a reasonable amount of time will be necessary to ensure the successful completion of the task in a timely manner. However, it would be time consuming if a robot interacts with every detected object in the environment to determine a substitute. In the next section, the research questions are discussed with a focus on the problems in dealing with the challenges in the object representation and substitute computations.

2   Research Question

One may wonder what is perceived as a tool. The common sense dictates that in a real-world a tool is some physical object and something one can use. As Samuel Butler [2] has put it "Nothing is tool unless during actual use". There are multiple definitions of a tool in the literature. For the proposed research, the definition offered by Parkar and Gibson [10] is adopted:

[Goal directed] manipulation of one detached object relative to another (and in some cases through a force field) involving subsequent change of state of one or both of the objects.

In other words, when an object is used to perform a certain function such that it changes the state of itself or both the objects, for example, hammering a nail with a hammer or eating food with a spoon, it is perceived as a tool. The definition offers a simplified account of what is considered as a tool in general. However, an actual tool use is quite an elaborate business involving complex physical and cognitive activities. Consider, for example a heel of a shoe. Though its primary function is to increase the height of a person, it can also be used for hammering a nail. This raises a question, how does one know that a heel can be used as a hammer. The answer lies in the representation of a tool which includes conceptual knowledge and functionalities of a tool, and the cognitive processes involved in the decision making [3]. Both of these factors leads to the following research questions.

2.1   How to Acquire and Represent a Knowledge About a Tool?

There is a consensus in the cognitive science literature that the properties of objects play a crucial role when a tool selection is involved. The challenge posed by this theory in the context of knowledge acquisition is twofold. The first challenge is how a robot can acquire the required knowledge. The visual perception can be used to detect and recognize object instances in the scene however the corresponding semantic information of the recognized object can be obtained from the external knowledge bases such as OpenCyc [5], RoboEarth [14], WordNet [15]. For instance, a rock can be visually recognized by the perception system in an online manner, however the semantic information such as rigidity, solid mass, surface topology can be obtained from WordNet for example. The viability of these sources including perception systems relies on the complexity of a required knowledge which unfolds the next problem.

It is clear that a sufficient knowledge is required to describe an object in terms of its properties and functionalities. The question is, what is the desired granularity of the knowledge to be acquired. In other words, whether knowledge should describe an object down to the smallest details. For example, if a rock is to be used in place of a hammer, the properties such as rigidity, solid mass, palm size may be sufficient to determine its suitability. However, if a heel of a shoe is to be used then in addition to rigidity, mass and palm size, properties such as heel on back side, higher mass on a heel side etc are required to determine its suitability. The granularity can also be seen in terms of the relevant and irrelevant features of an object with respect to the required function. For example, the color of a shoe is relevant to the choice of the clothes one wants to wear, but irrelevant if one wants to use a shoe for hammering. Apart from the relevance, the details may also include information about an object's geometrical properties such as shape, size; surface topology such as roughness, waviness; elasticity such as flexible, rigid; material such as wood, metal etc.

Given the different kinds of information to be included, knowledge about an object can not simply be seen as a set of assertions. This means that knowledge needs to be sorted into different classes of properties. Thus, to be able to express the knowledge systematically, it needs to represented formally. The research question, what is an appropriate representation for object properties, explores the representation approaches such as ontological or conceptual. The typical symbolic approach to represent ontological knowledge would be description logic, while in case of conceptual representation, an approach of conceptual spaces [6] would be an interesting option. Conceptual space is a representation that complements symbolic and sub-symbolic representation and uses geometrical structures to model similarity relations. Conceptual space is a multi-dimensional space where each axis in the space represents a quality dimension or a property of an object. A point in space is considered as an object while a region is regarded as a concept. The coordinates of a point in space are particular values of each dimension. The similarity between two objects is measured by the distance between their corresponding points in the space. Representing knowledge about objects in an adequate language is closely associated with the process of determining a substitute which leads to the second research question.

2.2   How to Determine a Reasonable Substitute?

There is an evidence that in case of a tool-selection, possible substitutes can be short-listed based on their similar physical appearances, for example, there is some similarity in the appearance of hammer and a shoe with a heel [4]. However this manner of tool-selection is based on the perception which may not be an adequate choice. For instance, a rock can also be used to hammer a nail, but its physical appearance is not similar to a hammer. The selection of a rock is more driven by the properties of a head of a hammer which are similar to that of the rock.

It is also important to note that appearance alone may not be a sufficient factor to select a substitute, for example, tobacco pipe has a similar appearance but it can not be used for hammering because there is a hole on a head of a pipe which can obstruct the hammering. Recall that not all properties of a substitute are relevant with respect to the required function. Thus the key issue here is how to select a substitute which are somewhat similar in appearance to the original tool and also has relevant properties with respect to the function. The main challenge in this case is how to determine the appearance similarity as well as identify relevant properties at the knowledge level.

The primary focus of this research is on developing a system which can compute one or more possible substitutes without interacting with the existing objects. Thus, the research will address the second research question by exploring the computational techniques in the area of machine learning and formal reasoning such as analogy reasoning to determine a substitute.

3   Related Work

The area of tool substitution has not received enough attention in the robotic research, although there have been attempts in the area of affordances where the focus is to learn the object affordances by performing a given set of actions on an object and learning from its effect on the environment. In this context, an affordance is defined as an opportunity for action to exert an effect on the environment or on some other object with the help of a tool [7]. By contrast, the proposed approach does not require a robot to learn to maneuver a tool, instead it relies on the assumption that a substitute can be used in a similar manner to the original tool which a robot already knows. In this section, work which explicitly addresses the problem of determining a substitute for an original tool is discussed.

In the approach proposed in [1], a substitute is determined by comparing the functional affordances and a conceptual similarity of the original tool with a possible substitute. The functional affordances [8] of an object are affordances that *help or aid to the user in doing something to achieve a goal*. The main focus of this work is to develop a robust and flexible planner where the requirement is that a planner should be able to cope with the unforeseen situations such as, if a required tool is missing then a substitute can be used to prevent a plan from failing. The required object related knowledge such as properties and functional affordances are modeled after dictionary definitions of the objects and expressed as OWL-DL ontologies while the lower-level representation of an object is represented using conceptual spaces in a sub-symbolic manner. How the objects are represented in conceptual spaces and how the conceptual similarity between objects is learned in the conceptual spaces are not explained in the paper, as according to the author it is still being investigated. As echoed by the author, another issue with this approach is object properties and functional affordances are provided off-line and not acquired autonomously or semi-autonomously. Thus, if an unknown object is introduced in the environment during the task execution, the knowledge base will not be updated, making the approach less flexible.

4 Computational Framework

Figure 1 shows a simplified illustration of a proposed reasoner. In the following, an exemplary scenario is described to explain the working of a reasoner. Consider a scenario in which a service robot is given a task of serving drinks. It is assumed that a robot is provided with a plan for serving and all the necessary knowledge required to complete the task including how to use a tray. During the plan execution, when a tray is found to be unavailable, the planner halts the execution and redirects a request to the reasoner to find a substitute. Along with the properties of a tray, the reasoner retrieves the properties of detected objects from a knowledge base. Recall that the properties of objects and of the original tool are required to determine the similarities between the two. To form a basis for similarity comparison, the relevant properties required in an object with respect to the function are identified. In the next step, the reasoner then compares the properties of the tray with the properties of other objects to determine the similarity. For example, in case of a conceptual space, those objects that are close to a tray with respect to some similarity measures, can be treated as viable substitutes. If more than one substitute is found in this step, then they are ranked according to the distance to the tray (recall conceptual spaces in Section 2). If the planner is able to replace a tray with a substitute successfully then this substitute can be used further for learning a general model of a substitute for a tray for serving. Such a model can be handy when a similar situation is encountered in which a tray is not available. In that case, existing objects can be checked against the model to determine the substitutability. The reasoner is intended to be a stand-alone system whose service can aid a robot during, for example, planning or affordance learning. For example, the learned affordance of an object can be transferred to the other similar looking objects, thereby avoiding the redundancy in the learning of the similar affordances. The framework shown in the Figure 1 will be evaluated initially in a simulated environment to examine its performance and later will be tested on a robotic system to analyze its applicability in a real-world environment.

5 Conclusion and Future Work

This is a work-in-progress report. In this extended abstract, a problem of tool selection from the possible set of objects is discussed and an approach to compute a tool substitution is suggested. In the coming months, the focus will be on experimenting with analogy reasoning techniques such as structure mapping engine [12], Heuristic Driven Theory Projection [13] to study their usefulness in determining the similarity between two tools and their suitability in the proposed reasoner.

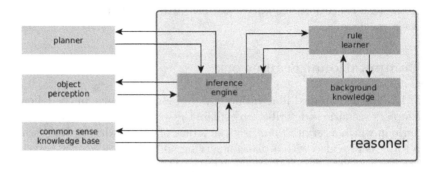

Fig. 1. The framework of a reasoner for tool substitution

References

1. Awaad, I., Kraetzschmar, G. K., Hertzberg, J.: Challenges in finding ways to get the job done. In: Planning and Robotics (PlanRob) Workshop at 24th International Conference on Automated Planning and Scheduling (2014)
2. Butler, S.: Tools, the note-books of samuel butler. In: Jones, H.F. (eds.), pp. 23–25 (1912)
3. Baber, C.: Introduction. In: Baber, C. (ed.) Cognition and Tool Use. Ch.1, pp. 1–15. Taylor and Francis, London (2003)
4. Baber, C.: Towards a theory of tool use. In: Baber, C. (ed.) Cognition and Tool Use, pp. 124–138. Taylor and Francis, London (2003)
5. http://www.opencyc.org/
6. Gaerdenfors, P.: How to make the semantic web more semantic. In: Varzi, A., Lieu, L. (eds.) Formal Ontology in Information Systems: Proceedings of the Third International Conference FOIS 2004, pp. 17–34. IOS Press, Amsterdam (2004)
7. Gibson, J.J.: The theory of affordances: perceiving, acting, and knowing. In: Shaw, R., Bransford, J. (eds.) Towards an Ecological Psychology, pp. 127–143. John Wiley & Sons Inc., Hoboken (1977)
8. Hartson, R.: Cognitive, physical, sensory, and functional affordances in interaction design. Behaviour and Information Technology **22**, 315–338 (2003)
9. Image courtesy: WikiHow. http://www.howwhywhere.com/Manually-Rewind-a-Cassette-Tape/
10. Parker, S.T., Gibson, K.R.: Object manipulation, tool use and sensorimotor intelligence as feeding adaptations in cebus monkeys and great apes. Journal of Human Evolution **6**(7), 623–641 (1977)
11. Quigley, M., Conley, K., Gerkey, B., FAust, J., Foote, T., Leibs, J., Berger, E., Wheeler, R., Ng, A.: ROS: an open-source robot operating system. In: Workshop on Open Source Software in International Conference on Robotics and Automation (2009)
12. Falkenhainer B., Forbus K. D., Gentner, D.: The Structure-Mapping Engine: Algorithm and Examples (Book). Metaphor and Symbolic Activity, vol. 41, issue 1, pp. 1–63. Elsevier Science Publishers Ltd., Essex (1989)

13. Schmidt, M., Krumnack, U., Gust, H.: Heuristic-driven theory projection: an overview: computational approaches to analogical reasoning: current trends. In: Studies in Computational Intelligence, vol. 548, pp. 163–194. Springer, Berlin Heidelberg (2014)
14. Tenorth, M., Perzylo, A., Lafrenz, R., Beetz, M.: The RoboEarth language: Representing and exchanging knowledge about actions, objects, and environments. IJCAI International Joint Conference on Artificial Intelligence **3**, 3091–3095 (2013)
15. Miller, G.A.: WordNet: A Lexical Database for English. Communications of the ACM **38**(11), 39–41 (1995)

Abductive Reasoning Using Tableau Methods for High-Level Image Interpretation

Yifan Yang[1]([⊠]), Jamal Atif[2], and Isabelle Bloch[1]

[1] Institut Mines Telecom, Telecom ParisTech, CNRS LTCI, Paris, France
[2] PSL, Université Paris-Dauphine, LAMSADE, UMR 7243, Paris, France
`yifan.yang@telecom-paristech.fr`

Abstract. Image interpretation is a dynamic research domain involving not only the detection of objects in a scene but also the semantic description considering context information in the whole scene. Image interpretation problem can be formalized as an abductive reasoning problem, i.e. an inference to the best explanation using a background knowledge. In this work, we present a framework using a tableau method for generating and selecting potential explanations of the given image when the background knowledge is encoded using a description that is able to handle spatial relations.

1 Introduction

High-level semantics extraction from an image is an important research area in artificial intelligence. Many related fields like image annotation, activity recognition and decision-support systems take advantage of semantic content. Scene understanding, which translates low level signal information into meaningful semantic information, belongs to one of the fundamental abilities of human beings. In this work, beyond a single object understanding based on low level features such as colors and forms, we focus on a complex description which relies on context information like spatial relations as well as prior knowledge on the application domain. Our aim is to extract high-level semantic information from a given image and translate it at a linguistic level. Concretely, we are interested in the interpretation of cerebral images with tumors. The high-level information corresponds to the presence of diverse types of pathologies as well as descriptions of brain structures and spatial relations among them in a brain image. For instance, according to different levels of anatomical prior knowledge on brain pathology, two possible descriptions of the image in Figure 1 could be:

- an abnormal structure is present in the brain,
- a peripheral non-enhanced tumor is present in the right hemisphere[1].

---

[1] We use the classical "left is right" convention for display. The "right" structure is on the left side in Figure 1 (i.e. on the right side of the brain).

© Springer International Publishing Switzerland 2015
S. Hölldobler et al. (Eds.): KI 2015, LNAI 9324, pp. 356–365, 2015.
DOI: 10.1007/978-3-319-24489-1_34

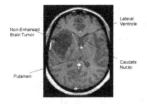

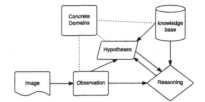

Fig. 1. A slice of a pathological brain volume (MRI acquisition), where some structures are annotated.

Fig. 2. A general schema of image interpretation task in this work.

In the context of this this work, the decision process is modeled as an abductive reasoning [1] using Description Logics. Abductive reasoning is a backward-chaining inference, consisting in generating hypotheses and finding the "best" explanation of a given observation. New knowledge should be added in order to positively entail the observation. Image interpretation can be expressed as an abductive reasoning mechanism. Figure 2 shows the major components of our framework. The main components encompass an observation of a given image, a prior knowledge base of the application domain and the reasoning service for the purpose of image interpretation. The given image is translated into symbolic representations in terms of logical formulas by segmentation and recognition of objects using image processing tools. The recognized structures are represented as individuals of concepts, and spatial relationships are computed and represented as role individuals. The future work will involve concrete domains. Concrete domains [6], considered as a real world model (e.g. image space) linked with abstract terminologies, is as well a useful part which benefits from complementary information of abstract level of knowledge in the image representation. Hypotheses are formulated with the help of the reasoning process taking both the observation and the background knowledge into account. The relations between the hypothesis and the reasoning are in two directions. One is backward-chaining for generating potential hypotheses. The other is forward-chaining reasoning to select satisfiable and preferred explanations.

To achieve our goal, we need to answer the following questions:

- *How to model the prior knowledge and formalize an appropriate representation in a given application domain? (Section 2)*
- *How to generate hypotheses to explain the observed scene? (Section 3 and 4)*
- *How to define a criterion to choose the "best" explanation in our case? (Section 3 and 4)*

2   Background and Related Work

Description Logics (DLs) are a family of knowledge representation formalisms [4]. We use $\mathcal{ALCHI}_{\mathcal{R}^+}$ including inverse roles, symmetric roles and transitive role axioms [11] in this paper. The role axioms are represented in a restricted form such as $r \equiv s^-$ (inverse roles) and $r \circ r \sqsubseteq r$ (transitive role axioms). A more complete overview of Description Logics can be found in [4].

The knowledge base used in our framework is built with three blocks: terminologies (TBox), role axioms (RBox) and assertions (ABox) ($\mathcal{K} = \{\mathcal{T}, \mathcal{R}, \mathcal{A}\}$). An example of a knowledge base referring to brain anatomy is as follows, where LVl and LVr denote left and right lateral ventricles, and left and right caudate nuclei are denoted by CNl and CNr. The general knowledge is represented in the TBox, which describes basic axioms of the background knowledge. The ABox represents the assertions, involving the facts in the observation (such as information extracted from an image). The complete knowledge base is given as follows:

$$
\begin{aligned}
TBox = \{ &Hemisphere \sqsubseteq \exists isPartOf.Brain \\
&BrainStructure \sqsubseteq \exists isPartOf.Brain \\
&BrainDisease \sqsubseteq \exists isPartOf.Brain \sqcap \neg BrainStructure \\
&Tumor \sqsubseteq BrainDisease \\
&LVl \sqsubseteq BrainStructure \sqcap \exists (rightOf \sqcap closeTo).CNl \\
&LVr \sqsubseteq BrainStructure \sqcap \exists (leftOf \sqcap closeTo).CNr \\
&CNl \sqsubseteq BrainStructure \\
&CNr \sqsubseteq BrainStructure \\
&PeripheralHemisphere \sqsubseteq Hemisphere \\
&CentralHemisphere \sqsubseteq Hemisphere \sqcap \neg PeripheralHemisphere \\
&PeripheralTumor \sqsubseteq Tumor \sqcap \exists isPartOf.PeripheralHemisphere \sqcap \exists farFrom.(LVl \sqcup LVr) \\
&SmallDeformingTumor \sqsubseteq Tumor \sqcap \exists closeTo.(CNl \sqcup CNr)\}
\end{aligned}
$$

$$
\begin{aligned}
RBox = \{ &rightOf \equiv leftOf^- \\
&above \equiv below^- \\
&closeTo \equiv closeTo^- \\
&farFrom \equiv farFrom^- \\
&isPartOf \circ isPartOf \sqsubseteq isPartOf \\
&hasPart \circ hasPart \sqsubseteq hasPart \\
&isPartOf \equiv hasPart^- \}
\end{aligned}
$$

$$
\begin{aligned}
ABox = \{ &a : CNl \\
&b : unknown \\
&c : Brain \\
&\langle a, b \rangle : leftOf, closeTo \\
&\langle b, c \rangle : isPartOf \}
\end{aligned}
$$

This knowledge base example demonstrates a practical way to represent brain anatomy. For instance, $LVl \sqsubseteq BrainStructure \sqcap \exists (rightOf \sqcap closeTo).CNl$ expresses that the left lateral ventricle belongs to the brain structure which is on the right of and close to the left caudate nucleus. In the RBox, inverse relations ($rightOf \equiv leftOf^-$) and transitive relations ($hasPart \circ hasPart \sqsubseteq hasPart$) are used to represent spatial relation properties. In the ABox, a, b, c are individuals corresponding to observed objects in the image. $a : CNl$ is a concept assertion and $\langle b, c \rangle : isPartOf$ is a role assertion, expressing that b is a part of c.

High level image interpretation is important in image analysis, for various tasks such as image annotation [17], event detection [14] and diagnostic problems [2,3]. Image interpretation combines image processing with artificial intelligence techniques to derive reasonable semantics.

Image interpretation task was regarded as an abduction problem in [2,9,15]. In [15], DL-safe rules were proposed to map high level concepts and occurrence objects in the scene and their relationships. The rules ensure the expressivity and preserve the decidability of the reasoning. However, only the concept defined in the rules can be inferred using this formalism. In [2], the image interpretation was formulated as a concept abduction problem. The DL is $\mathcal{EL}$. The knowledge base is processed using formal concept analysis and the abductive reasoning utilizes morphological operators. In [9], a probabilistic model is integrated into the abductive reasoning in order to facilitate the preference selection.

The tableau method was first adapted in Description Logics formalisms for a market matchmaking problem [7]. Colucci *et al.* modeled this problem as a concept abduction in the DL $\mathcal{ALN}$ [7], where the observations are the demand and the supply is treated as the explanation for the meet of the request. The tableau method has also been studied by Halland *et al.* in [10] for a TBox abduction problem. For a TBox abduction problem, a TBox axiom in the form $\phi = C \sqsubseteq D$ is an explanation enforcing the entailment of the observation, which is also in the form of a TBox subsumption form. Similar to the tableau method for the concept abduction, if the disjunction of two concepts A_1 and $\neg A_2$ can create a clash of the tableau, then $A_2 \sqsubseteq A_1$ is considered as a potential explanation.

Klarman *et al.* [13] present a tableau method for ABox abduction in $\mathcal{ALC}$. This method integrates first-order logic reasoning techniques. First, the background knowledge and the observation are transformed into first-order syntax. Then, a tableau in the context of the first-order logic is built and solutions are selected in the open branches. The results are transformed into Description Logic from the first-order logic in the end. In [8], Du *et al.* introduced a tractable approach to ABox abduction, called the query abduction problem. However, the potential hypotheses are restricted to atomic concepts and roles in the TBox.

Another ingredient in abductive reasoning is the selection of the "best" explanation. As a set of syntactical candidates generated using the tableau method, the selection relies on explicit restrictions for choosing the "best" explanation. Restrictions concern filtering out inappropriate hypotheses, for instance, inconsistent hypotheses ($\mathcal{H}_1$ such that $\mathcal{K} \cup \mathcal{H}_1 \models \bot$) and independent hypotheses ($\mathcal{H}_1$ entails the observation independently without background knowledge, such that $\mathcal{H}_1 \models \mathcal{O}$). These types of hypotheses need to be removed. In addition, minimality criteria are required to select the "best" among the filtered candidates. Though the desired candidates are selected, the solutions can be infinite. Therefore, defining minimality criteria is an important manner to find a preference among all the potential hypotheses. Bienvenu discussed a set of basic minimality criteria for abductive reasoning in DLs in [5] such as semantic minimality and cardinal minimality.

3 Abductive Reasoning Using Tableau Method

In this section, we will introduce how abduction is applied to image interpretation from two aspects (generation of hypotheses and selection of a preferred explanation).

Definition 1 (Concept Abduction). *Let $\mathcal{L}$ be a DL, $\mathcal{K} = \{\mathcal{T}, \mathcal{A}\}$ be a knowledge base in $\mathcal{L}$, C, D two concepts in $\mathcal{L}$ and suppose that they are satisfiable with* *respect to $\mathcal{K}$. The logical formalism of abduction in DLs is represented as follows: given an observation concept $\mathcal{O}$, a hypothesis is a concept $\mathcal{H}$ such that $\mathcal{K} \models \mathcal{H} \sqsubseteq \mathcal{O}$.*

As all observed objects in the ABox can be formulated by an appropriate concept, our problem is modeled as a concept abduction. $\mathcal{K} \models \mathcal{H} \sqsubseteq \mathcal{O}$. $\mathcal{H}$ is an explanation of the given observation $\mathcal{O}$ if $\mathcal{H}$ is subsumed by $\mathcal{O}$ w.r.t. $\mathcal{K}$. The subsumption problem can be converted into a test of satisfiability which requires to prove that $\mathcal{H} \sqcap \neg\mathcal{O}$ is unsatisfiable. According to the strategy proposed by Aliseda [1], a potential hypothesis $\mathcal{H}$ is the concept which makes the tableau of $\mathcal{H} \sqcap \neg\mathcal{O}$ closed as a consequence.

In the forward-chaining inference such as deduction, the corresponding axioms of the TBox are integrated in the tableau method using the normalization process [4]. The more general concept (in the right of a subsumption relation) can be obtained if the more specific concept is satisfied (in the left side of a subsumption relation). In Colucci's method, the authors employ this replacement strategy. In other words, the more specific concept cannot be inferred from the more general concept. For instance, a concept D can be inferred by getting a concept C with the axiom $C \sqsubseteq D$ in a deductive way since a model of the concept C is also a model of D. However, this is not suitable for a backward-chaining inference, which intends to find a concept C as a hypothesis for D. A possible solution is to add the internalized concept (see Definition 2) in the tableau.

Definition 2 (Internalized concept [4]). *Let $\mathcal{T}$ be a TBox and a set of axioms formulated as $C_i \sqsubseteq D_i$. The internalized concept of the TBox is defined as follows:*

$$C_\mathcal{T} \equiv \sqcap_{(C_i \sqsubseteq D_i \in \mathcal{T})}(\neg C_i \sqcup D_i)$$

For example, the internalized concept of the axiom $LVl \sqsubseteq BrainStructure \sqcap \exists(rightOf \sqcap closeTo).CNl$ is $\neg LVl \sqcup (BrainStructure \sqcap \exists(rightOf \sqcap closeTo).CNl)$.

If $C_i \sqsubseteq D_i$, then $\top \sqsubseteq \neg C_i \sqcup D_i$ and $C_\mathcal{T} \equiv \top$. As a consequence, all interpretations of the TBox $\mathcal{T}$ are equivalent to interpretations of the internalized concept $C_\mathcal{T}$. Therefore, every interpretation element belongs to $C_\mathcal{T}^\mathcal{I}$ and $C \equiv C \sqcap C_\mathcal{T}$ is proved.

We reformulate the subsumption checking in terms of satisfiability: the concept $\mathcal{H} \sqcap \neg\mathcal{O}$ is not satisfiable w.r.t. $\mathcal{T}$, where $\mathcal{H}$ is an explanation, $\mathcal{O}$ is an observation, $\mathcal{T}$ is a TBox. This problem can be reduced by testing the satisfiability of a concept $\mathcal{H} \sqcap \neg\mathcal{O} \sqcap C_\mathcal{T}$, where $C_\mathcal{T}$ is the internalized concept of $\mathcal{T}$. The concept $\mathcal{H}$ that causes unsatisfiability of $\mathcal{H} \sqcap \neg\mathcal{O} \sqcap C_\mathcal{T}$ is a potential hypothesis, i.e. the tableau built from this concept is closed. We follow this strategy and propose an extension of the work by Colucci *et al.* in [7].

Each interpretation element in the tableau has now four label functions: $\mathbf{T}(x)$, $\mathbf{F}(x)$, $\mathbf{T}(\langle x, y \rangle)$, $\mathbf{F}(\langle x, y \rangle)$, where x, y are interpretation elements in $\Delta^\mathcal{I}$. They are defined as follows:

Let $\mathcal{K} = \langle \mathcal{T}, \mathcal{R}, \mathcal{A} \rangle$ be a knowledge base, x, y interpretation elements, C, D two concepts and r, s two roles in the given DL, we have:

- $\mathbf{T}(x)$ represents a set of concepts such that x is one possible interpretation element: $C \in \mathbf{T}(x)$ iff $x \in C^{\mathcal{I}}$.
- $\mathbf{F}(x)$ represents a set of concepts such that x is not one possible interpretation element: $D \in \mathbf{F}(x)$ iff $x \notin D^{\mathcal{I}}$.
- $\mathbf{T}(\langle x, y \rangle)$ represents a set of roles between x and y: $r \in \mathbf{T}(\langle x, y \rangle)$ iff $\langle x, y \rangle \in r^{\mathcal{I}}$.
- $\mathbf{F}(\langle x, y \rangle)$ represents a set of unsatisfiable roles between x and y: $s \in \mathbf{F}(\langle x, y \rangle)$ iff $\langle x, y \rangle \notin s^{\mathcal{I}}$.

In the initialization step, the root node of the tableau is initialized with the concept $C_{\mathcal{T}} \sqcap \neg \mathcal{O}$. As $C_{\mathcal{T}} \sqcap \neg \mathcal{O}$ belongs to $\mathbf{T}(1)$, we add its negation to $\mathbf{F}(1)$. This technique avoids adding the negation before selecting concepts to generate contradictions in the tableau. We can prove the equivalence between $C \in \mathbf{T}(x)$ and $\neg C \in \mathbf{F}(x)$. Suppose that for $x \in \Delta^{\mathcal{I}}$, x is an interpretation element of a concept C, and x is also an interpretation individual of the concept $\neg C$. As a consequence, x is an interpretation of the concept $C \sqcap \neg C \equiv \bot$. There is no such interpretation. Thus, if $x \in C^{\mathcal{I}}$, then $x \notin (\neg C)^{\mathcal{I}}$, and conversely, $x \in C^{\mathcal{I}}$ is proved when $x \notin (\neg C)^{\mathcal{I}}$.

We assume that the concepts are expressed in a negation normal form (NNF). For a concept $C \in \mathcal{ALC}$, $\neg C$ in the NNF is denoted by $\overline{C}$. The expansion rules used in our work are:

1. Conjunction
    T) if $C \sqcap D \in \mathbf{T}(x)$, we add C and D in $\mathbf{T}(x)$.
    F) if $C \sqcup D \in \mathbf{F}(x)$, we add C and D in $\mathbf{F}(x)$.
2. Disjunction
    T) if $C \sqcup D \in \mathbf{T}(x)$, the branch is divided into two $(\mathbf{T}(x_1), \mathbf{T}(x_2))$. $\mathbf{T}(x_1) = \mathbf{T}(x) \cup \{C\}$ and $\mathbf{T}(x_2) = \mathbf{T}(x) \cup \{D\}$
    F) if $C \sqcap D \in \mathbf{F}(x)$, the branch is divided into two $(\mathbf{F}(x_1), \mathbf{F}(x_2))$. $\mathbf{F}(x_1) = \mathbf{F}(x) \cup \{C\}$ and $\mathbf{F}(x_2) = \mathbf{F}(x) \cup \{D\}$
3. Existential restriction
    T) if $\exists r.C \in \mathbf{T}(x)$ and there does not exist a y such that $r \in \mathbf{T}(\langle x, y \rangle)$ and $C \in \mathbf{T}(y)$, we create a new interpretation element y and then add r in $\mathbf{T}(\langle x, y \rangle)$, and C in $\mathbf{T}(y)$.
    F) if $\forall r.C \in \mathbf{F}(x)$ and there does not exist a y such that $r \in \mathbf{T}(\langle x, y \rangle)$ and $C \in \mathbf{F}(y)$, we create a new interpretation element y and then add r in $\mathbf{T}(\langle x, y \rangle)$, and C in $\mathbf{F}(y)$.
4. Universal restriction
    T) if $\forall r.C \in \mathbf{T}(x)$ and for all y such that $r \in \mathbf{T}(\langle x, y \rangle)$ and $C \notin \mathbf{T}(y)$, we add C in $\mathbf{T}(y)$.
    F) if $\exists r.C \in \mathbf{F}(x)$ and for all y such that $r \in \mathbf{T}(\langle x, y \rangle)$ and $C \notin \mathbf{F}(y)$, we add C in $\mathbf{F}(y)$.
5. Replacement of axioms in $\mathcal{T}$
    T) if $A \in \mathbf{T}(x)$ and $A \equiv C \in \mathcal{T}$, we add C in $\mathbf{T}(x)$.

T) if $\neg A \in \mathbf{T}(x)$ and $A \equiv C \in \mathcal{T}$, we add $\overline{C}$ in $\mathbf{T}(x)$.
F) if $\neg A \in \mathbf{F}(x)$ and $A \equiv C \in \mathcal{T}$, we add $\overline{C}$ in $\mathbf{F}(x)$.
F) if $A \in \mathbf{F}(x)$ and $A \equiv C \in \mathcal{T}$, we add C in $\mathbf{F}(x)$.
6. r^--rule
    T) if $r \in \mathbf{T}(\langle x, y \rangle)$, then $r^- \in \mathbf{T}(\langle y, x \rangle)$.
    F) if $r \in \mathbf{F}(\langle x, y \rangle)$, then $r^- \in \mathbf{F}(\langle y, x \rangle)$.
7. $\forall r_{trans}$-rule
    T) if $\forall r.C \in \mathbf{T}(x)$ and r is a transitive role, then for all y such that $r \in \mathbf{T}(\langle x, y \rangle)$, $\forall r.C \in \mathbf{T}(y)$.
    F) if $\exists r.C \in \mathbf{F}(x)$ and r is a transitive role, then for all y such that $r \in \mathbf{T}(\langle x, y \rangle)$, $\exists r.C \in \mathbf{F}(y)$.
8. $r_{\sqcap}$-rule
    T) if $r \sqcap s \in \mathbf{T}(\langle x, y \rangle)$, we add r and s in $\mathbf{T}(\langle x, y \rangle)$.
    F) if $r \sqcup s \in \mathbf{F}(\langle x, y \rangle)$, we add r and s in $\mathbf{F}(\langle x, y \rangle)$.

The contradiction is classified into two types: homogeneous clash and heterogeneous clash.

Definition 3 (Clash [7]). *A clash in a branch can be divided into two categories:*
1. *A branch is defined as a homogeneous clash if:*
    - $\bot \in \mathbf{T}(x)$ *or* $\top \in \mathbf{F}(x)$.
    - $\{A, \neg A\} \in \mathbf{T}(x)$ *or* $\{A, \neg A\} \in \mathbf{F}(x)$.
2. *A branch is defined as a heterogeneous clash if:*
    - $\{A \ or \ \neg A\} \in \mathbf{T}(x) \cap \mathbf{F}(x)$.

We illustrate this procedure on the brain MR image with a tumor (Figure 1) using the knowledge base described in Section 2. In this example, the observation is a concept for an unknown object considering the background knowledge: $\mathcal{O} \equiv \exists (leftOf^- \sqcap closeTo^-).CNl \sqcap \exists isPartOf.Brain^2$.

$$LVl \sqsubseteq BrainStructure \sqcap \exists(rightOf \sqcap closeTo).CNl$$
$$SmallDeformingTumor \sqsubseteq Tumor \sqcap \exists closeTo.(CNl \sqcup CNr).$$

By applying expansion rules, the construction process of the tableau is shown in Figure 3. We explain only the first part of the development of the tableau procedure. The hypotheses are generated from open branches. In this example, we have two sets of concepts for the expanded part:

$$H_1 = \{LVl, \ SmallDeformingTumor\}$$
$$H_2 = \{LVl, \ \forall closeTo.\neg CNr, \ \forall closeTo.CNl\}.$$

The concepts in these two sets are basic elements to build a hypothesis $\mathcal{H}$. We assume that the second part of the tableau is closed. Therefore, a hypothesis $\mathcal{H}$ is a conjunction of one concept from each set H_i. To avoid redundancy, we take the minimum hitting set in order to construct hypotheses from the candidate sets.

---

[2] We use image processing tools to recognize some known structures and to compute their spatial relationships. The description in logical formalism is given manually.

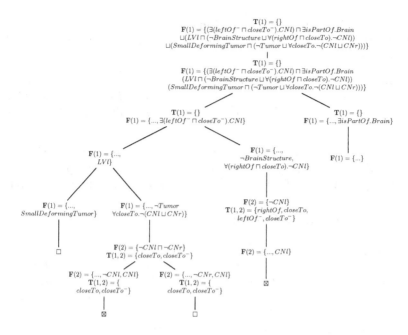

Fig. 3. The process of constructing the tableau by applying expansion rules.

Definition 4 (Hitting set). *Let $\{S_1, \ldots, S_n\}$ be a collection of sets. A hitting set T is a subset $T \subseteq \cup_{i=1}^{n} S_i$ such that T contains at least one element of each set in the collection $T \cap S_i \neq \emptyset$ $(1 \leq i \leq n)$. The minimal hitting set is a hitting set T_m if $\nexists$ hitting set T' such that $T' \subset T_m$.*

The inconsistent hypotheses ($\mathcal{K} \cup \mathcal{H} \models \bot$) and irrelevant hypotheses ($\mathcal{H} \models \mathcal{O}$) also need to be removed during the construction process. An exhaustive algorithm (Algorithm 1) is elaborated from the minimal hitting set algorithm [16].

Algorithm 1. Exhaustive search algorithm of selecting hitting sets.

1: **input:** A collection of sets $\{S_1, \ldots, S_n\}$
2: **output:** A collection of hitting sets $\mathcal{H}$
3: $\mathcal{H} = \emptyset$
4: Root node initialization.
5: **for** i from 1 to n **do**
6:    Create new children nodes for all concepts of S_i in every leaf node
7:    An intermediate hypothesis hyp_j is the conjunction of all the concepts in the same branch
8:    Delete the branch j if hyp_j is inconsistent w.r.t. the TBox
9: **end for**
10: The conjunction of all concepts in each branch j represents a potential hypothesis $\mathcal{H}_j$
11: **return:** $\mathcal{H} = \bigcup\{\mathcal{H}_j\}$

In order to choose a preferred solution among the hitting sets, two basic minimality criteria are used in our framework: subsumption criterion and cardinal minimality.

Definition 5 (Subsumption criterion). *For an abduction problem* $\mathcal{P} = \langle \mathcal{T}, \mathcal{H}, \mathcal{O} \rangle$, $\mathcal{H}_i$ *is a* $\sqsubseteq_{minimal}$ *explanation if there does not exist an explanation* $\mathcal{H}_j$ *for* $\mathcal{P}$ *such that* $\mathcal{H}_i \sqsubseteq \mathcal{H}_j$.

Definition 6 (Cardinal minimality criterion). *For an abduction problem* $\mathcal{P} = \langle \mathcal{T}, \mathcal{H}, \mathcal{O} \rangle$, *H is a set of concepts* $\{C_1, \cdots, C_n\}$ *and* $\mathcal{H} = C_1 \sqcap \cdots \sqcap C_n$. $\mathcal{H}_i$ *is a* $\leq_{minimal}$ *explanation if there does not exist an explanation* $\mathcal{H}_j$ *for* $\mathcal{P}$ *such that* $|H_i| \leq |H_j|$.

In our example, $\mathcal{H}_1 = LVl$ and $\mathcal{H}_2 = SmallDeformingTumor \sqcap \forall closeTo.\neg CNr$ are equally preferred if we choose the subsumption criterion. However, $\mathcal{H}_1 = LVl$ is preferred if we consider the cardinal minimality criterion.

4   Conclusions and Perspectives

We have exploited Description Logics and an associated tableau method for knowledge representation and reasoning in image interpretation. A first model of background knowledge of brain anatomy including spatial information is proposed. At this stage, we have adapted the tableau method for generating preferred hypotheses w.r.t. the TBox.

Several directions will be considered in the future. A first direction is to generate adaptive hypotheses iteratively. We have shown that the tableau method produces a large amount of hypotheses, however, most of them are irrelevant or unsatisfiable. In order to avoid getting these hypotheses, an iterative method will be considered. Instead of adding all internalized concepts into the tableau, only relevant axioms are added to corresponding branches that cause a closure. This action can avoid generating unsatisfiable hypotheses. Since the observation is a conjunction of the concepts, the partial hypotheses in each branch will be ordered according to the minimality criterion. The selection process for the "best" explanation will be directly embedded into the tableau construction process.

Concrete domains are necessary in image interpretation since they provide an interface between abstract logical level and concrete image space, because semantic truth models may not have corresponding regions in concrete domains. For example, a concept $CNl \sqcap \exists rightOf.CNr$ could be verified to be satisfiable w.r.t. to a defined TBox. However, this concept may not have a model in the image space. This aspect will also be studied in the future.

Fuzzy logic is also a useful ingredient in knowledge representation dealing with imprecision and vague information. This aspect has been proved to be important for spatial reasoning by combining fuzzy relations in the concrete domains to Description Logics for image interpretation [12]. Another strategy to integrate fuzzy set theory into knowledge representation is to add fuzzy values to terminological and assertional knowledge at the logical level. This part of the work will allow dealing directly with satisfaction degrees of spatial relations.

Acknowledgments. This work has been supported by the French ANR project LOGIMA.

References

1. Aliseda-Llera, A.: Seeking explanations: abduction in logic, philosophy of science and artificial intelligence. Ph.D. thesis, University of Amsterdam (1997)
2. Atif, J., Hudelot, C., Bloch, I.: Explanatory reasoning for image understanding using formal concept analysis and description logics. IEEE Transactions on Systems, Man, and Cybernetics: Systems **44**(5), 552–570 (2014)
3. Atif, J., Hudelot, C., Nempont, O., Richard, N., Batrancourt, B., Angelini, E., Bloch, I.: Grafip: a framework for the representation of healthy and pathological cerebral information. In: 4th IEEE International Symposium on Biomedical Imaging: From Nano to Macro, pp. 205–208 (2007)
4. Baader, F., Calvanese, D., McGuinness, D.L., Nardi, D., Patel-Schneider, P.F.: The Description Logic handbook: theory, implementation, and applications. Cambridge University Press (2003)
5. Bienvenu, M.: Complexity of abduction in the $\mathcal{EL}$ family of lightweight description logics. In: 11th International Conference on Principles of Knowledge Representation and Reasoning (KR08), pp. 220–230 (2008)
6. Lutz, C., Areces, C., Horrocks, I., Sattler, U.: Keys, nominals, and concrete domains. Journal of Artificial Intelligence Research **23**, 667–726 (2005)
7. Colucci, S., Di Noia, T., Di Sciascio, E., Donini, F.M., Mongiello, M.: A uniform tableaux-based approach to concept abduction and contraction in $\mathcal{ALN}$. In: 17th International Workshop on Description Logics (DL), vol. 104, pp. 158–167 (2004)
8. Du, J., Wang, K., Shen, Y.D.: A tractable approach to ABox abduction over description logic ontologies. In: 28th AAAI Conference on Artificial Intelligence (AAAI-14), pp. 1034–1040. Springer (2014)
9. Gries, O., Möller, R., Nafissi, A., Rosenfeld, M., Sokolski, K., Wessel, M.: A probabilistic abduction engine for media interpretation based on ontologies. In: Hitzler, P., Lukasiewicz, T. (eds.) RR 2010. LNCS, vol. 6333, pp. 182–194. Springer, Heidelberg (2010)
10. Halland, K., Britz, A., Klarman, S.: Tbox abduction in $\mathcal{ALC}$ using a DL tableau. In: 27th International Workshop on Description Logics (DL), pp. 556–566 (2014)
11. Horrocks, I., Sattler, U.: A description logic with transitive and inverse roles and role hierarchies. Journal of Logic and Computation **9**(3), 385–410 (1999)
12. Hudelot, C., Atif, J., Bloch, I.: A spatial relation ontology using mathematical morphology and description logics for spatial reasoning. In: ECAI 2008 Workshop on Spatial and Temporal Reasoning, pp. 21–25 (2008)
13. Klarman, S., Endriss, U., Schlobach, S.: Abox abduction in the description logic $\mathcal{ALC}$. Journal of Automated Reasoning **46**(1), 43–80 (2011)
14. Lavee, G., Rivlin, E., Rudzsky, M.: Understanding video events: a survey of methods for automatic interpretation of semantic occurrences in video. IEEE Transactions on Systems, Man, and Cybernetics, Part C: Applications and Reviews **39**(5), 489–504 (2009)
15. Neumann, B., Möller, R.: On scene interpretation with description logics. Image and Vision Computing **26**(1), 82–101 (2008)
16. Reiter, R.: A theory of diagnosis from first principles. Artificial intelligence **32**(1), 57–95 (1987)
17. Tousch, A.M., Herbin, S., Audibert, J.Y.: Semantic hierarchies for image annotation: A survey. Pattern Recognition **45**(1), 333–345 (2012)

Author Index

Printed in the United States
By Bookmasters